Blake's Britain

Major Cathedral Cities . . .
Minor Cathedral Cities . . . .

0   60   120 Miles
0   60   120 Kilometers

PENTLAND
Durness
John o'Groats
CAITHNESS

SCOTLAND

Staffa
(End of
Giant's
Causeway)

Beginning
of Giant's
Causeway

EDINBURGH

Tweed R.

NORTHUMBERLAND

Carlisle
CUMBERLAND   Durham
▲ *Skiddaw Mt.*   DURHAM

WESTMORLAND

ISLE   YORKSHIRE
OF
Sodor   MAN

ENGLAND
(ALBION)

LANCASHIRE

YORK

ANGLESEY

Asaph   FLINT   CHESHIRE   ▲ *Mam-Tor*   Lincoln
Bangor   Chester   DERBY   LINCOLN
CAERNARVON   ▲ *Mt. Penmaenmawr*   LINCOLN
DENBIGH   NOTTINGHAM
▲ *Mt. Snowdon*   MERIONETH   STAFFORD   NORFOLK
W A L E S   Lichfield   Norwich
RUT-
SHROPSHIRE   LEICESTER   LAND   Peterborough
MONTGOMERY   HUNT-   Ely
▲ *Mt. Plinlimmon*   WORCESTER   WARWICK   INGDON &
NORTHAMPTON   PETERBOROUGH
RADNOR   Worcester   CAMBRIDGE-   SUFFOLK
BRECONSHIRE   HEREFORD   SHIRE & ELY
St. David's   Hereford   *Severn R.*   BEDFORD
PEMBROKE   Gloucester   BEDFORD   HERTFORD   ESSEX
CARDIGAN   OXFORD   BUCKINGHAM   VERULAM
CARMARTHEN   GLOUCESTER   Oxford
MONMOUTH   *Thames R.*   LONDON
GLAMORGAN   Cotswold   Bath   Avebury   Rochester
Llandaff   Hills   BERKSHIRE   *Medway R.*
Bristol   Stonehenge   SURREY   Canterbury
Avon R.   KENT   Dover
SOMERSET   Salisbury   HAMPSHIRE   SUSSEX   *Cliffs*
WILTSHIRE   Winchester   Chichester
DEVON   Exeter   DORSET   *Selsey*   *Pagham*

CORNWALL

Land's End

Lizard Point

IRELAND
(ERIN)

F R A N C E

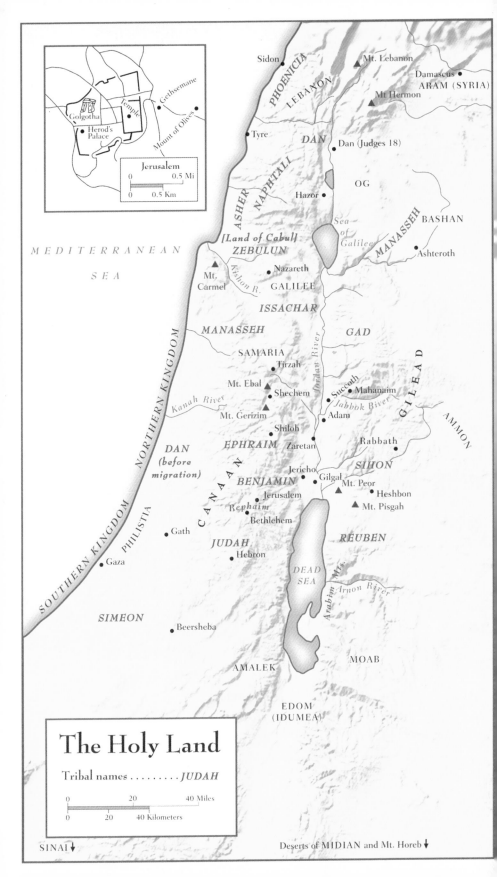

Jerusalem inset:

Golgotha
Herod's Palace
Temple
Gethsemane
Mount of Olives

Jerusalem

0   0.5 Mi
0   0.5 Km

Main map labels:

MEDITERRANEAN SEA

PHOENICIA
LEBANON
Sidon
Mt. Lebanon
Damascus
ARAM (SYRIA)
Mt Hermon
Tyre
DAN
Dan (Judges 18)
OG
Hazor
Sea of Galilee
BASHAN
MANASSEH
Ashteroth
ASHER
NAPHTALI
[Land of Cabull]
ZEBULUN
Nazareth
GALILEE
Mt. Carmel
Kishon R.
ISSACHAR
GAD
MANASSEH
SAMARIA
Tirzah
Mt. Ebal
Shechem
Succoth
Mahanaim
GILEAD
Kanah River
Mt. Gerizim
Jabbok River
Adam
AMMON
Shiloh
EPHRAIM
Zaretan
Rabbath
DAN (before migration)
BENJAMIN
Jericho
Gilgal
SIHON
Mt. Peor
Heshbon
Jerusalem
Mt. Pisgah
CANAAN
Rephaim
Bethlehem
REUBEN
PHILISTIA
Gath
JUDAH
Hebron
SOUTHERN KINGDOM
NORTHERN KINGDOM
Gaza
DEAD SEA
Arabim Mts.
Arnon River
SIMEON
Beersheba
AMALEK
MOAB
EDOM (IDUMEA)
SINAI ↓
Deserts of MIDIAN and Mt. Horeb ↓

The Holy Land

Tribal names . . . . *JUDAH*

0   20   40 Miles
0   20   40 Kilometers

The Editors

MARY LYNN JOHNSON is the coauthor, with Brian Wilkie, of *Blake's 'Four Zoas': The Design of a Dream* (1978) and coeditor, with Seraphia DeVille Leyda, of *Reconciliations: Studies in Honor of Richard Harter Fogle* (1983). Recent work has appeared in *The Cambridge Companion to William Blake* (2003), ed. Morris Eaves; *Physiognomy in Profile* (2005), ed. Melissa Percival and Graeme Tytler; and *Women Read William Blake* (2006), ed. Helen P. Bruder. Before serving as Special Assistant to the President of the University of Iowa (1983–2000), she held faculty positions at Delta State University, Louisiana State University, University of Illinois, and Georgia State University and was visiting professor at Coe College and Cornell College in Iowa.

JOHN E. GRANT is Professor Emeritus of English at the University of Iowa. Before joining the Iowa faculty, he taught at the University of Connecticut (1956–65). Most of his books and numerous essays consider William Blake's work as a writer and artist. He edited *Discussions of William Blake* (1961) and coedited, with David V. Erdman, *Blake's Visionary Forms Dramatic* (1970), and, with Edward J. Rose and Michael J. Tolley, *Blake's Designs for Edward Young's* Night Thoughts (1980). He is the honoree of the festschrift *Prophetic Character* (2002), ed. Alexander S. Gourlay.

A NORTON CRITICAL EDITION

BLAKE'S POETRY
AND DESIGNS

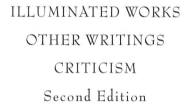

ILLUMINATED WORKS

OTHER WRITINGS

CRITICISM

Second Edition

Selected and Edited by

MARY LYNN JOHNSON

UNIVERSITY OF IOWA

JOHN E. GRANT

UNIVERSITY OF IOWA

W • W • NORTON & COMPANY • *New York* • *London*

Every effort has been made to contact the copyright holders of each of the selections. Rights holders of any selections not credited should contact W. W. Norton & Company, Inc. for a correction to be made in the next printing of our work.

Texts of Blake's illuminated works have been edited from transcriptions in the William Blake Archive of the Institute for Advanced Technology in the Humanities, University of Virginia, by permission of the editors, Morris Eaves, Robert Essick, and Joseph Viscomi. Texts of Blake's other writings are based on David V. Erdman, ed., *William Blake: Complete Poetry and Prose* (corr. ed., 1988), by permission of Virginia B. Erdman.

Images from Blake's work are published by permission of the libraries, museums, and archives acknowledged under "Illustrations."

The critical selections in "Twentieth- and Twenty-First-Century Perspectives," as excerpted, abridged, or otherwise edited for this edition, are published by permission of the authors and copyright holders acknowledged in the bibliographical notes to each essay.

The text of this book is composed in Fairfield Medium
with the display set in Bernhard Modern.
Composition by Binghamton Valley Composition.
Art file manipulation by Jay's Publishers Services.
Maps by Mary Lynn Johnson and Karen McHaney © 1978;
2007 revisions rendered by Mapping Specialists, Ltd.
Manufacturing by the Courier Companies—Westford Division.
Production manager: Benjamin Reynolds.

ISBN-13: 978-0-393-92498-5

W. W. Norton & Company, Inc., 500 Fifth Avenue,
New York, N.Y. 10110-0017
www.wwnorton.com

W. W. Norton & Company Ltd., Castle House,
75/76 Wells Street, London W1T 3QT

1 2 3 4 5 6 7 8 9 0

Contents

Other Writings   353

Criticism   495

Preface to the Second Edition

True to its title, this new edition of *Blake's Poetry and Designs* follows its predecessor (1979) in emphasizing visual as well as verbal aspects of Blake's self-published body of work in illuminated printing. This expanded selection, designed to be used in tandem with the magnificent William Blake Archive (www.blakearchive.org) and other online resources, presents newly annotated full texts of all the illuminated writings, including the epic-length *Jerusalem*; a rich sampling of images, sixteen in color and eighty-six in black and white; and a generous selection of Blake's most arresting poetry and prose in conventional printing and manuscript. Appearing for the first time in any edition is a letter rediscovered in 1997, now in the collection of Robert N. Essick. The chronology, bibliography, and other editorial materials have been reworked in light of scholarly discoveries of the past quarter century, and the "Criticism" section includes assessments of Blake's work from 1809 to 2003.

As explained in "Textual Technicalities," the thoroughly reedited—and now more lightly punctuated—reading texts are based both on our own study of original sources and on two distinguished editions that have won awards from the Modern Language Association's Committee on Scholarly Editions, one in print, one on the Internet. Texts of the illuminated writings are drawn in part from transcriptions in the William Blake Archive (1996–), edited by Morris Eaves, Robert N. Essick, and Joseph Viscomi; texts of other writings derive from David V. Erdman's *The Complete Poetry and Prose of William Blake* (1988). Large numbers set in boxes in the right margins of the reading texts refer to Blake's plate or page numbers, following a standardized system discussed in "Textual Technicalities" (p. 600). Rewritten headnotes provide brief thematic and factual introductions; revised footnotes—including those from the first edition that have been cited in subsequent scholarship—have been purged of interpretive material that is not strictly explanatory, in conformity with current practice in the Norton Critical Editions series.

We appreciate the opportunity, in this edition, to correct long-rankling 1979 glitches (which each of us secretly blames on the other) such as scrambled biblical citations (n. 9, p. 100) and anachronistic "internal combustion engines" (n. 9, p. 238). The sharp eyes of editors Carol Bemis and Brian Baker and copyeditor Candace Levy have made this edition factually sounder, better written, and typographically more pleasing than it would otherwise have been. Among others who have noted errors and oversights; recommended online or print resources; critiqued drafts; or provided encouragement, feedback, and advice, we thank Kristin Eager, Peter Schock, Harriet Kramer Linkin, Jennifer Davis Michael, Susan Wolfson, Richard Sha, Bill Van Pelt, Evan Radcliffe, George Donaldson, Justin Van Kleeck, David Christian, Judith Pascoe, Eric Gidal, Nelson Hilton, Morton D. Paley,

G. E. Bentley Jr., and participants in Neil Fraistat's seminar on editing Romantic texts at the 2004 meeting of the North American Society for the Study of Romanticism. For textual and pictorial advice and help at every stage, we are deeply indebted to Morris Eaves, Bob Essick, and Joseph Viscomi, editors of the William Blake Archive—especially to Joe, who greatly facilitated our publisher's use of images in the archive. For unfailing moral support and companionable cross-questioning of our annotations and the facts behind them, we thank our friend Sandy, Alexander S. Gourlay. For familial encouragement, we thank Michael E. ("Louie") Grant and his son Steven, Kenneth M. and Martha S. Grant and their daughter Kate, and Will Grant. And we thank each dear friend, sibling, and cousin, unnamed here, whose empathy and good cheer have uplifted us along the way.

Mary Lynn Johnson (Grant)
John E. Grant

Introduction

If you are encountering William Blake (1757–1827) for the first time in this edition, we welcome you to a great adventure. You will read the words of a poet, printmaker, and painter who calls on his contemporaries—and on "Children of the future Age" (p. 44 herein)—to join him in reimagining the world. "If the doors of perception were cleansed," the explorer-narrator of *The Marriage of Heaven and Hell* comes to realize, "every thing would appear to man as it is, infinite" (p. 75). With biblical prophecy as his model, Blake excoriates all social structures and belief systems that narrow perception and stifle the human spirit. "The Nature of my Work is Visionary or Imaginative," he writes of his painting *A Vision of the Last Judgment* (p. 434); "it is an Endeavor to Restore what the Ancients call the Golden Age." For Blake, visions of a lost paradise or a New Jerusalem are not escapist fantasies but insights into everyday reality as it could be if created anew by an awakened and energized people.

In whatever time Blake could spare from turning out commercial engravings to make a living, he labored mightily in his true vocation "under the dictates of our Angels" (p. 481), with his wife, Catherine, at his side. In all, he produced some fourteen hundred designs or engravings for other writers' books; more than a thousand prints, watercolors, and tempera pictures on biblical, literary, and historical subjects for patrons; and almost four hundred plates for his own books in a verbal-visual medium he invented himself, which he called "illuminated printing"—and which we might call graphic poetry. For these inventions he prepared templates or stereotypes on copper plates by inscribing his text-design composition in reverse, using an acid-resistant substance as ink; he then used an etching fluid to bite away the rest of the surface so as to leave words and images standing up in relief, as on a woodcut or a rubber stamp, ready to be inked and printed on paper, the right way around.

Blake was well prepared for his life's mission both by formal training in his craft and by self-education in the liberal arts. He came from a middle-class family of London shopkeepers: his father and oldest brother sold men's clothing; another brother was a gingerbread baker before joining the army. Luckily, his parents recognized their second son's gifts and stubborn independence and encouraged his artistic bent. At ten, he entered drawing school; at fourteen, he began a seven-year apprenticeship in engraving; at twenty-one, he was admitted as a student to the Royal Academy. For independent study, his father helped him purchase casts of antique sculptures, sixteenth-century prints, and books of poetry and philosophy. In poems written between the ages of twelve and twenty, published on his behalf by friends as *Poetical Sketches*, he revealed his youthful familiarity with earlier poets, especially Shakespeare, Spenser, and Pope. Steeped in the Bible and Milton, he read widely in philosophy, theology, history, and art theory and concerned himself deeply with the revolutionary events of his time, their causes and consequences.

Like other great artists, Blake had a profound intuitive grasp of human psychology. More explicitly than any English writer before him, he pointed out the interrelationship of individual and societal problems that link self-righteousness, hyperrationalism, sexual frustration, repression of energy, cruelty, injustice, and revolutionary violence. In his later works, he embodied these and other ills in the nightmare-ridden figure of the cosmic giant Albion, or universal humanity, who has fallen into the deadly sleep of mundane existence. In humanity's coma, the divine is a remote and forbidding sky-god; nature, a sterile heap of atoms; lovers and family members, enemies; and one's own innermost being, an unrecognized alien. To heal Albion and reunite the "Eternal Great Humanity Divine" (*Milton* **44**/39:27), Blake created illuminated epics aimed at restoring to the rational mind its estranged faculties of intuition, imagination, and feeling, thus liberating humanity from illusory oppositions between divine/human, spiritual/material, human/natural, self/other, male/female, and masculine/feminine elements within individuals. In everything Blake wrote and etched, he strove to arouse in each of us our full capacity to perceive, think, and act as whole persons belonging to the whole human race.

Selected works. This edition centers on the textual portion of Blake's illuminated works, his core achievement as a literary artist. These are the texts Blake considered important enough to coordinate with designs, etch on copper, print on paper (usually with color added), make into books, and offer for sale. We present this body of self-published writings in full, except for picture captions in the little emblem book *The Gates of Paradise* (1793, c. 1818–20). For a more general view of Blake's writings, we also offer selections from his best unpublished shorter poetry and his most energetic prose. Of works printed without designs in ordinary letterpress, we include selections from *Poetical Sketches* (1783, never sold) and *Descriptive Catalogue* (1809, sold at Blake's one-artist exhibition) but omit *The French Revolution* (1791, partially printed but never published). Of important manuscript works, we omit *Tiriel*, an early work, and represent the mature epic-length illustrated poem *Vala*, retitled *The Four Zoas*, by a brief sampling of self-contained episodes and passages of dialogue. To entice readers to move beyond the text to explore the crucial visual dimension of the illuminated books, we also include a generous selection of reproductions: seventeen in color, in the cover design and the sixteen-plate insert, and eighty-six in monochrome, interspersed throughout the main text, along with one illustration from the manuscript epic *The Four Zoas*.

Annotations and other aids. The reference system for Blake's illuminated books, involving alphabetical designations for copies and standardized numbers for the plates from which pages were printed, is explained in "Textual Technicalities" (p. 600). This section also explains the somewhat unorthodox editorial maneuvers required to produce in conventional typography a reading text that respects the idiosyncratic spelling, capitalization, and punctuation of Blake's handmade books. Since the advent of e-mail and text messaging, Blake's irregularities have perhaps become less of a barrier than they once appeared, as may be seen in the virtually unretouched lines of *All Religions Are One*, *Songs of Innocence and of Experience*, and the Notebook poems. After *Songs of Innocence and of Experience* (1794),

Blake's illuminated books become increasingly longer and more complex, more innovative in myth and form, and more densely allusive. We believe that twenty-first-century readers need some guidance but not so much as to miss the unsettling experience of utter disorientation, of being thrown back on one's own resources. As an aid to confidence building, we annotate earlier texts more heavily than later ones, emphasizing literary, biblical, and historical references that Blake could have expected his contemporaries to recognize; but instead of doubling the length of this book by teasing out the more arcane allusions of later works, we merely point out highlights. For substantial information or ideas attributable to a single scholar, we provide brief references (name, journal or book title, date), but usually we do not specify sources for well-established facts commonly noted in S. Foster Damon's *A Blake Dictionary* (1965, 1988) and commentaries in the Longman/Norton/Pearson Annotated English poets series by W. H. Stevenson (1971, 1989, 2007); the Rinehart edition by Hazard Adams (1970); the Penguin edition by Alicia Ostriker (1977); the annotated Princeton/Blake Trust facsimile series under the general editorship of David Bindman (1991–95); Henry Summerfield's *A Guide to the Books of William Blake for Innocent and Experienced Readers* (1998); and the online William Blake Archive (www.blakearchive.org) edited by Morris Eaves, Robert Essick, and Joseph Viscomi (1996–). The "Selected Bibliography" lists major reference books and general studies; more specialized books and articles cited in headnotes and footnotes are searchable by author in "Sources Cited in Editorial Notes," which supplements the bibliography. The chronology and maps provide orientation in time and space. The list of "Key Terms," which directs the reader to our fullest annotations of puzzling proper names in footnotes and headnotes, serves as a brief glossary of Blakean motifs.

Criticism. Although we cannot represent all important critics and schools of thought here, even those that have influenced us most, we provide a fair sampling over time of accessible, engaging interpretations that shed strong light on Blake's major works and encourage further exploration. Critical approaches that use Blake's writings to elucidate more general theories, rather than vice versa, are inherently unsuited to our purposes, but some in this category are listed in the "Selected Bibliography."

A final word. Blake has a way of attracting and repelling his readers at the same time. Nothing is out of bounds; he stops at nothing to shatter "mind-forg'd manacles." He writes soaring lyrics and crude jibes, obscure rants and startling punch lines. He can be inspirational, outrageous, inscrutable, funny, raunchy, offensive, and just plain weird—all in one passage. If you become more and more exasperated as you read, you are in good company. Distinguished scholars and enthusiasts of Blake have acknowledged the impulse to throw heavier books than this one across the room. But if you keep on reading, and especially if you let Blake's ideas and provocations get under your skin, you will experience the exhilaration of making your own discoveries not only about his works but about yourself. We hope that this edition will give you something to hang onto when you need it most, while staying out of Blake's way—and yours—as you explore the "wondrous worlds" that await you.

Abbreviations

Bentley edition	Bentley, G. E., Jr., ed, *William Blake's Writings*, 2 vols. (Oxford: Clarendon Press, 1978).
Blake Archive	William Blake Archive, ed. Morris Eaves, Robert N. Essick, and Joseph Viscomi. www.blakearchive.org.
Blake Trust/ Princeton University Press	Bindman, David, gen. ed., *Blake's Illuminated Books*. 6 vols. 1: Morton D. Paley, ed., *Jerusalem*; 2: Andrew Lincoln, ed., *Songs of Innocence and of Experience*; 3: Morris Eaves, Robert N. Essick, and Joseph Viscomi, eds., *The Early Illuminated Books*; 4: D. W. Dörrbecker, ed., *The Continental Prophecies*; 5: Essick and Viscomi, eds., *Milton a Poem and the Final Illuminated Works*; 6: David Worrall, ed., *The Urizen Books*. Princeton: The William Blake Trust and Princeton University Press, 1991–1995; see "Selected Bibliography."
Butlin	Butlin, Martin, *The Paintings and Drawings of William Blake*, 2 vols. (New Haven: Yale University Press, 1981).
Damon	Damon, S. Foster, *A Blake Dictionary: The Ideas and Symbols of William Blake*, rev. ed. with a new foreword by Morris Eaves (Hanover, NH: University Press of New England, 1988).
Erdman edition	Erdman, David V., ed., *The Complete Poetry and Prose of William Blake*, rev. ed., commentary by Harold Bloom (Berkeley: University of California Press, 1988).
Notebook	Erdman, David V., ed., with the assistance of Donald K. Moore, *The Notebook of William Blake: A Photographic and Typographic Facsimile* (1973; rev. Readex, 1977).
Ostriker	Ostriker, Alicia, ed., *William Blake: The Complete Poems* (Harmondsworth, Middlesex: Penguin, 1977; corr., 1986).
Stevenson	Stevenson, W. H., ed., *Blake: The Complete Poems*, 3rd ed. (New York: Longman, 2007).

Note on Illustrations

Each of Blake's illuminated works, and each page of those works, is meant to be seen as a whole. Although some designs appear without accompanying texts, few pages of text are altogether lacking in ornamentation. Often the interplay between visual and verbal images is elaborately orchestrated: some designs at least partly illustrate the texts they accompany, but—especially in longer works—full-page designs may appear at some distance from the most closely related narrative episodes or lines of verse. The placement of color images in the insert section is indicated by footnotes to the corresponding texts of the illuminated books. Within the size and format constraints of manageable page layout, images in black and white are placed near the texts with which Blake associated them on the pages indicated. Copy designations and plate numbers are explained in "Textual Technicalities," p. 599.

We are grateful to the libraries, museums, and archives acknowledged in the following list for permission to reproduce images from Blake's work in their collections. In the color section, variations from the original size, excluding framing lines, are noted in parentheses. Among black and white images, only the most drastic reductions are noted.

Color

1. *Songs of Innocence and of Experience* 1. Title page. Copy U. Princeton University Library, Department of Rare Books and Special Collections. (Enlarged from 11.2×7 cm.)
2. *Songs* 25. "Infant Joy." Copy Z. Lessing J. Rosenwald Collection, Library of Congress; Blake Archive.
3. *Songs* 39. "The Sick Rose." Copy Z. Lessing J. Rosenwald Collection, Library of Congress; Blake Archive.
4. *The Book of Thel* 2/ii. Title page. Copy N. Cincinnati Art Museum. Mr. and Mrs. John Emery, donors. (Reduced from 15.5×10.7 cm.)
5. *Visions of the Daughters of Albion* 1/i. Frontispiece. Copy P. Fitzwilliam Museum, The University of Cambridge; Bridgeman Archive. (Reduced from 17.1×11.9 cm.)
6. *Visions* 2/ii. Title page. Copy P. Fitzwilliam Museum, The University of Cambridge; Bridgeman Archive. (Reduced from 16.3×12.9 cm.)
7. *The Marriage of Heaven and Hell* 1. Title page. Copy G. The Houghton Library, Harvard University. (Reduced from 15.2×10.3 cm.)
8. *America a Prophecy* 2/ii. Title page. Copy O. Fitzwilliam Museum, The University of Cambridge; Bridgeman Archive. (Reduced from 23.5×16.7 cm.)

Black and White

Key Terms

ILLUMINATED WORKS

ALL RELIGIONS ARE ONE /
THERE IS NO NATURAL RELIGION (1788)

Blake's first illuminated works—*All Religions Are One* and *There Is No Natural Religion*—etched on plates smaller than half the size of a playing card, are explosive little manifestoes that deal with large questions indeed. What, in essence, is a human being? How does the mind acquire knowledge? Is truth derived from rational analysis of empirical data? Does the order of nature prove the existence of God? Through what faculty does humanity conceive the divine? Blake begins his lifelong effort to demolish tyrannical conceptions of divinity with these two tiny emblem books—one proclaiming the source of all religions to be the Poetic Genius, the guiding spirit of humanity; the other denying that humanity is limited to an aggregate of sensory perceptions. In format and organization, *All Religions Are One* resembles the condensed opening statement of a scientific or philosophical treatise; but instead of being followed by proofs, the grand assertion of the title and its seven numbered principles are allowed to stand alone, as if they were a set of axioms too self-evident to require support. In counterpoint, the resounding denial of *There Is No Natural Religion* is directed against the deistic and atheistic notion that "natural religion" is an enlightened alternative to the "revealed religion" of ecclesiastical and scriptural authority. The miniature books, taken together, lay the foundation for Blake's claim that true divinity originates within human nature as it awakens to its visionary capacity. Together, they reject the superstition and repressiveness of the established church as well as the rationalism and materialism of its critics. With prophetic certitude, they proclaim that the source of spiritual power and authority is the human imagination, nourished by the delights of the senses but unconfined by the world they perceive.

The frontispiece of *All Religions Are One*, an image in the tradition of Raphael's paintings of John the Baptist, identifies the strong and forthright voice behind both tractates: these are the words of a prophet who speaks truth and exposes error. As in Raphael's paintings, this new prophet looks directly at the reader-viewer and points with both hands, arms outstretched, toward a new revelation: presumably the contents of this very booklet. The caption, "The Voice of one crying in the Wilderness," after Isaiah 40:3, as quoted by John the Baptist in all four gospels, firmly places the contemporary prophet in the line of his biblical predecessors, just as John himself had been proclaimed a new Elijah (Matthew 11:14). The emblem of the pointing prophet serves not only as the frontispiece to Blake's first book but also as a portent of his larger mission as an artist.

To postulate the underlying unity of all religions was not unprecedented in scholarly speculation; but this public proclamation of a new doctrine is both heretical and politically radical, for it challenges the unique truth-claims of the Bible and the established church. Blake's name, not present at all in *All Religions Are One*, is obscured by paint on the frontispiece of most copies of *There Is No Natural Religion*, where it appears only in reverse printing. By what authority, then, does this new prophet dare to speak? The argument and all seven of the principles of *All Religions Are One* focus on "the Poetic Genius," a widely used term in discussions of poetry that Blake employs more generally, using *Poetic* in the original Greek sense of "making" and *Genius* in the Latin sense of "guiding spirit." What distinguishes humanity as a species is its innate capacity to create; it is by means of this core attribute—called "the true faculty of knowing" ("The Argument"), "the Spirit of Prophecy" (principle 5), and the "true man" (principle 7)—that humanity experiences what is real. In a later work, *The Marriage of Heaven and Hell* (1790), the prophets Isaiah and Ezekiel reaffirm that the Poetic Genius, humanity at its most imaginative, is the source of all perceptions of God and of regenerate humanity; in *Milton a Poem* (1804–18) the Poetic Genius inspires a series of transformations that bring the spirit of Milton back to earth to complete his prophetic mission through Blake.

If, as proclaimed in the first pamphlet, the Poetic Genius is the human essence and its only means of access to the divine, then by definition, as stated in the second pamphlet, "natural religion" is not a religion at all. *There Is No Natural Religion* consists of two sets of aphorisms (designated "a" and "b" by editors) under a single title. The first set exposes weaknesses in the common eighteenth-century liberal proposition that God is revealed through Nature, as perceived by the five senses of the human organism and reflected on by Reason. The second set denies that humanity is or should be limited to what it perceives through the five senses, a theme also treated at length in *The Marriage of Heaven and Hell*. Under such a narrow conception of human powers, derived from John Locke's theory that the mind is a blank tablet on which sensory data are registered, Reason is passive, capable merely of analyzing the "ratio" or relationships among previously accumulated sense-data. The revolutionary idea of the work, adumbrated in series a and made explicit in series b, is that a human being's desires become unlimited as his or her senses expand but that desires, once set free, can never be satisfied by sensory gratification alone. The tractate provides a further critique of Reason, a favorite eighteenth-century standard of judgment, and of "the bounded," probably intended to encompass the social evil of bondage as well as the intellectual fetters imposed by rigid philosophical systems. It is finally "the Poetic or Prophetic character" that keeps "the Philosophical & Experimental" character from repeating "the same dull round" ("Conclusion").

The colophon, or publisher's inscription, of *The Ghost of Abel* (1822), one of Blake's last illuminated works, looks back to the date of his first: "W Blake's Original Stereotype was 1788." In graphic style, both early tractates appear consistent with that date—a year before *The Book of Thel* and *Songs of Innocence*—although the earliest printed copies date from 1794–95, and Blake does not mention either booklet in his list of works for sale in 1793 (p. 378 herein). For *All Religions Are One*, our source text is Copy A (the only copy), printed in 1795, later embellished with framing lines and sold as a pair with Copy L of *There Is No Natural Religion*, also printed in 1795 and similarly embellished. Because no existing copy of *There Is No Natural Religion* contains a full set of pages, Blake's final intentions are unknowable; for this one work, therefore, instead of following a single source, we have drawn from Copies G and L to present the textual portion of all nineteen extant plates, in the hypothetical sequence proposed by Morris Eaves, Robert N. Essick, and Joseph Viscomi in *The Early Illuminated Books* (1993), volume 3 in the Blake Trust series edited by David Bindman.

To illustrate the effects of different degrees of editorial mediation discussed in "Textual Technicalities" (p. 599), we approximate Blake's own page layout, spelling, and punctuation in *All Religions Are One*, but present *There is No Natural Religion* in conventional prose lines.

ALL
RELIGIONS
are
ONE

The Voice of one crying in the
Wilderness[1]

The Argument

As the true meth-
-od of knowledge
is experiment
the true faculty
of knowing must
be the faculty which
experiences, This
faculty I treat of.

PRINCIPLE 2d

As all men are alike in
outward form, So (and
with the same infinite
variety) all are alike in
the Poetic Genius

PRINCIPLE 4.

As none by trave
ling over known
lands can find out
the unknown, So
from already ac-
quired knowledge
Man could not ac
quire more. there
-fore an universal
Poetic Genius exists

PRINCIPLE 1st

That the Poetic Genius is
the true Man. and that
the body or outward form
of Man is derived from the
Poetic Genius. Likewise
that the forms of all things
are derived from their
Genius.[2] which by the
Ancients was call'd an
Angel & Spirit & Demon.

PRINCIPLE 3d

No man can think
write or speak from his
heart but he must intend
truth. Thus all sects of
Philosophy are from the
Poetic Genius adapted
to the weaknesses of
every individual.

PRINCIPLE. 5.

The Religions of all Nati-
-ons are derived from each
Nations different reception
of the Poetic Genius which
is every where call'd the Spi
-rit of Prophecy.

1. Matthew 3:3; John the Baptist's quotation of Isaiah 40:3. Because no copy of this book bound by
   Blake himself is known to exist, the placement of this frontispiece cannot be certain.
2. Cf. "The tutelary god or attendant spirit allotted to every person at his birth" (*OED*).

PRINCIPLE 6

The Jewish & Chris-
tian Testaments are
An original derivation
from the Poetic Genius.
this is necessary from
the confined nature
of bodily sensation

PRINCIPLE 7th

As all men are alike
(tho' infinitely vari-
-ous) So all Religions
& as all similars have
one source.

The true Man is the
source he being the
Poetic Genius

THERE is NO NATURAL RELIGION[1]

[a]

The Argument

Man has no notion of moral fitness but from Education. Naturally he is
only a natural organ subject to Sense.

I

Man cannot naturally Percieve, but through his natural or bodily organs.

II

Man by his reasoning power can only compare & judge of what he has
already perciev'd.

III

From a perception of only 3 senses or 3 elements none could deduce a
fourth or fifth.

IV

None could have other than natural or organic thoughts if he had none but
organic perceptions.

V

Man's desires are limited by his perceptions; none can desire what he has
not perciev'd.

VI

The desires & perceptions of man untaught by any thing but organs of
sense, must be limited to objects of sense.

---

1. At the bottom of the frontispiece, in reverse lettering, "The Author & Printer W Blake" is barely leg-
ible in a few copies. Blake's own layout, resembling that of *All Religions Are One*, is normalized here.

[b]

I

Mans perceptions are not bounded by organs of perception; he percieves more than sense (tho' ever so acute) can discover.

II

Reason or the ratio of all we have already known is not the same that it shall be when we know more.

[III is missing]

IV

The bounded is loathed by its possessor. The same dull round even of a universe would soon become a mill with complicated wheels.[2]

V

If the many become the same as the few, when possess'd, More! More! is the cry of a mistaken soul, less than All cannot satisfy Man.

VI

If any could desire what he is incapable of possessing, despair must be his eternal lot.

VII

The desire of Man being Infinite the possession is Infinite & himself Infinite

Conclusion,

If it were not for the Poetic or Prophetic character, the Philosophic & Experimental would soon be at the ratio of all things & stand still, unable to do other than repeat the same dull round over again.

Application.

He who sees the Infinite in all things sees God. He who sees the Ratio only sees himself only.

Therefore

God becomes as we are, that we may be as he is.[3]

---

2. Although Blake seems at this point to associate the Infinite with the unbounded, in his *Descriptive Catalogue* of 1809 he adds the clarification that a "bounding line" in art and life is necessary to distinguish true vision from "the indefinite" (p. 431 herein).
3. Damon, *Blake Dictionary*, cites church fathers Athanasius and Irenaeus and reformer John Calvin, who use the past tense; in Blake, "the act is eternal and is always going on" (402).

SONGS OF INNOCENCE AND
OF EXPERIENCE (1789–94)

In Blake's *Songs*, the meaning of each gemlike illuminated page expands in relation to its many contexts; each poem, arresting in itself, means even more, and
means differently, when read as a text-design unit, and when read with other
poems. But with which others? In 1785, three of these songs popped up without titles in a zany satirical fragment known as *An Island in the Moon* (p. 360
herein), sung by characters named Obtuse Angle ("Holy Thursday"), Mrs. Nannicantipot ("Nurse's Song"), and Quid the Cynic ("The Little Boy Lost"). Then
these same three songs appeared with twenty others in the first printing of
Songs of Innocence in 1789. The impression made by all twenty-three songs
changed again whenever Blake rearranged the pages and again, in 1794, when
he paired *Songs of Innocence* with its darker companion or "contrary" collection *Songs of Experience* (also published separately) under a comprehensive
title page. Even after Blake began printing *Songs of Innocence and of Experience* as a single book in 1795, he continued to offer both *Innocence* and *Experience* on their own as late as 1818. In all, Blake produced some twenty-two
copies of *Innocence* alone, four of *Experience* alone, and twenty-seven copies
of the combined *Songs* (last printed in 1826, the year before his death), making this collection by far the most widely circulated of any of his writings.

As contexts multiply, interpretive possibilities for each poem expand almost
alarmingly. How are the words set visually amid figures above, below, surrounding, and interpenetrating the text? How is the whole text-design unit set
within the book? Is it part of a two-page spread? How does it resonate against
the preceding or following illuminated poem or full-page design? What does
the poem reveal about the "state" the speaker is in, Innocence or Experience?
Does the poem have a contrary or complementary poem in the companion volume? What is its dramatic situation, whether spoken by a specific character
like the Black Boy or in the larger voice of the presiding figure who opens each
series, the Piper or the Bard? Does it contribute to a broad narrative or thematic pattern interlinking all the songs? What is its position—especially with
respect to contiguous poems—in each of the different arrangements of *Songs*
established by Blake himself? Does it have literary or visual sources and
analogs in the work of other artists? What are its political, social, psychological, theological, philosophical, and (perhaps) biographical implications?
And—for those interested in studying variations among versions or editions of
Songs in printed or electronic facsimiles—how does a given rendering of an
illuminated page contribute to the distinctive character of the particular copy
of *Songs* in which it appears?

On the comprehensive title page that transforms two separate books into
complementary sections of a single work (color plate 1), Blake provided an
important framework for interpreting *Songs of Innocence and of Experience*
as a whole. At the bottom of the page, Adam and Eve are shown in the fiery
throes of their expulsion from Paradise. But above the flames the upward-
soaring bird and the tiny figures on the word "SONGS" offer other perspectives. The explanatory subtitle, "Shewing the Two Contrary States of the
Human Soul," affirms the importance of perspective in both volumes; in each
series, the spiritual state of each speaker, or singer, colors his or her perceptions.

On the title page of the *Innocence* series (p. 13 herein), the stage is set for a
world in which Piper, child, lamb, flower, mother, and shepherd will be the central figures: under a protective tree, a maternal teacher turns her book to encourage a boy and girl to read; and, within the title lettering above, a miniature piper

and others pursue their own innocent activities. To be innocent, though, is not always to be ignorant of the facts that girls and boys get lost, or have to live in orphanages or on the street, or are sold as slaves or chimney sweeps. The possibility of change and even of corruption always impinges: spring and summer die into winter, children should go indoors at nightfall, and shepherds are needed because there are wolves. Yet the primal state of innocence is a clear vision of the way life ought to be and indeed can be for many children and for gentle-hearted adults. These invincible innocents, despite their circumstances, retain their spiritual resilience and fresh outlook; with joy and contentment they love their enemies and dream of a better world. The cloud-borne child who inspires the "song about a Lamb" in the "Introduction" to *Innocence* offers an exemplary response to the whole volume of seemingly simple songs: he laughs on first hearing, then weeps, then weeps with joy. Similarly, the adult reader, especially after several re-readings, neither denies the appearance and reality of the innocent soul's happiness nor explains away signs of encroaching woe.

The voice that introduces, and in late copies also concludes, the *Experience* series is that of the Ancient Bard who "Present, Past, & Future sees." From this prophet's-eye perspective—which encompasses both Innocence and Experience not only from above but from within, as lived and breathed by the various singers—the fallen condition need not be permanent, if Earth could only respond to the divine summons to "return." But in the next poem, "Earth's Answer," the understandably bitter and defiant Earth strikes the keynote for the whole volume. Lacking the Bard's omniscient perspective, she voices the grief and despair of any "lapsed soul"—most of us, much of the time. For the singers who share her worldview, the state of Experience is so dark and self-enclosed that there appears no way out. The dominant images are of dark forests, sick flowers, threatening beasts, prematurely blighted and embittered children, the black and bloody city, and the poisonous dead Tree of Mystery that grows in the human brain. In this diseased and deathly world, parents and guardians, in league with "God & his Priest & his King," neglect, reject, or stifle the spirit of the young, under an evil system in which soldiers and harlots are as victimized as boys and girls. Yet here and there salutary bursts of energy break out in cries of the oppressed, as in the Chimney Sweeper's bitter exposé of the power structure that exploits him and the Little Vagabond's mischievous delight in proposing the alehouse as an alternative site of worship. Even on the gloomy title page of *Experience* (p. 29 herein), an airborne boy and girl fly and dance above the scene of mourning and transcend the curse of death visited upon Adam and Eve as they are driven from Eden on the title page of the combined *Songs of Innocence and of Experience*.

The relationship between Innocence and Experience, as contrary aspects of the human condition and as cycles of songs, is one not of static contrast but of many kinds of shifting tensions. The distinction between states is especially clear in contrasting poems with identical titles, such as "Holy Thursday," or those with sharply opposed titles, such as "The Lamb" and "The Tyger." Borderline characters under the pressure of transition, either barely clinging to innocent fantasies or fighting their way out of experiential delusions, reveal varying degrees of involvement in one state or the other. Large or small design elements may remind viewers of the contrary state beyond the speaker's range of perception, especially if there appears to be a striking mismatch between text and design: does the pictured Tyger, for example, belong in Experience or Innocence? And whole poems may take on new implications in the context of a different state. As Blake continued to produce *Songs*, he rearranged pages both within volumes and between them, changing the implications of "The School Boy," "The Voice of the Ancient Bard," "The Little Girl Lost," and "The Little Girl Found" by transferring them from *Innocence* to *Experience*. As early as 1795 he added a new poem, "To Tirzah," to *Experience*, a work that anticipates a major character and associated themes of much later epic-length poems.

In 1789, when Blake published *Songs of Innocence*, he was no thirty-two-year-old naif who took childlike joy in a nursery world, nor did he become, when he published *Songs of Experience* separately in 1793, a thirty-six-year-old cynic obsessed with suffering and oppression. In the productive period of 1789–93 Blake also published *The Book of Thel*, *The Marriage of Heaven and Hell*, *Visions of the Daughters of Albion*, *For Children: The Gates of Paradise*, and *America*. In these and later works he continued to explore themes related to the "contrary states." For example, the narrator of *The Marriage of Heaven and Hell* proclaims that "Without Contraries is no progression," and *Milton* and other poems distinguish between Contraries and Negations and between States and Individuals. Individuals are real and eternal; states are temporary conditions of error or illusion through which an individual may pass. In his own voice, Blake declared that "whenever any Individual Rejects Error & Embraces Truth a Last Judgment passes upon that Individual" (p. 436 herein). In *Songs*, Blake left it up to the reader to weigh the claims of Innocence and Experience against each other and to arrive, perhaps, at a larger way of seeing the world, neither naively nor cynically, that encompasses both states.

Blake's contemporary reputation as a poet (as opposed to a graphic artist) rested almost entirely on *Songs of Innocence and of Experience*: Wordsworth, Coleridge, and Lamb (who had heard "The Tyger" recited orally) admired individual poems; B. H. Malkin, father of one of Blake's pupils, published a selection in a memoir (1806); Henry Crabb Robinson translated and published several in a German magazine (1811); a few were anthologized in Britain. For Coleridge's comments, see p. 498 herein. For scholarly critical analyses of *Songs*, see Robert F. Gleckner, *The Piper and the Bard* (1959); Hazard Adams, *William Blake: A Reading of the Shorter Poems* (1963); D. G. Gillham, *Blake's Contrary States* (1966); Eban Bass, "Songs of Innocence and of Experience: The Thrust of Design" in *Blake's Visionary Forms Dramatic* (1970), ed. Erdman and Grant; Zachary Leader, *Reading Blake's Songs* (1981); Heather Glen, *Vision and Disenchantment* (1983); Stanley Gardner, *Blake's Innocence and Experience Retraced* (1986); Harold Pagliaro, *Selfhood and Redemption in Blake's Songs* (1987); and Michael Phillips, *The Creation of the Songs from Manuscript Draft to Illuminated Printing* (2000). *William Blake's Songs of Innocence and of Experience* (1987), ed. Harold Bloom, assembles previously published essays. *Approaches to Teaching Blake's Songs of Innocence and of Experience* (1989), ed. Robert F. Gleckner and Mark L. Greenberg, though in part factually outdated, remains of interest to students as well as teachers. There are even more articles on individual poems (some cited in the footnotes) than on the collection as a whole.

After 1818, in seven of the last eight printings of *Songs*, Blake arrived at a stable page sequence. A convenient way to explore shifts in meaning produced by his rearrangements of pages is to use the "next" and "previous" arrows of the online edition of *Songs* in the Blake Digital Text Project directed by Nelson Hilton at the University of Georgia (www.english.uga.edu/wblake/). The online William Blake Archive (www.blakearchive.org), ed. Morris Eaves, Robert Essick, and Joseph Viscomi, makes it possible to compare superb digital images of multiple copies on one screen, zoom in on details, and search for recurring visual motifs throughout Blake's illuminated oeuvre; the archive also provides transcriptions of the text and suggestions for further reading. An essential resource is Andrew Lincoln's generously annotated photographic facsimile edition of *Songs* Copy W, a late copy, volume 2 (1991) in the Blake Trust series; see also the beautiful hand-painted facsimiles in the older Blake Trust/Trianon Press series, ed. Geoffrey Keynes: an early version of *Songs of Innocence* alone (1954, Copy B) and a late version of the combined *Songs* (1955, Copy Z; photographically reproduced by

Orion Press, 1967; reprinted by Oxford University Press, 1971). From the same copies, Dover Press offers inexpensive reproductions of *Innocence* B (1971) and of the *Experience* portion of the combined *Songs* Z (1984). Images of Princeton University's Copy U, digitized by the University of Michigan, may be viewed online (catalog.princeton.edu): search on the book's title and click on the item dated 1794. Stanley Gardner, *The Tyger The Lamb and the Terrible Desart* (1998), reproduces Harvard University's Copy I and uncolored Copy b, printed by a friend after Blake's death.

It is easy to become overwhelmed by all these resources, especially if they lead to premature fretting over textual and pictorial minutiae. After all, Blake sold *Songs* one book at a time, to individuals, with no notion that anyone would someday compare copies image by image and line by line. Any single version of *Songs* offers more than enough to fill the mind with consideration of each illuminated poem, as it appears in any of its many possible contexts.

Our base text is Copy Z (1826 Library of Congress), closely compared with uncolored Copy b (posthumous) and with online Blake Archive facsimiles of Copies C (1794), AA (1826), and R (Blake's own copy, completed in 1795, touched up from time to time, and sold to his friend John Linnell in 1822). As noted in "Textual Technicalities," the erratic capitalization, spelling, and punctuation are Blake's, except for the occasional editorial period inserted to mark the end of a poem that lacks concluding punctuation.

SONGS Of *INNOCENCE* and Of *EXPERIENCE**   ⟦1⟧

Shewing the Two Contrary States of the Human Soul

SONGS OF *INNOCENCE*   ⟦3⟧

1789
The Author & Printer W Blake

Introduction   ⟦4⟧

Piping down the valleys wild
Piping songs of pleasant glee
On a cloud I saw a child.
And he laughing said to me.

Pipe a song about a Lamb;[1]   5
So I piped with merry chear,

---

* See color plate 1. This version of the title page (Princeton, Copy U), c.1818, is the only one in which the bird carries something in its beak, and it is one of the few in which the mouths of Adam and Eve are open, as if to protest their expulsion from Eden.
1. The carefree Piper (see design), a traditional figure in pastoral idylls, is inspired to become a singer, then a writer, of happy songs with profound undertones. Many songs of the innocent state express Christian themes in a natural setting or in images drawn from nature, as a child might understand them, apart from the institution of the Church. The "song about a Lamb"—foreshadowing lambs or lamblike children in "The Lamb," "Night," "The Little Black Boy," "The Chimney Sweeper," and "Holy Thursday"—calls to mind Jesus, Lamb of God (John 1:29, 1 Peter 1:19, Revelation 5:12), as the Passover lamb of Exodus 12:5, interpreted through Isaiah 53:7.

Piper pipe that song again—
So I piped, he wept to hear.

Drop thy pipe thy happy pipe,
Sing thy songs of happy chear,   10
So I sung the same again—
While he wept with joy to hear.

Piper sit thee down and write
In a book that all may read—
So he vanish'd from my sight,   15
And I pluck'd a hollow reed.

And I made a rural pen,
And I stain'd the water clear,
And I wrote my happy songs,
Every child may joy to hear.   20

The Shepherd. 5

How sweet is the Shepherds sweet lot,
From the morn to the evening he strays;
He shall follow his sheep all the day
And his tongue shall be filled with praise.

For he hears the lambs innocent call, 5
And he hears the ewes tender reply,
He is watchful while they are in peace,
For they know when their Shepherd is nigh.

The Ecchoing Green 6

The Sun does arise
And make happy the skies.
The merry bells ring
To welcome the Spring.
The sky-lark and thrush, 5
The birds of the bush,
Sing louder around.

To the bells chearful sound.
While our sports shall be seen
On the Ecchoing Green.   10

Old John with white hair
Does laugh away care,
Sitting under the oak,
Among the old folk,   7
They laugh at our play.   15
And soon they all say,
Such such were the joys.
When we all girls & boys.
In our youth-time were seen.
On the Ecchoing Green.   20

Till the little ones weary
No more can be merry
The sun does descend,

And our sports have an end:
Round the laps of their mothers.   25
Many sisters and brothers,
Like birds in their nest,
Are ready for rest:
And sport no more seen,
On the darkening Green.   30

The Lamb   8

Little Lamb who made thee
Dost thou know who made thee
Gave thee life & bid thee feed,
By the stream & o'er the mead;
Gave thee clothing of delight,   5
Softest clothing wooly bright;
Gave thee such a tender voice,
Making all the vales rejoice:
   Little Lamb who made thee
   Dost thou know who made thee   10

Little Lamb I'll tell thee,
Little Lamb I'll tell thee:
He is called by thy name,
For he calls himself a Lamb:[2]
He is meek & he is mild,   15
He became a little child:
I a child & thou a lamb,
We are called by his name.
   Little Lamb God bless thee.
   Little Lamb God bless thee.   20

2. Glen, *Vision and Disenchantment* (1983), 23–25, analyzes complex echoes of Charles Wesley's popular children's hymn, "Gentle Jesus, Meek and Mild." For a comprehensive discussion of Blake's use of popular hymns, citing valuable previous work, see Nelson Hilton in *Blake in the Nineties* (1999), ed. Clark and Worrall.

The Little Black Boy.   9

My mother bore me in the southern wild,
And I am black, but O! my soul is white.
White as an angel is the English child:
But I am black as if bereav'd of light.

My mother taught me underneath a tree   5
And sitting down before the heat of day.
She took me on her lap and kissed me,
And pointing to the east began to say.

Look on the rising sun: there God does live
And gives his light, and gives his heat away.   10
And flowers and trees and beasts and men recieve
Comfort in morning joy in the noon day.

And we are put on earth a little space,
That we may learn to bear the beams of love,
And these black bodies and this sun-burnt face   15
Is but a cloud, and like a shady grove.

For when our souls have learn'd the heat to bear   10
The cloud will vanish we shall hear his voice.
Saying: come out from the grove my love & care,
And round my golden tent like lambs rejoice.   20

Thus did my mother say and kissed me.
And thus I say to little English boy,
When I from black and he from white cloud free,
And round the tent of God like lambs we joy:

Ill shade him from the heat till he can bear,   25
To lean in joy upon our fathers knee.
And then I'll stand and stroke his silver hair,
And be like him and he will then love me.[3]

3. In 1788–89, as Blake prepared the first edition of *Innocence*, Parliament was holding hearings on the lucrative British involvement in the slave trade (finally outlawed in 1807; slavery itself was legal until 1833). On the complex ironies of the child's situation, as he struggles to reconcile his mother's teachings with the Christianity of his masters, see Alan Richardson, *Papers on Language and Literature* 26 (1990), 233–48. Damon (1924) notes imagery from Isaac Watts's 1709 hymn: "Nor is

For when our souls have learnd the heat to bear
The cloud will vanish we shall hear his voice.
Saying: come out from the grove my love & care,
And round my golden tent like lambs rejoice.

Thus did my mother say and kissed me,
And thus I say to little English boy.
When I from black and he from white cloud free,
And round the tent of God like lambs we joy:

Ill shade him from the heat till he can bear,
To lean in joy upon our fathers knee
And then Ill stand and stroke his silver hair.
And be like him and he will then love me.

The Blossom.   11

Merry Merry Sparrow
Under leaves so green
A happy Blossom
Sees you swift as arrow
Seek your cradle narrow   5
Near my Bosom.

Pretty Pretty Robin
Under leaves so green
A happy Blossom
Hears you sobbing sobbing   10
Pretty Pretty Robin
Near my Bosom.

---

my soul refined enough / To bear the beaming of his love." In early copies of the final design with
the Good Shepherd, both boys are lightly colored; in other copies, both are darker, of indeterminate heritage; in some late copies (V, W), the Black Boy retains his sharply contrasting original
color. Myra Glazer, *Colby Library Quarterly* 16 (1980), 220–36, discusses other variations.

The Chimney Sweeper $\boxed{12}$

When my mother died I was very young,
And my father sold me while yet my tongue,
Could scarcely cry weep weep weep weep.[4]
So your chimneys I sweep & in soot I sleep.

Theres little Tom Dacre,[5] who cried when his head   5
That curl'd like a lambs back, was shav'd, so I said.
Hush Tom never mind it, for when your head's bare,
You know that the soot cannot spoil your white hair.

And so he was quiet, & that very night,
As Tom was a sleeping he had such a sight,   10
That thousands of sweepers Dick, Joe, Ned & Jack
Were all of them lock'd up in coffins of black,

And by came an Angel who had a bright key
And he open'd the coffins & set them all free.
Then down a green plain leaping laughing they run   15
And wash in a river and shine in the Sun.

Then naked & white, all their bags left behind,
They rise upon clouds, and sport in the wind.
And the Angel told Tom if he'd be a good boy,
He'd have God for his father & never want joy.   20

And so Tom awoke and we rose in the dark
And got with our bags & our brushes to work.
Tho' the morning was cold, Tom was happy & warm
So if all do their duty, they need not fear harm.

The Little Boy lost[6] $\boxed{13}$

Father, father, where are you going
O do not walk so fast.
Speak father, speak to your little boy
Or else I shall be lost,

---

4. The child's ironically appropriate pronunciation of the street cry "Sweep!" In *Blake* (1966), ed. Frye, Martin K. Nurmi describes the sweeps' misery: hazards of suffocation in small coal-fire chimneys, skin permanently blackened with soot, legs bowed by the weight of heavy bags, and cancer of the scrotum. Children could be apprenticed to master sweeps at the age of five and were cast out in their early teens, when they grew too large for their claustrophobic tasks.
5. Tom's surname, the name of an almshouse (see map), probably indicates that he was a foundling. The older sweep's conclusion has generated much discussion: does this bleak notion of an acceptable life reflect limits of the child's viewpoint or of the state of Innocence itself? The same question applies to the last line of "The Little Black Boy."
6. Cf. the early version in *Island in the Moon*, p. 375 herein.

The night was dark no father was there   5
The child was wet with dew.
The mire was deep, & the child did weep
And away the vapour flew.

The Little Boy Found   `14`

The little boy lost in the lonely fen,
Led by the wand'ring light,
Began to cry, but God ever nigh,
Appeard like his father in white.

He kissed the child & by the hand led   5
And to his mother brought,
Who in sorrow pale, thro' the lonely dale
Her little boy weeping sought.

`15`

Laughing Song,

When the green woods laugh with the voice of joy
And the dimpling stream runs laughing by,
When the air does laugh with our merry wit,
And the green hill laughs with the noise of it.

When the meadows laugh with lively green   5
And the grasshopper laughs in the merry scene,
When Mary and Susan and Emily,
With their sweet round mouths sing Ha, Ha, He.

When the painted birds laugh in the shade
Where our table with cherries and nuts is spread   10
Come live & be merry and join with me,
To sing the sweet chorus of Ha, Ha, He.

A CRADLE SONG[7]

16

Sweet dreams form a shade.
O'er my lovely infants head,
Sweet dreams of pleasant streams,
By happy silent moony beams.

Sweet sleep with soft down.   5
Weave thy brows an infant crown.
Sweet sleep Angel mild,
Hover o'er my happy child.

Sweet smiles in the night,
Hover over my delight.   10
Sweet smiles Mothers smiles
All the livelong night beguiles.

Sweet moans, dovelike sighs,
Chase not slumber from thy eyes,
Sweet moans, sweeter smiles.   15
All the dovelike moans beguiles.

Sleep sleep happy child.
All creation slept and smil'd,
Sleep sleep, happy sleep,
While o'er thee thy mother weep   20

7. Modeled on "Cradle Hymn" in Watts's *Divine and Moral Songs* (1715), as discussed by Vivian de
Sola Pinto in *The Divine Vision* (1957) and Martha Winburn England in *Hymns Unbidden* (1966).
Blake's draft for a contrary song of the same title in his Notebook (p. 383 herein) was not published
in *Experience*.

Sweet babe in thy face.
Holy image I can trace.
Sweet babe once like thee.
Thy maker lay and wept for me

Wept for me for thee for all,   17 25
When he was an infant small.
Thou his image ever see.
Heavenly face that smiles on thee.

Smiles on thee on me on all,
Who became an infant small,   30
Infant smiles are his own smiles.
Heaven & earth to peace beguiles.

The Divine Image.   18

To Mercy Pity Peace and Love,
All pray in their distress:

And to these virtues of delight
Return their thankfulness.

For Mercy Pity Peace and Love,   5
Is God our father dear:
And Mercy Pity Peace and Love
Is Man his child and care.

For Mercy has a human heart
Pity, a human face: 10
And Love, the human form divine.[8]
And Peace, the human dress.

Then every man of every clime,
That prays in his distress,
Prays to the human form divine   15
Love Mercy Pity Peace.

And all must love the human form,
In heathen, turk or jew.[9]
Where Mercy, Love & Pity dwell
There God is dwelling too.   20

19

HOLY THURSDAY

Twas on a Holy Thursday their innocent faces clean
The children walking two & two in red & blue & green
Grey headed beadles walkd before with wands as white as snow
Till into the high dome of Pauls they like Thames waters flow[1]

8. In Pope's translation of Homer's *Odyssey* 10.278, "the human form divine" (echoing Milton's "human face divine" in *Paradise Lost* 3.44) vanishes when Circe changes men into swine. Cf. Michael J. Tolley, *Blake Newsletter* 2:4 (1969); and Paul Yoder in *Romantic Generations* (2001), ed. Ghislaine McDayter, Guinn Batten, and Barry Milligan.

9. In another Watts hymn, "Praise for the Gospel," as noted by Lincoln (1991), the singer is thankful "That I was born of *Christian* race, / And not a *Heathen*, or a *Jew*." In countering such attitudes, Blake adds "turk," which in his time was equivalent to "Muslim." Cf. his celebration of his irreverent friend Fuseli, nominally a Christian, as "both Turk & Jew" ("English Encouragement of Art"). Blake engraved a contrary song by this title for *Experience* (n. 8, p. 42 herein) but decided to replace it with "The Human Abstract."

1. Throughout the eighteenth century, Londoners thronged the streets to watch as many as six thousand destitute children in school uniforms march two by two from their charity schools (see map) to sing at annual springtime services thanking their benefactors; after 1782, the event took place in St. Paul's Cathedral. See David Fairer, *Eighteenth-Century Studies* 35:4 (2002), 535–62, building on work of Gleckner, *Modern Language Notes* 71 (1956), Glen (1983), and Gardner (1998).

O what a multitude they seemd these flowers of London town   5
Seated in companies they sit with radiance all their own
The hum of multitudes was there but multitudes of lambs
Thousands of little boys & girls raising their innocent hands

Now like a mighty wind[2] they raise to heaven the voice of song
Or like harmonious thunderings the seats of heaven among   10
Beneath them sit the aged men wise guardians of the poor
Then cherish pity, lest you drive an angel from your door.[3]

Night   20

The sun descending in the west.
The evening star does shine.
The birds are silent in their nest,
And I must seek for mine,
The moon like a flower,   5
In heavens high bower;
With silent delight,
Sits and smiles on the night.

Farewell green fields and happy groves,
Where flocks have took delight;   10
Where lambs have nibbled, silent moves
The feet of angels bright;
Unseen they pour blessing,
And joy without ceasing,
On each bud and blossom,   15
And each sleeping bosom.

They look in every thoughtless nest,
Where birds are coverd warm;
They visit caves of every beast,
To keep them all from harm: 20
If they see any weeping,
That should have been sleeping
They pour sleep on their head
And sit down by their bed.

When wolves and tygers howl for prey   21   25
They pitying stand and weep;

2. Recalls the Holy Spirit's presence in Acts 2:2.
3. Alludes to a motivation for charity: "for thereby some have entertained angels unawares" (Hebrews 13:2).

Seeking to drive their thirst away,
And keep them from the sheep.
But if they rush dreadful:
The angels most heedful,   30
Recieve each mild spirit,
New worlds to inherit.

And there the lions ruddy eyes,
Shall flow with tears of gold:
And pitying the tender cries,   35
And walking round the fold:
Saying: wrath by his meekness
And by his health, sickness,
Is driven away,
From our immortal day.   40

And now beside thee bleating lamb,
I can lie down and sleep;[4]
Or think on him who bore thy name
Graze after thee and weep.
For wash'd in lifes river,[5]   45
My bright mane for ever,
Shall shine like the gold,
As I guard o'er the fold.

Spring   22

Sound the Flute!
Now it's mute.
Birds delight
Day and Night.
Nightingale   5
In the dale
Lark in Sky
Merrily
Merrily Merrily to welcome in the Year

Little Boy   10
Full of joy.
Little Girl   23
Sweet and small,
Cock does crow
So do you.   15
Merry voice
Infant noise
Merrily Merrily to welcome in the Year

Little Lamb
Here I am,   20

4. Isaiah prophesies that the lion and lamb shall lie down together (11:6) and predators shall graze (65:25).
5. Prophesied in Ezekiel 47:9,12 and Revelation 22:1–2.

Come and lick
My white neck.
Let me pull
Your soft Wool.
Let me kiss   25
Your soft face.
Merrily Merrily we welcome in the Year.

Nurse's Song   24

When the voices of children are heard on the green
And laughing is heard on the hill,
My heart is at rest within my breast
And every thing else is still

Then come home my children, the sun is gone down   5
And the dews of night arise
Come come leave off play, and let us away
Till the morning appears in the skies
No no let us play, for it is yet day
And we cannot go to sleep   10
Besides in the sky, the little birds fly
And the hills are all coverd with sheep

Well well go & play till the light fades away
And then go home to bed
The little ones leaped & shouted & laugh'd   15
And all the hills ecchoed.

Infant Joy   25

I have no name
I am but two days old[6]—

---

6. Usually infants were baptized and given their Christian names three or more days after birth. On
this child's self-naming in the mother's imagination, see Stanley Gardner, *Blake's Innocence and
Experience Retraced* (1986), and Thomas Dilworth, *English Language Notes* 38 (2000), 43–47. For
the setting, see color plate 2.

What shall I call thee?
I happy am
Joy is my name,—
Sweet joy befall thee!   5

Pretty joy!
Sweet joy but two days old,
Sweet joy I call thee;
Thou dost smile.   10
I sing the while
Sweet joy befall thee.

A Dream   26

Once a dream did weave a shade,
O'er my Angel-guarded bed,
That an Emmet[7] lost it's way
Where on grass methought I lay.

Troubled wilderd and folorn   5
Dark benighted travel-worn,
Over many a tangled spray,
All heart-broke I heard her say.

O my children! do they cry
Do they hear their father sigh.   10
Now they look abroad to see,
Now return and weep for me.

Pitying I drop'd a tear;
But I saw a glow-worm near:
Who replied. What wailing wight.   15
Calls the watchman of the night.

I am set to light the ground,
While the beetle goes his round:
Follow now the beetles hum,
Little wanderer hie thee home.   20

On Anothers Sorrow   27

Can I see anothers woe,
And not be in sorrow too.
Can I see anothers grief.
And not seek for kind relief.

7. Ant. In this child's dreamworld, emmets live in two-parent families, not colonies. On mother fig-
ures in *Songs*, see Norma A. Greco, *Romanticism Past and Present* 10 (1986); Johnson in
Approaches (1989), ed. Gleckner and Greenberg; and Harriet Kramer Linkin in *Blake, Politics, and
History* (1998), ed. Di Salvo, Rosso, and Hobson.

Can I see a falling tear.   5
And not feel my sorrows share,
Can a father see his child,
Weep, nor be with sorrow fill'd.

Can a mother sit and hear
An infant groan an infant fear—   10
No no never can it be.
Never never can it be.

And can he who smiles on all[8]
Hear the wren with sorrows small.
Hear the small birds grief & care   15
Hear the woes that infants bear—

And not sit beside the nest
Pouring pity in their breast.
And not sit the cradle near
Weeping tear on infants tear.   20

And not sit both night & day,
Wiping all our tears away,[9]
O! no never can it be,
Never never can it be.

He doth give his joy to all,   25
He becomes an infant small.
He becomes a man of woe
He doth feel the sorrow too.

Think not, thou canst sigh a sigh,
And thy maker is not by.   30
Think not, thou canst weep a tear,
And thy maker is not near.

O! he gives to us his joy,
That our grief he may destroy
Till our grief is fled & gone   35
He doth sit by us and moan.[1]

8. In *Thel* 4/2:19, this is the Lilly's epithet for her heavenly visitor.
9. As promised in Revelation 7:17, 21:4.
1. In the "final order" of the plates followed here, *Innocence* ends with this poem: the "Sorrow" of "Another" in the title and the "moan" of the "maker" at the conclusion foreshadow the world of experience. But in the design (not reproduced), the tiny piper at the lower right reprises his signal appearances in the frontispiece and title page of *Innocence* (pp. 11–12 herein).

28

SONGS of EXPERIENCE   29

1794
The Author & Printer W Blake

Introduction.   30

Hear the voice of the Bard!
Who Present, Past, & Future sees[2]
Whose ears have heard,
The Holy Word,[3]
That walk'd among the ancient trees.   5

2. In *Jerusalem* **15**:8–9 the artisan-prophet Los, trying to awaken Albion, sees "the Past, Present & Future, existing all at once / Before me."
3. In John 1:1 Jesus is identified as the Word. In *Paradise Lost* 10.71–108, the Son rather than the Father calls Adam (discussed in Frye's 1957 commentary on "Introduction"; rpt. *Blake: A Collection of Critical Essays* [1966]). Dennis M. Welch, *English Studies* 76:3 (1995), 238–52, countering Michael Ackland, *Studies in Romanticism* (1980) and others, explores this point as a touchstone for interpreting such controversial poems as "The Tyger."

Calling the lapsed Soul
And weeping[4] in the evening dew:
That[5] might controll,
The starry pole;[6]
And fallen fallen light renew!   10

O Earth O Earth return![7]
Arise from out the dewy grass;
Night is worn,
And the morn
Rises from the slumberous mass.   15

4. Perhaps alluding to Jesus' tears over Lazarus (John 11:35) and his lament over Jerusalem (Matthew 23:37).
5. Ambiguous antecedent. Is it the Soul or the Word who could reverse the fallen state if only it chose to?
6. In Pope's translation of Homer's *Iliad*, Jupiter boasts: "Who shall the sovereign of the skies control? / Not all the gods that crown the starry pole" (8:472–73). In Edward Young's *The Last Day* 3.10, "the starry pole" is the muse's vantage point.
7. Echoing Jeremiah 22:29: "O earth, earth, earth, hear the word of the Lord" and Spenser's *Hymn of Heavenly Love*, 218–25: "Then rouze thyself, O Earth, out of thy soil . . . / And read through love His mercies manifold."

Turn away no more:
Why wilt thou turn away
The starry floor
The watry shore
Is giv'n thee till the break of day.[8]   20

EARTH'S Answer.   31

Earth rais'd up her head,
From the darkness dread & drear.
Her light fled;
Stony dread!
And her locks cover'd with grey despair,   5

Prison'd on watry shore
Starry Jealousy does keep my den[9]
Cold and hoar
Weeping o'er
I hear the Father of the ancient men   10

Selfish father of men
Cruel jealous selfish fear[1]
Can delight
Chain'd in night
The virgins of youth and morning bear,   15

Does spring hide its joy
When buds and blossoms grow?
Does the sower?
Sow by night?
Or the plowman in darkness plow?   20

Break this heavy chain,
That does freeze my bones around
Selfish! vain!

8. In Jeremiah 5:22 (cf. Job 38:8,11), the shore is a providential limit to the sea. Whether the stars
   form a floor or a ceiling as the Earth rotates is a matter of perspective.
9. Benighted Earth, personified as female but speaking for all of humanity, experiences her condition,
   limited by the "floor" and "shore," as imprisonment by an all-powerful paternalistic oppressor.
1. She hears the Holy Word's loving plea to "return" as the cold command of a remote, unfeeling
   "Father," the "jealous God" of the Ten Commandments (Exodus 20:5)

Eternal bane!
That free Love with bondage bound.[2]   25

The CLOD & the PEBBLE $\boxed{32}$

Love seeketh not Itself to please,
Nor for itself hath any care;
But for another gives its ease,
And builds a Heaven in Hells despair.

    So sung a little Clod of Clay,   5
    Trodden with the cattles feet:
    But a Pebble of the brook,
    Warbled out these metres meet.

Love seeketh only Self to please,
To bind another to its delight: 10
Joys in anothers loss of ease,
And builds a Hell in Heavens despite.[3]

HOLY THURSDAY[4] $\boxed{33}$

Is this a holy thing to see,
In a rich and fruitful land,
Babes reducd to misery
Fed with cold and usurous hand?

Is that trembling cry a song?   5
Can it be a song of joy?
And so many children poor?
It is a land of poverty!

And their sun does never shine.
And their fields are bleak & bare.   10
And their ways are fill'd with thorns
It is eternal winter there.

For where-e'er the sun does shine,
And where-e'er the rain does fall:
Babe can never hunger there,   15
Nor poverty the mind appall.

2. Understanding this pair of opening poems is complicated by perspectives introduced in the designs, showing a nude female, presumably Earth, stretched out on a floating couch ("Introduction") and a serpent with head raised and mouth wide open, undulating along the ground ("Earth's Answer").
3. The Clod's song recalls Saint Paul's praise of selfless love in 1 Corinthians 13; the Pebble's recalls Satan's defiant assertion in *Paradise Lost* 1.254–255: "The mind is its own place, and in itself / Can make a Heaven of Hell, a Hell of Heaven." Michael Ferber defends the Clod in *Prophetic Character* (2003), ed. Gourlay.
4. See n. 1, p. 22 herein.

The Little Girl Lost[5]   31   34

In futurity
I prophetic see.
That the earth from sleep,
(Grave the sentence deep)[6]

Shall arise and seek   5
For her maker meek:
And the desart wild
Become a garden mild.[7]

In the southern clime,
Where the summers prime,   10
Never fades away;
Lovely Lyca[8] lay.

Seven summers old
Lovely Lyca told,
She had wanderd long,   15
Hearing wild birds song.

Sweet sleep come to me
Underneath this tree;
Do father, mother weep.—
Where can Lyca sleep.   20

Lost in desart wild
Is your little child.
How can Lyca sleep.
If her mother weep.

5. This poem and "The Little Girl Found" first appeared in *Innocence*. In the context of *Experience*, the first two stanzas, set apart from the rest of the poem by a snake on a vine, are in the voice of the Bard of "Introduction."
6. A serious pun on the severity of Earth's suffering, the solemnity of the bardic voice, and the strenuousness of the engraving process.
7. Cf. Isaiah 35:1: "The desert shall rejoice, and blossom as the rose."
8. A mythological name not used elsewhere in Blake's published writings, perhaps derived from "wolf" in Latin. On the complex associations of Lyca's prolonged sleep, naked, under the lion king's protection and the broader motif of little girls lost, see Irene Chayes in *Blake* (1966), ed. Frye.

If her heart does ake,   25
Then let Lyca wake;
If my mother sleep,
Lyca shall not weep.

Frowning frowning night,
O'er this desart bright,   30
Let thy moon arise,
While I close my eyes.

Sleeping Lyca lay;
While the beasts of prey,
Come from caverns deep,   35
View'd the maid asleep

The kingly lion stood
And the virgin view'd,
Then he gambold round
O'er the hallowd ground: 40

Leopards, tygers play,   ⟦35⟧
Round her as she lay;
While the lion old,
Bow'd his mane of gold,

And her bosom lick.   45
And upon her neck,
From his eyes of flame,
Ruby tears there came;

While the lioness,
Loos'd her slender dress,   50
And naked they convey'd
To caves the sleeping maid.

The Little Girl Found

All the night in woe,
Lyca's parents go:
Over vallies deep,
While the desarts weep.

Tired and woe-begone,   5
Hoarse with making moan:
Arm in arm seven days,
They trac'd the desart ways.

Seven nights they sleep,
Among shadows deep: 10
And dream they see their child
Starv'd in desart wild.

Pale thro' pathless ways
The fancied image strays,
Famish'd, weeping, weak   36 15
With hollow piteous shriek

Rising from unrest,
The trembling woman prest,
With feet of weary woe;
She could no further go.   20

In his arms he bore,
Her arm'd with sorrow sore;
Till before their way,
A couching lion lay.

Turning back was vain,   25
Soon his heavy mane,
Bore them to the ground;
Then he stalk'd around,

Smelling to his prey.
But their fears allay,   30
When he licks their hands:
And silent by them stands.

They look upon his eyes
Fill'd with deep surprise;
And wondering behold,   35
A Spirit arm'd in gold.

On his head a crown
On his shoulders down,
Flow'd his golden hair,
Gone was all their care.   40

Follow me he said,
Weep not for the maid;
In my palace deep,
Lyca lies asleep.

Then they followed,   45
Where the vision led:
And saw their sleeping child,
Among tygers wild.

To this day they dwell
In a lonely dell,   50
Nor fear the wolvish howl,
Nor the lions growl.

The Chimney Sweeper   37

A little black thing among the snow:
Crying weep, weep, in notes of woe!
Where are thy father & mother? say?
They are both gone up to the church to pray.

Because I was happy upon the heath,   5
And smil'd among the winters snow:
They clothed me in the clothes of death,
And taught me to sing the notes of woe.

And because I am happy, & dance & sing,
They think they have done me no injury: 10
And are gone to praise God & his Priest & King
Who make up a heaven of our misery.

NURSES Song   38

When the voices of children are heard on the green
And whisprings are in the dale:
The days of my youth rise fresh in my mind,
My face turns green and pale.

Then come home my children, the sun is gone down   5
And the dews of night arise
Your spring & your day, are wasted in play
And your winter and night in disguise.[9]

The SICK ROSE   39

O Rose thou art sick.
The invisible worm.
That flies in the night
In the howling storm:

Has found out thy bed   5
Of crimson joy:
And his dark secret love
Does thy life destroy.[1]

---

9. Three of the eight lines are repeated from the counterpart poem in *Innocence*; the other five lines (and the design) reveal stark differences as implied by the body language of the boy's crossed forearms, the Nurse's bracketing of his head as she fusses with his hair, and the girl's absorption in her book.
1. Usually interpreted as corruption by a sexual aggressor (although in color plate 3 the female spirit emerging from the dying rose appears delighted). For a feminist counterview see Elizabeth Langland in *Critical Paths* (1987), ed. Miller, Bracher, and Ault, and for a political reading see Jon Mee, *Eighteenth-Century Life* 22:1 (1998).

THE FLY.[2]

Little Fly
Thy summers play,
My thoughtless hand
Has brush'd away.

Am not I   5
A fly like thee?
Or art not thou
A man like me?

For I dance
And drink & sing: 10
Till some blind hand
Shall brush my wing.[3]

If thought is life
And strength & breath;
And the want   15
Of thought is death;

Then am I
A happy fly,
If I live,
Or if I die.   20

2. In Blake's time *fly* referred also to the butterfly. The sequence of stanzas in Blake's two-column layout, with the fifth stanza centered below, is unambiguous in the stanza numbering of his draft
(Notebook 101).
3. Cf. *King Lear* 4.1.36–37: "As flies to wanton boys are we to the gods; / They kill us for their sport."
Grant, "Interpreting Blake's 'The Fly'" (1963; rpt. *Blake*, ed. Frye, 1966), notes the double enclosure formed by the nurse's arms and the dead tree.

The Angel   41

I Dreamt a Dream! what can it mean?
And that I was a maiden Queen:
Guarded by an Angel mild:
Witless woe, was ne'er beguil'd!

And I wept both night and day   5
And he wip'd my tears away
And I wept both day and night
And hid from him my hearts delight

So he took his wings and fled:
Then the morn blush'd rosy red: 10
I dried my tears & arm'd my fears,
With ten thousand shields and spears.

Soon my Angel came again:
I was arm'd, he came in vain;
For the time of youth was fled   15
And grey hairs were on my head.

The Tyger.⁴   42

Tyger Tyger. burning bright,
In the forests of the night:
What immortal hand or eye,
Could frame thy fearful symmetry?

In what distant deeps or skies.   5
Burnt the fire of thine eyes!
On what wings dare he aspire!
What the hand, dare sieze the fire?

And what shoulder, & what art,
Could twist the sinews of thy heart?   10
And when thy heart began to beat,
What dread hand? & what dread feet?⁵

What the hammer? what the chain,
In what furnace was thy brain?
What the anvil? what dread grasp,   15
Dare its deadly terrors clasp!

When the stars threw down their spears⁶
And water'd heaven with their tears:

---

4. For drafts, see p. 380 herein.
5. In one copy Blake altered "& what" to "Formd thy." In the letterpress text issued by his friend Thomas Malkin these words appeared as "forged thy," along with other slight variants.
6. Cf. Urizen's lament: "The stars threw down their spears and fled naked away / We fell" (*The Four Zoas*, V, 64:27–28), alluding to the apocalyptic fall of the stars (Revelation 6:13, 12:4; Daniel 8:10), and the war in Heaven (Revelation 12:7–8; *Paradise Lost* 5–6).

Did he smile his work to see?
Did he who made the Lamb make thee?[7]   20

Tyger, Tyger burning bright,
In the forests of the night:
What immortal hand or eye,
Dare frame thy fearful symmetry?

My Pretty ROSE TREE[8]   43

A flower was offerd to me;
Such a flower as May never bore.
But I said I've a Pretty Rose-tree,
And I passed the sweet flower o'er.

Then I went to my Pretty Rose-tree;   5
To tend her by day and by night.
But my Rose turnd away with jealousy:
And her thorns were my only delight.

AH! SUN-FLOWER

Ah Sun-flower! weary of time,
Who countest the steps of the Sun:
Seeking after that sweet golden clime
Where the travellers journey is done.

Where the Youth pined away with desire,   5
And the pale Virgin shrouded in snow:
Arise from their graves and aspire,
Where my Sun-flower wishes to go.[9]

7. The counterpart poem in *Innocence* obliquely alludes to Jesus as Lamb of God (see n. 2, p. 15 herein). For samplings of the many controversies in "Tyger studies" (Gleckner and Greenberg, 1989), see Winston Weathers, ed. *The Tyger* (1969), Grant, *Iowa Review* (1989), Bruce Borowsky (1996, www.english.uga.edu/wblake/songs/42/42bib.html), Bloom, ed. *William Blake* (2003), and Behrendt, p. 547 herein. Interpretations are further complicated by the unusually sharp disparity between impressions of the beast in the text and in the image (nonmenacing, viewed from the side). In two versions the Tyger actually smiles: Copies B (1794) and Y (c. 1825).
8. This poem and the two that follow, printed on the same plate, make up the only three-poem sequence that, of course, never changed in Blake's many rearrangements of the *Songs*.
9. In Ovid's *Metamorphoses* the nymph Clytie, rejected by Apollo, pines away until she becomes a heliotrope, a flower that always turns toward the sun. Grant, *Blake Studies* 5 (1974), 7–64, explores variations on the sunflower motif.

THE LILLY

The modest Rose puts forth a thorn:
The humble Sheep, a threatning horn:
While the Lilly white, shall in Love delight
Nor a thorn nor a threat stain her beauty bright.

The GARDEN of LOVE   44

I went to the Garden of Love.
And saw what I never had seen:
A Chapel was built in the midst,
Where I used to play on the green.

And the gates of this Chapel were shut,   5
And Thou shalt not writ over the door;[1]
So I turn'd to the Garden of Love,
That so many sweet flowers bore.

And I saw it was filled with graves,
And tomb-stones where flowers should be: 10
And Priests in black gowns, were walking their rounds,
And binding with briars, my joys & desires.

The Little Vagabond   45

Dear Mother, dear Mother, the Church is cold.
But the Ale-house is healthy & pleasant & warm;[2]
Besides I can tell where I am use'd well,
Such usage in heaven will never do well,

But if at the Church they would give us some Ale.   5
And a pleasant fire, our souls to regale;
We'd sing and we'd pray all the live-long day;
Nor ever once wish from the Church to stray.

Then the Parson might preach & drink & sing,
And we'd be as happy as birds in the spring: 10
And modest dame Lurch, who is always at Church,
Would not have bandy children nor fasting nor birch.

And God like a father rejoicing to see,
His children as pleasant and happy as he:

1. The negative commandments of the Decalogue contrast with instructions in Deuteronomy 6:4–9 to write "thou shalt love the Lord thy God," a positive commandment, "upon the posts of thy house, and on thy gates"; the point is repeated in *Europe* 15/12:28. Locked proprietary chapels and the locked pews rented by rich people in parish churches prompted Mrs. [Sarah] Trimmer, in *The Oeconomy of Charity* (1787, revised 1801) to observe: "It will be of little use to persuade the poor to go to their proper places of worship if when they do so, they either find the doors shut against their entrance, or no accommodation for them."
2. Laborers, including child laborers, regularly cheered themselves up in alehouses and gin mills before and after work. Some dissenting religious groups met in pubs.

Would have no more quarrel with the Devil or the Barrel   15
But kiss him & give him both drink and apparel.

46

LONDON

I wander thro' each charter'd street,[3]
Near where the charter'd Thames does flow
And mark in every face I meet
Marks of weakness, marks of woe.

In every cry of every Man,   5
In every Infants cry of fear.
In every voice; in every ban,[4]
The mind-forg'd manacles[5] I hear

How the Chimney-sweepers cry
Every blackning Church appalls,   10
And the hapless Soldiers sigh:
Runs in blood down Palace walls[6]

But most thro' midnight streets I hear
How the youthful Harlots curse[7]
Blasts the new-born Infants tear   15
And blights with plagues the Marriage hearse.

3. The "chartered rights of Englishmen" ultimately derive from the Magna Carta of 1215, but the
   ancient charters of London, which grant certain liberties, did not extend to most of the inhabitants.
   As Paine noted in *The Rights of Man* (1791), a charter actually operates by "taking rights away";
   see E. P. Thompson in *Interpreting Blake* (1978), ed. Michael Phillips, and Michael Ferber, "London and Its Politics" *ELH* 48 (1981). For drafts, see p. 379 herein.
4. A public prohibition or proclamation. Also "marriage banns," the required three-Sunday notice of
   forthcoming weddings in Anglican churches. Cf. "An Ancient Proverb" (p. 384 herein).
5. In linking individuals and institutions, Blake's compound adjective emphasizes confining mind-
   sets, primarily in the authorities of Church and State, perhaps also in the compliant victims. In his
   draft, Blake first wrote "german forged," a jab at the Hanoverian King George III.
6. The initial letters of this stanza spell out "HEAR" (Hilton, *Literal Imagination* [1983], p. 64).
7. The verbal curse becomes a metaphor for the plague of gonorrhea, which can cause blindness at
   birth. In London as elsewhere, then and now, impoverished girls seeking employment were tricked
   or lured into the sex trade. On the whole poem, Bloom (2003) excerpts eight essays; see also Morris Dickstein in *The Literary Freud* (1980), ed. Joseph H. Smith.

The Human Abstract.[8]   47

Pity would be no more,
If we did not make somebody Poor:
And Mercy no more could be,
If all were as happy as we;

And mutual fear brings peace;   5
Till the selfish loves increase.
Then Cruelty knits a snare,
And spreads his baits with care.

He sits down with holy fears,
And waters the ground with tears: 10
Then Humility takes its root
Underneath his foot.

Soon spreads the dismal shade
Of Mystery over his head;
And the Catterpiller and Fly,   15
Feed on the Mystery.

And it bears the fruit of Deceit,
Ruddy and sweet to eat;
And the Raven his nest has made
In its thickest shade.   20

The Gods of the earth and sea,
Sought thro' Nature to find this Tree[9]
But their search was all in vain;
There grows one in the Human Brain.[1]

8. Abstraction, which generalizes rather than particularizes, dehumanizes oneself and others. As a contrary for "The Divine Image" of *Innocence*, Blake first etched "A Divine Image" (in two quatrains): "Cruelty has a Human Heart / And Jealousy a Human Face; / Terror, the Human Form Divine / And Secrecy, the Human Dress. / The Human Dress, is forged Iron / The Human Form, a fiery Forge. / The Human Face, a Furnace seal'd / The Human Heart, its hungry Gorge."
9. I.e., the Tree of Mystery (see lines 13–14), derived from the tree of knowledge of good and evil (Genesis 2:9) and the name of the Whore of Babylon (Revelation 17:5), incorporating imagery of the poisonous upas tree of Java and the banyan tree, which grows by rerooting itself from its branches (cf. "The Poison Tree," *The Book of Ahania* 5/4:6, and *The Four Zoas* 119:1). It is repeatedly associated with the mystification that separates the human from the divine.
1. Blake was probably aware of the treelike structure of the cerebellum (described in Alan Richardson, *British Romanticism and the Science of Mind* [2001]).

INFANT SORROW[2]

48

My mother groand! my father wept.
Into the dangerous world I leapt:
Helpless, naked, piping loud:
Like a fiend hid in a cloud.

Struggling in my fathers hands: 5
Striving against my swadling bands:[3]
Bound and weary I thought best
To sulk upon my mothers breast.

A POISON TREE[4]

49

I was angry with my friend:
I told my wrath, my wrath did end.
I was angry with my foe:
I told it not, my wrath did grow.

And I waterd it in fears,   5
Night & morning with my tears:
And I sunned it with smiles,
And with soft deceitful wiles.

And it grew both day and night,
Till it bore an apple bright.   10
And my foe beheld it shine,
And he knew that it was mine.

2. See the draft of this poem, p. 381 herein.
3. Not present in the design.
4. First titled "Christian Forbearance."

And into my garden stole.
When the night had veild the pole;
In the morning glad I see;   15
My foe outstretchd beneath the tree.

A Little BOY Lost   50

Nought loves another as itself
Nor venerates another so.
Nor is it possible to Thought
A greater than itself to know:[5]

And Father, how can I love you,   5
Or any of my brothers more?
I love you like the little bird
That picks up crumbs around the door.

The Priest sat by and heard the child.
In trembling zeal he siez'd his hair: 10
He led him by his little coat;
And all admir'd the Priestly care.

And standing on the altar high,
Lo what a fiend is here! said he:
One who sets reason up for judge   15
Of our most holy Mystery.

The weeping child could not be heard.
The weeping parents wept in vain:
They strip'd him to his little shirt.
And bound him in an iron chain.   20

And burn'd him in a holy place,
Where many had been burn'd before:
The weeping parents wept in vain.
Are such things done on Albions shore.[6]

A Little GIRL Lost   51

Children of the future Age,
Reading this indignant page;
Know that in a former time,
Love! sweet Love! was thought a crime.[7]

5. In the spirit of the Clod (see p. 31 herein), the boy challenges Christian teachings of self-abnegation, beginning with the biblical admonition to love one's neighbor as oneself. According to St. Anselm, "God is the greatest thought it is possible to think"; but in annotating Swedenborg Blake disagrees: "Man can have no idea of anything greater than Man, as a cup cannot contain more than its capaciousness."
6. Although people were no longer burned for heresy, bonfires were made of subversive books like those of Paine. Stevenson recalls Watts's hymn "On Obedience to Parents": "Have ye not heard what dreadful plagues / Are threatened by the Lord, / To him that breaks his father's law / Or mocks his mother's word?"
7. This epigraph, in the voice of the Bard as a writer rather than a speaker, appears directly addressed to us—or is the "future Age" of more attentive readers yet to come?

In the Age of Gold,[8]   5
Free from winters cold:
Youth and maiden bright,
To the holy light,
Naked in the sunny beams delight.

Once[9] a youthful pair   10
Fill'd with softest care;
Met in garden bright.
Where the holy light,
Had just removd the curtains of the night.

There in rising day,   15
On the grass they play:
Parents were afar:
Strangers came not near:
And the maiden soon forgot her fear.

Tired with kisses sweet   20
They agree to meet,
When the silent sleep
Waves o'er heavens deep;
And the weary tired wanderers weep.

To her father white   25
Came the maiden bright:
But his loving look,
Like the holy book,
All her tender limbs with terror shook.

Ona! pale and weak!   30
To thy father speak:
O the trembling fear!
O the dismal care!
That shakes the blossoms of my hoary hair.

To Tirzah[1]   52

Whate'er is Born of Mortal Birth,
Must be consumed with the Earth
To rise from Generation[2] free;
Then what have I to do with thee?[3]

---

8. Primordial era of bliss, celebrated in classical literature, here enjoyed in the present tense (line 9).
   Blake once declared that his work is "an Endeavour to Restore what the Ancients called the Golden
   Age" (A Vision of the Last Judgment).
9. The temporal adverb introduces the narrative of the "former time" mentioned in the opening quatrain. Damon notes a buried allusion to Adam and Eve's pure "connubial love" before their fall (Paradise Lost 4.743).
1. This poem, not in the first printings of the combined Songs or of Experience alone, may have been
   added as early as 1795, according to Viscomi (1993), 238–239. The sinister character Tirzah—here
   the mother of the earthly and material body, the only mortal part of humanity—already has some
   of the attributes she will display prominently in Blake's later works.
2. Blake's term for the realm of mortal existence, in which the human body is merely the product of
   parental copulation. Opposed is the realm of renewed or resurrected life, when "Generation is
   swallowed up in Regeneration" (Milton 48/41:28). At best, "holy Generation" is an "Image of
   Regeneration" (Jerusalem 7:65).

The Sexes sprung from Shame & Pride[4]   5
Blow'd[5] in the morn; in evening died
But Mercy changd Death into Sleep;
The Sexes rose to work & weep.

Thou Mother of my Mortal part.
With cruelty didst mould my Heart   10
And with false self-decieving tears,
Didst bind my Nostrils Eyes & Ears.

Didst close my Tongue in senseless clay
And me to Mortal Life betray:
The Death of Jesus set me free,[6]   15
Then what have I to do with thee?

The School Boy[7]   53

I love to rise in a summer morn,
When the birds sing on every tree;
The distant huntsman winds his horn,
And the sky-lark sings with me.
O! what sweet company.   5

3. Both Elijah (1 Kings 17:18) and Jesus himself (Matthew 8:29) are confronted with variations on this question, but the crucial text is Jesus' rebuke to Mary before conducting the miracle at Cana in his own way and time (John 2:4).
4. In both Platonic myth and kabbalistic interpretations of Genesis 1 and 2, the primal human state is androgynous, and the separation of the sexes marks a descent to a lower state of being.
5. Bloomed.
6. In later writings Blake makes clear that Jesus sets people free not by atoning for their sins but by inspiring them through his exemplary act of self-sacrifice (cf. *Jerusalem* 96:13–45); the saving novelty of Jesus' teachings is his emphasis on forgiveness (cf. "The Everlasting Gospel"). The inscription about the raising of the "spiritual body" (see design) is from 1 Corinthians 15:44, a passage (beginning at 15:35) to which Blake repeatedly alludes; see also 1 Corinthians 12.
7. "School-Boy" in most copies. Transferred from *Innocence* to *Experience*. On the borderline between states, see Thomas Frosch in *Approaches* (1989), ed. Gleckner and Greenberg.

But to go to school in a summer morn,
O! it drives all joy away;
Under a cruel eye outworn,
The little ones spend the day,
In sighing and dismay.   10

Ah! then at times I drooping sit,
And spend many an anxious hour.
Nor in my book can I take delight,
Nor sit in learnings bower,
Worn thro' with the dreary shower.   15

How can the bird that is born for joy,
Sit in a cage and sing.
How can a child when fears annoy,
But droop his tender wing.
And forget his youthful spring.   20

O! father & mother, if buds are nip'd,
And blossoms blown away,
And if the tender plants are strip'd
Of their joy in the springing day,
By sorrow and cares dismay.   25

How shall the summer arise in joy.
Or the summer fruits appear,
Or how shall we gather what griefs destroy
Or bless the mellowing year,
When the blasts of winter appear.   30

The Voice of the Ancient Bard.[8]   54

Youth of delight come hither,
And see the opening morn,
Image of truth new born.
Doubt is fled & clouds of reason.
Dark disputes & artful teazing.   5
Folly is an endless maze,
Tangled roots perplex her ways,
How many have fallen there!
They stumble all night over bones of the dead:
And feel they know not what but care;   10
And wish to lead others when they should be led.

8. Transferred from *Innocence* to *Experience* but included in some later copies of the separately published *Innocence* volume. In the design (not included) a bearded harpist plays for young people,
mostly girls and women.

THE BOOK OF THEL (1789)

This early work, contemporary with *Songs of Innocence* (both are dated 1789 on their title pages), revolves around a troubled inquirer whose questions are never resolved. In all but two copies, the book opens with "Thel's Motto," a stark, undecorated set of riddles about knowing and asking; in two late copies, the motto concludes the work. On the title page (color plate 4) the main character, Thel, a shepherdess, watches an erotic encounter between two miniature human figures springing out of flamelike flowers (probably based on Erasmus Darwin's sexually explicit poem *The Loves of the Plants* [1789], reprinted in *The Botanic Garden* [1791]). The nude male flower-spirit vigorously propels himself toward his fully clothed female counterpart, resembling Thel herself, who appears shocked or repelled by her suitor's ardor. Still smaller figures, active and contemplative, nude and clothed, decorate letters of the title.

The narrative begins with Thel's withdrawal from her older sisters and her flock to bemoan the transience of beauty in nature. As she questions the natural objects around her about the meaning of life—life in general and her own life in particular—the creatures she addresses take on human form and speak about their places in the natural world. The Lilly (a virgin), the Cloud (a lover), and the Clod of Clay (a matron, mother of the infant Worm) assure the melancholy shepherdess that there is abundant meaning and purpose in all life, at all levels of sentience. Her mediations on death, worms, and decay recall the "graveyard poetry" of Edward Young's *Night Thoughts* (1743), Robert Blair's *The Grave* (1743), James Hervey's *Mediations among the Tombs* (1746), and Thomas Gray's "Elegy Written in a Country Churchyard"—all of which Blake was later to illustrate. Near the end of the story, Thel is granted the opportunity to enter the land of the dead "and return," but when she hears a voice from her own grave questioning why the senses are either too strong or too restrained, she flees terrified back to her former abode.

The implications of Thel's story, which repeatedly calls attention to her status as "virgin" and "maid," are strongly though not exclusively sexual. Why is Thel unhappy and what does she fear? Why do answers from the natural world leave her unsatisfied? Her unusual name prompts other speculations: although Blake had not yet studied Greek, scholars have pointed out its similarity to a Greek word meaning "wish," "will," or "desire" and to a different Greek word meaning "woman." The extra-narrative pictures at the top of plate 3/1 (p. 49 herein) and at the bottom of plate 8/6 (p. 54) provide a wider frame for her quest. In the end, her shrieking and running away have been interpreted as fear of entering mortal existence, or as a deficiency in her will and desire, or as a refusal to move on to the next stage of her earthly life. The unanswered questions of her motto and the final design that intervenes between her flight home and "The End" of her story leave open the possibility that in her terror she has at last found out something, from her own experience, that none of her fellow creatures could tell her.

Thel is the first of Blake's illuminated woks in the irregular septenary meter employed in most of his narrative poetry. For commentary on both printing history (updated in the Blake Archive notes) and content, see the facsimile edition of Copy J (Houghton Library) by Morris Eaves, Robert N. Essick, and Joseph Viscomi in *The Early Illuminated Books* (1993), volume 3 in the Blake Trust series. Nancy Bogan, *The Book of Thel: A Facsimile and a Critical Text* (1971) reproduces Copy M (New York Public Library). Other studies of interest include Mary Lynn Johnson, *Journal of English and Germanic Philology* 69 (1970), 258–77; Christopher Heppner, *Colby Library Quarterly* 13 (1977), 79–98; Annette S. Levitt, *Colby Library Quarterly* 14 (1978), 72–83; W. J. T. Mitchell, *Blake's Composite Art* (1978); Marjorie Levinson, *ELH* 47 (1980), 287–303;

Harriet Kramer Linkin, *Colby Library Quarterly* 23 (1987), 66–76; James E. Swearingen, *Eighteenth-Century Studies* 23 (1989–90), 123–39; Brian Wilkie, *Blake's Thel and Oothoon* (1990); A[lice] G. den Otter, *Studies in Romanticism* 30 (1991), 633–55; Gerda Norvig, *Studies in Romanticism* 34 (1995), 255–72; Helen P. Bruder, *William Blake and the Daughters of Albion* (1997); and Susan J. Wolfson in *Women Reading William Blake*, ed. Bruder (2006).

Our text is taken from Copy H (Library of Congress); color plate 4 is from Copy N (Cincinnati Museum of Art).

THE BOOK of THEL*   2/ii

The Author & Printer Willm Blake. 1789.

THEL's Motto,   1/i

Does the Eagle know what is in the pit?
Or wilt thou go ask the Mole:[1]
Can Wisdom be put in a silver rod?
Or Love in a golden bowl?[2]

3/1

THEL

I

The daughters of Mne Seraphim led round their sunny flocks,[1]
All but the youngest, she in paleness sought the secret air,
To fade away like morning beauty from her mortal day:

---

* See color plate 4. In most copies, "Thel's Motto," the frontispiece (plate 1 [Erdman plate i]), comes before the title page; in Copies N and O (1818), it is the last page.
1. Proverbially, the eagle is sharp-eyed and the mole is blind, but in *Visions of the Daughters of Albion* 8/5:39–40, the heroine Oothoon implies that the mole is a more reliable witness.
2. First drafted for *Tiriel* (see Erdman's edition, p. 815). Ecclesiastes 12:5–6 prophesies a bad time when "desire shall fail: because man goeth to his long home [the grave] . . . Or ever the silver cord be loosed, or the golden bowl be broken." A rod is a traditional symbol of authority.
1. Indicating a pastoral world, an Arcadia where even the queen, as Thel is called, is a shepherdess. "Mne": perhaps Mnemosyne, the Greek goddess of memory. "Seraphim": highest order of angels. Possibly Blake also knew that for the neoplatonic-kabbalistic magus Cornelius Agrippa (1486–1535) "Bne Seraphim" are sons of the seraphim, intelligences of the planet Venus (*Occult Philosophy* [trans. 1651], II. 22).

Down by the river of Adona[2] her soft voice is heard:
And thus her gentle lamentation falls like morning dew.   5

"O life of this our spring! why fades the lotus of the water?[3]
Why fade these children of the spring? born but to smile & fall.
Ah! Thel is like a watry bow, and like a parting cloud.
Like a reflection in a glass, like shadows in the water.
Like dreams of infants, like a smile upon an infant's face,   10
Like the dove's voice, like transient day, like music in the air:
Ah! gentle may I lay me down, and gentle rest my head.
And gentle sleep the sleep of death, and gentle hear the voice
Of him that walketh in the garden in the evening time."[4]

The Lilly of the valley[5] breathing in the humble grass   15
Answerd the lovely maid and said, "I am a watry weed,
And I am very small, and love to dwell in lowly vales;
So weak the gilded butterfly scarce perches on my head
Yet I am visited from heaven and he that smiles on all
Walks in the valley, and each morn over me spreads his hand   20
Saying, 'Rejoice thou humble grass, thou new-born lilly flower,
Thou gentle maid of silent valleys, and of modest brooks:
For thou shalt be clothed in light, and fed with morning manna;
Till summer's heat melts thee beside the fountains and the springs
To flourish in eternal vales': then why should Thel complain,   25
Why should the mistress of the vales of Har[6] utter a sigh?"   [4/2]

She ceasd & smild in tears, then sat down in her silver shrine.

Thel answerd, "O thou little virgin of the peaceful valley,
Giving to those that cannot crave, the voiceless, the o'ertired.[7]
Thy breath doth nourish the innocent lamb, he smells thy milky
    garments,   5
He crops thy flowers, while thou sittest smiling in his face,
Wiping his mild and meekin[8] mouth from all contagious taints.
Thy wine doth purify the golden honey, thy perfume,
Which thou dost scatter on every little blade of grass that springs
Revives the milked cow, & tames the fire-breathing steed.   10
But Thel is like a faint cloud kindled at the rising sun:
I vanish from my pearly throne, and who shall find my place?"[9]

2. The river Adonis in Lebanon is mentioned in *Paradise Lost* 1.450 in connection with amorous longings of women who mourn a dying god (cf. Ezekiel 8:14). Adonis is also the beautiful shepherd boy
   beloved by Venus. The Gardens of Adonis in Spenser's *Faerie Queene* 3.4 are an earthly paradise,
   the seed ground of mortality.
3. In *Odyssey* 9, the food of oblivion consumed by the Lotus (or Lotos) Eaters. The Egyptian lotus is
   an edible aquatic plant also called a water lily.
4. Thel's lamentation culminates in an allusion to Genesis 3:8, in which Adam and Eve hear "the
   voice of the Lord God walking in the garden, in the cool of the day." Cf. "the Holy Word" in the
   "Introduction" to *Experience*. In contrast, the contented Lilly says that God "smiles on all," and
   the Clod says that he "loves the lowly."
5. Compare "The Lilly" in *Experience*. In Song of Solomon 2:1, the bride is a "lily of the valleys"; in
   the Sermon on the Mount, God clothes the short-lived lilies of the field more beautifully even than
   Solomon in all his glory (Matthew 6:28–29).
6. In the early manuscript *Tiriel* (not included in this edition), old Har and his wife, Heva, live idly
   in pleasant gardens, nursed by Mnetha. In *The Song of Los* 3:30 and 4:5, Har appears to be king
   of a formerly paradisal state and the ancestor of a degenerate race.
7. The etched word is "o'erfired," perhaps related to the Lilly's taming of the "fire-breathing" steed
   (4/2:10).
8. Probably a variant of "meek."
9. Faintly echoing Job 7:10 and Revelation 20:11.

"Queen of the vales" the Lilly answerd, "ask the tender cloud,
And it shall tell thee why it glitters in the morning sky.
And why it scatters its bright beauty thro' the humid air.   15
Descend O little cloud & hover before the eyes of Thel."

The Cloud descended, and the Lilly bowd her modest head:
And went to mind her numerous charge among the verdant grass.

II.

"O little Cloud" the virgin said. "I charge thee tell to me,   5/3
Why thou complainest not when in one hour thou fade away:
Then we shall seek thee but not find: ah Thel is like to thee.
I pass away, yet I complain, and no one hears my voice."

The Cloud then shewd his golden head & his bright form emerg'd,   5
Hovering and glittering on the air before the face of Thel.

"O virgin know'st thou not, our steeds drink of the golden springs
Where Luvah[1] doth renew his horses: look'st thou on my youth,
And fearest thou because I vanish and am seen no more.
Nothing remains; O maid I tell thee, when I pass away,   10
It is to tenfold life, to love to peace and raptures holy:
Unseen descending, weigh my light wings upon balmy flowers;
And court the fair eyed dew, to take me to her shining tent;
The weeping virgin, trembling kneels before the risen sun,
Till we arise link'd in a golden band and never part;   15
But walk united, bearing food to all our tender flowers."

1. Another odd name introduced without explanation, its sound perhaps evoking "lover." In later
   works Luvah is one of humanity's Four Zoas or aspects, associated with emotion; his title is "the
   prince of Love" (*Four Zoas* I, 12:14; Erdman 334).

"Dost thou O little Cloud? I fear that I am not like thee;
For I walk through the vales of Har, and smell the sweetest
    flowers;
But I feed not the little flowers: I hear the warbling birds,
But I feed not the warbling birds; they fly and seek their food: 20
But Thel delights in these no more because I fade away,
And all shall say, without a use this shining woman liv'd,
Or did she only live, to be at death the food of worms?"

The Cloud reclind upon his airy throne and answer'd thus.

"Then if thou art the food of worms, O virgin of the skies,   25
How great thy use, how great thy blessing; every thing that lives,
Lives not alone, nor for itself:[2] fear not and I will call
The weak worm from its lowly bed, and thou shalt hear its voice.
Come forth, worm of the silent valley, to thy pensive queen."

The helpless worm arose, and sat upon the Lilly's leaf,   30
And the bright Cloud said on, to find his partner in the vale.

III.

Then Thel astonish'd view'd the Worm upon its dewy bed.   6/4

"Art thou a Worm? image of weakness, art thou but a Worm?
I see thee like an infant wrapped in the Lilly's leaf:[3]
Ah weep not little voice, thou can'st not speak, but thou can'st
    weep:

2. A refrain repeated by the Clod of Clay (6/4:10) and affirmed by (another?) Clod in "The Clod &
    the Pebble," *Songs of Experience*.
3. Reminiscent of the infant Jesus' swaddling clothes. A human-headed worm on an oak leaf (fron-
    tispiece to *Gates of Paradise*, not in this edition) is emblematic of the beginning of humanity's nat-
    ural "vegetative" life.

Is this a Worm? I see thee lay helpless & naked: weeping,   5
And none to answer, none to cherish thee with mother's smiles."

The Clod of Clay heard the Worm's voice, & raisd her pitying head;
She bowd over the weeping infant. and her life exhal'd
In milky fondness. Then on Thel she fix'd her humble eyes.

"O beauty of the vales of Har, we live not for ourselves.   10
Thou seest me the meanest thing, and so I am indeed;
My bosom of itself is cold, and of itself is dark,

But he that loves the lowly, pours his oil upon my head,   7/5
And kisses me, and binds his nuptial bands around my breast.
And says; 'Thou mother of my children, I have loved thee.
And I have given thee a crown that none can take away.'[4]
But how this is sweet maid, I know not, and I cannot know,   5
I ponder, and I cannot ponder; yet I live and love."

The daughter of beauty wip'd her pitying tears with her white veil,
And said. "Alas! I knew not this, and therefore did I weep:
That God would love a Worm I knew, and punish the evil foot[5]
That wilful, bruis'd its helpless form; but that he cherish'd it   10
With milk and oil, I never knew; and therefore did I weep,
And I complaind in the mild air, because I fade away,
And lay me down in thy cold bed, and leave my shining lot."

"Queen of the vales," the matron Clay answerd; "I heard thy sighs.
And all thy moans flew o'er my roof, but I have call'd them down: 15

4. Like that promised the faithful in 2 Timothy 4:8, 1 Peter 5:4, James 1:12, and Revelation 2:10.
5. Echoing the imagery, but not the point, of God's sentence on the serpent: Eve's offspring "shall bruise thy head, and thou shalt bruise his heel" (Genesis 3:15).

Wilt thou O Queen enter my house, 'tis given thee to enter,
And to return;[6] fear nothing, enter with thy virgin feet."

IV.

The eternal gates' terrific porter lifted the northern bar:[7] |8/6|
Thel enter'd in & saw the secrets of the land unknown:
She saw the couches of the dead, & where the fibrous roots
Of every heart on earth infixes deep its restless twists:
A land of sorrows & of tears where never smile was seen.   5

She wanderd in the land of clouds thro' valleys dark, listning
Dolours & lamentations: waiting oft beside a dewy grave
She stood in silence, listning to the voices of the ground,
Till to her own grave plot she came, & there she sat down,
And heard this voice of sorrow breathed from the hollow pit—   10

"Why cannot the Ear be closed to its own destruction?
Or the glistning Eye to the poison of a smile!
Why are Eyelids stord with arrows ready drawn,
Where a thousand fighting men in ambush lie?
Or an Eye of gifts & graces, show'ring fruits & coined gold!   15
Why a Tongue impress'd with honey from every wind?
Why an Ear, a whirlpool fierce to draw creations in?
Why a Nostril wide inhaling terror trembling & affright
Why a tender curb upon the youthful burning boy!
Why a little curtain of flesh[8] on the bed of our desire?"   20

The Virgin started from her seat, & with a shriek.
Fled back unhinderd till she came into the vales of Har.[9]

6. In classical mythology, the return journey from the underworld is difficult and dangerous, as in
   Aeneid VI and the story of Orpheus and Eurydice.
7. The land of the dead is often imagined as cold, to the north. The guardian of the gates of death is
   usually formidable, as in *Paradise Lost* 2.645 ff., where Sin and Death together are the porters.
   Blake probably also drew on images of porter and gates in *Faerie Queene* 3.4.31–32. In *Odyssey*
   8.145 ff., the Cave of the Sea Nymphs has two gates: that to the north for mortals, to the south for
   gods. Neoplatonic interpreters, who must have been known to Blake by the notes to Pope's translation of the *Odyssey* interpreted the northern door as an allegory of the way the soul enters the
   body (see Rodney M. Baine, *Philological Quarterly* 32 [1972], 957–951); in *Milton* 28/26:13 ff.,
   Los, the Zoa of productive imagination, is porter of both gates. The lettering style of this plate, and
   of the motto, differs from the rest of the text and may have been etched slightly later, perhaps to
   replace a rejected conclusion, before Blake issued the book in 1789 (see Eaves, et al. [1993]).
8. Probably referring to the hymen. Lines 19–20, which question restraints on the fifth sense, touch,
   as the conduit for sexual intimacy, were erased and painted over in Copies I (c. 1790) and J (c.
   1789), owned by the antiquarian bibliophiles Francis Douce (1757–1834) and Thomas Frognall
   Dibdin (1776–1847).
9. The tailpiece design of the reined serpent and its young riders is repeated, in reverse, on *America*
   13/11 (not printed herein).

VISIONS OF THE DAUGHTERS
OF ALBION (1793)

Both *The Book of Thel* and *Visions of the Daughters of Albion*, stories of crises in the lives of young women, open with the heroine in conversation with a humanized flower: the gowned Thel with the pale, virginal Lilly; the nude Oothoon with the glowing, open-hearted Marygold. In verbal and visual imagery the two works are opposed almost like the paired poems that reveal "Contrary States of the Human Soul" in *Songs of Innocence and of Experience*. Although *Visions* is primarily a critique of constraints on love and sexuality, it also denounces the enslavement of Africans and laboring children; and insofar as Oothoon is "the soft soul of America," it symbolically condemns exploitation of the unspoiled American land, its resources, and—by implication—its native people. In successive stages of fear, daring, guilt, and moral independence, Oothoon comes to recognize oppression as an interlocking system of the sort that the Chimney Sweeper of *Experience* identifies as "God & his Priest & King." Liberty, by contrast, is absolute: there is no such thing as freedom for only certain people, like white men.

The pivotal event in *Visions* is a rape, which takes place quickly, in only half a line (4/1:16). The rest of the work is devoted to tracing its causes, consequences, and implications—for the victim, Oothoon; her fiancé, Theotormon ("tormented by God"); and the rapist, Bromion ("thunderer"). Although *Visions* is not divided into formal sections, as *Thel* is, its intermittent narrative falls into three main parts, as noted by Stevenson. The first part (4/1:1–17) introduces the Daughters of Albion (referring to an ancient name for England) as a choral audience and recounts Oothoon's plucking of the flower, her joyous flight toward her beloved, and her rape. The second part, which covers Theotormon's binding and brooding over Oothoon and Bromion in his cave, consists mainly of declamations by the principal characters: Bromion (4/1:18–2:2 and 7/4:12–24), Oothoon (5/2:14–16, 5/2:20–6/3:20), and Theotormon (6/3:22–7/4:11). The third part (8/5:3–11/8:10) is a long, passionate oration on free love by Oothoon, still bound physically but now psychologically self-liberated. In their declarations the three characters constantly speak past one another, as though they were in an absurdist play; in the frontispiece (color plate 5) they appear forever locked in a Sartrean "No Exit" triangle. Although Oothoon never escapes from the two warped lovers who claim ownership of her, she finds strength—as their thoughts drift into philosophical questions about perception—to challenge their theology, break down their philosophical assumptions, and refuse her own victimhood. She rejects their definitions of her as an adulteress and a harlot; speaks past them to confront their creator and "mistaken Demon," Urizen; and concludes her oration with a rhapsody on the joys of love and the delights of inner freedom. At the end of the poem the Daughters of Albion continue to echo Oothoon's laments, unchanged by their visions of her experience, but in the final design, which appears after the words "The End" (p. 65 herein), two of the women look up as the free spirit of Oothoon soars above them. The epigraph on the title page (color plate 6), "The Eye sees more than the Heart knows," implies that even the Daughters of Albion could achieve a heightened level of consciousness if they could feel in their hearts the meaning of their visions and come to understand their own condition.

The best single source of images, commentary, and suggestions for further reading is Robert N. Essick's facsimile edition, published by the Huntington Library, of Copy E (2002), which builds on the excellent section on *Visions* (with a facsimile of Copy G) in *The Early Illuminated Books* (1993), ed. Eaves, Essick, and Viscomi, volume 3 in the Blake Trust series, *Blake's Illuminated*

Books, ed. David Bindman. Both should be studied in conjunction with the Blake Archive facsimiles (nine copies on view in 2007). Informative and/or provocative earlier studies of this controversial poem, cited in one or more of the resources recommended above, include earlier commentary by Jane E. Peterson, David Worrall, David Aers, Mark Bracher, David Punter, Laura Ellen Haigwood, Nelson Hilton, and Thomas Vogler, as well as Nancy Moore Goslee, *ELH* 57:1 (1990), 101–28; Harriet Kramer Linkin, *Blake: An Illustrated Quarterly* 23 (1990), 184–94, Brian Wilkie, *Blake's Thel and Oothoon* (1990), James A. Heffernan, *Studies in Romanticism* 30 (1991), 3–18, Tilottama Rajan in *The Mind in Creation* (1992), ed. J. Douglas Kneale, James E. Swearingen, *Journal of English and Germanic Philology* 91 (1992), 203–15; Steven Vine in *The Discourse of Slavery* (1994), ed. Carl Plasa and Betty J. Ring; Anne K. Mellor in *Huntington Library Quarterly* 58 (1996), 345–70; and Helen Bruder, *William Blake and the Daughters of Albion* (1997).

Our base text is Copy J (Library of Congress), compared with the Essick facsimile of Copy E and the Blake Archive facsimile of Copy P (Fitzwilliam Museum).

VISIONS of the Daughters of Albion*   2/ii

The Eye sees more than the Heart knows.
Printed by Willm Blake: 1793.

The Argument[1]   3/iii

I loved Theotormon
And I was not ashamed
I trembled in my virgin fears
And I hid in Leutha's vale![2]

I plucked Leutha's flower,   5
And I rose up from the vale;
But the terrible thunders tore
My virgin mantle in twain.

Visions   4/1

Enslav'd,[3] the Daughters of Albion weep: a trembling
   lamentation
Upon their mountains; in their valleys, sighs toward America.

---

*   See color plates 5 and 6. Blake placed the frontispiece (color plate 5) after the title page in one copy and at the end of the book in another; the closest text for the situation depicted (in which Oothoon's bonds are not visible) is *Visions* 5/2:5–7. The text most closely associated with the title page (color plate 6) is 4/1:14–15.

1. A prefatory "Argument," on the model of those in Milton's *Paradise Lost*, has traditionally been a prose summary introducing a complex epic action; but in *Visions* and *The Marriage of Heaven and Hell* it is a brief poetic introduction to a major theme of the larger work. Here "The Argument," which gives details not provided in the main narrative, appears to be Oothoon's own summary of her state of mind before Bromion's attack.

2. Not further identified in *Visions*. A temptress named Leutha appears in several later works; in *Milton* 12/11:28 ff, she enacts the part of Sin in *Paradise Lost* 2.766 ff.

3. Formed with exceptionally large letters, emphasizing Blake's analysis of the status of English women ("Daughters of Albion") and, by extension, anyone denied the rights that "free-born Englishmen" derived from the Magna Carta (1215).

The Argument

I loved Theotormon
And I was not ashamed
I trembled in my virgin fears
And I hid in Leutha's vale;

I plucked Leutha's Flower,
And I rose up from the vale;
But the terrible thunders tore
My virgin mantle in twain.

For the soft soul of America, Oothoon[4] wanderd in woe,
Along the vales of Leutha seeking flowers to comfort her;
And thus she spoke to the bright Marygold of Leutha's vale   5

> "Art thou a flower! art thou a nymph! I see thee now a flower;
> Now a nymph! I dare not pluck thee from thy dewy bed!"[5]

4. Perhaps from the root *oo* (egg), though in Blake's time applied only to geological formations. Here written in large letters. For Oothoon's further development, see *Europe* 17/14:21 ff., *Milton* 14/13 and 50/42:33, and *Jerusalem* 41/37:17. Her name is probably drawn from "Oithóna," a rape victim in one of the pseudo-Gaelic prose poems that James Macpherson, in *Fingal . . . with several other poems* (1762), presented as translations from the ancient bard Ossian; the name supposedly means "virgin of the wave." A two-syllable pronunciation of "Oothoon" (as opposed to separating the two sets of contiguous O's to form four syllables), with an accent on the first syllable, seems the best fit with Blake's irregular seven-measure line (seven strong syllables and any number of weak syllables).

5. Both the human and the vegetable forms of the Marygold, visible to Oothoon, are shown in the design (plate 3/iii), in accordance with Blake's emphasis on imaginative perception. Cf. "With my

The Golden nymph replied; "Pluck thou my flower
  Oothoon the mild
Another flower shall spring, because the soul of sweet delight
Can never pass away." She ceas'd & closd her golden shrine.   10

Then Oothoon pluck'd the flower saying, "I pluck thee from
  thy bed
Sweet flower, and put thee here to glow between my breasts
And thus I turn my face to where my whole soul seeks."

Over the waves she went in wing'd exulting swift delight;
And over Theotormon's reign,[6] took her impetuous course.   15

Bromion rent her with his thunders;[7] on his stormy bed
Lay the faint maid, and soon her woes appalld his thunders hoarse.

Bromion spoke. "Behold this harlot[8] here on Bromion's bed.
And let the jealous dolphins sport around the lovely maid:
Thy soft American plains are mine, and mine thy north & south: 20
Stampt with my signet are the swarthy children of the sun[9]
They are obedient, they resist not, they obey the scourge:
Their daughters worship terrors and obey the violent:

inward Eye 'tis an old Man grey / With my outward a Thistle across the way" in his verse epistle to Butts. Traditionally, from a male perspective, the plucking of a flower is a metaphor for "taking" a woman's virginity; Oothoon makes her own choice to seek her beloved.

6. I.e., the ocean. Etymologically, Theotormon's name suggests that he is tormented by God or by his idea of God as what Oothoon calls the "Father of Jealousy" (10/7:12; cf. the "new Religion from new Jealousy of Theotormon," *Milton* 24/22:38).

7. The rapist's name suggests the Greek word for "roarer." His attack is mythologized here as "thunders." In the late prophecies Bromion is Theotormon's brother, one of the sons of Los who usually work for liberation.

8. Although in the preceding line the omniscient narrator has continued to refer to Oothoon as a "maid," her rapist now paradoxically considers her "this harlot," an object, a possession. Under a moral system that blames the victim, the aftermath of rape is even worse than the attack; cf. Mary Wollstonecraft (whose life and writings may have contributed to Blake's inspiration for this work): "A woman who has lost her honour, imagines that she cannot fall lower, and as for recovering her former station, it is impossible; no exertion can wash this stain away. Losing thus every spur, and having no other means of support, prostitution becomes her only refuge . . . unless she possesses an uncommon portion of sense and loftiness" (*A Vindication of the Rights of Woman* [1792], 156).

9. The reference to the branding of slaves and the design on plate 35 are reminders that the assault on Oothoon includes the subjugation of African and Native Americans. Accompanying one of Blake's engravings, executed about 1791, of a family in John Gabriel Stedman's *Narrative of a Five Years Expedition against the revolted Negroes of Surinam* (1796) is a description of a supposedly happy slave, for whom "labour is no more than a healthy exercise," but who bears Stedman's brand on his chest: "J.G.S. in a cypher, by which his owner may ascertain his property."

Now thou maist marry Bromion's harlot, and protect the child   5/2
Of Bromion's rage, that Oothoon shall put forth in nine moons'
   time."[1]

Then storms rent Theotormon's limbs; he rolld his waves around.
And folded his black jealous waters round the adulterate pair
Bound back to back in Bromion's caves terror & meekness dwell.   5

At entrance Theotormon sits wearing the threshold hard
With secret tears; beneath him sound like waves on a desart shore
The voice of slaves beneath the sun, and children bought with
   money,
That shiver in religious caves beneath the burning fires
Of lust, that belch incessant from the summits of the earth.   10

Oothoon weeps not, she cannot weep! her tears are locked up;
But she can howl incessant writhing her soft snowy limbs.
And calling Theotormon's Eagles to prey upon her flesh.[2]

"I call with holy voice! Kings of the sounding air,
Rend away this defiled bosom that I may reflect   15
The image of Theotormon on my pure transparent breast."

The Eagles at her call descend & rend their bleeding prey;
Theotormon severely smiles, her soul reflects the smile;
As the clear spring mudded with feet of beasts grows pure & smiles.

The Daughters of Albion hear her woes, & eccho back her sighs.   20

"Why does my Theotormon sit weeping upon the threshold:
And Oothoon hovers by his side, perswading him in vain:

---

1. Bromion's boast that the rape has instantly impregnated Oothoon (a convention followed in countless plays and novels) emphasizes her state of bondage; pregnancy increased the market value of
   slaves.
2. A part of Prometheus' punishment for defying Zeus was to be perpetually devoured by an eagle (or
   a vulture).

I cry arise O Theotormon for the village dog
Barks at the breaking day, the nightingale has done lamenting,
The lark does rustle in the ripe corn, and the Eagle returns   25
From nightly prey, and lifts his golden beak to the pure east;
Shaking the dust from his immortal pinions to awake
The sun that sleeps too long. Arise my Theotormon I am pure.
Because the night is gone that clos'd me in its deadly black.
They told me that the night & day were all that I could see;[3]   30
They told me that I had five senses to inclose me up.
And they inclos'd my infinite brain into a narrow circle,
And sunk my heart into the Abyss, a red round globe hot burning
Till all from life I was obliterated and erased.
Instead of morn arises a bright shadow, like an eye   35
In the eastern cloud; instead of night a sickly charnel house;
That Theotormon hears me not! to him the night and morn
Are both alike: a night of sighs, a morning of fresh tears;

And none but Bromion can hear my lamentations.   6/3

With what sense is it that the chicken shuns the ravenous hawk?
With what sense does the tame pigeon measure out the expanse?
With what sense does the bee form cells? have not the mouse &
    frog
Eyes and ears and sense of touch? yet are their habitations   5
And their pursuits as different as their forms and as their joys:
Ask the wild ass why he refuses burdens: and the meek camel
Why he loves man: is it because of eye ear mouth or skin
Or breathing nostrils? No, for these the wolf and tyger have.
Ask the blind worm the secrets of the grave, and why her spires   10
Love to curl round the bones of death! and ask the rav'nous snake
Where she gets poison: & the wing'd eagle why he loves the sun
And then tell me the thoughts of man, that have been hid of old.

3. Unable to alter Theotormon's worldview, Oothoon shifts her focus to exploration of the relationship between sensory perception and our conception of reality, a pervasive theme in Blake.

Silent I hover all the night, and all day could be silent,
If Theotormon once would turn his loved eyes upon me;   15
How can I be defild when I reflect thy image pure?
Sweetest the fruit that the worm feeds on, & the soul prey'd on
    by woe
The new wash'd lamb ting'd with the village smoke & the bright
    swan
By the red earth of our immortal river: I bathe my wings,
And I am white and pure to hover round Theotormon's breast."   20

Then Theotormon broke his silence, and he answered.

"Tell me what is the night or day to one o'erflowd with woe?
Tell me what is a thought? & of what substance is it made?
Tell me what is a joy? & in what gardens do joys grow?
And in what rivers swim the sorrows? and upon what mountains   25
Wave shadows of discontent? and in what houses dwell the
    wretched   7/4
Drunken with woe forgotten, and shut up from cold despair,

Tell me where dwell the thoughts forgotten till thou call them
    forth
Tell me where dwell the joys of old! & where the ancient loves?
And when will they renew again & the night of oblivion past?   5
That I might traverse times & spaces far remote and bring
Comforts into a present sorrow and a night of pain.
Where goest thou O thought! to what remote land is thy flight?
If thou returnest to the present moment of affliction
Wilt thou bring comforts on thy wings, and dews and honey
    and balm;   10
Or poison from the desart wilds, from the eyes of the envier."[4]

Then Bromion said: and shook the cavern with his lamentation

"Thou knowest that the ancient trees seen by thine eyes have fruit;
But knowest thou that trees and fruits flourish upon the earth
To gratify senses unknown? trees beasts and birds unknown: 15
Unknown, not unpercievd, spread in the infinite microscope,
In places yet unvisited by the voyager, and in worlds
Over another kind of seas, and in atmospheres unknown.
Ah! are there other wars, beside the wars of sword and fire!
And are there other sorrows, beside the sorrows of poverty?   20
And are there other joys, beside the joys of riches and ease?
And is there not one law for both the lion and the ox?
And is there not eternal fire, and eternal chains?
To bind the phantoms of existence from eternal life?"[5]

Then Oothoon waited silent all the day, and all the night,   25

4. To Theotormon, thought is vague and shadowy; objects hardly exist for him; his only yearning is
  for an irrecoverable past.
5. To Bromion, the senses are insatiable, seeking gratification in other scales and dimensions. On
  "one law for both the lion and the ox," see also *Marriage* 24.

But when the morn arose, her lamentation renewd,   8/5
The Daughters of Albion hear her woes, & eccho back her sighs.

"O Urizen: Creator of men! mistaken Demon of heaven:[6]
Thy joys are tears! thy labour vain, to form men to thine image,
How can one joy absorb another? are not different joys   5
Holy, eternal, infinite! and each joy is a Love.

Does not the great mouth laugh at a gift? & the narrow eyelids
  mock
At the labour that is above payment, and wilt thou take the ape
For thy councellor? or the dog, for a schoolmaster to thy children?
Does he who contemns poverty, and he who turns with
  abhorrence   10
From usury: feel the same passion or are they moved alike?
How can the giver of gifts experience the delights of the
  merchant?
How the industrous citizen the pains of the husbandman.
How different far the fat fed hireling with hollow drum;
Who buys whole corn fields into wastes, and sings upon the
  heath: 15
How different their eye and ear! how different the world to them!
With what sense does the parson claim the labour of the farmer?
What are his nets & gins & traps, & how does he surround him
With cold floods of abstraction, and with forests of solitude,
To build him castles and high spires, where kings & priests may
  dwell.   20
Till she who burns with youth, and knows no fixed lot; is bound
In spells of law to one she loaths; and must she drag the chain

6. In this first reference to a recurrent character introduced at length in *Urizen*, Oothoon recognizes
   that the "Creator of men," as perceived by Theotormon, is a jealous, infernal god who vainly wishes
   for interchangeable creatures, all in his image; in later works, this "mistaken Demon of heaven"
   is revealed as the fallen faculty of reason, erroneously set up as the god of fallen humanity.
   Oothoon's situation bears a superficial resemblance to that of Macpherson's Oithóna, who is carried away by a rival (while her fiancé is away), imprisoned, and sexually abused in an island cave.
   But Oithóna, when rescued by her lover, disguises herself as a warrior and dies in battle avenging
   her honor, rather than challenging the system under which she has suffered.

Of life, in weary lust! must chilling murderous thoughts, obscure
The clear heaven of her eternal spring! to bear the wintry rage
Of a harsh terror driv'n to madness, bound to hold a rod   25
Over her shrinking shoulders all the day; & all the night
To turn the wheel of false desire: and longings that wake her
    womb
To the abhorred birth of cherubs in the human form
That live a pestilence & die a meteor & are no more.
Till the child dwell with one he hates, and do the deed he loaths   30
And the impure scourge force his seed into its unripe birth
E'er yet his eyelids can behold the arrows of the day.

Does the whale worship at thy footsteps as the hungry dog?
Or does he scent the mountain prey, because his nostrils wide
Draw in the ocean? does his eye discern the flying cloud   35
As the raven's eye? or does he measure the expanse like the vulture?
Does the still spider view the cliffs where eagles hide their young?
Or does the fly rejoice, because the harvest is brought in?
Does not the eagle scorn the earth & despise the treasures
    beneath?
But the mole knoweth what is there, & the worm shall tell it thee.[7]   40
Does not the worm erect a pillar in the mouldering church yard?
And a palace of eternity in the jaws of the hungry grave   9/6
Over his porch these words are written. Take thy bliss O Man!
And sweet shall be thy taste & sweet thy infant joys renew!

Infancy, fearless, lustful, happy! nestling for delight
In laps of pleasure; Innocence! honest, open, seeking   5
The vigorous joys of morning light; open to virgin bliss.[8]
Who taught thee modesty, subtil modesty! child of night & sleep
When thou awakest, wilt thou dissemble all thy secret joys
Or wert thou not awake when all this mystery was disclos'd!
Then com'st thou forth a modest virgin knowing to dissemble   10
With nets found under thy night pillow, to catch virgin joy,
And brand it with the name of whore: & sell it in the night,
In silence, ev'n without a whisper, and in seeming sleep,
Religious dreams and holy vespers, light thy smoky fires:
Once were thy fires lighted by the eyes of honest morn   15
And does my Theotormon seek this hypocrite modesty!
This knowing, artful, secret, fearful, cautious, trembling hypocrite.
Then is Oothoon a whore indeed! and all the virgin joys
Of life are harlots: and Theotormon is a sick man's dream
And Oothoon is the crafty slave of selfish holiness.   20

But Oothoon is not so, a virgin fill'd with virgin fancies
Open to joy and to delight where ever beauty appears
If in the morning sun I find it: there my eyes are fix'd

7. Cf. "Thel's Motto." The entire series of rhetorical questions, modeled on God's questions to Job, attacks the intertwined injustices of Urizen's system: the "hollow drum" of the recruiting officer, the "fat fed hireling" of the wealthy landowner, the tithes extracted from the laborer by the parson to build "castles and high spires" for the oppressors. Oothoon sees women as the ultimate victims of the system, oppressed by masculine authority (line 25), loveless love-making (line 27), continual pregnancy (line 28), infant mortality (line 29), alienation of the next generation (line 30), and stillbirth (line 31).
8. Oothoon welcomes this pre-Freudian insight, unlike the mother in the draft for "Cradle Song" (p. 383 herein).

In happy copulation; if in evening mild, wearied with work;   10/7
Sit on a bank and draw the pleasures of this free born joy.

   The moment of desire! the moment of desire! The virgin
That pines for man shall awaken her womb to enormous joys
In the secret shadows of her chamber; the youth shut up from   5
The lustful joy shall forget to generate, & create an amorous image
In the shadows of his curtains and in the folds of his silent pillow.
Are not these the places of religion? the rewards of continence!
The self enjoyings of self denial? Why dost thou seek religion?
Is it because acts are not lovely, that thou seekest solitude,   10
Where the horrible darkness is impressed with reflections of
   desire.[9]

Father of Jealousy, be thou accursed from the earth!
Why hast thou taught my Theotormon this accursed thing?
Till beauty fades from off my shoulders darken'd and cast out,
A solitary shadow wailing on the margin of non-entity.[1]   15

I cry, Love! Love! Love! happy happy Love! free as the mountain
   wind!
Can that be Love, that drinks another as a sponge drinks water?
That clouds with jealousy his nights, with weepings all the day:
To spin a web of age around him, grey and hoary! dark!
Till his eyes sicken at the fruit that hangs before his sight.   20
Such is self-love that envies all! a creeping skeleton
With lamplike eyes watching around the frozen marriage bed.

But silken nets and traps of adamant will Oothoon spread,
And catch for thee girls of mild silver, or of furious gold;
I'll lie beside thee on a bank & view their wanton play   25
In lovely copulation bliss on bliss with Theotormon;
Red as the rosy morning, lustful as the first born beam,

9. Oothoon's frankness here contrasts sharply with published medical and social directives to young
   ladies in Blake's time. Her address to Urizen has now exceeded its occasion and become a general
   discourse on love.
1. An important Blakean concept, here first introduced: the utter loss of one's identity and sense of
   reality.

Oothoon shall view his dear delight, nor e'er with jealous cloud
Come in the heaven of generous love; nor selfish blightings bring.[2]

Does the sun walk in glorious raiment, on the secret floor   30
Where the cold miser spreads his gold? or does the bright
    cloud drop
On his stone threshold? does his eye behold the beam that
    brings
Expansion to the eye of pity? or will he bind himself
Beside the ox to thy hard furrow? does not that mild beam blot
The bat, the owl, the glowing tyger, and the king of night.   5
The sea fowl takes the wintry blast for a cov'ring to her limbs:
And the wild snake, the pestilence to adorn him with gems & gold.
And trees, & birds. & beasts, & men behold their eternal joy.
Arise you little glancing wings, and sing your infant joy!
Arise and drink your bliss, for every thing that lives is holy!"[3]   10

Thus every morning wails Oothoon, but Theotormon sits
Upon the margind ocean conversing with shadows dire.

The Daughters of Albion hear her woes, & eccho back her sighs.

11/8

The End

2. One of the most debated passages (beginning at line 13) in Blake studies since the 1990s: is
   Oothoon voicing a male perspective on sexual liberation? Also see Ostriker (p. 560 herein) and
   Wright (p. 583 herein).
3. Affirmed also in the last line of *Marriage*, and in *America* 10/8:10 and *Four Zoas* II.34:80 (not
   included in this edition).

THE MARRIAGE OF HEAVEN AND HELL (1790)

The first thing a reader of this work notices is that it challenges established ideas of right and wrong. The second thing is that it does more than turn traditional values upside down. True, the devils are almost irresistible—quicker, wittier, bolder, and more exciting than the angels, who lose every argument. But the unnamed framer and narrator of *Marriage* is not himself a devil. He is an inquisitive, energetic Blake-like character who revels in self-education; he collects proverbs from Hell, converses with biblical prophets, observes disputes between angels and devils (and even challenges an angel himself), develops his own opinions, and confidently offers the public the wisdom he has gained. Page by page it becomes clearer that instead of abolishing or simply inverting conventional moral categories, the *Marriage* encourages exuberant exploration; what it attacks are unimaginative, simplistic value systems that automatically favor passive or repressive "good" over active or liberating "evil."

A reasonable guide to interpreting a puzzling work—especially one that, like the *Marriage*, is neither signed nor dated—is a consideration of its form: with what other literary works does it have affinities? What is its genre? One formal precedent for the *Marriage*'s wild mixture of styles is Swift's *Tale of a Tub* (1704), which satirically alternates allegory and philosophical "digressions." Another not-at-all-satirical precedent is *A Treatise on Heaven and Hell* (1758, trans. 1788), by the Swedish scientist, engineer, and mystic Emmanuel Swedenborg (1688–1772), a religious monograph that interrupts serious doctrinal exposition with (unintentionally) amusing references to conversations with angels and devils. In the hybrid of genres that constitutes the *Marriage*, parodies and burlesques of Swedenborg's religious writings, the Bible, and Milton's *Paradise Lost* point to satire; yet enthusiastic proclamations of a new age point to manifesto or prophecy.

The title page (color plate 7) depicts a swarm of embracing nude couples (some of uncertain gender) among flames and clouds that rise beneath the flat surface of ordinary life, in the top quarter of the page. In the work itself, however, the climactic event is not a "marriage," or even a reconciliation, between heaven and hell, but the conversion of an angel into a devil (plate **24**). The introductory poetic "Argument" emphasizes the changing terrain of the struggle between the "just man" and the "villain," and the opening page of the work proper reveals that labels like *heaven* and *hell*, imposed by "the religious," are time-bound; what endures in every age are the productive tensions that propel life forward. In Blake's own time, the "good" of the Age of Reason has held sway for so long that the "evil" of pent-up revolutionary energy is overdue for release. It so happens that 1757, the year in which Swedenborg announced the arrival of a "new heaven," was the year of Blake's birth; now in 1790, the year Blake penned onto plate **3** (Copy F) of *The Marriage of Heaven and Hell* (undated on the title page), both the Swedenborgian system and the author of this work have arrived at the messianic age of thirty-three. As if on cue, precisely on schedule, "the Eternal Hell revives"—but it is Blake's work, not Swedenborg's, that taps into the irrepressible spiritual, creative, sexual, and political energies of the day. With the outbreak of the French Revolution, English radicals believed that the world was on the brink of the millennium prophesied in the Book of Revelation, and the Apocalypse was beginning to unfold. In *The Marriage of Heaven and Hell*, after eighteen centuries of Christianity during which the dynamic new underground religion of the underclass in first-century Rome has become the tired old established religion of the ruling class, it is high time to acknowledge the disruptive and revolutionary aspects of Jesus' life and teachings.

The immediate satirical target of the *Marriage* is the thought of Sweden-borg, whose Church of the New Jerusalem had set up a congregation in London in 1787. On controversies within this community see Morton D. Paley, *Blake: An Illustrated Quarterly* 13 (1979). Blake was initially attracted to Swedenborg's idea of a "Divine Humanity," and in 1789, at the first session of the group's general conference, he and his wife, Catherine, signed a document approving Swedenborg's doctrines as "genuine Truths revealed from Heaven." Blake soon realized, however, that Swedenborg was actually a force for conservatism and that in aiming to abolish churches he had merely added a new one. The *Marriage's* "Memorable Fancies" (i.e., fantasies) ridicule Swedenborg's "Memorable Relations" (*True Christian Religion*, trans. 1781), prosaic accounts of his mystical experiences involving inhabitants of various levels of heaven and hell. Blake's stories resemble Swedenborg's in that they recount revelations that prepare the narrator to articulate his prophecies and credos. But Blake's narrator is a young contrarian who breaks out of the limits of this world to discover the value of "infernal" energies and to gain confidence, on the best authority, that "the voice of honest indignation is the voice of God."

Blake's celebration of "Contraries" (plates 3–6), in constant dynamic opposition, is in part a corrective to Swedenborg's belief that heaven and hell should remain in "equilibrium" (*A Treatise of Heaven and Hell*, sec. 536 ff.). In the *Marriage* as a whole, the theoretical ideal is neither a static balance nor a dialectical synthesis between Contraries but an invigorating, liberating, never-ending clash of ideas. The Gospel of Hell brings the "good news" that expanded sense perception (plates 6–13) reveals the infinity and energetic holiness of the ordinary world. This source of revelation, experienced also by the prophets Ezekiel and Isaiah, the cynic Diogenes, the psalmist David, the "North American tribes" (plates 12–13), the classical "ancient Poets" (plate 11), and such British poets as Milton at his most audacious (plate 6), is Poetic Genius, or the creative imagination. Poets and prophets, as creators, are always in opposition to priests and other systematizers who form religions from fossilized remains of the visions of others. The themes of Contraries and of expanded sense perception are brought together on plates 14–24 (see Nurmi, p. 554 herein).

The only poetry in the *Marriage* occurs in the free verse of the "Argument" at the beginning and in the quasi-biblical numbered verses of "The Song of Liberty" at the end. As Max Plowman pointed out in his 1927 Dent facsimile edition (of Copy I), the main prose text falls into six "chapters," most of which are set off by major designs rather than verbal headings. For a provocative commentary on all designs, see David V. Erdman et al., in *William Blake*, ed. Paley and Phillips (1973). More broadly, see the facsimile edition of Copy F by Eaves, Essick, and Viscomi in *The Early Illuminated Books* (1993) and of Bodleian Copy B by Michael Phillips (2007); Dan Miller, *Studies in Romanticism* 24 (1985), 491–509; Bloom's Chelsea House Modern Critical Interpretations collection (1987); Viscomi's series in *Huntington Library Quarterly* 48 (1997), 281–344, in *Lessons of Romanticism* (1998), ed. Robert Gleckner and Thomas Pfau, and in *Blake in the Nineties* (1999), ed. Clark and Worrall; Morton D. Paley, *Apocalypse and Millennium in English Romantic Poetry* (1999); Everett C. Frost in *Prophetic Character* (2002), ed. Gourlay; Ian Balfour, *The Rhetoric of Romantic Prophecy* (2002); and Peter Schock, *Romantic Satanism* (2003).

Our base text is Copy C, the Pierpont Morgan Library (William Blake Archive; partially reproduced in Erdman's *The Illuminated Blake*); the title page (color plate 7) is reproduced from Copy G, Houghton Library, Harvard.

THE MARRIAGE of HEAVEN and HELL* ☐1

☐2

The Argument[1]

Rintrah[2] roars & shakes his fires in the burdend air;
Hungry clouds swag[3] on the deep.

Once meek, and in a perilous path,
The just man kept his course along
5 The vale of death.
Roses are planted where thorns grow,[4]
And on the barren heath
Sing the honey bees.

Then the perilous path was planted:
10 And a river, and a spring
On every cliff and tomb;
And on the bleached bones[5]
Red clay[6] brought forth.

Till the villain left the paths of ease,
15 To walk in perilous paths, and drive
The just man into barren climes.

Now the sneaking serpent walks
In mild humility.
And the just man rages in the wilds
20 Where lions roam.[7]

Rintrah roars & shakes his fires in the
  burdend air;
Hungry clouds swag on the deep.

---

* See color plate 7 for the title page, which depicts embracing couples emerging from "heavenly" clouds and "hellish" flames, all beneath the earth's surface.

1. Usually an "Argument," such as those introducing the various books of *Paradise Lost*, is a prose preview of a verse narrative; here it is a poem that obliquely enacts themes that will be developed in prose sections of narrative and exposition.

2. Characteristically, without explanation, Blake suddenly introduces a newly invented, vaguely biblical-sounding proper name, as if alluding to some well-known ancient myth. But all that is revealed about Rintrah, in the identical first and last stanzas, is his anger. This character, along with Oothoon, Palamabron, and Bromion from *Visions*, will reappear in *Europe* among offspring of Los and Enitharmon ("O lion Rintrah raise thy fury" [11/8:2]), his position also in *The Four Zoas*, *Milton*, and *Jerusalem*.

3. Sink down, lie heavy (Johnson's *Dictionary*). Obsolete as a verb but surviving as a noun (meaning suspended garland, swath of drapery).

As a new heaven is begun, and it is now thirty-three years since its advent: the Eternal Hell revives. And lo! Swedenborg is the Angel sitting at the tomb; his writings are the linen clothes folded up.[8] Now is the dominion of Edom, & the return of Adam into Paradise; see Isaiah XXXIV & XXXV Chap:[9]

Without Contraries is no progression.[1] Attraction and Repulsion, Reason and Energy, Love and Hate, are necessary to Human existence.

From these contraries spring what the religious call Good & Evil. Good is the passive that obeys Reason. Evil is the active springing from Energy.

Good is Heaven. Evil is Hell.

---

4. As prophesied in Isaiah 35:1 (cf. citation on plate **3**).

5. Recalling Ezekiel's (37) vision of resurrection in the valley of dry bones.

6. The literal Hebrew meaning of Adam, who in plate 3 is said to return to Paradise.

7. As circumstances have changed from "Once" (2:3) through "Then" and "Till" to "Now," the apparent good of meekness and evil of rage have been transvalued (see Paley, *Energy and the Imagination*, Appendix A). The "just man," a conscientious pilgrim reminiscent of Christian in Bunyan's *Pilgrim's Progress*, has become an indignant prophet, while the sneaky, ease-loving "villain," having usurped the once-dangerous path, has become mild and humble. This conflict foreshadows the one between Devils and Angels in the body of the work. The just man's raging in the wilds (2:19) recalls the "voice of him that crieth in the wilderness" (Isaiah 40:3; later identified as John the Baptist in Matthew 3:3; cf. the epigraph to *All Religions Are One*).

8. If Swedenborg's writings are the grave clothes cast off by the risen Christ (John 20:4–13), his "new" heaven must have been rendered obsolete by the resurgence of "Eternal Hell"; cf. the childbirth scene on the clouds below. Jesus, as resurrected in Blake's book, shocks received opinion and thus appears diabolical to pious adherents of tradition-bound faiths.

9. The references to Isaiah 34 (on the devastation of the wrath of God and the curse on Edom, or Idumea) and 35 (on the return of the "ransomed" to Zion and the redemption of the world)

The voice of the Devil   4

All Bibles or sacred codes have been the causes of the following Errors.

1. That Man has two real existing principles Viz: a Body & a Soul.

2. That Energy, calld Evil, is alone from the Body, & that Reason, calld Good, is alone from the Soul.[2]

3. That God will torment Man in Eternity for following his Energies.

But the following Contraries to these are True

1. Man has no Body distinct from his Soul for that calld Body is a portion of Soul discernd by the five Senses, the chief inlets of Soul in this age.

2. Energy is the only life and is from the Body, and Reason is the bound or outward circumference of Energy.

3. Energy is Eternal Delight.

Those who restrain desire, do so because theirs is weak enough to   5
be restrained; and the restrainer or reason usurps its place & governs the unwilling.

And being restraind it by degrees becomes passive till it is only the shadow of desire.

The history of this is written in Paradise Lost, & the Governor or Reason is call'd Messiah.

And the original Archangel or possessor of the command of the heavenly host, is calld the Devil or Satan and his children are call'd Sin & Death.

But in the Book of Job Milton's Messiah is call'd Satan.[3]

For this history has been adopted by both parties.

It indeed appear'd to Reason as if Desire was cast out, but the Devil's account is, that the Messi
ah fell, & formed a heaven of what he stole from the Abyss.   6

This is shewn in the Gospel, where he prays to the Father to send the comforter or Desire[4] that Reason may have Ideas to build on, the Jehovah of the Bible being no other than he who dwells in flaming fire.

---

indicate that contemporary events in revolutionary France should be understood in the light of biblical prophecy. When Jacob, the smooth, devious man later renamed Israel, tricks his older twin brother Esau, the hairy, crude man known as Edom, out of both his birthright (Genesis 25:30) and his blessing (Genesis 27:19), their father Isaac promises that one day Edom will "have the dominion" (Genesis 27:40); in Isaiah 63 a man in red ("red" is the root meaning of both Adam and Edom) comes to take vengeance on Israel. Politically, Edom is the spirit of revolutionary France, which threatens conservative England. The idea that Adam, or redeemed humanity, will one day return to Paradise is a traditional Christian promise, as in Revelation 22:2; what is revolutionary is to say (see plate 14) that Paradise must and will be regained *now*, in the present moment.

1. Cf. "Contrary States of the Human Soul" in *Songs* 2, and the distinction between Contraries and Negations in *Milton* 46/40:33, *Jerusalem* 17:33. See also annotations to Lavater (Erdman 594) and Swedenborg (Erdman 604).

2. Despite the infernal partisanship of the narrator, some propositions in "The voice of the Devil," such as this claim that energy comes exclusively from the body, contradict Blake's ideas expressed elsewhere (cf. attacks on philosophical dualism in *All Religions Are One* and *There Is No Natural Religion*). In annotating Swedenborg's *Heaven and Hell* Blake cautioned that "Satan's blasphemies" in *Paradise Lost* are not those of Milton himself (Erdman 601).

3. In Book 6 the Messiah obeys God's command to restore order by putting down Satan's rebellion. The literal meaning of *Satan* is "adversary"; in Revelation 12:10, Satan is "the accuser of our brethren . . . [who] accused them . . . day and night." The connection here is that in the Bible Satan is the accuser of Job; in *Paradise Lost* the Messiah is the accuser of Adam and Eve.

4. An interpretation of Jesus' promise (John 14:16–17, 14:26) that the Father will send "another Comforter" for his disciples, the "Spirit of truth" or Holy Ghost. The sentence continues with an

Know that after Christ's death, he became Jehovah.

But in Milton; the Father is Destiny, the Son, a Ratio of the five senses, & the Holy-ghost, Vacuum![5]

Note. The reason Milton wrote in fetters when he wrote of Angels & God, and at liberty when of Devils & Hell, is because he was a true Poet and of the Devil's party without knowing it.[6]

A Memorable Fancy.

As I was walking among the fires of hell, delighted with the enjoyments of Genius; which to Angels look like torment and insanity, I collected some of their Proverbs: thinking that as the sayings used in a nation, mark its character, so the Proverbs of Hell, shew the nature of Infernal wisdom better than any description of buildings or garments.[7]

When I came home; on the abyss of the five senses, where a flat sided steep frowns over the present world, I saw a mighty Devil folded in black clouds, hovering on the sides of the rock, with corroding fires he wrote the following sentence now percieved by the   &boxed{7} minds of men, & read by them on earth.[8]

> How do you know but ev'ry Bird that cuts the airy way,
> Is an immense world of delight, clos'd by your senses five?[9]

Proverbs of Hell.[1]

In seed time learn, in harvest teach, in winter enjoy.
Drive your cart and your plow over the bones of the dead.
The road of excess leads to the palace of wisdom.
Prudence is a rich ugly old maid courted by Incapacity.
He who desires but acts not, breeds pestilence.   5
The cut worm forgives the plow.

---

outrageous claim that can be supported by biblical prooftexts from Moses' experiences at the burning bush (Exodus 3:2) and on Mount Sinai (Exodus 19:18) to the warning that Jesus' Second Coming will bring "flaming fire" upon his enemies (2 Thessalonians 1:8).

5. Cf. the Father's apparent endorsement of predestination (*Paradise Lost* 3. 183–84), the Son's physicality (*Paradise Lost* 3.282–86), and the Holy Spirit's absence from the main narrative. "Ratio": usually defined as "proportion," with additional meanings of "reason" and "sum," as in "Application," *There Is No Natural Religion.*

6. This point depends on contrasting the Satan of *Paradise Lost* 1–2, considered as a vividly imagined literary character, with the theologically correct abstract deity of *Paradise Lost* 3.

7. Parodying the tone of Swedenborg's "Memorable Relations" of conversations with angels and devils, especially in *True Christian Religion* (trans. 1781). The notion of collecting proverbs to gain insight into a nation's character is often attributed (without specific citation) to Bacon; Eaves et al. quote the biblical commentator Matthew Henry (1725): "[S]ome think we may judge of the Temper and Character of a Nation, by the Complexion of its vulgar Proverbs. . . . The Devil has his Proverbs, . . . which reflect Reproach on God and Religion" (*Early Illuminated Books,* 211 n.).

8. Alluding to the etching process in which corrosive acid bites inscribed lines into the surface of a metal plate. In Blake's relief-etching variation on this process, the inscriptions are acid resistant and the noninscribed surfaces are etched away by the acid.

9. Adapted from the pseudo-medieval *Bristowe Tragedie* ("How dydd I know that eve'ry darte, / That cutte the Airie waie / Myghte not find passage toe my harte, / And close mine eyes for aie?") by Thomas Chatterton (1752–1770), whose suicide at seventeen, in a garret, helped establish the Romantic idea of the misunderstood and rejected poet. "HOW," the first diabolically etched word, is clearly visible in the design.

1. These nuggets of infernal wisdom counter the prudent "heavenly" Proverbs of the Hebrew Bible and such cautionary folk sayings as "Look before you leap." Collections of tamer aphorisms, such as La Rochefoucauld's *Maxims,* were popular at the time. But Blake approvingly annotated his friend Fuseli's provocative translation of a bolder collection, Lavater's *Aphorisms on Man* (1788) (p. 453 herein). On contexts, see John Villalobos, *Studies in Philology* 87 (1990) 246ff. and Martin D. L. Lansverk, *The Wisdom of Many, The Vision of One* (1994). Line numbers, ignoring plate divisions, refer sequentially to the sixty-nine proverbs.

Dip him in the river who loves water.
A fool sees not the same tree that a wise man sees.
He whose face gives no light, shall never become a star.
Eternity is in love with the productions of time.   10
The busy bee has no time for sorrow.
The hours of folly are measur'd by the clock, but of wisdom:
    no clock can measure.
All wholsom food is caught without a net or a trap.
Bring out number weight & measure in a year of dearth.[2]
No bird soars too high, if he soars with his own wings.   15
A dead body revenges not injuries.
The most sublime act is to set another before you.
If the fool would persist in his folly he would become wise
Folly is the cloke of knavery.
Shame is Pride's cloke.   20

Prisons are built with stones of Law, Brothels with bricks of $\boxed{8}$
    Religion.
The pride of the peacock is the glory of God.
The lust of the goat is the bounty of God.
The wrath of the lion is the wisdom of God.
The nakedness of woman is the work of God.   25
Excess of sorrow laughs. Excess of joy weeps.
The roaring of lions, the howling of wolves, the raging of the
    stormy sea, and the destructive sword are portions of eternity
    too great for the eye of man.
The fox condemns the trap, not himself.
Joys impregnate, Sorrows bring forth.
Let man wear the fell of the lion, woman the fleece of the sheep.   30
The bird a nest, the spider a web, man friendship.
The selfish smiling fool, & the sullen frowning fool, shall be both
    thought wise, that they may be a rod.
What is now proved was once, only imagin'd.
The rat, the mouse, the fox, the rabbet watch the roots; the lion,
    the tyger, the horse, the elephant watch the fruits.
The cistern contains; the fountain overflows.   35
One thought, fills immensity.
Always be ready to speak your mind, and a base man will avoid you.
Every thing possible to be believ'd is an image of truth.
The eagle never lost so much time, as when he submitted to learn
    of the crow.

The fox provides for himself, but God provides for the lion. $\boxed{9}$
Think in the morning, Act in the noon, Eat in the evening, Sleep
    in the night.   40
He who has sufferd you to impose on him knows you.
As the plow follows words, so God rewards prayers.
The tygers of wrath are wiser than the horses of instruction.
Expect poison from the standing water.   45

---

2. Exactly this quantitative sequence appears in Andrew Marvell's "On Mr Milton's 'Paradise Lost'"
(1674) and in Edward Young's *Night Thoughts* (1745) IX.1078–81); cf. *Four Zoas* 9.33.23–24. See
Edward Tayler and Everett Frost, *Blake Newsletter* 5, no. 3 (1971) 213 ff.; and Philip Cox, *Notes
& Queries* 328, no. 40 (1993), 37–38.

You never know what is enough unless you know what is more
   than enough.
Listen to the fool's reproach! it is a kingly title!
The eyes of fire, the nostrils of air, the mouth of water, the beard
   of earth.
The weak in courage is strong in cunning.
The apple tree never asks the beech how he shall grow, nor the
   lion, the horse, how he shall take his prey.   50
The thankful reciever bears a plentiful harvest.
If others had not been foolish, we should be so.
The soul of sweet delight, can never be defil'd.
When thou seest an Eagle, thou seest a portion of Genius: lift up
   thy head!
As the catterpiller chooses the fairest leaves to lay her eggs on,
   so the priest lays his curse on the fairest joys.   55
To create a little flower is the labour of ages.
Damn, braces: Bless relaxes.
The best wine is the oldest, the best water the newest.
Prayers plow not! Praises reap not!
Joys laugh not! Sorrows weep not!   60

The head Sublime, the heart Pathos, the genitals Beauty, the   **10**
   hands & feet Proportion.
As the air to a bird or the sea to a fish, so is contempt to the
   contemptible.
The crow wish'd every thing was black, the owl, that every thing
   was white.
Exuberance is Beauty.
If the lion was advised by the fox, he would be cunning.   65
Improvement makes strait roads, but the crooked roads without
   Improvement, are roads of Genius.
Sooner murder an infant in its cradle than nurse unacted desires.
Where man is not nature is barren.
Truth can never be told so as to be understood, and not be believ'd.

                Enough! or Too much   70

The ancient Poets animated all sensible objects with Gods or 11
Geniuses, calling them by the names and adorning them with the
properties of woods, rivers, mountains, lakes, cities, nations, and whatever their enlarged & numerous senses could percieve.[3]

And particularly they studied the genius of each city & country, placing it under its mental deity.

Till a system was formed, which some took advantage of & enslav'd
the vulgar by attempting to realize or abstract the mental deities from
their objects; thus began Priesthood.

Choosing forms of worship from poetic tales.

And at length they pronouncd that the Gods had orderd such things.

Thus men forgot that All deities reside in the human breast.

A Memorable Fancy.   12

The Prophets Isaiah and Ezekiel dined with me, and I asked them
how they dared so roundly to assert, that God spoke to them; and
whether they did not think at the time, that they would be misunderstood, & so be the cause of imposition.[4]

Isaiah answer'd. "I saw no God, nor heard any, in a finite organical
perception; but my senses discover'd the infinite in every thing, and as
I was then perswaded, & remain confirm'd; that the voice of honest
indignation is the voice of God, I cared not for consequences but
wrote."

Then I asked: "does a firm perswasion that a thing is so, make it so?"

He replied, "All poets believe that it does, & in ages of imagination
this firm perswasion removed mountains; but many are not capable of
a firm perswasion of any thing."

Then Ezekiel said. "The philosophy of the east taught the first principles of human perception. Some nations held one principle for the
origin & some another. We of Israel taught that the Poetic Genius
(as you now call it) was the first principle and all the others merely
derivative, which was the cause of our despising the Priests &
Philosophers of other countries, and prophecying that all Gods
would at last be proved to originate in ours & to be the tributaries of the 13
Poetic Genius; it was this, that our great poet King David desired so fervently & invokes so patheticly, saying by this he conquers enemies &
governs kingdoms; and we so loved our God, that we cursed in his
name all the deities of surrounding nations, and asserted that they had
rebelled; from these opinions the vulgar came to think that all nations
would at last be subject to the jews."

"This," said he, "like all firm perswasions, is come to pass, for all
nations believe the jews' code and worship the jews' god, and what
greater subjection can be?"

I heard this with some wonder, & must confess my own conviction.
After dinner I ask'd Isaiah to favour the world with his lost works, he
said none of equal value was lost. Ezekiel said the same of his.

---

3. Jacob Bryant, whose work Blake knew as an apprentice, analyzes mythological roots of "Names of
   Cities, Lakes, and Rivers" in *A New System* (1774–76), 1.189ff.
4. This episode combines conventional scenes of the philosophic dinner, as in Plato's *Symposium*, and
   the encounter with the famous dead, as in *Gulliver's Travels* 3.7–8. The identification of the true
   God with the Poetic Genius or creative imagination first appears in *All Religions Are One*.

I also asked Isaiah what made him go naked and barefoot three years? He answerd, "the same that made our friend Diogenes the Grecian."[5]

I then asked Ezekiel, why he eat dung, & lay so long on his right & left side? He answerd, "the desire of raising other men into a perception of the infinite; this the North American tribes practise, & is he honest who resists his genius or conscience, only for the sake of present ease or gratification?"[6]

The ancient tradition that the world will be consumed in fire at the end of six thousand years is true, as I have heard from Hell.[7] |14|

For the cherub with his flaming sword is hereby commanded to leave his guard at tree of life, and when he does, the whole creation will be consumed, and appear infinite, and holy, whereas it now appears finite & corrupt.[8]

This will come to pass by an improvement of sensual enjoyment.

But first the notion that man has a body distinct from his soul, is to be expunged; this I shall do, by printing in the infernal method, by corrosives, which in Hell are salutary and medicinal, melting apparent surfaces away, and displaying the infinite which was hid.

If the doors of perception were cleansed every thing would appear to man as it is, infinite.

For man has closed himself up, till he sees all things thro' narrow chinks of his cavern.[9]

A Memorable Fancy |15|

I was in a Printing house in Hell & saw the method in which knowledge is transmitted from generation to generation.[1]

5. In Isaiah 20:2 this drastic behavior is a warning that the Egyptians and Ethiopians will be captured by the Assyrians. The Greek pre-Socratic philosopher Diogenes the Cynic (ca. 412–323 B.C.E.), recognized by Blake's Isaiah as a friend and fellow prophet, also went naked; he gave away his possessions, lived in a barrel, and went about with a lantern in broad daylight in search of an honest man. Even Saul, when he stripped off his clothes while briefly under divine inspiration, was taken for a prophet (1 Samuel 19:24).
6. In Ezekiel 4 the prophet is commanded to lie 390 days on his left side to represent the years of Israel's iniquity and 40 days on his right side to represent the years of Judah's iniquity. When he is commanded to bake and eat barley cakes "with" human dung, he prays to be spared and is then allowed to use cow's dung. Both Blake and Swedenborg apparently took this to mean that Ezekiel had to mix his barley cakes with dung rather than just use it for fuel (cf. Swedenborg's *True Christian Religion*, section 130). Ezekiel claims affinity with Native American medicine men who subject themselves to strict disciplines to produce visions that enlighten the whole community. In annotations to Watson Blake refers to "accounts of North American savages (as they are called)" without naming his source.
7. The traditional span of human history, in which a thousand years equals one day of God's time, extends for a "week" of thousand-year "days" corresponding to the six days of Creation, followed by a sabbatical millennium of Christ's reign on earth; all this is derived from Psalm 90:4, 2 Peter 3:8, Genesis 1, and Revelation 20:2–5; for the destruction of the world by fire, see 2 Peter 3:7, 12.
8. Blake probably forgot to write "the" before "tree." In Genesis 3:24 God stations cherubim (plural) "and a flaming sword which turned every way" to guard the tree of life; in Ezekiel 28:12–19 God directs the prophet to tell the "anointed cherub that covereth," who has "been in Eden the garden of God," that because of his pride and iniquity he will be devoured by fire. This prohibiting angel, the Covering Cherub, appears prominently in *Milton* 37 and *Jerusalem* 89.
9. This variation on Plato's myth of the cave (*Republic* 7) as an emblem of the skull recalls Locke's comparison of sensations to "windows by which light is let into" the "dark room" of the mind, which is like "a closet wholly shut out from light, with only some little openings left . . . to let in external visible resemblances . . . of things without" (*Essay Concerning Human Understanding* [1690], 2.11.17). Cf. Newton's "round Hole, about one third Part of an Inch broad, made in the Shut of a Window" in a "very dark Chamber" into which he admitted a single beam of light for experiments with a prism (*Opticks* [1704], I.I.ii).
1. Commentators agree that the first five chambers in this printing-house fantasy on the transmission of knowledge mark stages in the cleansing of the senses and the production of illuminated books. There is less agreement on the implications of the orderly sixth chamber.

In the first chamber was a Dragon-Man, clearing away the rubbish from a cave's mouth; within, a number of Dragons were hollowing the cave.

In the second chamber was a Viper folding round the rock & the cave, and others adorning it with gold silver and precious stones.

In the third chamber was an Eagle with wings and feathers of air, he caused the inside of the cave to be infinite, around were numbers of Eagle like men, who built palaces in the immense cliffs.

In the fourth chamber were Lions of flaming fire raging around & melting the metals into living fluids.

In the fifth chamber were Unnam'd forms, which cast the metals into the expanse.

There they were reciev'd by Men who occupied the sixth chamber, and took the forms of books & were arranged in libraries.

The Giants who formed this world into its sensual existence and now seem to live in it in chains, are in truth, the causes of its life & the sources of all activity, but the chains are the cunning of weak and tame minds, which have power to resist energy, according to the proverb, the weak in courage is strong in cunning.[2] |16|

Thus one portion of being, is the Prolific, the other, the Devouring; to the devourer it seems as if the producer was in his chains, but it is not so, he only takes portions of existence and fancies that the whole.

But the Prolific would cease to be Prolific unless the Devourer as a sea recieved the excess of his delights.

Some will say, Is not God alone the Prolific? I answer, God only Acts & Is, in existing beings or Men.

These two classes of men are always upon earth, & they should be enemies; whoever tries

to reconcile them seeks to destroy existence. |17|

Religion is an endeavour to reconcile the two.

Note. Jesus Christ did not wish to unite but to seperate them, as in the Parable of sheep and goats! & he says I came not to send Peace but a Sword.[3]

Messiah or Satan or Tempter was formerly thought to be one of the Antediluvians who are our Energies.

A Memorable Fancy[4]

An Angel came to me and said "O pitiable foolish young man! O horrible! O dreadful state! consider the hot burning dungeon thou art preparing for thyself to all eternity, to which thou art going in such career."

I said, "Perhaps you will be willing to shew me my eternal lot & we will

2. The narrator's quotation of a Proverb of Hell (9:49) leads into a devilish polarization of new contraries, Prolific and Devourer, that extend well beyond the economic opposition of producer and consumer.
3. Matthew 25:32–33 (on sheep and goats), 10:34 (on the sword; translated as "division" in Luke 12:51).
4. A variation on the traditional story patterns of a descent into hell and a flight into space (in this case, inner space), moving from recognizable Christian landmarks to a subterranean void in which horrific visions culminate in the approach of Leviathan. In Blake's engravings for the Book of Job (1825), this monstrous sea creature (Job 41) and Behemoth (Job 40), his counterpart on land, are seen to be apparitions of Job's frightened imagination (plate 15). Cf. Isaiah 27:1, Revelation 13:2.

contemplate together upon it and see whether your lot or mine is most desirable."

So he took me thro' a stable & thro' a church & down into the church vault at the end of which was a mill; thro' the mill we went, and came to a cave; down the winding cavern we groped our tedious way till a void boundless as a nether sky appeard beneath us, & we held by the roots of trees and hung over this immensity, but I said, "If you please we will commit ourselves to this void, and see whether providence is here also; if you will not I will?" But he answerd, "Do not presume O young-man but as we here remain behold thy lot which will soon appear when the darkness passes away."

So I remaind with him sitting in the twisted root of an oak. He was suspended in a fungus which hung with the head downward into the deep: [18]

By degrees we beheld the infinite Abyss, fiery as the smoke of a burning city; beneath us at an immense distance was the sun, black but shining round it were fiery tracks on which revolv'd vast spiders, crawling after their prey; which flew or rather swum in the infinite deep, in the most terrific shapes of animals sprung from corruption, & the air was full of them, & seemd composed of them; these are Devils, and are called Powers of the air. I now asked my companion which my eternal lot? he said, "between the black & white spiders."

But now, from between the black & white spiders a cloud and fire burst and rolled thro the deep, blackning all beneath, so that the nether deep grew black as a sea & rolled with a terrible noise: beneath us was nothing now to be seen but a black tempest, till looking east between the clouds & the waves, we saw a cataract of blood mixed with fire and not many stones' throw from us appeard and sunk again the scaly fold of a monstrous serpent. At last to the east, distant about three degrees[5] appeard a fiery crest above the waves. Slowly it reared like a ridge of golden rocks till we discovered two globes of crimson fire, from which the sea fled away in clouds of smoke, and now we saw, it was the head of Leviathan, his forehead was divided into streaks of green & purple like those on a tyger's forehead: soon we saw his mouth & red gills hang just above the raging foam tinging the black deep with beams of blood, advancing toward us with all the fury of a spiritual existence.   [19]

My friend the Angel climb'd up from his station into the mill; I remain'd alone, & then this appearance was no more, but I found myself sitting on a pleasant bank beside a river by moon light hearing a harper who sung to the harp, & his theme was, The man who never alters his opinion is like standing water, & breeds reptiles of the mind.

But I arose, and sought for the mill & there I found my Angel, who surprised asked me, how I escaped?

I answered. "All that we saw was owing to your metaphysics; for when you ran away, I found myself on a bank by moonlight hearing a harper. But now we have seen my eternal lot, shall I shew you yours?" He laughd at my proposal; but I by force suddenly caught him in my arms,

5. The longitudinal distance between London and Paris.

& flew westerly thro' the night, till we were elevated above the earth's shadow: then I flung myself with him directly into the body of the sun; here I clothed myself in white, & taking in my hand Swedenborg's volumes sunk from the glorious clime, and passed all the planets till we came to Saturn.[6] Here I staid to rest & then leap'd into the void, between Saturn & the fixed stars.

"Here" said I! "is your lot, in this space, if space it may be calld." Soon we saw the stable and the church, & I took him to the altar and open'd the Bible, and lo! it was a deep pit, into which I descended driving the Angel before me. Soon we saw seven houses of brick,[7] one we enterd; in it were a

number of monkeys, baboons, & all of that species chaind by the [20] middle, grinning and snatching at one another, but witheld by the shortness of their chains: however I saw that they sometimes grew numerous, and then the weak were caught by the strong and with a grinning aspect, first coupled with & then devourd, by plucking off first one limb and then another till the body was left a helpless trunk. This after grinning & kissing it with seeming fondness they devourd too; and here & there I saw one savourily picking the flesh off of his own tail; as the stench terribly annoyd us both we went into the mill, & I in my hand brought the skeleton of a body, which in the mill was Aristotle's Analytics.

So the Angel said: "Thy phantasy has imposed upon me & thou oughtest to be ashamed."

I answerd: "We impose on one another, & it is but lost time to converse with you whose works are only Analytics."

[Opposition is True Friendship][8]

6. Traditionally the outermost planet. Blake leaves the name uncapitalized.
7. Cf. the "seven churches of Asia" (Revelation 1:4). Another movement through landmarks of Christian history, this time descending through the "deep pit" of an open Bible.
8. This contrarian motto (beneath the serpent) was obliterated in our source text and, at least partially, in half of the copies of *Marriage;* but as can be seen in Copy B (reproduced herein), sometimes enough remains ("Opposition is True") to constitute a teasing alternative.

I have always found that Angels have the vanity to speak of   21
themselves as the only wise; this they do with a confident insolence
sprouting from systematic reasoning:[9]

Thus Swedenborg boasts that what he writes is new: tho' it is only
the Contents or Index of already publish'd books.

A man carried a monkey about for a shew, & because he was a little
wiser than the monkey, grew vain, and conciev'd himself as much wiser
than seven men. It is so with Swedenborg; he shews the folly of
churches & exposes hypocrites, till he imagines that all are religious,
& himself the single

one on earth that ever broke a net.   22

Now hear a plain fact: Swedenborg has not written one new truth:
Now hear another: he has written all the old falsehoods.

And now hear the reason. He conversed with Angels who are all religious, & conversed not with Devils who all hate religion, for he was
incapable thro' his conceited notions.

Thus Swedenborg's writings are a recapitulation of all superficial
opinions, and an analysis of the more sublime, but no further.

Have now another plain fact: Any man of mechanical talents may
from the writings of Paracelsus or Jacob Behmen,[1] produce ten thousand volumes of equal value with Swedenborg's, and from those of
Dante or Shakespear, an infinite number.

But when he has done this, let him not say that he knows better than
his master, for he only holds a candle in sunshine.

9. In the headpiece design, the right hand of a newly resurrected nude male rests on what looks like
 a sheet of paper, and his left knee rests on a rocklike skull; in Copy D, he is backed by a pyramid
 and a setting sun across the sea. A similar figure in *America* 6 (not included in this edition) has a
 skull beside his right hand. Blake reused the figure, atop a tomb, in his twelfth design for Blair's
 Grave (1808). Blake may have once intended this plate and the three following, etched first, to
 stand alone (Viscomi 1997).
1. Jakob Boehme (1575–1624), also called Behmen, German thosophist and shoemaker whose influential work was translated by William Law in 1761. Paracelsus (1493–1541), the pen name of a
 Swiss alchemist, theorist of the occult, and medical pioneer. Blake's letter-poem of September 12,
 1800 (p. 473), suggests that these two writers were greater influences on him than Swedenborg;
 but see later remarks on Swedenborg as "the Samson shorn by the Churches" (*Milton* **24**/22:50)
 and "The Spiritual Preceptor" (Erdman 546).

A Memorable Fancy

Once I saw a Devil in a flame of fire, who arose before an Angel that sat on a cloud, and the Devil utterd these words.

"The worship of God is, Honouring his gifts in other men, each according to his genius, and loving the greatest men best, those who envy or calumniate great men hate |23| God, for there is no other God."

The Angel hearing this became almost blue but mastering himself he grew yellow, & at last white pink & smiling,[2] and then replied,

"Thou Idolater, is not God One? & is not he visible in Jesus Christ? and has not Jesus Christ given his sanction to the law of ten commandments, and are not all other men fools, sinners, & nothings?"

The Devil answer'd: "Bray a fool in a morter with wheat, yet shall not his folly be beaten out of him:[3] if Jesus Christ is the greatest man, you ought to love him in the greatest degree; now hear how he has given his sanction to the law of ten commandments: did he not mock at the sabbath, and so mock the sabbath's God? murder those who were murderd because of him? turn away the law from the woman taken in adultery? steal the labor of others to support him? bear false witness when he omitted making a defence before Pilate? covet when he pray'd for his disciples, and when he bid them shake off the dust of their feet against such as refused to lodge them? I tell you, no virtue can exist without breaking these ten commandments:[4] Jesus was all virtue, and acted from impulse, not from rules. |24|

When he had so spoken: I beheld the Angel who stretched out his arms embracing the flame of fire & he was consumed and arose as Elijah.[5]

Note. This Angel, who is now become a Devil, is my particular friend: we often read the Bible together in its infernal or diabolical sense which the world shall have if they behave well.

I have also: The Bible of Hell:[6] which the world shall have whether they will or no.

One Law for the Lion & Ox is Oppression[7]

---

2. Recalling the changing colors of the embarrassed archangel Raphael in *Paradise Lost* 8.619, when Adam asks how angels make love.
3. A paraphrase of Proverbs 27:22. "Bray": to crush, as with a mortar and pestle.
4. The commandments Jesus broke or reinterpreted, according to the incidents cited by the devil, are the fourth (Matthew 12:2–13), sixth (John 16:2; Matthew 2:16–18), seventh (John 8:1–11), eighth (Matthew 10:9–10); ninth (Matthew 27:12–14), and tenth (John 17:9–10; Matthew 10:14). The connection between Jesus' virtue and his violation of conventional morality is further explored in Blake's manuscript poem "The Everlasting Gospel" (c. 1818).
5. The Angel's transformative embrace of the flame anticipates Blake's concept of self-annihilation. Cf. *Jerusalem* 96:35. The prophet Elijah, separated from his successor Elisha by a "chariot of fire" and caught up into heaven in a whirlwind (2 Kings 2:11), was named a forerunner of the Messiah (Malachi 4:5), identified by some with John the Baptist (Matthew 11:14). This conversion is as close as this work comes to the "marriage" named in the title.
6. Refers to "A Song of Liberty" and probably also to the biblically formatted "Lambeth books" of *Urizen*, *Ahania*, and *Los*. Cf. the title page drafted for Volume I, "in Nocturnal Visions collected" (Erdman 674).
7. Cf. *Visions* 7/4:22. The design above this caption (p. 81), a bestial king crawling through a forest,

One Law for the Lion & Ox is Oppression

A Song of Liberty[8]   25

1. The Eternal Female groand! it was heard over all the Earth:

2. Albion's coast is sick, silent; the American meadows faint!

3. Shadows of Prophecy shiver along by the lakes and the rivers and mutter across the ocean? France rend down thy dungeon.[9]

4. Golden Spain burst the barriers of old Rome;

5. Cast thy keys[1] O Rome into the deep down falling, even to eternity down falling,

6. And weep.

7. In her trembling hands she took the new born terror howling:

8. On those infinite mountains of light now barr'd out by the atlantic sea,[2] the new born fire stood before the starry king!

---

is identified in Blake's series of large color prints (1799–1805) as the mad king Nebuchadnezzar of Babylon who "did eat grass as oxen" (illustrated in Blake's design 299 for Young's *Night Thoughts*) and whose nails grew "like birds' claws" (Daniel 4:30–33), historically associated with King George III's episodic dementia.

8. The Eternal Female, the new born terror (verse 7), and the starry king (verse 8) appear in *America* and *Europe* as Enitharmon, Orc, and Urizen, archetypal figures of the American and French revolutions. Urthona, whose dens are mentioned in verse 16, is ultimately identified with Los, another major character who appears first in *Europe*.

9. The Bastille, destroyed in 1789, one of the political and social allusions that would have been instantly recognizable to Blake's contemporaries.

1. The keys of Christ's kingdom, given to St. Peter (Matthew 16:19); symbol of papal authority. The French National Assembly's Civil Constitution of the Clergy Act (1790) abolished eighty-three bishropics and confiscated papal property.

2. Covering the lost continent of Atlantis. Cf. *America* **12**/10:6.

9. Flag'd with grey brow'd snows and thunderous visages the jealous wings wav'd over the deep.

10. The speary hand burned aloft, unbuckled was the shield, forth went the hand of jealousy among the flaming hair, and hurl'd the new born wonder thro' the starry night. |26|

11. The fire, the fire, is falling!

12. Look up! look up! O citizen of London, enlarge thy countenance; O Jew, leave counting gold! return to thy oil and wine; O African! black African! (go, winged thought widen his forehead.)[3]

13. The fiery limbs, the flaming hair, shot like the sinking sun into the western sea.

14. Wak'd from his eternal sleep, the hoary element roaring fled away;[4]

15. Down rushd beating his wings in vain the jealous king; his grey brow'd councellors, thunderous warriors, curl'd veterans among helms, and shields, and chariots, horses, elephants: banners, castles, slings and rocks,

16. Falling, rushing, ruining! buried in the ruins, on Urthona's dens.

17. All night beneath the ruins, then, their sullen flames faded, emerge round the gloomy king,

18. With thunder and fire: leading his starry hosts thro' the waste wilderness

he promulgates his ten commands, glancing his beamy eyelids |27| over the deep in dark dismay,

19. Where the son of fire in his eastern cloud, while the morning plumes her golden breast,

20. Spurning the clouds written with curses, stamps the stony law to dust, loosing the eternal horses from the dens of night, crying

Empire is no more! and now the lion & wolf shall cease.[5]

Chorus

Let the Priests of the Raven of dawn, no longer in deadly black, with hoarse note curse the sons of joy.[6] Nor his accepted brethren whom, tyrant, he calls free: lay the bound or build the roof.[7] Nor pale religious letchery call that virginity, that wishes but acts not!

For every thing that lives is Holy[8]

---

3. These exclamations probably urge abandonment of confining ethnic stereotypes. Lavater's *Essays on Physiognomy* (1789–98), for which Blake provided four engravings, claimed that the developing brain shapes and determines the size of the skull: in a free society, both the Londoner and the African would develop wider foreheads with the expansion of revolutionary consciousness, and revolutionary change would liberate Jews from their traditional occupations in Europe.
4. The sea disappears at the Apocalypse (Revelation 21:1). Imagery of verses 13–20 anticipates the recurring conflict between an aged king of night and a fiery youth of dawn in *America* 10/8:3–5, *Europe* 13/10:14, and *Urizen* 28.
5. In larger lettering than the rest of the song; repeated in *America* 8/6:15.
6. The commas indicate rhetorical pauses, not the interruption of a parenthetical phrase—that is, "no longer" modifies "curse" as well as "in deadly black."
7. On political factions among Freemasons, "Free and Accepted Brethren," see Schuchard in *Blake and the Nineties* (1999), ed. Clark and Worrall.
8. Drafted in marginalia to Lavater and reiterated in *Visions* 10/8:10 and *America* 10/8:13.

AMERICA: A PROPHECY (1793)

America, "Printed by William Blake in the year 1793" and offered for sale in October of that year, appeared in a momentous period that overlaps with Year 1 of the French revolutionary calendar. The year began with Louis XIV's execution in January, followed by Britain's declaration of war against the French revolutionary government in February, the radical Jacobins' ascendancy over the moderate Girondins in May, the assassination of Marat and the rise of Robespierre in July, and the onset of the Reign of Terror in September. Little wonder that English sympathizers like Blake found it increasingly difficult to justify support for revolutionary change. Not only difficult but dangerous: the British Parliament passed harsh laws against seditious publications, informants reported on their neighbors, and police cracked down on all forms of political dissent. The upheavals of 1789–93 in France, coming so soon after those of 1775–81 in what became the United States, threatened the stability of monarchies everywhere and raised questions about the causes underlying all revolutions. At a time of urgent political debate about events unfolding in France, Blake sought a larger, more visionary understanding of the shape of history. How does revolution arise? Why does it recur? Why and how does it spread from one country to another? Are the American and French revolutions different, or are they manifestations of the same spirit of renewal? How should Britain conduct itself in a revolutionary age?

As the first of Blake's works to be subtitled "A Prophecy" (the other is *Europe*), *America* proclaims itself the utterance of a prophet, but its subject is recent history, not the future. Prophecy of this sort makes connections between past and present, provides insights into underlying motives, raises alarms about likely consequences, and envisions fresh possibilities, but it does not predict an inevitable future. Blake's most straightforward definition of a prophet appears in his 1798 marginalia to Watson: "Prophets, in the modern sense of the word, have never existed. Jonah was no prophet in the modern sense, for his prophecy of Nineveh failed" (p. 458 herein); instead of making ironclad forecasts, true prophets point out that "If you go on So, the result is So." Above all, prophets like Isaiah and Ezekiel, as Blake represents them in *The Marriage of Heaven and Hell*, recognize that "the voice of honest indignation is the voice of God" and speak out fearlessly to alert their contemporaries to the implications of what is going on around them. This Blake does through his own myth of clashing titanic forces of rebellion and repression.

Blake's earlier work *The French Revolution* (not in this edition), set in ordinary type but never published, is a more conventional poetic narrative of the revolution between 1789 and 1791—well before the Terror. Blake also designed a title page for a work to be called *The American War*, possibly a projected poetic history of some of the same events that appear in mythic form in *America: A Prophecy*. *America* begins with a narrative "Preludium" (plates 3/1–4/2) on an outbreak of repressed energy followed by the pain of new growth. A "terrible boy," the fiery, resentful "red Orc," suddenly breaks his chains at the age of fourteen and sexually assaults a mute, dark, virginal "nameless female," clad only in a helmet and armed with a bow and arrows, who has been bringing his food. The woman, in mingled suffering and joy, gains the ability to speak, declares that her attacker is "the image of God" who takes different forms in different nations, identifies herself with the "American plains," and proclaims that she is undergoing "eternal death . . . the torment long foretold." References to recognizable historical figures begin in the work proper, but the forces that set them in motion are the giant antagonists Orc and Urizen, mythical "spiritual forms" associated with rebellious energy and restrictive rationality. Urizen operates through the "guardian Prince of Albion," who resembles the repressive

King George III but is not quite identical with him, while Orc spurs on Washington and other American patriots. Leaders of both sides are represented as magnified human beings standing on their respective coastlines, signaling and shouting across the Atlantic. As agents of Orc and Urizen, they are like Trojan War heroes manipulated by the gods of Homer's *Iliad*.

Although none of Blake's illuminated works is named after Orc, *America* may be thought of as his book: he precipitates most of the action. In the "Preludium," his first action is a *reaction* to his having been enchained during his first fourteen years. Whether the name Orc derives from "orc" (sea monster), "Orcus" (hell, also a giant in Spenser), "cor" (heart), or "orchis" (testicle), or all of these, this furious and libidinous figure struggles against political oppression, sexual repression, religious authority, and all rational constraints and restraints on all forms of energy. In the myth of Orc, Blake establishes an identity between psychological and sociological expressions of rage and lust: Orc is the pent-up energy and desire in human nature and human history that, if held down too long, inevitably erupts in violent action. In *America*, Orc's gorgeous rhetoric of rebellion and new life overpowers the empty fulminations of Albion's Angel, agent of Urizen. But in *Europe*, the sequel, Orc's revolutionary spirit is subdued until the very end, when "in the vineyards of red France appear'd the light of his fury" (**18**/15:2).

America is the first of Blake's "Lambeth books," so called by scholars because their title pages display this place of publication, a section of London on the south side of the Thames (see map) where the Blakes lived in the 1790s. The other Lambeth books are *Europe, The Song of Los, Urizen, Ahania,* and *The Book of Los. America* is also the first of the subgroup nicknamed "continental prophecies," which include *Europe* and the "Asia" and "Africa" sections of *The Song of Los.* Among the numerous verbal bridges between *America* and other illuminated books, the most important are to "The Song of Liberty" at the end of *The Marriage of Heaven and Hell,* a condensed account of an Orc-like newborn who challenges a "jealous king" and "stamps the stony law to dust." The concluding words of the Chorus, "For every thing that lives is Holy," repeated by Oothoon in *Visions of the Daughters of Albion* (11/8:10), reappear in *America* **10**/8:13. The first line of the main body of *America* (3:1), "The Guardian Prince of Albion burns in his nightly tent," is also the last line of "Africa" in *The Song of Los;* the "Preludium" of *Europe* is a kind of sequel to the "Preludium" of *America; America* **18**/16:15 prophesies the French reception of Orc's furious light, confirmed in *Europe* **18**/15:2, and the same inflammatory influence is traced in "Asia" (*Song of Los* **6**:6), as if Blake foresaw in 1793 the geopolitical transformations beginning in the mid-twentieth century. The "howling" of Albion's Guardian in *America* (**17**/15:8) continues in *Europe* (**15**/12:12, 14), echoed by reactionary forces throughout the Continent (*Europe* **15**/12:21) and spreading east, where in "Asia" it is heard by other kings (*Song of Los* **6**:2).

For *America,* as for the other "continent" works, Blake used copperplates measuring about nine by seven inches, to make books much larger than other illuminated works except *Jerusalem.* Only four of the fifteen copies of *America* are colored. The designs in *America* are beautifully woven into the text in a more complex way than in earlier works. Earlier versions of four plates as well as some preliminary drawings provide a fuller record than usual about how Blake's thoughts changed on the best way to render his material. For example, in most copies, including our source text, he masked the lines about the Bard's smashing of his harp at the end of the "Preludium" (1:18–21; printed in n. 8, p. 87 herein), but two of the three copies in which these lines appear are late copies. Minor pictorial and textual variants among the published copies round out indications of the care with which Blake considered and refined this work about the origins and fate of freedom in history.

D. W. Dörrbecker's facsimile edition of Copy H (uncolored), British Museum, in *The Continental Prophecies*, volume 4 of the Blake Trust series, includes helpful commentary. David V. Erdman's section on "The American War" in *Blake: Prophet against Empire* and his "America: New Expanses" in *Visionary Forms Dramatic* have inspired (or provoked) useful essays by Minna Doskow, *Blake Studies* 8:2 (1979), David E. James, *Studies in Romanticism* 18 (1979), 235–52; Ronald Schliefer, *Studies in English Literature* 19:4 (1979), 569–88; Stephen C. Behrendt, *Eighteenth Century: Theory and Interpretation* 27:1 (1986), 379–97; Michael Ferber in *History & Myth* (1990), ed. Behrendt (1990); William Richey in *Blake, Politics, and History* (1998), ed. Di Salvo et al.; Saree Makdisi in *Romantic Generations* (2001), ed. McDayter, Batten, and Milligan; and work by Mee (p. 574 herein) and Makdisi (p. 576 herein). For the fullest consideration of multitudinous issues surrounding the figure of Orc, see Christopher Z. Hobson, *The Chained Boy: Orc and Blake's Idea of Revolution* (1999). For other facsimiles, see Copy M in the older Blake Trust Series, ed. Geoffrey Keynes (the source of an inexpensive Dover reprint, 1984); Copies E, A, M, and O, with more to come, in the online William Blake Archive, ed. Eaves, Essick, and Viscomi; and Copy L in the New York Public Library's digital gallery (digitalgallery.nypl.org).

Our text and black and white images are taken from Copy E, Library of Congress, from Blake's first print run of this work (1793); the color plate is from Copy O (1821), Fitzwilliam Museum.

AMERICA a PROPHECY*   2/ii

Lambeth[1]
Printed by William Blake in the year 1793.

Preludium   3/1

---

* See color plate 8: male and female figures in the clouds concentrate on books, probably of prophecy; on earth below, a woman embraces a dead soldier on a battlefield.

1. Section of London south of the Thames (see map); Blake's home, 1790–1800.

The shadowy daughter of Urthona stood before red Orc,[2]   3/1
When fourteen suns[3] had faintly journey'd o'er his dark abode;
His food she brought in iron baskets, his drink in cups of iron;
Crown'd with a helmet & dark hair the nameless female stood;
A quiver with its burning stores, a bow like that of night,[4]   5
When pestilence is shot from heaven; no other arms she need:
Invulnerable tho' naked, save where clouds roll round her loins,
Their awful folds in the dark air; silent she stood as night;
For never from her iron tongue could voice or sound arise;
But dumb till that dread day when Orc assay'd his fierce embrace.   10

"Dark virgin," said the hairy youth, "thy father stern abhorr'd;[5]
Rivets my tenfold chains while still on high my spirit soars;
Sometimes an eagle screaming in the sky, sometimes a lion,
Stalking upon the mountains, & sometimes a whale I lash
The raging fathomless abyss, anon a serpent[6] folding   15
Around the pillars of Urthona, and round thy dark limbs,
On the Canadian wilds I fold, feeble my spirit folds.
For chaind beneath I rend these caverns; when thou bringest food
I howl my joy: and my red eyes seek to behold thy face
In vain! these clouds roll to & fro, & hide thee from my sight."   20

Silent as despairing love, and strong as jealousy,   4/2
The hairy shoulders rend the links, free are the wrists of fire;
Round the terrific loins he siez'd the panting struggling womb;
It joy'd: she put aside her clouds & smiled her first-born smile;

2. "Urthona" (cf. "Song of Liberty," verse 16, *Marriage* 25): In Blake's later writings, an alter ego of
   the blacksmith-artist-prophet Los. The "shadowy daughter," associated with the unrealized potential of Nature, the fertile land and abundant resources of the New World, resembles the "shadowy
   female" in *Europe* 4/1:1–4. "Orc" (for possible derivations, see headnote) is anticipated in "the new
   born terror," "fire," and "wonder" of "Song of Liberty" (*Marriage* 25–26), later identified as the first-
   born son of Los and Enitharmon (*Urizen* VII.1 [20:6]). As rebel and enchained victim, Orc resembles Prometheus; as cosmic warrior, he is associated with Mars and his red planet. His being "hairy"
   (3/1:11, 4/2:2) and "red" emphasizes his similarity to the biblical Esau, the resentful outcast also
   named Edom, whose long-expected "dominion" is proclaimed in *Marriage* 3.
3. Interval between Rousseau's *Social Contract* (1762) and the Declaration of Independence (1776)
   and between the Battle of Bunker Hill (1775) and the fall of the Bastille (1789).
4. I.e., with accoutrements recalling other mythical virgins: a helmet (3/1:4) associated with Athena,
   the Valkyries, and McPherson's Oithóna (see n. 4, p. 57) and a bow and quiver (3/1:5) associated
   with Diana. Her implements evoke the Iron Age.
5. In later works Blake links Urthona with Orc's father, Los, who binds his son with the "Chain of
   Jealousy" (*Urizen* VII.4 [20:25]; cf. this book's cover and design on *America* 3/1), but here there
   is no indication that the "shadowy female" and Orc have the same father.
6. One of Blake's first fourfold arrays, here of creatures associated with the four elements; for the shadowy female, the serpent, eagle, lion, and whale, are totems of Canada, Mexico, Peru, and the South
   Seas (4/2:12). In Blake's work, the serpent is also associated with the tempter in Eden (10/8:1), the
   phallus, and the spirit of revolution (cf. the widely disseminated images of Franklin's self-renewing
   "Join or Die" emblem of 1754 and the "Don't Tread on Me" Gadsden rattlesnake flag of 1775).

As when a black cloud shews its light'nings to the silent deep,   5

Soon as she saw the terrible boy then burst the virgin cry.

"I know thee, I have found thee, & I will not let thee go;
Thou art the image of God who dwells in darkness of Africa:
And thou art fall'n to give me life in regions of dark death.[7]
On my American plains I feel the struggling afflictions   10
Endur'd by roots that writhe their arms into the nether deep:
I see a serpent in Canada, who courts me to his love;
In Mexico an Eagle, and a Lion in Peru;
I see a Whale in the South-sea, drinking my soul away.
O what limb rending pains I feel, thy fire & my frost   15
Mingle in howling pains, in furrows by thy lightnings rent;
This is eternal death; and this the torment long foretold."[8]

A PROPHECY   5/3

The Guardian Prince of Albion burns in his nightly tent[9]
Sullen fires across the Atlantic glow to America's shore:
Piercing the souls of warlike men, who rise in silent night,
Washington, Franklin, Paine & Warren, Gates, Hancock & Green[1]
Meet on the coast glowing with blood from Albion's fiery Prince.   5

7. Cf. "Africa," *Song of Los* **3**:21 and the reference to slavery in *Visions* **4**/1:21. The female, speaking as a fertile land, suggests in her idolatry of Orc that he is a vegetation god "fall'n to give me life." Her refusal to let him go echoes Song of Solomon 3:4.
8. In three copies—one early and two late—this scene is undercut by a renunciation: "The stern Bard ceas'd, asham'd of His own song; enraged he swung / His harp aloft sounding, then dash'd its shining frame against / A ruin'd pillar in glittering fragments; silent he turn'd away, / And wanderd down the vales of Kent in sick & drear lamentings." In all other copies these four lines were masked to prevent them from printing.
9. Repeated as the last line of "Africa" in *Song of Los*. As representatives of the British establishment, "Guardian Prince of Albion" and "Albion's Angel" (7/5:1), are virtually interchangeable.
1. General Nathaniel Greene (1742–1786), member of the Continental Congress and later of the U.S. Congress, was known for his brilliant tactics as cavalry commander. In the British popular imagination of the American Revolution, Washington (1732–1799) and Franklin (1706–1790) were heroic icons, unlike the English-born radical Thomas Paine (1737–1809). Paine's *Common Sense* and *Crisis* (1776) inspired American resistance; his *Rights of Man* (1791–92) justified the French Revolution, led to his conviction for treason against Britain (December 1792). According to legend, Blake warned Paine to flee to France, where he was in fact seated as a "citizen of the world" in the National Convention; soon afterward he was jailed by Robespierre and narrowly escaped the guillotine. Blake defended Paine's *The Age of Reason* (1794–96), considered blasphemous in challenging Christian superstition, as well as *Common Sense*: "Is it a greater miracle to feed five thousand men with five loaves than to overthrow all the armies of Europe with a small pamphlet?" (Marginalia to Watson, see p. 458 herein). Joseph Warren (1741–1775) of Boston was killed at Bunker Hill (1775). General Horatio Gates (1728?–1806) received Burgoyne's surrender at Saratoga (1777) but was later disgracefully defeated by Cornwallis (1780). John Hancock (1737–1793) of Boston, president of the Continental Congress, penned the first and largest signature on the Declaration of Independence.

Washington spoke; "Friends of America look over the Atlantic sea;
A bended bow is lifted in heaven, & a heavy iron chain[2]
Descends link by link from Albion's cliffs across the sea to bind
Brothers & sons of America, till our faces pale and yellow;
Heads deprest, voices weak, eyes downcast, hands work-bruis'd,   10
Feet bleeding on the sultry sands, and the furrows of the whip
Descend to generations that in future times forget.————"

The strong voice ceas'd; for a terrible blast swept over the heaving sea;
The eastern cloud rent; on his cliffs stood Albion's wrathful Prince,
A dragon form clashing his scales; at midnight he arose,   15
And flam'd red meteors round the land of Albion beneath.
His voice, his locks, his awful shoulders, and his glowing eyes
Appear to the Americans upon the cloudy night.   6/4

Solemn heave the Atlantic waves between the gloomy nations
Swelling, belching from its deeps red clouds & raging fires.
Albion is sick. America faints! enrag'd the Zenith grew,
As human blood shooting its veins all round the orbed heaven,   5
Red rose the clouds from the Atlantic in vast wheels of blood
And in the red clouds rose a Wonder o'er the Atlantic sea;
Intense! naked! a Human fire fierce glowing, as the wedge
Of iron heated in the furnace; his terrible limbs were fire
With myriads of cloudy terrors, banners dark & towers   10
Surrounded; heat but not light went thro' the murky atmosphere.

The King of England looking westward trembles at the vision.[3]

Albion's Angel stood beside the Stone of night,[4] and saw   7/5
The terror like a comet, or more like the planet red
That once inclos'd the terrible wandering comets in its sphere.
Then Mars thou wast our center, & the planets three flew round
Thy crimson disk; so e'er the Sun was rent from thy red sphere;[5]   5
The Spectre glowd his horrid length staining the temple long
With beams of blood; & thus a voice came forth, and shook the temple:

"The morning comes, the night decays, the watchmen leave
    their stations;   8/6
The grave is burst, the spices shed, the linen wrapped up;
The bones of death, the cov'ring clay, the sinews shrunk & dry'd,   10
Reviving shake, inspiring move, breathing! awakening![6]
Spring like redeemed captives when their bonds & bars are burst;

2. Although the historical Washington was a slaveholder, the mythic Washington freely employs
   imagery of African-American slavery to deplore the subjugation of Anglo-Americans to British rule.
3. I.e., American defiance as a "Human fire" (6/4:7) in the west: the rebel Orc, full of "heat without
   light" (6/4:11), violence without wisdom. In an early version of this plate, withdrawn perhaps
   because of its explicitness, George III (1738–1820), who reigned 1760–1811, and his "Lords &
   Commons" are mentioned by name.
4. In the spirit of 2 Corinthians 3:3, the "Stone" is associated both with the stony law of the Decalogue and with papal authority (cf. Matthew 16:18). For dissenting Protestants, the British equivalent to the papacy was the king's position as Defender of the (Anglican) Faith. In later writings
   Blake especially associates stones with Druidism, thought to be a religion of human sacrifice (cf.
   Europe 13/10:21–23, 13/10:26).
5. On this mythical early solar system centered on Mars, seen from the perspective of Albion's Angel,
   see Ferber in Blake: An Illustrated Quarterly 15 (1981–82), 136.
6. Recalling resurrection imagery from the Gospels and Ezekiel's (37:1) rousing of the dry bones. The
   design at the top of the page (not included in this edition) reprises the resurrection scene on Marriage 21 (p. 79 herein).

Let the slave grinding at the mill[7] run out into the field;
Let him look up into the heavens & laugh in the bright air;
Let the inchained soul shut up in darkness and in sighing,   15
Whose face has never seen a smile in thirty weary years,
Rise and look out, his chains are loose, his dungeon doors are open.
And let his wife and children return from the opressor's scourge;
They look behind at every step & believe it is a dream.
Singing, 'The Sun has left his blackness, & has found a fresher
    morning   20
And the fair Moon rejoices in the clear & cloudless night;
For Empire is no more, and now the Lion & Wolf shall cease.' "[8]

9/7

In thunders ends the voice. Then Albion's Angel wrathful burnt
Beside the Stone of Night; and like the Eternal Lion's howl
In famine & war, reply'd. "Art thou not Orc, who serpent-form'd
Stands at the gate of Enitharmon to devour her children;
Blasphemous Demon, Antichrist, hater of Dignities;   5
Lover of wild rebellion, and transgresser of God's Law;
Why dost thou come to Angels' eyes in this terrific form?"[9]

7. Opening a passage on liberation (cf. Isaiah 42:7) that is repeated at the apocalyptic conclusion of
  Four Zoas 9 (134:18–34; not included in this edition). Cf. Samson's regeneration after having been
  made to grind "at the mill with slaves" (Milton's *Samson Agonistes* 41, referring to his task in Judges
  16:21). Though factories were becoming widespread, Blake's frequent use of "mill" generally
  reflects the older technology of the grain mill.
8. Cf. "Song of Liberty," verse 20 (*Marriage* 27). The first line of the released prisoners' song (8/6:20)
  is repeated in *Four Zoas* 9 (138:20).
9. Cf. "All that we saw was owing to your metaphysics" (*Marriage* 19). Orc as a child-devouring serpent (9/7:3–4) recalls the dragon in Revelation 12:4 and Chronos in Hesiod's *Theogony*. The
  Antichrist (9/7:5; cf. 1 John 2:18, 4:3 and 2 John 1:7), regularly cited in contemporary radical
  Protestant denunciations of political and ecclesiastical abominations, becomes Blake's ultimate
  personification of the closed-in, other-repelling selfhood (*Jerusalem* 89).

The terror answerd: "I am Orc, wreath'd round the accursed
    tree:
The times are ended; shadows pass, the morning 'gins to break;
The fiery joy, that Urizen perverted to ten commands,
What night he led the starry hosts thro' the wide wilderness:
That stony law I stamp to dust:[1] and scatter religion abroad

`10/8`

5

To the four winds as a torn book, & none shall gather the leaves;
But they shall rot on desart sands, & consume in bottomless
    deeps,
To make the desarts blossom, & the deeps shrink to their
    fountains,[2]
And to renew the fiery joy, and burst the stony roof,
That pale religious letchery, seeking Virginity,
May find it in a harlot, and in coarse-clad honesty
The undefil'd tho' ravish'd in her cradle night and morn:
For every thing that lives is holy,[3] life delights in life;
Because the soul of sweet delight can never be defil'd.[4]
Fires inwrap the earthly globe, yet man is not consumd;
Amidst the lustful fires he walks; his feet become like brass,
His knees and thighs like silver, & his breast and head like gold."[5]

10

15

"Sound! sound! my loud war-trumpets & alarm my Thirteen
    Angels!
Loud howls the eternal Wolf! the eternal Lion lashes his tail!
America is darkned; and my punishing Demons terrified

`11/9`

---

1. Cf. "Song of Liberty," verse 20 (*Marriage* **27**).
2. Signs of renewal: the desert blooms in Isaiah 35:1; the fountains of the deep are stopped at the end
    of Noah's flood (Genesis 8:2), and in the New Jerusalem there is "no more sea" (Revelation 21:1).
3. Cf. *Visions* **11**/8:10 and the Chorus of "The Song of Liberty" (*Marriage* **27**).
4. Cf. "Proverbs of Hell" (line 53, *Marriage* **9**).
5. Cf. the fourth figure "like the Son of God" who joins Daniel's three faithful friends to walk through
    Nebuchadnezzar's fiery furnace unharmed (Daniel 3:25–27) and Nebuchadnezzar's dream of an
    image with a head of gold, breast and arms of silver, belly and thighs of brass, legs of iron, and feet
    partly of clay (Daniel 2:31–35).

Crouch howling before their caverns deep like skins dry'd in the
    wind.
They cannot smite the wheat, nor quench the fatness of the earth,   5
They cannot smite with sorrows, nor subdue the plow and spade,
They cannot wall the city, nor moat round the castle of princes.
They cannot bring the stubbed oak to overgrow the hills.
For terrible men stand on the shores, & in their robes I see
Children take shelter from the lightnings; there stands
    Washington   10
And Paine and Warren with their foreheads reard toward the east
But clouds obscure my aged sight. A vision from afar!
Sound! sound! my loud war-trumpets & alarm my thirteen Angels:
Ah vision from afar! Ah rebel form that rent the ancient
Heavens! Eternal Viper self-renew'd, rolling in clouds   15
I see thee in thick clouds and darkness on America's shore.
Writhing in pangs of abhorred birth; red flames the crest
    rebellious
And eyes of death; the harlot womb oft opened in vain
Heaves in enormous circles, now the times are return'd upon
    thee,
Devourer of thy parent, now thy unutterable torment renews.   20
Sound! sound! my loud war trumpets & alarm my thirteen Angels,
Ah terrible birth! a young one bursting! where is the weeping
    mouth?
And where the mother's milk? instead those ever-hissing jaws
And parched lips drop with fresh gore; now roll thou in the clouds
Thy mother lays her length outstretch'd upon the shore beneath.   25
Sound! sound! my loud war-trumpets & alarm my thirteen Angels!
Loud howls the eternal Wolf: the eternal Lion lashes his tail!"

Thus wept the Angel voice & as he wept the terrible blasts   <u>12/10</u>
Of trumpets blew a loud alarm across the Atlantic deep.
No trumpets answer; no reply of clarions or of fifes,
Silent the Colonies remain and refuse the loud alarm.

On those vast shady hills between America & Albion's shore;   5
Now barr'd out by the Atlantic sea: call'd Atlantean hills;[6]
Because from their bright summits you may pass to the Golden
    world
An ancient palace, archetype of mighty Emperies,
Rears its immortal pinnacles, built in the forest of God
By Ariston the king of beauty for his stolen bride.[7]   10

Here on their magic seats the thirteen Angels[8] sat perturb'd
For clouds from the Atlantic hover o'er the solemn roof,

6. The lost paradisal island of Atlantis, described in Plato's *Timaeus* and *Critias*, now sunk beneath
    the Atlantic, no longer links England and America (cf. "Song of Liberty," verse 8, *Marriage* 25); dis-
    cussed by Michael Holley in *Colby Library Quarterly* 30 (1994).
7. The story of Ariston (Greek: "the best"), who reappears in "Africa," *Song of Los* 3:4, is derived from
    Herodotus' tale of a king of Sparta who stole the beautiful wife of his friend.
8. As leading spirits of the Colonies rather than historical figures, the "Angels" gather for a council
    that leads to their rebellion (14/12:1) on the lines of the angelic insurgency in Milton's *Paradise
    Lost* 5.710 ff.).

Fiery the Angels rose, & as they rose deep thunder roll'd   13/11
Around their shores; indignant burning with the fires of Orc
And Boston's Angel cried aloud as they flew thro' the dark night,

He cried: "Why trembles honesty and like a murderer,
Why seeks he refuge from the frowns of his immortal station,   5
Must the generous tremble & leave his joy, to the idle: to the
    pestilence!
That mock him? who commanded this, what God? what Angel!
To keep the gen'rous from experience till the ungenerous
Are unrestraind performers of the energies of nature;
Till pity is become a trade, and generosity a science   10
That men get rich by, & the sandy desart is giv'n to the strong.
What God is he, writes laws of peace, & clothes him in a tempest,
What pitying Angel lusts for tears, and fans himself with sighs,
What crawling villain preaches abstinence & wraps himself
In fat of lambs? no more I follow, no more obedience pay."   15

So cried he, rending off his robe[9] & throwing down his scepter 14/12
In sight of Albion's Guardian, and all the thirteen Angels
Rent off their robes to the hungry wind, & threw their golden
    scepters
Down on the land of America; indignant they descended
Headlong from out their heav'nly heights, descending swift as fires   5
Over the land; naked & flaming are their lineaments seen

9. Boston's Angel, having voiced sentiments shared by, among others, John Adams (1735–1826) and
his more radical cousin Samuel Adams (1722–1803), takes the lead in stripping off the guberna-
torial robes of a royal appointee.

In the deep gloom. By Washington & Paine & Warren they stood
And the flame folded roaring fierce within the pitchy night
Before the Demon red, who burnt towards America,
In black smoke, thunders and loud winds, rejoicing in its terror   10
Breaking in smoky wreaths from the wild deep, & gath'ring thick
In flames as of a furnace on the land from North to South.

What time the thirteen Governors that England sent convene $\boxed{15/13}$
In Bernard's[1] house, the flames coverd the land; they rouze,
    they cry
Shaking their mental chains, they rush in fury to the sea[2]
To quench their anguish; at the feet of Washington down fall'n
They grovel on the sand and writhing lie, while all   5
The British soldiers thro' the thirteen states sent up a howl
Of anguish: threw their swords & muskets to the earth & ran
From their encampments and dark castles seeking where to hide
From the grim flames; and from the visions of Orc, in sight
Of Albion's Angel; who, enrag'd, his secret clouds open'd   10
From north to south, and burnt outstretchd on wings of wrath
    cov'ring
The eastern sky, spreading his awful wings across the heavens;
Beneath him rolld his num'rous hosts, all Albion's Angels camp'd,
Darkend the Atlantic mountains & their trumpets shook the
    valleys,
Arm'd with diseases of the earth to cast upon the Abyss,   15
Their numbers forty millions, must'ring in the eastern sky.[3]

In the flames stood & view'd the armies drawn out in the sky $\boxed{16/14}$
Washington Franklin Paine & Warren Allen Gates & Lee:[4]
And heard the voice of Albion's Angel give the thunderous command.
His plagues obedient to his voice flew forth out of their clouds
Falling upon America, as a storm to cut them off,   5
As a blight cuts the tender corn when it begins to appear.
Dark is the heaven above, & cold & hard the earth beneath;
And as a plague wind fill'd with insects cuts off man & beast;
And as a sea o'erwhelms a land in the day of an earthquake;

Fury! rage! madness! in a wind swept through America   10
And the red flames of Orc that folded roaring fierce around
The angry shores, and the fierce rushing of th' inhabitants together;
The citizens of New-York close their books & lock their chests;

1. Sir Francis Bernard (1712–1779), royal governor of New Jersey (1758–60) and of Massachusetts (1760–69), was replaced by Thomas Hutchinson (1711–1780; acting 1769–70, governor 1771–74) before the Revolutionary War began but remained notorious as a tool of British control. The royal governors' official residence was Province House in Boston.
2. Cf. "mind-forg'd manacles" in "London" and the drowning of the devil-possessed swine in Mark 5:13.
3. Repressive British laws and their military enforcement are mythologized as biological warfare on the scale of biblical plagues. In the mythical mode of hyperbole the troop strength of "forty millions" is greater than the entire population of the British isles.
4. Cf. 5/3:4; here Hancock and Greene are replaced by the Revolutionary commanders Ethan Allen (1748–1789), who led the Green Mountain Boys to capture Fort Ticonderoga (1775), and Henry "Light-Horse Harry" Lee (1756–1818), known for surprise attacks in capturing the fort at Paulus Hook (1779) and in the Carolina campaign. Or perhaps this seventh name belongs to the patriot Richard Henry Lee (1732–1794), author of two addresses to the British people protesting oppression of the Colonies. The pamphleteer and lieutenant colonel Charles Lee (1731–1782) has also been proposed, but his misdeeds led to a court-martial and a public reprimand from Washington.

The mariners of Boston drop their anchors and unlade;
The scribe of Pensylvania casts his pen upon the earth;   15
The builder of Virginia throws his hammer down in fear.[5]

Then had America been lost, o'erwhelm'd by the Atlantic,[6]
And Earth had lost another portion of the infinite,
But all rush together in the night in wrath and raging fire.
The red fires rag'd! the plagues recoil'd! then rolld they back with
    fury   20

On Albion's Angels: then the Pestilence began in streaks of red   17/15
Across the limbs of Albion's Guardian, the spotted plague smote
    Bristol's
And the Leprosy London's Spirit, sickening all their bands:[7]
The millions sent up a howl of anguish and threw off their
    hammerd mail,
And cast their swords & spears to earth, & stood a naked multitude.   5
Albion's Guardian writhed in torment on the eastern sky
Pale quivring toward the brain his glimmering eyes, teeth chattering
Howling & shuddering his legs quivering; convuls'd each muscle &
    sinew
Sick'ning lay London's Guardian, and the ancient miter'd York[8]
Their heads on snowy hills, their ensigns sick'ning in the sky.   10

The plagues creep on the burning winds driven by flames of Orc,
And by the fierce Americans rushing together in the night
Driven o'er the Guardians of Ireland and Scotland and Wales
They spotted with plagues forsook the frontiers & their banners seard
With fires of hell, deform their ancient heavens with shame & woe,   15
Hid in his caves the Bard of Albion[9] felt the enormous plagues.
And a cowl of flesh grew o'er his head & scales on his back & ribs;
And rough with black scales all his Angels fright their ancient heavens.
The doors of marriage are open, and the Priests in rustling scales
Rush into reptile coverts, hiding from the fires of Orc,   20
That play around the golden roofs in wreaths of fierce desire,
Leaving the females naked and glowing with the lusts of youth,

For the female spirits of the dead pining in bonds of religion
Run from their fetters reddening, & in long drawn arches sitting:
They feel the nerves of youth renew, and desires of ancient times,   25
Over their pale limbs as a vine when the tender grape appears.[1]

5. Citizens of the diverse colonies, including commercial-minded New Yorkers, drop their local concerns
   in shock and then "rush together" (16/14:19) to make common cause against the British "plagues," or
   harsh measures against the Colonies, so that the most serious damage falls back on Britain. "Unlade":
   reference to the Boston Tea Party. Historically, neither the Pennsylvanian writer-printer Franklin nor
   the Virginia "builder" Jefferson (architect of his home and of the university) expressed despair or fear.
6. Another allusion to the myth of Atlantis.
7. Opposition to British policy on America was particularly intense in trade-dependent Bristol and
   London, the first cities to experience negative consequences from the war.
8. The established church is represented by the mitre-wearing bishop of London (better known as the
   archbishop of Canterbury, whose palace is in the London borough of Lambeth) and the archbishop
   of York.
9. Perhaps referring to William Whitehead (1715–1785), poet laureate (1757–85), who supported
   the American War to subdue the Colonies. On the archetypal Bard's repudiation of the poetry of
   liberation, see no. 8, p. 87 herein.
1. In Song of Solomon 7:12 the "tender grape" is a sign of sexual ripeness. This vision of sexually liberated British women had no historical basis during the American Revolution, but in 1793 the

18/16

Over the hills, the vales, the cities, rage the red flames fierce;
The Heavens melted from north to south; and Urizen who sat
Above all heavens in thunders wrap'd, emerg'd his leprous head
From out his holy shrine, his tears in deluge piteous
Falling into the deep sublime! flag'd with grey-brow'd snows   5
And thunderous visages, his jealous wings wav'd over the deep;
Weeping in dismal howling woe he dark descended howling
Around the smitten bands, clothed in tears & trembling
    shudd'ring cold.
His stored snows he poured forth, and his icy magazines
He open'd on the deep, and on the Atlantic sea white shiv'ring.   10
Leprous his limbs, all over white, and hoary was his visage.
Weeping in dismal howlings before the stern Americans
Hiding the Demon red with clouds & cold mists from the earth;
Till Angels & weak men twelve years[2] should govern o'er the strong;
And then their end should come, when France reciev'd the
    Demon's light.   15

Stiff shudderings shook the heav'nly thrones! France Spain & Italy
In terror view'd the bands of Albion, and the ancient Guardians
Fainting upon the elements, smitten with their own plagues
They slow advance to shut the five gates of their law-built heaven
Filled with blasting fancies and with mildews of despair   20
With fierce disease and lust, unable to stem the fires of Orc;
But the five gates[3] were consum'd, & their bolts and hinges melted
And the fierce flames burnt round the heavens, & round the
    abodes of men.

rights of women, as a consequence and corollary of the French Revolution, were much discussed, especially as set forth in Wollstonecraft's *Vindication* (1792). Erdman suggests, in addition, that the furor in 1781 about the legality of certain chapel marriages and a failed bill to legalize secular civil marriages were the first cracks in the stony code of law.

2. Roughly, the period between the Declaration of Independence and the outbreak of the French Revolution. Possibly the interval between 1781, the American victory at Yorktown, and 1793, the execution of Louis XVI in the year of this "Prophecy."

3. The portals of the five senses; cf. *Marriage* 14 and *Europe* 3/iii. In *America*, Orc opens these gates permanently though he himself is temporarily obscured. In the design depicting the land of America in female form, with hair like Niagara Falls, miniature American citizens engage in what appear to be sexual (near her feet), pastoral (on her leg), scholarly (on her head), and religious (on her back) activities; there is even a small piper, wearing a hat, leaning on a tree that branches out of her belt. At the left the forests are undergoing metamorphosis (like Daphne, into vegetated form? or the reverse?). The terminal word, *FINIS*, is clearly visible in the tailpiece design in uncolored copies, on the back of a serpent weaving among thorns, near two tiny human figures moving in contrary directions.

EUROPE: A PROPHECY (1794)

As *America* can be thought of as "The Book of Orc," so its companion prophecy may be considered "The Book of Enitharmon." Enitharmon, mother of Orc, is everything that breeds revolution but simultaneously keeps it from developing. A spirit of queenly hauteur pervades the poem; the great Female triumphs over all. During the dark night of eighteen Christian centuries, shifting images form and disappear in Enitharmon's dreaming mind. European civilization remains at a standstill; Orc is silent and motionless. *Europe* is a prophecy for a revolutionary era because it demonstrates how much there is to rebel against and how sorely this languorous, effeminate society is in need of a cataclysmic awakening.

As the work unfolds, the language becomes more oblique and compressed, in Blake's later style. It opens slowly, with four (or five) preliminary pages before the main text begins on plate 6/3. In all but two copies, the first page is an imposing frontispiece (color plate 9), one of Blake's best-known and most successful designs, popularly called the "Ancient of Days" (from Daniel 7:9; not Blake's title). This is the false deity Urizen, humanity's limited conception of God as the ultimate circumscriber and measurer; with his left hand, he reaches down to define and control the globe (cf. Proverbs 8:27). The title page (color plate 10) depicts a serpent coiled and upreared like the rattlesnake on the American revolutionary flag, "Don't Tread on Me"—a force too wily to be contained or regulated, even by the design area of the page. A third page (the first page in one copy), which occurs in only two of nine printings of the book issued by Blake himself, serves as an unconventional invocation to the muse, who turns out to be a coolly insolent Fairy. After the Fairy page, or directly after the title page in most copies, comes the two-page "Preludium" about a "nameless shadowy female," apparently the same personage who was raped by Orc in the "Preludium" to *America*. All the prefatory pages display repressed and wasted energy, particularly sexual energy. The Fairy, a detached observer of the human scene, finds it strange that "cavern'd Man" fails fully to open his five senses, especially sexual touch. The shadowy female in the Preludium complains that she must continually—and futilely—give birth to fiery terrors, Orc's offspring, only to have them set in final form by Enitharmon and claimed as her property.

Who is this mighty Enitharmon? What is the source of her power? Her characterization as charming tyrant bears considerable resemblance to Wollstonecraft's contemporaneous portrait of Marie Antoinette (guillotined in 1793) in her *Historical and Moral View of the French Revolution* (1794). More broadly, in *The Book of Urizen* (another work of 1794) Enitharmon is a personification of Pity, the by-product of humanity's self-limitation; as the female counterpart and spouse of Urizen's adversary Los and mother of their firstborn Orc, she is at the apex of the Oedipal triangle. Here in *Europe*, from the heights of her "crystal house," she rules her husband and their numerous sons and daughters (including the shadowy female) without lifting a finger, luxuriating in their attentions, languidly supervising their sports, pleased that they display aspects of her dominance that have overspread Europe. For Enitharmon, Orc's birth is not the dawn of a new era but the beginning of a night when men yield up their power to women. During her sleep, time is collapsed so that to her the birth of Christ, marking the beginning of the European calendar, is the same event as the birth of revolution eighteen hundred years later. She calls on Orc to arise, but she keeps him bound by sending her other sons, Rintrah and Palamabron, to disseminate her doctrine that woman's love is sin, and therefore irresistibly desirable. Her curse on sex underlies Mariolatry, the chivalric code, and all the means by which women, denied independence and autonomy, turn men's authority against them and wield power underhandedly. Her daughters excel in manipulating chastity, jealousy, and seductiveness to their advantage—except for Oothoon, who, as narrated in *Visions of the Daughters of Albion*, has given up "woman's secrecy" (**17**/14:22).

In the poem proper, everything revolves around Enitharmon's dream, a time when revolutionary energy is held in check. The first third of the poem prepares for the dream, the middle portion recounts it, and the final third describes the dreamer's awakening and its aftermath. This circular movement, like the compasses in the frontispiece and the serpent's coils on the title page (color plate 10), exemplify "revolution" in its negative sense, a re-turning of the cycle of tyrant and oppressed. The first and third sections are linked by the repeated command "Arise," as Enitharmon calls the roll of her children to enlist their aid in suppressing, distracting, and deferring humanity's rebellious spirit. Orc, the first to be called, is the last to respond; he arises only at the end of the eighteen-hundred-year dream. This delay probably signifies the historical transformation of Jesus from religious and social revolutionary, as in *The Marriage of Heaven and Hell*, to the mild-mannered deity of state religion; it seems that Jesus' birth, instead of igniting worldwide revolutionary change, has led to the establishment of repressive European religious and political institutions. After eighteen hundred years, the time is again ripe for revolution: when Enitharmon awakens, Orc responds to her call but escapes her influence; as dawn breaks, he shoots down from her heights into "the vineyards of red France," leaving his mother to groan in dismay. The secular messiah may have come at last, but the millennium has not arrived; what Orc brings immediately is war, death, destruction, and terror. The closing lines strongly imply that even Los the artist, who with his sons had played on the harp at the opening of the poem, will become a warrior if that is the only way to make the new revolution succeed.

For a range of comments on *Europe* see Detlef Dörrbecker's Blake Trust facsimile edition of copy B in *The Continental Prophecies* (1995); Michael J. Tolley in *Blake's Visionary Forms Dramatic* (1970); John Howard, *Infernal Poetics* (1984); Stephen C. Behrendt, *Blake: An Illustrated Quarterly* 21 (1987–88); James E. Swearingen, *Clio* 20 (1991); Helen P. Bruder, *William Blake and the Daughters of Albion* (1997); Michael Ferber and Peter Otto, both in *Blake, Politics, and History* (1998); Andrew Lincoln in *Studies in Romanticism* 38 (1999); and Nancy Goslee in *Women Reading William Blake* (2006), ed. Bruder. For other facsimiles, see the composite of Copies B and G in the older Blake Trust series (1969; source of a Dover reprint, 1984); Copies B, E, H, and K, in the online Blake Archive; and Copy F in the New York Public Library Digital Gallery (digitalgallery.nypl.org).

Our text is based on Copy H, from Blake's 1795 printing, compared with transcriptions of other copies in the Blake Archive and with the Bentley and Erdman editions; the pages, though arranged in the order of Copy H, are identified by Bentley/Erdman numbers (for example, the title page is **2**/ii).

EUROPE a PROPHECY   **2**/ii

Lambeth
Printed by Will: Blake: 1794

"Five windows light the cavern'd Man;[1] thro' one he breathes
the air;   **3**/iii
Thro' one, hears music of the spheres; thro' one, the eternal vine
Flourishes, that he may recieve the grapes; thro' one can look,

---

1. An image derived from both Plato's cave and Locke's theory that the mind contains only what is imprinted on it by sense impressions. Cf. "narrow chinks of his cavern" (*Marriage* 14). In seven of the nine versions of *Europe*, the introductory page is not present, and the poem opens with the "Preludium."

And see small portions of the eternal world that ever groweth;
Thro' one, himself pass out what time he please, but he will not;   5
For stolen joys are sweet, & bread eaten in secret pleasant."[2]

So sang a Fairy mocking as he sat on a streak'd Tulip,[3]
Thinking none saw him: when he ceas'd I started from the trees:
And caught him in my hat as boys knock down a butterfly.
"How know you this" said I "small Sir? where did you learn this
   song?"[4]   10
Seeing himself in my possession thus he answerd me:
"My master, I am yours, command me, for I must obey."

"Then tell me, what is the material world, and is it dead?"
He laughing answer'd: "I will write a book on leaves of flowers,
If you will feed me on love-thoughts, & give me now and then   15
A cup of sparkling poetic fancies; so when I am tipsie,
I'll sing to you to this soft lute; and shew you all alive
The world, when every particle of dust breathes forth its joy."

I took him home in my warm bosom; as we went along
Wild flowers I gatherd; & he shew'd me each eternal flower: 20
He laugh'd aloud to see them whimper because they were pluck'd,[5]
They hover'd round me like a cloud of incense: when I came
Into my parlour and sat down, and took my pen to write;
My Fairy sat upon the table, and dictated EUROPE.

PRELUDIUM   4/1

The nameless shadowy female rose from out the breast
   of Orc:
Her snaky hair brandishing in the winds of Enitharmon;
And thus her voice arose.

"O mother Enitharmon wilt thou bring forth other sons?
To cause my name to vanish, that my place may not be found,   5
For I am faint with travel![6]
Like the dark cloud disburdend in the day of dismal thunder.

My roots are brandish'd in the heavens, my fruits, in earth beneath
Surge, foam, and labour into life, first born & first consum'd!

2. Proverbs 9:17. Touch, the fifth sense (line 5), enabling sexual contact, is potentially an outlet as
   well as an inlet for the closed-in self.
3. In Johnson's *Rasselas*, chapter 9, Imlac the tutor advises the ideal poet not to "number the streaks
   of the tulip" but to remark "general properties and large appearances." In doing the opposite, Blake
   encounters the singing Fairy, who as a nature-spirit finds human follies and preoccupations laughable.
   Poems with Blake's fairies include "I will tell you," "The Fairy," and "Long John Brown & Little
   Mary Bell"; see John Adlard, *The Sports of Cruelty* (1972).
4. Cf. "Where hadst thou this terrible Song" (*Milton* 14/13:50).
5. The Fairy introduces the author to a fully alive world, sensitive to both joy (line 18) and pain. The
   flowers' whimpering, laughed off by the Fairy, would be understood by Oothoon's Marygold (*Visions*
   4/1:6–10) and Thel's Lilly (*Thel* 3/1:21–25), life-affirming flowers who consider their own deaths
   part of a larger cycle.
6. Travail, the labor of childbirth; but perhaps the shadowy female's "turban" (line 12) also indicates
   a journey from the East. Her complaint centers on excessive fertility, not only her own but that of
   her mother, Enitharmon (4/1:4, 4/1:11). No longer the armed nude warrior of the "Preludium" to
   America, she adopts imagery of an upside-down tree (lines 8–9), apparently giving birth from her
   head (line 12) and bosom (5/2:9) to Orc's fiery progeny.

Consumed and consuming!   10
Then why shouldst thou accursed mother bring me into life?

I wrap my turban of thick clouds around my lab'ring head:
And fold the sheety waters as a mantle round my limbs.
Yet the red sun and moon,
And all the overflowing stars rain down prolific pains.   15

Unwilling I look up to heaven! unwilling count the stars!   5/2
Sitting in fathomless abyss of my immortal shrine.
I sieze their burning power
And bring forth howling terrors, all devouring fiery kings.

Devouring & devoured roaming on dark and desolate mountains   5
In forests of eternal death, shrieking in hollow trees.
Ah mother Enitharmon!
Stamp not with solid form this vig'rous progeny of fires.

I bring forth from my teeming bosom myriads of flames.
And thou dost stamp them with a signet, then they roam abroad   10
And leave me void as death;
Ah! I am drown'd in shady woe, and visionary joy.

And who shall bind the infinite with an eternal band?
To compass it with swaddling bands? and who shall cherish it
With milk and honey?   15
I see it smile & I roll inward & my voice is past."[7]

She ceast & rolld her shady clouds
Into the secret place.

A PROPHECY   6/3

The deep of winter came;
        What time the secret child,
Descended thro' the orient gates of the eternal day;[8]
War ceas'd, & all the troops like shadows fled
        to their abodes.   5

Then Enitharmon saw her sons & daughters rise around.
Like pearly clouds they meet together in the crystal house;[9]
And Los, possessor of the moon, joy'd in the peaceful night:
Thus speaking while his num'rous sons shook their bright fiery
        wings.[1]

7. Although Enitharmon has so far enslaved (stamped with her signet) all of these offspring, her daughter envisions someday delivering an "infinite" newborn who cannot be swaddled (cf. Luke 2:12 and "Infant Sorrow"). On "milk and honey" (5/2:15), see God's promise to Moses in Exodus 3:8.
8. Echoing the opening lines of Milton's "On the Morning of Christ's Nativity," in which Christ's birth overturns the old order (see Tolley in Blake's Visionary Forms Dramatic [1970], ed. Erdman and Grant). The French Republic had proclaimed the Year One in September 1792, the end of the Christian era (see the chronology); in the Marriage Blake himself dated the beginning of the New Age as 1790.
9. Perhaps alluding to the Ice Palace of Catherine the Great (Thomas McClean, dissertation, University of Iowa, 2004). Most commentators consider Marie Antoinette the likely historical counterpart to Enitharmon.
1. Blake uses no quotation marks here. We attribute the following passage, through 7/4:14, to Los; but as "possessor of the moon" he may stop at 6/3:15, or at 7/4:2, leaving lines 7/4:1–2 to a narrator or to his sons, who would continue with 7/4:3–9. Then Enitharmon may speak lines 7/4:10–14.

"Again the night is come   10
That strong Urthona takes his rest,
And Urizen unloos'd from chains
Glows like a meteor in the distant north
Stretch forth your hands and strike the elemental strings!
Awake the thunders of the deep,   15

The shrill winds wake!   7/4
Till all the sons of Urizen look out and envy Los;
Sieze all the spirits of life and bind
Their warbling joys to our loud strings
Bind all the nourishing sweets of earth   5
To give us bliss, that we may drink the sparkling wine of Los
And let us laugh at war,
Despising toil and care.
Because the days and nights of joy, in lucky hours renew.

Arise O Orc from thy deep den,   10
First born of Enitharmon rise!
And we will crown thy head with garlands of the ruddy vine;
For now thou art bound;
And I may see thee in the hour of bliss, my eldest born."

The horrent Demon rose, surrounded with red stars of fire,   15
Whirling about in furious circles round the immortal fiend.

Then Enitharmon down descended into his red light,[2]
And thus her voice rose to her children, the distant heavens
 reply.

"Now comes the night of Enitharmon's joy,   8/5
Who shall I call? Who shall I send?
That Woman, lovely Woman![3] may have dominion?
Arise O Rintrah thee I call! & Palamabron thee![4]
Go: tell the human race that Woman's love is Sin: 5
That an Eternal life awaits the worms of sixty winters
In an allegorical abode where existence hath never come:
Forbid all Joy, & from her childhood shall the little female
Spread nets in every secret path.

My weary eyelids draw towards the evening, my bliss is yet
 but new![5]   10

Arise O Rintrah eldest born: second to none but Orc: 11/8
O lion Rintrah raise thy fury from thy forests black;
Bring Palamabron horned priest, skipping upon the
 mountains:
And silent Elynittria the silver bowed queen:
Rintrah where hast thou hid thy bride!   5
Weeps she in desert shades?
Alas my Rintrah! bring the lovely jealous Ocalythron.

Arise my son! bring all thy brethren O thou king of fire.
Prince of the sun I see thee with thy innumerable race;
Thick as the summer stars:[6]   10
But each ramping his golden mane shakes,[7]
And thine eyes rejoice because of strength O Rintrah furious
 king."

Enitharmon slept,   12/9
Eighteen hundred years: Man was a Dream!
The night of Nature and their harps unstrung:[8]
She slept in middle of her nightly song.
Eighteen hundred years, a female dream!   5

2. Orc's association with imagery of Mars ("red light") and Dionysius ("ruddy vine," 7/4:12) anticipates the purifying energies of the Second Coming, in which Christ, wearing a vesture dipped in blood, smites the nations and treads the winepress of God's wrath (Revelation 19:11–15; Isaiah 63:3).
3. A catch-phrase from Thomas Otway's *Venice Preserv'd*, 1.1 (1682): "O Woman! lovely Woman! Nature made thee / To temper Man: We had been Brutes without you"; picked up by (among others) Wollstonecraft (*Maria*, 1788; *The Wrongs of Woman*, 1798), Cowper, Byron, Clare, and Austen.
4. Rintrah, a roarer and shaker in *Marriage* 2, is here a furious king rather than a prophet, and his brother Palamabron is a priest. In *Milton* both are loyal, hardworking sons of the artist-prophet Los.
5. Plates 9/6 and 10/7 (not included in this edition) depict Famine (two women waiting for a pot to boil, a sick or dead child at their feet) and Plague (a bellman and three victims, in front of a door inscribed "LORD HAVE MERCY ON US").
6. Enitharmon's vision of descendants innumerable as stars (cf. the shadowy female's complaint, 5/2:1) recalls God's promise to Abraham (Genesis 22:17).
7. Echoes Milton's description of the newly created lion who "rampant shakes his brinded mane" in *Paradise Lost* 7.467. "Ramping": rearing upright, showing fierceness. Cf. the "ramping and roaring lions" of Psalm 22:13 (Coverdale trans., *Book of Common Prayer*), which John Wesley applied metaphorically to mobs from which he narrowly escaped in 1743 and 1748.
8. Apparently the harps played by Los and his sons (6/3:14, 7/4:4).

Shadows of men in fleeting bands upon the winds:
Divide the heavens of Europe:
Till Albion's Angel smitten with his own plagues fled with his
  bands.[9]
The cloud bears hard on Albion's shore:
Fill'd with immortal demons of futurity: 10
In council gather the smitten Angels of Albion

9. Cf. *America* 16/14:20–17/15:1.

The cloud bears hard upon the council house; down rushing
On the heads of Albion's Angels.[1]

One hour they lay buried beneath the ruins of that hall;
But as the stars rise from the salt lake they arise in pain,   15
In troubled mists o'erclouded by the terrors of strugling times.

In thoughts perturb'd they rose from the bright ruins silent $\boxed{13/10}$
    following
The fiery King, who sought his ancient temple serpent-form'd[2]
That stretches out its shady length along the Island white.
Round him roll'd his clouds of war; silent the Angel went,
Along the infinite shores of Thames to golden Verulam.[3]   5
There stand the venerable porches that high-towering rear
Their oak-surrounded pillars, form'd of massy stones, uncut
With tool; stones precious, such eternal in the heavens,
Of colours twelve, few known on earth, give light in the opake,
Plac'd in the order of the stars,[4] when the five senses whelm'd   10
In deluge o'er the earth-born man; then turn'd the fluxile eyes
Into two stationary orbs, concentrating all things.
The ever-varying spiral ascents to the heavens of heavens
Were bended downward; and the nostrils' golden gates shut
Turn'd outward, barr'd and petrify'd against the infinite.[5]   15

Thought chang'd the infinite to a serpent; that which pitieth:
To a devouring flame; and man fled from its face and hid
In forests of night; then all the eternal forests were divided
Into earths rolling in circles of space, that like an ocean rush'd
And overwhelmed all except this finite wall of flesh.   20
Then was the serpent temple form'd, image of infinite
Shut up in finite revolutions, and man became an Angel;
Heaven a mighty circle turning; God a tyrant crown'd.

Now arriv'd the ancient Guardian at the southern porch,
That planted thick with trees of blackest leaf, & in a vale   25
Obscure, inclos'd the Stone of Night;[6] oblique it stood, o'erhung
With purple flowers and berries red;[7] image of that sweet south,

1. Associated by Erdman, *Prophet against Empire*, with the collapse of Parliament, touched on in a cancelled plate of *America*.
2. Blake's earliest reference to megalithic ruins in Avebury, near Stonehenge (see map), widely believed to be remains of a serpent-shaped Druid temple (see color plate 16; see also Peter F. Fisher, *JEGP* 58 [1959], and A. L. Owen, *The Famous Druids* [1962]). According to Blake's sources, the Druids were originally biblical patriarchs whose religion became corrupted by human sacrifice and nature worship. In Blake's myth a huge serpent temple spreads over all of Britain, wherever human victims of war and oppression are sacrificed. To the degree that Christians interpret the Crucifixion as a blood sacrifice and approve of wars and executions, they practice Druidism, in Blake's sense of the word.
3. Variant spelling of Verulamium, the Latin name for St. Alban's, home of Francis Bacon. Blake repeatedly attacked Bacon, father of the scientific method, for valuing sensory data above prophetic vision.
4. The oaks identify Verulam as a Druid site. The zodiac arrangement alludes to the mechanistic order of the heavens. "Stones, uncut / With tool" describe the altar that God directs Moses to build (Exodus 20:25). "Stones . . . of colours twelve" derive both from Aaron's breastplate (Exodus 28:17) and the twelve foundations of the walls of the New Jerusalem (Revelation 21:19–20).
5. In the fallen state the five senses have shrunk, hardened, and turned opaque. This and the following verse paragraph are in the condensed, allusive style of Blake's later works.
6. The human skull after the shrinking of the once-infinite senses (lines 10–15); cf. the religious and political stoniness of 14/11:1 and *America* 7/5:1.
7. Identifying features of the common woody nightshade (Stevenson), popularly confused with deadly nightshade.

Once open to the heavens and elevated on the human neck,
Now overgrown with hair and coverd with a stony roof,
Downward 'tis sunk beneath th' attractive north, that round the
    feet   30
A raging whirlpool draws the dizzy enquirer to his grave.

Albion's Angel rose upon the Stone of Night.   14/11
He saw Urizen on the Atlantic:
And his brazen Book,
That Kings & Priests had copied on Earth
Expanded from North to South.   5

  And the clouds & fires pale rolld round in the night of
    Enitharmon   15/12
Round Albion's cliffs & London's walls; still Enitharmon slept!
Rolling volumes of grey mist involve Churches, Palaces, Towers:
For Urizen unclaspd his Book! feeding his soul with pity.
The youth of England hid in gloom curse the paind heavens;
    compell'd   5
Into the deadly night to see the form of Albion's Angel.
Their parents brought them forth & aged ignorance preaches
    canting,
On a vast rock, perciev'd by those senses that are clos'd from
    thought:
Bleak, dark, abrupt, it stands & overshadows London city.
They saw his boney feet on the rock, the flesh consum'd in
    flames: 10
They saw the Serpent temple lifted above, shadowing the Island
    white:
They heard the voice of Albion's Angel howling in flames of Orc,
Seeking the trump of the last doom.

Above the rest the howl was heard from Westminster louder &
    louder;
The Guardian of the secret codes forsook his ancient mansion,   15
Driven out by the flames of Orc; his furr'd robes & false locks[8]
Adhered and grew one with his flesh, and nerves & veins shot
    thro' them
With dismal torment sick hanging upon the wind: he fled
Groveling along Great George Street[9] thro' the Park gate; all
    the soldiers
Fled from his sight; he drag'd his torments to the wilderness.   20

Thus was the howl thro Europe![1]
For Orc rejoic'd to hear the howling shadows
But Palamabron shot his lightnings trenching down his wide back
And Rintrah hung with all his legions in the nether deep.

8. Regalia worn in both the upper house of Parliament and the Courts of Law at Westminster. Erdman identifies the "Guardian" as Thurlow, lord high chancellor and keeper of the seal, dismissed
   by the king in June 1792.
9. Ironically bearing the king's name, this street is near Parliament (see map).
1. Heard by the kings of Asia in *The Song of Los* 6:1–2.

Enitharmon laugh'd in her sleep to see (O woman's triumph)   25
Every house a den, every man bound; the shadows are filld
With spectres, and the windows wove over with curses of iron:
Over the doors Thou shalt not; & over the chimneys Fear is written:
With bands of iron round their necks, fasten'd into the walls.
The citizens: in leaden gyves the inhabitants of suburbs   30
Walk heavy: soft and bent are the bones of villagers.

Between the clouds of Urizen the flames of Orc roll heavy
Around the limbs of Albion's Guardian, his flesh consuming.
Howlings & hissings, shrieks & groans, & voices of despair
Arise around him in the cloudy   35
Heavens of Albion, Furious

The red limb'd Angel siez'd—in horror and torment; |16/13|
The Trump of the last doom; but he could not blow the iron
    tube!
Thrice he assay'd presumptuous to awake the dead to Judgment.

A mighty Spirit leap'd from the land of Albion,
Nam'd Newton; he siez'd the Trump, & blow'd the enormous blast!   5
Yellow as leaves of Autumn the myriads of Angelic hosts,
Fell thro' the wintry skies seeking their graves;
Rattling their hollow bones in howling and lamentation.[2]

    Then Enitharmon woke nor knew that she had slept
And eighteen hundred years were fled   10
As if they had not been.
She calld her sons & daughters
To the sports of night,
Within her crystal house;
And thus her song proceeds.   15

"Arise Ethinthus! tho' the earth-worm call;
Let him call in vain;
Till the night of holy shadows
And human solitude is past!

Ethinthus queen of waters, how thou shinest in the sky: |17/14|
My daughter how do I rejoice! for thy children flock around
Like the gay fishes on the wave, when the cold moon drinks the
    dew.
Ethinthus! thou art sweet as comforts to my fainting soul:
For now thy waters warble round the feet of Enitharmon.   5

Manathu-Varcyon! I behold thee flaming in my halls,
Light of thy mother's soul! I see thy lovely eagles round;
Thy golden wings are my delight, & thy flames of soft delusion.

Where is my lureing bird of Eden! Leutha silent love!
Leutha, the many colour'd bow delights upon thy wings;   10

2. When Newton displaces Albion's Angel in prematurely blowing the Last Trump to awaken the dead
   (1 Corinthians 15:52), all the angels in heaven are overcome by his law of gravity (Bloom, *Blake's
   Apocalypse* 117).

Soft soul of flowers Leutha!
Sweet smiling pestilence! I see thy blushing light:
Thy daughters many changing,
Revolve like sweet perfumes ascending O Leutha silken queen!

Where is the youthful Antamon, prince of the pearly dew,   15
O Antamon, why wilt thou leave thy mother Enitharmon?
Alone I see thee crystal form,
Floting upon the bosomd air:
With lineaments of gratified desire.[3]
My Antamon the seven churches of Leutha seek thy love,   20

I hear the soft Oothoon in Enitharmon's tents:
Why wilt thou give up woman's secrecy my melancholy child?
Between two moments bliss is ripe:
O Theotormon robb'd of joy, I see thy salt tears flow
Down the steps of my crystal house.   25

Sotha & Thiralatha, secret dwellers of dreamful caves,
Arise and please the horrent fiend with your melodious songs.
Still all your thunders golden hoofd, & bind your horses black.
Orc! smile upon my children!
Smile son of my afflictions.   30
Arise O Orc and give our mountains joy of thy red light."

She ceas'd, for All were forth at sport beneath the solemn moon
Waking the stars of Urizen with their immortal songs,
That nature felt thro' all her pores the enormous revelry.
Till morning ope'd the eastern gate.   35
Then every one fled to his station, & Enitharmon wept.

But terrible Orc, when he beheld the morning in the east,
Shot from the heights of Enitharmon;   18/15
And in the vineyards of red France appear'd the light of his fury.[4]

The sun glow'd fiery red!
The furious terrors flew around!
On golden chariots raging, with red wheels dropping with blood;   5
The Lions lash their wrathful tails!
The Tigers couch upon the prey & suck the ruddy tide;
And Enitharmon groans & cries in anguish and dismay.

Then Los arose, his head he reard in snaky thunders clad:
And with a cry that shook all nature to the utmost pole,   10
Call'd all his sons to the strife of blood.

FINIS

---

3. Cf. "What is it men in women do require," Notebook (p. 389 herein).
4. On the widely held expectation that the American Revolution would spread over the world, see the
famous sermon by Dr. Richard Price (November 4, 1789) commemorating England's Glorious Revolution (1688): "Behold kingdoms . . . starting from sleep, breaking their fetters, and claiming justice from their oppressors! Behold, the light you have struck out, after setting AMERICA free,
reflected to FRANCE, and there kindled into a blaze that lays despotism in ashes, and warms and
illuminates Europe."

THE SONG OF LOS (1795)

The cycle of poems tracing the west-to-east movement of revolution over the continents begins with the prophecies *America* (1793) and *Europe* (1794) and ends with the songs "Africa" and "Asia" in *The Song of Los* (1795). Instead of being arrayed chronologically, however, the four "continent" poems are related through repeated phrases and images, as described in the headnote to *America*. The first two lines of the introductory stanza of "Africa" also serve as an introduction to "Asia," as an unidentified mortal bard offers fellow human beings the very song that Los, the "Eternal Prophet," sang at a banquet in Eternity. The "I" who sings Los's *Song* in the world of time and space, like the "I" who invokes the Eternals to dictate "swift winged words" at the beginning of *Urizen*, is hardly distinguishable from the visionary-prophet-artist-author himself, who identifies himself on the title page only as printer.

After the first line of the introductory stanzas, the title character of *The Song of Los* is mentioned only twice in "Africa," as progenitor of a "terrible race" (4:13) of "children" (3:9) who knowingly or unknowingly act as Urizen's agents. The "Africa" section recounts the progressive degeneration of the human race as Rintrah, Palamabron, and most of the other sons summoned by Enitharmon in *Europe* serve Urizen's purposes by bestowing false doctrines on the world's religious and intellectual leaders. Despite the title, the African continent is rarely named directly, but it is implicitly the site of the earliest biblical stories (3:6–10) as well as the original source of Hindu, Muslim, and other world religions and philosophies. Blake was aware of legends of Greek philosophers' studies in Egypt, an argument for African origins of European culture, and he appears to reaffirm the key ideas of his 1788 tractate, *All Religions Are One*: the true universal religion derives only from insights of the "Poetic Genius," the "true Man," not from isolated and unaided rationality, the tyrannical mechanistic dictates of Urizen. But after Los's misguided sons and daughters have done their worst, and the human race is firmly bound down to earth, it is Urizen, weeping, who springs back into direct action: as an alternative to religion, he gives "a Philosophy of Five Senses" to Newton and Locke, who are closely associated with Rousseau and Voltaire (4:16–18). The song "Africa" ends where *America* begins—"The Guardian Prince of Albion burns in his nightly tent"—perhaps implying that the tyranny of corrupt and binding religions and the sterility of mechanistic philosophy have made inevitable a worldwide revolution in which the people of Africa will also be liberated.

The "Asia" section of Los's *Song* deals with responses to revolution rather than its causes. Alarmed by the disturbance in Europe, the kings of Asia call for constrictive economic, religious, and demographic measures of the kind practiced by European monarchs to stave off social change. (In 1795 Blake may or may not have considered that the British Empire, as it expanded its influence into India and Ceylon [now Sri Lanka], was, from an Asian perspective, among the reactionary rulers of that continent.) Hearing the Asian kings' outcry, Urizen returns to Jerusalem, sacred city of three world religions, and tries to cover the whole area with clouds and darkness—apparently to hide the bleached bones of Adam and Noah, who were the first to fall under Urizen's law in "Africa." But when Orc rises over Europe (7:26–28) like the pillar of fire that guided the Israelites in the Exodus and like the fiery flying serpent that presages abundance and safety (Isaiah 14:29–30), a universal resurrection occurs, blending imagery from Ezekiel's vision of reanimation in the Valley of Dry Bones with a transfiguration of old Mother Earth. In contrast to the "nameless Female"— the personification of Earth in the preludia to *America* and *Europe* who appears first as a virgin and then as a teeming but dissatisfied producer of Orc's abortive offspring—the insatiable Grave experiences a regenerative orgasm and becomes a fruitful womb. The sexual renewal of the final stanza, foreshadowed in the sexual awakening of the "female spirits of the dead, pining in bonds of religion" near the end of *America* (17/15:19–26), implies that Orc's revolutionary changes will eventually fulfill the whole world's longings.

But what of Los, after whom this work is named? In *Europe*, when Los calls his sons to "strike the elemental strings" (6/3:13), their songs have no observable influence on the power struggles of Urizen, Orc, and Enitharmon; and at the end of the work Los abruptly summons them to the "strife of blood" (18/15:11), apparently in preparation for joining the revolution as a warrior. In *The Book of Urizen*, which like *Europe* is dated 1794, and in later works, Los is a positive through flawed creative force; as "Eternal Prophet," artisan, husband, and father, he does his best, despite intermittent self-doubt and constrained vision, to combat error and illusion. Here, in *The Song of Los*, the Eternal Prophet is less effective than in *Urizen*, but more effective than in *Europe*. Even though Los is hardly more than a name in the text, he comes into his own in the designs, as is especially evident in the contrast between the full-page frontispiece and tailpiece designs (not included here; to compare multiple versions of each, see the online Blake Archive). The opening design shows a devotee, seen from the rear, abjectly bending over an altar beneath a huge, mysterious orb covered in illegible symbols—probably the dead sun of Urizen's material universe. By contrast, the closing illustration shows a nude, muscular Los, hammer at the ready, musing over an equally large orb, deep red, radiating energy—a completely different conception of our visible universe, or of the spiritual sun—which the Eternal Prophet is in process of shaping into art.

For commentary and a compendium of earlier perspectives on the work, see Detlef Dörrbecker, *The Continental Prophecies* (1995), volume 4 in the Blake Trust facsimile series (which reproduces Copy A; the Blake Trust/Trianon Press series [1975] reproduces Copy B; Copy D and others appear in the Blake Archive). Among Dörrbecker's useful citations are John Howard, *Infernal Poetics* (1984) and essays by David V. Erdman, *Studies in Romanticism* 16 (1977), 179–88; James McCord, *Colby Library Quarterly* 20 (1984), 22–35; Dörrbecker (on copy F), *Huntington Library Quarterly* 52 (1989), 43–72; and Stephen Behrendt (particularly in relation to *America* and *Europe*) in *Papers on Language and Literature* 28 (1992), 379–97; since augmented by Tilottama Rajan, *Huntington Library Quarterly* 58 (1997), 383–411, and Saree Makdisi (see p. 576) and in *Blake, Nation and Empire* (2006), ed. Clark and Worrall.

Our source text is Copy B, one of six impressions produced in Blake's first and only printing of this work.

The Song of Los   2

Lambeth Printed by W Blake 1795

AFRICA   3

I will sing you a song of Los, the Eternal Prophet:
He sung it to four harps at the tables of Eternity.
    In heart-formed Africa.
Urizen faded! Ariston[1] shudderd!
    And thus the Song began.   5

---

1. Greek *aristos*: "best." Cf. *America* 12/10:10. Reactions to Los's song in "Eternity" in this framing stanza (3:4) parallel those to Urizen's law on earth in the song proper (3:10). As "Africa" proceeds, figures from biblical, classical, Hindu, Islamic, Norse, and English-French traditions are increasingly restricted by "Laws & Religions" (4:14), invented by Urizen and disseminated by the children of Los and Enitharmon.

Adam stood in the garden of Eden:
And Noah on the mountains of Ararat:
They saw Urizen give his Laws to the Nations
By the hands of the children of Los.

Adam shuddered! Noah faded! black grew the sunny African[2]   10
When Rintrah gave Abstract Philosophy to Brama[3] in the East.
    (Night spoke to the Cloud!
"Lo these Human form'd spirits in smiling hipocrisy, War
Against one another: so let them War on: slaves to the eternal
        Elements.")
Noah shrunk beneath the waters;   15
Abram fled in fires from Chaldea;
Moses beheld upon Mount Sinai forms of dark delusion;

            To Trismegistus, Palamabron gave an abstract Law:[4]
            To Pythagoras Socrates & Plato.[5]

Times rolled on o'er all the sons of Har, time after time   20
Orc on Mount Atlas howld, chain'd down with the Chain
    of Jealousy.
Then Oothoon hoverd over Judah & Jerusalem
And Jesus heard her voice (a man of sorrows); he recievd
A Gospel from wretched Theotormon.[6]

The human race began to wither, for the healthy built   25
Secluded places, fearing the joys of Love,
And the disease'd only propagated:
So Antamon call'd up Leutha from her valleys of delight:
And to Mahomet a loose Bible[7] gave.
But in the North, to Odin, Sotha gave a Code of War,   30
Because of Diralada, thinking to reclaim his joy.[8]

2. Noah's cursed son Ham, condemned with his descendants to serve his brothers and their descendants (Genesis 9:22–27), was regarded in European tradition as the ancestor of black people.
3. Blake knew of the Indian god through Charles Wilkins's 1785 translation of the *Bhagvat-Geeta* (see
   n. 1, p. 431 herein). For more on the eighteenth-century mythographic, religious, and political
   implications of Blake's use of this material, represented as coeval with the Bible, see David Weir,
   Brahma in the West (2003). As transmitter of this text, Rintrah appears in a role perhaps more easily reconciled with *Europe* (8/5 and 11/8) than with his appearance in the "Argument" to *Marriage*.
4. Palamabron (cf. *Europe* (11/8:3) continues his brother Rintrah's dispensation of "abstract" teachings, this time in law, in the form of Greek religious philosophy. The legendary Hermes Trismegistus ("thrice greatest Hermes"), identified (by Cicero) with Thoth, Egyptian god of speech
   and writing, was supposed to have written secret sealed ("Hermetic") books of ancient wisdom
   (actually from the third century C.E.), including the alchemical "Smaragdine [Emerald] Table,"
   smashed by Los in *Jerusalem* 91:34.
5. The Greek philosopher, mathematician, and musician Pythagoras (b. about 576 B.C.E.), famous for
   his geometrical proofs, mathematical theory of musical harmony, and fabled magical powers, was
   supposed to have learned secrets in Egypt and the East. Even the classical philosophers Socrates
   and Plato, intentionally or not, were founders of quasi-religions.
6. Here the apparent critique of Christianity as an organized religion depends on prior knowledge of
   Visions 1–2, in which Oothoon, after being raped, is rejected by her moralistic lover, Theotormon.
7. I.e., the Qu'ran, or Koran. A well-known etymology for *Qu'ran* at the time was "a collection of loose
   sheets" (Stevenson), though the derivation was disputed by George Sale, whose landmark 1734
   translation was published in a new edition (1795) sold by Blake's employer Joseph Johnson. In context, especially if prior knowledge of Antamon's and Leutha's association with "lineaments of
   gratified desire" (*Europe* 17/14:19) is assumed, "loose" would have broader associations.
8. Sotha (cf. *Europe* 17/14:26; apparently "Diralada" is an alternate spelling of "Thiralatha") gives the
   Norse god Odin (or Woden) the war-loving religion of pre-Christian Europe. As usual, Blake provides only bits and pieces of the myth he has created as a premise for Los's *Song*.

These were the Churches: Hospitals: Castles: Palaces: 4
Like nets & gins & traps to catch the joys of Eternity
        And all the rest a desart;
Till like a dream Eternity was obliterated & erased.

Since that dread day when Har and Heva[9] fled,   5
Because their brethren & sisters liv'd in War & Lust;
And as they fled they shrunk
    Into two narrow doleful forms:
    Creeping in reptile flesh upon
    The bosom of the ground: 10
    And all the vast of Nature shrunk
    Before their shrunken eyes.

Thus the terrible race of Los & Enitharmon gave
Laws & Religions to the sons of Har, binding them more
And more to Earth: closing and restraining: 15
Till a Philosophy of Five Senses was complete.
Urizen wept & gave it into the hands of Newton & Locke.

        Clouds roll heavy upon the Alps round Rousseau &
            Voltaire:[1]
        And on the mountains of Lebanon round the deceased
            Gods
        Of Asia; & on the desarts of Africa round the Fallen
            Angels.   20
        The Guardian Prince of Albion burns in his nightly
            tent.[2]

                        ASIA   6

        The kings of Asia heard
The howl rise up from Europe![1]
And each ran out from his Web;
From his ancient woven Den;
For the darkness of Asia was startled   5
At the thick-flaming, thought-creating fires of Orc.

And the Kings of Asia stood
And cried in bitterness of soul:

    "Shall not the King call for Famine from the heath?[2]

9. "Heva": Eve. In the early manuscript poem *Tiriel* (not included in this edition), the ancestral figures Har and Heva are senile, doting parents of the title character, who curses all his children; here
  they have fled from "War & Lust," later strongly associated with Orc.
1. With the dominance of nature-based philosophical ideas in Blake's time, from Newton and Locke in
  England to Voltaire and Rousseau in Geneva, humanity's spiritual degeneration has reached its nadir.
2. Identical to *America* 3:1.
1. Cf. *Europe* 14/11:21. Civilization was thought by Europeans to have spread from east to west; revolution, having begun in America, is spreading from west to east.
2. The cry of the Asian kings satirizes the sort of British economic policies and gross inequities
  between classes detailed in E. P. Thompson, *The Making of the English Working Classes* (1963; rev.
  ed. 1988). In the bread shortage of 1795 country people blocked grain shipments, while city people
  blamed millers and middlemen for adulterating flour and holding it back to inflate prices, creating
  "an Artificiall Famine in a Land of plenty."

Nor the Priest, for Pestilence from the fen?   10
To restrain! to dismay! to thin!
The inhabitants of mountain and plain;
In the day of full-feeding prosperity;
And the night of delicious songs.

    Shall not the Councellor throw his curb   15
Of Poverty on the laborious?
To fix the price of labour:
To invent allegoric riches:[3]

And the privy admonishers of men
Call for fires in the City   20
For heaps of smoking ruins,
In the night of prosperity & wantonness[4]

To turn man from his path,
To restrain the child from the womb,

To cut off the bread from the city, | 7 |
That the remnant may learn to obey,

That the pride of the heart may fail;
That the lust of the eyes may be quench'd:[5]
That the delicate ear in its infancy   5
May be dull'd; and the nostrils clos'd up:
To teach mortal worms the path
That leads from the gates of the Grave."

    Urizen heard them cry;
And his shudd'ring waving wings   10
Went enormous above the red flames,
Drawing clouds of despair thro' the heavens
Of Europe as he went:
And his Books of brass iron & gold
Melted over the land as he flew,   15
Heavy-waving, howling, weeping.

      And he stood over Judea;
And stay'd in his ancient place:
And stretch'd his clouds over Jerusalem.

      For Adam, a mouldering skeleton   20
Lay bleach'd on the garden of Eden;
And Noah as white as snow
On the mountains of Ararat.

---

3. Any form of invisible money—credit, stocks, interest—that is negotiable by the rich but unavailable to the poor; also the promise of riches in heaven that consoles the poor.
4. Lines 20–22 are repeated in *Milton* 5/f:40–41. In the early 1790s mobs of "Church and King" arsonists who attacked English sympathizers with the French Revolution were ignored, encouraged, or even hired by authorities; the house of Joseph Priestley was burned in Birmingham in 1791. In London, the Privy Council was occupied with the grain crisis from May to December 1795.
5. Ironic paraphrase of 1 John 2:16; the senses are being narrowed as humanity accepts a religion of asceticism for the sake of the life hereafter.

Then the thunders of Urizen bellow'd aloud
From his woven darkness above.   25

Orc, raging in European darkness,
Arose like a pillar of fire above the Alps,
Like a serpent of fiery flame!
          The sullen Earth
                Shrunk!   30

Forth from the dead dust rattling bones to bones
Join: shaking convuls'd the shivring clay breathes[6]
And all flesh naked stands: Fathers and Friends;
Mothers & Infants; Kings & Warriors:

          The Grave shrieks with delight, & shakes   35
          Her hollow womb, & clasps the solid stem;
          Her bosom swells with wild desire:
          And milk & blood & glandous wine,
          In rivers rush & shout & dance,
          On mountain, dale and plain.   40

          The SONG of LOS is Ended.
          Urizen Wept.[7]

THE BOOK OF URIZEN (1794)

Blake delivered magnificently on his promise, or threat, to give the world "The Bible of Hell" (*Marriage* 24)—whether we want it or not—beginning with "A Song of Liberty" and continuing with book after antiestablishment book saturated in biblical language, imagery, and themes. In three of these works—*The ~~First~~ Book of Urizen* (Blake removed *First* from one late title page and from parts of the copy followed here), *The Book of Ahania*, and *The Book of Los*—Blake went so far as to imitate even the double-columned biblical page layout and its division into chapters and verses. *Urizen*, the first volume of Blake's "diabolical" Bible, is modeled on the "angelic" Genesis (known as "The First Book of Moses" on the theory that Moses himself wrote the five books of the Pentateuch); and like Genesis, *Urizen* is a chronicle of beginnings. In the spirit of *All Religions Are One*, Blake absorbs images and ideas from a great variety of sources, including Hesiod's *Theogony* (which he later helped to illustrate), Ovid's *Metamorphoses*, the Norse mythology of P. H. Mallet's *Northern Antiquities* (trans.1770), the multicultural mythic syntheses of Jacob Bryant's *A New System* (1774–76), and the work of such speculative philosophers and occultists as Jacob Boehme ("Behmen" in *Marriage* 22). But in his countermyth to the familiar creation story, there is no Prime Mover; the created world is not "something" made out of "nothing" but a finite and erroneous perception of the infinite fullness of being. In *Urizen* and its companion books, as in heterodox Jewish and Christian interpretive traditions that produced the Kabbalah and Gnostic texts, the creation and fall are the same event: the fall occurs at the instant the infinite divine mind chooses to limit itself. Instead of starting with a formless void and filling it with "the heaven and the earth" (Genesis 1:1),

---

6. Cf. the resurrection of the dry bones in Ezekiel 37:1–10.
7. Ironically alluding to "Jesus wept," the shortest verse in the Bible (John 11:35); Urizen's weeping, anticipated in 4:17, is not over a friend's death but over the resurrection of humanity.

Urizen starts with everything, with plenitude; but in defining himself as a separate being he demarcates whatever is finite, the not-everything, as his personal property. As he weighs and measures his holdings, he reduces even that finitude to a vacuumed-out void. All he ever "creates" is this inner emptiness, which must be sealed off from the full, fluctuating life of the "myriads" in Eternity.

The Book of Urizen is *about* Urizen but not *by* him. The "I" of the Preludium invokes the "Eternals" who "dictate" the work. As David Worrall notes in his introduction to *The Urizen Books*, volume 6 in the Blake Trust series (1995), *The Book of Urizen* explores "when, why and how man's ideas of God and religion came into existence" (p. 20)—*man's* ideas, indeed, for in *Urizen* as in Genesis there is no feminine or female consciousness in the beginning; only belatedly is a female entity derived from a secondary fissure within the all-male primordial divine/human persona. Urizen's initial act of anticreation generates the error of perceiving life as finite and corrupt, and the primal separation of self from other, subject from object, mind from matter, and finite from infinite precipitates a cascade of further separations: joy from pain; moral from immoral; time from eternity; human from animal, vegetable, and mineral; and the subdivision of matter into the four elements. These separations alarm Los, the rather ineffectual bard introduced in *Europe*, who has now become the "Eternal Prophet" (10:7, 15), the arch-opponent of the "primeval Priest" ("Preludium"), Urizen. Suffering from the pain of Urizen's having been "rent from his side" (6:4) and recognizing that the Eternals will not reverse the separation, Los takes action to contain Urizen's withdrawal but inadvertently makes matters worse: time is subdivided into hours, days, and years; and the body is subdivided into the five senses and the separate organic functions. Still worse, Los begins to disintegrate internally. His concern over the still-further-confined Urizen becomes "Pity" and takes on a separate existence as Enitharmon, Los's female counterpart, an objectification not only of his own emotions but also of the feminine side of his personality, an aspect of himself that he now projects with fear, distrust, and loathing onto the other half of the emerging human race. This alienation of the sexes results in yet another division, this time along generational lines, as the child Orc arouses his father's jealousy and is chained down by both parents.

The name *Urizen* probably derives from the Greek word for "limit," the root of our word "horizon" (Dorothy Plowman, 1929 Dent facsimile). Because Urizen personifies the error of reducing all reality to what can be manipulated by cold, calculating rationality, his name has long been taken as a pun on "Your Reason" (Damon 1924), and further puns have multiplied in scholarly commentary (Hilton, p. 573 herein). Both Urizen and his antagonist Urthona (Los's eternal name) may recall Uranus, the primeval father of the Titans in Greek mythology. In acting as primal lawgiver, both physical and moral, Urizen imposes a uniform standard under "One King, one God, one Law," which has the unintended and unforeseen consequence of forcing what would otherwise be productively opposed energies or virtues into incommensurable contradictions. For example, his "Laws of peace of love of unity / Of pity compassion forgiveness" (4:34–35) appear to reassert the sterling virtues of "Mercy Pity Peace and Love" celebrated in "The Divine Image" of *Songs of Innocence*. But "Mercy no more could be, / If all were as happy as we," as is recognized in the contrary poem "The Human Abstract," in *Songs of Experience*. The manifestation of these virtues—and, even worse, Urizen's attempt to legislate them—indicates that his world, estranged from the full communal life of the Eternals, has sunk deeply into the either/or, self/other oppositions of the fallen state. In the book's concluding image, a bearded Urizen and all he has tried to create are caught in the net of his own reasonings, his own authoritarian code; that is why his fiery son Fuzon pronounces the entire planet earth "Egypt," a state of slavery, and summons the "children" personifying the other elements to abandon it.

An unusual feature of *Urizen* is that ten of its twenty-eight pages (in the fullest form of the book) are large designs without text, an integral component of its meaning impossible to incorporate into a text-based edition; as always, we advise supplementing a study of our sampling of images (including this book's cover and color plates 11 and 12) with the complete facsimiles available in print and electronic formats. A further unique feature of this book is that, in its eight known versions, the full-page designs are interspersed among the other pages in eight different sequences; and even the text pages are not all in the same order (or all present) in the various versions of the book. As of 2007, the simplest brief description of differing sequences is to be found in the online Blake Archive. Worrall's detailed standard-order table in the Blake Trust facsimile edition (1995) of Copy D (p. 149), though flawed by minor inconsistencies, provides an informative overview. Copy A, one of two now in the Paul Mellon collection of the Yale Center for British Art, is the source of the Dent facsimile edited by Dorothy Plowman (1929). Copy G (Library of Congress), one of six currently available in the online Blake Archive, was the source of the Blake Trust / Trianon Press facsimile edited by Keynes (1958), reprinted by Dover (1997); it has also been published in the Shambala series edited by Kay Parkhurst Easson and Roger R. Eason (1978) and as a compact disk (Octavo 2001), with a commentary by Nicolas Barker. For the context of politicized religious discourse, see Worrall's introduction. On the effect of differing page sequences, see Robert N. Essick, *Studies in Bibliography* 39 (1986), 230–235); Helen B. Ellis in *Colby Library Quarterly* 23 (1987), 99–107; and John Pierce (2003). For further interpretive insights, see Leslie Tannenbaum (1982); John Howard (1984); Paul Mann in *Unnam'd Forms* (1986), ed. Hilton and Vogler; Jerome J. McGann in *Studies in Romanticism* 25 (1986), 303–324; Angela Esterhammer in *Blake and the Nineties* (1999), ed. Clark and Worrall; and Terence Allan Hoagwood, *Politics, Philosophy, and the Production of Romantic Texts* (1996).

Our text is taken from Copy A (Yale Center for British Art), which contains all twenty-eight plates with the textual portion in an order closest to the standard "ideal" sequence of the Bentley, Erdman, and Keynes editions (though numbered differently). Blake produced this copy, along with five others (variously colored and arranged) in his first print run of the book (1794), but altered and renumbered pages as he rethought his plans for a sequel. Although *First* remains on the title page, Blake removed the word from both the Preludium and the conclusion. Our page width cannot accommodate Blake's double-columned biblical format, but we emphasize his biblical chapter-verse organization by keeping verses together across column and plate boundaries. Marginal plate numbers refer to the standard order only.

THE FIRST BOOK of *URIZEN*[*] $\boxed{1}$

LAMBETH. Printed by Will Blake 1794

PRELUDIUM $\boxed{2}$
TO THE BOOK OF *URIZEN*

Of the primeval Priest's assum'd power,
When Eternals spurn'd back his religion;

---

[*] See color plate 11, where "FIRST" has been deleted. Urizen sits on an open book, quill in one hand, etching tool or small paintbrush in the other, blindly copying blots and blurs onto books at each side. Behind him loom the dual tombstone-like tablets of the Mosaic Law. See Eaves, p. 586 herein, and W. J. T. Mitchell in *The Visionary Hand* (1973), ed. Essick.

And gave him a place in the north,
Obscure, shadowy, void, solitary.

Eternals I hear your call gladly,   5
Dictate swift winged words, & fear not
To unfold your dark visions of torment.[1]

Chap: I   3

1. Lo, a shadow of horror is risen
In Eternity! Unknown, unprolific?
Self-closd, all-repelling; what Demon
Hath form'd this abominable void
This soul-shudd'ring vacuum? Some said   5
"It is Urizen,"[2] But unknown, abstracted
Brooding secret, the dark power hid.

2. Times on times he divided, & measur'd[3]
Space by space in his ninefold darkness
Unseen, unknown; changes appeard   10
Like[4] desolate mountains rifted furious
By the black winds of perturbation.

3. For he strove in battles dire
In unseen conflictions with shapes
Bred from his forsaken wilderness,   15
Of beast, bird, fish, serpent & element,
Combustion, blast, vapour and cloud.

4. Dark revolving in silent activity:
Unseen in tormenting passions;
An activity unknown and horrible;   20
A self-contemplating shadow,
In enormous labours occupied.

5. But Eternals beheld his vast forests.
Age on ages he lay, clos'd, unknown,
Brooding shut in the deep; all avoid   25
The petrific abominable chaos.

6. His cold horrors silent, dark Urizen
Prepar'd; his ten thousands of thunders
Rang'd in gloom'd array stretch out across
The dread world, & the rolling of wheels   30
As of swelling seas, sound in his clouds

1. The epic-style "Preludium" previews the main action, invokes the muse (the "Eternals"), and appropriates the stock Homeric phrase "winged words" (translated circuitously by Chapman and Pope, though Pope's editors provided the literal meaning in footnotes). In the large headpiece design (not included in this edition), a flying woman guides an airborne child. Under a separate impression Blake wrote "Teach these souls to fly."
2. One of Blake's rare insertions of quotation marks; another is Chapter V, verse 11 (19:2–4).
3. Cf. "Bring out number, weight, & measure in a year of dearth" ("Proverbs of Hell," *Marriage* 9). In this chapter Urizen splits the finite from the infinite.
4. Changed to "In his" in Copy G, the latest version.

In his hills of stor'd snows, in his mountains
Of hail & ice; voices of terror,
Are heard, like thunders of autumn,
When the cloud blazes over the harvests.   35

Chap: II.

1. Earth was not: nor globes of attraction
The will of the Immortal expanded
Or contracted his all flexible senses.[5]
Death was not, but eternal life sprung.

2. The sound of a trumpet the heavens   40
Awoke & vast clouds of blood roll'd
Round the dim rocks of Urizen, so nam'd
That solitary one in Immensity.

3. Shrill the trumpet: & myriads of Eternity[6]
Muster around the bleak desarts   [4]
Now fill'd with clouds, darkness & waters
That roll'd perplex'd labring & utter'd
Words articulate, bursting in thunders
That roll'd on the tops of his mountains.   5

4. "From the depths of dark solitude,[7] From
The eternal abode in my holiness,
Hidden, set apart in my stern counsels
Reserv'd for the days of futurity,
I have sought for a joy without pain,   10
For a solid without fluctuation.
Why will you die O Eternals?
Why live in unquenchable burnings?

5. First I fought with the fire; consum'd
Inwards, into a deep world within:[8]   15
A void immense, wild dark & deep
Where nothing was: Nature's wide womb
And self balanc'd stretch'd o'er the void
I alone, even I! the winds merciless
Bound; but condensing, in torrents   20
They fall & fall; strong, I repell'd
The vast waves, & arose on the waters
A wide world of solid obstruction.[9]

5. At this point Urizen is still "Immortal"; his senses are still flexible; the rules of Newtonian celestial mechanics do not yet govern his cosmos.
6. This line is scratched through but not obliterated in our source, Copy A. It provides a subject for the verb *Muster* in the next line, which begins a new page (plate 4) on Urizen's motivations, a page omitted from five of the eight versions of *Urizen*, including the latest.
7. With the trumpet, clouds, and thunderous words of verse 3, recalling Moses's encounters with God on Sinai (Exodus 19:16–19, 20:18–21).
8. Urizen's contentions turn the fire of vitality inward (later to become his rebellious son Fuzon).
9. When Urizen has subdued fire, air, and water, the fourth element appears: the massive earth, the solid objective world for which he has striven. "Self balanc'd" (4:18) recalls *Paradise Lost* 7.242.

6. Here alone I in books formd of metals[1]
Have written the secrets of wisdom 25
The secrets of dark contemplation
By fightings and conflicts dire.
With terrible monsters Sin-bred:
Which the bosoms of all inhabit;
Seven deadly Sins of the soul. 30

7. Lo! I unfold my darkness; and on
This rock, place with strong hand the Book
Of eternal brass, written in my solitude.

8. Laws of peace, of love, of unity;
Of pity, compassion, forgiveness. 35
Let each chuse one habitation;
His ancient infinite mansion:
One command, one joy, one desire,
One curse, one weight, one measure
One King, one God, one Law."[2] 40

Chap: III.

1. The voice ended, they saw his pale visage
Emerge from the darkness; his hand
On the rock of eternity unclasping
The Book of brass. Rage siez'd the strong.

2. Rage, fury, intense indignation 45
In cataracts of fire blood & gall
In whirlwinds of sulphurous smoke:
And enormous forms of energy;
~~In living creations appear'd~~ | 5 |
~~In the flames of eternal fury,~~[3]

3. Sund'ring, dark'ning, thund'ring!
Rent away with a terrible crash
Eternity roll'd wide apart 5
Wide asunder rolling
Mountainous all around
Departing; departing: departing:
Leaving ruinous fragments of life
Hanging frowning cliffs & all between 10
An ocean of voidness unfathomable.

1. Cf. *Europe* 14/11:3 and *Ahania* 3:73–74:1. Blake places the second syllable of "metals" on a separate line (perhaps to emphasize *me*; see Hilton, *Literal Imagination*, p. 250 herein).
2. Perhaps a parody of "one body, . . . one Spirit, . . . one hope . . . One Lord, one faith, one baptism, one God" (Ephesians 4:4–6); cf. the final line of *Marriage* 24: "One Law for the Lion & Ox is Oppression" and *Visions* 7/4:22. The seven deadly sins (verse 6)—pride, avarice, envy, wrath, lust, gluttony, and sloth—were first codified by Pope Gregory I (c. 540–604).
3. In Copy A, our source text, the first two lines of plate **5** are lightly crossed out, as is the last line on plate **3**, so that the narrative would have made sense if Blake had decided to remove plate **4**, as he did in five copies (but not this one). The mass of unintelligible shapes in the open book of the design is different in each copy. A separate impression (Butlin 261.8) is captioned "The Book of my Remembrance" (Malachi 3:16).

4. The roaring fires ran o'er the heav'ns
In whirlwinds & cataracts of blood
And o'er the dark desarts of Urizen
Fires pour thro' the void on all sides   15
~~On Urizen's self-begotten armies.~~[4]

5. But no light from the fires, all was darkness
In the flames of Eternal fury.

6. In fierce anguish & quenchless flames
To the desarts and rocks He[5] ran raging   20
To hide, but He could not; combining
He dug mountains & hills in vast strength
He piled them in incessant labour,
In howlings & pangs & fierce madness
Long periods in burning fires labouring   25
Till hoary, and age-broke, and aged,
In despair and the shadows of death.

7. And a roof vast petrific around,
On all sides He fram'd: like a womb;
Where thousands of rivers in veins   30
Of blood pour down the mountains to cool
The eternal fires beating without
From Eternals; & like a black globe
View'd by sons of Eternity, standing

4. In our source text Blake painted over this line (present in other copies) and covered it with a vine.
5. Blake etched and printed the pronoun *they* (in four occurrences), but after printing the word he
erased *t* and *y* in all copies to convert the plural (referring to "armies") to singular (referring to
"Urizen"), with a capital *H* at the beginning of lines 5:22–23. In Copy A, our source text, the capital *H* also appears midsentence in lines 20–21 and 29.

On the shore of the infinite ocean   35
Like a human heart strugling & beating
The vast world of Urizen appear'd.

8. And Los round the dark globe of Urizen,[6]
Kept watch for Eternals to confine
The obscure separation alone;   40
For Eternity stood wide apart,
As the stars are apart from the earth. $\boxed{6}$

9. Los wept howling around the dark Demon:
And cursing his lot for in anguish,
Urizen was rent from his side:[7]
And a fathomless void for his feet: 5
And intense fires for his dwelling.

10. But Urizen laid in a stony sleep
Unorganiz'd, rent from Eternity.

11. The Eternals said: "What is this? Death.
Urizen is a clod of clay."   10

12: Los howld in a dismal stupor, $\boxed{7}$
Groaning! gnashing! groaning!
Till the wrenching apart was healed.

13: But the wrenching of Urizen heal'd not
Cold, featureless, flesh or clay   5
Rifted with direful changes
He lay in a dreamless night

14: Till Los rouz'd his his fires affrighted
At the formless unmeasurable death.

Chap: IV[a]:[8] $\boxed{8}$

1: Los smitten with astonishment
Frightend at the hurtling bones

2: And at the surging sulphureous
Perturbed Immortal mad raging

3: In whirlwinds & pitch & nitre   5
Round the furious limbs of Los.

6. In the same moment that the heart becomes distinct from the brain, Los appears.
7. The former Eternals Urizen and Los are so closely connected that Urizen's self-separation also involves Los, who experiences it as a ripping away of part of his own body; other details from Los's point of view appear in *The Book of Los.* The two-word formula "X wept" in verse 9, sometimes (as here) extended adverbially, occurs repeatedly at crucial points in the *Urizen* books. Cf. n. 7, p. 112. In *Urizen* see also Los's weeping in **13**:48, and Enitharmon's in **20**:22.
8. By accident (almost certainly), Blake gave the number IV to two different chapters, which editors distinguish, in brackets, as *a* and *b*. He omitted Chapter IV[a] from two copies but kept both chapters in the other six copies, perhaps reflecting his awareness of German biblical scholars' discoveries that Genesis was woven from earlier sources, as reported in English by Dr. Alexander Geddes (see Tannenbaum and McGann in the headnote).

4: And Los formed nets & gins
And threw the nets round about.

5: He watch'd in shuddring fear
The dark changes & bound every change   10
With rivets of iron & brass;

6. And these were the changes of Urizen.

Chap: IV[b].   [10]

1. Ages on ages roll'd over him!
In stony sleep ages roll'd over him!
Like a dark waste stretching chang'able
By earthquakes riv'n, belching sullen fires.
On ages roll'd, ages in ghastly   5
Sick torment; around him in whirlwinds
Of darkness the eternal Prophet howl'd
Beating still on his rivets of iron
Pouring sodor of iron; dividing
The horrible night into watches.   10

2. And Urizen (so his eternal name)
His prolific delight obscurd more & more
In dark secresy, hiding in surgeing
Sulphureous fluid his phantasies.
The Eternal Prophet heavd the dark bellows.   15
And turn'd restless the tongs; and the hammer
Incessant beat; forging chains new & new
Numb'ring with links, hours days & years.

3. The eternal mind bounded began to roll
Eddies of wrath ceaseless round & round   20
And the sulphureous foam surgeing thick
Settled, a lake, bright, & shining clear:
White as the snow on the mountains cold.

4. Forgetfulness, dumbness, necessity!
In chains of the mind locked up,   25
Like fetters of ice shrinking together
Disorganiz'd, rent from Eternity.
Los beat on his fetters of iron:
And heated his furnaces & pour'd
Iron sodor and sodor of brass.   30

5. Restless turnd the immortal inchain'd
Heaving dolorous! anguish'd! unbearable
Till a roof shaggy wild inclos'd
In an orb, his fountain of thought.

6. In a horrible dreamful slumber;   35
Like the linked infernal chain;
A vast Spine writh'd in torment

Upon the winds; shooting pain'd
Ribs, like a bending cavern
And bones of solidness, froze   40
Over all his nerves of joy.
And a first Age passed over,
And a state of dismal woe.

7. From the caverns of his jointed Spine,   11
Down sunk with fright a red
Round globe hot burning deep
Deep down into the Abyss;
Panting: Conglobing, Trembling   5
Shooting out ten thousand branches
Around his solid bones.
And a second Age passed over,
And a state of dismal woe.

8. In harrowing fear rolling round;   10
His nervous brain shot branches
Round the branches of his heart.
On high into two little orbs
And fixed in two little caves
Hiding carefully from the wind,   15
His Eyes beheld the deep,

And a third Age passed over;
And a state of dismal woe.

9. The pangs of hope began,
In heavy pain striving, struggling.   20
Two Ears in close volutions
From beneath his orbs of vision
Shot spiring out and petrified
As they grew. And a fourth Age passed[9]
And a state of dismal woe.   25

10. In ghastly torment sick;
Hanging upon the wind;
Two Nostrils bent down to the deep,   13
And a fifth Age passed over;
And a state of dismal woe.

11. In ghastly torment sick;
Within his ribs bloated round,   5
A craving Hungry Cavern:
Thence arose his channeld Throat,
And like a red flame a Tongue
Of thirst & of hunger appeard.
And a sixth Age passed over: 10
And a state of dismal woe.

12. Enraged & stifled with torment
He threw his right Arm to the north
His left Arm to the south
Shooting out in anguish deep,   15
And his Feet stampd the nether Abyss
In trembling & howling & dismay.
And a seventh Age passed over;
And a state of dismal woe.[1]

Chap: V.

1. In terrors Los shrunk from his task;   20
His great hammer fell from his hand.
His fires beheld, and sickening,
Hid their strong limbs in smoke.
For with noises ruinous loud;
With hurtlings & clashings & groans   25
The Immortal endurd his chains,
Tho' bound in a deadly sleep.

2. All the myriads of Eternity;
All the wisdom & joy of life:
Roll like a sea around him.   30

9. This break in the pattern of refrain that ends other "ages" of creation/fall is caused at least in part
by contingencies of spacing. In the design, p. 121 herein, the round object at bottom right is the
head of Los's hammer, seen end-forward.
1. Los's endeavor to confine Urizen within space and time (verse 1), the human lifespan (verse 2),
and then in the mortal body (verses 3–12) ironically parallels Genesis 1–2. For another perspective on Urizen's confinement, see color plate 12.

Except what his little orbs
Of sight by degrees unfold.

3. And now his eternal life
Like a dream was obliterated.

4. Shudd'ring, the Eternal Prophet smote   35
With a stroke, from his north to south region.
The bellows & hammer are silent now
A nerveless silence, his prophetic voice
Siez'd; a cold solitude & dark void
The Eternal Prophet & Urizen clos'd.   40

5. Ages on ages rolld over them
Cut off from life & light, frozen
Into horrible forms of deformity,
Los suffer'd his fires to decay
Then he look'd back with anxious desire   45
But the space undivided by existence
Struck horror into his soul.

6. Los wept obscur'd with mourning:
His bosom earthquak'd with sighs;
He saw Urizen deadly black,   50
In his chains bound, & Pity began.

7. In anguish dividing & dividing
For pity divides the soul[2]
In pangs eternity on eternity
Life in cataracts pourd down his cliffs.   55
The void shrunk the lymph into Nerves
Wand'ring wide on the bosom of night
And left a round globe of blood
Trembling upon the Void.

8. The globe of life blood trembled $\boxed{18}$
Branching out into roots:
Fib'rous, writhing upon the winds:
Fibres of blood, milk and tears:
In pangs, eternity on eternity,   5
At length in tears & cries imbodied
A female form trembling and pale
Waves before his deathy face.

9. All Eternity shudderd at sight
Of the first female now separate[3]   10
Pale as a cloud of snow
Waving before the face of Los.

---

2. Cf. "Pity would be no more / If we did not make somebody Poor" ("The Human Abstract"). Los
becomes separate from his own tender feelings, personified and objectified as "female." (The plate
numbers skip from 13 to 18 between verses 7 and 8 because most intervening plates are full-page
designs.)
3. This "first female," called Enitharmon in the next chapter (20:6), shares some characteristics with
Pandora, the first woman in Hesiodic myth, and others with Milton's Eve. In Chapter VI, as Los and
Enitharmon identify themselves with their sexual roles, they lose sight of their common humanity.

10. Wonder, awe, fear, astonishment
Petrify the eternal myriads;
At the first female form now separate   15
They call'd her Pity, and fled.   19

11. "Spread a Tent with strong curtains around them.
Let cords & stakes bind in the Void
That Eternals may no more behold them."

12. They began to weave curtains of darkness.
They erected large pillars round the Void   5
With golden hooks fastend in the pillars
With infinite labour the Eternals
A woof wove, and called it Science.

Chap: VI.

1. But Los saw the Female & pitied:
He embrac'd her, she wept, she refus'd   10

In perverse and cruel delight
She fled from his arms, yet he followd.

2. Eternity shudder'd when they saw
Man begetting his likeness
On his own divided image.   15

3. A time passed over, the Eternals
Began to erect the tent;
When Enitharmon sick,
Felt a Worm within her womb.

4. Yet helpless it lay like a Worm   20
In the trembling womb
To be moulded into existence.

5. All day the worm lay on her bosom
All night within her womb
The worm lay till it grew to a serpent   25
With dolorous hissings & poisons
Round Enitharmon's loins folding.

6. Coild within Enitharmon's womb
The serpent grew casting its scales,
With sharp pangs the hissings began   30
To change to a grating cry,
Many sorrows and dismal throes.
Many forms of fish, bird & beast
Brought forth an Infant form
Where was a worm before.[4]   35

7. The Eternals their tent finished
Alarm'd with these gloomy visions
When Enitharmon groaning
Produc'd a man Child to the light.[5]

8. A shriek ran thro' Eternity: 40
And a paralytic stroke;
At the birth of the Human shadow.

9. Delving earth in his resistless way;
Howling, the Child with fierce flames
Issu'd from Enitharmon.   45

10. The Eternals closed the tent
They beat down the stakes, the cords.

4. On Blake's use of medical and embryological research, see Carmen S. Kreiter, *Studies in Roman-ticism* 4 (1965), 110–18; F. B. Curtis, *Blake Studies* 8 (1979), 187–99; Tristanne J. Connolly, *William Blake and the Body* (2002); and George H. Gilpin, *Studies in Romanticism* 43 (2004), 35–56. Enitharmon experiences her pregnancy as a parasitic illness.
5. Alluding to the Apocalyptic "woman clothed with the sun" who "brought forth a man child, who was to rule all nations (Revelation 12:1–5, echoing Isaiah 66:7): i.e., the Messiah.

Thus the Eternal Prophet was divided[6] $\boxed{15}$
Before the death image of Urizen
For in changeable clouds and darkness
In a winterly night beneath,
The Abyss of Los stretch'd immense: 5
And now seen, now obscur'd to the eyes
Of Eternals, the visions remote

Of the dark seperation appear'd.
As glasses discover Worlds
In the endless Abyss of space.   10
So the expanding eyes of Immortals
Beheld the dark visions of Los,
And the globe of life blood trembling.

Urizen C: VII $\boxed{20}$

Stretch'd for a work of eternity;
No more Los beheld Eternity.

11. In his hands he siez'd the infant
He bathed him in springs of sorrow
He gave him to Enitharmon.   5

1. They named the child Orc, he grew
Fed with milk of Enitharmon.

2. Los awoke her; O sorrow & pain!
A tight'ning girdle grew
Around his bosom. In sobbings   10
He burst the girdle in twain,
But still another girdle
Opressd his bosom. In sobbings
Again he burst it. Again
Another girdle succeeds   15
The girdle was form'd by day;
By night was burst in twain.

3. These falling down on the rock
Into an iron Chain
In each other link by link lock'd.   20

4. They took Orc to the top of a mountain.
O how Enitharmon wept!
They chain'd his young limbs to the rock
With the Chain of Jealousy
Beneath Urizen's deathful shadow.[7]   25

5. The dead heard the voice of the child
And began to awake from sleep

6. In Copy B (Pierpont Morgan Library), what appears here as an expansion of Chapter VI, verse 10, continues Chapter V, verse 7 (plate 13), on the separation of Urizen and Los, leading to the "globe of life blood" (plate 18).

7. The chaining of Orc, not represented visually, casts retrospective light on the Preludium design of *America* 3/1. For Los's formation of the chain from his own jealousy, see the cover of this book.

All things heard the voice of the child
And began to awake to life.

6. And Urizen craving with hunger   30
Stung with the odours of Nature
Explor'd his dens around.

7. He form'd a line & a plummet
To divide the Abyss beneath.
He form'd a dividing rule: 35

8. He formed scales to weigh;
He formed massy weights;
He formed a brazen quadrant:
He formed golden compasses[8]
And began to explore the Abyss   40
And he planted a garden of fruits.

9. But Los encircled Enitharmon
With fires of Prophecy
From the sight of Urizen & Orc.

10. And she bore an enormous race.   45

Chap. VIII.

1. Urizen explor'd his dens
Mountain, moor, & wilderness,
With a globe of fire[9] lighting his journey
A fearful journey, annoy'd
By cruel enormities; forms   50
Of life on his forsaken mountains.   23

2. And his world teemd vast enormities
Frightning: faithless; fawning
Portions of life; similitudes
Of a foot, or a hand, or a head   5
Or a heart, or an eye, they swam mischevous
Dread terrors! delighting in blood.

3. Most Urizen sicken'd to see
His eternal creations appear,
Sons & daughters of sorrow on mountains[1]   10
Weeping! wailing! first Thiriel appear'd
Astonish'd at his own existence
Like a man from a cloud born, & Utha

---

8. Urizen, awakened by Orc's protest, explores his environment by further measuring and quantify-
ing it (cf. the compass on the frontispiece to *Europe* [color plate 9]).
9. Presumably the material sun, which Blake (following Swedenborg) distinguished from the spiritual sun; used like Diogenes' lantern. Cf. Los's explorations illuminated by the spiritual sun in
Jerusalem 1 and 97.
1. The offspring named here are personifications of the four elements (cf. Urizen's struggle in Chapter II) or productions of subhuman nature (as in Hesiod's *Theogony*). Urizen apparently generates
these children without a mate (cf. "self-begotten" in the canceled line of 5:16). His consort, Ahania, is not introduced until the book that bears her name.

From the waters emerging, laments!
Grodna rent the deep earth howling   15
Amaz'd! his heavens immense cracks
Like the ground parch'd with heat; then Fuzon
Flam'd out! first begotten, last born.
All his eternal sons in like manner
His daughters from green herbs & cattle   20
From monsters, & worms of the pit.

4. He in darkness clos'd, view'd all his race
And his soul sicken'd! he curs'd
Both sons & daughters; for he saw
That no flesh nor spirit could keep   25
His iron laws one moment.[2]

5. For he saw that life liv'd upon death
The Ox in the slaughter house moans   25
The Dog at the wintry door
And he wept, & he called it Pity
And his tears flowed down on the winds.[3]

6. Cold he wander'd on high, over their cities   5
In weeping & pain & woe!
And where-ever he wanderd in sorrows
Upon the aged heavens
A cold shadow follow'd behind him
Like a spider's web, moist, cold, & dim   10
Drawing out from his sorrowing soul
The dungeon-like heaven dividing,
Where ever the footsteps of Urizen
Walk'd over the cities in sorrow.

7. Till a Web dark & cold, throughout all   15
The tormented element stretch'd
From the sorrows of Urizen's soul.

None could break the Web, no wings of fire,[4]

8. So twisted the cords, & so knotted   20
The meshes; twisted like to the human brain

9. And all calld it, The Net of Religion.

Chap: IX

1. Then the Inhabitants of those Cities:
Felt their Nerves change into Marrow

2. Cf. Paul's quotation of Deuteronomy 27:26: "For as many as are of the works of the law are under the curse: for it is written, Cursed is every one that continueth not in all things which are written in the book of the law to do them" (Galatians 3:10 ff.).
3. This sequence of cursing and weeping recalls Los's behavior toward him in binding (8:10) and pitying (13:48–51).
4. Line 18 (blank here) is painted over with a decorative vine in this copy; in other copies: "And the Web is a Female in embrio." The Web of Religion is to the distortions of priestcraft (*Marriage* 11) and Mystery ("The Human Abstract") as the Tent of Science (19:2–9) is to the distortions of abstract reasoning.

And hardening Bones began   25
In swift diseases and torments,
In throbbings & shootings & grindings
Thro' all the coasts; till weaken'd
The Senses inward rush'd shrinking,
Beneath the dark net of infection.[5]   30

2. Till the shrunken eyes clouded over
Discern'd not the woven hipocrisy
But the streaky slime in their heavens
Brought together by narrowing perceptions
Appeard transparent air; for their eyes   35
Grew small like the eyes of a man
And in reptile forms shrinking together[6]
Of seven feet stature they remaind.

3. Six days they shrunk up from existence
And on the seventh day they rested.   40
And they bless'd the seventh day, in sick hope:
And forgot their eternal life.

4. And their thirty cities divided[7]
In form of a human heart
No more could they rise at will   45
In the infinite void, but bound down
To earth by their narrowing perceptions
They lived a period of years   [28]
Then left a noisom body
To the jaws of devouring darkness.

5. And their children wept, & built
Tombs in the desolate places,   5
And form'd laws of prudence, and call'd them
The eternal laws of God.

6. And the thirty cities remain
Surrounded by salt floods, now call'd
Africa: its name was then Egypt.[8]   10

7. The remaining sons of Urizen
Beheld their brethren shrink together

---

5. As with the materialization of Urizen's body in Chapter IV[b], the senses begin to contract as the nerves harden. Because of their "narrowing perceptions," those caught under the Net of Religion (25:21) cannot register its distortions.
6. Shrinking into "reptile forms" recalls the fate of the devils in *Paradise Lost* 10.504–84. At this still relatively early stage of the creation/fall, those caught under the Net have not yet shrunk to average human dimensions (cf. "There were giants in the earth in those days"; Genesis 6:4). The degenerative stages of anticreation have shrunk from "ages" (10:42–13:19) to "days" (25:39 ff.), clinched by the parody of Genesis 2:2–3.
7. Jair gave his thirty sons thirty cities in Gilead (Judges 10:4). Alexander the Great named thirty (or more) cities after himself, beginning with Alexandria in Egypt.
8. In taking the shape of a human heart (25:44) in Africa the cities become identified with "heart-formed Africa" (*Song of Los* 3:3), both as a continent and as a phase of history. Egypt, renamed Africa, encompasses two enslaved peoples: the ancient Israelites and the Africans of Blake's time. Those trapped in Egypt are occupied with the building of tombs and making of laws.

Beneath the Net of Urizen;
Perswasion was in vain;

For the ears of the inhabitants,   15
Were wither'd, & deafen'd, & cold.
And their eyes could not discern,
Their brethren of other cities.[9]

8. So Fuzon call'd all together   20
The remaining children of Urizen:
And they left the pendulous earth:[1]
They called it Egypt, & left it.

9. And the salt ocean rolled englob'd.[2]

The End of the book of Urizen.

THE BOOK OF AHANIA (1794)

Perhaps first planned as "The Second Book of Urizen," this sequel to the Genesis book of Blake's "Bible of Hell" contains only scattered allusions to the Exodus announced at the end of *The Book of Urizen*. The first four chapters are concerned with the primal conflict between Urizen and his self-generated son, Fuzon; the fifth and final chapter centers on Urizen's "Unseen, unbodied, unknown" female counterpart Ahania, who bewails her outcast state and the loss of her former joys as Urizen's consort. In this infernal variation on the theme of Exodus, Urizen acts as God the lawgiver, and Fuzon plays the part of Moses the liberator (but not receiver of the law); his fiery beam substitutes for the pillar of fire that guides the children of Israel through the dark wilderness. The story picks up from the end of *Urizen*, when with his band of the "remaining sons of Urizen" Fuzon left the element of earth, renamed Egypt, to its fate under Urizen's Net of Religion. Now, at the beginning of *Ahania*, instead of leading his followers out of bondage, Fuzon rides to battle "on a chariot," as if leading Pharaoh's pursuing army; and in the next chapter he actually proclaims himself God. All the action takes place in an imaginary no-man's-land, a mental space that recalls the desert between Egypt and the Promised Land.

From 1794 on, Blake frequently explores attributes of his primary male characters both through their "sons," whose personalities and actions reveal the primary character's contradictory elements, and through their female counterparts, who embody their emotive and sometimes more devious aspects. In *Ahania* Urizen's character is reflected through Fuzon, the first-begotten son who embodies his suppressed fiery energy, his pent-up lust and rage, and through Ahania, the compliant wife whose memory retains an indelible image of Urizen at his best. Modeled in part on the goddess Athena and on the biblical personification of divine Wisdom as female (Proverbs 8:22–31; translated "Sophia" in Greek), Ahania expresses and reveals the gentle and graceful side of reason, intellectual pursuits at their most delightful.

9. With constricted senses, those under the Net are cut off from the rest of humanity as well as from Eternity.
1. Echoing Milton's "pendulous round earth" (*Paradise Lost* 4.1000).
2. Emphasizing the shape of earth in empty space, a mechanistic perspective that Blake takes as characteristic of the fallen state.

Although Fuzon bears an obvious resemblance to Orc, the two are different kinds of rebels. In *Ahania*, Fuzon personifies pure defiance, the dead-end drive to depose a tyrant and seize power for its own sake. In *America*, by contrast, Orc personifies invigorating, life-promoting revolutionary energy, the irrepressible urge to destroy old constraints to make way for new growth. When Orc tramples Urizen's law to dust and scatters the torn book of religion abroad, he does so to make the desert bloom (*America* 9/7:12). Probably the reason Fuzon disappears from Blake's cast of characters after *Ahania* is that his presence in the same work with Orc would be redundant. In Blake's larger myth sexual and revolutionary energies are forces for change that originate in the imaginative faculty, not the rational one. Orc, son of Los, can change the world; Fuzon, son of Urizen, can at most merely usurp his father's powers. Nevertheless, in his limited role as the fiery reaction unconsciously produced by cold rationality, Fuzon is superb. He has been developed far beyond his original scope in *Urizen* **24**:17 as the personification of fire, one of the four elements internalized by Urizen in his struggle to master his environment.

Although almost everything Blake wrote has political implications in one way or another, Fuzon's conflict with his father in *Ahania* has more to do with resistance to religious and psychosexual oppression than with political rebellion. During a struggle for phallic supremacy modeled on the conflict between Uranus and his rebellious son Cronus in Hesiod's *Theogony*, Fuzon castrates Urizen and separates him from Ahania, his soul (or Emanation, to use Blake's later term). In retaliation, Urizen slays Fuzon and nails his corpse on the Tree of Mystery that grows out of his own thoughts, as in "The Human Abstract," and on this tree the crucified corpse is reanimated. This dreadful tale blends elements of the father-son relationship between Saturn and Cronos, Cronos and Zeus, David and Absalom, and especially Jehovah and Jesus. In later epics, as Blake repeatedly returned to the crucifixion story with refinements and reinterpretations, Orc is always the crucified one, but his suffering is eventually transformed into meaningful self-sacrifice by Jesus. In *Ahania*, the struggle between Urizen and Fuzon is waged with fantastic weapons drawn from the loins of the combatants: a huge thunderstone that lengthens into a laserlike beam, a shieldlike disk with a cutting edge, a gigantic bow, resembling a slingshot or catapult, made of a dead serpent's ribs, and a poisoned rock-projectile that falls to earth in the form of Mount Sinai, where Moses received the Ten Commandments.

The true victim of this terrible conflict is Ahania, bereft of both son and husband. She is a shadowy being, described first as her husband's invisible satellite, then as a mere voice in the void around Fuzon's tree. But her lament offers a glimpse of what the mind ought to be and could be, even now. In a song that abounds with images of luxury and fertility, Ahania recalls her former life with Urizen as a joyous time of productive intellectual inquiry, excitement, and fulfillment. She remembers Urizen as a virile and generous lover, father of many children, sower of "the seed of eternal science" in the human soul—certainly not the stony, austere, life-denying despot who tries to control everyone and everything in *Urizen* and *Ahania*. In the end, in a world reduced to barren rocks, chains, bones, and the jealousy and selfishness of her beloved, Ahania's wail blends with that of the benighted Earth in "Earth's Answer."

Following the precedent of *Urizen*, both *Ahania* and *The Book of Los* are laid out in double columns like the Holy Bible. These two books, each existing only in one copy, stand apart from the other illuminated books in that they were etched in conventional intaglio, a less laborious process than relief etching. Although both books have elaborately color-printed frontispieces, title pages, and terminal designs, the text pages are virtually undecorated. Neither work appears in Blake's lists of books for sale (pp. 377, 491 herein).

For insight into political dimensions of this work see Worrall, ed., *The Urizen Books* (1995), volume 6 in the Blake Trust series of facsimile editions; for other important aspects, see Morton D. Paley, *Bulletin of the New York Public Library* 70 (1966): 27–33; Steven C. Behrendt in *Blake, Politics, and History* (1998), ed. DiSalvo et al.; Hatsuko Niimi, *Blake: An Illustrated Quarterly* 34:2 (2000), 46–54; and comments by Leslie Tannenbaum, *Biblical Tradition . . .* (1982), and John Howard, *Infernal Poetics* (1984).

As Copy A is the only known printing of this book, it is, of course, our source text.

THE BOOK of AHANIA   2/1

LAMBETH Printed by W Blake 1795

AHANIA   3/2

Chap: I[st]

1: Fuzon on a chariot iron-wing'd
On spiked flames rose; his hot visage
Flam'd furious! sparkles his hair & beard
Shot down his wide bosom and shoulders.
On clouds of smoke rages his chariot   5
And his right hand burns red in its cloud
Moulding into a vast globe his wrath
As the thunder-stone is moulded[1]
Son of Urizen's silent burnings.

2: "Shall we worship this Demon of smoke,"   10
Said Fuzon, "this abstract non-entity
This cloudy God seated on waters
Now seen, now obscur'd; King of sorrow?"

3: So he spoke, in a fiery flame,
On Urizen frowning indignant,   15
The Globe of wrath shaking on high.
Roaring with fury, he threw
The howling Globe: burning it flew
Lengthning into a hungry beam. Swiftly

4: Oppos'd to the exulting flam'd beam   20
The broad Disk of Urizen upheav'd
Across the Void many a mile.

5: It was forg'd in mills where the winter
Beats incessant; ten winters the disk
Unremitting endur'd the cold hammer.   25

6: But the strong arm that sent it, remember'd
The sounding beam;[2] laughing it tore through
That beaten mass: keeping its direction
The cold loins of Urizen dividing.

---

1. Round rocks or meteorites, called thunderstones, were thought to be products of lightning.
2. Latinate inversion: the beam remembers the arm that sent it; the history and personification of weapons are epic conventions.

7: Dire shriek'd his invisible Lust;   30
Deep groan'd Urizen! stretching his awful hand.
Ahania (so name his parted soul)[3]
He siez'd on his mountains of Jealousy,
He groand anguishd & called her Sin,
Kissing her and weeping over her: 35
Then hid her in darkness in silence;
Jealous tho' she was invisible.

8: She fell down a faint shadow wandring
In chaos and circling dark Urizen,
As the moon anguishd circles the earth;   40
Hopeless! abhorrd! a death-shadow,
Unseen, unbodied, unknown,
The mother of Pestilence.

9: But the fiery beam of Fuzon
Was a pillar of fire to Egypt[4]   45
Five hundred years wandring on earth
Till Los siezd it and beat in a mass
With the body of the sun.

Chap: II:[d]   4/3

1: But the forehead of Urizen gathering,
And his eyes pale with anguish, his lips
Blue & changing; in tears and bitter
Contrition he prepar'd his Bow,

2: Form'd of Ribs: that in his dark solitude   5
When obscur'd in his forests fell[5] monsters
Arose. For his dire Contemplations
Rush'd down like floods from his mountains
In torrents of mud settling thick
With Eggs of unnatural production   10
Forthwith hatching; some howl'd on his hills
Some in vales; some aloft flew in air.

3: Of these: an enormous dread Serpent
Scaled and poisonous horned
Approach'd Urizen even to his knees   15
As he sat on his dark rooted Oak.

4: With his horns he push'd furious.
Great the conflict & great the jealousy
In cold poisons: but Urizen smote him.

5: First he poison'd the rocks with his blood   20
Then polish'd his ribs, and his sinews

---

3. Cf. Enitharmon's origin and Los's response to her in *Urizen* 18:9–16 and 19:10–16.
4. Cf. Exodus 13:21, where a pillar of fire leads the Israelites in the wilderness after they leave Egypt.
5. Fierce, cruel, deadly. Blake's syntax is garbled but it is clear that these ribs are from the Serpent in 4/3:13, one of the "fell monsters" hatched from eggs of Urizen's "dire Contemplations"; cf. "reptiles of the mind" (*Marriage* 19).

Dried; laid them apart till winter;
Then a Bow black prepar'd; on this Bow.
A poisoned rock plac'd in silence:
He utter'd these words to the Bow.   25

6: "O Bow of the clouds of secresy:
O nerve of that lust form'd monster!
Send this rock swift, invisible thro'
The black clouds, on the bosom of Fuzon."

7: So saying, In torment of his wounds,   30
He bent the enormous ribs slowly;
A circle of darkness! then fixed
The sinew in its rest: then the Rock
Poisonous source! plac'd with art, lifting difficult
Its weighty bulk: silent the rock lay,   35

8: While Fuzon his tygers unloosing
Thought Urizen slain by his wrath.
"I am God," said he, "eldest of things!"

9: Sudden sings the rock, swift & invisible
On Fuzon flew, enter'd his bosom;   40
His beautiful visage, his tresses,[6]
That gave light to the mornings of heaven
Were smitten with darkness, deform'd
And outstretch'd on the edge of the forest.

10: But the rock fell upon the Earth,   45
Mount Sinai, in Arabia.

Chap: III:

1: The Globe shook; and Urizen seated
On black clouds his sore wound anointed
The ointment flow'd down on the void
Mix'd with blood; here the snake gets her poison.   50

2: With difficulty & great pain; Urizen
Lifted on high the dead corse:
On his shoulders he bore it to where
A Tree hung over the Immensity.

3: For when Urizen shrunk away   55
From Eternals, he sat on a rock
Barren; a rock which himself
From redounding fancies had petrified.
Many tears fell on the rock,
Many sparks of vegetation;   60
Soon shot the pained root
Of Mystery, under his heel:
It grew a thick tree; he wrote

---

6. Recalling Absalom's hair (2 Samuel 14:25 ff.); see Paley, *Energy and Imagination*, p. 83.

In silence his book of iron:
Till the horrid plant bending its boughs   65
Grew to roots when it felt the earth
And again sprung to many a tree.[7]

4: Amaz'd started Urizen! when
He beheld himself compassed round
And high roofed over with trees.   70
He arose but the stems stood so thick
He with difficulty and great pain
Brought his Books, all but the Book
Of iron, from the dismal shade.   [5/4]

5: The Tree still grows over the Void
Enrooting itself all around
An endless labyrinth of woe!

6: The corse of his first begotten   5
On the accursed Tree of Mystery:
On the topmost stem of this Tree
Urizen nail'd Fuzon's corse.

Chap: IV:

1: Forth flew the arrows of pestilence
Round the pale living Corse on the tree.[8]   10

2: For in Urizen's slumbers of abstraction
In the infinite ages of Eternity:
When his Nerves of Joy melted & flow'd
A white Lake on the dark blue air
In perturb'd pain and dismal torment   15
Now stretching out, now swift conglobing.

3: Effluvia vapor'd above
In noxious clouds; these hover'd thick
Over the disorganiz'd Immortal,
Till petrific pain scurfd o'er the Lakes[9]   20
As the bones of man, solid & dark.

4: The clouds of disease hover'd wide
Around the Immortal in torment
Perching around the hurtling bones
Disease on disease, shape on shape.   25
Winged screaming in blood & torment.

5: The Eternal Prophet beat on his anvils
Enrag'd in the desolate darkness

7. Recalling the legendary upas tree that reroots itself (like the banyan) and poisons everything around it. See n. 9, p. 42.
8. Recalling St. Sebastian's martyrdom, Apollo's plague-carrying arrows in *Iliad* 1.47–61, and (by contrast) Moses' display of a brazen serpent on a pole to cure Israelites bitten by fiery serpents (Numbers 21:9; traditionally viewed by Christians as a "type" or foreshadowing of the Crucifixion [John 3:14]).
9. Cf. *Paradise Lost* 1.672, where "scurfed" (encrusted) is an aspect of corruption in Hell.

He forg'd nets of iron around
And Los threw them around the bones.   30

6: The shapes screaming flutter'd vain:
Some combin'd into muscles & glands
Some organs for craving and lust
Most remain'd on the tormented void:
Urizen's army of horrors.   35

7: Round the pale living Corse on the Tree
Forty years[1] flew the arrows of pestilence.

8: Wailing and terror and woe
Ran thro' all his dismal world:
Forty years all his sons & daughters   40
Felt their skulls harden; then Asia
Arose in the pendulous deep.

9: They reptilize upon the Earth.

10: Fuzon groand on the Tree.

Chap: V

1: The lamenting voice of Ahania   45
Weeping upon the void.
And round the Tree of Fuzon:
Distant in solitary night
Her voice was heard, but no form
Had she; but her tears from clouds   50
Eternal fell round the Tree.

2: And the voice cried: "Ah Urizen! Love!
Flower of morning! I weep on the verge
Of Non-entity;[2] how wide the Abyss
Between Ahania and thee!   55

3: I lie on the verge of the deep.
I see thy dark clouds ascend,
I see thy black forests and floods,
A horrible waste to my eyes!

4: Weeping I walk over rocks   60
Over dens & thro' valleys of death.
Why didst thou despise Ahania
To cast me from thy bright presence
Into the World of Loneness?

5: I cannot touch his hand: 65
Nor weep on his knees, nor hear

---

1. The length of time that the Israelites wandered in the wilderness before being allowed to enter the Promised Land (Exodus 16:35; Numbers 14:33); in Hebrew symbolism, forty is one of the numbers (like seven) that represents completeness.
2. Cf. Oothoon's lament in *Visions* 9/6:15.

His voice & bow, nor see his eyes
And joy, nor hear his footsteps, and
My heart leap at the lovely sound!
I cannot kiss the place   70
Whereon his bright feet have trod,
But I wander on the rocks   6/5
With hard necessity.

6: Where is my golden palace
Where my ivory bed[3]
Where the joy of my morning hour   5
Where the sons of eternity, singing

7: To awake bright Urizen my king:
To arise to the mountain sport,
To the bliss of eternal valleys:

8: To awake my king in the morn: 10
To embrace Ahania's joy
On the bredth of his open bosom:
From my soft cloud of dew to fall
In showers of life on his harvests.

9: When he gave my happy soul   15
To the sons of eternal joy:
When he took the daughters of life
Into my chambers of love:

10: When I found babes of bliss on my beds
And bosoms of milk in my chambers   20
Fill'd with eternal seed
O! eternal births sung round Ahania
In interchange sweet of their joys.

11: Swell'd with ripeness & fat with fatness
Bursting on winds my odors.   25
My ripe figs and rich pomegranates[4]
In infant joy at thy feet
O Urizen sported and sang;

12: Then thou with thy lap full of seed[5]
With thy hand full of generous fire   30
Walked forth from the clouds of morning
On the virgins of springing joy,
On the human soul to cast
The seed of eternal science,

13: The sweat poured down thy temples   35
To Ahania return'd in evening

---

3. Cf. Psalm 45:8, a "Song of loves."
4. Recalling the sexual imagery of Song of Solomon (e.g., 2:13, 4:3, 6:7–11, 7:12, 8:2) and the produce of the Promised Land in Deuteronomy 8:8.
5. Repeated (or drafted) in "Thou hast a lap full of seed," Notebook.

The moisture awoke to birth
My mothers-joys, sleeping in bliss.

14: But now alone over rocks, mountains
Cast out from thy lovely bosom: 40
Cruel jealousy! selfish fear![6]
Self-destroying: how can delight,
Renew in these chains of darkness
Where bones of beasts are strown
On the bleak and snowy mountains   45
Where bones from the birth are buried
Before they see the light.

FINIS

THE BOOK OF LOS (1795)

The third book of Blake's "Bible of Hell" is not a sequel to *Urizen* like *Ahania* but an intersecting, overlapping, and sometimes contradictory version of the same primordial events, as experienced by the "Eternal Prophet" Los. As in *Urizen*, the formation of the material world and the development of the body and the senses take place simultaneously. Los's alternative narrative is introduced by a new character, Eno, "aged Mother," whose sense of the past provides a framework for all that follows. Her memory goes back to "Times remote!" before fundamental human impulses and passions were deemed "impure," apparently a reference to Urizen and his commandments although she does not mention his name. In this fluid, protean early epoch, the fallen world's vices of Covet, Envy, Wrath, and Wantonness—all reactions to deprivation—were so abundantly fulfilled that they expressed themselves in harmless, even benevolent ways. Eno's oration ends with no conclusion or transition except for a wavy line separating stanzas 5 and 6, at which point the narrative proper begins. No new narrator appears, but the omniscient narrative voice—later revealed by the pronoun *our* to be a mortal like us (4:39)—is like that of the narrator of *Urizen* who in the "Preludium" invokes the "dark visions" of "Eternals."

As the main story opens, Los appears "bound in a chain," in the midst of living, organized, intelligent, but plague-bearing "flames of desire," already in a fallen state, compelled to watch Urizen's shadow. He comes to consciousness at about the point of his first appearance in *The Book of Urizen*, in Chapter III, when he "Kept watch" around Urizen's "dark globe," waiting for the Eternals to take action (5:38–40). In *Urizen*, Los binds others with iron links and fetters forged on his anvil or with the Chain of Jealousy that bursts from his bosom; in *Los*, he immediately flings off his chains in fury, rises into "non-entity," and stamps out a space for himself within the raging flames; he does not consume the fires "Inwards," as Urizen does in his book (4:15). Instead of separating the waters above from the waters below to create the firmament, as in Genesis, or anticreating a "soul-shudd'ring vacuum" or a "petrific abominable chaos," as in *Urizen*, Los forms a void "between fire and fire." Within this void appears the "solid without fluctuation" that Urizen, in withdrawing from the Eternals' "unquenchable burnings," had sought to form in the book bearing his name. In

---

6. See "Earth's Answer," *Songs* 31.

the retelling of the creation story in *The Book of Los*, error arises not from reason alone but from a failure of imagination; the Eternal Prophet rather than the Eternal Priest is to blame for the fall from spirit into matter. By elevating his thoughts and overcoming his wrath, Los is able to change the angle of his fall but not to arrest it. He takes on a weighty human body and, as in *Urizen*, deepens the fall by the further binding of Urizen, and by hammering Newtonian particles of light into the fiery orb of the material sun. In the end, the product of his imaginings is only the "Human Illusion," an erroneous conception of humanity as mind contained and confined in the flesh.

Quite by design, the trilogy of *Urizen*, *Ahania*, and *Los* is marked by contradictions, gaps, partial cross-references, and other loose ends. Blake was keenly aware of similar inconsistencies within the Bible itself, beginning with the incompletely interwoven alternative accounts of humanity's creation in Genesis 1:26–28 and 2:4–25, now known as the J (Jehovah) and E (Elohim) narrative strands (see Leslie Tannenbaum, *Biblical Tradition in Blake's Early Prophecies* [1982]). In Blake's time, the ground was shifting under traditional notions of biblical authority. Comparative mythographers like Jacob Bryant, who in *A New System* (1774–76) interpreted Egyptian, Indian, Greco-Roman, Nordic, and Celtic myths as garbled evidence of biblical authenticity, inadvertently provided support for speculation about the basis for Judeo-Christian stories. Of greater concern, in a movement that came to be called the Higher Criticism, German scholars had begun to uncover evidence of multiple textual layers indicating that stories of the creation and the deluge derived from other Middle Eastern cultures. And from another direction such Deists as Thomas Paine (in *The Age of Reason* [1794–95]) were using internal contradictions within the Bible to question its claim to divine inspiration. Blake followed these controversies intently and came to believe that the "Divinity of the books in the Bible [does not] consist either in who they were written by, or at what time, or in the historical evidence . . . but in the Sentiments & Examples" (Marginalia on Watson, p. 459 herein.)

For general accounts of *The Book of Los* and companion works, the "Lambeth prophecies" or the smaller grouping of "Urizen books," see John Howard, *Infernal Poetics* (1984) and Andrew Lincoln (in *Cambridge Companion* [2003]); for remarks emphasizing political and economic aspects of the work, see David Worrall's notes in volume 6 of the Blake Trust facsimile edition and Dennis M. Welch's essay in *ANQ* (formerly *American Notes and Queries*) 12 (1999): 6–12.

Los, like *Ahania*, was etched quickly in conventional intaglio rather than in relief. Our text is based on the one and only impression of the work, Copy A in the British Museum.

THE BOOK of LOS   2

LAMBETH Printed by W Blake 1795

Chap. I   3

1: Eno aged Mother,
Who the chariot of Leutha guides,
Since the day of thunders in old time

2: Sitting beneath the eternal Oak
Trembled and shook the stedfast Earth   5
And thus her speech broke forth.

3: "O Times remote!
When Love & Joy were adoration:
And none impure were deem'd.
Not Eyeless Covet   10
Nor Thin-lip'd Envy
Nor Bristled Wrath
Nor Curled Wantonness

4: But Covet was poured full:
Envy fed with fat of lambs: 15
Wrath with lions' gore:
Wantonness lulld to sleep
With the virgin's lute,
Or sated with her love.

5: Till Covet broke his locks & bars.   20
And slept with open doors:
Envy sung at the rich man's feast:
Wrath was follow'd up and down
By a little ewe lamb
And Wantonness on his own true love   25
Begot a giant race:"

6: Raging furious the flames of desire
Ran thro' heaven & earth, living flames
Intelligent, organiz'd; arm'd
With destruction & plagues. In the midst   30
The Eternal Prophet bound in a chain
Compell'd to watch Urizen's shadow

7: Rag'd with curses & sparkles of fury
Round the flames roll as Los hurls his chains
Mounting up from his fury, condens'd   35
Rolling round & round, mounting on high
Into vacuum: into non-entity
Where nothing was! dash'd wide apart
His feet stamp the eternal fierce-raging
Rivers of wide flame; they roll round   40
And round on all sides making their way
Into darkness and shadowy obscurity.

8: Wide apart stood the fires; Los remain'd
In the void between fire and fire.
In trembling and horror they beheld him.   45
They stood wide apart, driv'n by his hands
And his feet which the nether abyss
Stamp'd in fury and hot indignation.

9: But no light from the fires; all was   50
Darkness round Los: heat was not; for bound up $\boxed{4}$
Into fiery spheres from his fury
The gigantic flames trembled and hid.

10: Coldness, darkness, obstruction, a Solid
Without fluctuation,[1] hard as adamant   5
Black as marble of Egypt; impenetrable
Bound in the fierce raging Immortal.
And the seperated fires froze in
A vast solid without fluctuation,
Bound in his expanding clear senses.   10

Chap: II

1: The Immortal stood frozen amidst
The vast rock of eternity; times
And times: a night of vast durance:
Impatient, stifled, stiffend, hardned.

2: Till impatience no longer could bear   15
The hard bondage, rent; rent, the vast solid
With a crash from immense to immense

3: Crack'd across into numberless fragments.
The Prophetic wrath, strug'ling for vent
Hurls apart, stamping furious to dust   20
And crumbling with bursting sobs; heaves
The black marble on high into fragments.

4: Hurl'd apart on all sides, as a falling
Rock; the innumerable fragments away
Fell asunder; and horrible vacuum   25
Beneath him & on all sides round.

5: Falling, falling! Los fell & fell
Sunk precipitant heavy down down
Times on times, night on night, day on day
Truth has bounds, Error none; falling, falling: 30
Years on years, and ages on ages
Still he fell thro' the void, still a void
Found for falling day & night without end.
For tho' day or night was not; their spaces
Were measurd by his incessant whirls   35
In the horrid vacuity bottomless.[2]

6: The Immortal revolving; indignant
First in wrath threw his limbs, like the babe
New born into our world:[3] wrath subsided
And contemplative thoughts first arose.   40
Then aloft his head rear'd in the Abyss
And his downward-borne fall chang'd oblique.

1. This phrase, repeated in line 9, echoes *Urizen* 4:11.
2. In *The Four Zoas, Milton,* and *Jerusalem* merciful limits are set to the fall (cf. the "starry floor" and "watry shore" of "Introduction" to *Experience*), but the three Lambeth books of the "Bible of Hell" are more pessimistic. The word *vacuity* (cf. Satan's journey through chaos in *Paradise Lost* 2.932 ff.) appears only six times in Blake's work, first in this cluster on plates **4** and **5** and then in a similar context *Four Zoas* Night 6 (not included in this edition).
3. Cf. "Infant Sorrow."

7: Many ages of groans; till there grew
Branchy forms, organizing the Human
Into finite inflexible organs.   45

8: Till in process from falling he bore
Sidelong on the purple air, wafting
The weak breeze in efforts oerwearied

9: Incessant the falling Mind labour'd
Organizing itself: till the Vacuum   50
Became element, pliant to rise,
Or to fall, or to swim, or to fly:
With ease searching the dire vacuity.

Chap: III

1: The Lungs heave incessant, dull and heavy
For as yet were all other parts formless   55
Shiv'ring: clinging around like a cloud
Dim & glutinous as the white Polypus
Driv'n by waves & englob'd on the tide.

2: And the unformed part crav'd repose.
Sleep began: the Lungs heave on the wave   60
Weary overweigh'd, sinking beneath
In a stifling black fluid he woke.

3: He arose on the waters but soon
Heavy falling his organs like roots
Shooting out from the seed, shot beneath;   65
And a vast world of waters around him
In furious torrents began.

4: Then he sunk, & around his spent Lungs
Began intricate pipes that drew in
The spawn of the waters. Outbranching   70
An immense Fibrous form, stretching out | 5 |
Thro' the bottoms of immensity raging.

5: He rose on the floods: then he smote
The wild deep with his terrible wrath,
Seperating the heavy and thin.   5

6: Down the heavy sunk; cleaving around
To the fragments of solid; up rose
The thin, flowing round the fierce fires
That glow'd furious in the expanse.

Chap: IV:

1: Then Light first began; from the fire's   10
Beams, conducted by fluid so pure[4]

---

4. Ether, the rarified element of the upper air in medieval cosmologies, adapted by Newton to explain
   how light waves can be transmitted in a vacuum. Blake considered Newton's mechanistic corpus-
   cular theory of light antivisionary (see "Mock on, Mock on, Voltaire, Rousseau," p. 393).

Flow'd around the Immense: Los beheld
Forthwith writhing upon the dark void
The Back bone of Urizen appear
Hurtling upon the wind   15
Like a serpent! like an iron chain
Whirling about in the Deep.

2: Upfolding his Fibres together
To a Form of impregnable strength
Los, astonish'd and terrified, built   20
Furnaces; he formed an Anvil
A Hammer of adamant then began
The binding of Urizen day and night.

3: Circling round the dark Demon, with howlings
Dismay & sharp blightings; the Prophet   25
Of Eternity beat on his iron links.

4: And first from those infinite fires
The light that flow'd down on the winds
He siez'd; beating incessant, condensing
The subtil particles in an Orb.   30

5: Roaring indignant the bright sparks
Endur'd the vast Hammer; but unwearied
Los beat on the Anvil: till glorious
An immense Orb of fire he fram'd.[5]

6: Oft he quench'd it beneath in the Deeps   35
Then surveyd the all bright mass. Again
Siezing fires from the terrific Orbs
He heated the round Globe, then beat
While roaring his Furnaces endur'd
The chaind Orb in their infinite wombs.   40

7: Nine ages completed their circles
When Los heated the glowing mass, casting
It down into the Deeps: the Deeps fled
Away in redounding smoke; the Sun
Stood self-balanc'd. And Los smild with joy.   45
He the vast Spine of Urizen siez'd
And bound down to the glowing illusion.

8: But no light, for the Deep fled away
On all sides, and left an unform'd
Dark vacuity: here Urizen lay   50
In fierce torments on his glowing bed

---

5. Los, whose name is an anagram of *Sol*, is frequently depicted as the forger of the sun. Blake derived
the distinction between the material sun and the spiritual sun or human imagination (cf. *A Vision
of the Last Judgment*) from Swedenborg. For Blake's account of his intensely personal vision of
Los standing in the sun and blocking his path, see his second November 22, 1802, letter to Butts
(p. 477 herein).

9: Till his Brain in a rock, & his Heart
In a fleshy slough formed four rivers[6]
Obscuring the immense Orb of fire
Flowing down into night: till a Form   55
Was completed, a Human Illusion
In darkness and deep clouds involvd.

The End of the
Book of LOS

MILTON: A POEM (1804; c. 1810–18)

The book *Milton* is a searching critique of the life, writings, and cultural influence of the poet Blake admired most. It is both the only illuminated work that he named after a publicly recognizable figure and the only one in which Blake, as "William," appears under his own name as a character. Milton the hero—a clear-eyed muscular nude, seen from the rear—strides away from the viewer directly into the title page (color plate 13) through flames and billowing smoke, right foot forward, pushing apart the syllables of his name (and the poem's title) with one hand, brushing aside authorial credits with the other. His left foot, flexed to take another step, is poised above an inscription from *Paradise Lost* (1.26): "To Justify the Ways of God to Men." In choosing the second part of Milton's twofold statement of epic purpose as his epigraph, Blake perhaps implies that Milton achieved only his first goal, to "assert Eternal Providence" (*Paradise Lost* 1.25). Now, through Blake's poem, Milton returns to our world to reenvision God and his ways and complete his life's mission.

Although no one before Blake had written an odyssey about a poet-hero on a quest of world-shaking significance, there were good reasons for imagining Milton in this way. For most literary-minded Europeans in the eighteenth century, Milton was the foremost poet of Christianity and, in his personal life, a model Christian who opposed tyranny, purified religion, defended free expression (in his pamphlet *Aeropagetica*), and labored mightily, despite his blindness, in his poetic vocation. In Britain, where even the poorest book owners kept *Paradise Lost* and Bunyan's *Pilgrim's Progress* alongside the Bible, Milton's work was associated with both individual and national salvation. A poet of such eminence of course attracted criticism as well, such as Samuel Johnson's unflattering biography (1778) and Voltaire's witty attack, through his character Pococurante, in *Candide* (1759). Milton's stormy relations with the first of his three wives, and with his three daughters, as well as his scandalous pamphlets supporting divorce on grounds of incompatibility were part of his legend; and his characterizations of Eve and Dalila seemed antifeminist even by eighteenth-century standards.

According to Blake's Devil in *The Marriage of Heaven and Hell* (5–6), Milton's chief error was to relegate revolutionary energy to the realm of the diabolic: his abstractly reasonable father-God is merely "Destiny," or predestination; his Messiah, a "Governor" who coolly puts down challenges to divine authority and takes the side of Reason in accusing humankind, is no better than God's cynical wagering partner Satan in the Book of Job; and his Holy Ghost, invoked under the name of the heavenly muse Urania, is effectually nonexistent ("Vaccuum"). In *Milton*,

---

6. Four rivers flow out of Eden (Genesis 2:10–14); in classical myth there are also four rivers in Hades, adapted by Dante for his *Inferno* (canto 14). The description of the veins and arteries as rivers prefigures Blake's myth of the giant man Albion who contains within himself the physical universe.

the true Satan is Milton's own "Selfhood." This ultimate inhibitor, prideful self-righteousness—nothing at all like the Devil in *The Marriage*—comes between humanity and divinity, the masculine and the feminine, moral rectitude and exuberant sexuality. Imprisoned in his self-righteousness, England's great literary, religious, and political iconoclast has himself become an icon; the champion of liberty has become, through his critical legacy, an instrument of oppression; the theorist of sensory and spiritual fulfillment in marriage has become, in practice, an agent of misogyny; the purifier of corrupt state religion has become contaminated with his own puritanism. Only by rejecting this false identity can Milton the poet—rewritten in (and as) *Milton* the poem—reclaim the energy, including sexual energy, of Blake's Orc (the flawed but vital faculty misidentified as Satan in *Paradise Lost*), shake off the restraints of Urizen (misidentified as God), rejoin his Emanation Ololon (a composite of his poems, his loving impulses, and his three wives and three daughters), and pass down to Blake his reinvigorated imaginative powers. This he accomplishes under the inspiration of the "Bard's Song"—one third of the poem—that moves him to give up his "Elect" status and undergo the "Self-annihilation" of reuniting with his female counterpart.

Even though some innovative cosmological symbols, such as the Vortex, are explained as part of the narrative, most of the plot is almost impossible to follow. Eternity, or Eden, a condition of Being outside time and space, is presupposed. As the realm of life after death, it resembles traditional conceptions of heaven, but it is also a state of cosmic consciousness in the here and now. In the fallen world, time, space, and Eternity are intertwined so that the same event, depending on the observer's perspective, is described in varied and apparently contradictory ways, and events widely separated in ordinary space and time also occur simultaneously, in a single inspired "moment" of redemptive action. From the perspective of Blake the character, this moment of inspiration occurs in the three places he lived while undergoing or writing about these experiences: Lambeth, Felpham, and South Molton Street. And the characters are almost as hard to keep straight as the plot, largely because a single name may be given to a host of personalities who take on different characteristics in different circumstances and on different planes of existence—as if, in a production of *Hamlet*, one group of actors were to perform the hero's role according to varied critical interpretations of the play and another group were to play the combined roles of Ophelia and Gertrude according to Hamlet's ambivalent responses to womankind. One actor in each group would also portray male and female members of the audience and another pair would portray Shakespeare and the important women in his life.

The hero, on the model of Christ who "into himself descended" to be tested in *Paradise Regained* (see Wittreich, *Angel of Apocalypse* [1975]), journeys into the depths of his own identity; on the same journey, he enters into Blake's being as a falling star that crashes into his left foot. As Milton moves toward Blake on one plane of reality, Blake moves toward Milton in another, while in yet another dimension Ololon undertakes a complementary salvific mission of her own, as she gives up the "Female Will," the equivalent of Milton's selfishness on the sexual plane, and seeks reunion with her lover. In cinema-style jump-cuts, flashbacks, flash-forwards, and speeded-up and stop-motion replays, each poet participates in the self-transformation of the other, and both gain insight into unresolved contradictions in the historical Milton's life, work, and critical reputation that have impeded the transmission of his prophetic legacy to Blake's generation. In a climactic scene in Blake's garden at Felpham, Ololon and Milton are reconciled in mutual forgiveness, whereupon they are united with "One Man Jesus the Saviour," on the verge of the apocalypse. As the poem ends, Blake returns to his "Vegetable Body" empowered to continue his own work; Albion stirs in his sleep, and the Last Harvest and Vintage approaches.

The title page of *Milton*, like that of *Jerusalem*, is dated 1804, an important year in Blake's life (see the chronology and the headnote to *Jerusalem*). But the first three copies or versions of the work are printed on paper watermarked 1808; the fourth is on paper watermarked 1815. According to Viscomi, *Blake and the Idea of the Book* (1993), forty-five pages of Copies A, B, and C, constituting the first "edition," were probably printed in one session in 1811. Years later, Blake added gold paint, framing lines, and five new pages to Copy C but made the critical decision to withdraw the preface. This version probably reached its final form in 1818, as did Copy D, which also lacks the preface but contains a sixth new page (the added pages are identified a–f in Bentley's edition). In experimenting with the expanded forty-nine-page Copy C, Blake resorted to repeated erasures and marked duplicate numbers with asterisks. Whether Blake improved *Milton* by trading the prose and verse "Preface" for the added pages is debatable. Set as a hymn by C. Hubert Hastings Parry in 1916, the "Jerusalem" stanzas have ever since found a wider British public, across the political spectrum, even than *Paradise Lost*, the epic that *Milton a Poem* was designed to complete.

Most commentaries on *Milton* are addressed to advanced scholars, but first-time readers will find help in Harold Bloom's *Blake's Apocalypse* (p. 590 herein) and Susan Fox's *Poetic Form in Blake's* Milton (1976) and in essays by Edward J. Rose, *Blake Studies* 1 (1968), 16–38; W. J. T. Mitchell in *Blake's Sublime Allegory* (1973), ed. Curran and Wittreich; Joseph Wittreich in *Milton Studies* (1978), 51–82; Brian Wilkie in *Blake's Visionary Forms Dramatic* (1970), ed. Erdman and Grant; Thomas Vogler in *Unnam'd Forms* (1986), ed. Hilton and Vogler; Julia W. Wright in *Milton and the Imperial Vision* (1999), ed. Rajan and Sauer, and her *Milton* chapter in *Blake, Nationalism, and the Politics of Alienation* (2004). For a general introduction partially overlapping with this one, see Johnson in *The Cambridge Companion to William Blake* (2003), ed. Eaves; for comprehensive annotations of difficult passages, see Essick and Viscomi in the *Milton* volume of the Blake Trust facsimile series (1993). For help with names, see Damon's *Dictionary* and the cross-references in "Key Terms."

As with all of Blake's illuminated books, we cannot emphasize enough the importance of studying *Milton* as a whole—that is, as a "marriage" of text and design, if often a turbulent one. For color images, see the online Eaves-Essick-Viscomi Blake Archive, the Essick-Viscomi Blake Trust facsimile edition (1993) of Copy C, Keynes's Blake Trust/Trianon Press facsimile edition (1967) of Copy D, and the Shambala facsimile edition of Copy B by Kay Parkhurst Easson and Roger R. Easson (1978).

Our text follows the fifty-page Copy D, as paginated by Blake (corresponding to the numeration of Erdman's *Illuminated Blake* and the bracketed numbers in the Erdman edition); after a forward slash we also provide the Erdman edition's primary numbers (1–43), which omit full-page designs but are essential for scholarly citation.

MIL TON a Poem in 12 Books[1]

1/i

The Author & Printer W Blake 1804
To Justify the Ways of God to Men[2]

---

1. Although the title page (color plate 13) proclaims a twelve-book poem on the model of *Paradise Lost*, *Milton* (M) turned out to be only two books long (*12* is partly converted to 2 in Copies A and B). For the significance of the 1804 date, shared with *Jerusalem* (J), see the chronology.
2. From *Paradise Lost* (PL) 1.26 (where the first word is "And"; see the headnote). A theodicy, or justification of God's ways, explains why evil and suffering exist in a world designed by an all-good, all-powerful creator. Blake now undertakes Milton's uncompleted task (see Bloom, p. 590 herein).

The Stolen and Perverted Writings of Homer & Ovid: of Plato & Cicero,[4] which all Men ought to contemn: are set up by artifice against the Sublime of the Bible. But when the New Age is at leisure to Pronounce; all will be set right: & those Grand Works of the more ancient & consciously & professedly Inspired Men, will hold their proper rank, & the Daughters of Memory shall become the Daughters of Inspiration.[5] Shakspeare & Milton were both curbd by the general malady & infection from the silly Greek & Latin slaves of the Sword.

Rouze up O Young Men of the New Age! set your foreheads against the ignorant Hirelings! For we have Hirelings in the Camp, the Court, & the University: who would if they could, for ever depress Mental & prolong Corporeal War.[6] Painters! on you I call! Sculptors! Architects! Suffer not the fashionable Fools to depress your powers by the prices they pretend to give for contemptible works or the expensive advertizing boasts that they make of such works; believe Christ & his Apostles that there is a Class of Men whose whole delight is in Destroying.[7] We do not want either Greek or Roman Models if we are but just & true to our own Imaginations, those Worlds of Eternity in which we shall live for ever; in Jesus our Lord.

> And did those feet in ancient time,
> Walk upon England's mountains green:
> And was the holy Lamb of God,
> On England's pleasant pastures seen!
>
> And did the Countenance Divine,   5
> Shine forth upon our clouded hills?
> And was Jerusalem builded here,
> Among these dark Satanic Mills?[8]
>
> Bring me my Bow of burning gold:
> Bring me my Arrows of desire;   10

---

3. This important preface, which we have inserted in brackets, appears only in Copies A and B (plate i in the Erdman edition, p. 95). Because it is not present in Copies C and D (our source), we include it only as a supplement. For plate 1, the title page, see color plate 13.
4. Derived from the claim that the classics are poor imitations of Hebrew poetry and prophecy (cf. Christ's rebuke to Satan in *Paradise Regained* 4.334 ff.).
5. In the preface to *The Reason of Church Government* II, Milton rejects "Dame Memory and her Siren daughters," the classical muses whose mother was Mnemosyne ("memory" in Greek), in favor of the Spirit who inspired the prophets. But in *Paradise Lost*, Milton's invocations of the Holy Spirit through such circumlocutions as the "Heav'nly born" Urania (7.1 ff.) reveal what Blake considered an excessive deference to classical models. In the poem *Milton* (15/14:29), the hero discovers that he has fallen under the sway of the wrong muses.
6. In *On Virgil* Blake deplores the glorification of war and empire in classical tradition. Although Milton rejected classical military heroism (*PL* 9. 13–47), he justified the violence of Cromwell's English Revolution (see essays by Wright cited in the headnote). By 1808 (the watermark date of the first three copies of *Milton*), the Napoleonic Wars had been going on for six years and were to continue for seven more. Except for the brief Peace of Amiens in 1802, England and France were at war continuously from 1793 to 1815 (see the chronology).
7. Probably the Pharisees, scribes, and chief priests (Matthew 12:14; Mark 11:18).
8. At a time before steam-driven factories were common, "mills" evoked windmills, watermills, and (for Blake, especially) treadmills driven by animals or men working on a circular track, as Milton's Samson labors "Eyeless in Gaza at the Mill with slaves" (*Samson Agonistes*, line 41); see the letter of October 23, 1804. Blake associated mills with mechanistic systems generally ("Public Address"), "the same dull round" of reductive reasoning (*There Is No Natural Religion*), and Newtonian celestial mechanics.

Bring me my Spear: O clouds unfold!
Bring me my Chariot of fire!

I will not cease from Mental Fight,
Nor shall my Sword sleep in my hand:[9]
Till we have built Jerusalem,   15
In England's green & pleasant Land.[1]

Would to God that all the Lord's people were Prophets.[2]
                                        Numbers XI. ch 29 v.

MILTON   2
Book the First

Daughters of Beulah![3] Muses who inspire the Poet's Song
Record the journey of immortal Milton thro' your Realms
Of terror & mild moony lustre, in soft sexual delusions
Of varied beauty, to delight the wanderer and repose
His burning thirst & freezing hunger! Come into my hand   5
By your mild power; descending down the Nerves of my right arm
From out the Portals of my Brain, where by your ministry
The Eternal Great Humanity Divine planted his Paradise,[4]
And in it caus'd the Spectres of the Dead to take sweet forms
In likeness of himself. Tell also of the False Tongue! vegetated   10
Beneath your land of shadows: of its sacrifices, and
Its offerings; even till Jesus, the image of the Invisible God
Became its prey; a curse, an offering, and an atonement,[5]
For Death Eternal in the heavens of Albion, & before the Gates
Of Jerusalem his Emanation, in the heavens beneath Beulah.   15

Say first! what mov'd Milton,[6] who walkd about in Eternity
One hundred years, pondring the intricate mazes of Providence[7]

9. After Israel's return from captivity, each rebuilder of Jerusalem "had his sword girded by his side, and so builded" (Nehemiah 4:18). Cf. spiritual warfare in Ephesians 6:10–20; 2 Corinthians 10:4; 1 Timothy 6:12; and Michael Ferber in *Blake in the Nineties* (1999), ed. Clark and Worrall.

1. Cf. prefatory hymns to *Jerusalem* chapters II and IV. On the *Milton* hymn see Nancy Goslee, *Studies in Romanticism* 13 (1974), 105–125; and Ferber, *Blake: An Illustrated Quarterly* 34:3 (2000–01), 82–94.

2. Quoting Moses, Blake also alludes to Milton's echo in *Areopagitica*, his 1644 tractate on the freedom of the press: "For now the time seems come, wherein Moses, the great prophet, may sit in heaven rejoicing to see that memorable and glorious wish of his fulfilled, when not only our seventy elders, but all the Lord's people, are become prophets."

3. These Muses, the "Daughters of Inspiration" of the Preface (i), do not descend from heaven but arise from the poet's brain (*M* 2:7). Their realm Beulah ("married" in Hebrew) is the promised new name of the redeemed Zion (Isaiah 62:4) and, in Bunyan's *Pilgrim's Progress* II, a delightful place of temporary repose where "the Shining Ones commonly walked, because it was upon the borders of heaven" (cf. *M* 33/30:2; *J* 5:54). At least one of the daughters, Leutha, later takes part in the action (*M* 12/11:28).

4. Literally a "garden." Eden is real not in remote history but within the mind of the inspired poet.

5. The doctrine of Original Sin, promulgated by the False Tongue (Psalm 120:2–4; cf. *J* 14:4–7), leads to the doctrine of the Atonement; note echoes of Colossians 1:15 and Galatians 3:13. Although Milton was so theologically radical as to reject the doctrine of the Trinity, his view of the atonement was the traditional one that God demands man's death as payment for sin but accepts Jesus' sacrifice as a substitute (see n. 6, p. 158 herein). Under such a God, for Blake, the crucifixion is reduced to "Druidical" blood sacrifice. H. C. Robinson reported that Blake considered atonement in the "ordinary Calvinistic sense" a "horrible doctrine; if another pay your debt, I do not forgive it" (p. 514 herein); see Romans 5:11, the only New Testament reference to atonement. See also Florence Sandler, *Blake Studies* 5 (1972), 13–57; Johnson, *Blake Studies* 6 (1973), 11–17; Lawrence Mathews, *Wascana Review* 15 (1980), 72–86.

6. Cf. Milton's formulaic invocation: "[S]ay first what cause / Mov'd our Grand Parents . . ." (*PL* 1.28–29).

7. Milton died in 1674; did his unhappiness begin only after he had spent his first three decades, in human time, in his limited heaven? His convoluted debt-and-payment theological reasoning is as labyrinthine as that of his fallen angels, "in wandering mazes lost" (*PL* 2.561).

Unhappy tho in heav'n, he obey'd, he murmur'd not, he was silent
Viewing his Sixfold Emanation[8] scatter'd thro' the deep
In torment! To go into the deep her to redeem & himself perish?   20
What cause at length mov'd Milton to this unexampled deed?
A Bard's prophetic Song![9] for sitting at eternal tables,
Terrific among the Sons of Albion in chorus solemn & loud
A Bard broke forth! all sat attentive to the awful man.

Mark well my words! they are of your eternal salvation: 25

Three Classes[1] are Created by the Hammer of Los, & Woven
By Enitharmon's Looms when Albion was slain upon his
   Mountains   3
And in his Tent, thro envy of Living Form, even of the Divine
   Vision
And of the sports of Wisdom in the Human Imagination
Which is the Divine Body of the Lord Jesus, blessed for ever.
Mark well my words, they are of your eternal salvation: 5

Urizen lay in darkness & solitude, in chains of the mind lock'd up.[2]
Los siezd his Hammer & Tongs; he labourd at his resolute Anvil
Among indefinite Druid rocks & snows of doubt & reasoning.

Refusing all Definite Form, the Abstract Horror roofd, stony hard.
And a first Age passed over & a State of dismal woe: 10

Down sunk with fright a red round Globe hot burning, deep
Deep down into the Abyss, panting: conglobing: trembling
And a second Age passed over & a State of dismal woe.

Rolling round into two little Orbs & closed in two little Caves
The Eyes beheld the Abyss: lest bones of solidness freeze over all   15
And a third Age passed over & a State of dismal woe.

From beneath his Orbs of Vision, Two Ears in close volutions
Shot spiring out in the deep darkness & petrified as they grew
And a fourth Age passed over & a State of dismal woe.

Hanging upon the wind, Two Nostrils bent down into the Deep   20
And a fifth Age passed over & a State of dismal woe.

In ghastly torment sick, a Tongue of hunger & thirst flamed out
And a sixth Age passed over & a State of dismal woe.

Enraged & stifled without & within: in terror & woe, he threw his
Right Arm to the north, his left Arm to the south, & his Feet   25
Stampd the nether Abyss in trembling & howling & dismay
And a seventh Age passed over & a State of dismal woe.

---

8. In corporeal form, his three wives and three daughters.
9. This song extends from the opening refrain at 2:25 (reiterated seven more times) through
14/13:44.
1. Not identified until 7:1–3 (see n. 3, p. 153 herein); reiterated at 4:4, 5:13, 5:38, 6:32–35,
27/25:26–39. The following page (plate 3, Bentley "b") was added to Copies C and D.
2. Beginning a reprise (through 3:34) of the creation/confinement story in *Urizen* 10–18.

Terrified Los stood in the Abyss & his immortal limbs
Grew deadly pale; he became what he beheld: for a red
Round Globe sunk down from his Bosom into the Deep. In pangs   30
He hoverd over it trembling & weeping, suspended it shook
The nether Abyss in temblings; he wept over it, he cherish'd it
In deadly sickening pain: till separated into a Female pale
As the cloud that brings the snow: all the while from his Back
A blue fluid exuded in Sinews hardening in the Abyss   35
Till it separated into a Male Form howling in Jealousy.

Within labouring, beholding Without: from Particulars to Generals
Subduing his Spectre, they Builded the Looms of Generation.
They Builded Great Golgonooza Times on Times Ages on Ages.
First Orc was Born then the Shadowy Female: then All Los's
    Family   40
At last Enitharmon brought forth Satan, Refusing Form, in vain
The Miller of Eternity made subservient to the Great Harvest
That he may go to his own Place Prince of the Starry Wheels

Beneath the Plow of Rintrah & the harrow of the Almighty   4
In the hands of Palamabron, Where the Starry Mills of Satan
Are built beneath the Earth & Waters of the Mundane Shell.
Here the Three Classes of Men take their Sexual texture Woven
The Sexual is Threefold: the Human is Fourfold.   5

"If you account it Wisdom when you are angry to be silent, and
Not to shew it: I do not account that Wisdom but Folly.
Every Man's Wisdom is peculiar to his own Individuality.
O Satan my youngest born, art thou not Prince of the Starry Hosts
And of the Wheels of Heaven, to turn the Mills day & night?   10
Art thou not Newton's Pantocrator[3] weaving the Woof of Locke?
To Mortals thy Mills seem every thing & the Harrow of Shaddai[4]
A scheme of Human conduct invisible & incomprehensible
Get to thy Labours at the Mills & leave me to my wrath."

Satan was going to reply, but Los roll'd his loud thunders.   15

"Anger me not! thou canst not drive the Harrow in pity's paths.
Thy Work is Eternal Death, with Mills & Ovens & Cauldrons.
Trouble me no more; thou canst not have Eternal Life."

---

3. Ruler of all (Greek; see 2 Corinthians 6:18, Revelation 19:6); the "Universal Ruler" in Newton's
   Principia (trans. 1686), associated with compasses in church iconography and on the *Principia*
   frontispiece. Cf. Martin K. Nurmi in *The Divine Vision* (1957), ed. Vivian de Sola Pinto; Paul
   Miner, *Notes and Queries* 8 (1961), 15–16.
4. Almighty (Hebrew; cf. 4:1); a name for God revealed to Abraham (Genesis 17:1, Exodus 6:3)
   before Yahweh ("Jehovah") was revealed to Moses; in Blake's work, the fourth of seven "Eyes" of
   God (see 14/13:22–23). To mortals under the reductive Mills of the deceptive Satan, God can be
   no more than the mechanistic deity of Newtonian physics and Lockean philosophy. The reason for
   Los's anger emerges on plate 7: his noncreative "son" Satan, who should operate the Mills, wishes
   to usurp the Almighty's Harrow or cultivator, the implement assigned to Palamabron. The third
   farming tool is the Plow, assigned to Rintrah and driven also by Los. In 1 Kings 19:19 Elijah casts
   his prophetic mantle upon Elisha, his successor, at the plow; in Hosea 10:11 the prophet declares
   that "Judah shall plow, and Jacob shall break his clods"; in Luke 9:62, Jesus warns against looking
   back after beginning to plow.

So Los spoke! Satan trembling obeyd weeping along the way.
Mark well my words, they are of your eternal Salvation.   20

Between South Molton Street[5] & Stratford Place: Calvary's foot
Where the Victims were preparing for Sacrifice, their Cherubim
Around their loins pour forth their arrows & their bosoms beam
With all colours of precious stones, & their inmost palaces
Resounded with preparation of animals wild & tame   25
(Mark well my words! Corporeal Friends are Spiritual Enemies)
Mocking Druidical Mathematical Proportion of Length Bredth
    Highth
Displaying Naked Beauty! with Flute & Harp & Song.

Palamabron with the fiery Harrow in morning returning[6]   [5]
From breathing fields, Satan fainted beneath the artillery.[7]
Christ took on Sin in the Virgin's Womb, & put it off on the Cross.
All pitied the piteous & was wrath with the wrathful & Los
    heard it.

And this is the manner of the Daughters of Albion in their beauty   5
Every one is threefold in Head & Heart & Reins,[8] & every one
Has three Gates into the Three Heavens of Beulah which shine
Translucent in their Foreheads & their Bosoms & their Loins
Surrounded with fires unapproachable: but whom they please

5. Blake's home, 1803–21 (see map), included in this added plate (Bentley "a") that appears only in
   Copies C and D; the shorter (forty-five-page) version (Copies A and B) refers to Blake's homes in
   Lambeth (1790–1800) and Felpham (1800–03). Apparently the "moment" of encountering Milton
   extends over time and space (see **22**/20:60, **38**/36:23). Nearby Tyburn, the site of public executions
   (1196–1783), was to Blake a latter-day British Stonehenge or Calvary, a place of Druid sacrifice.
6. Beginning a new page (Bentley "f") unique to this copy; a story of how Satan took charge of the
   world, "correcting" the one in *Paradise Lost*. For biographical elements of the Palamabron-Satan
   conflict, stemming from Blake's unhappiness under Hayley's patronage in Felpham, see letters of
   January 10, 1803 (p. 479) and April 25, 1803 (p. 483).
7. See **5**:43, **11**/10:17, **14**/13:37.
8. Kidneys; biblically, a seat of emotions (cf. Psalm 7:9; Proverbs 23:16).

They take up into their Heavens in intoxicating delight.   10
For the Elect cannot be Redeemd, but Created continually
By Offering & Atonement in the cruelties of Moral Law
Hence the three Classes of Men take their fix'd destinations
They are the Two Contraries & the Reasoning Negative.

While the Females prepare the Victims, the Males at Furnaces   15
And Anvils dance the dance of tears & pain, loud lightnings
Lash on their limbs as they turn the whirlwinds loose upon
The Furnaces, lamenting around the Anvils & this their Song:

"Ah weak & wide astray! Ah shut in narrow doleful form
Creeping in reptile flesh upon the bosom of the ground   20
The Eye of Man a little narrow orb closd up & dark
Scarcely beholding the great light conversing with the Void
The Ear, a little shell in small volutions shutting out
All melodies & comprehending only Discord and Harmony
The Tongue a little moisture fills, a little food it cloys   25
A little sound it utters & its cries are faintly heard
Then brings forth Moral Virtue the cruel Virgin Babylon.

Can such an Eye judge of the stars? & looking thro its tubes
Measure the sunny rays that point their spears on Udanadan
Can such an Ear filld with the vapours of the yawning pit,   30
Judge of the pure melodious harp struck by a hand divine?
Can such closed Nostrils feel a joy? or tell of autumn fruits
When grapes & figs burst their covering to the joyful air
Can such a Tongue boast of the living waters? or take in
Ought but the Vegetable Ratio & loathe the faint delight   35
Can such gross Lips percieve? alas! folded within themselves
They touch not ought but pallid turn & tremble at every wind."

Thus they sing Creating the Three Classes among Druid Rocks
Charles calls on Milton for Atonement. Cromwell is ready.
James calls for fires in Golgonooza, for heaps of smoking ruins[9]   40
In the night of prosperity and wantonness which he himself
    Created
Among the Daughters of Albion, among the Rocks of the Druids
When Satan fainted beneath the arrows of Elynittria
And Mathematic Proportion was subdued by Living Proportion.

From Golgonooza the spiritual Four-fold London eternal |6|
In immense labours & sorrows, ever building, ever falling,
Thro Albion's four Forests which overspread all the Earth,
From London Stone to Blackheath east: to Hounslow west:
To Finchley north: to Norwood south:[1] and the weights   5
Of Enitharmon's Loom play lulling cadences on the winds of
    Albion
From Caithness in the north, to Lizard-point & Dover in the south.

---

9. Milton, Latin secretary under Cromwell, helped justify the execution of Charles I. The link between James II and the Great Fire of London (1666), which was blamed on Catholics, is ahistorical. James privately converted to Catholicism in 1672 and lived abroad until the death of Charles II in 1685.
1. Frequently mentioned suburbs (see 28/26:19, 39/35:13), along with placenames in 6:9–11 (see London map). For landmarks in 6:7, see "Blake's Britain" map.

Loud sounds the Hammer of Los, & loud his Bellows is heard
Before London to Hampstead's breadths & Highgate's heights to
Stratford & old Bow: & across to the Gardens of Kensington   10
On Tyburn's Brook: loud groans Thames beneath the iron Forge
Of Rintrah & Palamabron, of Theotormon & Bromion, to forge the
  instruments
Of Harvest: the Plow & Harrow to pass over the Nations.

The Surrey hills glow like the clinkers of the furnace: Lambeth's
  Vale
Where Jerusalem's foundations began; where they were laid in
  ruins   15
Where they were laid in ruins from every Nation & Oak Groves
  rooted.

Dark gleams before the Furnace-mouth a heap of burning ashes.
When shall Jerusalem return & overspread all the Nations?
Return: return to Lambeth's Vale O building of human souls.
Thence stony Druid Temples overspread the Island white   20
And thence from Jerusalem's ruins, from her walls of salvation
And praise: thro the whole Earth were reard from Ireland
To Mexico & Peru west, & east to China & Japan; till Babel
The Spectre of Albion frownd over the Nations in glory & war.
All things begin & end in Albion's ancient Druid rocky shore   25
But now the Starry Heavens are fled from the mighty limbs of
  Albion.[2]

Loud sounds the Hammer of Los, loud turn the Wheels
  of Enitharmon
Her Looms vibrate with soft affections, weaving the Web of Life
Out from the ashes of the Dead; Los lifts his iron Ladles
With molten ore: he heaves the iron cliffs in his rattling chains   30
From Hyde Park to the Alms-houses of Mile-end & old Bow.
Here the Three Classes of Mortal Men take their fixd destinations
And hence they overspread the Nations of the whole Earth & hence
The Web of Life is woven: & the tender sinews of life created
And the Three Classes of Men regulated by Los's hammer.   35

The first, The Elect from before the foundation of the World: | 7 |
The second, The Redeem'd. The Third, The Reprobate & Form'd
To destruction from the mother's womb:[3] follow with me my plow!

Of the first class was Satan: with incomparable mildness;
His primitive tyrannical attempts on Los: with most endearing love   5

2. Quoted (with the line above) in *J* 27. The spread of Druid temples from Jerusalem's ruined "walls
   of salvation / and praise" (lines 21–22; cf. Isaiah 60:18) is a recurrent theme in *Jerusalem*.
3. Midpoint of a line formed from two half-deleted lines. (Blake also deleted a link between plates 6
   and 7: "and woven / By Enitharmons Looms, & Spun beneath the Spindle of Tirzah.") The Three
   Classes, derived from Calvinist theology, are ironically inverted: the Elect (Romans 8:29–33),
   instead of being predestined for salvation, are self-righteous condemners of others; the Reprobate
   (2 Corinthians 13:5), instead of being damned, are fiercely independent contrarians—like Jesus in
   Marriage—who occasionally release a cleansing wrath; the Redeemed (Galatians 3:13; Revelation
   5:9), instead of considering themselves purchased by Jesus' blood, are moved by pity and fear, troubled by the Elect. In the terms of 5:13–14, the wrathful Reprobate and pitying Redeemed are creative Contraries; the pseudo-mild Elect is a destructive Negation. Cf. Blake's troubles with Hayley
   (pp. 480–85 herein).

He soft intreated Los to give to him Palamabron's station;
For Palamabron returnd with labour wearied every evening
Palamabron oft refus'd; and as often Satan offer'd
His service till by repeated offers and repeated intreaties
Los gave to him the Harrow of the Almighty; alas blamable　　　10
Palamabron, fear'd to be angry lest Satan should accuse him of
Ingratitude, & Los believe the accusation thro Satan's extreme
Mildness. Satan labour'd all day; it was a thousand years.
In the evening returning terrified overlabourd & astonish'd
Embrac'd soft with a brother's tears Palamabron, who also wept.　　　15

Mark well my words! they are of your eternal salvation.

Next morning Palamabron rose: the horses of the Harrow
Were maddend with tormenting fury, & the servants of the Harrow,
The Gnomes, accus'd Satan, with indignation fury and fire.
Then Palamabron reddening like the Moon in an eclipse,　　　20
Spoke saying, "You know Satan's mildness and his self-imposition,
Seeming a brother, being a tyrant, even thinking himself a brother
While he is murdering the just; prophetic I behold
His future course thro' darkness and despair to eternal death.
But we must not be tyrants also! he hath assum'd my place　　　25
For one whole day, under pretence of pity and love to me:
My horses hath he maddend! and my fellow servants injur'd:
How should he, he know the duties of another? O foolish
　　　forbearance
Would I had told Los all my heart! but patience O my friends.
All may be well: silent remain, while I call Los and Satan."　　　30

Loud as the wind of Beulah that unroots the rocks & hills
Palamabron call'd! and Los & Satan came before him
And Palamabron shew'd the horses & the servants. Satan wept,
And mildly cursing Palamabron, him accus'd of crimes
Himself had wrought. Los trembled; Satan's blandishments almost　　　35
Perswaded the Prophet of Eternity that Palamabron
Was Satan's enemy, & that the Gnomes being Palamabron's friends
Were leagued together against Satan thro' ancient enmity.
What could Los do? how could he judge, when Satan's self believ'd
That he had not oppres'd the horses of the Harrow, nor the
　　　servants.　　　40

So Los said, "Henceforth Palamabron, let each his own station
Keep: nor in pity false, nor in officious brotherhood, where
None needs, be active." Mean time Palamabron's horses
Rag'd with thick flames redundant, & the Harrow maddend with
　　　fury.
Trembling Palamabron stood, the strongest of Demons trembled:　　　45
Curbing his living creatures; many of the strongest Gnomes,
They bit in their wild fury, who also maddend like wildest beasts.

Mark well my words; they are of your eternal salvation.

Mean while wept Satan before Los, accusing Palamabron;　　　 8

Himself exculpating with mildest speech, for himself believ'd
That he had not opress'd nor injur'd the refractory servants.

But Satan returning to his Mills (for Palamabron had serv'd
The Mills of Satan as the easier task) found all confusion   5
And back return'd to Los, not fill'd with vengeance but with tears,
Himself convinc'd of Palamabron's turpitude. Los beheld
The servants of the Mills drunken with wine and dancing wild
With shouts and Palamabron's songs, rending the forests green
With ecchoing confusion, tho' the Sun was risen on high.   10

Then Los took off his left sandal placing it on his head,[4]
Signal of solemn mourning: when the servants of the Mills
Beheld the signal they in silence stood, tho' drunk with wine.
Los wept! But Rintrah also came, and Enitharmon on
His arm lean'd tremblingly observing all these things   15

And Los said, "Ye Genii of the Mills! the Sun is on high
Your labours call you! Palamabron is also in sad dilemma;
His horses are mad! his Harrow confounded! his companions
     enrag'd.
Mine is the fault! I should have remember'd that pity divides the
     soul
And man, unmans: follow with me my Plow; this mournful day   20
Must be a blank in Nature: follow with me, and tomorrow again
Resume your labours, & this day shall be a mournful day."

Wildly they follow'd Los and Rintrah, & the Mills were silent
They mourn'd all day this mournful day of Satan & Palamabron:
And all the Elect & all the Redeem'd mourn'd one toward another   25
Upon the mountains of Albion among the cliffs of the Dead.

They Plow'd in tears! incessant pourd Jehovah's rain, & Molech's[5]
Thick fires contending with the rain thunder'd above, rolling
Terrible over their heads; Satan wept over Palamabron
Theotormon & Bromion contended on the side of Satan   30
Pitying his youth and beauty; trembling at eternal death:
Michael contended against Satan in the rolling thunder
Thulloh[6] the friend of Satan also reprovd him; faint their reproof.

But Rintrah who is of the reprobate: of those form'd to destruction
In indignation, for Satan's soft dissimulation of friendship!   35
Flam'd above all the plowed furrows, angry red and furious,
Till Michael sat down in the furrow weary dissolv'd in tears.
Satan who drave the team beside him, stood angry & red
He smote Thulloh & slew him, & he stood terrible over Michael
Urging him to arise: he wept! Enitharmon saw his tears   40
But Los hid Thulloh from her sight, lest she should die of grief.
She wept: she trembled! she kissed Satan; she wept over Michael

4. Masashi Suzuki, *Journal of English and Germanic Philology* 100 (2001), 40–56, relates this bizarre
   gesture to Ruth 4:7 (also cited by Ostriker).
5. Miltonic devil based on a Canaanite idol; for his place in Blake's larger scheme, see **14**/13:19.
6. The only appearance of a character invented to balance Michael, traditional antagonist of Satan
   (Jude 1:9; Revelation 12:7; *PL* 6).

She form'd a Space for Satan & Michael & for the poor infected.
Trembling she wept over the Space, & clos'd it with a tender Moon.

Los secret buried Thulloh, weeping disconsolate over the moony
   Space   45

But Palamabron called down a Great Solemn Assembly,
That he who will not defend Truth, may be compelled to
Defend a Lie, that he may be snared & caught & taken.

And all Eden descended into Palamabron's tent   [9]
Among Albion's Druids & Bards, in the caves beneath Albion's
Death Couch, in the caverns of death, in the corner of the Atlantic.
And in the midst of the Great Assembly Palamabron pray'd:
"O God protect me from my friends, that they have not power
   over me   5
Thou hast giv'n me power to protect myself from my bitterest
   enemies."

Mark well my words, they are of your eternal salvation.

Then rose the Two Witnesses, Rintrah & Palamabron:
And Palamabron appeal'd to all Eden, and recievd
Judgment: and Lo! it fell on Rintrah and his rage: 10
Which now flam'd high & furious in Satan against Palamabron
Till it became a proverb in Eden: Satan is among the Reprobate.[7]

Los in his wrath curs'd heaven & earth, he rent up Nations
Standing on Albion's rocks among high-reard Druid temples
Which reach the stars of heaven & stretch from pole to pole.   15
He displacd continents, the oceans fled before his face
He alter'd the poles of the world, east, west & north & south
But he clos'd up Enitharmon from the sight of all these things.

For Satan flaming with Rintrah's fury hidden beneath his own
   mildness
Accus'd Palamabron before the Assembly of ingratitude! of malice: 20
He created Seven deadly Sins drawing out his infernal scroll,
Of Moral laws and cruel punishments upon the clouds of Jehovah
To pervert the Divine voice in its entrance to the earth
With thunder of war & trumpets sound, with armies of disease
Punishments & deaths musterd & number'd; Saying "I am God
   alone   25
There is no other! let all obey my principles of moral individuality
I have brought them from the uppermost innermost recesses
Of my Eternal Mind, transgressors I will rend off for ever,
As now I rend this accursed Family from my covering."

Thus Satan rag'd amidst the Assembly! and his bosom grew   30
Opake against the Divine Vision: the paved terraces of
His bosom inwards shone with fires, but the stones becoming
   opake!

7. Cf. "Is Saul also among the prophets?" (1 Samuel 19:24).

Hid him from sight, in an extreme blackness and darkness,
And there a World of deeper Ulro was open'd, in the midst
Of the Assembly. In Satan's bosom a vast unfathomable Abyss.   35

Astonishment held the Assembly in an awful silence: and tears
Fell down as dews of night, & a loud solemn universal groan
Was utter'd from the east & from the west & from the south
And from the north; and Satan stood opake immeasurable
Covering the east with solid blackness, round his hidden heart   40
With thunders utterd from his hidden wheels: accusing loud
The Divine Mercy, for protecting Palamabron in his tent.

Rintrah rear'd up walls of rocks and pourd rivers & moats
Of fire round the walls: columns of fire guard around
Between Satan and Palamabron in the terrible darkness.   45

And Satan not having the Science of Wrath, but only of Pity:
Rent them asunder, and wrath was left to wrath, & pity to pity.
He sunk down a dreadful Death, unlike the slumbers of Beulah.

The Separation was terrible: the Dead was repos'd on his Couch
Beneath the Couch of Albion, on the seven mountains of Rome   50
In the whole place of the Covering Cherub, Rome Babylon &
    Tyre.[8]
His Spectre raging furious descended into its Space.

Then Los & Enitharmon knew that Satan is Urizen[9]   11/10
Drawn down by Orc & the Shadowy Female into Generation.
Oft Enitharmon enterd weeping into the Space, there appearing
An aged Woman raving along the Streets (the Space is named
Canaan[1]) then she returnd to Los weary frighted as from dreams.   5

The nature of a Female Space is this: it shrinks the Organs
Of Life till they become Finite & Itself seems Infinite.

And Satan vibrated in the immensity of the Space! Limited
To those without but Infinite to those within: it fell down and
Became Canaan: closing Los from Eternity in Albion's Cliffs   10
A mighty Fiend against the Divine Humanity mustring to War.

"Satan! Ah me! is gone to his own place," said Los! "their God
I will not worship in their Churches, nor King in their Theatres.
Elynittria![2] whence is this jealousy running along the mountains?
British Women were not Jealous when Greek & Roman were
    jealous.   15
Every thing in Eternity shines by its own Internal light: but thou
Darkenest every Internal light with the arrows of thy quiver

8. Home of the "Covering Cherub," a personification of ultimate error derived from Ezekiel 28:16,
   most fully revealed in *Jerusalem* 89; see n. 7, p. 195 herein. The earliest readers of Revelation 17
   understood "Babylon" as a code name for the Roman Empire; in the Protestant tradition, Babylon
   is the Church of Rome.
9. Beginning a plate (Bentley "c") present only in Copies C and D. Plate **10**, a full-page design, depicts
   Satan's fiery outburst, witnessed by Rintrah and Palamabron (cf. *M* **12**/11:11).
1. The original name of the land promised to Abraham (Genesis 12). Within this finite space, our
   world, Satan demands to be worshiped as God.
2. Partnered in *Europe* 11/8:1–7 with Palamabron, as is Ocalythron (*M* 11/10:19) with Rintrah.

Bound up in the horns of jealousy to a deadly fading Moon
And Ocalythron binds the Sun into a Jealous Globe:
That every thing is fixd Opake without Internal light."   20

So Los lamented over Satan, who triumphant divided the Nations.

He set his face against Jerusalem to destroy the Eon of Albion   12/11

But Los hid Enitharmon from the sight of all these things,
Upon the Thames whose lulling harmony repos'd her soul:
Where Beulah lovely terminates in rocky Albion:
Terminating in Hyde Park, on Tyburn's awful brook.   5

And the Mills of Satan were separated into a moony Space
Among the rocks of Albion's Temples, and Satan's Druid sons
Offer the Human Victims throughout all the Earth, and Albion's
Dread Tomb immortal on his Rock overshadowd the whole Earth:[3]
Where Satan making to himself Laws from his own identity,   10
Compell'd others to serve him in moral gratitude & submission
Being call'd God: setting himself above all that is called God.[4]
And all the Spectres of the Dead calling themselves Sons of God
In his Synagogues worship Satan under the Unutterable Name.[5]

And it was enquir'd: Why in a Great Solemn Assembly   15
The Innocent should be condemn'd for the Guilty? Then an Eternal
        rose

Saying. "If the Guilty should be condemn'd, he must be an Eternal
        Death
And one must die for another throughout all Eternity.[6]
Satan is fall'n from his station & never can be redeem'd
But must be new created continually moment by moment   20
And therefore[7] the Class of Satan shall be calld the Elect, & those
Of Rintrah, the Reprobate, & those of Palamabron the Redeem'd
For he is redeem'd from Satan's Law, the wrath falling on Rintrah,
And therefore Palamabron dared not to call a solemn Assembly
Till Satan had assum'd Rintrah's wrath in the day of mourning   25
In a feminine delusion of false pride self-deciev'd."

So spake the Eternal and confirm'd it with a thunderous oath.

But when Leutha[8] (a Daughter of Beulah) beheld Satan's
        condemnation

---

3. Satan's machinery of human sacrifice and Albion's death-sleep overshadow the earth through
   Christian imperialism, in the form of the British Empire. Cf. the spread of Druidic religion over
   the ruins of Jerusalem (M 6:14–26).
4. This echo of 2 Thessalonians 2:4 identifies Satan as the "son of perdition" who is revealed at the
   end of time.
5. YHWH (Yahweh); in rabbinical tradition too holy to be spoken aloud (n. 1, p. 350 herein).
6. Cf. the explanation of Milton's God the Father that Man must die for his sin "unless for him / Some
   other able, and as willing, pay / The rigid satisfaction, death for death" (PL 3:210–12), to which
   the Son replies: "Behold mee then, mee for him, life for life / I offer, on mee let thine anger fall"
   (3:236–237).
7. The Eternal's "If . . . must . . . therefore" chain of reasoning may allude to the illogic of traditional
   Christian teachings on God's wrath.
8. This character, mentioned briefly in Visions 4/1:4, Europe 17/14:9, and Book of Los 3:2, is modeled, in part, on Sin, daughter-wife of Satan in Paradise Lost 2. Her sudden appearance and offer

She down descended into the midst of the Great Solemn Assembly
Offering herself a Ransom for Satan, taking on her, his Sin.   30

Mark well my words, they are of your eternal salvation!

And Leutha stood glowing with varying colours immortal,
    heart-piercing
And lovely: & her moth-like elegance shone over the Assembly.

At length standing upon the golden floor of Palamabron
She spake: "I am the Author of this Sin! by my suggestion   35
My Parent power Satan has committed this transgression.
I loved Palamabron & I sought to approach his Tent,
But beautiful Elynittria with her silver arrows repelld me.

For her light is terrible to me. I fade before her immortal
    beauty. | 13/12 |
O wherefore doth a Dragon-form forth issue from my limbs[9]
To sieze her new born son? Ah me! the wretched Leutha!
This to prevent, entering the doors of Satan's brain night after night[1]
Like sweet perfumes I stupified the masculine perceptions   5
And kept only the feminine awake, hence rose his soft
Delusory love to Palamabron: admiration join'd with envy
Cupidity unconquerable! my fault, when at noon of day
The Horses of Palamabron call'd for rest and pleasant death:
I sprang out of the breast of Satan, over the Harrow beaming   10
In all my beauty! that I might unloose the flaming steeds
As Elynittria use'd to do; but too well those living creatures
Knew that I was not Elynittria, and they brake the traces.
But me, the servants of the Harrow saw not: but as a bow
Of varying colours on the hills; terribly rag'd the horses.   15
Satan astonishd, and with power above his own controll
Compell'd the Gnomes to curb the horses, & to throw banks of sand
Around the fiery flaming Harrow in labyrinthine forms.
And brooks between to intersect the meadows in their course.
The Harrow cast thick flames: Jehovah thunderd above: 20
Chaos & ancient night[2] fled from beneath the fiery Harrow:
The Harrow cast thick flames & orb'd us round in concave fires
A Hell of our own making; see, its flames still gird me round.
Jehovah thunder'd above! Satan in pride of heart
Drove the fierce Harrow among the constellations of Jehovah   25
Drawing a third part[3] in the fires as stubble north & south
To devour Albion and Jerusalem, the Emanation of Albion,
Driving the Harrow in Pity's paths. 'Twas then, with our dark fires

---

of atonement introduces a new psychological dimension to the Satan-Palamabron conflict and
foreshadows, negatively, the role Milton's own feminine counterpart is to play in Book 2.

9. Instead of hell-hounds bred by Milton's Sin (*PL* 2.650), Leutha gives birth to an apocalyptic child-
devouring dragon (Revelation 12:1–4).
1. Leutha's nightly forays into Satan's brain recall those of Milton's Satan in tempting the sleeping
Eve (*PL* 4.799) and inhabiting the sleeping Serpent (*PL* 9.187).
2. Cf. Milton's "Chaos and old Night," rulers of the void between heaven and hell (*PL* 1.543, 2.894ff.,
2.959ff.); primal cosmic parents in Greek mythology. The two reappear in *M* 19/17:24–25,
22/20:33, and 44/39:29–30.
3. Milton's fallen angels constitute "the third part of Heav'n's Sons" (*PL* 2.692). Cf. the Dragon's
drawing down "a third part of the stars of heaven" with his tail (Revelation 12:4; Daniel 8:10).

Which now gird round us (O eternal torment) I form'd the Serpent
Of precious stones & gold turn'd poisons on the sultry wastes.   30
The Gnomes in all that day spar'd not; they curs'd Satan bitterly.
To do unkind things in kindness! with power armd, to say
The most irritating things in the midst of tears and love.
These are the stings of the Serpent! thus did we by them; till thus
They in return retaliated, and the Living Creatures maddend.   35
The Gnomes labourd. I weeping hid in Satan's inmost brain;
But when the Gnomes refus'd to labour more, with blandishments
I came forth from the head of Satan! back the Gnomes recoil'd.
And call'd me Sin, and for a sign portentous held me.⁴ Soon
Day sunk and Palamabron return'd, trembling I hid myself   40
In Satan's inmost Palace of his nervous fine wrought Brain:
For Elynittria met Satan with all her singing women.
Terrific in their joy & pouring wine of wildest power
They gave Satan their wine: indignant at the burning wrath.
Wild with prophetic fury his former life became like a dream   45
Cloth'd in the Serpent's folds, in selfish holiness demanding purity
Being Most impure, self-condemn'd to eternal tears, he drove
Me from his inmost Brain & the doors clos'd with thunders' sound.
O Divine Vision who didst create the Female: to repose
The Sleepers of Beulah: pity the repentant Leutha. My   50
Sick Couch bears the dark shades of Eternal Death infolding   14/13
The Spectre of Satan; he furious refuses to repose in sleep
I humbly bow in all my Sin before the Throne Divine.
Not so the Sick-one; Alas what shall be done him to restore?
Who calls the Individual Law, Holy: and despises the Saviour,   5
Glorying to involve Albion's Body in fires of eternal War—"

Now Leutha ceas'd: tears flow'd: but the Divine Pity supported her.

"All is my fault! We are the Spectre of Luvah the murderer.
Of Albion: O Vala! O Luvah! O Albion! O lovely Jerusalem
The Sin was begun in Eternity, and will not rest to Eternity   10
Till two Eternitys meet together, Ah! lost! lost! lost! for ever!"

So Leutha spoke. But when she saw that Enitharmon had
Created a New Space to protect Satan from punishment;
She fled to Enitharmon's Tent & hid herself. Loud raging
Thundered the Assembly dark & clouded, and they ratify'd   15
The kind decision of Enitharmon & gave a Time to the Space,
Even Six Thousand years; and sent Lucifer⁵ for its Guard.
But Lucifer refus'd to die & in pride he forsook his charge
And they elected Molech, and when Molech was impatient

---

4. Echoing *Paradise Lost* 2.760–761. Leutha's emergence from Satan's brain recalls the Athena-like birth of Sin (*PL* 2.758); cf. *M* 13/12:10.
5. Morning star, literally "light-bearer" (Latin translation of Isaiah 14:12), the first of Blake's "Seven Eyes of God" *M* 25/23:51; cf. *J* 55:31) or "Seven Angels of the Presence" (*M* 17/15:3), historical stages in humanity's evolving conception of God in the fallen world. The others are Molech (for whom children are burned alive; Leviticus 18:21, 2 Kings 23:10); Elohim ("gods"; Genesis 1); Shaddai ("Almighty"; Exodus 6:2), Pahad [Pachad] ("fear"; Genesis 31:42), Jehovah or Yahweh ("Lord God," "I Am"; Genesis 2:4, Exodus 3:14), and Jesus or "the Lamb" (John 1:29). "Six Thousand Years": traditional timespan from Eden to the Apocalypse, to be followed by a seventh millennium of Christ's rule on earth (Revelation 20), which ends with the Last Judgment and the new heaven and new earth (Revelation 21).

The Divine hand found the Two Limits: first of Opacity, then
    of Contraction   20
Opacity was named Satan, Contraction was named Adam.[6]
Triple Elohim came: Elohim wearied fainted: they elected Shaddai.
Shaddai angry, Pahad descended: Pahad terrified, they sent Jehovah
And Jehovah was leprous; loud he call'd, stretching his hand to
    Eternity
For then the Body of Death[7] was perfected in hypocritic holiness,   25
Around the Lamb, a Female Tabernacle woven in Cathedron's
    Looms.[8]
He died as a Reprobate, he was Punish'd as a Transgressor!
Glory! Glory! Glory! to the Holy Lamb of God
I touch the heavens as an instrument to glorify the Lord!

The Elect shall meet the Redeem'd, on Albion's rocks they shall
    meet   30
Astonish'd at the Transgressor,[9] in him beholding the Saviour.
And the Elect shall say to the Redeemd, "We behold it is of Divine
Mercy alone! of Free Gift and Election that we live.
Our Virtues & Cruel Goodnesses, have deserv'd Eternal Death."
Thus they weep upon the fatal Brook of Albion's River.   35

But Elynittria met Leutha in the place where she was hidden.
And threw aside her arrows, and laid down her sounding Bow;
She sooth'd her with soft words & brought her to Palamabron's bed.
In moments new created for delusion, interwoven round about,
In dreams she bore the shadowy Spectre of Sleep, & namd him
    Death.   40
In dreams she bore Rahab the mother of Tirzah & her sisters
In Lambeth's vales; in Cambridge & in Oxford, places of Thought
Intricate labyrinths of Times and Spaces unknown, that Leutha
    lived
In Palamabron's Tent, and Oothoon was her charming guard.

The Bard ceas'd. All consider'd and a loud resounding murmur   45
Continu'd round the Halls; and much they question'd the immortal
Loud voicd Bard, and many condemn'd the high tone'd Song
Saying "Pity and Love are too venerable for the imputation
Of Guilt." Others said. "It is true! if the acts have been perform'd

---

6. The fall is arrested just short of the point of no return, at the limits of Satan's imperviousness to
   divine illumination (opacity) and Adam's confinement within the finite material body and lifespan
   (contraction). Donald Ault, *Blake's Visionary Physics* (1973), notes Blake's transformation of Newton's conception of mathematical limits. According to Los's fuller exposition in *Jerusalem*
   42:29–35, there is no limit of expansion or of translucence.
7. Cf. Paul's "Who shall deliver me from the body of this death" (Romans 7:24), here associated with
   Jesus' incarnation and his cast-off mortal body (cf. "O Christians Christians! tell me Why / You rear
   it on your Altars high," in *For the Sexes: The Gates of Paradise*).
8. Associated earlier with Enitharmon's weaving the Three Classes (3:1) and the world of Generation
   (3:38). "Cathedron": the name of the looms (*Four Zoas* 8; 100:3, E372), evocative of *Catherine* and
   cathedral (cf. 26/24:35; 28/26:35–36; *J* 59:23–25). "Female Tabernacle" (cf. *J* 88:19): associated
   with both the genitalia and the Holy of Holies (*J* 30/44:34–35), as in Blake's drawing in *Four Zoas*
   44 (not included in this edition).
9. A prophecy of reconciliation: when the Elect discover that Jesus, "numbered with the transgressors" (Isaiah 53:12, Mark 15:28), was among the Reprobate, they will repent their besetting sin of
   self-righteousness and recognize "Election" as the "Free Gift" of Mercy, not their birthright as
   members of a moral elite.

Let the Bard himself witness. Where hadst thou this terrible
  Song ?"   50

The Bard replied. "I am Inspired! I know it is Truth! for I Sing
According to the inspiration of the Poetic Genius   15/14
Who is the eternal all-protecting Divine Humanity
To whom be Glory & Power & Dominion Evermore Amen."

Then there was great murmuring in the Heavens of Albion
Concerning Generation & the Vegetative power & concerning   5
The Lamb the Saviour: Albion trembled to Italy Greece & Egypt
To Tartary & Hindostan & China & to Great America
Shaking the roots & fast foundations of the Earth in doubtfulness
The loud voic'd Bard terrify'd took refuge in Milton's bosom.

Then Milton rose up from the heavens of Albion ardorous!   10
The whole Assembly wept prophetic, seeing in Milton's face
And in his lineaments divine the shades of Death & Ulro.
He took off the robe of the promise,[1] & ungirded himself from the
  oath of God.

And Milton said, "I go to Eternal Death! The Nations still
Follow after the detestable Gods of Priam;[2] in pomp   15
Of warlike selfhood, contradicting and blaspheming.
When will the Resurrection come; to deliver the sleeping body
From corruptibility: O when Lord Jesus wilt thou come?
Tarry no longer; for my soul lies at the gates of death.
I will arise and look forth for the morning of the grave.   20
I will go down to the sepulcher to see if morning breaks!
I will go down to self annihilation and eternal death,
Lest the Last Judgment come & find me unannihilate
And I be siez'd & giv'n into the hands of my own Selfhood.
The Lamb of God is seen thro' mists & shadows, hov'ring   25
Over the sepulchers in clouds of Jehovah & winds of Elohim
A disk of blood, distant; & heav'ns & earth's roll dark between.
What do I here before the Judgment? without my Emanation?
With the daughters of memory, & not with the daughters
  of inspiration?
I in my Selfhood am that Satan: I am that Evil One!   30
He is my Spectre! in my obedience to loose him from my Hells
To claim the Hells, my Furnaces, I go to Eternal Death."[3]

And Milton said, "I go to Eternal Death!" Eternity shudder'd
For he took the outside course, among the graves of the dead
A mournful shade. Eternity shudderd at the image of eternal death.   35

Then on the verge of Beulah he beheld his own Shadow;
A mournful form double; hermaphroditic: male & female

1. Cf. the "garments of salvation" and "robe of righteousness" in Isaiah 61:10. Milton's stripping off
  these garments is depicted on plate **16** (not included in this edition).
2. King of Troy. Milton's Christian epics have not freed the world from Homeric gods of war.
3. Having recognized himself in the self-deceptive, self-righteous Satan of the Bard's song, Milton
  resolves to free up and reclaim the energy he had poured into his erroneous representation of evil
  in *Paradise Lost* (cf. *Marriage* **4–5**) and reunite with his Emanation or estranged authentic being,
  his capacity to love and create, personified as female.

In one wonderful body,[4] and he enterd into it
In direful pain for the dread shadow, twenty-seven-fold[5]
Reachd to the depths of direst Hell, & thence to Albion's land: 40
Which is this earth of vegetation on which now I write.

The Seven Angels of the Presence wept over Milton's Shadow!

As when a man dreams, he reflects not that his body sleeps,   17/15
Else he would wake; so seem'd he entering his Shadow: but
With him the Spirits of the Seven Angels of the Presence[6]
Entering; they gave him still perceptions of his Sleeping Body;
Which now arose and walk'd with them in Eden, as an Eighth   5
Image Divine tho' darken'd; and tho walking as one walks
In sleep; and the Seven comforted and supported him.

Like as a Polypus that vegetates beneath the deep![7]
They saw his Shadow vegetated underneath the Couch
Of death: for when he enterd into his Shadow: Himself: 10
His real and immortal Self: was as appeard to those
Who dwell in immortality, as One sleeping on a couch
Of gold; and those in immortality gave forth their Emanations
Like Females of sweet beauty, to guard round him & to feed
His lips with food of Eden in his cold and dim repose!   15
But to himself he seemd a wanderer lost in dreary night.

Onwards his Shadow kept its course[8] among the Spectres; call'd
Satan, but swift as lightning passing them, startled the shades
Of Hell beheld him in a trail of light as of a comet[9]
That travels into Chaos: so Milton went guarded within.   20

The nature of infinity is this: That every thing has its
Own Vortex;[1] and when once a traveller thro Eternity
Has passd that Vortex, he percieves it roll backward behind
His path, into a globe itself infolding; like a sun:
Or like a moon, or like a universe of starry majesty,   25
While he keeps onwards in his wondrous journey on the earth
Or like a human form, a friend with whom he livd benevolent.
As the eye of man views both the east & west encompassing
Its vortex; and the north & south, with all their starry host;

4. Apparently encompassing his unresolved, unproductive, self-contradictory views on sexuality, the
   nature of women, and the women in his family; cf. 21/19:33, 41/37.
5. Or 3×3×3, a number of incompletion (cf. 19/17:24, 41/37:35). With the addition of one
   (40/36:9), it becomes a multiple of seven, the biblical number representing perfection.
6. Eternal identities (24/22:1, 35/32:2, 44/39:3; cf. Isaiah 63:9) of the seven historically conceived
   images of God (14/13:7–27); see n. 5, p. 160 herein. Milton's "real and immortal Self" (17/15:11),
   presently protected within his Sleeping Body, will become the Eighth (17/15:5).
7. Here introduced as a simile, the Polypus becomes (in 26/24:38, 31/29:31, 38/34:31, 40/36:13,
   43/38:2) a hideous symbol of the entrapping "vegetated" systems of Ulro, the lowest plane of non-
   spiritual materialistic existence (see n. 3, p. 226 herein).
8. The Shadow's journey recalls that of Milton's Satan to the gate of Hell (PL 2.629) and then through
   Chaos (PL 2.891).
9. Recalls Satan's trail (PL 2.708; plate 32). In Book 2, Ololon follows in Milton's track (M 39/35:47)
   as Sin and Death follow in Satan's.
1. Blake's fullest exposition of a cosmological system derived from Descartes, discussed by Mark
   Greenberg, Colby Library Quarterly 14 (1978), 198–212, and in books by Frye, Adams, and Ault
   (see "Selected Bibliography"). For analogies with quantum physics and Zen teachings, see Mark
   Lussier, Romantic Dynamics (2000). Passage through the narrow point of intersection between one
   helix and another reorients one's sense of time, space, and being.

Also the rising sun & setting moon he views surrounding   30
His corn-fields and his valleys of five hundred acres square.
Thus is the earth one infinite plane, and not as apparent
To the weak traveller confin'd beneath the moony shade.
Thus is the heaven a vortex passd already, and the earth
A vortex not yet pass'd by the traveller thro' Eternity.   35

First Milton saw Albion upon the Rock of Ages,[2]
Deadly pale outstretchd and snowy cold, storm coverd;
A Giant form of perfect beauty outstretchd on the rock
In solemn death: the Sea of Time & Space thunderd aloud
Against the rock, which was inwrapped with the weeds of death.   40
Hovering over the cold bosom, in its vortex Milton bent down
To the bosom of death, what was underneath soon seemd above,
A cloudy heaven mingled with stormy seas in loudest ruin;
But as a wintry globe descends precipitant thro' Beulah
    bursting,
With thunders loud and terrible: so Milton's shadow fell   45
Precipitant loud thundring into the Sea of Time & Space.

Then first I saw him in the Zenith as a falling star,[3]
Descending perpendicular, swift as the swallow or swift;
And on my left foot falling on the tarsus,[4] enterd there;
But from my left foot a black cloud[5] redounding spread over
    Europe.   50

Then Milton knew that the Three Heavens of Beulah were beheld
By him on earth in his bright pilgrimage of sixty years
In those three females whom his Wives, & those three whom his
    Daughters   ┌─────────┐
                                                         │ 19/17 │
Had represented and containd, that they might be resum'd └─────────┘
By giving up of Selfhood: & they distant view'd his journey
In their eternal spheres, now Human, tho' their Bodies remain
    clos'd
In the dark Ulro till the Judgment: also Milton knew: they and   5
Himself was Human, tho' now wandering thro Death's Vale
In conflict with those Female forms, which in blood & jealousy
Surrounded him, dividing & uniting without end or number.

He saw the Cruelties of Ulro, and he wrote them down
In iron tablets: and his Wives' & Daughters' names were these: 10
Rahab and Tirzah, & Milcah & Malah & Noah & Hoglah.[6]

2. See n. 2, p. 268 herein. "Albion": see headnote to *Jerusalem*, p. 205 herein.
3. Echoing Milton's description of Mulciber's fall (*PL* 1.745); also a portent of the end of time
   (cf. Matthew 24:29; Revelation 9:1).
4. Ankle. Milton enters Blake through the lowest part of his body, on the left, traditionally the inferior (*gauche*, sinister) side (depicted on plate **32**); the narrative thread continues on 23/21:4. In
   Blake Studies 6 (1973), 73–87, Erdman links "tarsus" with Tarsus, home of the Pharisee Saul, who
   became the apostle Paul after encountering Jesus on the Damascus Road (Acts 9:3). Cf. "tarsus"
   of the eyelid, Dennis Welsh, *Religion and Literature* 18 (1986), 1–15.
5. Reappears in 23/21:36; see also **20**/21:20–21.
6. All but Rahab are brotherless daughters of Zelophehad who established the right of female inheritance (Numbers 27:1–11 and 36:10); see also "To Tirzah." Rahab, who shares her name with a
   primeval male dragon (Psalm 89:10; Isaiah 51:9), is a harlot of Jericho who harbored Hebrew
   spies preparing for the Israelite conquest (Joshua 2:11). In Christian tradition, she is a righteous
   pagan who prefigures the Church (Hebrews 11:31; James 2:25), which, in its worldly form is, for

They sat rangd round him as the rocks of Horeb round the land
Of Canaan: and they wrote in thunder smoke and fire
His dictate; and his body was the Rock Sinai; that body,
Which was on earth born to corruption: & the six Females   15
Are Hor & Peor & Bashan & Abarim & Lebanon & Hermon[7]
Seven rocky masses terrible in the Desarts of Midian.

But Milton's Human Shadow continu'd journeying above
The rocky masses of The Mundane Shell; in the Lands
Of Edom & Aram & Moab & Midian & Amalek.   20

The Mundane Shell[8] is a vast Concave Earth: an immense
Hardend shadow of all things upon our Vegetated Earth
Enlarg'd into dimension & deform'd into indefinite space,
In Twenty-seven Heavens and all their Hells; with Chaos
And Ancient Night; & Purgatory. It is a cavernous Earth   25
Of labyrinthine intricacy, twenty-seven folds of opakeness
And finishes where the lark mounts; here Milton journeyed
In that Region calld Midian among the Rocks of Horeb
For travellers from Eternity pass outward to Satan's seat,
But travellers to Eternity pass inward to Golgonooza.[9]   30

Los the Vehicular terror beheld him, & divine Enitharmon
Call'd all her daughters, Saying. "Surely to unloose my bond
Is this Man come! Satan shall be unloosd upon Albion."

Los heard in terror Enitharmon's words: in fibrous strength
His limbs shot forth like roots of trees against the forward path   35
Of Milton's journey. Urizen beheld the immortal Man,
And Tharmas Demon of the Waters, & Orc, who is Luvah.   20/18

The Shadowy Female[1] seeing Milton, howl'd in her lamentation
Over the Deeps, outstretching her Twenty seven Heavens over
   Albion.

Blake, the Whore of Babylon (Revelation 17); see G. A. Rosso in *Prophetic Character* (2002), ed.
    Gourlay.
7. Mountains and hills in lands hostile to the Israelites (see map). Horeb (19/17:12, 28), where
    Moses struck water from the rock (Exodus 17:6), is another name for Sinai (19/17:14), where he
    received the commandments (Exodus 3:1). Midian (appearing also in 19/17:20, with other hostile
    lands and tribes) was exterminated for tempting Israel into idolatry (Numbers 31). The rocky scene
    of dictation combines elements of the issuing of the Ten Commandments to Moses and the blind
    Milton's dictation of *Paradise Lost* to his daughters.
8. A major symbol of the material world mentioned on nine succeeding pages; depicted schematically
    in 36/35; elaborately described in 38/34:31–46. The ancient conception of the universe as a pri-
    mordial egg appears in Plato's *Symposium* and may be extrapolated from the image of the Holy
    Spirit as a brooding dove (*PL* 1.20–22). At first Milton is outside and Ololon is within the egg
    (23/21:30), but Milton's descent (38/34:40–42) cracks the shell between them.
9. In one arena of action Milton is retracing Moses' journey in the Exodus, but as a traveler from Eter-
    nity he is paradoxically passing "outward" to confront the Satan within; in another arena, incar-
    nated within Blake, he moves beyond the law as Blake, joined with Los, journeys "inward," toward
    Eternity, to Golgonooza (24/22:27), city of art, the "spiritual fourfold London" (in another dimen-
    sion, represented by a star near the center of London on the map). As if on a surreal Möbius strip,
    each poet spirals along a Vortex that intersects with and reorients the other (17/15:22 ff.).
1. Here, on another of the pages added to Copies C and D (Bentley "d"), Orc's female counterpart,
    Vala, appears at her least distinct level of being; cf. the "Shadowy Daughter of Urthona" in *Amer-
    ica* 1 and the "nameless shadowy female" in *Europe* 1. The narrator's "sweet Shadow of Delight"
    (40/36, 40/36:31) appears to be an aspect of Catherine Blake. For the Shadowy Female's needle-
    work, see Paley in *Blake's Sublime Allegory* (1973), ed. Curran and Wittreich.

And thus the Shadowy Female howls in articulate howlings

"I will lament over Milton in the lamentations of the afflicted   5
My Garments shall be woven of sighs & heart broken lamentations
The misery of unhappy Families shall be drawn out into its border
Wrought with the needle with dire sufferings poverty pain & woe
Along the rocky Island & thence throughout the whole Earth
There shall be the sick Father & his starving Family! there   10
The Prisoner in the stone Dungeon & the Slave at the Mill
I will have Writings written all over it in Human Words
That every Infant that is born upon the Earth shall read
And get by rote as a hard task of a life of sixty years
I will have Kings inwoven upon it, & Councellors & Mighty Men   15
The Famine shall clasp it together with buckles & Clasps
And the Pestilence shall be its fringe & the War its girdle
To divide into Rahab & Tirzah that Milton may come to our tents
For I will put on the Human Form & take the Image of God
Even Pity & Humanity but my Clothing shall be Cruelty   20
And I will put on Holiness as a Breastplate & as a helmet[2]
And all my ornaments shall be of the gold of broken hearts
And the precious stones of anxiety & care & desperation & death
And repentance for sin & sorrow & punishment & fear
To defend me from thy terrors O Orc! my only beloved!"   25

Orc answerd. "Take not the Human Form O loveliest. Take not
Terror upon thee! Behold how I am & tremble lest thou also
Consume in my Consummation; but thou maist take a Form
Female & lovely, that cannot consume in Man's consummation.
Wherefore dost thou Create & Weave this Satan for a Covering?   30
When thou attemptest to put on the Human Form, my wrath
Burns to the top of heaven against thee in Jealousy & Fear.
Then I rend thee asunder, then I howl over thy clay & ashes.
When wilt thou put on the Female Form as in times of old
With a Garment of Pity & Compassion like the Garment of God?   35
His garments are long sufferings for the Children of Men
Jerusalem is his Garment & not thy Covering Cherub O lovely
Shadow of my delight who wanderest seeking for the prey."

So spoke Orc when Oothoon & Leutha hoverd over his Couch
Of fire in interchange of Beauty & Perfection, in the darkness   40
Opening interiorly into Jerusalem & Babylon shining glorious
In the Shadowy Female's bosom. Jealous her darkness grew:
Howlings filld all the desolate places in accusations of Sin
In Female beauty shining in the unformd void & Orc in vain
Stretch'd out his bands of fire, & wooed: they triumph in his pain.   45

Thus darkend the Shadowy Female tenfold & Orc tenfold
Glowd on his rocky Couch against the darkness; loud thunders
Told of the enormous conflict. Earthquake beneath: around:
Rent the Immortal Females, limb from limb & joint from joint,
And moved the fast foundations of the Earth to wake the Dead.   50

---

2. The Shadowy Female's helmet and breastplate pervert the metaphors of Isaiah 59:17, Ephesians
6:17, and 1 Thessalonians 5:8; cf. Aaron's breastplate in Exodus 28:15 ff.

Urizen emerged from his Rocky Form & from his Snows,

And he also darkend his brows: freezing dark rocks between   21/19
The footsteps, and infixing deep the feet in marble beds:
That Milton labourd with his journey, & his feet bled sore
Upon the clay now chang'd to marble; also Urizen rose,
And met him on the shores of Arnon;[3] & by the streams of the
    brooks.   5

Silent they met, and silent strove among the streams of Arnon
Even to Mahanaim,[4] when with cold hand Urizen stoop'd down
And took up water from the river Jordan:[5] pouring on
To Milton's brain the icy fluid from his broad cold palm.
But Milton took of the red clay of Succoth,[6] moulding it with
    care   10
Between his palms: and filling up the furrows of many years
Beginning at the feet of Urizen, and on the bones
Creating new flesh on the Demon cold, and building him,
As with new clay a Human form in the Valley of Beth Peor.[7]

Four Universes round the Mundane Egg remain Chaotic   15
One to the North, named Urthona: One to the South, named
    Urizen:
One to the East, named Luvah: One to the West, named Tharmas.
They are the Four Zoa's[8] that stood around the Throne Divine:
But when Luvah assum'd the World of Urizen to the South:
And Albion was slain upon his mountains, & in his tent;   20
All fell towards the Center in dire ruin, sinking down.
And in the South remains a burning fire; in the East a void.
In the West, a world of raging waters; in the North a solid,
Unfathomable! without end. But in the midst of these,
Is built eternally the Universe of Los and Enitharmon: 25
Towards which Milton went, but Urizen oppos'd his path.

The Man and Demon strove many periods. Rahab beheld
Standing on Carmel;[9] Rahab and Tirzah trembled to behold
The enormous strife, one giving life, the other giving death
To his adversary, and they sent forth all their sons & daughters 30
In all their beauty to entice Milton across the river.

The Twofold form Hermaphroditic: and the Double-sexed;
The Female-male & the Male-female, self-dividing stood

3. East-west river flowing into the Dead Sea (see the "Blake's Holy Land" map); separating Moab
(Numbers 21:13) from the Amorites, whose land was conquered and claimed by the Israelites
(Numbers 21:25; Joshua 12:1, 12:6).
4. Near the Jabbok river, where Jacob had a vision of angels (Genesis 32:1–2) before wrestling with
an angel (Genesis 32:22–30); cf. *Paradise Lost* 9:213 ff.
5. Flowing north to south, where Jesus was baptized (Matthew 3:6).
6. Where the artisan Hiram cast brass ornaments and furnishings for Solomon's temple (1 Kings
7:46). God molded red clay (the literal meaning of "Adam") into human flesh (cf. *Marriage* 2; Genesis 2:7). In the design (18/16), perhaps depicting an alternate version of this struggle, Milton's
right foot divides the word *Self-hood* in the inscription.
7. Where the Israelites rested (Deuteronomy 3:27–29) before entering the Promised Land, and where
Moses was buried (Deuteronomy 34:6).
8. Blake's plural (with apostrophe); Greek: "living creatures"; see note to *The Four Zoas*, p. 408.
9. Mountain locale of the contest between Elijah and Baal's prophets (1 Kings 18:19; see map).

Before him in their beauty, & in cruelties of holiness!
Shining in darkness, glorious upon the deeps of Entuthon,[1]   35

Saying, "Come thou to Ephraim![2] behold the Kings of Canaan!
The beautiful Amalekites, behold the fires of youth
Bound with the Chain of jealousy by Los & Enitharmon;
The banks of Cam: cold learning's streams: London's
    dark-frowning towers;
Lament upon the winds of Europe in Rephaim's Vale.[3]   40
Because Ahania, rent apart into a desolate night,
Laments! & Enion wanders like a weeping inarticulate voice
And Vala labours for her bread & water among the Furnaces.
Therefore bright Tirzah triumphs: putting on all beauty.
And all perfection, in her cruel sports among the Victims,   45
Come bring with thee Jerusalem with songs on the Grecian Lyre:
In Natural Religion! in experiments on Men,
Let her be Offerd up to Holiness! Tirzah numbers her;
She numbers with her fingers every fibre ere it grow;
Where is the Lamb of God? where is the promise of his coming?[4]   50
Her shadowy Sisters form the bones, even the bones of Horeb:
Around the marrow: and the orbed scull around the brain!
His Images are born for War! for Sacrifice to Tirzah!
To Natural Religion! to Tirzah the Daughter of Rahab the Holy!
She ties the knot of nervous fibres, into a white brain!   55
She ties the knot of bloody veins, into a red hot heart![5]
Within her bosom Albion lies embalmd, never to awake
Hand is become a rock! Sinai & Horeb, is Hyle & Coban:
Scofield[6] is bound in iron armour before Reuben's Gate!
She ties the knot of milky seed into two lovely Heavens,   60
Two yet but one: each in the other sweet reflected! these   `22/20`
Are our Three Heavens beneath the shades of Beulah, land of
    rest!
Come then to Ephraim & Manasseh O beloved-one!
Come to my ivory palaces[7] O beloved of thy mother!
And let us bind thee in the bands of War & be thou King   5
Of Canaan and reign in Hazor[8] where the Twelve Tribes meet."

So spoke they as in one voice: Silent Milton stood before
The darkend Urizen; as the sculptor silent stands before
His forming image; he walks round it patient labouring.
Thus Milton stood forming bright Urizen, while his Mortal part   10

1. A state of error and confusion (cf. 28/26:25). These mixed-gender sons and daughters are trying
   to tempt Milton to cross over and become king of Canaan (Exodus 15:15), also the land of the
   Amelekites (Numbers 14:43). The latter-day equivalents are Cambridge (21/19:39; cf 14/13:42),
   where the historical Milton studied, and London, where he lived and wrote.
2. With Manasseh (22/20:3), Israelite half-tribes descended from Joseph's sons by his Egyptian wife
   (Genesis 41:51–52), given territory in the Promised Land (Joshua 16:17; see map). Ephraim
   turned against David (Isaiah 7:2, 7:5) and fell into idolatry (Hosea 4:17). Both eventually belonged
   to the breakaway Northern Kingdom of Israel under Jeroboam (1 Kings 12:19 ff.), hostile to Judah.
3. Where David defeated the Philistines (2 Samuel 5:18, 23:13); traditionally associated with ghosts
   of giants (Damon's *Dictionary*); cf. *Jerusalem* 48:41.
4. Taunt of the scoffers in 2 Peter 3:4.
5. Forming the head, heart, and loins for sacrifice in war and religion; c.f. *Jerusalem* 67:2 ff. Tirzah
   is also the capital city of the Northern Kingdom (1 Kings 15–16), opposing Jerusalem in the south.
6. See *Jerusalem* 4:25–27.
7. Recalls Psalm 45.
8. A defeated Canaanite stronghold (Joshua 11).

Sat frozen in the rock of Horeb: and his Redeemed portion
Thus form'd the Clay of Urizen; but within that portion
His real Human walkd above in power and majesty
Tho darkend; and the Seven Angels of the Presence attended him.

O how can I with my gross tongue that cleaveth to the dust,[9]   15
Tell of the Four-fold Man, in starry numbers[1] fitly orderd
Or how can I with my cold hand of clay! But thou O Lord
Do with me as thou wilt! for I am nothing, and vanity.
If thou chuse to elect a worm, it shall remove the mountains.
For that portion namd the Elect: the Spectrous body of Milton: 20
Redounding from my left foot into Los's Mundane space,
Brooded over his Body in Horeb against the Resurrection
Preparing it for the Great Consummation; red the Cherub on
    Sinai
Glow'd; but in terrors folded round his clouds of blood.

Now Albion's sleeping Humanity began to turn upon his Couch;   25
Feeling the electric flame of Milton's awful precipitate descent.
Seest thou the little winged fly, smaller than a grain of sand?
It has a heart like thee; a brain open to heaven & hell,
Withinside wondrous & expansive; its gates are not clos'd,
I hope thine are not: hence it clothes itself in rich array;   30
Hence thou art cloth'd with human beauty O thou mortal man.
Seek not thy heavenly father then beyond the skies:
There Chaos dwells & ancient Night & Og & Anak[2] old:
For every human heart has gates of brass & bars of adamant,
Which few dare unbar because dread Og & Anak guard the gates   35
Terrific! and each mortal brain is walld and moated round
Within: and Og & Anak watch here; here is the Seat
Of Satan in its Webs; for in brain and heart and loins
Gates open behind Satan's Seat to the City of Golgonooza
Which is the spiritual fourfold London, in the loins of Albion.   40

Thus Milton fell thro Albion's heart, travelling outside of
    Humanity
Beyond the Stars in Chaos in Caverns of the Mundane Shell.

But many of the Eternals rose up from eternal tables
Drunk with the Spirit,[3] burning round the Couch of death they
    stood
Looking down into Beulah: wrathful, fill'd with rage!   45
They rend the heavens round the Watchers in a fiery circle:
And round the Shadowy Eighth: the Eight close up the Couch
Into a tabernacle, and flee with cries down to the Deeps:
Where Los opens his three wide gates, surrounded by raging fires;
They soon find their own place & join the Watchers of the Ulro.[4]   50

9. Blake as narrator (cf. 15/14:41) again breaks in, this time to renew his prayer for divine aid (cf. PL
   3:1 ff. and 7:1 ff.). Like Moses (Exodus 4:10) and Isaiah (6:5), he feels inadequate in prophetic
   utterance ("tongue") as well as in visual-verbal artistry ("hand," 22/20:17).
1. Poetry (metrical units).
2. A father of giants (Numbers 13:33); cf. 35/31:49. Og is a giant king of Bashan (Deuteronomy 3:11).
3. Cf. Ephesians 5:18. These Eternals are later associated with Ololon (23/21:16). They see that Milton, at his "real Human" level (22/20:13–14), the Eighth, has joined the Seven Angels of the Presence (15/14:42), or "Watchers" (cf. Daniel 4:13).
4. Blake's lowest state of sheer materiality.

Los saw them and a cold pale horror coverd o'er his limbs.
Pondering he knew that Rintrah & Palamabron might depart:
Even as Reuben & as Gad; gave up himself to tears.
He sat down on his anvil-stock; and leand upon the trough.
Looking into the black water, mingling it with tears.   55

At last when desperation almost tore his heart in twain
He recollected an old Prophecy in Eden recorded,
And often sung to the loud harp at the immortal feasts
That Milton of the Land of Albion should up ascend
Forwards from Ulro from the Vale of Felpham, and set free   60
Orc from his Chain of Jealousy. He started at the thought

And down descended into Udan-Adan;[5] it was night: $\boxed{23/21}$
And Satan sat sleeping upon his Couch in Udan-Adan:
His Spectre slept, his Shadow woke; when one sleeps th'other
    wakes.

But Milton entering my Foot;[6] I saw in the nether
Regions of the Imagination; also all men on Earth,   5
And all in Heaven, saw in the nether regions of the Imagination
In Ulro beneath Beulah, the vast breach of Milton's descent.
But I knew not that it was Milton, for man cannot know
What passes in his members till periods of Space & Time
Reveal the secrets of Eternity: for more extensive   10
Than any other earthly things, are Man's earthly lineaments.

And all this Vegetable World appeard on my left Foot,
As a bright sandal formd immortal of precious stones & gold:
I stooped down & bound it on to walk forward thro' Eternity.

There is in Eden a sweet River, of milk & liquid pearl,[7]   15
Namd Ololon;[8] on whose mild banks dwelt those who Milton
    drove
Down into Ulro: and they[9] wept in long resounding song
For seven days of eternity, and the river's living banks
The mountains waild! & every plant that grew, in solemn sighs
    lamented.

When Luvah's bulls each morning drag the sulphur Sun out of
    the Deep   20
Harnessd with starry harness black & shining kept by black slaves
That work all night at the starry harness. Strong and vigorous
They drag the unwilling Orb: at this time all the Family
Of Eden heard the lamentation, and Providence began.

5. Another strange psycho-cosmic space (**25**/23:60, **28**/26:49, **29**/27:50). In *Four Zoas* 8 (113:24) called
   a "Lake not of Waters but of Spaces"; associated with the Forests of Entuthon Benython (**28**/26:25).
6. Cf. **17**/15:49, **22**/20:21; such repetitions, replaying critical events from new angles, help provide
   cohesiveness in a work without narrative chronology.
7. See *Paradise Lost* 3.519, 4.237.
8. Ololon, like Milton, takes different forms according to the perspectives of the character and the
   viewer.
9. The riverbank inhabitants who take responsibility for having driven Milton into the lower world;
   they descend into Beulah as a family (**33**/30:4) but enter Blake's garden in the Mundane Shell in
   the form of a twelve-year old girl (**40**/36:17).

But when the clarions of day sounded they drownd the
  lamentations   25
And when night came all was silent in Ololon: & all refusd to
  lament
In the still night fearing lest they should others molest.

Seven mornings Los heard them, as the poor bird within the shell
Hears its impatient parent bird; and Enitharmon heard them:
But saw them not, for the blue Mundane Shell inclosd them in.   30

And they lamented that they had in wrath & fury & fire
Driven Milton into the Ulro; for now they knew too late
That it was Milton the Awakener: they had not heard the Bard,
Whose song calld Milton to the attempt; and Los heard these
  laments.
He heard them call in prayer all the Divine Family;   35
And he beheld the Cloud of Milton stretching over Europe.

But all the Family Divine collected as Four Suns
In the Four Points of heaven East, West & North & South
Enlarging and enlarging till their Disks approachd each other:
And when they touch'd closed together Southward in One Sun   40
Over Ololon: and as One Man, who weeps over his brother,
In a dark tomb, so all the Family Divine wept over Ololon.

Saying, "Milton goes to Eternal Death!" so saying, they groan'd
  in spirit
And were troubled![1] and again the Divine Family groaned in spirit!

And Ololon said, "Let us descend also, and let us give   45
Ourselves to death in Ulro among the Transgressors.
Is Virtue a Punisher? O no! how is this wondrous thing?
This World beneath, unseen before: this refuge from the Wars
Of Great Eternity! unnatural refuge! unknown by us till now!
Or are these the pangs of repentance? let us enter into them."   50

Then the Divine Family said, "Six Thousand Years are now
Accomplish'd in this World of Sorrow; Milton's Angel knew
The Universal Dictate; and you also feel this Dictate.
And now you know this World of Sorrow, and feel Pity. Obey
The Dictate! Watch over this World, and with your brooding
  wings,[2]   55
Renew it to Eternal Life: Lo! I am with you alway[3]
But you cannot renew Milton he goes to Eternal Death."

So spake the Family Divine as One Man even Jesus
Uniting in One with Ololon & the appearance of One Man
Jesus the Saviour appeard coming in the Clouds of Ololon![4]   60

---

1. Alluding to Jesus' weeping and groaning in spirit over Lazarus (John 11:33–35)
2. Cf. the dovelike brooding of Milton's Holy Spirit (*PL* 1.19–22), which blends Genesis 1:2 with
   Matthew 3:16.
3. Jesus' promise to his disciples (Matthew 28:20).
4. Alluding to the clouds in which Jesus appears at the Second Coming (Mark 13:26); cf *M* 39/35:41.

Tho driven away with the Seven Starry Ones into the Ulro   24/22
Yet the Divine Vision remains Every-where For-ever. Amen.
And Ololon lamented for Milton with a great lamentation.

While Los heard indistinct in fear, what time I bound my sandals
On; to walk forward thro' Eternity, Los descended to me: 5
And Los behind me stood; a terrible flaming Sun: just close
Behind my back; I turned round in terror, and behold,
Los stood in that fierce glowing fire; & he also stoop'd down
And bound my sandals on in Udan-Adan; trembling I stood
Exceedingly with fear & terror, standing in the Vale   10
Of Lambeth: but he kissed me and wishd me health.
And I became One Man with him arising in my strength:
Twas too late now to recede. Los had enterd into my soul:
His terrors now posses'd me whole! I arose in fury & strength.[5]

"I am that Shadowy Prophet who Six Thousand Years ago   15
Fell from my station in the Eternal bosom. Six Thousand Years
Are finishd. I return! both Time & Space obey my will.
I in Six Thousand Years walk up and down: for not one Moment
Of Time is lost, nor one Event of Space unpermanent
But all remain: every fabric of Six Thousand Years   20
Remains permanent: tho' on the Earth where Satan
Fell, and was cut off all things vanish & are seen no more
They vanish not from me & mine, we guard them first & last.
The generations of men run on in the tide of Time
But leave their destind lineaments permanent for ever & ever."   25
So spoke Los as we went along to his supreme abode.

Rintrah and Palamabron met us at the Gate of Golgonooza[6]
Clouded with discontent, & brooding in their minds terrible
    things.

They said, "O Father most beloved! O merciful Parent!
Pitying and permitting evil, tho strong & mighty to destroy.[7]   30
Whence is this Shadow terrible? wherefore dost thou refuse
To throw him into the Furnaces: knowest thou not that he
Will unchain Orc? & let loose Satan, Og, Sihon & Anak,
Upon the Body of Albion? for this he is come! behold it written
Upon his fibrous left Foot black! most dismal to our eyes.   35
The Shadowy Female shudders thro' heaven in torment
    inexpressible!
And all the Daughters of Los prophetic wail: yet in deceit,
They weave a new Religion from new Jealousy of Theotormon!
Milton's Religion is the cause: there is no end to destruction!
Seeing the Churches at their Period in terror & despair: 40
Rahab created Voltaire; Tirzah created Rousseau;[8]

---

5. The Bard's entrance into Milton, and Milton's into Blake, involve all three poets in Blake's vision of Los, the Eternal Prophet and the spirit of Time (see design, 47/43). Cf. Blake's encounter with Los in Felpham (p. 477 herein).
6. City of art—all art, everywhere, through all time—that preserves and renews the archetypal acts of the human race.
7. The core question of Christian theodicy applied here to the perceived threat of Milton's reappearance on earth through Blake.
8. Cf. M 46/40:12, Jerusalem 66:12, and "Mock on."

Asserting the Self-righteousness against the Universal Saviour,
Mocking the Confessors & Martyrs, claiming Self-righteousness;
With cruel Virtue: making War upon the Lamb's Redeemed;
To perpetuate War & Glory, to perpetuate the Laws of Sin: 45
They perverted Swedenborg's Visions in Beulah & in Ulro;
To destroy Jerusalem as a Harlot & her Sons as Reprobates;
To raise up Mystery the Virgin Harlot Mother of War,
Babylon the Great, the Abomination of Desolation![9]
O Swedenborg! strongest of men, the Samson shorn by the
     Churches!   50
Shewing the Transgresors in Hell, the proud Warriors in Heaven:
Heaven as a Punisher & Hell as One under Punishment:
With Laws from Plato & his Greeks to renew the Trojan Gods,
In Albion; & to deny the value of the Saviour's blood.
But then I rais'd up Whitefield, Palamabron raisd up Westley,[1]   55
And these are the cries of the Churches before the two Witnesses
'Faith in God the dear Saviour who took on the likeness of men:
Becoming obedient to death, even the death of the Cross.[2]
The Witnesses lie dead in the Street of the Great City.
No Faith is in all the Earth: the Book of God is trodden under
     Foot: 60
He sent his two Servants Whitefield & Westley; were they
     Prophets
Or were they Idiots or Madmen? shew us Miracles!'

Can you have greater Miracles than these? Men who devote   [25/23]
Their life's whole comfort to intire scorn & injury & death?
Awake thou sleeper on the Rock of Eternity, Albion awake!
The trumpet of Judgment hath twice sounded: all Nations are
     awake
But thou art still heavy and dull: Awake Albion awake!   5
Lo Orc arises on the Atlantic. Lo his blood and fire
Glow on America's shore: Albion turns upon his Couch
He listens to the sounds of War, astonishd and confounded:
He weeps into the Atlantic deep, yet still in dismal dreams
Unwakend! and the Covering Cherub[3] advances from the East: 10
How long shall we lay dead in the Street of the great City
How long beneath the Covering Cherub give our Emanations?
Milton will utterly consume us & thee our beloved Father
He hath enterd into the Covering Cherub, becoming one with
Albion's dread Sons; Hand, Hyle & Coban surround him as   15
A girdle; Gwendolen & Conwenna as a garment woven
Of War & Religion; let us descend & bring him chained
To Bowlahoola O father most beloved! O mild Parent!
Cruel in thy mildness, pitying and permitting evil
Tho strong and mighty to destroy, O Los our beloved Father!"   20

9. An apocalyptic manifestation of evil; see n. 1, p. 217.
1. The great Methodist evangelists George Whitefield (1714–70, pronounced "Whitfield") and John
   Wesley (1703–91, a name Blake consistently misspelled and presumably pronounced "Westley")
   are identified with the two martyred witnesses of Revelation 11:3 (cf. Revelation 6:10, 11:8). Rintrah identifies himself with the fiery Calvinist Whitefield; Palamabron, with the more temperate
   Wesley, champion of "free grace." "Witnesses" (24:56) may be in the possessive case.
2. Echoes Philippians 2:7–8. Rintrah's quotation of the Churches' "cries" may end here.
3. See n. 7, p. 195 herein.

Like the black storm, coming out of Chaos, beyond the stars:
It issues thro the dark & intricate caves of the Mundane Shell
Passing the planetary visions, & the well adorned Firmament
The Sun rolls into Chaos & the Stars into the Desarts;
And then the storms become visible, audible & terrible,   25
Covering the light of day, & rolling down upon the mountains,
Deluge all the country round. Such is a vision of Los;
When Rintrah & Palamabron spake; and such his stormy face
Appeard, as does the face of heaven, when coverd with thick
   storms
Pitying and loving tho in frowns of terrible perturbation.   30

But Los dispersd the clouds even as the strong winds of Jehovah,
And Los thus spoke. "O noble Sons, be patient yet a little:
I have embracd the falling Death, he is become One with me.
O Sons we live not by wrath, by mercy alone we live!
I recollect an old Prophecy in Eden recorded in gold; and oft   35
Sung to the harp: That Milton of the land of Albion
Should up ascend forward from Felpham's Vale & break the Chain
Of jealousy from all its roots;[4] be patient therefore O my Sons
These lovely Females form sweet night and silence and secret
Obscurities to hide from Satan's Watch-Fiends Human loves   40
And graces; lest they write them in their Books, & in the Scroll
Of mortal life, to condemn the accused: who at Satan's Bar
Tremble in Spectrous Bodies continually day and night
While on the Earth they live in sorrowful Vegetations.
O when shall we tread our Wine-presses in heaven; and Reap   45
Our wheat with shoutings of joy, and leave the Earth in peace?
Remember how Calvin and Luther in fury premature
Sow'd War and stern division between Papists & Protestants
Let it not be so now! O go not forth in Martyrdoms & Wars.
We were plac'd here by the Universal Brotherhood & Mercy   50
With powers fitted to circumscribe this dark Satanic death
And that the Seven Eyes of God may have space for Redemption.
But how this is as yet we know not, and we cannot know;
Till Albion is arisen; then patient wait a little while,
Six Thousand years are passd away; the end approaches fast;   55
This mighty one is come from Eden, he is of the Elect,
Who died from Earth & he is returnd before the Judgment. This
   thing
Was never known that one of the holy dead should willing return.
Then patient wait a little while till the Last Vintage is over:
Till we have quenchd the Sun of Salah in the Lake of Udan Adan.   60
O my dear Sons! leave not your Father, as your brethren left me.
Twelve Sons successive fled away in that thousand years of
   sorrow

Of Palamabron's Harrow, & of Rintrah's wrath & fury: 26/24
Reuben & Manazzoth[5] & Gad & Simeon & Levi,

---

4. Repeated from 22/20:59–61.
5. Made-up Hebrew-sounding name (noted by Stevenson), changed to a genuine biblical name in 26/24:6 (alternate of "Manasseh," 22/20:3). The twelve tribes of Israel, descended from Jacob's sons, are here identified as the twelve sons of Los who fled from Eternity; in *Jerusalem* they are the sons of Albion.

And Ephraim & Judah were Generated, because
They left me, wandering with Tirzah: Enitharmon wept
One thousand years, and all the Earth was in a watry deluge.   5
We calld him Menassheh because of the Generations of Tirzah
Because of Satan: & the Seven Eyes of God continually
Guard round them, but I the Fourth Zoa am also set
The Watchman of Eternity, the Three are not! & I am preserved.
Still my four mighty ones are left to me in Golgonooza   10
Still Rintrah fierce, and Palamabron mild & piteous
Theotormon filld with care, Bromion loving Science.
You O my Sons still guard round Los. O wander not & leave me
Rintrah, thou well rememberest when Amalek & Canaan
Fled with their Sister Moab into the abhorred Void   15
They became Nations in our sight beneath the hands of Tirzah.
And Palamabron thou rememberest when Joseph an infant;
Stolen from his nurse's cradle wrapd in needle-work
Of emblematic texture, was sold to the Amalekite,
Who carried him down into Egypt where Ephraim & Menassheh   20
Gatherd my Sons together in the Sands of Midian.
And if you also flee away and leave your Father's side,
Following Milton into Ulro, altho your power is great
Surely you also shall become poor mortal vegetations
Beneath the Moon of Ulro: pity then your Father's tears.   25
When Jesus raisd Lazarus from the Grave I stood & saw
Lazarus who is the Vehicular Body of Albion the Redeemd,
Arise into the Covering Cherub who is the Spectre of Albion
By martyrdoms to suffer: to watch over the Sleeping Body
Upon his Rock beneath his Tomb. I saw the Covering Cherub   30
Divide Four-fold into Four Churches[6] when Lazarus arose.
Paul, Constantine, Charlemaine, Luther; behold they stand
     before us
Stretchd over Europe & Asia. Come O Sons, come, come away
Arise O Sons give all your strength against Eternal Death
Lest we are vegetated, for Cathedron's Looms weave only Death   35
A Web of Death: & were it not for Bowlahoola & Allamanda[7]
No Human Form but only a Fibrous Vegetation
A Polypus of soft affections without Thought or Vision
Must tremble in the Heavens & Earths thro all the Ulro space.
Throw all the Vegetated Mortals into Bowlahoola,   40
But as to this Elected Form who is returnd again
He is the Signal that the Last Vintage now approaches
Nor Vegetation may go on till all the Earth is reapd."

So Los spoke. Furious they descended to Bowlahoola &
     Allamanda
Indignant, unconvincd by Los's arguments & thunders rolling   45
They saw that wrath now swayd and now pity absorbd him
As it was, so it remaind & no hope of an end.

6. Historical stages of division and decline, from Paul to Luther; aspects of the Covering Cherub who
   blocks access to vision (see n. 7, p. 195). To the extent that the Christian church confuses a reanimated dead body (Lazarus) with the "spiritual body" (I Corinthians 15:44; cf. "To Tirzah"), it is
   the antithesis of Blake's idea of true Christianity.
7. Allegorical places not as clearly and fully developed as Golgonooza. Bowlahoola (associated by
   some with the bowels) is "Law" (26/24:48). Allamanda (perhaps the alimentary canal) is "Commerce" (29/27:43). See Damon's *Dictionary*.

Bowlahoola is namd Law, by mortals, Tharmas founded it:
Because of Satan, before Luban in the City of Golgonooza.
But Golgonooza is namd Art & Manufacture by mortal men. 50

In Bowlahoola Los's Anvils stand & his Furnaces rage;
Thundering the Hammers beat & the Bellows blow loud
Living self moving mourning lamenting & howling incessantly
Bowlahoola thro all its porches feels, tho' too fast founded
Its pillars & porticoes to tremble at the force 55
Of mortal or immortal arm: and softly lilling flutes
Accordant with the horrid labours make sweet melody.
The Bellows are the Animal Lungs: the hammers the Animal
  Heart
The Furnaces the Stomach for digestion, terrible their fury.
Thousands & thousands labour, thousands play on instruments 60
Stringed or fluted to ameliorate the sorrows of slavery.
Loud sport the dancers in the dance of death, rejoicing in carnage.
The hard dentant Hammers are lulld by the flutes lula lula,
The bellowing Furnaces blare by the long sounding clarion
The double drum drowns howls & groans, the shrill fife
  shrieks & cries: 65
The crooked horn mellows the hoarse raving serpent,[8] terrible,
  but harmonious.

Bowlahoola is the Stomach in every individual man.

Los is by mortals nam'd Time, Enitharmon is nam'd Space
But they depict him bald & aged who is in eternal youth
All powerful and his locks flourish like the brows of morning. 70
He is the Spirit of Prophecy, the ever apparent Elias.[9]
Time is the mercy of Eternity; without Time's swiftness
Which is the swiftest of all things: all were eternal torment:
All the Gods of the Kingdoms of Earth labour in Los's Halls.
Every one is a fallen Son of the Spirit of Prophecy. 75
He is the Fourth Zoa, that stood around the Throne Divine.

Loud shout the Sons of Luvah, at the Wine-presses as Los
  descended
With Rintrah & Palamabron in his fires of resistless fury.

27/25

The Wine-press on the Rhine[1] groans loud, but all its central
  beams
Act more terrific in the central Cities of the Nations
Where Human Thought is crushd beneath the iron hand of
  Power. 5

---

8. Curved (double-S-shaped) horn, invented in France (1590); used in England in eighteenth-century
   military bands.
9. Another name for Elijah. After this prophet is swept up into Heaven in a whirlwind, his spirit passes
   to Elisha (2 Kings 2:9 ff.) and is rekindled in John the Baptist (Matthew 11:4, cf. Malachi 4:6).
   Elijah and Moses join Jesus at his transfiguration (Matthew 17:3).
1. Border between France and Germany, a wine-producing region and for centuries the site of warfare (though not in the Napoleonic era). The winepress as instrument of God's wrath, interpreted
   as warfare, derives from Isaiah 63:1–6 and Revelation 14:19–20.

There Los puts all into the Press, the Opressor & the Opressed
Together, ripe for the Harvest & Vintage & ready for the Loom.

They sang at the Vintage. "This is the Last Vintage! & Seed
Shall no more be sown upon Earth, till all the Vintage is over
And all gatherd in, till the Plow has passd over the Nations   10
And the Harrow & heavy thundering Roller upon the mountains."

And loud the Souls howl round the Porches of Golgonooza
Crying "O God deliver us to the Heavens or to the Earths,
That we may preach righteousness & punish the sinner with
    death."
But Los refused, till all the Vintage of Earth was gatherd in.   15

And Los stood & cried to the Labourers of the Vintage in voice
    of awe.

"Fellow Labourers! The Great Vintage & Harvest is now upon
    Earth.
The whole extent of the Globe is explored: Every scatterd Atom
Of Human Intellect now is flocking to the sound of the Trumpet.
All the Wisdom which was hidden in caves & dens, from ancient   20
Time; is now sought out from Animal & Vegetable & Mineral.
The Awakener is come, outstretchd over Europe! the Vision of
    God is fulfilled.
The Ancient Man upon the Rock of Albion Awakes,
He listens to the sounds of War astonishd & ashamed;
He sees his Children mock at Faith and deny Providence;   25
Therefore you must bind the Sheaves not by Nations or Families
You shall bind them in Three Classes; according to their Classes
So shall you bind them. Separating What has been Mixed[2]
Since Men began to be Wove into Nations by Rahab & Tirzah
Since Albion's Death & Satan's Cutting-off from our awful Fields;   30
When under pretence to benevolence the Elect Subdud All
From the Foundation of the World. The Elect is one Class: You
Shall bind them separate: they cannot Believe in Eternal Life
Except by Miracle & a New Birth. The other two Classes;
The Reprobate who never cease to Believe, and the Redeemd,   35
Who live in doubts & fears perpetually tormented by the Elect,
These you shall bind in a twin-bundle for the Consummation—
But the Elect must be saved [from] fires of Eternal Death,
To be formed into the Churches of Beulah that they destroy not
    the Earth
For in every Nation & every Family the Three Classes are born   40
And in every Species of Earth, Metal, Tree, Fish, Bird & Beast,
We form the Mundane Egg, that Spectres coming by fury or amity
All is the same, & every one remains in his own energy.
Go forth Reapers with rejoicing; you sowed in tears
But the time of your refreshing cometh, only a little moment   45
Still abstain from pleasure & rest, in the labours of eternity

---

2. An elaboration of the harvest imagery of Joel 3:13, Micah 4:12–13, Revelation 14:15, amplified by
the parable of the wheat and the tares (Matthew 13:24–30).

And you shall Reap the whole Earth, from Pole to Pole! from
    Sea to Sea
Begining at Jerusalem's Inner Court, Lambeth[3] ruin'd and given
To the detestable Gods of Priam, to Apollo: and at the Asylum[4]
Given to Hercules, who labour in Tirzah's Looms for bread   50
Who set Pleasure against Duty: who Create Olympic crowns
To make Learning a burden & the Work of the Holy Spirit: Strife.
To Thor & cruel Odin[5] who first reard the Polar Caves
Lambeth mourns, calling Jerusalem; she weeps & looks abroad
For the Lord's coming, that Jerusalem may overspread all Nations. 55
Crave not for the mortal & perishing delights, but leave them
To the weak, and pity the weak as your infant care; Break not
Forth in your wrath lest you also are vegetated by Tirzah
Wait till the Judgement is past, till the Creation is consumed
And then rush forward with me into the glorious spiritual   60
Vegetation; the Supper of the Lamb & his Bride;[6] and the
Awaking of Albion our friend and ancient companion."

So Los spoke. But lightnings of discontent broke on all sides
    round
And murmurs of thunder rolling heavy long & loud over the
    mountains
While Los calld his Sons around him to the Harvest & the Vintage. 65

Thou[7] seest the Constellations in the deep & wondrous Night
They rise in order and continue their immortal courses
Upon the mountains & in vales with harp & heavenly song
With flute & clarion; with cups & measures filld with foaming
    wine.
Glittring the streams reflect the Vision of beatitude,   70
And the calm Ocean joys beneath & smooths his awful waves!

These are the Sons of Los, & these the Labourers of the
    Vintage   28/26
Thou seest the gorgeous clothed Flies that dance & sport in
    summer
Upon the sunny brooks & meadows: every one the dance
Knows in its intricate mazes of delight artful to weave:
Each one to sound his instruments of music in the dance,   5
To touch each other & recede; to cross & change & return:
These are the Children of Los; thou seest the Trees on mountains
The wind blows heavy, loud they thunder thro' the darksom sky
Uttering prophecies & speaking instructive words to the sons
Of men: These are the Sons of Los! These the Visions of Eternity 10
But we see only as it were the hem of their garments
When with our vegetable eyes we view these wond'rous Visions.

3. Probably referring to Lambeth Palace, residence of the archbishop of Canterbury, near the Blakes'
   home at 13 Hercules Buildings (see map).
4. The Royal Asylum for Female Orphans employed the girls in textile work. Apollo Gardens was a
   run-down amusement park (see map).
5. The Norse gods, known to Blake through P. H. Mallet, *Northern Antiquities* (trans. 1770), are
   "detestable gods of Priam" by other names.
6. See Revelation 19:9, 21:2.
7. Suddenly the reader/viewer is addressed directly, by a fellow mortal (see "we" at **28/26:**11–12); but the
   perspective, from this point through "End of the First Book" appears to be omniscient, or nearly so.

There are Two Gates[8] thro which all Souls descend. One
    Southward
From Dover Cliff to Lizard Point, the other toward the North
Caithness & rocky Durness, Pentland & John Groat's House.[9]   15

The Souls descending to the Body, wail on the right hand
Of Los; & those deliverd from the Body, on the left hand
For Los against the east his force continually bends
Along the Valleys of Middlesex from Hounslow to Blackheath:
Lest those Three Heavens of Beulah should the Creation destroy   20
And lest they should descend before the north & south Gates.
Groaning with pity, he among the wailing Souls laments.

And these the Labours of the Sons of Los in Allamanda:
And in the City of Golgonooza: & in Luban: & around
The Lake of Udan-Adan, in the Forests of Entuthon Benython   25
Where Souls incessant wail, being piteous Passions & Desires
With neither lineament nor form but like to watry clouds
The Passions & Desires descend upon the hungry winds,
For such alone Sleepers remain meer passion & appetite;
The Sons of Los clothe them & feed & provide houses & fields.   30

And every Generated Body in its inward form,
Is a garden of delight & a building of magnificence,
Built by the Sons of Los in Bowlahoola & Allamanda
And the herbs & flowers & furniture & beds & chambers
Continually woven in the Looms of Enitharmon's Daughters   35
In bright Cathedron's golden Dome with care & love & tears.
For the various Classes of Men are all markd out determinate
In Bowlahoola; & as the Spectres choose their affinities
So they are born on Earth, & every Class is determinate
But not by Natural but by Spiritual power alone. Because   40
The Natural power continually seeks & tends to Destruction
Ending in Death: which would of itself be Eternal Death
And all are Class'd by Spiritual, & not by Natural power.

And every Natural Effect has a Spiritual Cause, and Not
A Natural: for a Natural Cause only seems, it is a Delusion   45
Of Ulro: & a ratio of the perishing Vegetable Memory.

But the Wine-press of Los is eastward of Golgonooza, before
    the Seat   29/27
Of Satan. Luvah laid the foundation & Urizen finish'd it in
    howling Woe.
How red the sons & daughters of Luvah! here they tread the
    grapes,
Laughing & shouting, drunk with odours, many fall oerwearied
Drownd in the wine is many a youth & maiden: those around   5
Lay them on skins of Tygers & of the spotted Leopard & the Wild
    Ass
Till they revive, or bury them in cool grots, making lamentation.

8. See Baine, cited in n. 7, p. 54 herein.
9. From the far southwest tip of Cornwall to the northeast tip of Scotland, near the Orkney Islands
   (see "Blake's Britain" map).

This Wine-press is call'd War on Earth, it is the Printing-Press
Of Los; and here he lays his words in order above the mortal brain
As cogs are formd in a wheel to turn the cogs of the adverse wheel.   10

Timbrels & violins sport round the Wine-presses; the little Seed;
The sportive Root, the Earth-worm, the gold Beetle; the wise
     Emmet;
Dance round the Wine-presses of Luvah: the Centipede is there:
The ground Spider with many eyes: the Mole clothed in velvet
The ambitious Spider in his sullen web; the lucky golden Spinner;   15
The Earwig armd: the tender Maggot emblem of immortality:
The Flea: Louse: Bug: the Tape-Worm: all the Armies of Disease:
Visible or invisible to the slothful vegetating Man.
The slow Slug: the Grasshopper that sings & laughs & drinks:
Winter comes, he folds his slender bones without a murmur.   20
The cruel Scorpion is there: the Gnat: Wasp: Hornet & the
     Honey Bee:
The Toad & venomous Newt; the Serpent clothd in gems & gold:
They throw off their gorgeous raiment: they rejoice with loud
     jubilee
Around the Wine-presses of Luvah, naked & drunk with wine.

There is the Nettle that stings with soft down; and there   25
The indignant Thistle: whose bitterness is bred in his milk:
Who feeds on contempt of his neighbour: there all the idle Weeds
That creep around the obscure places shew their various limbs,
Naked in all their beauty dancing round the Wine-presses.

But in the Wine-presses the Human grapes sing not, nor dance   30
They howl & writhe in shoals of torment; in fierce flames
     consuming,
In chains of iron & in dungeons circled with ceaseless fires.
In pits & dens & shades of death: in shapes of torment & woe.
The plates & screws & wracks & saws & cords & fires & cisterns
The cruel joys of Luvah's Daughters lacerating with knives   35
And whips their Victims & the deadly sport of Luvah's Sons.

They dance around the dying, & they drink the howl & groan
They catch the shrieks in cups of gold, they hand them to one
     another:
These are the sports of love, & these the sweet delights of amorous
     play
Tears of the grape, the death sweat of the cluster, the last sigh   40
Of the mild youth who listens to the lureing songs of Luvah.

But Allamanda, calld on Earth Commerce, is the Cultivated land
Around the City of Golgonooza in the Forests of Entuthon:
Here the Sons of Los labour against Death Eternal; through all
The Twenty-seven Heavens of Beulah in Ulro, Seat of Satan,   45
Which is the False Tongue beneath Beulah: it is the Sense of
     Touch:
The Plow goes forth in tempests & lightnings & the narrow cruel
In blights of the east; the heavy Roller follows in howlings of woe.

Urizen's sons here labour also; & here are seen the Mills
Of Theotormon, on the verge of the Lake of Udan-Adan: 50
These are the starry voids of night & the depths & caverns of earth.
These Mills are oceans, clouds & waters ungovernable in their fury.
Here are the stars created & the seeds of all things planted
And here the Sun & Moon recieve their fixed destinations.

But in Eternity the Four Arts: Poetry, Painting, Music,   55
And Architecture which is Science: are the Four Faces of Man.
Not so in Time & Space: there Three are shut out, and only
Science remains thro Mercy: & by means of Science, the Three
Become apparent in time & space, in the Three Professions

That Man may live upon Earth till the time of his awaking,[1]
And from these Three, Science derives every Occupation of Men.
And Science is divided into Bowlahoola & Allamanda.

Some Sons of Los surround the Passions with porches of iron
    & silver $\boxed{30/28}$
Creating form & beauty around the dark regions of sorrow,
Giving to airy nothing a name and a habitation[2]
Delightful! with bounds to the Infinite putting off the Indefinite
Into most holy forms of Thought: (such is the power of inspiration)   5
They labour incessant; with many tears & afflictions:
Creating the beautiful House for the piteous sufferer.

Others, Cabinets richly fabricate of gold & ivory;
For Doubts & fears unform'd & wretched & melancholy
The little weeping Spectre stands on the threshold of Death   10
Eternal; and sometimes two Spectres like lamps quivering
And often malignant they combat (heart-breaking sorrowful &
    piteous).
Antamon[3] takes them into his beautiful flexible hands,
As the Sower takes the seed, or as the Artist his clay
Or fine wax, to mould artful a model for golden ornaments,   15
The soft hands of Antamon draw the indelible line:
Form immortal with golden pen; such as the Spectre admiring
Puts on the sweet form; then smiles Antamon bright thro his
    windows.
The Daughters of beauty look up from their Loom & prepare
The integument soft for its clothing with joy & delight.   20

But Theotormon & Sotha stand in the Gate of Luban anxious.
Their numbers are seven million & seven thousand & seven
    hundred.
They contend with the weak Spectres, they fabricate soothing
    forms.
The Spectre refuses, he seeks cruelty, they create the crested Cock.

---

1. Line 60, "Poetry in Religion: Music, Law: Painting, in Physic & Surgery," appears only in Copy A;
   erased from other copies.
2. Variation on Theseus' formula for poetry in *Midsummer Night's Dream* V.i.14–17 (cf. **39/35**:49).
3. An artistic son of Los, along with Sotha (**30/28**:21), Ozoth (**30/28**:29), and others (**30/28**:44) not
   developed elsewhere in Blake's work.

Terrified the Spectre screams & rushes in fear into their Net   25
Of kindness & compassion & is born a weeping terror.
Or they create the Lion & Tyger in compassionate thunderings
Howling the Spectres flee: they take refuge in Human lineaments.

The Sons of Ozoth within the Optic Nerve stand fiery glowing
And the number of his Sons is eight millions & eight.   30
They give delights to the man unknown; artificial riches
They give to scorn, & their posessors to trouble & sorrow & care,
Shutting the sun, & moon, & stars, & trees, & clouds, & waters,
And hills, out from the Optic Nerve & hardening it into a bone
Opake, and like the black pebble on the enraged beach.   35
While the poor indigent is like the diamond which tho cloth'd
In rugged covering in the mine, is open all within
And in his hallowd center holds the heavens of bright eternity.
Ozoth here builds walls of rocks against the surging sea
And timbers crampt with iron cramps bar in the joys of life   40
From fell destruction in the Spectrous cunning or rage. He Creates
The speckled Newt, the Spider & Beetle, the Rat & Mouse,
The Badger & Fox: they worship before his feet in trembling fear.

But others of the Sons of Los build Moments & Minutes & Hours
And Days & Months & Years & Ages & Periods; wondrous buildings   45
And every Moment has a Couch of gold for soft repose,
(A Moment equals a pulsation of the artery),
And between every two Moments stands a Daughter of Beulah
To feed the Sleepers on their Couches with maternal care.
And every Minute has an azure Tent with silken Veils.   50
And every Hour has a bright golden Gate carved with skill.
And every Day & Night has Walls of brass & Gates of adamant,
Shining like precious stones & ornamented with appropriate
    signs:
And every Month, a silver paved Terrace builded high:
And every Year, invulnerable Barriers with high Towers.   55
And every Age is Moated deep with Bridges of silver & gold.
And every Seven Ages is Incircled with a Flaming Fire.
Now Seven Ages is amounting to Two Hundred Years.
Each has its Guard, each Moment Minute Hour Day Month &
    Year,
All are the work of Fairy hands of the Four Elements.   60
The Guard are Angels of Providence on duty evermore.
Every Time less than a pulsation of the artery
Is equal in its period & value to Six Thousand Years.

For in this Period the Poet's Work is Done: and all the Great | 31/29 |
Events of Time start forth & are concievd in such a Period
Within a Moment: a Pulsation of the Artery.

The Sky is an immortal tent built by the Sons of Los
And every Space that a Man views around his dwelling-place: 5
Standing on his own roof, or in his garden on a mount
Of twenty-five cubits in height, such space is his Universe;
And on its verge the Sun rises & sets, the Clouds bow

To meet the flat Earth[4] & the Sea in such an orderd Space:
The Starry heavens reach no further but here bend and set,   10
On all sides & the two Poles turn on their valves of gold:
And if he move his dwelling-place, his heavens also move,
Wher'eer he goes & all his neighbourhood bewail his loss:
Such are the Spaces called Earth & such its dimension:
As to that false appearance which appears to the reasoner,   15
As of a Globe rolling thro Voidness, it is a delusion of Ulro.
The Microscope knows not of this nor the Telescope; they alter
The ratio of the Spectator's Organs but leave Objects untouchd.
For every Space larger than a red Globule of Man's blood
Is visionary: and is created by the Hammer of Los   20
And every Space smaller than a Globule of Man's blood opens
Into Eternity of which this vegetable Earth is but a shadow:
The red Globule is the unwearied Sun by Los created
To measure Time and Space to mortal Men, every morning.
Bowlahoola & Allamanda are placed on each side   25
Of that Pulsation & that Globule, terrible their power.

But Rintrah & Palamabron govern over Day & Night
In Allamanda & Entuthon Benython where Souls wail:
Where Orc incessant howls, burning in fires of Eternal Youth,
Within the vegetated mortal Nerves; for every Man born is
    joined
                                                                        30
Within into One mighty Polypus, and this Polypus is Orc.

But in the Optic vegetative Nerves Sleep was transformed
To Death in old time by Satan the father of Sin & Death
And Satan is the Spectre of Orc & Orc is the generate Luvah.

But in the Nerves of the Nostrils, Accident being formed   35
Into Substance & Principle, by the cruelties of Demonstration
It became Opake & Indefinite; but the Divine Saviour
Formed it into a Solid by Los's Mathematic power.
He named the Opake Satan: he named the Solid Adam.[5]

And in the Nerves of the Ear, (for the Nerves of the Tongue are
    closed)
                                                                        40
On Albion's Rock Los stands creating the glorious Sun each
    morning
And when unwearied in the evening he creates the Moon
Death to delude, who all in terror at their splendor leaves
His prey while Los appoints, & Rintrah & Palamabron guide
The Souls clear from the Rock of Death, that Death himself may
    wake
                                                                        45
In his appointed season when the ends of heaven meet.

Then Los conducts the Spirits to be Vegetated, into
Great Golgonooza, free from the four iron pillars of Satan's
    Throne

4. The earth as directly experienced, rather than as intellectually constructed. Similarly, Milton chose
    to incorporate features of the Ptolemaic system into the cosmology of *Paradise Lost* even though
    he knew of Galileo's discoveries validating the Copernican system.
5. Limits of opacity and contraction in 14/13:20.

(Temperance, Prudence, Justice, Fortitude, the four pillars
    of tyranny)[6]
That Satan's Watch-Fiends touch them not before they Vegetate.   50

But Enitharmon and her Daughters take the pleasant charge,
To give them to their lovely heavens till the Great Judgment Day
Such is their lovely charge. But Rahab & Tirzah pervert
Their mild influences; therefore the Seven Eyes of God walk
    round
The Three Heavens of Ulro, where Tirzah & her Sisters   55
Weave the black Woof of Death upon Entuthon Benython
In the Vale of Surrey where Horeb terminates in Rephaim.
The stamping feet of Zelophehad's Daughters are coverd with
    Human gore
Upon the treddles of the Loom, they sing to the winged shuttle:
The River rises above his banks to wash the Woof: 60
He takes it in his arms: he passes it in strength thro his current.
The veil of human miseries is woven over the Ocean
From the Atlantic to the Great South Sea, the Erythrean.[7]

Such is the World of Los the labour of six thousand years.
Thus Nature is a Vision of the Science of the Elohim.   65

End of the First Book.

6. The four cardinal virtues of the Catholic Church; cf. Thomas Aquinas, *Summa Theologica* 2.2.Q47–170.
7. The Red Sea, which flows into the Indian Ocean, or "the great Southern sea," according to Blake's probable source (Essick and Viscomi, 1993): Jacob Bryant's *New System* 3 (1776), 185–186.

Milton.   33/30
Book the Second.

How wide the Gulf & Unpassable between Simplicity and Insipidity[1]
Contraries are Positives A Negation is not a Contrary

There is a place where Contrarieties are equally True
This place is called Beulah.[2] It is a pleasant lovely Shadow
Where no dispute can come. Because of those who Sleep.
Into this place the Sons & Daughters of Ololon descended
With solemn mourning into Beulah's moony shades & hills   5
Weeping for Milton: mute wonder held the Daughters of Beulah
Enrapturd with affection sweet and mild benevolence.

Beulah is evermore Created around Eternity; appearing
To the Inhabitants of Eden, around them on all sides.
But Beulah to its Inhabitants appears within each district   10
As the beloved infant in his mother's bosom round incircled
With arms of love & pity & sweet compassion. But to
The Sons of Eden the moony habitations of Beulah,
Are from Great Eternity a mild & pleasant Rest.

And it is thus Created. Lo the Eternal Great Humanity   15
To whom be Glory & Dominion Evermore Amen[3]
Walks among all his awful Family seen in every face
As the breath of the Almighty, such are the words of man to man
In the great Wars of Eternity, in fury of Poetic Inspiration,
To build the Universe stupendous: Mental forms Creating.   20

But the Emanations trembled exceedingly, nor could they
Live, because the life of Man was too exceeding unbounded
His joy became terrible to them they trembled & wept
Crying with one voice, "Give us a habitation & a place
In which we may be hidden under the shadow of wings[4]   25
For if we who are but for a time, & who pass away in winter
Behold these wonders of Eternity we shall consume:
But you O our Fathers & Brothers, remain in Eternity
But grant us a Temporal Habitation; do you speak
To us; we will obey your words as you obey Jesus   30
The Eternal who is blessed for ever & ever. Amen."

So spake the lovely Emanations; & there appeard a pleasant
Mild Shadow above: beneath: & on all sides round.

Into this pleasant Shadow all the weak & weary   34/31
Like Women & Children were taken away as on wings

1. The design (not included in this edition) incorporates the mottoes (this line and the next) in mirror writing above and below "Milton."
2. A dreamy "threefold" state (cf. 4:5) of sexual fulfillment (for biblical and literary sources, see n. 3,
   p. 148). Blake's four levels of vision, from fourfold to single, are set forth, without names, in
   descending order at the end of his letter-poem to Butts of November 22, 1802 (p. 479 herein).
   Here inhabitants of Beulah are represented as women and children; inhabitants of Eden as men.
   But see "sisters" in *Jerusalem* 38/34:9–22.
3. Derived from 1 Peter 5:11 and Revelation 1:6. Cf. the end of the Bard's song (M 15/14:3).
4. An image from David's prayer for protection (Psalm 17:8).

Of dovelike softness, & shadowy habitations prepared for them.
But every Man returnd & went still going forward thro'
The Bosom of the Father in Eternity, on Eternity.
Neither did any lack or fall into Error without   5
A Shadow to repose in all the Days of happy Eternity.
Into this pleasant Shadow Beulah, all Ololon descended
And when the Daughters of Beulah heard the lamentation
All Beulah wept, for they saw the Lord coming in the Clouds   10
And the Shadows of Beulah terminate in rocky Albion.

And all Nations wept in affliction Family by Family:
Germany wept towards France & Italy: England wept & trembled
Towards America: India rose up from his golden bed:
As one awakend in the night: they saw the Lord coming   15
In the Clouds of Ololon with Power & Great Glory!⁵

And all the Living Creatures of the Four Elements wail'd
With bitter wailing: these in the aggregate are named Satan
And Rahab: they know not of Regeneration, but only of
     Generation.
The Fairies, Nymphs, Gnomes & Genii of the Four Elements   20
Unforgiving & unalterable: these cannot be Regenerated
But must be Created, for they know only of Generation.
These are the Gods of the Kingdoms of the Earth: in contrarious
And cruel opposition: Element against Element, opposed in War
Not Mental, as the Wars of Eternity, but a Corporeal Strife   25
In Los's Halls, continual labouring in the Furnaces of Golgonooza.
Orc howls on the Atlantic: Enitharmon trembles: All Beulah weeps.

Thou hearest the Nightingale begin the Song of Spring;
The Lark sitting upon his earthy bed: just as the morn
Appears; listens silent; then springing from the waving Corn-field!
     loud
He leads the Choir of Day! trill, trill, trill, trill,   30
Mounting upon the wings of light into the Great Expanse:
Reecchoing against the lovely blue & shining heavenly Shell:
His little throat labours with inspiration; every feather
On throat & breast & wings vibrates with the effluence Divine.   35
All Nature listens silent to him & the awful Sun
Stands still upon the Mountain looking on this little Bird
With eyes of soft humility, & wonder love & awe.
Then loud from their green covert all the Birds begin their Song
The Thrush, the Linnet & the Goldfinch, Robin & the Wren   40
Awake the Sun from his sweet reverie upon the Mountain:
The Nightingale again assays his song, & thro the day,
And thro the night warbles luxuriant; every Bird of Song
Attending his loud harmony with admiration & love.
This is a Vision of the lamentation of Beulah over Ololon!   45

Thou percievest the Flowers put forth their precious Odours!
And none can tell how from so small a center comes such sweets

5. A sign of the end of time (Matthew 24:30); cf. M 23/21:60 and 39/35:41.

Forgetting that within that Center Eternity expands
Its ever during doors,[6] that Og & Anak fiercely guard.
First eer the morning breaks joy opens in the flowery bosoms   50
Joy even to tears, which the Sun rising dries; first the Wild Thyme
And Meadow-sweet downy & soft waving among the reeds,
Light springing on the air lead the sweet Dance: they wake
The Honeysuckle sleeping on the Oak: the flaunting beauty
Revels along upon the wind; the White-thorn lovely May   55
Opens her many lovely eyes: listening, the Rose still sleeps.
None dare to wake her; soon she bursts her crimson curtaind bed
And comes forth in the majesty of beauty; every Flower:
The Pink, the Jessamine, the Wall-flower, the Carnation
The Jonquil, the mild Lilly opes her heavens! every Tree,   60
And Flower & Herb soon fill the air with an innumerable Dance
Yet all in order sweet & lovely. Men are sick with Love!
Such is a Vision of the lamentation of Beulah over Ololon.

And Milton oft sat up on the Couch of Death & oft conversed[7]   35/32
In vision & dream beatific with the Seven Angels of the
    Presence.

"I have turned my back upon these Heavens builded on cruelty.
My Spectre still wandering thro' them follows my Emanation,
He hunts her footsteps thro' the snow & the wintry hail & rain.[8]   5
The idiot Reasoner laughs at the Man of Imagination
And from laughter proceeds to murder by undervaluing calumny."

Then Hillel[9] who is Lucifer replied over the Couch of Death
And thus the Seven Angels instructed him & thus they converse.

"We are not Individuals but States: Combinations of Individuals[1]   10
We were Angels of the Divine Presence: & were Druids in
    Annandale
Compelld to combine into Form by Satan, the Spectre of Albion,
Who made himself a God &, destroyed the Human Form Divine.
But the Divine Humanity & Mercy gave us a Human Form
Because we were combind in Freedom & holy Brotherhood[2]   15
While those combind by Satan's Tyranny first in the blood of War
And Sacrifice & next, in Chains of imprisonment: are Shapeless
    Rocks
Retaining only Satan's Mathematic Holiness, Length: Bredth &
    Highth,
Calling the Human Imagination: which is the Divine Vision &
    Fruition

6. Cf. "Heaven's "ever-during gates" (*PL* 7.206).
7. This page (Bentley "c"), absent from copies A and B, appears after 36/33 in copy C.
8. Cf. "My Spectre," Notebook (p. 391 herein).
9. A variation on "helel," the day-star, translated "Lucifer" (Isaiah 14:12), the first of the Seven Eyes
    of God. Here he apparently speaks for all seven, who as a group are generally reliable.
1. This distinction, analogous to that between the sin and the sinner, allows for universal salvation:
    annihilation of states replaces damnation of individuals.
2. In the margin alongside lines 14–15 Blake inscribed Hebrew letters that may be transliterated
    Khrbm, not a real word but perhaps an attempted pun on *cherubim* and *kerabim* (multitudes), fol-
    lowed by "as multitudes" and "Vox Populi" (voice of the people).

In which Man liveth eternally: madness & blasphemy, against   20
Its own Qualities, which are Servants of Humanity, not Gods or
    Lords.
Distinguish therefore States from Individuals in those States.
States Change: but Individual Identities never change nor cease:
You cannot go to Eternal Death in that which can never Die.
Satan & Adam are States Created into Twenty-seven Churches   25
And thou O Milton art a State about to be Created
Called Eternal Annihilation that none but the Living shall
Dare to enter: & they shall enter triumphant over Death
And Hell & the Grave! States that are not, but ah! Seem to be.

Judge then of thy Own Self: thy Eternal Lineaments explore: 30
What is Eternal & what Changeable? & what Annihilable!

The Imagination is not a State: it is the Human Existence itself
Affection or Love becomes a State, when divided from Imagination
The Memory is a State always, & the Reason is a State
Created to be Annihilated & a new Ratio Created.   35
Whatever can be Created can be Annihilated; Forms cannot.
The Oak is cut down by the Ax, the Lamb falls by the Knife
But their Forms Eternal Exist, For-ever. Amen Hallelujah!"

Thus they converse with the Dead watching round the Couch
    of Death.
For God himself enters Death's Door always with those that enter   40
And lays down in the Grave with them, in Visions of Eternity
Till they awake & see Jesus & the Linen Clothes lying
That the Females had Woven for them, & the Gates of their
    Father's House
And the Divine Voice was heard in the Songs of Beulah Saying | 36/33 |

"When I first Married you, I gave you all my whole Soul,
I thought that you would love my loves & joy in my delights
Seeking for pleasures in my pleasures O Daughter of Babylon.
Then thou wast lovely, mild & gentle, now thou art terrible   5
In jealousy & unlovely in my sight, because thou hast cruelly
Cut off my loves in fury till I have no love left for thee.
Thy love depends on him thou lovest & on his dear loves
Depend thy pleasures which thou hast cut off by jealousy.
Therefore I shew my jealousy & set before you Death.   10
Behold Milton descended to Redeem the Female Shade
From Death Eternal; such your lot, to be continually Redeem'd
By death & misery of those you love & by Annihilation.
When the Sixfold Female percieves that Milton annihilates
Himself: that seeing all his loves by her cut off: he leaves   15
Her also: intirely abstracting himself from Female loves
She shall relent in fear of death: She shall begin to give
Her maidens to her husband: delighting in his delight.
And then & then alone begins the happy Female joy
As it is done in Beulah, & thou O Virgin Babylon Mother of
    Whoredoms   20
Shalt bring Jerusalem in thine arms in the night watches; and

No longer turning her a wandering Harlot in the streets
Shalt give her into the arms of God your Lord & Husband."³

Such are the Songs of Beulah in the Lamentations of Ololon.

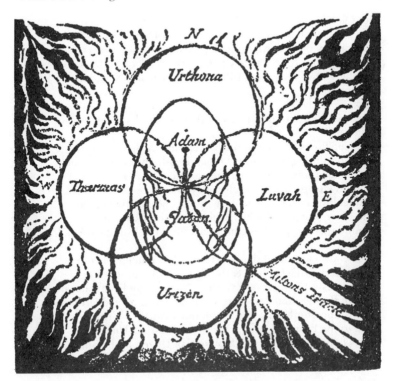

And all the Songs of Beulah sounded comfortable notes   38/34
To comfort Ololon's lamentation, for they said
"Are you the Fiery Circle that late drove in fury & fire
The Eight Immortal Starry-Ones down into Ulro dark⁴
Rending the Heavens of Beulah with your thunders &
     lightnings?   5
And can you thus lament & can you pity & forgive?
Is terror changd to pity O wonder of Eternity!"

And the Four States of Humanity in its Repose
Were shewed them.⁵ First of Beulah a most pleasant Sleep
On Couches soft, with mild music, tended by Flowers of
     Beulah,   10
Sweet Female forms, winged or floating in the air spontaneous;
The Second State is Alla & the third State Al-Ulro;
But the Fourth State is dreadful; it is named Or-Ulro:
The First State is in the Head, the Second is in the Heart:

3. Modeled on the patriarchs' wives' bestowal of their handmaidens on their husbands (Genesis 16,
   30). Cf. Oothoon's rhapsody on capturing "girls" for her lover (*Visions* 10/7:23–29). On the extent
   to which Blake, in critiquing Milton's misogyny, falls into the same trap, see Ostriker (p. 560 herein).
4. See **22**/20:45–46; **23**/21:31–34.
5. Ololon is still plural; see also "They" in line 50.

The Third in the Loins & Seminal Vessels & the Fourth   15
In the Stomach & Intestines terrible, deadly, unutterable
And he whose Gates are opend in those Regions of his Body
Can from those Gates view all these wondrous Imaginations.[6]

But Ololon sought the Or-Ulro & its fiery Gates
And the Couches of the Martyrs: & many Daughters of Beulah   20
Accompany them down to the Ulro with soft melodious tears,
A long journey & dark thro Chaos in the track of Milton's course
To where the Contraries of Beulah War beneath Negation's
    Banner.

Then view'd from Milton's Track they see the Ulro: a vast
    Polypus
Of living fibres down into the Sea of Time & Space growing   25
A self-devouring monstrous human Death Twenty-seven fold.
Within it sit Five Females & the nameless Shadowy Mother
Spinning it from their bowels with songs of amorous delight
And melting cadences that lure the Sleepers of Beulah down
The River Storge[7] (which is Arnon) into the Dead Sea: 30
Around this Polypus Los continual builds the Mundane Shell.

Four Universes round the Universe of Los remain Chaotic,
Four intersecting Globes, & the Egg form'd World of Los
In midst; stretching from Zenith to Nadir, in midst of Chaos.
One of these Ruind Universes is to the North named Urthona;   35
One to the South, this was the glorious World of Urizen;
One to the East, of Luvah; One to the West; of Tharmas.
But when Luvah assumed the World of Urizen in the South
All fell towards the Center sinking downward in dire Ruin.

Here in these Chaoses the Sons of Ololon took their abode   40
In Chasms of the Mundane Shell which open on all sides round
Southward & by the East within the Breach of Milton's descent
To watch the time, pitying & gentle to awaken Urizen.
They stood in a dark land of death of fiery corroding waters
Where lie in evil death the Four Immortals pale and cold   45
And the Eternal Man even Albion upon the Rock of Ages.
Seeing Milton's Shadow, some Daughters of Beulah trembling
Returnd, but Ololon remaind before the Gates of the Dead.

And Ololon looked down into the Heavens of Ulro in fear
They said. "How are the Wars of Man which in Great Eternity   50
Appear around, in the External Spheres of Visionary Life
Here renderd Deadly within the Life & Interior Vision
How are the Beasts & Birds & Fishes, & Plants & Minerals

---

6. This array of four states, apparently linking Beulah to Ulro, is not mentioned elsewhere. Blake's comprehensive fourfold paradigm, set forth by name only in the description of four sets of four gates in *Jerusalem* 12–13, is understood to consist of Eden (an invigorating, fully human life of creativity and fellowship), Beulah (a relaxing sexual paradise), Generation (the everyday world of subjects and objects), and Ulro (a hell of spiritless materiality). Generation is also a fallen reflection of "Regeneration" or Eden (J 7:65), and Ulro is a shattered Beulah (cf. "The Crystal Cabinet"). See Frye's essay on p. 524 herein and his *Fearful Symmetry*; also Adams, *William Blake*.
7. Parental love (Greek).

Here fixd into a frozen bulk subject to decay & death?
Those Visions of Human Life & Shadows of Wisdom &
   Knowledge   55

Are here frozen to unexpansive deadly destroying terrors.   39/35
And War & Hunting:[8] the Two Fountains of the River of Life
Are become Fountains of bitter Death & of corroding Hell
Till Brotherhood is changd into a Curse & a Flattery
By Differences between Ideas, that Ideas themselves, (which are   5
The Divine Members) may be slain in offerings for sin.
O dreadful Loom of Death! O piteous Female forms compelld
To weave the Woof of Death, On Camberwell Tirzah's Courts,
Malah's on Blackheath, Rahab & Noah dwell on Windsor's
   heights,
Where once the Cherubs of Jerusalem spread to Lambeth's Vale   10
Milcah's Pillars shine from Harrow to Hampstead, where Hoglah
On Highgate's heights magnificent Weaves over trembling
   Thames
To Shooters Hill and thence to Blackheath the dark Woof! Loud
Loud roll the Weights & Spindles over the whole Earth, let down
On all sides round to the Four Quarters of the World, eastward on 15
Europe to Euphrates & Hindu, to Nile & back in Clouds
Of Death across the Atlantic to America North & South."

So spake Ololon in reminiscence astonishd, but they
Could not behold Golgonooza without passing the Polypus
A wondrous journey not passable by Immortal feet, & none   20
But the Divine Saviour can pass it without annihilation.
For Golgonooza cannot be seen till, having passd the Polypus,
It is viewed on all sides round by a Four-fold Vision
Or till you become Mortal & Vegetable in Sexuality;
Then you behold its mighty Spires & Domes of ivory & gold.   25

And Ololon examined all the Couches of the Dead.
Even of Los & Enitharmon & all the Sons of Albion
And his Four Zoas terrified & on the verge of Death.
In midst of these was Milton's Couch, & when they saw Eight
Immortal Starry-Ones, guarding the Couch in flaming fires   30
They thunderous utterd all a universal groan falling down
Prostrate before the Starry Eight asking with tears forgiveness
Confessing their crime with humiliation and sorrow.[9]

O how the Starry Eight rejoic'd to see Ololon descended!
And now that a wide road[1] was open to Eternity,   35
By Ololon's descent thro Beulah to Los & Enitharmon,

For mighty were the multitudes of Ololon, vast the extent
Of their great sway, reaching from Ulro to Eternity
Surrounding the Mundane Shell outside in its Caverns

---

8. Intellectual activities (debate and research?) in Eternity (*Jerusalem* 98).
9. Modeled on Eve's prostration before Adam (*PL* 10.393), cf. Leutha's repentance (12/11:35; 13/12:8–11).
1. The opposite of that built by Sin and Death in *Paradise Lost* 9.393.

And through Beulah, and all silent forbore to contend   40
With Ololon for they saw the Lord in the Clouds of Ololon.

There is a Moment in each Day that Satan cannot find[2]
Nor can his Watch Fiends find it, but the Industrious find
This Moment & it multiply, & when it once is found
It renovates every Moment of the Day if rightly placed.   45
In this Moment Ololon descended to Los & Enitharmon
Unseen beyond the Mundane Shell Southward in Milton's track.

Just in this Moment when the morning odours rise abroad
And first from the Wild Thyme, stands a Fountain in a rock
Of crystal flowing into two Streams; one flows thro Golgonooza   50
And thro Beulah to Eden beneath Los's western Wall
The other flows thro the Aerial Void & all the Churches
Meeting again in Golgonooza beyond Satan's Seat.

The Wild Thyme is Los's Messenger to Eden, a mighty Demon
Terrible deadly & poisonous, his presence in Ulro dark.   55
Therefore he appears only a small Root creeping in grass
Covering over the Rock of Odours his bright purple mantle
Beside the Fount above the Lark's nest in Golgonooza.
Luvah slept here in death & here is Luvah's empty Tomb.
Ololon sat beside this Fountain on the Rock of Odours.[3]   60

Just at the place to where the Lark mounts, is a Crystal Gate
It is the enterance of the First Heaven named Luther: for
The Lark is Los's Messenger thro the Twenty-seven Churches
That the Seven Eyes of God who walk even to Satan's Seat
Thro all the Twenty-seven Heavens may not slumber nor sleep   65
But the Lark's Nest is at the Gate of Los, at the eastern
Gate of wide Golgonooza & the Lark is Los's Messenger.

When on the highest lift of his light pinions he arrives | 40/36 |
At that bright Gate, another Lark meets him & back to back
They touch their pinions tip tip: and each descend
To their respective Earths & there all night consult with Angels
Of Providence & with the Eyes of God all night in slumbers   5
Inspired: & at the dawn of day send out another Lark
Into another Heaven to carry news upon his wings.
Thus are the Messengers dispatchd till they reach the Earth
    again
In the East Gate of Golgonooza, & the Twenty-eighth bright
Lark met the Female Ololon descending into my Garden.   10
Thus it appears to Mortal eyes & those of the Ulro Heavens
But not thus to Immortals; the Lark is a mighty Angel.

For Ololon step'd into the Polypus within the Mundane Shell
They could not step into Vegetable Worlds without becoming

---

2. Cf. the poet's moment of inspiration, within a pulsation of the artery (31/29:3)
3. Both the Wild Thyme and the Lark (cf. *M* **34**/31:29) have Shakespearean associations: the flower
   covering Titania's bower (*Midsummer Night's Dream* 2.1.249; cf. Milton's "Lycidas" 40) and the
   dawn-bird singing "at heaven's gate" (Sonnet 29).

The enemies of Humanity except in a Female Form   15
And as One Female, Ololon and all its mighty Hosts
Appear'd: a Virgin of twelve years[4] nor time nor space was
To the perception of the Virgin Ololon, but as the
Flash of lightning but more quick the Virgin in my Garden
Before my Cottage stood, for the Satanic Space is delusion.   20

For when Los joind with me he took me in his firy whirlwind.
My Vegetated portion was hurried from Lambeth's shades
He set me down in Felpham's Vale & prepard a beautiful
Cottage for me that in three years I might write all these
  Visions[5]
To display Nature's cruel holiness: the deceits of Natural
  Religion.   25
Walking in my Cottage Garden, sudden I beheld
The Virgin Ololon & address'd her as a Daughter of Beulah:

"Virgin of Providence fear not to enter into my Cottage
What is thy message to thy friend: What am I now to do?
Is it again to plunge into deeper affliction? behold me   30
Ready to obey, but pity thou my Shadow of Delight[6]
Enter my Cottage, comfort her, for she is sick with fatigue."

The Virgin answerd. "Knowest thou of Milton who
  descended   ┌─────────┐
Driven from Eternity; him I seek! terrified at my Act   │ 41/37 │
In Great Eternity which thou knowest! I come him to seek!"   └─────────┘

So Ololon utterd in words distinct the anxious thought.
Mild was the voice, but more distinct than any earthly,   5
That Milton's Shadow heard & condensing all his Fibres
Into a strength impregnable of majesty & beauty infinite
I saw he was the Covering Cherub[7] & within him Satan
And Rahab, in an outside which is fallacious! within
Beyond the outline of Identity, in the Selfhood deadly   10
And he appeard the Wicker Man of Scandinavia[8] in whom
Jerusalem's children consume in flames among the Stars.

---

4. Neither hesitant like Thel nor a victim of rape like Oothoon, but hardly old enough to be called a "virgin," Ololon is shortly to give up her virginity (**49/40**:3). Male or female virginity on the sexual plane corresponds to Selfhood on the human plane.
5. Blake may have brought a draft of this work back to London (cf. letter of April 25, 1803, p. 483 herein); but see the headnote on the dating of the fiinished book.
6. Catherine Blake, whose health suffered at Felpham.
7. The full manifestation of ultimate evil (foreshadowed in 9:51, **20/18**:37, **25/23**:10 ff.; **26/24**:28 ff.), based on Ezekiel's (28) condemnation of the Prince of Tyre as one who had claimed to be God, perfect in wisdom and beauty, who had been in Eden, who was covered with every precious stone, who had been upon the holy mountain (Horeb/Sinai) and had walked up and down in the midst of the stones of fire—imagery that is strikingly similar to the precious stones and fire associated with God himself (Exodus 24:10; Deuteronomy 4:24, 9:3; Psalm 18:8; Hebrews 12:29). This image of holiness, probably also to be identified with the cherubim guarding Eden (Genesis 3:24) and those covering the mercy seat above the Ark of the Covenant (Exodus 25:20) in the Holy of Holies (1 Kings 6:23–28), stands between fallen humanity and Divine Humanity and prevents the return to Eden and recognition of the divinity within, which is the Holy Spirit or human imagination.
8. Described in Caesar's *Commentaries: Gallic Wars* 6:16 as a figure "of immense size whose limbs, woven out of twigs, they fill with living men and set on fire"; see *Jerusalem* 47.3 ff.

Blakes Cottage at Felpham.

Descending down into my Garden, a Human Wonder of God
Reaching from heaven to earth a Cloud & Human Form
I beheld Milton with astonishment & in him beheld   15
The Monstrous Churches of Beulah, the Gods of Ulro dark
Twelve monstrous dishumanizd terrors, Synagogues of Satan.
A Double Twelve & Thrice Nine: such their divisions.

And these their Names & their Places within the Mundane Shell
In Tyre & Sidon I saw Baal & Ashtaroth. In Moab, Chemosh;   20
In Ammon, Molech: loud his Furnaces rage among the Wheels
Of Og, & pealing loud the cries of the Victims of Fire!
And pale his Priestesses infolded in Veils of Pestilence, border'd
With War; Woven in Looms of Tyre & Sidon by beautiful
     Ashtaroth.
In Palestine Dagon, Sea Monster! worshipd o'er the Sea.   25
Thammuz in Lebanon & Rimmon in Damascus curtaind
Osiris: Isis: Orus: in Egypt: dark their Tabernacles on Nile
Floating with solemn songs, & on the Lakes of Egypt nightly
With pomp, even till morning break & Osiris appear in the sky
But Belial of Sodom & Gomorrha, obscure Demon of Bribes   30
And secret Assasinations, not worshipd nor adord; but
With the finger on the lips & the back turnd to the light
And Saturn, Jove & Rhea of the Isles of the Sea remote.
These Twelve Gods are the Twelve Spectre Sons of the Druid
     Albion.

And these the names of the Twenty-seven Heavens & their
     Churches[9]
         35
Adam, Seth, Enos, Cainan, Mahalaleel, Jared, Enoch,
Methuselah, Lamech: these are Giants mighty Hermaphroditic
Noah, Shem, Arphaxad, Cainan the second, Salah, Heber,
Peleg, Reu, Serug, Nahor, Terah, these are the Female-Males

9. Among the twelve gods and their "Churches" (line 16) or "Synagogues" (line 17), the six from the
Bible (lines 20–26) include several who also appear as devils in *Paradise Lost*. For the chief Greek
god Zeus, Blake consistently preferred the Roman names Jupiter or Jove (line 33). Astaroth (lines
20 and 24), Isis (line 27), and Rhea (line 33) were female deities.

A Male within a Female hid as in an Ark & Curtains,   40
Abraham, Moses, Solomon, Paul, Constantine, Charlemaine
Luther, these seven are the Male-Females, the Dragon Forms,
Religion hid in War, a Dragon red & hidden Harlot.[1]

All these are seen in Milton's Shadow who is the Covering
    Cherub
The Spectre of Albion in which the Spectre of Luvah inhabits   45
In the Newtonian Voids between the Substances of Creation.

For the Chaotic Voids outside of the Stars are measured by
The Stars, which are the boundaries of Kingdoms, Provinces
And Empires of Chaos invisible to the Vegetable Man
The Kingdom of Og is in Orion: Sihon is in Ophiucus   50
Og has Twenty-seven Districts; Sihon's Districts Twenty-one
From Star to Star, Mountains & Valleys, terrible dimension
Stretchd out, compose the Mundane Shell, a mighty Incrustation
Of Forty-eight deformed Human Wonders of the Almighty
With Caverns whose remotest bottoms meet again beyond   55
The Mundane Shell in Golgonooza, but the Fires of Los rage
In the remotest bottoms of the Caves, that none can pass
Into Eternity that way, but all descend to Los
To Bowlahoola & Allamanda & to Entuthon Benython.

The Heavens are the Cherub, the Twelve Gods are Satan   60

And the Forty-eight Starry Regions are Cities of the Levites   43/38
The Heads of the Great Polypus, Four-fold twelve enormity
In mighty & mysterious comingling enemy with enemy
Woven by Urizen into Sexes from his mantle of years.
And Milton collecting all his fibres into impregnable strength   5
Descended down a Paved work of all kinds of precious stones
Out from the eastern sky; descending down into my Cottage
Garden: clothed in black, severe & silent he descended.[2]
The Spectre of Satan stood upon the roaring sea & beheld
Milton within his sleeping Humanity! trembling & shuddring   10
He stood upon the waves, a Twenty-seven-fold mighty Demon
Gorgeous & beautiful: loud roll his thunders against Milton
Loud Satan thunderd, loud & dark upon mild Felpham shore
Not daring to touch one fibre he howld round upon the Sea.

I also stood in Satan's bosom & beheld its desolations!   15
A ruind Man: a ruind building of God not made with hands;[3]
Its plains of burning sand, its mountains of marble terrible:
Its pits & declivities flowing with molten ore & fountains
Of pitch & nitre: its ruind palaces & cities & mighty works;

1. Alluding to the "great red dragon" (Revelation 12:3, 9) and the Whore of Babylon (Revelation 17).
   The three sets of nine (three and its multiples are incomplete numbers in Blake's schema) trace
   stages in the development of Judaism and Christianity from Eden to Protestant Europe.
2. This aspect of Milton in Puritan dress, descending down a "Paved work of . . . precious stones" (cf.
   Exodus 24:10), is the Covering Cherub, everything that impedes him in art and love, now coming
   face to face with the true Satan, his own Selfhood.
3. Blake himself experiences the inner desolation of Satan (cf. the "Hell within" of PL 4.20). The
   "house not made with hands" (2 Corinthians 5:1) should be the spiritual body.

Its furnaces of affliction in which his Angels & Emanations   20
Labour with blackend visages among its stupendous ruins
Arches & pyramids & porches, colonades & domes:
In which dwells Mystery Babylon, here is her secret place
From hence she comes forth on the Churches in delight
Here is her Cup filld with its poisons, in these horrid vales   25
And here her scarlet Veil woven in pestilence & war:
Here is Jerusalem bound in chains, in the Dens of Babylon.

In the Eastern porch of Satan's Universe Milton stood & said

"Satan! my Spectre! I know my power thee to annihilate
And be a greater in thy place, & be thy Tabernacle,   30
A covering for thee to do thy will, till one greater comes
And smites me as I smote thee & becomes my covering.
Such are the Laws of thy false Heavns! but Laws of Eternity
Are not such: know thou: I come to Self Annihilation.
Such are the Laws of Eternity that each shall mutually   35
Annihilate himself for others' good, as I for thee.
Thy purpose & the purpose of thy Priests & of thy Churches
Is to impress on men the fear of death; to teach
Trembling & fear, terror, constriction; abject selfishness.
Mine is to teach Men to despise death & to go on   40
In fearless majesty annihilating Self, laughing to scorn
Thy Laws & terrors, shaking down thy Synagogues as webs.
I come to discover before Heavn & Hell the Self righteousness
In all its Hypocritic turpitude, opening to every eye
These wonders of Satan's holiness shewing to the Earth   45
The Idol Virtues of the Natural Heart, & Satan's Seat
Explore in all its Selfish Natural Virtue & put off
In Self annihilation all that is not of God alone:
To put off Self & all I have ever & ever Amen.[4]

Satan heard! Coming in a cloud, with trumpets & flaming fire   50
Saying "I am God the judge of all, the living & the dead[5]
Fall therefore down & worship me, submit thy supreme
Dictate, to my eternal Will & to my dictate bow.
I hold the Balances of Right & Just & mine the Sword
Seven Angels bear my Name & in those Seven I appear   55
But I alone am God & I alone in Heavn & Earth
Of all that live dare utter this, others tremble & bow
Till All Things become One Great Satan, in Holiness $\boxed{44/39}$
Oppos'd to Mercy, and the Divine Delusion Jesus be no more."

Suddenly around Milton on my Path, the Starry Seven
Burnd terrible! my Path became a solid fire, as bright
As the clear Sun & Milton silent came down on my Path.   5
And there went forth from the Starry limbs of the Seven: Forms
Human; with Trumpets innumerable, sounding articulate
As the Seven spake; and they stood in a mighty Column of Fire

4. If Milton should try to annihilate Satan as an external being, he would succeed only in becoming another layer of concealment over evil, a church of "Milton's Religion" (24/22:39).
5. Satan responds by trying even harder to imitate the conventional image of God (see also 44/49:23–28), but Milton can no longer be deceived.

Title page for *Songs of Innocence and of Experience* (1794), plate 1. Copy U, c. 1818.

Details of Adam's and Eve's responses to their fiery expulsion from Paradise vary in the twenty-four copies of *Songs* that Blake issued between 1794 and 1826 (see p. 8). In some, only the backs of the couple's heads can be seen; in others, one face or the other appears to register resignation, pain, despair, or even outrage; and in still others, only Eve looks out while Adam's face remains buried in his arms. This 1818 version is the only one in which the soaring bird carries an egg-shaped object in its beak, perhaps a piece of fruit.

"Infant Joy." *Songs of Innocence and of Experience*, plate 25. Copy Z, 1826.

The text alone gives no hint of the floral setting or the attending fairy. In five versions of *Songs* (and two versions of *Innocence* alone), the protective flame-shaped blossom and the drooping bud are colored blue. For references to critical commentary, see note 6 on p. 25 herein.

"The Sick Rose." *Songs of Innocence and of Experience*, plate 39. Copy Z, 1826.

In all versions of this design, the gowned figures on the upper stems, apparently humanized rosebuds, contrast with the open-armed nude, whose lower body has been seized by the worm in the mature rose. The rose's color, red in most copies, ranges from white to pink to intense crimson, and leaves vary from yellow to green. In this copy, an open area between thorny rose stems at the upper right has been transformed into a third wormy pest, and the wormlike swath extending from the figure on the right clings to another stem. In many copies, the caterpillar at the upper left is distinctly segmented (in Copy AA [1826], it is blue), but the creature in the open rose looks more like an earthworm. See note 1, p. 36.

Title page for *The Book of Thel* (1789), plate **2**/ii, Copy N, c. 1815.

Standing under a bent, vine-entwined willow sapling, the virginal shepherdess Thel observes a dramatic moment of amorous pursuit and resistance among spirits of flamelike flowers, an episode unrecorded in the text. In various copies of this work, Thel's expression ranges from curious to slightly frowning to pensive. Her frame of vision does not encompass the two birds and the flying sprite above her, or the seven miniature occupants of the letters of the title. For further discussion, see p. 49.

Frontispiece for *Visions of the Daughters of Albion* (1793), plate 1/i, Copy P, c. 1818.

In this tableau of constraint, which Blake placed last in two late copies, the heroine Oothoon is oppressed by both her rapist Bromion and her beloved Theotormon. Bromion, his hair standing on end, apparently reacts to something outside the picture frame; Theotormon folds "his black jealous waters round the adulterate pair / Bound black to back in Bromion's caves" where "terror & meekness dwell" (*Visions* **5**/2). Oothoon's wrists, as noted on p. 56, are not visible in the design.

Title page for *Visions of the Daughters of Albion*, Plate 2/ii. Copy P, c. 1818.

Oothoon flees across the ocean, the realm of her lover Theotormon, while look-ing back at a self-hugging bearded and winged figure in flames, presumably the law-giver Urizen, "Creator of men! mistaken Demon of heaven!" (*Visions* 8/5:3), or perhaps Bromion, who "rent her with his thunders" (**4**/3:16). Or Bromion may be at the upper right, the cross-legged, cloud-borne male figure who appears to be orchestrating the storm. The ecstatic dancers and other female denizens of the clouds at left are not mentioned in the poem (introduced on p. 55).

Title page for *The Marriage of Heaven and Hell* (1790), plate 1. Copy G, c. 1818.

In the foreground of the subsurface area, two embracing nudes—one emerging from flames, the other from clouds—will presumably join the couples, individuals, and threesomes who rise toward clouds at the upper right, beneath the root of a dead tree. On the thin surface area occupying the top third of the design, two contrasting couples appear unaware of the eight soaring birds overhead. (For additional contexts, see p. 66.)

Title page for *America a Prophecy* (1793), plate 1/ii. Copy 0, 1821.

Below the clouds, on a rainy battlefield, a woman kisses a fallen warrior, clothed in medieval armor, still grasping his sword; his shoulders and feet rest on the bodies of other dead soldiers. Above, between the main words of the title, studious seated female and male figures, perhaps a sibyl and a prophet, appear absorbed in their books while youthful figures point elsewhere. The nude young woman who springs toward the upper right may be showing the old man—and Blake's readers—the way into the poem (introduced on p. 85).

Surrounding Felpham's Vale, reaching to the Mundane Shell,
    Saying

"Awake Albion awake! reclaim thy Reasoning Spectre. Subdue   10
Him to the Divine Mercy, Cast him down into the Lake
Of Los, that ever burneth with fire, ever & ever Amen!
Let the Four Zoas awake from Slumbers of Six Thousand Years."

Then loud the Furnaces of Los were heard! & seen as Seven
    Heavens
Stretching from south to north over the mountains of Albion.   15

Satan heard; trembling round his Body, he incircled it
He trembled with exceeding great trembling & astonishment
Howling in his Spectre round his Body, hungring to devour
But fearing for the pain for if he touches a Vital,
His torment is unendurable: therefore he cannot devour: 20
But howls round it as a lion round his prey continually.[6]
Loud Satan thunderd, loud & dark upon mild Felpham's Shore
Coming in a Cloud with Trumpets & with Fiery Flame,
An awful Form eastward from midst of a bright Paved-work
Of precious stones by Cherubim surrounded: so permitted   25
(Lest he should fall apart in his Eternal Death) to imitate
The Eternal Great Humanity Divine surrounded by
His Cherubim & Seraphim in ever happy Eternity.
Beneath sat Chaos: Sin on his right hand Death on his left
And Ancient Night spread over all the heavn his Mantle of Laws   30
He trembled with exceeding great trembling & astonishment.

Then Albion rose up in the Night of Beulah on his Couch
Of dread repose seen by the visionary eye; his face is toward
The east, toward Jerusalem's Gates: groaning he sat above
His rocks. London & Bath & Legions[7] & Edinburgh   35
Are the four pillars of his Throne; his left foot near London
Covers the shades of Tyburn: his instep from Windsor
To Primrose Hill stretching to Highgate & Holloway,
London is between his knees: its basements fourfold.
His right foot stretches to the sea on Dover cliffs, his heel   40
On Canterbury's ruins; his right hand covers lofty Wales
His left Scotland; his bosom girt with gold involves
York, Edinburgh, Durham & Carlisle & on the front
Bath, Oxford, Cambridge Norwich; his right elbow
Leans on the Rocks of Erin's Land, Ireland ancient nation;   45
His head bends over London: he sees his embodied Spectre
Trembling before him with exceeding great trembling & fear;
He views Jerusalem & Babylon, his tears flow down.
He movd his right foot to Cornwall, his left to the Rocks of
    Bognor
He strove to rise to walk into the Deep but strength failing   50

6. Cf. 1 Peter 5:8. Although Satan realizes that he is about to be annihilated, he cannot defend him-
    self, because Milton's inmost selfishness is a part of himself.
7. Named by the Romans; formerly an archbishopric in Glamorganshire (combined with Bath in J
    41/37:1). Usually the four major cathedral cities are London (or Canterbury), Verulam, York, and
    Edinburgh (J 46/41:24); see "Blake's Britain" map. For 44/39:37–38, see London map.

Forbad & down with dreadful groans he sunk upon his Couch
In moony Beulah. Los his strong Guard walks round beneath
    the Moon.

Urizen faints in terror striving among the Brooks of Arnon
With Milton's Spirit: as the Plowman or Artificer or Shepherd
While in the labours of his Calling sends his Thought abroad   55
To labour in the ocean or in the starry heaven, So Milton
Labourd in Chasms of the Mundane Shell, tho here before
My Cottage midst the Starry Seven, where the Virgin Ololon
Stood trembling in the Porch: loud Satan thunderd on the
    stormy Sea
Circling Albion's Cliffs in which the Four-fold World resides   60
Tho seen in fallacy outside: a fallacy of Satan's Churches.

Before Ololon Milton stood & percievd the Eternal Form   46/40
Of that mild Vision; wondrous were their acts by me unknown
Except remotely; and I heard Ololon say to Milton

"I see thee strive upon the Brooks of Arnon; there a dread
And awful Man I see, oercoverd with the mantle of years.   5
I behold Los & Urizen. I behold Orc & Tharmas;
The Four Zoa's of Albion & thy Spirit with them striving
In Self annihilation giving thy life to thy enemies.
Are those who contemn Religion & seek to annihilate it
Become in their Feminine portions the causes & promoters   10
Of these Religions, how is this thing? this Newtonian
    Phantasm
This Voltaire & Rousseau: this Hume & Gibbon & Bolingbroke
This Natural Religion! this impossible absurdity!
Is Ololon the cause of this? O where shall I hide my face?
These tears fall for the little-ones: the Children of Jerusalem,   15
Lest they be annihilated in thy annihilation."

No sooner she had spoke but Rahab Babylon appeard
Eastward upon the Paved work across Europe & Asia
Glorious as the midday Sun in Satan's bosom glowing:
A Female hidden in a Male, Religion hidden in War   20
Namd Moral Virtue; cruel two-fold Monster shining bright
A Dragon red & hidden Harlot which John in Patmos saw.[8]

And all beneath the Nations innumerable of Ulro
Appeard the Seven Kingdoms of Canaan & Five Baalim
Of Philistea, into Twelve divided, calld after the Names   25
Of Israel: as they are in Eden. Mountain, River & Plain
City & sandy Desart intermingled beyond mortal ken.

But turning toward Ololon in terrible majesty Milton
Replied. "Obey thou the Words of the Inspired Man
All that can be annihilated must be annihilated,   30
That the Children of Jerusalem may be saved from slavery.
There is a Negation, & there is a Contrary;

8. John had visions "in the isle . . . called Patmos" (Revelation 1:9).

The Negation must be destroyd to redeem the Contraries.
The Negation is the Spectre; the Reasoning Power in Man;
This is a false Body: an Incrustation over my Immortal
Spirit; a Selfhood, which must be put off & annihilated alway.[9]   35
To cleanse the Face of my Spirit by Self-examination,[1]

47

9. Cf. **35**/32:22–23, **35**/32:30–36. Milton has found Selfhood to be a state, a Negation, and therefore annihilable; when Ololon's turn comes in **48**/41:30 ff., she finds virginity to be an annihilable
   state, and when she frees herself from this Negation she meets Milton as his Contrary.
1. Plate **47**, a full-page design depicting Blake's encounter with Los in Book 1 (**24**/22:4–1), was
   moved to Book 2 in Copies C and D.

To bathe in the Waters of Life; to wash off the Not Human,   48/41
I come in Self-annihilation & the grandeur of Inspiration;
To cast off Rational Demonstration by Faith in the Saviour
To cast off the rotten rags of Memory by Inspiration
To cast off Bacon, Locke & Newton from Albion's covering   5
To take off his filthy garments, & clothe him with Imagination
To cast aside from Poetry, all that is not Inspiration
That it no longer shall dare to mock with the aspersion of Madness
Cast on the Inspired, by the tame high finisher of paltry Blots,
Indefinite, or paltry Rhymes; or paltry Harmonies;   10
Who creeps into State Government like a catterpiller to destroy;
To cast off the idiot Questioner who is always questioning,
But never capable of answering; who sits with a sly grin
Silent plotting when to question, like a thief in a cave;
Who publishes doubt & calls it knowledge; whose Science is
    Despair,   15
Whose pretence to knowledge is Envy, whose whole Science is
To destroy the wisdom of ages to gratify ravenous Envy;
That rages round him like a Wolf day & night without rest.
He smiles with condescension; he talks of Benevolence & Virtue
And those who act with Benevolence & Virtue, they murder time
    on time.   20
These are the destroyers of Jerusalem, these are the murderers
Of Jesus, who deny the Faith & mock at Eternal Life:
Who pretend to Poetry that they may destroy Imagination:
By imitation of Nature's Images drawn from Remembrance.
These are the Sexual Garments, the Abomination of Desolation   25
Hiding the Human lineaments as with an Ark & Curtains
Which Jesus rent: & now shall wholly purge away with Fire
Till Generation is swallowd up in Regeneration."

Then trembled the Virgin Ololon & replyd in clouds of despair

"Is this our Feminine Portion, the Six-fold Miltonic Female?   30
Terribly this Portion trembles before thee O awful Man.
Altho' our Human Power can sustain the severe contentions
Of Friendship, our Sexual cannot: but flies into the Ulro.
Hence arose all our terrors in Eternity! & now remembrance
Returns upon us! are we Contraries O Milton, Thou & I?   35
O Immortal! how were we led to War the Wars of Death?
Is this the Void Outside of Existence, which if enterd into
Becomes a Womb? & is this the Death Couch of Albion?   49/42
Thou goest to Eternal Death & all must go with thee."

So saying, the Virgin divided Six-fold & with a shriek
Dolorous that ran thro all Creation, a Double Six-fold Wonder!
Away from Ololon² she divided & fled into the depths   5
Of Milton's Shadow as a Dove upon the stormy Sea.

2. As Ololon's virginity and Milton's Shadow are cast off, and Milton joins the Eight who become one
with Jesus, more signs of the apocalypse appear: "the moon became as blood" (Revelation 6:12; cf.
Joel 2:31), and Ololon becomes Jesus' "vesture dipped in blood" (Revelation 19:13), "written within
and without " (Ezekiel 2:10).

Then as a Moony Ark Ololon descended to Felpham's Vale
In clouds of blood, in streams of gore, with dreadful thunderings
Into the Fires of Intellect that rejoic'd in Felpham's Vale
Around the Starry Eight: with one accord the Starry Eight became   10
One Man Jesus the Saviour, wonderful! round his limbs
The Clouds of Ololon folded as a Garment dipped in blood
Written within & without in woven letters: & the Writing
Is the Divine Revelation in the Litteral expression:
A Garment of War, I heard it namd the Woof of Six Thousand
      Years.   15

And I beheld the Twenty-four Cities of Albion
Arise upon their Thrones to Judge the Nations of the Earth.
And the Immortal Four in whom the Twenty-four appear
      Four-fold
Arose around Albion's body: Jesus wept & walked forth
From Felpham's Vale clothed in Clouds of blood, to enter into   20
Albion's Bosom, the bosom of death & the Four surrounded him
In the Column of Fire in Felpham's Vale; then to their mouths
      the Four
Applied their Four Trumpets & them sounded to the Four winds.

Terror struck in the Vale. I stood at that immortal sound,
My bones trembled. I fell outstretchd upon the path   25
A moment, & my Soul returnd into its mortal state
To Resurrection & Judgment in the Vegetable Body
And my sweet Shadow of Delight stood trembling by my side.

Immediately the Lark mounted with a loud trill from Felpham's
      Vale
And the Wild Thyme from Wimbleton's green & impurpled Hills   30
And Los & Enitharmon rose over the Hills of Surrey
Their clouds roll over London with a south wind, soft Oothoon
Pants in the Vales of Lambeth weeping oer her Human Harvest.
Los listens to the Cry of the Poor Man: his Cloud
Over London in volume terrific, low bended in anger.   35

Rintrah & Palamabron view the Human Harvest beneath;
Their Wine-presses & Barns stand open; the Ovens are prepar'd
The Waggons ready: terrific Lions & Tygers sport & play;
All Animals upon the Earth are prepard in all their strength

To go forth to the Great Harvest & Vintage of the Nations.[3]   50/43

Finis

3. Although the apocalypse has not yet fully occurred (see conclusions of *The Four Zoas* and *Jerusalem*), the resumption of the Great Harvest and Vintage (interrupted by events in the Bard's song) indicates the approach of the end of time (cf. Revelation 14:14–20). For a discussion of the concluding design, see Grant in *Milton Reconsidered* (1976), ed. John Karl Franson.

JERUSALEM: THE EMANATION OF THE GIANT ALBION (1804; c. 1821)

Jerusalem, Blake's longest and most carefully finished work in illuminated printing, the crowning achievement of his career, brings his myth of the fall and recovery of the Divine Humanity to its fullest development. In twice as many pages as the longest version of *Milton*, and on pages twice as large, *Jerusalem* fulfills the promise of apocalypse with which *Milton* ends. Although long stretches of the poem offer scarcely any readerly amenities, numerous biblical, classical, and Miltonic allusions provide a measure of reassurance, as does the work's deceptively orderly framework of four chapters of twenty-five pages each. From the beginning it is clear that Albion, who is both Britain and a cosmic human-divine being, has become estranged from his beloved Emanation Jerusalem, his soul, his best self—a condition of error represented geographically by the separation between biblical and English place names for what should be one landscape in the mind. Jerusalem, "a City yet a Woman," is both the spiritual capital of the British people and the eternal spirit of Liberty in religion and society; she should be the biblical "Bride of the Lamb," but for most of the poem she is a friendless outcast, enslaved and condemned as a harlot.

Flashbacks reveal that Albion has been seduced by the world of appearances, in the form of the beautiful but destructive nature-force Vala, who takes the part of Babylon against Jerusalem. Having hidden Jerusalem from the Divine Vision and succumbed to the delusion that "By demonstration, man alone can live, and not by faith," Albion now imagines God only as a remote, jealous lawgiver, a being totally other than humankind. In self-defense against his own alienated divine nature, he shrinks and turns inward; his body of earth and stars is scattered away from him; and he sinks into the coma of finite human time and material existence. Nightmarishly replaying variations on the recurring evils of war, empire, cruelty, and exploitation, his troubled mind generates a phantasmagoria of personages drawn from British prehistory, biblical prophecy, public events, and personal myth who materialize and vanish, struggle and fail, love and despair, dominate others and are victimized in their turn. In this radically nonlinear narrative, the same or closely similar events happen over and over, sometimes with different participants or viewed from different perspectives. As Fred Dortort notes in *The Dialectic of Vision: A Contrary Reading of Jerusalem* (1998), "The second chapter appears to contain more events than the first (in a process that continues and dramatically accelerates through Chapters 3 and 4) because in the course of reading each successive chapter readers develop an ever-increasing backlog of past references that add their resonances to the examination of new material" (p. 99). As new events and new contexts proliferate and characters break apart, the narrative spins its wheels; its chief suspense lies in whether and by what means Albion will awake, break out of his selfish isolation, recognize his divine nature, reconcile himself with his Emanation, the new Jerusalem—eventually revealed as his daughter—and release her to become the Bride of the Lamb who is celebrated in Revelation 21:9–14.

Each of the work's four chapters is introduced by a frontispiece and a preface, and each preface—part prose, part verse—is addressed to a particular audience: To the Public, To the Jews, To the Deists, and To the Christians. In the general preface and in first-person interjections throughout, Blake unequivocally claims that Jesus himself, in a spirit of acceptance and forgiveness, has directly and personally inspired and even dictated the illuminated poem. Instead of courting the audience's favor and outlining major themes, as would be expected in a conventional introduction, all four prefaces confront and even harass the reader, from unexpected angles. The first addresses the generic "Dear Reader" of the general Public as a fellow Christian who is "wholly One" with the author "in Jesus our Lord." But *Dear* has been obliterated, and the words *Sheep* and *Goats* at the top of the page, recalling Matthew 25:31–33, warn that Judgment Day has arrived: what happens next depends on the spirit in which this book is received. The second preface addresses Jews as fellow believers in one religion, now divided, and links the myth of cosmic man in the Jewish kabbalah with British myths of primordial Christianity. By both acknowledging Jews as "the true Christians" and simultaneously urging them to "follow Jesus," Blake implies that the conversion of the Jews, traditionally a precursor to the apocalypse, has already taken place or has never been necessary at all. The third preface charges the Deists, who deplore superstition and idolatry, with worshiping an idol of their own: the God of this World, or things as they are. In explaining away the problem of evil by redefining natural man as good, Deists have become enemies of "Universal Nature"—the very standard they claim to revere—and are themselves the causes of the wars that they blame on the religious extremism of "monks and Methodists." In rejecting Christianity, Deists have rejected its central tenet of forgiveness of sins and have cut themselves off from the source of spiritual rebirth. Finally, the fourth preface urges avowedly Christian readers—with whom most members of Blake's potential audience would want to identify themselves—to cease condemning the "Mental Gifts" of others and, instead, to engage in the positive, productive action of assiduously cultivating their own talents and laboring in art and science to build up Jerusalem within the nation of England. The cumulative effect of all four prefaces is to promote Christianity as the spirit of mutual forgiveness that releases a society's energies into constructive communal activity. Each individual has a patriotic duty to engage in "some Mental pursuit" toward building the new Jerusalem, the ideal community in Revelation, in the here and now.

Although Blake was so little a patriot, in some senses of the word, that he was tried for sedition in 1804—an experience that contributed to the bitter symbolism of the villainous "Sons of Albion" in *Jerusalem*—he made his country the protagonist and central focus of his master work. He draws so persuasively on the rich complex of Anglocentric "histories" that had been developed by eighteenth-century speculative mythographers that at times he appears actually to endorse "British Israelite" theories that early man was an ancient Briton and that the biblical patriarchs were Druids. But amid the geopolitical realities of the early nineteenth century, the symbolic claim that "All things begin and end in Albion's ancient Druid Rocky shore" was no overstatement: what the British chose to do, how they spent their money, where they sent their troops and their merchants, did in fact affect the lives of people around the world. Thus a spiritual awakening of the most powerful industrial and military country in the world might well be imagined as the apocalyptic event that would reunify the warring nations and shake humanity out of its crippling self-limitations.

Blake traces Albion's self-divisions into a legion of negative characters who, in various alliances and rivalries, act out the symptoms of their progenitor's illness. The twelve Daughters of Albion, offspring or fragments of Vala generally named after royal women in British legend, take delight in torturing and dominating Albion and other male characters. Unlike the silent chorus of nameless oppressed Englishwomen who echo Oothoon's sighs in *Visions of the Daughters of Albion*, they join Blake's mythical figures Vala, Rahab, and Tirzah in tormenting and defaming their rival Jerusalem. The twelve Sons of Albion, sometimes interwoven with the twelve tribes of Israel, are named after Blake's own artistic, philosophical, and political enemies; for example, accusers or judges in Blake's trial for seditious utterance ("Damn the King"). But Blake's real target throughout is the ultimate principle behind such actions. Another Son—based on the coeditors John, Robert, and Leigh Hunt, whose journal *The Examiner* attacked Blake's one-artist show in 1809—is named "Hand," for Leigh Hunt's graphic signature, a printer's hand with a pointing finger. This character, the monstrous triple-headed universal satanic Accuser depicted on plate 93, not only sent the historical Socrates and Jesus to their deaths but continues to attack champions of intellectual and spiritual free- dom as sinners and criminals. Throughout, Blake's aim is not just to settle personal scores but to expand specific instances from his own experience into a myth of the kind of thing that happens over and over when a country sick- ens, loses its soul, and rejects its spirit of liberty and forgiveness.

Beset though he is by all these enemies, Albion also has a few important allies. The benevolent Erin, or Ireland, and the merciful Daughters of Beulah (a biblical state of harmony) open time and space to eternity and protect the outcast Jerusalem. The masculine Friends of Albion, bearing names of the cathedral cities of England, try without success to bear up their fallen comrade and bring him back to Eden, and the immortal human form of London offers its whole being to Albion. In the background, barely perceptible to a few in the main action, the Divine Family from which Albion has separated himself remains on constant standby alert—watching, waiting, hoping; ready to support any movement Albion may make toward recovery.

Of all Albion's fallen constituents, headed by the four "Zoas" or living creatures—Urizen, Tharmas, Luvah or Orc, and Urthona or Los—only the tire- less Los, the creative blacksmith, retains his power of action; he emerges as the poem's true hero, precipitator of most events and continuous agent of change. Despite the cynicism of his Spectre, who embodies both his pride and his self- doubt, and his consort, Enitharmon, who thwarts him almost as much as she helps him, Los persists in building Golgonooza, city of art (represented by a star on the map of "Blake's London"), upon and within the continuously disintegrat- ing physical city of London. Even at his worst, in the persona of his Spectre, Los-Urthona is the Zoa who "kept the Divine Vision in time of trouble." Largely through Los's efforts, all the evils of the poem are at last condensed in Chap- ter 4 into a single concrete abomination, a fearsome hermaphroditic dragon, the Antichrist or Covering Cherub. Only at this point is Los able to enlist in full the help of his Spectre and his Emanation in his last-ditch labors to save Albion. When Albion awakes to see Jesus on the verge of death "in the likeness & simil- itude of Los my Friend," he throws himself without a thought for his own safety into the furnaces of affliction, which instantly turn into "Fountains of Living Waters flowing from the Humanity Divine." The illusion is broken, and the poem ends with the restored and reintegrated Albion's re-entrance into the vibrant communal life of Eternity.

Blake, like his character Los, labored at intervals over the years to give form to his *Jerusalem*. He probably began in 1804, the date of the title page (the year of his trial and acquittal); by 1807, he had developed sixty of the one hundred plates; in 1812, he exhibited "Detached Specimens," probably full-page designs, at the Water Colour Society; in 1820, he printed his first edition of three complete copies (A, C, and D, all uncolored); in 1821, he produced two versions in color: Copy E—the source of our reading text—and Copy B, con- sisting of the first chapter only; and in the last months of his life he fulfilled an order for the uncolored Copy F (Viscomi, *Blake and the Idea of the Book* [1993], 313, 338–61); see also Aileen Ward, *Blake; An Illustrated Quarterly* 39 (2006), 183–85. The large format of *Jerusalem*—practically the same size as *America*, *Eu- rope*, and *The Song of Los*—provides ample space for powerful designs, large and small. The reproductions seen in color plates 14–16, taken from Copy E, give some idea of Blake's accomplishment in the work as a whole; but the splen- dor of this book and the depth of its visual dimension cannot be appreciated without viewing every page, as presented in the Blake Trust/Princeton Univer- sity Press facsimile edited and superbly annotated by Morton D. Paley (1991);

the online digital Blake Archive edited by Eaves, Essick, and Viscomi; or the handcolored Blake Trust/Trianon Press facsimile edited by Geoffrey Keynes (1951). Minna Doskow's *William Blake's Jerusalem* (1982) provides a facsimile of Copy C (first issued by the Blake Trust in 1952) along with a guide for the general reader (first undertaken by Joseph Wicksteed in *William Blake's Jerusalem* [1953]); more specialized studies include E. J. Rose's view of the "Opened Center" in *Studies in English Literature, 1500–1900* 5 (1965), 587–606; Stuart Curran, "Structures of *Jerusalem*" in *Blake's Sublime Allegory* (1973), ed. Curran and Wittreich; Paley, *The Continuing City* (1983); Joanne Witke, *Blake's Prophetic Epic* (1986); and Dortort, *Dialectic of Vision*, mentioned earlier. In Chapter 2 Blake varied the order of pages; we follow the sequence of Copy E, our source text, as in the Bentley edition. This is also the order of Copies D (1821) and F (1827) in its original form, as sleuthed out by Viscomi ([1993], 357–60); therefore, it represents Blake's final intention. Erdman's numbering, which follows the alternative sequence of Copies A and C (B consists of Chapter 1 only), is provided after a forward slash. On the changing sequences, see Paul Yoder, *Studies in Romanticism* 41 (2002), and the pre-Viscomi work of Paley, *Continuing City* 294 ff., and De Luca, *Words of Eternity* 126 ff.

A final pointer: despite the marvelous designs, *Jerusalem* is at times so text heavy, especially in a typographic edition like this one, that some pages present an impenetrable "wall of words," in De Luca's apt phrase (p. 591 herein). Blake's motto for the preface "To the Christians" offers both encouragement and a practical guide: "I give you the end of a golden string, / Only wind it into a ball: / It will lead you in at Heaven's gate, / Built in Jerusalem's wall." There are many ways to enter the poem but no royal road to understanding it. Our advice is simply to start with whichever thread of meaning first catches your eye, follow that lead as far as it takes you; pick up the next loose end you see, and keep on exploring the book in your own way. If you try the opposite approach and insist on unsnarling each knotty passage line by line, you'll find yourself tangled in a self-trapping thicket even worse than the one growing in the "Human Brain" in *Songs* 47 (p. 42 herein). Don't fret about what doesn't make sense to you at any given moment. If one knot is too stubborn to unravel after a reasonable effort, drop it; skip around a bit until something else intrigues you; keep following the glint of that golden string just ahead, winding as you go—and the walls will start opening before you.

1

Jerusalem

2

The Emanation of The Giant Albion

1804 Printed by W. Blake Sth Molton S^t.[1]

SHEEP   GOATS[2] 3

To the Public

After my three years' slumber[3] on the banks of the Ocean, I again display my Giant forms to the Public: My former Giants & Fairies having reciev'd the highest reward possible: the love and friendship of those with whom to be connected, is to be blessed, I cannot doubt that this more consolidated & extended Work will be as kindly received. The Enthusiasm of the following Poem, the Author hopes[4] no Reader will think presumptuousness or arrogance when he is reminded that the Ancients acknowledged their love to their Deities, to the full as Enthusiatically as I have who Acknowledge mine for my Saviour and Lord, for they were wholly absorb'd in their Gods. I also hope the Reader will be with me, wholly One in Jesus our Lord, who is the God of Fire and Lord of Love to whom the Ancients look'd and saw his day afar off, with trembling & amazement.[5]

The Spirit of Jesus is continual forgiveness of Sin: he who waits to be righteous before he enters into the Saviour's kingdom, the Divine Body; will never enter there. I am perhaps the most sinful of men![6] I pretend not to holiness: yet I pretend to love, to see, to converse with daily, as man with man; & the more to have an interest in the Friend of Sinners. Therefore Dear Reader, forgive what you do not approve, & love me for this energetic exertion of my talent.

> Reader! lover of books! lover of heaven.
> And of that God from whom all books are given,
> Who in mysterious Sinai's awful cave,
> To Man the wond'rous art of writing gave.[7]
> Again he speaks in thunder and in fire!   5
> Thunder of Thought, & flames of fierce desire:
> Even from the depths of Hell his voice I hear,
> Within the unfathomd caverns of my Ear.
> Therefore I print: nor vain my types[8] shall be:

1. Incised, not etched, along the bottom of the plate—a late addition? Work continued until about 1820, but the symbolic date 1804 (for both *Jerusalem* and *Milton*) marks Blake's acquittal and his resumption of illuminated printing and prophetic art at 17 South Molton Street in London (see map and the chronology). Among inscriptions in the stonework of the frontispiece—visible in a proof copy but later obliterated—are the following: "There is a Void, outside of Existence, which if entered into / Englobes itself & becomes a Womb, such was Albions Couch"; "Half Friendship is the bitterest Enmity said Los / As he enterd the Door of Death for Albions sake Inspired / The long sufferings of God are not for ever there is a Judgment"; "Every Thing has its Vermin O Spectre of the Sleeping Dead" (reversed writing).
2. All versions of *Jerusalem* open with a defective preface, the result of Blake's gouging out whole words and phrases (see print facsimiles and the online Blake Archive), leaving "wounds that could never heal" (Paley). Even in the beautifully finished Copy E, the fifth of six impressions that the author himself produced and offered "To the Public," Blake allowed the marred opening pages to stand. Nevertheless, we depart from our source (Copy E) to offer readers in a "New Age" (p. 147 herein) a fresh start, based on Erdman's reconstruction of the unspoiled original plate (*Complete Poetry* 145–156). "Sheep" and "Goats" (upper right and upper left), incised after the etching process, and probably after the mutilation, imply (notes Wicksteed) that we as readers, facing this page, are ourselves under judgment (cf. Matthew 25:33).
3. Residence in Felpham, September 1800 to September 1803; see the April 25, 1803, letter to Butts (p. 483 herein). Blake deleted "love," "friendship," and "blessed" in this sentence.
4. After "hopes," Blake deleted the rest of the sentence—the largest gap on the page. For consistency with other past-tense verbs that distinguish the time of the "Ancients" from Blake's own time, we have added a final "d" to Erdman's restoration of "acknowledge."
5. In this sentence Blake deleted "of Fire" and "of Love," and at the end of the next paragraph he deleted "Dear," "forgive," and "love."
6. The apostle Paul claimed to be the chief of sinners (1 Timothy 1:15).
7. The tradition that God taught Moses alphabetic writing, discussed in Essick, *Blake and the Language of Adam* (1989) and (briefly) in John B. Pierce, *The Wond'rous Art* (2003), derives from stories that both God (Exodus 24:12, 31:18, 34:1) and Moses (Exodus 24:4, 34:27) wrote down the commandments. Blake proclaims that the true gift of the true God is not Mosaic law but the art of the written word. Blake deleted both occurrences of "lover" in line 1 and everything after "whom" in line 2.
8. (1) Mythic archetypes; (2) relief-etched "stereotypes" (see *The Death of Abel*; cf. William St. Clair, *The Reading Nation in the Romantic Period* [2004] on commercial stereotypes); (3) reworkings of

Heaven, Earth & Hell, henceforth shall live in
    harmony   10

Of the Measure,[9] in which the following Poem is written

We who dwell on Earth can do nothing of ourselves, every thing is conducted by Spirits, no less than Digestion or Sleep. To Note the last words
of Jesus, Εδοθη μοι πασα εξουσια εν ουρανω χαι επι γης.[1]

When this Verse was first dictated to me I consider'd a Monotonous
Cadence like that used by Milton & Shakspeare & all writers of English
Blank Verse derived from the modern bondage of Rhyming; to be a necessary and indispensible part of Verse. But I soon found that in the
mouth of a true Orator such monotony was not only awkward, but as
much a bondage as rhyme itself. I therefore have produced a variety in
every line, both of cadences & number of syllables. Every word and every
letter is studied and put into its fit place: the terrific numbers are
reserved for the terrific parts, the mild & gentle, for the mild & gentle
parts, and the prosaic, for inferior parts; all are necessary to each other.
Poetry Fetter'd, Fetters the Human Race. Nations are Destroy'd, or
Flourish, in proportion as Their Poetry Painting and Music, are
Destroy'd or Flourish! The Primeval State of Man, was Wisdom, Art, and
Science.

Μονος ο Ιεςους[2]   **4**

Jerusalem
Chap: 1

Of the Sleep of Ulro! and of the passage through
Eternal Death! and of the awaking to Eternal Life

This theme calls me in sleep night after night, & ev'ry morn
Awakes me at sun-rise, then I see the Saviour over me
Spreading his beams of love, & dictating the words of this
    mild song.[3]

"Awake! awake O sleeper of the land of shadows, wake! expand!

Old Testament anticipatory "types" linked to New Testament "antitypes" (cf. Moses' brazen ser-
pent/the crucifixion [John 3:14–15] and Jonah's emergence from fish's belly/the resurrection
[Matthew 12:39–40, 16:4]).

9. Cf. Milton's prefatory note on "The Verse" for *Paradise Lost* (*PL*), justifying his use of blank verse.
   Blake claims both that the poem was "dictated" and that he has purposefully "produced" rhythmic
   and stylistic variety.

1. Blake deleted this sentence. The Greek passage, "All power is given unto me in heaven and in
   earth" (Matthew 28:18), is not Jesus' dying utterance but part of the commission to his disciples
   that ends the Gospel. The final sentence (Matthew 28:20) is quoted in *J* 60:67 and 62:29.

2. "Only Jesus" or "Jesus alone," probably alluding both to Matthew 17:8, the disappearance of Elijah and Moses after Jesus' transfiguration, and John 8:9 (received text), Jesus' forgiveness of the
   woman taken in adultery after her accusers depart. Blake, self-taught, wrote Greek without
   accents, points, or breathings and freely used unorthodox spellings: for "Jesus," instead of the correct spelling Ιησους, he substituted an epsilon (resembling "e") for the eta and used the terminal
   form of the sigma, resembling "s," in the middle of the word.

3. Following epic convention, Blake opens by stating his theme and invoking his muse. As Milton
   broke with classical tradition to call on the higher muse of the Holy Spirit (*PL* 1.6, 1.20–21), who
   visits him nightly (7.28–29, 9.21–24) and "dictates" the poem, so Blake now breaks with Miltonic
   tradition to proclaim Jesus as his inspiration (**5**:16 ff.).

I am in you and you in me, mutual in love divine:
Fibres of love from man to man thro Albion's pleasant land.
In all the dark Atlantic vale down from the hills of Surrey
A black water accumulates, return Albion! return!⁴   10
Thy brethren call thee, and thy fathers, and thy sons,
Thy nurses and thy mothers, thy sisters and thy daughters
Weep at thy soul's disease, and the Divine Vision is darkend:
Thy Emanation that was wont to play before thy face,
Beaming forth with her daughters into the Divine bosom,
Where hast thou hidden thy Emanation lovely Jerusalem
From the vision and fruition of the Holy-one?
I am not a God afar off,⁵ I am a brother and friend;
Within your bosoms I reside, and you reside in me:
Lo! we are One; forgiving all Evil; Not seeking recompense!⁶   20
Ye are my members O ye sleepers of Beulah, land of shades!"

But the perturbed Man away turns down the valleys dark;⁷

"Phantom of the over heated brain! shadow of immortality!
Seeking to keep my soul a victim to thy Love! which binds
Man the enemy of man into deceitful friendships;
Jerusalem is not! her daughters are indefinite;
By demonstration, man alone can live, and not by faith.
My mountains are my own, and I will keep them to myself:
The Malvern and the Cheviot, the Wolds, Plinlimmon &
    Snowdon⁸   30
Are mine. Here will I build my Laws of Moral Virtue:
Humanity shall be no more: but war & princedom & victory!"

So spoke Albion in jealous fears, hiding his Emanation
Upon the Thames and Medway, rivers of Beulah: dissembling
His jealousy before the throne divine, darkening, cold!

The banks of the Thames are clouded! the ancient porches of
    Albion are
Darken'd! they are drawn thro' unbounded space, scatter'd upon
The Void in incoherent despair! Cambridge & Oxford & London
Are driven among the starry Wheels, rent away and dissipated,
In Chasms & Abysses of sorrow, enlarg'd without dimension,
    terrible
Albion's mountains run with blood, the cries of war & of tumult
Resound into the unbounded night, every Human perfection
Of mountain & river & city, are small & wither'd & darken'd.
Cam is a little stream! Ely is almost swallowd up!

4. The Saviour's opening summons to the poet to "awake" (cf. Ephesians 5:14; Judges 5:12) and his
   affirmation of oneness (cf. John 15:4, 17:21; 1 John 4:13) merge with the Divine Vision's summons
   to Albion, or to all humanity. Ulro (opening line) is the world as we know it at the lowest level of
   consciousness; mere physicality, the delusion that nothing exists except matter.
5. The angry deity in Jeremiah 23:23, denouncing false prophets, says the opposite: "Am I a God at
   hand . . . and not a God afar off? (cf. Acts 17:27: "not far from every one of us").
6. The all-forgiving Saviour who is speaking—the divine humanity within all people ("in you and you
   in me" [4:7, cf. John 15:4, 17:21–23])—requires no "recompense," or atonement through blood
   sacrifice.
7. Blake obliterated line 23: "Saying, 'We are not One: we are Many, thou most simulative.'"
8. British mountains and hilly areas (wolds); see map. Albion's claim of absolute possession echoes
   that of Pharaoh in Ezekiel 29:3 (Ostriker). On "over heated brain," cf. *Macbeth* 2.1.39.

Lincoln & Norwich stand trembling on the brink of Udan-Adan!   10
Wales and Scotland shrink themselves to the west and to the
    north!
Mourning for fear of the warriors in the Vale of Entuthon-Benython
Jerusalem is scatterd abroad like a cloud of smoke thro' non-entity:
Moab & Ammon & Amalek & Canaan & Egypt & Aram[9]
Recieve her little-ones for sacrifices and the delights of cruelty.

Trembling I sit day and night, my friends are astonish'd at me[1]
Yet they forgive my wanderings, I rest not from my great task!
To open the Eternal Worlds, to open the immortal Eyes
Of Man inwards into the Worlds of Thought: into Eternity
Ever expanding in the Bosom of God, the Human Imagination.   20
O Saviour pour upon me thy Spirit of meekness & love:
Annihilate the Selfhood in me, be thou all my life!
Guide thou my hand which trembles exceedingly upon the rock
    of ages,[2]
While I write of the building of Golgonooza, & of the terrors of
    Entuthon:
Of Hand & Hyle & Coban, of Kwantok, Peachey, Brereton, Slayd &
    Hutton:
Of the terrible sons & daughters of Albion, and their Generations.

Scofield: Kox, Kotope and Bowen,[3] revolve most mightily upon
The Furnace of Los: before the eastern gate bending their fury.
They war, to destroy the Furnaces, to desolate Golgonooza:
And to devour the Sleeping Humanity of Albion in rage & hunger.   30
They revolve into the Furnaces Southward & are driven forth
    Northward
Divided into Male and Female forms time after time.
From these Twelve all the Families of England spread abroad.

The Male is a Furnace of beryll; the Female is a golden Loom;
I behold them and their rushing fires overwhelm my Soul;
In London's darkness; and my tears fall day and night,
Upon the Emanations of Albion's Sons! the Daughters of Albion
Names anciently rememberd, but now contemn'd as fictions:
Although in every bosom they controll our Vegetative powers.

These are united into Tirzah and her Sisters, on Mount Gilead: 40
Cambel & Gwendolen & Conwenna & Cordella & Ignoge.

9. Sprinkled among British and biblical place names of recognizable significance (e.g., centers of
learning and culture [5:3], enemies of Israel [5:14]) are puzzling made-up names (5:10, 5:12; cf.
M 27/26:25) that tend to accumulate meaning as the poem unfolds, or in relation to other illuminated books. Golgonooza (5:24), for instance, is a city of art constructed in, on, beneath, above,
and around the physical city of London.
1. Blake's deeply personal interjections, like Milton's in *Paradise Lost*, go beyond a formulaic reitera-
tion of his opening invocation to restate and reframe his theme at critical moments in the poem
(cf. 15:6 ff.).
2. Later Albion's place of repose (48:4). For the biblical context, see n. 2, p. 268.
3. "Hand": the three Hunt brothers with a pointing-finger logo (see headnote), whose journal *The
Examiner* ridiculed Blake's work (see Robert Hunt's review, p. 497 herein). "Hyle": probably a combination of Hayley and *hyle*, Greek for "matter." "Coban": unidentified. "Kwantok" (Quantock),
"Peachey" (Peechy), "Brereton": judges at Blake's indictment or his trial. "Slayd": unidentified.
"Hutton" (Hulton): lieutenant who countersigned charges. "Scofield" (Scolfield or Schofield) and
"Kox" (Cock, 5:37): soldiers who brought charges of sedition and assault. "Kotope": unidentified.
"Bowen": lawyer, perhaps a prosecutor. These twelve sometimes exchange identities with the twelve
tribes of Israel but ally themselves with Israel's enemies.

And these united into Rahab in the Covering Cherub[4] on
   Euphrates:
Gwiniverra & Gwinefred, & Gonorill & Sabrina beautiful;
Estrild, Mehetabel & Ragan, lovely Daughters of Albion.[5]
They are the beautiful Emanations of the Twelve Sons of Albion.

The Starry Wheels revolv'd heavily over the Furnaces;
Drawing Jerusalem in anguish of maternal love,
Eastward, a pillar of a cloud with Vala upon the mountains
Howling in pain, redounding from the arms of Beulah's Daughters,[6]
Out from the Furnaces of Los above the head of Los,   50
A pillar of smoke writhing afar into Non-Entity, redounding
Till the cloud reaches afar outstretch'd among the Starry Wheels
Which revolve heavily in the mighty Void above the Furnaces.

O what avail the loves & tears of Beulah's lovely Daughters
They hold the Immortal Form in gentle bands & tender tears
But all within is open'd into the deeps of Entuthon Benython
A dark and unknown night, indefinite, unmeasurable, without end.
Abstract Philosophy warring in enmity against Imagination
Which is the Divine Body of the Lord Jesus, blessed for ever.
And there Jerusalem wanders with Vala upon the mountains,   60
Attracted by the revolutions of those Wheels the Cloud of smoke:
Immense, and Jerusalem & Vala weeping in the Cloud
Wander away into the Chaotic Void, lamenting with her Shadow
Among the Daughters of Albion, among the Starry Wheels:
Lamenting for her children, for the sons & daughters of Albion

Los heard her lamentations in the deeps afar! his tears fall
Incessant before the Furnaces, and his Emanation divided in pain.
Eastward toward the Starry Wheels. But Westward a black Horror,
His Spectre driv'n by the Starry Wheels of Albion's sons,
   black and   6
Opake divided from his back; he labours and he mourns![7]

For as his Emanation divided, his Spectre also divided
In terror of those starry wheels: and the Spectre stood over Los

4. For the Church Fathers, the prideful Covering Cherub (Ezekiel 28:16) was Lucifer, Satan himself. For Blake, this ultimate evil is the Selfhood that blocks love and forgiveness, the monstrous self-righteousness revealed in 89 and vanquished in Albion's self-sacrifice in 96 and thereafter; cf. *Milton* 41/37:8 and n. 7, p. 195 herein.

5. All but three of the Daughters are named after royal women in legendary British history. "Gwinefred": a Welsh virgin martyr. "Mehetabel": wife of an Edomite king, a descendant of Esau in Genesis 36:39 (cf. the British princess Methahel noted in Michael Mason's 1988 Oxford Authors edition of Blake). "Cambel": perhaps a princess Kambreda (Damon), or possibly the female co-founder of the Scots clan Campbell, which is named for her father rather than her husband. The twelve operate in two groups headed by biblical figures: five under the prudish Tirzah and seven under the wanton Rahab; see *Milton* 19/17:11 and n. 6, p. 164 herein.

6. Opposing the Daughters of Albion, these protective female spirits (muses in *Milton* 2:1) personify the idyllic "married" land of the redeemed Zion (Isaiah 62:4); see n. 3, p. 145. Jerusalem, as "a pillar of a cloud" (5 48; cf. Exodus 13:21), is obscured by Vala, as "a pillar of smoke" (5:51) from Los's furnaces.

7. As in *Urizen* 19 Los's expression of pity (this time for the outcast Jerusalem) precipitates self-division. His Emanation, Enitharmon, emerges from his breast as an exterior female manifestation of his yearnings and sexual conflicts, while his Spectre, the hypermasculine hardened outer shell of his personality, emerges from his back as a personification of all that blocks him as an artist: self-doubt, discouragement, repression, counterproductivity, resistance to inspiration, self-centeredness. In *The Four Zoas*, Los accepts his Spectre as another self and is reunited with him; but in *Jerusalem*, Los masters his Spectre and forces him to help build Golgonooza. The conflict is pictured in the design for plate 6. Cf. Blake's account of his own "spectrous Fiend" (p. 489 herein).

Howling in pain: a blackning Shadow, blackning dark & opake
Cursing the terrible Los: bitterly cursing him for his friendship
To Albion, suggesting murderous thoughts against Albion.

Los rag'd and stamp'd the earth in his might & terrible wrath!
He stood and stampd the earth! then he threw down his hammer
    in rage &
In fury; then he sat down and wept, terrified! Then arose   10
And chaunted his song, labouring with the tongs and hammer:
But still the Spectre divided, and still his pain increas'd!

In pain the Spectre divided: in pain of hunger and thirst:
To devour Los's Human Perfection, but when he saw that Los

Was living: panting like a frighted wolf, and howling   7
He stood over the Immortal, in the solitude and darkness:
Upon the darkning Thames, across the whole Island westward.
A horrible Shadow of Death, among the Furnaces: beneath
The pillar of folding smoke; and he sought by other means
To lure Los: by tears, by arguments of science & by terrors:
Terrors in every Nerve, by spasms & extended pains:
While Los answer'd unterrified to the opake blackening Fiend.

And thus the Spectre spoke: "Wilt thou still go on to destruction?
Till thy life is all taken away by this deceitful Friendship?   10
He drinks thee up like water! like wine he pours thee

Into his tuns: thy Daughters are trodden in his vintage
He makes thy Sons the trampling of his bulls, they are plow'd
And harrowd for his profit, lo! thy stolen Emanation
Is his garden of pleasure! all the Spectres of his Sons mock thee
Look how they scorn thy once admired palaces: now in ruins
Because of Albion! because of deceit and friendship! For Lo!
Hand has peopled Babel & Nineveh! Hyle, Ashur & Aram;[8]
Coban's son is Nimrod: his son Cush is adjoind to Aram,
By the Daughter of Babel, in a woven mantle of pestilence & war.   20
They put forth their spectrous cloudy sails; which drive their
     immense
Constellations over the deadly deeps of indefinite Udan-Adan.
Kox is the Father of Shem & Ham & Japheth, he is the Noah
Of the Flood of Udan-Adan. Hutn is the Father of the Seven
From Enoch to Adam; Schofield is Adam who was New-
Created in Edom. I saw it indignant, & thou art not moved!
This has divided thee in sunder: and wilt thou still forgive?
O! thou seest not what I see! what is done in the Furnaces.
Listen I will tell thee what is done in moments to thee unknown:
Luvah was cast into the Furnaces of affliction[9] and sealed.   30
And Vala fed in cruel delight, the Furnaces with fire:
Stern Urizen beheld; urgd by necessity to keep
The evil day afar, and if perchance with iron power
He might avert his own despair: in woe & fear he saw
Vala incircle round the Furnaces where Luvah was clos'd:
With joy she heard his howlings, & forgot he was her Luvah,
With whom she liv'd in bliss in times of innocence & youth!
Vala comes from the Furnace in a cloud, but wretched Luvah
Is howling in the Furnaces, in flames among Albion's Spectres,
To prepare the Spectre of Albion to reign over thee O Los.   40
Forming the Spectres of Albion according to his rage:
To prepare the Spectre sons of Adam, who is Scofield: the Ninth
Of Albion's sons, & the father of all his brethren in the Shadowy
Generation. Cambel & Gwendolen wove webs of war & of
Religion, to involve all Albion's sons, and when they had
Involv'd Eight; their webs roll'd outwards into darkness
And Scofield the Ninth remain on the outside of the Eight
And Kox, Kotope, & Bowen, One in him, a Fourfold Wonder
Involv'd the Eight–Such are the Generations of the Giant Albion.
To separate a Law of Sin, to punish thee in thy members."   50

Los answer'd, "Altho' I know not this! I know far worse than this:
I know that Albion hath divided me, and that thou O my Spectre.
Hast just cause to be irritated: but look stedfastly upon me:
Comfort thyself in my strength; the time will arrive,
When all Albion's injuries shall cease, and when we shall
Embrace him tenfold bright, rising from his tomb in immortality.
They have divided themselves by Wrath, they must be united by

8. From this point on, the onrushing density of biblical allusion makes detailed annotation impracti-
   cable. In general, the Sons of Albion, now Spectres, dominate territories hostile to biblical Israel.
   Some biblical genealogies (Genesis 5, 10:8) are reversed: Cush is the father of Nimrod, not his son;
   the seven generations in 7:25 should run from Adam to Enoch.
9. Used for refining in Isaiah 48:10. Luvah is the male counterpart of Vala (cf. *Four* Zoas **64**:29–30);
   elsewhere, the Zoa of Love and Passion, or Orc in his unfallen state.

Pity: let us therefore take example & warning O my Spectre.
O that I could abstain from wrath! O that the Lamb
Of God would look upon me and pity me in my fury.   60
In anguish of regeneration! in terrors of self annihilation:
Pity must join together those whom wrath has torn in sunder.
And the Religion of Generation which was meant for the
      destruction
Of Jerusalem, become her covering, till the time of the End.
O holy Generation! Image of regeneration!
O point of mutual forgiveness between Enemies!
Birthplace of the Lamb of God incomprehensible!
The Dead despise & scorn thee, & cast thee out as accursed:
Seeing the Lamb of God in thy gardens & thy palaces:
Where they desire to place the Abomination of Desolation.[1]   70
Hand sits before his furnace: scorn of others & furious pride:
Freeze round him to bars of steel & to iron rocks beneath
His feet: indignant self-righteousness like whirlwinds of the north:
Rose up against me thundering from the Brook of Albion's River | 8 |
From Ranelagh & Strumbolo, from Cromwell's gardens & Chelsea[2]
The place of wounded Soldiers, but when he saw my Mace
Whirld round from heaven to earth, trembling he sat; his cold
Poisons rose up: & his sweet deceits coverd them all over
With a tender cloud. As thou art now; such was he O Spectre
I know thy deceit & thy revenges, and unless thou desist
I will certainly create an eternal Hell for thee. Listen!
Be attentive: be obedient! Lo the Furnaces are ready to recieve
      thee,
I will break thee into shivers: & melt thee in the furnaces of death.   10
I will cast thee into forms of abhorrence & torment if thou
Desist not from thine own will, & obey not my stern command:
I am closd up from my children! my Emanation is dividing
And thou my Spectre art divided against me. But mark
I will compell thee to assist me in my terrible labours. To beat
These hypocritic Selfhoods on the Anvils of bitter Death.
I am inspired! I act not for myself: for Albion's sake
I now am what I am! a horror and an astonishment
Shuddring the heavens to look upon me: Behold what cruelties
Are practised in Babel & Shinar, & have approachd to Zion's Hill."[3]   20

While Los spoke, the terrible Spectre fell shuddring before him
Watching his time with glowing eyes to leap upon his prey.
Los opend the Furnaces in fear, the Spectre saw to Babel & Shinar
Across all Europe & Asia; he saw the tortures of the Victims:
He saw now from the outside what he before saw & felt from within.

1. Citing Daniel 12:11, Jesus refers to this loathsome evil (Matthew 24:15)—usually interpreted as an
   idol in the Holy of Holies of the Temple in Jerusalem—as a portent of the end of time. The phrase
   (cf. *Milton* [M] 24/22:49, 48/41:25), repeated in 10:16 and 75:19, is identified in annotations to
   Watson's *Apology* with "State Religion, which is the source of all Cruelty" (p. 459 herein). If "everything that lives is Holy" (*Marriage* 27; cf. *Visions* 11/8:10 *America* 10/8:13), an especially set-aside
   holy place is itself abominable. The fallen world of Generation is the "Image" (7:65; deleted or
   badly printed in Copy E) of spiritual regeneration, a temporary haven for the outcast Jerusalem.
2. "Ranelagh," "Strombolo," "Cromwell's gardens": public places of amusement; "Chelsea": home for
   disabled veterans (see map).
3. Or "promontory" (12:27, 29/43:4, 80:36): temple site in Jerusalem; in Christian metaphor, a name
   for heaven. "Babel and Shinar": Babylonian territories inimical to Israel.

He saw that Los was the sole, uncontrolld Lord of the Furnaces.
Groaning he kneeld before Los's iron-shod feet on London Stone,[4]
Hungring & thirsting for Los's life yet pretending obedience.
While Los pursud his speech in threatnings loud & fierce.

"Thou art my Pride & Self-righteousness; I have found thee out: 30
Thou art reveald before me in all thy magnitude & power
Thy Uncircumcised pretences to Chastity must be cut in sunder![5]
Thy holy wrath & deep deceit cannot avail against me
Nor shalt thou ever assume the triple-form of Albion's Spectre
For I am one of the living: dare not to mock my inspired fury
If thou wast cast forth from my life! if I was dead upon the
    mountains
Thou mightest be pitied & lovd: but now I am living; unless
Thou abstain ravening I will create an eternal Hell for thee.
Take thou this Hammer & in patience heave the thundering Bellows
Take thou these Tongs: strike thou alternate with me: labour
    obedient   40
Hand & Hyle & Koban: Skofeld, Kox & Kotope labour mightily
In the Wars of Babel & Shinar, all their Emanations were
Condensd. Hand has absorbd all his Brethren in his might
All the infant Loves & Graces were lost, for the mighty Hand
Condens'd his Emanations into hard opake substances;   9
And his infant thoughts & desires into cold, dark, cliffs of death.
His hammer of gold he siez'd; and his anvil of adamant.
He siez'd the bars of condens'd thoughts, to forge them:
Into the sword of war! into the bow and arrow:
Into the thundering cannon and into the murdering gun
I saw the limbs form'd for exercise, contemn'd: & the beauty of
Eternity, look'd upon as deformity & loveliness as a dry tree:
I saw disease forming a Body of Death around the Lamb
Of God, to destroy Jerusalem & to devour the body of Albion   10
By war and stratagem to win the labour of the husbandman:

Awkwardness arm'd in steel: folly in a helmet of gold:
Weakness with horns & talons: ignorance with a rav'ning beak!
Every Emanative joy forbidden as a Crime:
And the Emanations buried alive in the earth with pomp of
    religion:
Inspiration deny'd; Genius forbidden by laws of punishment:
I saw terrified; I took the sighs & tears & bitter groans:
I lifted them into my Furnaces; to form the spiritual sword[6]
That lays open the hidden heart: I drew forth the pang
Of sorrow red hot: I workd it on my resolute anvil: 20
I heated it in the flames of Hand, & Hyle, & Coban
Nine times; Gwendolen & Cambel & Gwineverra

4. Ancient London landmark, the point from which Romans measured distances (set in Saint
   Swithin's church wall, 1798, now destroyed, on what is now Cannon Street; reset after World War
   II in the wall of the Bank of China). For Blake it is the remains of a Druid sacrificial altar (see map).
5. On Blake's circumcision symbolism (removing the "excrementitious / Husk" of the isolated self, the
   male equivalent of the hymen), see E. J. Rose, *Studies in Romanticism* 8 (1968).
6. The "sword of the Spirit, which is the word of God" (Ephesians 6:17), part of the "whole armor"
   of the Christian; see n. 9, p. 148 herein.

Are melted into the gold, the silver, the liquid ruby,
The crysolite, the topaz, the jacinth, & every precious stone.[7]
Loud roar my Furnaces and loud my hammer is heard:
I labour day and night, I behold the soft affections
Condense beneath my hammer into forms of cruelty
But still I labour in hope, tho' still my tears flow down.
That he who will not defend Truth, may be compelld to defend
A Lie: that he may be snared and caught and snared and taken[8]   30
That Enthusiasm and Life may not cease: arise Spectre arise!"

Thus they contended among the Furnaces with groans & tears;
Groaning the Spectre heavd the bellows, obeying Los's frowns;
Till the Spaces of Erin[9] were perfected in the furnaces
Of affliction, and Los drew them forth, compelling the harsh
    Spectre,
Into the Furnaces & into the valleys of the Anvils of Death | 10 |
And into the mountains of the Anvils & of the heavy Hammers
Till he should bring the Sons & Daughters of Jerusalem to be
The Sons & Daughters of Los that he might protect them from
Albion's dread Spectres: storming, loud, thunderous & mighty
The Bellows & the Hammers move compell'd by Los's hand.

And this is the manner of the Sons of Albion in their strength
They take the Two Contraries which are calld Qualities, with
    which
Every Substance is clothed, they name them Good & Evil.
From them they make an Abstract, which is a Negation[1]   10
Not only of the Substance from which it is derived
A murderer of its own Body: but also a murderer
Of every Divine Member: it is the Reasoning Power
An Abstract objecting power,[2] that Negatives every thing.
This is the Spectre of Man; the Holy Reasoning Power
And in its Holiness is closed the Abomination of Desolation.[3]

Therefore Los stands in London building Golgonooza
Compelling his Spectre to labours mighty; trembling in fear
The Spectre weeps, but Los unmovd by tears or threats remains.

"I must Create a System, or be enslav'd by another Man's   20
I will not Reason & Compare: my business is to Create."

So Los, in fury & strength: in indignation & burning wrath
Shuddring the Spectre howls, his howlings terrify the night.
He stamps around the Anvil, beating blows of stern despair

---

7. Wisdom (Job 28:18, Proverbs 8:11) and a virtuous woman (Proverbs 3:15, 31:10) are more precious than rubies. Other gems appear in Aaron's breastplate (Exodus 28:17–20) and in the foundations of the New Jerusalem (Revelation 21:19–20).
8. Cf. *Milton* 8:47–48 and Isaiah 8:15.
9. For more on the redemptive female spirit Erin, an idealized personification of revolutionary activity in Ireland, who leads the Daughters of Beulah in protecting the stricken Albion (11:8) see Catherine L. McClenahan in *Prophetic Character* (2002), ed. Gourlay, and Essick in *Blake, Nation, and Empire* (2006), ed. Clark and Worrall.
1. See *Milton* 46/40:32–36. "Contraries": see *Marriage* 3. The relation between Negations and Contraries is further developed in J 17:33–39.
2. Both resisting and objectifying (Hilton, p. 573 herein). Cf. "The Human Abstract."
3. See 7:70, **75**:19. For an early warning against reliance on reason alone, apart from the "Poetic Genius," see the 1788 tractates (p. 3 herein).

He curses Heaven & Earth, Day & Night & Sun & Moon
He curses Forest Spring & River, Desart & sandy Waste
Cities & Nations, Families & Peoples, Tongues & Laws
Driven to desperation by Los's terrors & threatning fears.

Los cries, "Obey my voice & never deviate from my will
And I will be merciful to thee: be thou invisible to all   30
To whom I make thee invisible, but chief to my own Children
O Spectre of Urthona: Reason not against their dear approach
Nor them obstruct with thy temptations of doubt & despair.
O Shame O strong & mighty Shame I break thy brazen fetters.
If thou refuse, thy present torments will seem southern breezes
To what thou shalt endure if thou obey not my great will."

The Spectre answer'd, "Art thou not ashamd of those thy Sins
That thou callest thy Children? lo the Law of God commands
That they be offered upon his Altar; O cruelty & torment
For thine are also mine! I have kept silent hitherto   40
Concerning my chief delight: but thou hast broken silence
Now I will speak my mind! Where is my lovely Enitharmon
O thou my enemy, where is my Great Sin? She is also thine.
I said: 'now is my grief at worst: incapable of being
Surpassed': but every moment it accumulates more & more
It continues accumulating to eternity; the joys of God advance
For he is Righteous: he is not a Being of Pity & Compassion
He cannot feel Distress: he feeds on Sacrifice & Offering:
Delighting in cries & tears & clothed in holiness & solitude.
But my griefs advance also, for ever & ever without end.   50
O that I could cease to be! Despair! I am Despair
Created to be the great example of horror & agony! also my
Prayer is vain. I called for compassion: compassion mockd.
Mercy & pity threw the grave stone over me & with lead
And iron, bound it over me for ever: Life lives on my
Consuming: & the Almighty hath made me his Contrary
To be all evil, all reversed & for ever dead: knowing
And seeing life, yet living not; how can I then behold
And not tremble; how can I be beheld & not abhorrd?"

So spoke the Spectre shuddring, & dark tears ran down his
   shadowy face   60
Which Los wiped off, but comfort none could give! or beam of
   hope
Yet ceasd he not from labouring at the roarings of his Forge
With iron & brass Building Golgonooza in great contendings
Till his Sons & Daughters came forth from the Furnaces
At the sublime Labours for Los compelld the invisible Spectre
To labours mighty, with vast strength, with his mighty chains. |11|
In pulsations of time, & extensions of space, like Urns of
   Beulah,
With great labour upon his anvils, & in his ladles the Ore
He lifted, pouring it into the clay ground prepar'd with art;[4]

4. Where ornaments for Solomon's temple in Jerusalem were formed (1 Kings 7:46; cf. *M* 21/19:10; analog for relief etching.

Striving with Systems to deliver Individuals from those Systems:
That whenever any Spectre began to devour the Dead,
He might feel the pain as if a man gnawd his own tender nerves.

Then Erin came forth from the Furnaces, & all the Daughters
    of Beulah
Came from the Furnaces, by Los's mighty power for Jerusalem's
Sake: walking up and down among the Spaces of Erin: 10
And the Sons and Daughters of Los came forth in perfection lovely!
And the Spaces of Erin reach'd from the starry heighth, to the
    starry depth.

Los wept with exceeding joy & all wept with joy together:
They feard they never more should see their Father, who
Was built in from Eternity, in the Cliffs of Albion.

But when the joy of meeting was exhausted in loving embrace:
Again they lament. "O what shall we do for lovely Jerusalem?⁵
To protect the Emanations of Albion's mighty ones from cruelty?
Sabrina & Ignoge begin to sharpen their beamy spears
Of light and love: their little children stand with arrows of gold: 20
Ragan is wholly cruel, Scofield is bound in iron armour!
He is like a mandrake in the earth before Reuben's gate:⁶
He shoots beneath Jerusalem's walls to undermine her foundations;
Vala is but thy Shadow, O thou loveliest among women!
A shadow animated by thy tears O mournful Jerusalem!

Why wilt thou give to her a Body whose life is but a Shade?   [12]
Her joy and love, a shade! a shade of sweet repose:
But animated and vegetated, she is a devouring worm:
What shall we do for thee O lovely mild Jerusalem?"

And Los said, "I behold the finger of God in terrors!
Albion is dead! his Emanation is divided from him!
But I am living! yet I feel my Emanation also dividing
Such thing was never known! O pity me, thou all-piteous-one!
What shall I do! or how exist, divided from Enitharmon?
Yet why despair! I saw the finger of God go forth   10
Upon my Furnaces, from within the Wheels of Albion's Sons:
Fixing their Systems, permanent: by mathematic power
Giving a body to Falshood that it may be cast off for ever.
With Demonstrative Science piercing Apollyon⁷ with his own bow:
God is within & without! he is even in the depths of Hell":⁸

Such were the lamentations of the Labourers in the Furnaces:

5. Echo of Song of Solomon 8:8 ("[W]hat shall we do for our sister"). See also 12:4.
6. The earthbound, vegetated forces of Albion's degenerate progeny undermine foundations of spiritual
    renewal embodied in the city/woman Jerusalem. Mandrakes, roots with vaguely human shapes, were
    considered aphrodisiacs and remedies for infertility. In a rivalry analogous to that between Jerusalem
    and Vala, the barren Rachel, one of Jacob's two wives, gives her fertile sister, Leah, a night with Jacob
    in exchange for mandrakes found by Leah's son Reuben (Genesis 30). This son, who also beds his
    own father's concubine (Genesis 35:22), becomes Blake's archetype of earthly, sensuous man.
7. Apocalyptic angel of the bottomless pit (Revelation 9:11) who unleashes plagues of locusts and
    scorpions.
8. Los's reference to God's omnipresence, even in hell, derives from Psalm 138:8.

And they appeard within & without incircling on both sides
The Starry Wheels of Albion's Sons, with Spaces for Jerusalem:
And for Vala the shadow of Jerusalem: the ever mourning shade:
On both sides, within & without beaming gloriously: 20

Terrified at the sublime Wonder, Los stood before his Furnaces.
And they stood around, terrified with admiration at Erin's Spaces
For the Spaces reachd from the starry heighth, to the starry
     depth;
And they builded Golgonooza: terrible eternal labour!

What are those golden builders doing? where was the
     burying-place
Of soft Ethinthus? near Tyburn's fatal Tree?[9] is that
Mild Zion's hill's most ancient promontory; near mournful
Ever weeping Paddington? is that Calvary and Golgotha?
Becoming a building of pity and compassion? Lo!
The stones are pity, and the bricks, well wrought affections;   30
Enameld with love & kindness, & the tiles engraven gold,
Labour of merciful hands: the beams & rafters are forgiveness:
The mortar & cement of the work, tears of honesty: the nails,
And the screws & iron braces, are well wrought blandishments,
And well contrived words, firm fixing, never forgotten,
Always comforting the remembrance: the floors, humility,
The cielings, devotion: the hearths, thanksgiving:
Prepare the furniture O Lambeth in thy pitying looms!
The curtains, woven tears & sighs, wrought into lovely forms
For comfort; there the secret furniture of Jerusalem's chamber   40
Is wrought: Lambeth! the Bride the Lamb's Wife loveth thee;
Thou art one with her & knowest not of self in thy supreme joy
Go on, builders in hope: tho Jerusalem wanders far away,
Without the gate of Los: among the dark Satanic wheels.

Fourfold the Sons of Los in their divisions: and fourfold
The great City of Golgonooza: fourfold toward the north
And toward the south fourfold, & fourfold toward the east & west
Each within other toward the four points: that toward
Eden, and that toward the World of Generation.
And that toward Beulah, and that toward Ulro;   50
Ulro is the space of the terrible starry wheels of Albion's sons:
But that toward Eden is walled up, till time of renovation:
Yet it is perfect in its building, ornaments & perfection.

And the Four Points are thus beheld in Great Eternity
West, the Circumference: South, the Zenith: North,
The Nadir; East, the Center, unapproachable for ever.
These are the four Faces towards the Four Worlds of Humanity

---

9. Site of public executions (c. 1200–1783) near South Molton Street (see map); in Blake's work, a latter-day site of Druidical human sacrifice. Before executions were moved indoors to Newgate in 1783, the forger W. W. Ryland, whom Blake had rejected as an engraving master because he had a "hanging look," became the last person executed at Tyburn (Peter Linebaugh, *Albion's Fatal Tree* [1975]). Ethinthus is a daughter of Enitharmon in *Europe* 17/14:1–2. "Golden builders": see *Jerusalem* 27:25 and n. 6, p. 240.

In every Man. Ezekiel saw them by Chebar's flood.[1]
And the Eyes are the South, and the Nostrils are the East.
And the Tongue is the West, and the Ear is the North.   60

And the North Gate of Golgonooza toward Generation:
Has four sculpturd Bulls terrible before the Gate of iron,
And iron, the Bulls: and that which looks toward Ulro,
Clay bak'd & enamel'd, eternal glowing as four furnaces:
Turning upon the Wheels of Albion's sons with enormous power.
And that toward Beulah four, gold. silver, brass, & iron;
And that toward Eden, four, form'd of gold, silver, brass, & iron.   13

The South, a golden Gate, has four Lions terrible, living!
That toward Generation, four, of iron carv'd wondrous:
That toward Ulro, four, clay bak'd, laborious workmanship
That toward Eden, four; immortal gold, silver, brass & iron.

The Western Gate fourfold is closd: having four Cherubim
Its guards, living, the work of elemental hands, laborious task!
Like Men, hermaphroditic, each winged with eight wings
That towards Generation, iron: that toward Beulah, stone:
That toward Ulro, clay: that toward Eden, metals.   10
But all clos'd up till the last day, when the graves shall yield their
    dead.

The Eastern Gate, fourfold; terrible & deadly its ornaments:
Taking their forms from the Wheels of Albion's sons; as cogs
Are formd in a wheel, to fit the cogs of the adverse wheel.

That toward Eden, eternal ice, frozen in seven folds
Of forms of death: and that toward Beulah, stone:
The seven diseases of the earth are carved terrible.
And that toward Ulro, forms of war; seven enormities;
And that toward Generation, seven generative forms.

And every part of the City is fourfold; & every inhabitant, fourfold.   20
And every pot & vessel & garment & utensil of the houses,
And every house, fourfold; but the third Gate in every one
Is closd as with a threefold curtain of ivory & fine linen & ermine,
And Luban stands in middle of the City, a moat of fire
Surrounds Luban, Los's Palace & the golden Looms of Cathedron.[2]
And sixty-four thousand Genii, guard the Eastern Gate:
And sixty-four thousand Gnomes, guard the Northern Gate:

1. Where the prophet sees a vision of four "living creatures" (Ezekiel 1; cf. Greek plural *zoa*, trans-lated "beasts" in Revelation 4:6–9), each with four faces and four wings, moving on wheels within wheels in all directions, bearing the throne of "the appearance of the likeness" of divine glory. This fourfold vision, along with the foursquare city of Revelation 21:16, is the prototype of such four-fold schema as the four seasons, four elements, four cardinal directions, four senses (taste and touch, both requiring contact, are united), four Gospels and their evangelists, the Four Zoas and their Emanations, and the four states of being (see the dagger note to *Four Zoas*). On the charac-teristics of the four states, see n. 6, p. 192 herein. Dimensions become surreal as Circumference, Center, Zenith, and Nadir are assigned points of the compass. The direction toward Eden is "walled up," and the "Western Gate fourfold" is closed (13:6).
2. Where the fabric of human life is woven (cf. *Milton* 13:26). "Luban": a gateway elsewhere associ-ated with the female genitalia.

And sixty-four thousand Nymphs, guard the Western Gate:
And sixty-four thousand Fairies, guard the Southern Gate:[3]

Around Golgonooza lies the land of death eternal! a Land   30
Of pain and misery and despair and ever brooding melancholy;
In all the Twenty-seven Heavens,[4] numberd from Adam to Luther;
From the blue Mundane Shell, reaching to the Vegetative Earth.

The Vegetative Universe opens like a flower from the Earth's center:
In which is Eternity. It expands in Stars to the Mundane Shell
And there it meets eternity again, both within and without,[5]
And the abstract Voids between the Stars are the Satanic Wheels.

There is the Cave; the Rock; the Tree; the Lake of Udan Adan;[6]
The Forest, and the Marsh, and the pits of bitumen deadly:
The Rocks of solid fire: the Ice valleys: the Plains   40
Of burning sand: the rivers, cataract & Lakes of Fire:
The Islands of the fiery Lakes: the Trees of Malice; Revenge;
And black Anxiety; and the Cities of the Salamandrine men:
(But whatever is visible to the Generated Man
Is a Creation of mercy & love, from the Satanic Void.)
The land of darkness flamed but no light, & no repose:
The land of snows of trembling, & of iron hail incessant:
The land of earthquakes: and the land of woven labyrinths:
The land of snares & traps & wheels & pit-falls & dire mills:
The Voids, the Solids, & the land of clouds & regions of waters: 50
With their inhabitants; in the Twenty-seven Heavens beneath
     Beulah:
Self-righteousnesses conglomerating against the Divine Vision:
A Concave Earth wondrous. Chasmal. Abyssal. Incoherent:
Forming the Mundane Shell: above; beneath: on all sides
     surrounding
Golgonooza; Los walks round the walls night and day.

He views the City of Golgonooza, & its smaller Cities:
The Looms & Mills & Prisons & Work-houses of Og & Anak:[7]
The Amalekite: the Canaanite: the Moabite; the Egyptian:
And all that has existed in the space of six thousand years:
Permanent, & not lost not lost nor vanishd, & every little act,   60
Word, work, & wish that has existed, all remaining still
In those Churches ever consuming & ever building by the Spectres
Of all the inhabitants of Earth wailing to be Created;
Shadowy to those who dwell not in them, meer possibilities:
But to those who enter into them they seem the only substances

3. Elemental spirits: Genii (fire), Gnomes (earth), Nymphs (water), Fairies (air). Cf. *Milton* **34**/31:20, partly anticipated in the mock-epic machinery of Pope's *The Rape of the Lock*. Sixty-four thousand is a multiple of four cubed (4^3), a perfect number in Blake's system (Ostriker). See also George Mills Harper, "The Divine Tetrad in *Jerusalem*," in *William Blake*, ed. Rosenfeld (1969).
4. False ideas of the supernal realm throughout history, falling short of the ideal fourfold multiple of seven; see n. 5, p. 163, and n. 5, p. 309.
5. True eternity lies deep within earthly existence and at the highest reach of the human imagination.
6. Mentioned in **5**:10 and **7**:22, this lake "not of Waters but of spaces" (*The Four Zoas* **8**:224, not included in this edition) is associated with a strictly material universe, barren of spirit or imagination.
7. Telescoping time and space, Blake places London's centers of misery within the territories of biblical Israel's enemies.

For every thing exists & not one sigh nor smile nor tear,
One hair nor particle of dust, not one can pass away.[8]   14

He views the Cherub at the Tree of Life, also the Serpent,
Orc the first born coild in the south: the Dragon Urizen:
Tharmas the Vegetated Tongue even the Devouring Tongue:
A threefold region, a false brain; a false heart:
And false bowels: altogether composing the False Tongue,
Beneath Beulah: as a watry flame revolving every way[9]
And as dark roots and stems: a Forest of affliction; growing
In seas of sorrow. Los also views the Four Females:
Ahania, and Enion, and Vala, and Enitharmon lovely.   10
And from them all the lovely beaming Daughters of Albion.
Ahania & Enion & Vala are three evanescent shades:
Enitharmon is a vegetated mortal Wife of Los:
His Emanation, yet his Wife till the sleep of death is past.

Such are the Buildings of Los: & such are the Woofs of
    Enitharmon!

And Los beheld his Sons, and he beheld his Daughters:
Every one a translucent Wonder: a Universe within,
Increasing inwards, into length, and breadth, and heighth:
Starry & glorious: and they every one in their bright loins:
Have a beautiful golden gate which opens into the vegetative
    world: 20
And every one a gate of rubies & all sorts of precious stones

8. Los's imaginative encompassing of all that has ever existed is expressed in language recalling
   both Jesus' assurance that every hair is numbered (Matthew 10:30) and Newton's law of the
   conservation of matter. "Six thousand years" (line 59): traditionally, the period from Creation to
   Apocalypse.
9. The cherub whose flaming sword "turned every way" to guard the tree of life (Genesis 3:24; cf.
   Marriage 14) takes different forms in the various Zoas.

In their translucent hearts, which opens into the vegetative world:
And every one a gate of iron dreadful and wonderful.
In their translucent heads, which opens into the vegetative world
And every one has the three regions Childhood: Manhood: & Age.
But the gate of the tongue: the western gate in them is clos'd.
Having a wall builded against it, and thereby the gates
Eastward & Southward & Northward are incircled with flaming
    fires.
And the North is Breadth, the South is Heighth & Depth:
The East is Inwards; & the West is Outwards every way.   30
And Los beheld the mild Emanation Jerusalem eastward bending
Her revolutions toward the Starry Wheels in maternal anguish
Like a pale cloud arising from the arms of Beulah's Daughters:
In Entuthon Benython's deep Vales beneath Golgonooza.
And Hand & Hyle rooted into Jerusalem by a fibre   15
Of strong revenge & Skofeld Vegetated by Reuben's Gate
In every Nation of the Earth till the Twelve Sons of Albion
Enrooted into every Nation: a mighty Polypus growing
From Albion over the whole Earth: such is my awful Vision.

I see the Four-fold Man. The Humanity in deadly sleep
And its fallen Emanation. The Spectre & its cruel Shadow
I see the Past, Present & Future, existing all at once
Before me;[1] O Divine Spirit sustain me on thy wings!
That I may awake Albion from his long & cold repose.   10
For Bacon & Newton sheathd in dismal steel their terrors hang
Like iron scourges over Albion, Reasonings like vast Serpents
Infold around my limbs, bruising my minute articulations.

I turn my eyes to the Schools & Universities of Europe
And there behold the Loom of Locke whose Woof rages dire
Washd by the Water-wheels of Newton. Black the cloth
In heavy wreathes folds over every Nation; cruel Works
Of many Wheels I view, wheel without wheel, with cogs tyrannic
Moving by compulsion each other: not as those in Eden: which
Wheel within Wheel[2] in freedom revolve in harmony & peace.   20

I see in deadly fear in London Los raging round his Anvil
Of death: forming an Ax of gold: the Four Sons of Los
Stand round him cutting the Fibres from Albion's hills[3]
That Albion's Sons may roll apart over the Nations
While Reuben enroots his brethren[4] in the narrow Canaanite
From the Limit Noah to the Limit Abram in whose Loins

---

1. Direct authorial address (cf. line 21 and *J* 4:5), echoing "Introduction" to *Experience*. Here Humanity, Emanation, Spectre, and Shadow make up the "Four-fold Man." In this poem, only Los/Urthona and Luvah from *The Four Zoas* quaternary (see dagger note, p. 408 herein) have major roles; the others are hardly mentioned at all.
2. Visionary wheels within wheels (Ezekiel 1:16) contrast with gear-driven industrial machinery (run by human cogs in a larger socioeconomic machine; cf. 13:13–14), and with what Blake considered the soul-grinding mechanistic reasoning of Locke (on the mind) and Newton (on the cosmos).
3. Los's helpers strike at the fibrous roots and tentacles of the "Polypus" (15:4, 18:40)—both a sea creature and a cancerous lesion—that stems from Albion to his vegetated sons (cf. Paul Miner, *Texas Studies in Literature and Language* 2 [1960]).
4. Developed in Chapter 2 (31/45:43 ff.).

Reuben in his Twelve-fold majesty & beauty shall take refuge
As Abraham flees from Chaldea shaking his goary locks.[5]
But first Albion must sleep, divided from the Nations.

I see Albion sitting upon his Rock in the first Winter   30
And thence I see the Chaos of Satan & the World of Adam
When the Divine Hand went forth on Albion in the mid Winter
And at the place of Death when Albion sat in Eternal Death
Among the Furnaces of Los in the Valley of the Son of Hinnom.[6]

Hampstead Highgate Finchley Hendon Muswell hill: rage loud |16|
Before Bromion's iron Tongs & glowing Poker reddening fierce
Hertfordshire glows with fierce Vegetation! in the Forests
The Oak frowns terrible, the Beech & Ash & Elm enroot
Among the Spiritual fires: loud the Corn fields thunder along
The Soldier's fife; the Harlot's shriek; the Virgin's dismal groan
The Parent's fear: the Brother's jealousy: the Sister's curse
Beneath the Storms of Theotormon & the thundring Bellows
Heaves in the hand of Palamabron who in London's darkness
Before the Anvil watches the bellowing flames: thundering   10
The Hammer loud rages in Rintrah's strong grasp swinging loud
Round from heaven to earth down falling with heavy blow
Dead on the Anvil, where the red hot wedge groans in pain.
He quenches it in the black trough of his Forge: London's River
Feeds the dread Forge, trembling & shuddering along the Valleys.

Humber & Trent roll dreadful before the Seventh Furnace
And Tweed & Tyne anxious give up their Souls for Albion's sake
Lincolnshire Derbyshire Nottinghamshire Leicestershire
From Oxfordshire to Norfolk on the Lake of Udan Adan
Labour within the Furnaces, walking among the Fires   20
With Ladles huge & iron Pokers over the Island white.

Scotland pours out his Sons to labour at the Furnaces
Wales gives his Daughters to the Looms; England: nursing
     Mothers
Gives to the Children of Albion & to the Children of Jerusalem.
From the blue Mundane Shell even to the Earth of Vegetation
Throughout the whole Creation which groans to be deliverd[7]
Albion groans in the deep slumbers of Death upon his Rock.

Here Los fixd down the Fifty-two Counties of England & Wales
The Thirty-six of Scotland, & the Thirty-four of Ireland
With mighty power, when they fled out at Jerusalem's Gates   30
Away from the Conflict of Luvah & Urizen, fixing the Gates
In the Twelve Counties of Wales & thence Gates looking every way
To the Four Points: conduct to England & Scotland & Ireland

---

5. Abraham, "father of a great multitude," is God's new name for Abram, born in Ur of the Chaldees (Genesis 11:31). Banquo's ghost shakes his "gory locks" in *Macbeth* 3.3.
6. Place of human sacrifice, where children are burned alive as offerings to the idol Molech (Jeremiah 7:31; 2 Kings 23:10; 2 Chronicles 28:3, 33:6).
7. A sign of the end of time (cf. Romans 8:22), with an implied comparison to the pangs of childbirth.

And thence to all the Kingdoms & Nations & Families of the Earth.
The Gate of Reuben in Carmarthenshire: the Gate of Simeon in
Cardiganshire; & the Gate of Levi in Montgomeryshire
The Gate of Judah Merionethshire: the Gate of Dan Flintshire
The Gate of Napthali, Radnorshire: the Gate of Gad
    Pembrokeshire
The Gate of Asher, Carnarvonshire the Gate of Issachar
    Brecknokshire
The Gate of Zebulun, in Anglesea & Sodor, so is Wales divided.   40
The Gate of Joseph, Denbighshire; the Gate of Benjamin
    Glamorganshire
For the protection of the Twelve Emanations of Albion's Sons
And the Forty Counties of England are thus divided in the Gates
Of Reuben: Norfolk, Suffolk, Essex; Simeon: Lincoln York
    Lancashire;
Levi: Middlesex Kent Surrey; Judah: Somerset Glouster Wiltshire;
Dan: Cornwal Devon Dorset; Napthali: Warwick Leicester
    Worcester;
Gad: Oxford Bucks Harford; Asher: Sussex Hampshire Berkshire;
Issachar: Northampton Rutland Nottgham; Zebulun: Bedford
    Huntgn Camb;
Joseph: Stafford Shrops Heref; Benjamin: Derby Cheshire
    Monmouth;
And Cumberland Northumberland Westmoreland & Durham are   50
Divided in the Gates of Reuben Judah Dan & Joseph
And the Thirty-six Counties of Scotland divided in the Gates
Of Reuben: Kincard Haddntn Forfar; Simeon: Ayr Argyll Banff;
Levi: Edinburh Roxbro Ross; Judah: Abrdeen Berwik Dumfries;
Dan: Bute Caitnes Clakmanan; Napthali: Nairn Invernes Linlithgo;
Gad: Peebles Perth Renfru; Asher: Sutherlan Sterling Wigtoun;
Issachar: Selkirk Dumbartn Glasgo; Zebulun: Orkney Shetland
    Skye;
Joseph: Elgin Lanerk Kinros; Benjamin: Kromarty Murra
    Kirkubriht,[8]
Governing all by the sweet delights of secret amorous glances
In Enitharmon's Halls builded by Los & his mighty Children.   60

All things acted on Earth are seen in the bright Sculptures of
Los's Halls & every Age renews its powers from these Works
With every pathetic story possible to happen from Hate or
Wayward Love & every sorrow & distress is carved here,
Every Affinity of Parents, Marriages & Friendships are here
In all their various combinations wrought with wondrous Art
All that can happen to Man in his pilgrimage of seventy years
Such is the Divine Written Law of Horeb & Sinai:
And such the Holy Gospel of Mount Olivet & Calvary:[9]

His Spectre divides & Los in fury compels it to divide: 17
To labour in the fire, in the water, in the earth, in the air.

8. This (slightly altered and heavily abbreviated) list of British counties assigned to the twelve tribes
   of Israel—a clear example of "prosaic" versification for "inferior parts" (p. 211 herein)—is modeled
   on Homeric epic catalogs (of ships or troops) and biblical genealogies and censuses.
9. Los's archetypes encompass the entire law and gospel as well as secular history.

To follow the Daughters of Albion as the hound follows the scent
Of the wild inhabitant of the forest, to drive them from his own:
To make a way for the Children of Los to come from the Furnaces.
But Los himself against Albion's Sons his fury bends, for he
Dare not approach the Daughters openly lest he be consumed
In the fires of their beauty & perfection & be Vegetated beneath
Their Looms, in a Generation of death & resurrection to
    forgetfulness.
They wooe Los continually to subdue his strength: he continually   10
Shews them his Spectre: sending him abroad over the four points
    of heaven
In the fierce desires of beauty & in the tortures of repulse! He is
The Spectre of the Living pursuing the Emanations of the Dead.
Shuddring they flee: they hide in the Druid Temples in cold
    chastity:
Subdued by the Spectre of the Living & terrified by undisguisd
    desire.

For Los said: "Tho my Spectre is divided: as I am a Living Man
I must compell him to obey me wholly! that Enitharmon may not
Be lost: & lest he should devour Enitharmon: Ah me!
Piteous image of my soft desires & loves: O Enitharmon!
I will compell my Spectre to obey: I will restore to thee thy
    Children.   20
No one bruises or starves himself to make himself fit for labour:

Tormented with sweet desire for these beauties of Albion
They would never love my power if they did not seek to destroy
Enitharmon: Vala would never have sought & loved Albion
If she had not sought to destroy Jerusalem: such is that false
And Generating Love: a pretence of love to destroy love:
Cruel hipocrisy unlike the lovely delusions of Beulah:
And cruel forms, unlike the merciful forms of Beulah's Night,

They know not why they love nor wherefore they sicken & die
Calling that Holy Love: which is Envy Revenge & Cruelty   30
Which separated the stars from the mountains: the mountains
    from Man
And left Man a little grovelling Root, outside of Himself.
Negations are not Contraries: Contraries mutually Exist:
But Negations Exist Not: Exceptions & Objections & Unbeliefs
Exist not: nor shall they ever be Organized for ever & ever:
If thou separate from me, thou art a Negation: a meer
Reasoning & Derogation from me, an Objecting & cruel Spite
And Malice & Envy: but my Emanation, Alas! will become
My Contrary: O thou Negation, I will continually compell
Thee to be invisible to any but whom I please, & when   40
And where & how I please, and never! never! shalt thou be
    Organized
But as a distorted & reversed Reflexion in the Darkness
And in the Non Entity: nor shall that which is above
Ever descend into thee: but thou shalt be a Non Entity for ever
And if any enter into thee, thou shalt be an Unquenchable Fire

And he shall be a never dying Worm,[1] mutually tormented by
Those that thou tormentest, a Hell & Despair For ever & ever."

So Los in secret with himself communed & Enitharmon heard
In her darkness & was comforted: yet still she divided away
In gnawing pain from Los's bosom in the deadly Night;   50
First as a red Globe of blood trembling beneath his bosom[2]
Suspended over her he hung: he infolded her in his garments
Of wool: he hid her from the Spectre, in shame & confusion of
Face;[3] in terrors & pains of Hell & Eternal Death, the
Trembling Globe shot forth Self-living & Los howld over it:
Feeding it with his groans & tears day & night without ceasing:
And the Spectrous Darkness from his back divided in temptations,
And in grinding agonies in threats: stiflings: & direful strugglings.

"Go thou to Skofield: ask him if he is Bath or if he is Canterbury
Tell him to be no more dubious: demand explicit words   60
Tell him: I will dash him into shivers, where & at what time
I please: tell Hand & Skofield they are my ministers of evil
To those I hate; for I can hate also as well as they!"

From every-one of the Four Regions of Human Majesty,   18
There is an Outside spread Without, & an Outside spread Within
Beyond the Outline of Identity both ways, which meet in One:
An orbed Void of doubt, despair, hunger, & thirst & sorrow.
Here the Twelve Sons of Albion join'd in dark Assembly,
Jealous of Jerusalem's children, asham'd of her little-ones
(For Vala produc'd the Bodies, Jerusalem gave the Souls)
Became as Three Immense Wheels, turning upon one-another
Into Non-Entity, and their thunders hoarse appall the Dead
To murder their own Souls, to build a Kingdom among the Dead.   10

"Cast! Cast ye Jerusalem forth![4] The Shadow of delusions!
The Harlot daughter! Mother of pity and dishonourable
    forgiveness
Our Father Albion's sin and shame! But father now no more!
Nor sons! nor hateful peace & love, nor soft complacencies
With transgressors meeting in brotherhood around the table,
Or in the porch or garden. No more the sinful delights
Of age and youth and boy and girl and animal and herb,
And river and mountain, and city & village, and house & family,
Beneath the Oak & Palm, beneath the Vine and Fig-tree.
In self-denial! But War and deadly contention Between   20
Father and Son, and light and love! All bold asperities
Of Haters met in deadly strife, rending the house & garden
The unforgiving porches, the tables of enmity, and beds
And chambers of trembling & suspition, hatreds of age & youth

1. The undying worm and unquenchable fire are ultimate punishments in Isaiah 66:24 and Mark
   9:44,9:48.
2. An elaboration of *Urizen* 18; cf. *M* 3:28–36.
3. Derived from Psalm 44:15 and Daniel 9:7; cf. letter to Butts, p. 481 herein.
4. Cf. the allegory of Sarah and Hagar in Galatians 4:21–31 (Paley) and such sexually charged con-
   demnations of the faithless Jerusalem/Israel as Jeremiah 2–3, Lamentations 1–2, Ezekiel 16 and
   23, and Hosea 2.

And boy & girl, & animal & herb, & river & mountain
And city & village, and house & family, That the Perfect
May live in glory, redeem'd by Sacrifice of the Lamb
And of his children, before sinful Jerusalem. To build
Babylon the City of Vala, the Goddess Virgin-Mother.
She is our Mother! Nature! Jerusalem is our Harlot-Sister   30
Return'd with Children of pollution, to defile our House
With Sin and Shame. Cast! Cast her into the Potter's field.[5]
Her little-ones She must slay upon our Altars: and her aged
Parents must be carried into captivity, to redeem her Soul
To be for a Shame & a Curse, and to be our Slaves for ever."

So cry Hand & Hyle the eldest of the fathers of Albion's
Little-ones: to destroy the Divine Saviour; the Friend of Sinners,
Building Castles in desolated places, and strong Fortifications.
Soon Hand mightily devour'd & absorb'd Albion's Twelve Sons.
Out from his bosom a mighty Polypus, vegetating in darkness.[6]   40
And Hyle & Coban were his two chosen ones for Emissaries
In War; forth from his bosom they went and return'd.
Like Wheels from a great Wheel reflected in the Deep.
Hoarse turn'd the Starry Wheels, rending a way in Albion's Loins
Beyond the Night of Beulah. In a dark & unknown Night.
Outstretch'd his Giant beauty on the ground in pain & tears;

His Children exil'd from his breast, pass to and fro before him   19
His birds are silent on his hills, flocks die beneath his branches
His tents are fall'n! his trumpets, and the sweet sound of his harp
Are silent on his clouded hills, that belch forth storms & fire,
His milk of Cows, & honey of Bees, & fruit of golden harvest,
Is gather'd in the scorching heat, & in the driving rain:
Where once he sat he weary walks in misery and pain:
His Giant beauty and perfection fallen into dust:
Till from within his witherd breast grown narrow with his woes:
The corn is turn'd to thistles & the apples into poison: 10
The birds of song to murderous crows, his joys to bitter groans!
The voices of children in his tents to cries of helpless infants:
And self-exiled from the face of light & shine of morning,
In the dark world a narrow house! he wanders up and down.
Seeking for rest and finding none! and hidden far within,
His Eon[7] weeping in the cold and desolated Earth.

All his Affections now appear withoutside: all his Sons,
Hand, Hyle & Coban, Guantok, Peachey, Brereton, Slayd &
  Hutton,
Scofeld, Kox, Kotope & Bowen; his Twelve Sons: Satanic Mill!
Who are the Spectres of the Twentyfour, each Double-form'd: 20
Revolve upon his mountains groaning in pain: beneath
The dark incessant sky, seeking for rest and find none:
Raging against their Human natures, ravning to gormandize

5. Nonconsecrated burial ground, bought with Judas's rejected blood money (Matthew 27:7).
6. Cf. those emerging from Albion's bosom (J 32/46:10), depicted in J 50.
7. In this context, not an era of time but a synonym for "Emanation" (cf. 40/36:41, 19:16, and *Milton* 12/11:1), a term from Bryant's *New System*.

The Human majesty and beauty of the Twentyfour.
Condensing them into solid rocks with cruelty and abhorrence
Suspition & revenge, & the seven diseases of the Soul
Settled around Albion and around Luvah in his secret cloud.
Willing the Friends endur'd, for Albion's sake, and for
Jerusalem his Emanation shut within his bosom;
Which hardend against them more and more; as he builded
    onwards   30
On the Gulph of Death in self-righteousness, that roll'd
Before his awful feet, in pride of virtue for victory:
And Los was roofd in from Eternity in Albion's Cliffs
Which stand upon the ends of Beulah, and withoutside, all
Appear'd a rocky form against the Divine Humanity.

Albion's Circumference was clos'd: his Center began darkning
Into the Night of Beulah, and the Moon of Beulah rose
Clouded with storms: Los his strong Guard walked round beneath
    the Moon
And Albion fled inward among the currents of his rivers.

He found Jerusalem upon the River of his City soft repos'd   40
In the arms of Vala, assimilating in one with Vala[8]
The Lilly of Havilah: and they sang soft thro' Lambeth's vales,[9]
In a sweet moony night & silence that they had created
With a blue sky spread over with wings and a mild moon.
Dividing & uniting into many female forms: Jerusalem
Trembling! then in one comingling in eternal tears,
Sighing to melt his Giant beauty, on the moony river.

But when they saw Albion fall'n upon mild Lambeth's vale:
Astonish'd! Terrified! they hover'd over his Giant limbs.
Then thus Jerusalem spoke, while Vala wove the veil of tears:
Weeping in pleadings of Love, in the web of despair:

"Wherefore hast thou shut me into the winter of human life
And clos'd up the sweet regions of youth and virgin innocence:
Where we live, forgetting error, not pondering on evil:
Among my lambs & brooks of water, among my warbling birds:
Where we delight in innocence before the face of the Lamb;
Going in and out before him in his love and sweet affection."   10

Vala replied weeping & trembling, hiding in her veil:

"When winter rends the hungry family and the snow falls:
Upon the ways of men hiding the paths of man and beast,

---

8. Not yet registering Albion's fall, the eternal, spiritual Jerusalem and the temporal, physical Vala
   enjoy unrestrained intimacy—probably depicted on plate 28 (p. 243), first etched as an image of
   male-female copulation. The subliminal eroticism of their embrace, as they compete for Albion's
   affections, is probably meant to be disturbing; it is not yet clear that the Emanation Jerusalem, in
   the unfallen state, is Albion's daughter rather than his wife or lover (Blake may have changed his
   mind in the years of his work on the poem). On Vala, see Ostriker, p. 566 herein.
9. Before moving to Felpham the Blakes lived in the London section of Lambeth (see map), as
   recorded on the title pages of Blake's earlier prophetic books. Havilah is watered by Pison, one of
   the four rivers of Eden (Genesis 2:10–11).

Then mourns the wanderer: then he repents his wanderings & eyes
The distant forest; then the slave groans in the dungeon of stone.
The captive in the mill of the stranger, sold for scanty hire.
They view their former life: they number moments over and over:
Stringing them on their remembrance as on a thread of sorrow.
Thou art my sister and my daughter! thy shame is mine also!
Ask me not of my griefs! thou knowest all my griefs."   20

Jerusalem answer'd with soft tears over the valleys.

"O Vala what is Sin? that thou shudderest and weepest
At sight of thy once lov'd Jerusalem! What is Sin but a little
Error & fault that is soon forgiven; but mercy is not a Sin
Nor pity nor love nor kind forgiveness! O! if I have Sinned
Forgive & pity me; O! unfold thy Veil in mercy & love!

Slay not my little ones, beloved Virgin daughter of Babylon
Slay not my infant loves & graces, beautiful daughter of Moab.
I cannot put off the human form, I strive but strive in vain.
When Albion rent thy beautiful net of gold and silver twine;   30
Thou hadst woven it with art, thou hadst caught me in the bands
Of love; thou refusedst to let me go! Albion beheld thy beauty
Beautiful thro' our Love's comeliness, beautiful thro' pity.
The Veil shone with thy brightness in the eyes of Albion.
Because it inclosd pity & love; because we lov'd one-another!
Albion lov'd thee! he rent thy Veil! he embrac'd thee! he lov'd thee!
Astonish'd at his beauty & perfection, thou forgavest his furious
    love
I redounded from Albion's bosom in my virgin loveliness.
The Lamb of God reciev'd me in his arms; he smil'd upon us:
He made me his Bride & Wife: he gave thee to Albion.   40
Then was a time of love! O why is it passed away!"[1]

Then Albion broke silence and with groans reply'd:

"O Vala! O Jerusalem! do you delight in my groans   21
You O lovely forms, you have prepared my death-cup:
The disease of Shame covers me from head to feet; I have no hope
Every boil upon my body is a separate & deadly Sin.[2]
Doubt first assaild me, then Shame took possession of me
Shame divides Families. Shame hath divided Albion in sunder!
First fled my Sons, & then my Daughters, then my Wild
    Animations
My Cattle next, last ev'n the Dog of my Gate. The Forests fled,
The Corn-fields, & the breathing Gardens outside separated,
The Sea; the Stars; the Sun; the Moon! drivn forth by my disease.   10
All is Eternal Death unless you can weave a chaste
Body over an unchaste Mind! Vala! O that thou wert pure!
That the deep wound of Sin might be clos'd up with the Needle,
And with the Loom: to cover Gwendolen & Ragan with costly
    Robes

1. Reworking of Ezekiel 16:8 ff.
2. Variation on the affliction of sore boils in Job 2:7, further developed in J 29/43:64.

Of Natural Virtue, for their Spiritual forms without a Veil
Wither in Luvah's Sepulcher. I thrust him from my presence
And all my Children followd his loud howlings into the Deep.
Jerusalem! dissembler Jerusalem! I look into thy bosom!
I discover thy secret places: Cordella! I behold
Thee whom I thought pure as the heavens in innocence & fear: 20
Thy Tabernacle taken down, thy secret Cherubim disclosed
Art thou broken? Ah me Sabrina, running by my side:
In childhood what wert thou? unutterable anguish! Conwenna
Thy cradled infancy is most piteous. O hide, O hide!
Their secret gardens were made paths to the traveller:
I knew not of their secret loves with those I hated most.
Nor that their every thought was Sin & secret appetite.
Hyle sees in fear, he howls in fury over them, Hand sees
In jealous fear; in stern accusation with cruel stripes
He drives them thro' the Streets of Babylon before my face: 30
Because they taught Luvah to rise into my clouded heavens
Battersea and Chelsea mourn for Cambel & Gwendolen!
Hackney and Holloway sicken for Estrild & Ignoge!
Because the Peak, Malvern & Cheviot Reason in Cruelty
Penmaenmawr & Dhinas-bran Demonstrate in Unbelief
Manchester & Liverpool are in tortures of Doubt & Despair
Malden & Colchester Demonstrate: I hear my Children's voices
I see their piteous faces gleam out upon the cruel winds
From Lincoln & Norwich, from Edinburgh & Monmouth.
I see them distant from my bosom scourgd along the roads   40
Then lost in clouds; I hear their tender voices! clouds divide
I see them die beneath the whips of the Captains! they are taken
In solemn pomp into Chaldea across the bredths of Europe
Six months they lie embalmd in silent death: worshipped,[3]
Carried in Arks of Oak before the armies in the spring
Bursting their Arks they rise again to life! they play before
The Armies: I hear their loud cymbals & their deadly cries
Are the Dead cruel? are those who are infolded in moral Law
Revengeful? O that Death & Annihilation were the same!"

Then Vala answerd spreading her scarlet Veil over Albion,[4]   50

"Albion thy fear has made me tremble; thy terrors have
    surrounded me,   22
Thy Sons have naild me on the Gates piercing my hands & feet:
Till Skofield's Nimrod the mighty Huntsman Jehovah came
With Cush his Son & took me down. He in a golden Ark
Bears me before his Armies tho my Shadow hovers here.[5]
The flesh of multitudes fed & nourishd me in my childhood

3. Apparently written "warshipped," a visual pun noted by Hilton and adopted by Erdman, Paley, and the Blake Archive. Albion laments that his daughters are worshiped as vegetation goddesses in arks carried before armies (cf. the Israelites' carrying the Ark of the Covenant into battle in 1 Samuel 4:3–6).
4. Filling Albion's field of vision, the woven fabric of Vala's Veil, the emblem of illusory entrapment in the natural world, conflates imagery of flesh and blood (circulatory network, hymen, placenta) with the veil over the ark of the covenant (Exodus 26:31–33), the tabernacle hangings (Exodus 26:36), and the Whore of Babylon's robes (Revelation 17:4). Cf. Paul Miner, Criticism 3 (1961), 46–61 and Blake's own escape from "the Web & the Veil" of London (p. 473 herein).
5. Vala claims that Nimrod and Cush (whose genealogy in Genesis 10:6–10 is reversed) carry her martyred body in an even grander version of the ark (cf. n. 3).

My morn & evening food were prepard in Battles of Men.
Great is the cry of the Hounds of Nimrod along the Valley
Of Vision, they scent the odor of War in the Valley of Vision.
All Love is lost! terror succeeds & Hatred instead of Love[6]   10
And stern demands of Right & Duty instead of Liberty
Once thou wast to me the loveliest Son of heaven; but now
Where shall I hide from thy dread countenance & searching eyes
I have looked into the secret Soul of him I loved
And in the dark recesses found Sin & can never return."

Albion again utterd his voice beneath the silent Moon:

"I brought Love into light of day to pride in chaste beauty
I brought Love into light & fancied Innocence is no more."

Then spoke Jerusalem "O Albion! my Father Albion
Why wilt thou number every little fibre of my Soul   20
Spreading them out before the Sun like stalks of flax to dry?
The Infant Joy is beautiful, but its anatomy
Horrible ghast & deadly! nought shalt thou find in it
But dark despair & everlasting brooding melancholy!"

Then Albion turnd his face toward Jerusalem & spoke.

"Hide thou Jerusalem in impalpable voidness, not to be
Touchd by the hand nor seen with the eye: O Jerusalem,
Would thou wert not & that thy place might never be found
But come O Vala with knife & cup! drain my blood
To the last drop! then hide me in thy Scarlet Tabernacle   30
For I see Luvah whom I slew. I behold him in my Spectre
As I behold Jerusalem in thee O Vala dark and cold."

Jerusalem then stretchd her hand toward the Moon & spoke.

"Why should Punishment Weave the Veil with Iron Wheels of
    War
When Forgiveness might it Weave with Wings of Cherubim?"

Loud groand Albion from mountain to mountain & replied,

"Jerusalem! Jerusalem! deluding shadow of Albion! | 23 |
Daughter of my phantasy! unlawful pleasure! Albion's curse!
I came here with intention to annihilate thee! But
My soul is melted away. Inwoven within the Veil
Hast thou again knitted the Veil of Vala, which I for thee
Pitying rent in ancient times,[7] I see it whole and more
Perfect, and shining with beauty!" "But thou! O wretched
    Father!"

---

6. Several lines of Vala's speech, and that of Jerusalem (below), are adapted from a dialogue between
   Enion and Tharmas in *Four Zoas*, Night 1.
7. Splitting the veil that conceals the ark (at Jesus' crucifixion, Matthew 27:51); shattering illusion.
   Albion later uses the reknit veil as a net (**23**:23) and as a shroud (**23**:36).

Jerusalem reply'd, like a voice heard from a sepulcher:
"Father! once piteous! Is Pity a Sin? Embalm'd in Vala's bosom
In an Eternal Death for Albion's sake, our best beloved: 10
Thou art my Father & my Brother: Why hast thou hidden me,
Remote from the divine Vision: my Lord and Saviour."

Trembling stood Albion at her words in jealous dark despair

He felt that Love and Pity are the same; a soft repose!
Inward complacency of Soul: a Self-annihilation!

"I have erred! I am ashamed! and will never return more;
I have taught my children sacrifices of cruelty: what shall I answer?
I will hide it from Eternals! I will give myself for my Children!
Which way soever I turn, I behold Humanity and Pity!"

He recoil'd: he rush'd outwards; he bore the Veil whole away   20
His fires redound from his Dragon Altars in Errors returning
He drew the Veil of Moral Virtue, woven for Cruel Laws,
And cast it into the Atlantic Deep, to catch the Souls of the Dead.
He stood between the Palm tree & the Oak of weeping[8]
Which stand upon the edge of Beulah; and there Albion sunk
Down in sick pallid languor! These were his last words, relapsing!
Hoarse from his rocks, from caverns of Derbyshire & Wales
And Scotland, utter'd from the Circumference into Eternity.

"Blasphemous Sons of Feminine delusion! God in the dreary Void[9]
Dwells from Eternity, wide separated from the Human Soul   30
But thou deluding Image by whom imbu'd the Veil I rent,
Lo here is Vala's Veil whole, for a Law, a Terror & a Curse!
And therefore God takes vengeance on me: from my clay-cold
    bosom
My children wander trembling victims of his Moral Justice.
His snows fall on me and cover me while in the Veil I fold
My dying limbs. Therefore O Manhood, if thou art aught
But a meer Phantasy, hear dying Albion's Curse!
May God who dwells in this dark Ulro & voidness, vengeance take,
And draw thee down into this Abyss of sorrow and torture,
Like me thy Victim. O that Death & Annihilation were the same!"   40

What have I said? What have I done? O all-powerful Human
    Words!   24
You recoil back upon me in the blood of the Lamb slain in his
    Children.
Two bleeding Contraries equally true are his Witnesses against me.
We reared mighty Stones! we danced naked around them:
Thinking to bring Love into light of day, to Jerusalem's shame:
Displaying our Giant limbs to all the winds of heaven! Sudden

---

8. The "Palm of Suffering" flanks Albion's tomb in 59:5, along with the "Oak of Weeping" (burial place of Rebekah's nurse; Genesis 35:8, gloss to King James Version).
9. Albion's "last words" run from here through 24:60. Shifting between first and third person and interspersing side remarks to others, Albion variously addresses Jesus or the Divine Image (which includes his own best self) as "deluding Image" (23:31), "Manhood" (23:36), "Human Imagination . . . Divine Body" (24:23), and "Lamb of God" (24:53)

Shame siezd us, we could not look on one-another for abhorrence.
  The Blue
Of our immortal Veins & all their Hosts fled from our Limbs,
And wanderd distant in a dismal Night clouded & dark:
The Sun fled from the Briton's forehead: the Moon from his
  mighty loins,   10
Scandinavia fled with all his mountains filld with groans.

O what is Life & what is Man, O what is Death? Wherefore
Are you my Children natives in the Grave to where I go?
Or are you born to feed the hungry ravenings of Destruction
To be the sport of Accident! to waste in Wrath & Love a weary
Life in brooding cares & anxious labours, that prove but chaff.
O Jerusalem Jerusalem I have forsaken thy Courts
Thy Pillars of ivory & gold: thy Curtains of silk & fine
Linen: thy Pavements of precious stones: thy Walls of pearl
And gold, thy Gates of Thanksgiving, thy Windows of Praise:[1]   20
Thy Clouds of Blessing; thy Cherubims of Tender-mercy
Stretching their Wings[2] sublime over the Little-ones of Albion.
O Human Imagination O Divine Body I have Crucified,
I have turned my back upon thee into the Wastes of Moral Law:
There Babylon is builded in the Waste, founded in Human
  desolation.
O Babylon thy Watchman stands over thee in the night
Thy severe Judge all the day long proves thee O Babylon
With provings of destruction, with giving thee thy heart's desire.
But Albion is cast forth to the Potter, his Children to the
  Builders,
To build Babylon because they have forsaken Jerusalem.   30
The Walls of Babylon are Souls of Men: her Gates the Groans
Of Nations: her Towers are the Miseries of once happy Families.
Her Streets are paved with Destruction, her Houses built with
  Death
Her Palaces with Hell & the Grave; her Synagogues with
  Torments
Of ever-hardening Despair squard & polishd with cruel skill.
Yet thou wast lovely as the summer cloud upon my hills
When Jerusalem was thy heart's desire in times of youth & love.
Thy Sons came to Jerusalem with gifts, she sent them away
With blessings on their hands & on their feet, blessings of gold,
And pearl & diamond: thy Daughters sang in her Courts: 40
They came up to Jerusalem; they walked before Albion
In the Exchanges of London every Nation walkd[3]
And London walkd in every Nation mutual in love & harmony.
Albion coverd the whole Earth, England encompassd the Nations,
Mutual each within other's bosom in Visions of Regeneration;
Jerusalem coverd the Atlantic Mountains & the Erythrean.
From bright Japan & China to Hesperia,[4] France & England.

---

1. The Jerusalem whom Albion has forsaken is the promised Zion that is to "call thy walls Salvation,
  and thy gates Praise" (Isaiah 60:18).
2. The cherubim who cover the mercy seat on the ark of the covenant (Exodus 25:18–20).
3. Cf. 27:85 and n. 7, p. 242 herein.
4. Italy, "country of the west."

Mount Zion lifted his head in every Nation under heaven:
And the Mount of Olives was beheld over the whole Earth:
The footsteps of the Lamb of God were there: but now no more   50
No more shall I behold him, he is closd in Luvah's Sepulcher.
Yet why these smitings of Luvah, the gentlest mildest Zoa?
If God was Merciful this could not be: O Lamb of God
Thou art a delusion and Jerusalem is my Sin! O my Children
I have educated you in the crucifying cruelties of Demonstration
Till you have assum'd the Providence of God & slain your Father.
Dost thou appear before me who liest dead in Luvah's Sepulcher[5]
Dost thou forgive me! thou who wast Dead & art Alive?
Look not so merciful upon me O thou Slain Lamb of God
I die! I die in thy arms tho Hope is banishd from me."   60

Thundring the Veil rushes from his hand Vegetating Knot by
Knot. Day by Day. Night by Night: loud roll the indignant
   Atlantic
Waves & the Erythrean, turning up the bottoms of the Deeps.

25

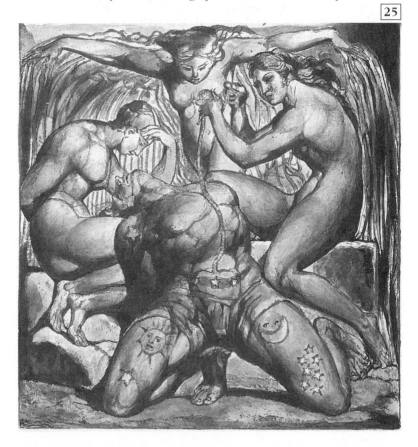

5. The vegetation god Luvah, Vala's former lover (7:36–37) and Urizen's opponent (16:31), was slain
by Albion (22:31) and placed in this sepulcher (21:16), in which Jesus now appears. Steeped in
guilt but rejecting forgiveness, the cosmic man succumbs to an agonizing death (cf. 22:29–30), as
depicted in the scene of torture by Vala and her confederates (J 25) that concludes Chapter 1.

And there was heard a great lamenting in Beulah: all the Regions
Of Beulah were moved as the tender bowels are moved: & they
    said:

"Why did you take Vengeance O ye Sons of the mighty Albion?
Planting these Oaken Groves: Erecting these Dragon Temples?[6]
Injury the Lord heals but Vengeance cannot be healed:
As the Sons of Albion have done to Luvah: so they have in him
Done to the Divine Lord & Saviour, who suffers with those that
    suffer;
For not one sparrow can suffer & the whole Universe not suffer
    also,
In all its Regions, & its Father & Saviour not pity and weep.[7]
But Vengeance is the destroyer of Grace & Repentance in the
    bosom   10
Of the Injurer; in which the Divine Lamb is cruelly slain;
Descend O Lamb of God & take away the imputation of Sin
By the Creation of States & the deliverance of Individuals
    Evermore Amen."

Thus wept they in Beulah over the Four Regions of Albion
But many doubted & despaird & imputed Sin & Righteousness
To Individuals & not to States, and these Slept in Ulro.

SUCH VISIONS HAVE APPEARED TO ME   26
AS I MY ORDERD RACE HAVE RUN
JERUSALEM IS NAMED LIBERTY
AMONG THE SONS OF ALBION[8]

To the Jews.   27

Jerusalem the Emanation of the Giant Albion! Can it be? Is it a
Truth that the Learned have explored? Was Britain the Primitive Seat
of the Patriarchal Religion? If it is true: my title-page is also True, that
Jerusalem was & is the Emanation of the Giant Albion. It is True, and
cannot be controverted. Ye are united O ye Inhabitants of Earth in One
Religion, The Religion of Jesus: the most Ancient, the Eternal: & the
Everlasting Gospel[9]—The Wicked will turn it to Wickedness, the
Righteous to Righteousness. Amen! Huzza! Selah![1]

---

6. Antiquarians of Blake's time believed that Druids worshiped in oak groves and that they built a temple shaped like a serpent (here called a "Dragon") in and around what is now the town of Avebury,
   near Stonehenge (see color plate 16).
7. Cf. the sparrow's fall in Matthew 10:29.
8. Written along the sides and between the figures in the chapter's frontispiece (not included in this
   edition): a nude man in flames labeled HAND, arms outstretched, looks back at a gowned woman
   labeled JERUSALEM, who raises her hands in distress.
9. On Blake's view of this original—and ultimate—dispensation to all humanity (Revelation 14:6) as
   the "religion of Jesus," as opposed to the timebound "old" and "new" testaments, see *Descriptive
   Catalogue* V (p. 429 herein) and the dagger note (p. 445) to his "Everlasting Gospel" Notebook
   fragments. On Blake's view of Judaism, see Karen Shabetei, *ELH* 63 (1996); Spector (2001); Leslie
   Tannenbaum in *British Romanticism and the Jews* (2002), ed. Spector; and Roger Whitsun, *Romanticism on the Net* 40 (2005).
1. Hebrew interjection of uncertain meaning (e.g., Psalms 3 and 4), here grouped with Amen (let it
   be) and the English Huzza (hooray) as an exclamation of approval.

"All things Begin & End in Albion's Ancient Druid Rocky Shore."[2]
Your Ancestors derived their origin from Abraham, Heber, Shem, and
Noah, who were Druids: as the Druid Temples (which are the Patriarchal
Pillars & Oak Groves) over the whole Earth witness to this day.[3]
You have a tradition, that Man anciently contain'd in his mighty limbs all
things in Heaven & Earth:[4] this you recieved from the Druids.
"But now the Starry Heavens are fled from the mighty limbs of Albion."
Albion was the Parent of the Druids; & in his Chaotic State of Sleep
Satan & Adam & the whole World was Created by the Elohim.[5]

The fields from Islington to Marybone,[6]
To Primrose Hill and Saint John's Wood:
Were builded over with pillars of gold,
And there Jerusalem's pillars stood.

Her Little-ones ran on the fields   5
The Lamb of God among them seen
And fair Jerusalem his Bride:
Among the little meadows green.

Pancrass & Kentish-town repose
Among her golden pillars high;   10
Among her golden arches which
Shine upon the starry sky.

The Jews-harp-house & the Green Man;[7]
The Ponds where Boys to bathe delight:
The fields of Cows by Willan's farm: 15
Shine in Jerusalem's pleasant sight.

She walks upon our meadows green:
The Lamb of God walks by her side:
And every English Child is seen,
Children of Jesus & his Bride.   20

2. With the line beginning "But now" (below), a rare example of quotation marks supplied by Blake
himself, explicating his own text (Milton 6:25–26) on the Divine Humanity's fall; see also J
32/46:15, 34/30:20, 75:27).
3. William Stukeley (1687–1765) and other antiquarians identified the British Druids with the
Hebrew patriarchs. According to Blake's Descriptive Catalogue, Abraham is "called to succeed the
Druidical age" to end human sacrifice. Heber, a descendant of Jacob's son Asher (Genesis 46:17),
and Shem, Noah's son and Abraham's ancestor (Genesis 10), are reminders of changes in the patriarchal religion over time.
4. On the primordial Adam Kadmon of mystical Jewish tradition, see Sheila A. Spector, "Wonders
Divine": The Development of Blake's Kabbalistic Myth (2001). Christianized kabbalistic lore was
disseminated, e.g., by Jacques Basnage (1643–1725), History of the Jews (trans. 1708).
5. In Genesis 1, the name of God, a Hebrew plural; also, in Gnostic tradition, the lower manifestation of the deity who, himself fallen, creates the material world; the third of Blake's "Seven Eyes
of God," or stages in humankind's slowly evolving recognition of the Divine Humanity, from Lucifer
and Molech through Jehovah to Jesus (see M 14/13:17–25).
6. In Blake's layout this poem is arranged in a double column. As anticipated in 12:25, imagery for
the building of Jerusalem (the soul) and Golgonooza (art) is drawn from John Nash's renovation
(1813–23) that incorporated outlying villages into London; transformed the slum of Paddington;
and created splendid terraces, roadways, and parks; see Stanley Gardner, Blake (1969). For landmark references, see the "Blake's London" map.
7. The Jews-harp-house (named for a musical instrument) was a tea garden, the Green Man (named
for a legendary fertility spirit) was a pie house; both were absorbed into Nash's Regent's Park, along
with Willan's Farm, where Blake used to play as a boy; see Paul Miner, Bulletin of the New York
Public Library (1958). Regent Street, leading from the Prince Regent's home in Carleton House
to Picadilly Circus, was colonnaded in gleaming cream-colored stucco, as if in "pillars of gold."

Forgiving trespasses and sins
Lest Babylon with cruel Og,[8]
With Moral & Self-righteous Law
Should Crucify in Satan's Synagogue![9]

What are those golden Builders doing   25
Near mournful ever-weeping Paddington
Standing above that mighty Ruin
Where Satan the first victory won,

Where Albion slept beneath the Fatal Tree
And the Druid's golden Knife,   30
Rioted in human gore,
In Offerings of Human Life?

They groan'd aloud on London Stone
They groan'd aloud on Tyburn's Brook.[1]
Albion gave his deadly groan.   35
And all the Atlantic Mountains shook.

Albion's Spectre from his Loins
Tore forth in all the pomp of War:
Satan his name: in flames of fire
He stretch'd his Druid Pillars far,   40

Jerusalem fell from Lambeth's Vale
Down thro Poplar & Old Bow;
Thro Malden & across the Sea,[2]
In War & howling death & woe,

The Rhine was red with human blood: 45
The Danube rolld a purple tide;
On the Euphrates Satan stood:
And over Asia stretch'd his pride.

He witherd up sweet Zion's Hill.
From every Nation of the Earth;   50
He witherd up Jerusalem's Gates,
And in a dark Land gave her birth.

He witherd up the Human Form,
By laws of sacrifice for sin:

8. The giant king of Bashan (Deuteronomy 3:11) is an enemy of Israel (cf. 22/20:33). Babylon the Whore opposes Jerusalem.
9. Members of early Christian churches who "say they are Jews, and are not" (Revelation 2:9, 3:9); the "worldly church" (Damon) that trusts in law, not vision.
1. London remnants of the satanic Druid altar on which Albion is tortured reach from the Tyburn gallows in the west to London Stone at the historic city center. In the next several stanzas Albion's Spectre or Selfhood, Satan himself, spreads British Druidism worldwide while shrinking and withering the human spirit into a small, faraway geographical space. Cf. James L. Swauger: "Old World dolmens occur in a band stretching from the British Isles and the Scandinavian countries, Germany, France, Portugal, and Spain east across Italy and North Africa into the Near East and the Caucasus, India, and on to Korea and Japan" (*Anchor Bible Dictionary* [1992], 2:221).
2. From nearby eastern villages (see map) and a port (correctly spelled "Maldon") on the English Channel, the perspective zooms out and pans east toward rivers of wartorn Europe and biblical Babylon.

Till it became a Mortal Worm: 55
But O! translucent all within.

The Divine Vision still was seen
Still was the Human Form, Divine
Weeping in weak & mortal clay
O Jesus still the Form was thine.   60

And thine the Human Face & thine
The Human Hands & Feet & Breath
Entering thro' the Gates of Birth
And passing thro' the Gates of Death.

And O thou Lamb of God, whom I   65
Slew in my dark self-righteous pride:
Art thou returnd to Albion's Land!
And is Jerusalem thy Bride?

Come to my arms & never more
Depart; but dwell for ever here: 70
Create my Spirit to thy Love:
Subdue my Spectre to thy Fear.

Spectre of Albion! warlike Fiend!
In clouds of blood & ruin roll'd:
I here reclaim³ thee as my own   75
My Selfhood; Satan! armd in gold.

Is this thy soft Family-Love
Thy cruel Patriarchal pride
Planting thy Family alone
Destroying all the World beside?⁴   80

A man's worst enemies are those
Of his own house & family;⁵
And he who makes his law a curse,
By his own law shall surely die.⁶

In my Exchanges⁷ every Land   85
Shall walk, & mine in every Land,
Mutual shall build Jerusalem:
Both heart in heart & hand in hand.

If Humility is Christianity; you O Jews are the true Christians; If your tradition that Man contained in his Limbs, all Animals, is True & they were separated from him by cruel Sacrifices; and when compulsory cruel Sacrifices

---

3. Meaning both "acknowledge" and "recover"; apparently spoken in Blake's authorial voice, which soon
   blends into Albion's voice. Cf. Milton's words to his own Satan in *Milton* 15/14:30 and 43/38:29 ff.
4. Equating British and Jewish claims of inherent exclusivity as a people.
5. Repeated in 41:25–26; cf. Micah 7:6 and Matthew 10:36.
6. Cf. Galatians 3:10.
7. Stock and currency markets associated with money-handling occupations open to European Jews
   (cf. *Marriage*, "Song of Liberty," verse 12); fallen metaphors of worldwide spiritual interchange,
   mourned in Albion's dying speech of Chapter 1 (24:42–45).

had brought Humanity into a Feminine Tabernacle, in the loins of Abraham & David;[8] the Lamb of God, the Saviour became apparent on Earth as the Prophets had foretold? The Return of Israel is a Return to Mental Sacrifice & War.[9] Take up the Cross O Israel & follow Jesus.

Jerusalem.
Chap: 2.

Every ornament of perfection, and every labour of love,
In all the Garden of Eden, & in all the golden mountains
Was become an envied horror, and a remembrance of jealousy:
And every Act a Crime, and Albion the punisher & judge.

And Albion spoke from his secret seat and said

"All these ornaments are crimes. They are made by the labours
Of loves: of unnatural consanguinities and friendships
Horrid to think of when enquired deeply into; and all
These hills & valleys are accursed witnesses of Sin.
I therefore condense them into solid rocks, stedfast!   10
A foundation and certainty and demonstrative truth:
That Man be separate from Man, & here I plant my seat."

Cold snows drifted around him: ice coverd his loins around.
He sat by Tyburn's brook, and underneath his heel, shot up!
A deadly Tree, he nam'd it Moral Virtue, and the Law
Of God who dwells in Chaos hidden from the human sight.

8. Referring to the Jewish emphasis on genealogy, perpetuated in the Christian claim that Jesus (or his earthly father Joseph) descended from David (Matthew 1).
9. Cf. *Milton* [i], p. 147 herein.

The Tree spread over him its cold shadows, (Albion groand)
They bent down, they felt the earth and again enrooting
Shot into many a Tree! an endless labyrinth of woe![1]

From willing sacrifice of Self to sacrifice of (miscall'd) Enemies   20
For Atonement: Albion began to erect twelve Altars,
Of rough unhewn rocks[2] before the Potter's Furnace
He nam'd them Justice and Truth. And Albion's Sons
Must have become the first Victims, being the first transgressors
But they fled to the mountains to seek ransom: building A Strong
Fortification against the Divine Humanity and Mercy,
In Shame & Jealousy to annihilate Jerusalem!

Then the Divine Vision like a silent Sun appeard above $\boxed{29/43}$
Albion's dark rocks: setting behind the Gardens of Kensington
On Tyburn's River, in clouds of blood: where was mild Zion Hill's
Most ancient promontory, and in the Sun a Human Form appeard
And thus the Voice Divine went forth upon the rocks of Albion

"I elected Albion for my glory; I gave to him the Nations
Of the whole Earth. He was the Angel of my Presence: and all
The Sons of God were Albion's Sons: and Jerusalem was my joy.
The Reactor[3] hath hid himself thro envy. I behold him.
But you cannot behold him till he be reveald in his System.   10
Albion's Reactor must have a Place prepard: Albion must Sleep
The Sleep of Death till the Man of Sin & Repentance be reveald,
Hidden in Albion's Forests he lurks; he admits of no Reply
From Albion; but hath founded his Reaction into a Law
Of Action, for Obedience to destroy the Contraries of Man.
He hath compelld Albion to become a Punisher & hath possessd
Himself of Albion's Forests & Wilds: and Jerusalem is taken!
The City of the Woods in the Forest of Ephratah[4] is taken!
London is a stone of her ruins; Oxford is the dust of her walls!
Sussex & Kent are her scatterd garments! Ireland her holy place!   20
And the murderd bodies of her little ones are Scotland and Wales.
The Cities of the Nations are the smoke of her consummation.
The Nations are her dust! ground by the chariot wheels
Of her lordly conquerors, her palaces levelld with the dust.
I come that I may find a way for my banished ones to return
Fear not O little Flock I come: Albion shall rise again."

So saying, the mild Sun inclosd the Human Family.

Forthwith from Albion's darkning locks came two Immortal forms
Saying "We alone are escaped.[5] O merciful Lord and Saviour,

1. Cf. "The Human Abstract."
2. Cf. the twelve stones commemorating the ark's passage over the Jordan (Joshua 4:8, 4:20) and Joshua's (8:30 ff.) altar of uncut stones displaying the Law; here associated with Druid ruins.
3. Required by Newton's laws (Paley); Albion's unrecognized negation, or Spectre, his Selfhood, also called Satan. The speaker is the Divine Vision in the form of the spiritual sun, or the "Sun of righteousness" (Malachi 4:2) as Messiah.
4. Alternate name for Bethlehem (Genesis 35:19; Psalm 132:6; Micah 5:2), in the vicinity of Jerusalem.
5. In their opening and closing words these two fugitive witnesses—Los's Spectre (under his "eternal" name Urthona) and his Emanation, Enitharmon—echo reporters of disasters in Job 1:13–19.

We flee from the interiors of Albion's hills and mountains!   30
From his Valleys Eastward: from Amalek Canaan & Moab,
Beneath his vast ranges of hills surrounding Jerusalem.
Albion walkd on the steps of fire before his Halls
And Vala walkd with him in dreams of soft deluding slumber.
He looked up & saw the Prince of Light with splendor faded
Then Albion ascended mourning into the porches of his Palace
Above him rose a Shadow from his wearied intellect:
Of living gold, pure, perfect, holy: in white linen pure he hoverd
A sweet entrancing self-delusion a watry vision of Albion
Soft exulting in existence; all the Man absorbing!   40

Albion fell upon his face prostrate before the watry Shadow
Saying 'O Lord whence is this change: thou knowest I am nothing!'
And Vala trembled & coverd her face! & her locks were spread on
    the pavement.

We heard astonishd at the Vision & our hearts trembled within us;
We heard the voice of slumberous Albion, and thus he spake,
Idolatrous to his own Shadow words of eternity uttering!

'O I am nothing when I enter into judgment with thee!
If thou withdraw thy breath I die & vanish into Hades
If thou dost lay thine hand upon me behold I am silent!
If thou withhold thine hand; I perish like a fallen leaf: 50
O I am nothing: and to nothing must return again:
If thou withdraw thy breath, Behold I am oblivion.'

He ceasd; the shadowy voice was silent: but the cloud hoverd over
    their heads
In golden wreathes, the sorrow of Man; & the balmy drops fell
    down.
And lo! that son of Man that Shadowy Spirit of mild Albion:
Luvah descended from the cloud; in terror Albion rose:
Indignant rose the awful Man, & turnd his back on Vala.

We heard the voice of Albion starting from his sleep!

'Whence is this voice crying Enion: that soundeth in my ears?
O cruel pity! O dark deceit: can love seek for dominion?'   60

And Luvah strove to gain dominion over Albion.
They strove together above the Body where Vala was inclosd
And the dark Body of Albion left prostrate upon the crystal
    pavement,
Coverd with boils from head to foot: the terrible smitings of Luvah.

Their long testimony on the causes of humanity's fall (ending at **29**:79), which embeds dialogue among Albion, Vala, and others, returns to Albion's situation at the opening of Chapter 1. From their perspective, the cosmic man has separated himself from his true divine nature and abased himself before a shadowy idol of his own making, an abstract concept of holiness that turns out to be the fallen Luvah, Zoa of passion, the Prince of Light as the natural sun. In line 28, Erdman emends "locks" to "rocks," crediting Joanne Witke.

Then frownd the fallen Man, and put forth Luvah from his
   presence
Saying. 'Go and Die the Death of Man, for Vala the sweet
   wanderer.
I will turn the volutions of your ears outward, and bend your
   nostrils
Downward, and your fluxile eyes englob'd roll round in fear:
Your withring lips and tongue shrink up into a narrow circle,
Till into narrow forms you creep: go take your fiery way: 70
And learn what tis to absorb the Man you Spirits of Pity & Love.'

They heard the voice and fled swift as the winter's setting sun
And now the human blood foamd high. The Spirits Luvah & Vala
Went down the Human Heart where Paradise & its joys abounded,
In jealous fears & fury & rage, & flames roll round their fervid feet:
And the vast form of Nature like a serpent playd before them.
And as they fled in folding fires & thunders of the deep:
Vala shrunk in like the dark sea that leaves its slimy banks
And from her bosom Luvah fell far as the east and west.
And the vast form of Nature like a serpent rolld between   80
Whether of Jerusalem's or Vala's ruins congenerated we know not:
All is confusion: all is tumult, & we alone are escaped."
So spoke the fugitives; they joind the Divine Family, trembling.
And the Two that escaped were the Emanation of Los & his
Spectre: for whereever the Emanation goes, the Spectre $\boxed{30/44}$
Attends her as her Guard, & Los's Emanation is named
Enitharmon, & his Spectre is named Urthona: they knew
Not where to flee: they had been on a visit to Albion's Children
And they strove to weave a Shadow of the Emanation
To hide themselves: weeping & lamenting for the Vegetation
Of Albion's Children, fleeing thro Albion's vales in streams of gore,

Being not irritated by insult, bearing insulting benevolences
They percieved that corporeal friends are spiritual enemies.[6]   10
They saw the Sexual Religion in its embryon Uncircumcision
And the Divine hand was upon them bearing them thro darkness
Back safe to their Humanity as doves to their windows:
Therefore the Sons of Eden praise Urthona's Spectre in Songs
Because he kept the Divine Vision in time of trouble.

They wept & trembled: & Los put forth his hand, & took them in,
Into his Bosom; from which Albion shrunk in dismal pain;
Rending the fibres of Brotherhood & in Feminine Allegories
Inclosing Los: but the Divine Vision appeard with Los
Following Albion into his Central Void among his Oaks.   20

And Los prayed and said, "O Divine Saviour arise
Upon the Mountains of Albion as in ancient time. Behold!
The Cities of Albion seek thy face, London groans in pain
From Hill to Hill & the Thames laments along the Valleys
The little Villages of Middlesex & Surrey hunger & thirst

6. One of the stock phrases of *Milton* (4:26); cf. the April 25, 1803, letter to Butts.

The Twenty-eight Cities of Albion stretch their hands to thee:
Because of the Opressors of Albion in every City & Village:
They mock at the Labourer's limbs! they mock at his starvd
    Children.
They buy his Daughters that they may have power to sell his Sons:
They compell the Poor to live upon a crust of bread by soft mild
    arts;   30
They reduce the Man to want: then give with pomp &
    ceremony—
The praise of Jehovah is chaunted from lips of hunger & thirst!
Humanity knows not of Sex: wherefore are Sexes in Beulah?
In Beulah the Female lets down her beautiful Tabernacle;
Which the Male enters magnificent between her Cherubim:[7]
And becomes One with her mingling condensing in Self-love
The Rocky Law of Condemnation & double Generation, & Death.
Albion hath enterd the Loins, the place of the Last Judgment:
And Luvah hath drawn the Curtains around Albion in Vala's bosom.
The Dead awake to Generation! Arise O Lord, & rend the Veil!"   40

So Los in lamentations followd Albion. Albion coverd
His western heaven with rocky clouds of death & despair.   31/45

Fearing that Albion should turn his back against the Divine Vision
Los took his globe of fire to search the interiors of Albion's
Bosom,[8] in all the terrors of friendship, entering the caves
Of despair & death, to search the tempters out, walking among
Albion's rocks & precipices! caves of solitude & dark despair,
And saw every Minute Particular of Albion degraded & murderd
But saw not by whom; they were hidden within in the minute
    particulars[9]
Of which they had possessd themselves; and there they take up
The articulations of a man's soul, and laughing throw it down   10
Into the frame, then knock it out upon the plank, & souls are
    bak'd
In bricks to build the pyramids of Heber & Terah.[1] But Los
Searchd in vain: closd from the minutia he walkd, difficult.
He came down from Highgate thro Hackney & Holloway towards
    London
Till he came to old Stratford & thence to Stepney & the Isle
Of Leutha's Dogs, thence thro the narrows of the River's side

7. In the ideal fourfold state of Eden, the human and divine, male and female, are one; in Los's prayer, the division between the sexes in the lower threefold "married" state of Beulah is expressed in imagery of the division between man and God see n. 4, p. 234 herein and temple the ark. Although Beulah is a state of sexual fulfillment, Los fears that the male's self-love leads to the fallen sexuality of the still lower twofold state of Generation, which by implication leads to the lowest state of all, the absolute materiality of Ulro.
8. See the frontispiece to *Jerusalem*, in which Los's attire resembles Blake's "plain black suit and *rather* broad-brimmed, but not quakerish hat," worn in 1825 (Gilchrist 283).
9. This recurrent term, "minute particulars"—as opposed to the indefinite, the abstract, and the general—reappears in connection with slavery and brick making in 89:17, in the brain of the Covering Cherub.
1. Blending the enslaved Hebrews' brick making in Egypt (Exodus 1:14, 5:7) with the building of the tower of Babel (Genesis 11:1–4) and the names of Abraham's distant ancestor and his father (Genesis 11:14, 11:26).

And saw every minute particular, the jewels of Albion, running
  down
The kennels[2] of the streets & lanes as if they were abhorrd.
Every Universal Form was become barren mountains of Moral
Virtue: and every Minute Particular hardend into grains of sand: 20
And all the tendernesses of the soul cast forth as filth & mire,
Among the winding places of deep contemplation intricate
To where the Tower of London frownd dreadful over Jerusalem:
A building of Luvah builded in Jerusalem's eastern gate to be
His secluded Court: thence to Bethlehem where was builded
Dens of despair in the house of bread: enquiring in vain
Of stones and rocks he took his way, for human form was none:
And thus he spoke, looking on Albion's City with many tears
"What shall I do! what could I do, if I could find these Criminals
I could not dare to take vengeance; for all things are so
  constructed   30
And builded by the Divine hand, that the sinner shall always
  escape,
And he who takes vengeance alone is the criminal of Providence:
If I should dare to lay my finger on a grain of sand
In way of vengeance: I punish the already punished; O whom
Should I pity if I pity not the sinner who is gone astray!
O Albion, if thou takest vengeance; if thou revengest thy wrongs
Thou art for ever lost! What can I do to hinder the Sons
Of Albion from taking vengeance? or how shall I them perswade?"

So spoke Los, travelling thro darkness & horrid solitude:
And he beheld Jerusalem in Westminster & Marybone   40
Among the ruins of the Temple: and Vala who is her Shadow,
Jerusalem's Shadow bent northward over the Island white.
At length he sat on London Stone, & heard Jerusalem's voice.

"Albion I cannot be thy Wife. Thine own Minute Particulars
Belong to God alone, and all thy little ones are holy.
They are of Faith & not of Demonstration: wherefore is Vala
Clothd in black mourning upon my river's currents? Vala awake!
I hear thy shuttles sing in the sky, and round my limbs
I feel the iron threads of love & jealousy & despair."

Vala reply'd. "Albion is mine: Luvah gave me to Albion   50
And now recieves reproach & hate. Was it not said of old
Set your Son before a man & he shall take you & your sons
For slaves: but set your Daughter before a man and She
Shall make him & his sons & daughters your slaves for ever:
And is this Faith? Behold the strife of Albion & Luvah
Is great in the east. Their spears of blood rage in the eastern heaven.
Urizen is the champion of Albion, they will slay my Luvah:
And thou O harlot daughter! daughter of despair art all
This cause of these shakings of my towers on Euphrates.

2. Gutters, open sewers. Los's vain search for the murderers takes him from northern to eastern parts
  of greater London toward the estuary of the Thames; then he circles west and back to the central
  landmark of London Stone (see map). "Isle Of Leutha's Dogs" (lines 15–16): Isle of Dogs in the
  Thames (cf. 83:82); Leutha appears in *Milton* 12/11:28.

Here is the House of Albion, & here is thy secluded place   60
And here we have found thy sins: & hence we turn thee forth,
For all to avoid thee: to be astonishd at thee for thy sins:
Because thou art the impurity & the harlot: & thy children!
Children of whoredoms: born for Sacrifice: for the meat & drink
Offering: to sustain the glorious combat & the battle & war
That Man may be purified by the death of thy delusions."

So saying she her dark threads cast over the trembling River;
And over the valleys; from the hills of Hertfordshire to the hills
Of Surrey across Middlesex & across Albion's House
Of Eternity! Pale stood Albion at his eastern gate,   70
Leaning against the pillars, & his disease rose from his skirts.   32/46
Upon the Precipice he stood: ready to fall into Non- Entity.

Los was all astonishment & terror: he trembled sitting on the Stone
Of London: but the interiors of Albion's fibres & nerves were
   hidden
From Los; astonishd he beheld only the petrified surfaces!

And saw his Furnaces in ruins, for Los is the Demon of the
    Furnaces,
He saw also the Four Points of Albion reversd inwards.
He siezd his Hammer & Tongs, his iron Poker & his Bellows,
Upon the valleys of Middlesex, Shouting loud for aid Divine.

In stern defiance came from Albion's bosom Hand, Hyle, Koban,[3]   10
Gwantok, Peachy, Brertun, Slaid, Huttn Skofeld, Kock, Kotope
Bowen, Albion's Sons: they bore him a golden couch into the porch
And on the Couch reposd his limbs, trembling from the bloody field.
Rearing their Druid Patriarchal rocky Temples around his limbs.
(All things begin & end in Albion's Ancient Druid Rocky Shore.)

Turning his back to the Divine Vision, his Spectrous $\boxed{33/29}$
Chaos before his face appeard: an Unformed Memory.

Then spoke the Spectrous Chaos to Albion darkning cold
From the back & loins where dwell the Spectrous Dead

"I am your Rational Power O Albion & that Human Form
You call Divine is but a Worm seventy inches long
That creeps forth in a night & is dried in the morning sun
In fortuitous concourse[4] of memorys accumulated & lost.
It plows the Earth in its own conceit. It overwhelms the Hills
Beneath its winding labyrinths, till a stone of the brook   10
Stops it in midst of its pride among its hills & rivers.
Battersea & Chelsea mourn. London & Canterbury tremble.
Their place shall not be found, as the wind passes over[5]
The ancient Cities of the Earth remove as a traveller.
And shall Albion's Cities remain when I pass over them
With my deluge of forgotten remembrances over the tablet?"

So spoke the Spectre to Albion. He is the Great Selfhood
Satan: Worshipd as God by the Mighty Ones of the Earth
Having a white Dot calld a Center from which branches out
A Circle in continual gyrations. This became a Heart   20
From which sprang numerous branches varying their motions
Producing many Heads three or seven or ten, & hands & feet
Innumerable at will of the unfortunate contemplator
Who becomes his food; such is the way of the Devouring Power.

And this is the cause of the appearance in the frowning Chaos.
Albion's Emanation which he had hidden in Jealousy
Appeard now in the frowning Chaos prolific upon the Chaos
Reflecting back to Albion in Sexual Reasoning Hermaphroditic.[6]

---

3. Pictured on plate 50 (p. 272 herein).
4. Cicero's phrase for the random collision of atoms (*On the Nature of the Gods* I.xxvi.66), applied
here to chance encounters among fleeting memories. Cf. Locke's theory that thought arises from
the random bombardment of atoms that stream off objects and register as sense impressions on
the blank tablet of the mind.
5. Cf. Psalm 103:16–17 on the transience of human life: "For the wind passeth over it, and it is gone;
and the place thereof shall know it no more."
6. Not the true Jerusalem but a reflected illusion (identified as Vala, line 35).

Albion spoke. "Who art thou that appearest in gloomy pomp
Involving the Divine Vision in colours of autumn ripeness   30
I never saw thee till this time, nor beheld life abstracted
Nor darkness immingled with light on my furrowd field
Whence camest thou: who art thou O loveliest? The Divine Vision
Is as nothing before thee. Faded is all life and joy."

Vala replied in clouds of tears, Albion's garment embracing,

"I was a City & a Temple built by Albion's Children.
I was a Garden planted with beauty. I allured on hill & valley
The River of Life to flow against my walls & among my trees.
Vala was Albion's Bride & Wife in great Eternity,
The loveliest of the daughters of Eternity, when in day-break   40
I emanated from Luvah over the Towers of Jerusalem
And in her Courts among her little Children offering up
The Sacrifice of fanatic love! Why loved I Jerusalem:
Why was I one with her, embracing in the Vision of Jesus?
Wherefore did I loving create love, which never yet
Immingled God & Man, when thou & I hid the Divine Vision
In cloud of secret gloom, which behold involve me round about?
Know me now Albion; look upon me. I alone am Beauty.
The Imaginative Human Form is but a breathing of Vala.
I breathe him forth into the Heaven from my secret Cave   50
Born of the Woman to obey the Woman O Albion the mighty,
For the Divine appearance is Brotherhood, but I am Love
Elevate into the Region of Brotherhood with my red fires."   34/30

"Art thou Vala?" replied Albion, "image of my repose.
O how I tremble! how my members pour down milky fear!
A dewy garment covers me all over, all manhood is gone:
At thy word & at thy look death enrobes me about
From head to feet, a garment of death & eternal fear
Is not that Sun thy husband & that Moon thy glimmering Veil?
Are not the Stars of heaven thy Children! art thou not Babylon?
Art thou Nature Mother of all! is Jerusalem thy Daughter?
Why have thou elevate inward; O dweller of outward chambers,   10
From grot & cave beneath the Moon, dim region of death
Where I laid my Plow in the hot noon, where my hot team fed
Where implements of War are forged, the Plow to go over the
    Nations
In pain girding me round like a rib of iron in heaven! O Vala
In Eternity they neither marry nor are given in marriage.[7]
Albion the high Cliff of the Atlantic is become a barren Land."

Los stood at his Anvil: he heard the contentions of Vala.
He heavd his thundring Bellows upon the valleys of Middlesex
He opend his Furnaces before Vala. Then Albion frownd in anger
On his Rock; ere yet the Starry Heavens were fled away   20

7. From Matthew 22:30.

From his awful Members, and thus Los cried aloud
To the Sons of Albion & to Hand the eldest Son of Albion:

"I hear the screech of Childbirth loud pealing & the groans
Of Death in Albion's clouds dreadful utterd over all the Earth.
What may Man be? who can tell! but what may Woman be?
To have power over Man from Cradle to corruptible Grave.
There is a Throne in every Man, it is the Throne of God
This Woman has claimd as her own & Man is no more!
Albion is the Tabernacle of Vala & her Temple
And not the Tabernacle & Temple of the Most High   30
O Albion why wilt thou Create a Female Will?
To hide the most evident God in a hidden covert, even
In the shadows of a Woman & a secluded Holy Place
That we may pry after him as after a stolen treasure
Hidden among the Dead & mured up from the paths of life?
Hand! art thou not Reuben enrooting thyself into Bashan[8]
Till thou remainest a vaporous Shadow in a Void! O Merlin!
Unknown among the Dead where never before Existence came,
Is this the Female Will O ye lovely Daughters of Albion, To
Converse concerning Weight & Distance in the Wilds of Newton &
    Locke?"   40

So Los spoke standing on Mam-Tor looking over Europe & Asia[9]
The Graves thunder beneath his feet from Ireland to Japan.

Reuben slept in Bashan like one dead in the valley
Cut off from Albion's mountains & from all the Earth's summits
Between Succoth & Zaretan beside the Stone of Bohan[1]
While the Daughters of Albion divided Luvah into three Bodies.
Los bended his Nostrils down to the Earth, then sent him over
Jordan to the Land of the Hittite: every-one that saw him
Fled! they fled at his horrible Form: they hid in caves
And dens, they looked on one-another & became what they
    beheld.   50

Reuben return'd to Bashan, in despair he slept on the Stone.
Then Gwendolen divided into Rahab & Tirza in Twelve Portions.
Los rolled his Eyes into two narrow circles, then sent him
Over Jordan; all terrified fled; they became what they beheld.

"If Perceptive Organs vary: Objects of Perception seem to vary:
If the Perceptive Organs close: their Objects seem to close also:
Consider this O mortal Man: O worm of sixty winters," said Los
"Consider Sexual Organization & hide thee in the dust."[2]

8. Hand, Albion's eldest son, is identified with Jacob/Israel's oldest son Reuben (ruled by his mother
   Leah; see n. 6, p. 221 herein) and associated with Arthur's magician Merlin (bewitched and imprisoned by his lover Vivien); reiterated in J 56:3–4. Instead of crossing the Jordan to claim an inheritance in the Promised Land, Reuben and two of his brothers insist on settling in fertile land on
   the east side, south of Bashan (Numbers 32; see map). Los's notion of the proper place of woman
   derives, in part, from 1 Corinthians 11.
9. Standing on a mountain in England's Peak District (see map), Los looks east.
1. Border between territories of Benjamin and Judah, named after a son of Reuben (Joshua 15:6,
   18:17).
2. The last five words echo a prophecy of repentance in Isaiah 2:10.

Then the Divine hand found the Two Limits, Satan and Adam,[3]
In Albion's bosom: for in every Human bosom those Limits stand.
And the Divine voice came from the Furnaces, as multitudes
      without
Number! the voices of the innumerable multitudes of Eternity.
And the appearance of a Man was seen in the Furnaces:[4]
Saving those who have sinned from the punishment of the Law,
(In pity of the punisher whose state is eternal death,)
And keeping them from Sin by the mild counsels of his love.

"Albion goes to Eternal Death: In Me all Eternity
Must pass thro' condemnation, and awake beyond the Grave: 10
No individual can keep these Laws, for they are death
To every energy of man, and forbid the springs of life;

3. See J 42:29–35 and n. 6, p. 161 herein.
4. A fourth, in form "like the Son of God" (Daniel 3:25), joins Shadrach, Meshach, and Abednego as
   they walk unhurt in Nebuchadnezzar's fiery furnace; cf. **60:5, 62:35**.

Albion hath enterd the State Satan! Be permanent O State![5]
And be thou for ever accursed! that Albion may arise again:
And be thou created into a State! I go forth to Create
States; to deliver Individuals evermore! Amen."

So spoke the voice from the Furnaces, descending into
    Non-Entity.

Reuben return'd to his place, in vain he sought beautiful
    Tirzah
For his Eyelids were narrowd, & his Nostrils scented the
    ground.
And Sixty Winters Los raged in the Divisions of Reuben:
Building the Moon of Ulro, plank by plank & rib by rib.[6]
Reuben slept in the Cave of Adam, and Los folded his Tongue
Between Lips of mire & clay, then sent him forth over Jordan.
In the love of Tirzah he said "Doubt is my food day & night"—
All that beheld him fled howling and gnawed their tongues
For pain: they became what they beheld. In reasonings Reuben
    returned
To Heshbon. Disconsolate he walked thro Moab & he stood   10
Before the Furnaces of Los in a horrible dreamful slumber,
On Mount Gilead looking toward Gilgal: and Los bended
His Ear in a spiral circle outward; then sent him over Jordan.

36/32

The Seven Nations[7] fled before him.They became what they
    beheld.
Hand, Hyle & Coban fled; they became what they beheld.
Gwantock & Peachy hid in Damascus beneath Mount Lebanon,
Brereton & Slade in Egypt, Hutton & Skofeld & Kox
Fled over Chaldea in terror in pains in every nerve,
Kotope & Bowen became what they beheld, fleeing over the
    Earth
And the Twelve Female Emanations fled with them agonizing.   20

Jerusalem trembled seeing her Children drivn by Los's Hammer
In the visions of the dreams of Beulah on the edge of Non-Entity.
Hand stood between Reuben & Merlin, as the Reasoning Spectre
Stands between the Vegetative Man & his Immortal Imagination.

And the Four Zoa's clouded rage East & West & North & South.
They change their situations, in the Universal Man.
Albion groans, he sees the Elements divide before his face.
And England who is Brittannia divided into Jerusalem & Vala[8]

---

5. In *Milton* 35/32:10–38, States are annihilated when Individuals, who are eternal, reject them. Here Jesus makes the State of Satan permanent to arrest Albion's death and disintegration and then, for Albion's sake, passes into Non-Entity.
6. Los is trying to contain the fall by making an ark out of Ulro, the realm of materiality (cf. Nicholas O. Warner, *Blake: An Illustrated Quarterly* 14 ([1980], 44–59), and binding the sensual, vegetated Reuben into the finite human body and lifespan. Reuben keeps returning to the east side of the Jordan, and the sons of Albion flee into heathen territory.
7. Displaced Canaanite peoples (Deuteronomy 7:1; Acts 13:19).
8. This is the first and only foreshadowing of the "wife" who is to be resurrected in **94**:20.

And Urizen assumes the East, Luvah assumes the South
In his dark Spectre ravening from his open Sepulcher.   30

And the Four Zoa's who are the Four Eternal Senses of Man
Became Four Elements separating from the Limbs of Albion.
These are their names in the Vegetative Generation.

And Accident & Chance were found hidden in Length Bredth &
    Highth
And they divided into Four ravening deathlike Forms
Fairies & Genii & Nymphs & Gnomes of the Elements.
These are States Permanently Fixed by the Divine Power
The Atlantic Continent sunk round Albion's cliffy shore
And the Sea poured in amain upon the Giants of Albion
As Los bended the Senses of Reuben. Reuben is Merlin   40
Exploring the Three States of Ulro; Creation; Redemption, &
    Judgment.

And many of the Eternal Ones laughed after their manner.

"Have you known the Judgment that is arisen among the
Zoa's of Albion? where a Man dare hardly to embrace
His own Wife for the terrors of Chastity that they call
By the name of Morality; their Daughters govern all
In hidden deceit! they are Vegetable only fit for burning,
Art & Science cannot exist but by Naked Beauty displayd."

Then those in Great Eternity who contemplate on Death
Said thus, "What seems to Be: Is; To those to whom   50
It seems to Be, & is productive of the most dreadful
Consequences to those to whom it seems to Be: even of
Torments, Despair, Eternal Death; but the Divine Mercy
Steps beyond and Redeems Man in the Body of Jesus Amen.
And Length Bredth Highth again Obey the Divine Vision
    Hallelujah."

And One stood forth from the Divine Family & said $\boxed{37/33}$

"I feel my Spectre rising upon me! Albion! arouze thyself!
Why dost thou thunder with frozen Spectrous wrath against us?
The Spectre is, in Giant Man; insane, and most deform'd.
Thou wilt certainly provoke my Spectre against thine in fury!
He has a Sepulcher hewn out of a Rock ready for thee:[9]
And a Death of Eight thousand years forg'd by thyself, upon
The point of his Spear! if thou persistest to forbid with Laws
Our Emanations, and to attack our secret supreme delights."

So Los spoke: But when he saw blue death in Albion's feet,   10
Again he join'd the Divine Body, following merciful:
While Albion fled more indignant: revengeful covering

9. Cf. the tomb that Joseph of Arimathea provided for Jesus (Matthew 27:60).

His face and bosom with petrific hardness, and his hands   38/34
And feet, lest any should enter his bosom & embrace
His hidden heart; his Emanation wept & trembled within him:
Uttering not his jealousy, but hiding it as with

Iron and steel, dark and opake, with clouds & tempests brooding:
His strong limbs shudderd upon his mountains high and dark.

Turning from Universal Love petrific as he went,
His cold against the warmth of Eden rag'd with loud
Thunders of deadly war (the fever of the human soul)
Fires and clouds of rolling smoke! but mild the Saviour follow'd
    him,   10
Displaying the Eternal Vision! the Divine Similitude!
In loves and tears of brothers, sisters, sons, fathers, and friends
Which if Man ceases to behold, he ceases to exist:

Saying, "Albion! Our wars are wars of life, & wounds of love,
With intellectual spears, & long winged arrows of thought:
Mutual in one another's love and wrath all renewing

We live as One Man; for contracting our infinite senses
We behold multitude: or expanding: we behold as one,
As One Man all the Universal Family; and that One Man
We call Jesus the Christ; and he in us, and we in him.   20
Live in perfect harmony in Eden the land of life.
Giving, recieving, and forgiving each other's trespasses.
He is the Good shepherd, he is the Lord and master:
He is the Shepherd of Albion, he is all in all.
In Eden: in the garden of God: and in heavenly Jerusalem.
If we have offended, forgive us, take not vengeance against us,"

Thus speaking; the Divine Family follow Albion:
I see them in the Vision of God upon my pleasant valleys,[1]

I behold London; a Human awful wonder of God!
He says: "Return, Albion, return! I give myself for thee: 30
My Streets are my Ideas of Imagination.
Awake Albion, awake! and let us awake up together.
My Houses are Thoughts: my Inhabitants; Affections.
The children of my thoughts, walking within my blood-vessels,
Shut from my nervous form which sleeps upon the verge of Beulah
In dreams of darkness, while my vegetating blood in veiny pipes,
Rolls dreadful thro' the Furnaces of Los, and the Mills of Satan.
For Albion's sake, and for Jerusalem thy Emanation
I give myself, and these my brethren give themselves for Albion."

So spoke London, immortal Guardian! I heard in Lambeth's
   shades: 40
In Felpham I heard and saw the Visions of Albion.
I write in South Molton Street what I both see and hear
In regions of Humanity, in London's opening streets.

I see thee awful Parent Land in light, behold I see!
Verulam![2] Canterbury! venerable parent of men,
Generous immortal Guardian golden clad! for Cities
Are Men, fathers of multitudes, and Rivers & Mountins
Are also Men; every thing is Human, mighty! sublime!
In every bosom a Universe expands, as wings
Let down at will around, and call'd the Universal Tent.   50
York, crown'd with loving kindness, Edinburgh, cloth'd
With fortitude as with a garment of immortal texture
Woven in looms of Eden, in spiritual deaths of mighty men
Who give themselves in Golgotha, Victims to Justice; where
There is in Albion a Gate of precious stones and gold
Seen only by Emanations, by vegetations viewless,
Bending across the road of Oxford Street; it from Hyde Park
To Tyburn's deathful shades admits the wandering souls
Of multitudes who die from Earth: this Gate cannot be found

---

1. Blake's authorial voice again, as revealed by references to his previous and present London addresses and the Felpham sojourn (38/34:40–42).
2. The rationalist Francis Bacon was dubbed Baron Verulam, after the Latin name of his birthplace, Saint Albans, site of the first British Christian martyrdom (cf. *Europe* 16/13). Verulam, Canterbury, Edinburgh (as center of the non-episcopal Church of Scotland), and York lead the personified cathedral cities.

By Satan's Watch-fiends tho' they search numbering every grain 39/35
Of sand on Earth every night, they never find this Gate.
It is the Gate of Los.[3] Withoutside is the Mill, intricate, dreadful
And fill'd with cruel tortures; but no mortal man can find the Mill
Of Satan,[4] in his mortal pilgrimage of seventy years,
For Human beauty knows it not: nor can Mercy find it! But
In the Fourth region of Humanity, Urthona namd
Mortality begins to roll the billows of Eternal Death
Before the Gate of Los. Urthona here is named Los.
And here begins the System of Moral Virtue, named Rahab.   10
Albion fled thro' the Gate of Los, and he stood in the Gate.

Los was the friend of Albion who most lov'd him. In
    Cambridgeshire
His eternal station, he is the twenty-eighth, & is four-fold.
Seeing Albion had turn'd his back against the Divine Vision,
Los said to Albion, "Whither fleest thou?" Albion reply'd,

"I die! I go to Eternal Death! the shades of death
Hover within me & beneath, and spreading themselves outside
Like rocky clouds, build me a gloomy monument of woe:
Will none accompany me in my death? or be a Ransom for me
In that dark Valley? I have gird round my cloke, and on my feet   20
Bound these black shoes of death, & on my hands, death's iron
    gloves
God hath forsaken me, & my friends are become a burden
A weariness to me, & the human footstep is a terror to me."

Los answerd, troubled: and his soul was rent in twain:
"Must the Wise die for an Atonement? does Mercy endure
    Atonement?
No! It is Moral Severity, & destroys Mercy in its Victim."[5]
So speaking not yet infected with the Error & Illusion

Los shudder'd at beholding Albion, for his disease   40/36
Arose upon him pale and ghastly: and he call'd around
The Friends of Albion: trembling at the sight of Eternal Death.
The four appear'd with their Emanations in fiery
Chariots: black their fires roll beholding Albion's House of Eternity.
Damp couch the flames beneath and silent, sick, stand shuddering
Before the Porch of sixteen pillars: weeping every one
Descended and fell down upon their knees round Albion's knees,
Swearing the Oath of God! with awful voice of thunders round
Upon the hills & valleys, and the cloudy Oath roll'd far and wide.   10

---

who try to save Albion (see map); in 46:24 London replaces Canterbury. In reality, Canterbury
(founded 597) and York (founded 625; 664) are the only archbishoprics in the Church of England;
and Verulam, which has no cathedral, is in the archdiocese of Canterbury.
3. A visionary space near Blake's home in South Molton Street (see map), the gate through which Los
and the Cathedral Cities attempt to move Albion back into Eden (44/39:3). The self-giving of Golgotha counters the Druid sacrifice of the Tyburn gallows. Satan's Watch-fiends find neither this passage to Eden nor the sexual gateway into Beulah in Lambeth, Blake's home in the 1790s (41/37:15);
similarly, they search in vain for the redemptive moment of inspiration in *Milton* 39/35:42–45.
4. The Mill, the "same dull round" (*No Natural Religion* [b] IV,) of reductive logic and celestial
mechanics, is identified with Satan in *Milton* 3:41–42).
5. On Los's position here, see n. 5, p. 148.

"Albion is sick!" said every Valley, every mournful Hill
And every River: "our brother Albion is sick to death.
He hath leagued himself with robbers! he hath studied the arts
Of unbelief! Envy hovers over him! his Friends are his abhorrence!
Those who give their lives for him are despised!
Those who devour his soul, are taken into his bosom!
To destroy his Emanation is their intention:
Arise! awake O Friends of the Giant Albion
They have perswaded him of horrible falshoods!
They have sown errors over all his fruitful fields!"   20

The Twenty-four heard! they came trembling on watry chariots,
Borne by the Living Creatures of the third procession
Of Human Majesty; the Living Creatures wept aloud as they
Went along Albion's roads, till they arriv'd at Albion's House.

O! how the torments of Eternal Death waited on Man;
And the loud-rending bars of the Creation ready to burst:
That the wide world might fly from its hinges, & the immortal
      mansion
Of Man for ever be possess'd by monsters of the deeps:
And Man himself become a Fiend, wrap'd in an endless curse,
Consuming and consum'd for-ever in flames of Moral Justice.   30

For had the Body of Albion fall'n down, and from its dreadful ruins
Let loose the enormous Spectre on the darkness of the deep,
At enmity with the Merciful & fill'd with devouring fire,
A nether-world must have reciev'd the foul enormous spirit,
Under the presence of Moral Virtue, fill'd with Revenge and Law.[6]
There to eternity chain'd down, and issuing in red flames
And curses, with his mighty arms brandish'd against the heavens
Breathing cruelty blood & vengeance, gnashing his teeth with pain
Torn with black storms, & ceaseless torrents of his own consuming
      fire:[7]
Within his breast his mighty Sons chaind down & fill'd with
      cursings: 40
And his dark Eon, that once fair crystal form divinely clear:
Within his ribs producing serpents whose souls are flames of fire.
But, glory to the Merciful-One, for he is of tender mercies!
And the Divine Family wept over him as One Man.

And these the Twenty-four in whom the Divine Family
Appear'd; and they were One in Him, A Human Vision!
Human Divine, Jesus the Saviour, blessed for ever and ever.

Selsey,[8] true friend! who afterwards submitted to be devourd
By the waves of Despair, whose Emanation rose above

---

6. This "might-have-been" scenario, blocked by Los's efforts, recalls the Christian doctrine of hell as
presented in *Paradise Lost*.
7. See Deuteronomy 4:24; Hebrews 12:29; and Blake's inscription on a painting, *Epitome of Hervey's
Meditations among the Tombs* (Butlin 770): "God out of Christ is a Consuming Fire."
8. The list of the lesser cathedral cities begins with the sunken town of Selsey, near Blake's temporary home in Felpham (see map); after Selsey's inundation, its bishopric was transferred to Chichester in 1075. Blake's tinkerings with history, such as ignoring the ruined state of Sodor's
cathedral on the Isle of Man, help round the total of twenty-four lesser and four greater cathedral
cities to twenty-eight, a multiple of the "complete" numbers four and seven.

The flood, and was nam'd Chichester, lovely mild & gentle! Lo!   50
Her lambs bleat to the sea-fowls' cry, lamenting still for Albion.

Submitting to be call'd the son of Los the terrible vision:
Winchester stood devoting himself for Albion: his tents
Outspread with abundant riches, and his Emanations
Submitting to be call'd Enitharmon's daughters, and be born
In vegetable mould: created by the Hammer and Loom
In Bowlahoola & Allamanda where the Dead wail night & day.

(I call them by their English names: English, the rough basement,
Los built the stubborn structure of the Language, acting against
Albion's melancholy, who must else have been a Dumb despair.)   60

Gloucester and Exeter and Salisbury and Bristol: and benevolent
    Bath.
Bath who is Legions; he is the Seventh, the physician and $\boxed{41/37}$
The poisoner:[9] the best and worst in Heaven and Hell:
Whose Spectre first assimilated with Luvah in Albion's
    mountains
A triple octave he took, to reduce Jerusalem to twelve
To cast Jerusalem forth upon the wilds to Poplar & Bow:
To Malden & Canterbury in the delights of cruelty:
The Shuttles of death sing in the sky to Islington & Pancrass
Round Marybone to Tyburn's River, weaving black melancholy as
    a net,
And despair as meshes closely wove over the west of London,
Where mild Jerusalem sought to repose in death & be no more.   10
She fled to Lambeth's mild Vale and hid herself beneath
The Surrey Hills where Rephaim terminates: her Sons are siez'd
For victims of sacrifice; but Jerusalem cannot be found! Hid
By the Daughters of Beulah: gently snatch'd away: and hid in
    Beulah.

There is a Grain of Sand in Lambeth that Satan cannot find
Nor can his Watch Fiends find it: tis translucent & has many
    Angles
But he who finds it will find Oothoon's palace, for within
Opening into Beulah every angle is a lovely heaven
But should the Watch Fiends find it, they would call it Sin
And lay its Heavens & their inhabitants in blood of punishment   20
Here Jerusalem & Vala were hid in soft slumberous repose
Hid from the terrible East, shut up in the South & West.

The Twenty-eight trembled in Death's dark caves, in cold despair
They kneeld around the Couch of Death in deep humiliation

---

9. Stevenson cites Merlin's prophecy, reported by Geoffrey of Monmouth, that Bath's healing waters will grow cold and "bring forth death." The spa city of Bath, developed by the Romans, has no cathedral but is recognized in the title of the "Bishop of Bath and Wells." "Legions": city (*urbs legionum*) where Arthur was crowned; not actually near Bath. In the design depicting the despairing Albion, the mirror-writing on the scroll penned by the small figure (the poet?) reads: "Each Man is in his Spectre's power / Untill the arrival of that hour, / When his Humanity awake / And cast his Spectre into the Lake."

And tortures of self condemnation while their Spectres ragd within:
The Four Zoa's in terrible combustion clouded rage
Drinking the shuddering fears & loves of Albion's Families
Destroying by selfish affections the things that they most admire
Drinking & eating, & pitying & weeping, as at a trajic scene,
The soul drinks murder & revenge, & applauds its own holiness.   30

They saw Albion endeavouring to destroy their Emanations.

Thus Albion sat, studious of others in his pale disease: 42
Brooding on evil: but when Los opend the Furnaces before him:
He saw that the accursed things were his own affections,
And his own beloveds: then he turn'd sick: his soul died within him.
Also Los sick & terrified beheld the Furnaces of Death
And must have died, but the Divine Saviour descended
Among the infant loves & affections, and the Divine Vision wept
Like evening dew on every herb upon the breathing ground.

Albion spoke in his dismal dreams; "O thou deceitful friend
Worshipping mercy & beholding thy friend in such affliction: 10
Los! thou now discoverest thy turpitude to the heavens.
I demand righteousness & justice. O thou ingratitude!
Give me my Emanations back, food for my dying soul!
My daughters are harlots! my sons are accursed before me.
Enitharmon is my daughter: accursed with a father's curse:
O! I have utterly been wasted! I have given my daughters to
    devils."

So spoke Albion in gloomy majesty, and deepest night
Of Ulro rolld round his skirts from Dover to Cornwall.

Los answerd. "Righteousness & justice I give thee in return
For thy righteousness! but I add mercy also, and bind   20
Thee from destroying these little ones; am I to be only
Merciful to thee and cruel to all that thou hatest?
Thou wast the Image of God surrounded by the Four Zoa's.
Three thou hast slain: I am the Fourth, thou canst not destroy me.
Thou art in Error; trouble me not with thy righteousness.
I have innocence to defend and ignorance to instruct:
I have no time for seeming; and little arts of compliment
In morality and virtue: in self-glorying and pride.
There is a limit of Opakeness, and a limit of Contraction:
In every Individual Man, and the limit of Opakeness   30
Is named Satan: and the limit of Contraction is named Adam,
But when Man sleeps in Beulah, the Saviour in mercy takes
Contraction's Limit, and of the Limit he forms Woman: That
Himself may in process of time be born Man to redeem.
But there is no Limit of Expansion! there is no Limit of
    Translucence
In the bosom of Man for ever from eternity to eternity.
Therefore I break thy bonds of righteousness; I crush thy
    messengers!
That they may not crush me and mine: do thou be righteous,
And I will return it; otherwise I defy thy worst revenge:
Consider me as thine enemy: on me turn all thy fury   40
But destroy not these little ones, nor mock the Lord's anointed:[1]
Destroy not by Moral Virtue the little ones whom he hath chosen!
The little ones whom he hath chosen in preference to thee.
He hath cast thee off for ever; the little ones he hath anointed!
Thy Selfhood is for ever accursed from the Divine presence."

So Los spoke: then turn'd his face & wept for Albion.

Albion replied. "Go: Hand & Hyle! sieze the abhorred friend:
As you have siezd the Twenty-four rebellious ingratitudes;
To atone for you, for spiritual death! Man lives by deaths of Men.
Bring him to justice before heaven here upon London stone,   50
Between Blackheath & Hounslow, between Norwood & Finchley.
All that they have is mine: from my free genrous gift.
They now hold all they have: ingratitude to me!
To me their benefactor calls aloud for vengeance deep."

Los stood before his Furnaces awaiting the fury of the Dead:
And the Divine hand was upon him, strengthening him mightily.

The Spectres of the Dead cry out from the deeps beneath
Upon the hills of Albion; Oxford groans in his iron furnace

---

1. David, anointed as Saul's successor (1 Samuel 16:13), refused during the king's lifetime to raise his hand against "the Lord's anointed" (1 Samuel 24:10, 26:23) and executed the Amelekite who killed Saul (2 Samuel 1:16). Jesus warns against despising or harming his "little ones" (Matthew 18:6, 18:10, 18:14).

Winchester in his den & cavern; they lament against
Albion: they curse their human kindness & affection   60
They rage like wild beasts in the forests of affliction
In the dreams of Ulro they repent of their human kindness.

"Come up, build Babylon, Rahab is ours & all her multitudes
With her in pomp and glory of victory. Depart
Ye twenty-four into the deeps! let us depart to glory!"

Their Human majestic forms sit up upon their Couches
Of death: they curb their Spectres as with iron curbs
They enquire after Jerusalem in the regions of the dead.
With the voices of dead men, low, scarcely articulate,
And with tears cold on their cheeks they weary repose.   70

"O when shall the morning of the grave appear, and when
Shall our salvation come? we sleep upon our watch
We cannot awake! and our Spectres rage in the forests
O God of Albion where art thou! pity the watchers!"

Thus mourn they, Loud the Furnaces of Los thunder upon
The clouds of Europe & Asia, among the Serpent Temples!

And Los drew his Seven Furnaces around Albion's Altars
And as Albion built his frozen Altars, Los built the Mundane Shell.
In the Four Regions of Humanity East & West & North & South,
Till Norwood & Finchley & Blackheath & Hounslow coverd the
    whole Earth.   80
This is the Net & Veil of Vala, among the Souls of the Dead.

They saw their Wheels rising up poisonous against Albion   43/38
Urizen, cold & scientific: Luvah, pitying & weeping:
Tharmas, indolent & sullen: Urthona, doubting & despairing,
Victims to one another & dreadfully plotting against each other
To prevent Albion walking about in the Four Complexions.

They saw America clos'd out by the Oaks of the western shore;
And Tharmas dash'd on the Rocks of the Altars of Victims in Mexico.
"If we are wrathful Albion will destroy Jerusalem with rooty Groves
If we are merciful, ourselves must suffer destruction on his Oaks:
Why should we enter into our Spectres to behold our own
    corruptions?   10
O God of Albion descend! deliver Jerusalem from the Oaken
    Groves!"

Then Los grew furious raging; "Why stand we here trembling around
Calling on God for help; and not ourselves in whom God dwells,
Stretching a hand to save the falling Man: are we not Four
Beholding Albion upon the Precipice ready to fall into Non-Entity:
Seeing these Heavens & Hells conglobing in the Void. Heavens over
    Hells
Brooding in holy hypocritic lust, drinking the cries of pain
From howling victims of Law; building Heavens Twenty-seven-fold.

Swelld & bloated General Forms, repugnant to the Divine
Humanity, who is the Only General and Universal Form   20
To which all Lineaments tend & seek with love & sympathy.
All broad & general principles belong to benevolence
Who protects minute particulars, every one in their own identity.
But here the affectionate touch of the tongue is closd in by deadly
    teeth
And the soft smile of friendship & the open dawn of benevolence
Become a net & a trap, & every energy renderd cruel,
Till the existence of friendship & benevolence is denied:
The wine of the Spirit & the vineyards of the Holy-One.
Here: turn into poisonous stupor & deadly intoxication:
That they may be condemnd by Law & the Lamb of God be slain!   30
And the two Sources of Life in Eternity, Hunting and War,
Are become the Sources of dark & bitter Death & of corroding Hell:
The open heart is shut up in integuments of frozen silence
That the spear that lights it forth may shatter the ribs & bosom.
A pretence of Art, to destroy Art! a pretence of Liberty
To destroy Liberty, a pretence of Religion to destroy Religion.
Oshea and Caleb fight: they contend in the valleys of Peor[2]
In the terrible Family Contentions of those who love each other:
The Armies of Balaam weep—no women come to the field.
Dead corses lay before them, & not as in Wars of old.   40
For the Soldier who fights for Truth calls his enemy his brother!
They fight & contend for life, & not for eternal death!
But here the Soldier strikes, & a dead corse falls at his feet.
Nor Daughter nor Sister nor Mother come forth to embosom the
    Slain!
But Death! Eternal Death! remains in the Valleys of Peor.
The English are scatterd over the face of the Nations: are these
Jerusalem's children? Hark! hear the Giants of Albion cry at night
"We smell the blood of the English! we delight in their blood on our
    Altars![3]
The living & the dead shall be ground in our rumbling Mills
For bread of the Sons of Albion; of the Giants Hand & Scofield.'   50
Scofeld & Kox are let loose upon my Saxons! they accumulate
A World in which Man is by his Nature the Enemy of Man,
In pride of Selfhood unwieldy stretching out into Non Entity
Generalizing Art & Science till Art & Science is lost.
Bristol & Bath, listen to my words, & ye Seventeen: give ear!
It is easy to acknowledge a man to be great & good while we
Derogate from him in the trifles & small articles of that goodness;
Those alone are his friends who admire his minutest powers.
Instead of Albion's lovely mountains & the curtains of Jerusalem
I see a Cave, a Rock, a Tree deadly and poisonous, unimaginative: 60
Instead of the Mutual Forgivenesses, the Minute Particulars, I see

---

2. The mountain on which the seer Balaam refuses, for the third time, to follow the order of Balak,
   king of Moab, to curse the Israelites (Numbers 23:28); see also the idol Baal-peor (Numbers 25)
   and Beth-peor associated with Moses' burial (Deuteronomy 34:6). Oshea (Joshua), representing
   the tribe of Ephraim, and Caleb, representing Judah, are actually allies; as the only members of
   their generation who oppose returning to Egypt, they alone survive the forty years in the wilderness and enter into the Promised Land to receive an inheritance (Numbers 13–14; Joshua 14).
3. Cf. the threat overheard by Jack the Giant-killer: "Fe fi foh fum / I smell the blood of an Englishman /
   Be he alive or be he dead / I'll grind his bones to make my bread."

Pits of bitumen ever burning: artificial Riches of the Canaanite
Like Lakes of liquid lead: instead of heavenly Chapels, built
By our dear Lord: I see Worlds crusted with snows & ice;
I see a Wicker Idol woven round Jerusalem's children, I see
The Canaanite, the Amalekite, the Moabite, the Egyptian:
By Demonstrations the cruel Sons of Quality & Negation
Driven on the Void in incoherent despair into Non Entity.
I see America closd apart, & Jerusalem driven in terror
Away from Albion's mountains, far away from London's spires!   70
I will not endure this thing! I alone withstand to death,
This outrage! Ah me! how sick & pale you all stand round me!
Ah me! pitiable ones! do you also go to death's vale?
All you my Friends & Brothers! all you my beloved Companions!
Have you also caught the infection of Sin & stern Repentance?
I see Disease arise upon you! yet speak to me and give
Me some comfort: why do you all stand silent? I alone
Remain in permanent strength. Or is all this goodness & pity,
      only
That you may take the greater vengeance in your Sepulcher?"

So Los spoke. Pale they stood around the House of Death: 80
In the midst of temptations & despair: among the rooted Oaks:
Among reared Rocks of Albion's Sons, at length they rose
With one accord in love sublime, & as on Cherubs' wings   44/39
They Albion surround with kindest violence to bear him back
Against his will thro Los's Gate to Eden: Four-fold; loud!
Their Wings waving over the bottomless Immense: to bear
Their awful charge back to his native home: but Albion dark,
Repugnant; rolld his Wheels backward into Non-Entity.
Loud roll the Starry Wheels of Albion into the World of Death
And all the Gate of Los, clouded with clouds redounding from
Albion's dread Wheels, stretching out spaces immense between
That every little particle of light & air, became Opake   10
Black & immense, a Rock of difficulty & a Cliff
Of black despair; that the immortal Wings labourd against
Cliff after cliff, & over Valleys of despair & death:
The narrow Sea between Albion & the Atlantic Continent:
Its waves of pearl became a boundless Ocean bottomless,
Of grey obscurity, filld with clouds & rocks & whirling waters
And Albion's Sons ascending & descending in the horrid Void.

But as the Will must not be bended but in the day of Divine
Power: silent calm & motionless, in the mid-air sublime.
The Family Divine hover around the darkend Albion.   20

Such is the nature of the Ulro: that whatever enters
Becomes Sexual, & is Created, and Vegetated, and Born.
From Hyde Park spread their vegetating roots beneath Albion
In dreadful pain the Spectrous Uncircumcised Vegetation,
Forming a Sexual Machine: an Aged Virgin Form.
In Erin's Land toward the north, joint after joint & burning
In love & jealousy immingled & calling it Religion
And feeling the damps of death they with one accord delegated Los,

Conjuring him by the Highest that he should Watch over them
Till Jesus shall appear: & they gave their power to Los   30
Naming him the Spirit of Prophecy, calling him Elijah.

Strucken with Albion's disease they become what they behold;
They assimilate with Albion in pity & compassion:[4]
Their Emanations return not: their Spectres rage in the Deep
The Slumbers of Death came over them around the Couch of Death
Before the Gate of Los & in the depths of Non Entity
Among the Furnaces of Los: among the Oaks of Albion.

Man is adjoind to Man by his Emanative portion:
Who is Jerusalem in every individual Man: and her
Shadow is Vala, builded by the Reasoning power in Man.   40
O search & see: turn your eyes inward: open O thou World
Of Love & Harmony in Man: expand thy ever lovely Gates.

They wept into the deeps a little space; at length was heard
The voice of Bath, faint as the voice of the Dead in the House
   of Death

Bath, healing City! whose wisdom in midst of Poetic   45/40
Fervor; mild spoke thro' the Western Porch, in soft gentle tears

"O Albion mildest Son of Eden! clos'd is thy Western Gate.
Brothers of Eternity! this Man whose great example
We all admir'd & lov'd, whose all benevolent countenance, seen
In Eden, in lovely Jerusalem, drew even from envy
The tear: and the confession of honesty, open & undisguis'd
From mistrust and suspition,The Man is himself become
A piteous example of oblivion. To teach the Sons
Of Eden, that however great and glorious; however loving   10
And merciful the Individuality; however high
Our palaces and cities, and however fruitful are our fields,
In Selfhood, we are nothing: but fade away in morning's breath.
Our mildness is nothing: the greatest mildness we can use
Is incapable and nothing: none but the Lamb of God can heal
This dread disease: none but Jesus: O Lord descend and save.
Albion's Western Gate is clos'd: his death is coming apace!
Jesus alone can save him; for alas we none can know
How soon his lot may be our own. When Africa in sleep
Rose in the night of Beulah, and bound down the Sun & Moon   20
His friends cut his strong chains, & overwhelm'd his dark
Machines in fury & destruction, and the Man reviving repented.
He wept before his wrathful brethren, thankful & considerate
For their well timed wrath. But Albion's sleep is not
Like Africa's; and his machines are woven with his life.
Nothing but mercy can save him! nothing but mercy interposing
Lest he should slay Jerusalem in his fearful jealousy
O God descend! gather our brethren, deliver Jerusalem
But that we may omit no office of the friendly spirit,

---

4. The Cathedral Cities, unable to force Albion back through Los's "Gate to Eden" (44/39:2), suc-
   cumb to his illness.

Oxford take thou these leaves of the Tree of Life:⁵ with eloquence   30
That thy immortal tongue inspires; present them to Albion:
Perhaps he may recieve them, offerd from thy loved hands."

So spoke, unhear'd by Albion, the merciful Son of Heaven
To those whose Western Gates were open, as they stood weeping
Around Albion: but Albion heard him not; obdurate! hard!
He frown'd on all his Friends, counting them enemies in his
    sorrow.

And the Seventeen conjoining with Bath, the Seventh:
In whom the other Ten shone manifest, a Divine Vision!
Assimilated and embrac'd Eternal Death for Albion's sake.⁶

And these the names of the Eighteen combining with those Ten   40

Bath, mild Physician of Eternity, mysterious power   46/41
Whose springs are unsearchable & knowledg infinite.
Hereford, ancient Guardian of Wales, whose hands
Builded the mountain palaces of Eden, stupendous works!
Lincoln, Durham & Carlisle, Councellors of Los.
And Ely, Scribe of Los, whose pen no other hand
Dare touch! Oxford, immortal Bard! with eloquence
Divine, he wept over Albion: speaking the words of God
In mild perswasion: bringing leaves of the Tree of Life.

"Thou art in Error Albion. The Land of Ulro: 10
One Error not remov'd will destroy a human Soul.
Repose in Beulah's night, till the Error is remov'd
Reason not on both sides, Repose upon our bosoms
Till the Plow of Jehovah and the Harrow of Shaddai⁷
Have passed over the Dead, to awake the Dead to Judgment."
But Albion turn'd away refusing comfort.

Oxford trembled while he spoke, then fainted in the arms
Of Norwich, Peterboro, Rochester, Chester awful, Worcester,
Litchfield, Saint David's, Landaff, Asaph, Bangor, Sodor,
Bowing their heads devoted: and the Furnaces of Los   20
Began to rage, thundering loud the storms began to roar
Upon the Furnaces, and loud the Furnaces rebellow beneath.

And these the Four in whom the twenty-four appear'd four-fold:
Verulam, London, York, Edinburgh, mourning one towards another
"Alas!—The time will come, when a man's worst enemies
Shall be those of his own house and family: in a Religion
Of Generation, to destroy by Sin and Atonement, happy Jerusalem.
The Bride and Wife of the Lamb. O God thou art Not an Avenger!"

---

5. At the end of time, when the New Jerusalem appears, the tree of life, no longer denied to humanity (cf. *Marriage* 14), is to provide not only fruit but leaves "for the healing of the nations" (Revelation 22:2; cf. Ezekiel 47:12).
6. With Bath as their leader, the Cathedral Cities willingly sacrifice themselves.
7. Jehovah (traditional English spelling of the ineffable name transliterated YHWH) and Shaddai
   ("Almighty") are Hebrew names of God, two of Blake's "Seven Eyes" of God.

From Camberwell to Highgate where the mighty Thames shudders
    along, |47|
Where Los's Furnaces stand, where Jerusalem & Vala howl;
Luvah tore forth from Albion's Loins, in fibrous veins, in rivers
Of blood over Europe: a Vegetating Root in grinding pain,
Animating the Dragon Temples, soon to become that Holy Fiend
The Wicker Man of Scandinavia in which cruelly consumed
The Captives reard to heaven howl in flames among the stars[8]
Loud the cries of War on the Rhine & Danube, with Albion's Sons,
Away from Beulah's hills & vales break forth the Souls of the Dead.
With cymbal, trumpet, clarion; & the scythed chariots of Britain.[9] 10

And the Veil of Vala is composed of the Spectres of the Dead.

Hark! the mingling cries of Luvah with the Sons of Albion.
Hark! & Record the terrible wonder! that the Punisher
Mingles with his Victim's Spectre, enslaved and tormented,
To him whom he has murderd, bound in vengeance & enmity.
Shudder not, but Write, & the hand of God will assist you!"
Therefore I write Albion's last words. "Hope is banish'd from me."[1]

These were his last words, and the merciful Saviour in his arms |48|
Reciev'd him, in the arms of tender mercy and repos'd
The pale limbs of his Eternal Individuality
Upon the Rock of Ages.[2] Then, surrounded with a Cloud:
In silence the Divine Lord builded with immortal labour.
Of gold & jewels a sublime Ornament, a Couch of repose,
With Sixteen pillars: canopied with emblems & written verse,
Spiritual Verse, order'd & measur'd, from whence, time shall reveal,
The Five books of the Decalogue, the books of Joshua & Judges,
Samuel, a double book & Kings, a double book, the Psalms
    & Prophets   10
The Four-fold Gospel, and the Revelations everlasting.[3]
Eternity groan'd & was troubled, at the image of Eternal Death!

Beneath the bottoms of the Graves, which is Earth's central joint,
There is a place where Contrarieties are equally true:[4]
(To protect from the Giant blows in the sports of intellect,

8. According to Caesar's *Commentaries on the Gallic Wars* 6.16, the Druid priests of the Gauls in Britain burned wicker "figures of vast size" filled with living men; they believe their gods cannot be propitiated "unless the life of a man be offered for the life of a man" (see also **43**/38:65).
9. Legendarily, the Britons used "Chariots phang'd at the Axle with Iron Sithes" against Caesar (Milton, *History of Britain* [1670], book. 2). Historically, the Persian king Darius, despite his scythed chariots, was defeated by Alexander the Great in 330 B.C.E.
1. Cf. **24**:59. Lines 25–26 repeat **27**:81–82 (cf. Matthew 10:36).
2. Alternate translation of "strength" in Isaiah 26:4, applied by Christians to Jesus; cf. the hymn by Augustus Toplady (1740–78) first published in his *Gospel Magazine* (1776) and widely reprinted thereafter.
3. Exactly the books that Swedenborg (*Arcana Cœlestia* #10325) considered to have a "spiritual sense" that the rest of the Bible lacks. The first five books, traditionally attributed to Moses as author, center on the law (Decalogue = Ten Commandments). To arrive at a foursquare total of sixteen, Blake uses the traditional comprehensive title "Prophets" for all seventeen prophetic books individually listed by Swedenborg (perhaps extended to include his favorite, the "Wisdom" book of Job, omitted by Swedenborg).
4. In *Milton* **33**/30:1 this place is Beulah, located on "all sides" of Eternity. Although Jerusalem now leaves Beulah to enter Erin's newly opened spaces, she is still under the Daughters' protection in the "Ends" of this dreamy realm (line 52).

Thunder in the midst of kindness, & love that kills its beloved:
Because Death is for a period, and they renew tenfold.)
From this sweet Place Maternal Love awoke Jerusalem.
With pangs she forsook Beulah's pleasant lovely shadowy Universe
Where no dispute can come; created for those who Sleep.   20

Weeping was in all Beulah, and all the Daughters of Beulah
Wept for their Sister the Daughter of Albion, Jerusalem:
When out of Beulah the Emanation of the Sleeper descended
With solemn mourning out of Beulah's moony shades and hills:
Within the Human Heart, whose Gates closed with solemn
    sound.

And this the manner of the terrible Separation:
The Emanations of the grievously afflicted Friends of Albion
Concenter in one Female form an Aged pensive Woman.
Astonish'd! lovely! embracing the sublime shade: the Daughters
    of Beulah
Beheld her with wonder! With awful hands she took   30
A Moment of Time, drawing it out with many tears & afflictions
And many sorrows: oblique across the Atlantic Vale
Which is the Vale of Rephaim[5] dreadful from East to West,
Where the Human Harvest waves abundant in the beams of Eden
Into a Rainbow of jewels and gold, a mild Reflection from
Albion's dread Tomb, Eight thousand and five hundred years
In its extension. Every two hundred years has a door to Eden.
She also took an Atom of Space, with dire pain opening it a
    Center
Into Beulah: trembling the Daughters of Beulah dried
Her tears. She ardent embrac'd her sorrows, occupied in labours   40
Of sublime mercy in Rephaim's Vale. Perusing Albion's Tomb
She sat: she walk'd among the ornaments solemn mourning.
The Daughters attended her shudderings, wiping the death sweat.
Los also saw her in his seventh Furnace, he also terrified
Saw the finger of God go forth upon his seventh Furnace:[6]
Away from the Starry Wheels to prepare Jerusalem a place.
When with a dreadful groan the Emanation mild of Albion,
Burst from his bosom[7] in the Tomb like a pale snowy cloud,
Female and lovely, struggling to put off the Human form
Writhing in pain. The Daughters of Beulah in kind arms reciev'd   50
Jerusalem: weeping over her among the Spaces of Erin,
In the Ends of Beulah, where the Dead wail night & day.

And thus Erin spoke to the Daughters of Beulah, in soft tears

"Albion the Vortex of the Dead! Albion the Generous!
Albion the mildest son of Heaven! The Place of Holy Sacrifice!

---

5. Valley southwest of Jerusalem where David defeated the Philistines (2 Samuel 5:17–25); elsewhere
   translated "giants" (Joshua 15:8) and "the dead" (Psalm 88:10).
6. This benevolent intervention also occurs in 12:5.
7. Jerusalem is usually described as Albion's soul, a lovely woman who should be the bride of the
   Lamb. Here she bursts forth as a sort of daughter to Albion, rather than a consort. On the female
   aspect of the Divine Presence or *shekhinah*, see Spector, 2001. On Erin, see n. 9, p. 219.

Where Friends Die for each other: will become the Place.
Of Murder, & Unforgiving, Never-awaking Sacrifice of Enemies.
The Children must be sacrific'd! (a horror never known
Till now in Beulah) unless a Refuge can be found
To hide them from the wrath of Albion's Law that freezes sore   60
Upon his Sons & Daughters, self-exiled from his bosom.
Draw ye Jerusalem away from Albion's Mountains
To give a Place for Redemption, let Sihon and Og[8]
Remove Eastward to Bashan and Gilead, and leave

The secret coverts of Albion & the hidden places of America.   49
Jerusalem Jerusalem! why wilt thou turn away?[9]
Come ye O Daughters of Beulah, lament for Og & Sihon
Upon the Lakes of Ireland from Rathlin to Baltimore;
Stand ye upon the Dargle from Wicklow to Drogheda
Come & mourn over Albion the White Cliff of the Atlantic
The Mountain of Giants; all the Giants of Albion are become
Weak! witherd! darkend! & Jerusalem is cast forth from Albion.
They deny that they ever knew Jerusalem, or ever dwelt in Shiloh
The Gigantic roots & twigs of the vegetating Sons of Albion   10
Filld with the little-ones are consumed in the Fires of their Altars
The vegetating Cities are burned & consumed from the Earth:
And the Bodies in which all Animals & Vegetations, the Earth &
    Heaven,
Were containd in the All Glorious Imagination are witherd &
    darkend:
The golden Gate of Havilah, and all the Garden of God,
Was caught up with the Sun in one day of fury and war:
The Lungs, the Heart, the Liver, shrunk away far distant from Man
And left a little slimy substance floating upon the tides.
In one night the Atlantic Continent was caught up with the Moon,
And became an Opake Globe far distant clad with moony beams,   20
The Visions of Eternity, by reason of narrowed perceptions,
Are become weak Visions of Time & Space, fix'd into furrows of
    death;
Till deep dissimulation is the only defence an honest man has left.
O Polypus of Death! O Spectre over Europe and Asia
Withering the Human Form by Laws of Sacrifice for Sin!
By Laws of Chastity & Abhorrence I am witherd up.
Striving to Create a Heaven in which all shall be pure & holy
In their Own Selfhoods, in Natural Selfish Chastity to banish Pity
And dear Mutual Forgiveness; & to become One Great Satan
Inslavd to the most powerful Selfhood; to murder the Divine
    Humanity   30
In whose sight all are as the dust & who chargeth his Angels
    with folly;[1]

8. Kings defeated by the Israelites (Numbers 21:21–35); probably because Sihon was defeated immediately before Og, the last "remnant of the giants" (Deuteronomy 3:11), Blake associates him with
   the giants as well (J 89:47 ff.).
9. Cf. Jesus' lament over Jerusalem (Matthew 23:37) and the Bard's call to Earth in "Introduction"
   to *Songs of Experience*.
1. Echoing Job. 4:18.

Ah! weak & wide astray! Ah shut in narrow doleful form!
Creeping in reptile flesh upon the bosom of the ground:
The Eye of Man, a little narrow orb, closd up & dark.
Scarcely beholding the Great Light; conversing with the ground:
The Ear, a little shell, in small volutions shutting out
True Harmonies, & comprehending great, as very small:
The Nostrils, bent down to the earth & clos'd with senseless flesh.
That odours cannot them expand, nor joy on them exult:
The Tongue, a little moisture fills, a little food it cloys,   40
A little sound it utters, & its cries are faintly heard.
Therefore they are removed; therefore they have taken root
In Egypt & Philistea: in Moab & Edom & Aram:
In the Erythrean Sea their Uncircumcision in Heart & Loins
Be lost for ever & ever. Then they shall arise from Self,
By Self Annihilation into Jerusalem's Courts & into Shiloh,[2]
Shiloh the Masculine Emanation among the Flowers of Beulah.
Lo Shiloh dwells over France, as Jerusalem dwells over Albion.
Build & prepare a Wall & Curtain for America's shore!
Rush on: Rush on: Rush on! ye vegetating Sons of Albion   50
The Sun shall go before you in Day; the Moon shall go
Before you in Night.[3] Come on! Come on! Come on! The Lord
Jehovah is before, behind, above, beneath, around.
He has builded the arches of Albion's Tomb binding the Stars
In merciful Order, bending the Laws of Cruelty to Peace.
He hath placed Og & Anak, the Giants of Albion for their Guards:
Building the Body of Moses in the Valley of Peor: the Body
Of Divine Analogy; and Og & Sihon in the tears of Balaam
The Son of Beor, have given their power to Joshua & Caleb,[4]
Remove from Albion, far remove these terrible surfaces.   60
They are beginning to form Heavens & Hells in immense
Circles; the Hells for food to the Heavens: food of torment,
Food of despair: they drink the condemnd Soul & rejoice
In cruel holiness, in their Heavens of Chastity & Uncircumcision.
Yet they are blameless & Iniquity must be imputed only
To the State they are enterd into that they may be deliverd:
Satan is the State of Death, & not a Human existence:
But Luvah is named Satan because he has enterd that State,
A World where Man is by Nature the enemy of Man
Because the Evil is Created into a State, that Men   70
May be deliverd time after time evermore. Amen.
Learn therefore O Sisters to distinguish the Eternal Human
That walks about among the stones of fire in bliss & woe[5]
Alternate! from those States or Worlds in which the Spirit
   travels:

2. City smitten for its failure to protect the ark of the covenant (1 Samuel 4:3, Psalm 78:60, Jeremiah 7:12); also a name for the Messiah (Genesis 49:10–12).
3. As the pillars of cloud and fire guided the Israelites (Exodus 13:21).
4. Defeat of the giants Og (Deuteronomy 3:11) and Anak (Numbers 13:33, Joshua 11:21), Moses' burial (Deuteronomy 34:6), and Balaam's travails (Numbers 22–24) lead up to the entrance of Joshua and Caleb into the Promised Land.
5. The Covering Cherub also walks "in the midst of the stones of fire" (Ezekiel 28:14). This ultimate state of error, solidifying all that blocks Albion from the Divine Vision of true humanity, is revealed in 89. On the importance of distinguishing the "State" from the Individual within it, cf. *Milton* 35/32:10, 22–29.

This is the only means to Forgiveness of Enemies
Therefore remove from Albion these terrible Surfaces
And let wild seas & rocks close up Jerusalem away from

The Atlantic Mountains where Giants dwelt in Intellect;   50
Now given to stony Druids, and Allegoric Generation
To the Twelve Gods of Asia. the Spectres of those who Sleep:
Sway'd by a Providence oppos'd to the Divine Lord Jesus:
A murderous Providence! A Creation that groans, living on
    Death.
Where Fish & Bird & Beast & Man & Tree & Metal & Stone
Live by Devouring, going into Eternal Death continually:
Albion is now possess'd by the War of Blood! the Sacrifice
Of envy Albion is become, and his Emanation cast out:
Come Lord Jesus, Lamb of God descend! for if; O Lord!   10
If thou hadst been here, our brother Albion had not died.[6]
Arise sisters! Go ye & meet the Lord, while I remain—
Behold the foggy mornings of the Dead on Albion's cliffs!
Ye know that if the Emanation remains in them:
She will become an Eternal Death, an Avenger of Sin
A Self-righteousness: the proud Virgin-Harlot! Mother of War!
And we also & all Beulah, consume beneath Albion's curse."

6. Echoing both Mary and Martha (John 11:21, 11:32), before the resurrection of their brother Lazarus.
7. The Daughters' prayer, reiterated in the last line, significantly alters the traditional Anglican liturgy based on John 1:29: "Lamb of God, that takest away the sins of the world, / Have mercy upon us"; cf. "take away the imputation of Sin" at **25**:12.
8. Modeled on "[L]et not the sun go down on your wrath" (Ephesians 4:26), another rejection of "remembrance of sin." Cf. the apostle's repudiation of atonement rituals because "in those sacrifices there is a remembrance again made of sins every year" (Hebrews 10:3). On the "hideous orifice" in the chest of the triple-headed Hand, depicted on this last plate of chapter 2, see **70**:1–14; Hand as triple Accuser is also shown in **93**. Cf. the "Triple Headed Gog-Magog Giant" (**98**:52).

So Erin spoke to the Daughters of Beulah. Shuddering
With their wings they sat in the Furnace, in a night
Of stars, for all the Sons of Albion appeard distant stars,   20
Ascending and descending into Albion's sea of death.
And Erin's lovely Bow enclos'd the Wheels of Albion's Sons.

Expanding on wing, the Daughters of Beulah replied in sweet
    response

"Come O thou Lamb of God and take away the remembrance
    of Sin[7]
To Sin & to hide the Sin in sweet deceit is lovely!!
To Sin in the open face of day is cruel & pitiless! But
To record the Sin for a reproach: to let the Sun go down
In a remembrance of the Sin; is a Woe & a Horror[8]
A brooder of an Evil Day, and a Sun rising in blood.
Come then O Lamb of God and take away the remembrance
    of Sin."   30

    End of Chap. 2[d].

| Rahab is an
Eternal State[9] | To the Deists. | The Spiritual States of   **52**
the Soul are All Eternal
Distinguish between the
Man, & his present State[9] |

He never can be a Friend to the Human Race who is the Preacher of Natural Morality or Natural Religion.[1] He is a flatterer who means to betray,
to perpetuate Tyrant Pride & the Laws of that Babylon which he foresees
shall shortly be destroyed with the Spiritual and not the Natural Sword: He
is in the State named Rahab: which State must be put off before he can be
the Friend of Man.

You O Deists profess yourselves the Enemies of Christianity: and you are
so: you are also the Enemies of the Human Race & of Universal Nature. Man
is born a Spectre or Satan & is altogether an Evil, & requires a New Selfhood
continually & must continually be changed into his direct Contrary. But
your Greek Philosophy (which is a remnant of Druidism) teaches that Man
is Righteous in his Vegetated Spectre; an Opinion of fatal & accursed consequence to Man, as the Ancients saw plainly by Revelation to the intire
abrogation of Experimental Theory, and many believed what they saw, and
Prophecied of Jesus.[2]

---

9. States are established so that individuals, who are eternal, may pass through them (cf. *Milton* 35/32:10–38); Although Rahab (see 5:42) is an Eternal State" identified with "Moral Virtue" (39/35:10), the conclusion of the opening paragraph indicates that it too can be "put off."
1. Assumes a divine order in nature discernible to rational beings, independent of the "revealed reli-gion" of Scripture (see headnote, p. 3)."Natural Morality," the rationalist's answer to original sin, assumes the innate goodness of human nature and attributes evil to corrupt social institutions. In Blake's work, any god derived from nature is a bloodthirsty, unforgiving tyrant, and true morality lies in the struggle to overcome one's own pride and self-righteousness.
2. For Christians of Blake's time, the primary instance of such a prophecy was Virgil's "messianic" Fourth Eclogue.

Man must & will have Some Religion; if he has not the Religion of Jesus, he will have the Religion of Satan, & will erect the Synagogue of Satan, calling the Prince of this World,[3] God; and destroying all who do not worship Satan under the Name of God! Will any one say, Where are those who worship Satan under the Name of God! Where are they? Listen! Every Religion that Preaches Vengeance for Sin is the Religion of the Enemy & Avenger; and not the Forgiver of Sin, and their God is Satan, Named by the Divine Name. Your Religion O Deists: Deism, is the Worship of the God of this World by the means of what you call Natural Religion and Natural Philosophy, and of Natural Morality or Self-Righteousness, the Selfish Virtues of the Natural Heart. This was the Religion of the Pharisees who murderd Jesus. Deism is the same & ends in the same.

Voltaire Rousseau Gibbon Hume[4] charge the Spiritually Religious with Hypocrisy! but how a Monk or a Methodist either, can be a Hypocrite; I cannot concieve. We are Men of like passions with others & pretend not to be holier than others:[5] therefore, when a Religious Man falls into Sin, he ought not to be calld a Hypocrite: this title is more properly to be given to a Player who falls into Sin; whose profession is Virtue & Morality & the making Men Self-Righteous. Foote in calling Whitefield, Hypocrite; was himself one:[6] for Whitefield pretended not to be holier than others: but confessed his Sins before all the World. Voltaire! Rousseau! You cannot escape my charge that you are Pharisees & Hypocrites, for you are constantly talking of the Virtues of the Human Heart, and particularly of your own, that you may accuse others & especially the Religious, whose errors, you by this display of pretended Virtue, chiefly design to expose. Rousseau thought Men Good by Nature; he found them Evil & found no friend. Friendship cannot exist without Forgiveness of Sins continually. The Book written by Rousseau calld his Confessions is an apology & cloke for his sin & not a confession.[7]

But you also charge the poor Monks & Religious with being the causes of War: while you acquit & flatter the Alexanders & Caesars, the Lewis's & Fredericks:[8] who alone are its causes & its actors. But the Religion of Jesus, Forgiveness of Sin, can never be the cause of a War nor of a single Martyrdom.

3. Jesus' name for Satan (John 12:31, 14:30, 16:11); cf. "God of this World" (2 Corinthians 4:4) in "Everlasting Gospel" and Epilogue to *Gates of Paradise*. (see n. 6, p. 343). Throughout *Jerusalem*, the true "religion of Jesus" is mutual forgiveness. "Synagogue of Satan": see n. 9, p. 241.
4. Rationalist philosophers and historians of religion—two French, two English (augmented by Bolingbroke in *Milton* 46/40:12). Although Gibbon is not usually considered a Deist, his *Decline and Fall of the Roman Empire* (esp. chapters 15–16) casts a harsh light on early Christianity.
5. Those claiming to be "holier than thou" are condemned in Isaiah 65:5; cf. the injunction "not to think of himself more highly than he ought to think" (Romans 12:3) and the echo of 1 Timothy in "To the Public". With "We," the author/narrator firmly identifies himself as a Christian, echoing Paul and Barnabus (Acts 14:15).
6. In attacking the "license to perform" for nontheatrical presenters, the actor-playwright Samuel Foote pilloried the Methodist evangelist George Whitefield in *The Minor* (1760; in print through the 1790s). As Paley notes, both Blake and Methodists were attacked in Hunt's *Examiner*; in *Milton* (24/22:55), Whitefield and Wesley appear as the "two witnesses" of Revelation.
7. Rousseau's *Confessions* (1782–88), unlike Saint Augustine's, does not culminate in repentance or conversion. In Christian writing generally, an "apology" is a reasoned defense, not an admission of error.
8. I.e., Frederick the Great of Prussia. "Lewis's": Louis XIV, XV, and XVI of France.

Those who Martyr others or who cause War are Deists, but never can be
Forgivers of Sin. The Glory of Christianity is, To Conquer by Forgiveness.
All the Destruction therefore, in Christian Europe has arisen from Deism,
which is Natural Religion.

>   I saw a Monk of Charlemaine
>   Arise before my sight
>   I talkd with the Grey Monk[9] as we stood
>   In beams of infernal light
>
>   Gibbon arose with a lash of steel   5
>   And Voltaire with a wracking wheel
>   The Schools in clouds of learning rolld
>   Arose with War in iron & gold.[1]
>
>   "Thou lazy Monk" they sound afar,
>   "In vain condemning glorious War   10
>   And in your Cell you shall ever dwell
>   Rise War & bind him in his Cell."
>
>   The blood red ran from the Grey Monk's side
>   His hands & feet were wounded wide
>   His body bent, his arms & knees   15
>   Like to the roots of ancient trees.
>
>   When Satan first the black bow bent
>   And the Moral Law from the Gospel rent
>   He forgd the Law into a Sword
>   And spilld the blood of mercy's Lord.   20
>
>   Titus! Constantine! Charlemaine![2]
>   O Voltaire! Rousseau! Gibbon! Vain
>   Your Grecian Mocks & Roman Sword
>   Against this image of his Lord!
>
>   For a Tear is an Intellectual thing;   25
>   And a Sigh is the Sword of an Angel King
>   And the bitter groan of a Martyr's woe
>   Is an Arrow from the Almightie's Bow.

9. Cf. "The Grey Monk." This vision of a martyred pacifist spans the ages: in Charlemaine's eighth
century, the predominant monastic order was Benedictine; the Franciscan order, to which Grey Fri-
ars belonged, was not founded until 1209.
1. Although the rack and wheel are associated with the twelfth-century Inquisition that continued in
Spain to Blake's time, the torturers are philosophers of the Age of Reason. In *Decline and Fall*, Gibbon challenges accounts of tortured saints unconfirmed by pagan historians. "Schools": associated
with Scholasticism, a theological method and system emphasizing logic, syllogistic argumentation,
and deductive reasoning. In Blake's layout, this poem's first six stanzas appear in double columns,
with the last stanza centered beneath.
2. Frankish warrior-king (742–814) who conquered the Saxons, consolidated western territories, and
was crowned emperor of the Holy Roman Empire, without approval from Constantinople. Titus
(c. 40–81 C.E.): Roman emperor who destroyed the Temple and sacked Jerusalem (depicted on his
Arch in Rome). Constantine (280–337): Roman emperor who changed the empire's religion to
Christianity, moved the capital to Byzantium (Constantinople), and claimed to conquer enemies
under the sign of the Cross. The three emperors mark eras in the takeover of "the religion of Jesus,"
mutual forgiveness, by warmongering state religion.

53

Jerusalem
Chap. 3

But Los, who is the Vehicular Form of strong Urthona
Wept vehemently over Albion where Thames' currents spring
From the rivers of Beulah; pleasant river! soft, mild, parent stream.
And the roots of Albion's Tree enterd the Soul of Los
As he sat before his Furnaces clothed in sackcloth of hair
In gnawing pain dividing him from his Emanation;
Inclosing all the Children of Los time after time.
Their Giant forms condensing into Nations & Peoples & Tongues
Translucent the Furnaces, of Beryll & Emerald immortal:
And Seven-fold each within other; incomprehensible   10
To the Vegetated Mortal Eyes perverted & single vision.
The Bellows are the Animal's Lungs, the Hammers, the Animal
    Heart
The Furnaces, the Stomach for Digestion; terrible their fury
Like seven burning heavens rang'd from South to North.

Here on the banks of the Thames Los builded Golgonooza,
Outside of the Gates of the Human Heart, beneath Beulah
In the midst of the rocks of the Altars of Albion. In fears
He built it, in rage & in fury. It is the Spiritual Fourfold
London: continually building & continually decaying desolate!
In eternal labours: loud the Furnaces & loud the Anvils   20
Of Death thunder incessant around the flaming Couches of
The Twentyfour Friends of Albion and round the awful Four
For the protection of the Twelve Emanations of Albion's Sons
The Mystic Union of the Emanation in the Lord; Because
Man, divided from his Emanation, is a dark Spectre
His Emanation is an ever-weeping melancholy Shadow.
But she is made receptive of Generation thro' mercy

In the Potter's Furnace, among the Funeral Urns of Beulah
From Surrey hills, thro' Italy and Greece, to Hinnom's vale.

In Great Eternity, every particular Form gives forth or Emanates   54
Its own peculiar Light & the Form is the Divine Vision
And the Light is his Garment. This is Jerusalem in every Man,
A Tent & Tabernacle of Mutual Forgiveness, Male & Female
     Clothings.
And Jerusalem is called Liberty among the Children of Albion.

But Albion fell down, a Rocky fragment from Eternity hurld
By his own Spectre, who is the Reasoning Power in every Man,
Into his own Chaos which is the Memory between Man & Man.

The silent broodings of deadly revenge springing from the
All powerful parental affection fills Albion from head to foot,   10
Seeing his Sons assimilate with Luvah, bound in the bonds
Of spiritual Hate, from which springs Sexual Love as iron chains.
He tosses like a cloud outstretchd among Jerusalem's Ruins
Which overspread all the Earth, he groans among his ruind
     porches.

But the Spectre like a hoar frost & a Mildew rose over Albion
Saying, "I am God O Sons of Men! I am your Rational Power!
Am I not Bacon & Newton & Locke who teach Humility to Man!
Who teach Doubt & Experiment & my two Wings Voltaire:
     Rousseau.
Where is that Friend of Sinners[3] that Rebel against my Laws!
Who teaches Belief to the Nations, & an unknown Eternal Life?   20
Come hither into the Desart & turn these stones to bread.[4]
Vain foolish Man! wilt thou believe without Experiment?
And build a World of Phantasy upon my Great Abyss!
A World of Shapes in craving lust & devouring appetite?"

So spoke the hard cold constrictive Spectre; he is named Arthur
Constricting into Druid Rocks round Canaan Agag & Aram
     & Pharoh.

Then Albion drew England into his bosom in groans & tears
But she stretchd out her starry Night in Spaces against him, like
A long Serpent, in the Abyss of the Spectre which augmented

3. From Matthew 11:19: "friend of publicans [tax-collectors for the Roman empire] and sinners."
4. The Spectre identifies himself with Satan, who tempted Jesus in the wilderness (Matthew 4:3).

The Night with Dragon wings coverd with stars, & in the Wings   30
Jerusalem & Vala appeard: & above between the Wings
  magnificent
The Divine Vision dimly appeard in clouds of blood weeping.

When those who disregard all Mortal Things saw a Mighty-One   55
Among the Flowers of Beulah still retain his awful strength
They wonderd: checking their wild flames & Many gathering
Together into an Assembly; they said, "Let us go down
And see these changes!" Others said, "If you do so prepare
For being driven from our fields, what have we to do with the
  Dead?
To be their inferiors or superiors we equally abhor;
Superior, none we know: inferior none: all equal share
Divine Benevolence & joy, for the Eternal Man
Walketh among us, calling us his Brothers & his Friends: 10
Forbidding us that Veil which Satan puts between Eve & Adam:
By which the Princes of the Dead enslave their Votaries
Teaching them to form the Serpent of precious stones & gold
To sieze the Sons of Jerusalem & plant them in One Man's Loins
To make One Family of Contraries: that Joseph may be sold
Into Egypt: for Negation; a Veil the Saviour born & dying rends."[5]

But others said: "Let us to him who only Is, & who
Walketh among us, give decision. Bring forth all your fires!"

So saying, an eternal deed was done: in fiery flames
The Universal Concave[6] raged, such thunderous sounds as never   20
Were sounded from a mortal cloud, nor on Mount Sinai old
Nor in Havilah where the Cherub rolld his redounding flame.[7]

Loud! loud! the Mountains lifted up their voices, loud the
  Forests,
Rivers thunderd against their banks, loud Winds furious fought
Cities & Nations contended in fires & clouds & tempests.
The Seas raisd up their voices & lifted their hands on high
The Stars in their courses fought,[8] the Sun! Moon! Heaven:
  Earth.
Contending for Albion & for Jerusalem his Emanation
And for Shiloh, the Emanation of France & for lovely Vala.

Then far the greatest number were about to make a Separation   30
And they Elected Seven, calld the Seven Eyes of God;[9]
Lucifer, Molech, Elohim, Shaddai, Pahad, Jehovah, Jesus.

---

5. I.e., the veil in the temple, torn at the Crucifixion (Matthew 27:51), metaphorically associated with the hymen (see n. 4, p. 234 herein) and hence with the virgin birth.
6. Possible error for "Conclave," the assembly; otherwise, the concave interior of the illusory sky-dome, the Mundane Shell (59:7); see n. 8, p. 165 herein.
7. The "flaming sword" blocking humanity's return to Paradise (Genesis 3:24), always in Blake's work wielded by only one cherub (cf. *Marriage* 14). Havilah is encompassed by one of the rivers of Eden (Genesis 2:11).
8. Echoing Judges 5:20.
9. Messengers (Zechariah 4:10) or manifestations of God through history; n. 5, p. 160 herein. In *Milton*, the Eighth Eye is Milton; here, it is Albion.

They namd the Eighth, he came not, he hid in Albion's
   Forests
But first they said: (& their Words stood in Chariots in array
Curbing their Tygers with golden bits & bridles of silver & ivory)

"Let the Human Organs be kept in their perfect Integrity
At will Contracting into Worms, or Expanding into Gods
And then behold! what are these Ulro Visions of Chastity
Then as the moss upon the tree: or dust upon the plow:
Or as the sweat upon the labouring shoulder; or as the chaff   40
Of the wheat-floor or as the dregs of the sweet wine-press
Such are these Ulro Visions, for tho we sit down within
The plowed furrow, listning to the weeping clods till we
Contract or Expand Space at will: or if we raise ourselves
Upon the chariots of the morning, Contracting or Expanding
   Time!
Every one knows, we are One Family: One Man blessed for ever."

Silence remaind & every one resumd his Human Majesty
And many conversed on these things as they labourd at the furrow
Saying; "It is better to prevent misery, than to release from misery
It is better to prevent error, than to forgive the criminal!   50
Labour well the Minute Particulars, attend to the Little-ones!
And those who are in misery cannot remain so long
If we do but our duty: labour well the teeming Earth."

They Plow'd in tears, the trumpets sounded before the golden
   Plow
And the voices of the Living Creatures were heard in the clouds of
   heaven
Crying; "Compell the Reasoner to Demonstrate with unhewn
   Demonstrations
Let the Indefinite be explored, and let every Man be Judged
By his own Works, Let all Indefinites be thrown into
   Demonstrations
To be pounded to dust & melted in the Furnaces of Affliction:
He who would do good to another, must do it in Minute
   Particulars   60
General Good is the plea of the scoundrel hypocrite & flatterer:
For Art & Science cannot exist but in minutely organized
   Particulars
And not in generalizing Demonstrations of the Rational Power,
The Infinite alone resides in Definite & Determinate Identity
Establishment of Truth depends on destruction of Falshood
   continually
On Circumcision: not on Virginity, O Reasoners of Albion."

So cried they at the Plow. Albion's Rock frowned above
And the Great Voice of Eternity rolled above terrible in clouds
Saying "Who will go forth for us! & Who shall we send before
   our face?"[1]

---

1. The call to prophetic mission (cf. Isaiah 6:8).

Then Los heaved his thund'ring Bellows on the Valley of
    Middlesex
And thus he chaunted his Song: the Daughters of Albion reply

"What may Man be? who can tell! But what may Woman be?
To have power over Man from Cradle to corruptible Grave.
He who is an Infant, and whose Cradle is a Manger[2]
Knoweth the Infant sorrow: whence it came, and where it goeth:
And who weave it a Cradle of the grass[3] that withereth away.
This World is all a Cradle for the erred wandering Phantom:
Rock'd by Year, Month, Day & Hour; and every two Moments
Between dwells a Daughter of Beulah, to feed the Human
    Vegetable.
Entune: Daughters of Albion, your hymning Chorus mildly!   10
Cord of affection thrilling extatic on the iron Reel:
To the golden Loom of Love! to the moth-labour'd Woof
A Garment and Cradle weaving for the infantine Terror:
For fear; at entering the gate into our World of cruel
Lamentation: it flee back & hide in Non-Entity's dark wild
Where dwells the Spectre of Albion: destroyer of Definite Form.
The Sun shall be a Scythed Chariot of Britain: the Moon; a Ship
In the British Ocean! Created by Los's Hammer; measured out
Into Days & Nights & Years & Months, to travel with my feet   20
Over these desolate rocks of Albion; O daughters of despair:
Rock the Cradle, and in mild melodies tell me where found
What you have enwoven with so much tears & care? so much
Tender artifice: to laugh: to weep: to learn: to know;
Remember! recollect! what dark befel in wintry days."

"O it was lost for ever! and we found it not: it came
And wept at our wintry Door: Look! look! behold! Gwendolen
Is become a Clod of Clay! Merlin is a Worm of the Valley!"

Then Los uttered with Hammer & Anvil; "Chaunt! revoice!
I mind not your laugh: and your frown I not fear! and   30
You must my dictate obey from your gold-beam'd Looms; trill
Gentle to Albion's Watchman, on Albion's mountains; reeccho
And rock the Cradle while! Ah me! Of that Eternal Man
And of the cradled Infancy in his bowels of compassion:
Who fell beneath his instruments of husbandry & became
Subservient to the clods of the furrow! The cattle and even
The emmet and earth-Worm are his superiors & his lords."

Then the response came warbling from trilling Looms in Albion
"We Women tremble at the light therefore! hiding fearful
The Divine Vision with Curtain & Veil & fleshly Tabernacle."   40
Los utter'd; swift as the rattling thunder upon the mountains
"Look back into the Church Paul! Look! Three Women around
The Cross; O Albion why didst thou a Female Will Create?"

2. Cf. "Infant Sorrow" and "Cradle Song"; from *Experience*. Jesus himself has experienced birth into
  a strictly natural world, unredeemed by imagination. J 56:3–4 reprises 34/30:25–26.
3. Refers literally to the wicker cradle used throughout Europe, metaphorically the "grass" of Psalm
  103:15, Isaiah 40:8, and James 1:10; Paley also notes the infant Moses' ark of bulrushes (Exodus 2:3),
  as depicted by Blake (Butlin 773). For more on imagery of fibers and weaving, see Hilton, *Literal
  Imagination* (1993), 79 ff., and Paley in *Blake's Sublime Allegory* (1973), ed. Curran and Wittreich.

York　　London

And the voices of Bath & Canterbury & York & Edinburgh Cry
Over the Plow of Nations in the strong hand of Albion thundering along
Among the fires of the Druid & the deep black rethundering Waters
Of the Atlantic which poured in impetuous loud loud louder & louder.
And the Great Voice of the Atlantic howled over the Druid Altars:
Weeping over his Children in Stone-henge in Malden & Colchester.
Round the Rocky Peak of Derbyshire London Stone & Rosamonds Bower

What is a Wife & what is a Harlot? What is a Church? & What
Is a Theatre? are they Two & not One? can they Exist Separate?
Are not Religion & Politics the Same Thing? Brotherhood is Religion
O Demonstrations of Reason Dividing Families in Cruelty & Pride!

But Albion fled from the Divine Vision, with the Plow of Nations enflaming
The Living Creatures maddend and Albion fell into the Furrow, and
The Plow went over him & the Living was Plowed in among the Dead
But his Spectre rose over the starry Plow. Albion fled beneath the Plow
Till he came to the Rock of Ages. & he took his Seat upon the Rock.
Wonder seizd all in Eternity: to behold the Divine Vision. open
The Center into an Expanse, & the Center rolled out into an Expanse.

Jerusalem

And the voices of Bath & Canterbury & York & Edinburgh Cry $\boxed{57}$
Over the Plow of Nations in the strong hand of Albion
   thundering along
Among the Fires of the Druid & the deep black rethundering
   Waters
Of the Atlantic which poured in impetuous loud loud, louder &
   louder
And the Great Voice of the Atlantic howled over the Druid Altars:
Weeping over his Children in Stone-henge in Malden & Colchester.
Round the Rocky Peak of Derbyshire London Stone & Rosamond's
   Bower.[4]

"What is a Wife & what is a Harlot? What is a Church? & What
Is a Theatre? are they Two & not One? can they Exist Separate?
Are not Religion & Politics the Same Thing? Brotherhood is
   Religion
O Demonstrations of Reason Dividing Families in Cruelty & Pride!"   10

But Albion fled from the Divine Vision, with the Plow of Nations
   enflaming
The Living Creatures maddend and Albion fell into the Furrow, and
The Plow went over him & the Living was Plowed in among the Dead
But his Spectre rose over the starry Plow. Albion fled beneath the
   Plow
Till he came to the Rock of Ages, & he took his Seat upon the
   Rock.
Wonder siezd all in Eternity! to behold the Divine Vision open
The Center into an Expanse, & the Center rolled out into an
   Expanse.

In beauty the Daughters of Albion divide & unite at will, $\boxed{58}$
Naked & drunk with blood, Gwendolen dancing to the timbrel[5]
Of War: reeling up the Street of London she divides in twain
Among the Inhabitants of Albion, the People fall around.
The Daughters of Albion divide & unite in jealousy & cruelty.
The Inhabitants of Albion at the Harvest & the Vintage
Feel their Brain cut round beneath the temples shrieking
Bonifying into a Scull, the Marrow exuding in dismal pain
They flee over the rocks bonifying: Horses; Oxen; feel the knife.
And while the Sons of Albion by severe War & Judgment bonify   10
The Hermaphroditic Condensations are divided by the Knife
The obdurate Forms are cut asunder by Jealousy & Pity.

Rational Philosophy and Mathematic Demonstration
Is divided in the intoxications of pleasure & affection
Two Contraries War against each other in fury & blood,
And Los fixes them on his Anvil, incessant his blows!
He fixes them with strong blows, placing the stones & timbers.

---

4. Labyrinthine underground hideaway in Woodford, Oxfordshire, built by Henry II for his mistress,
   called "Fair Rosamond" in a folk ballad.
5. Orgiastic rites amalgamating images of Hebrew timbrel and dance, drunkenness of Greco-Roman
   Bacchantes, nakedness of ancient Britons, and Aztec excision of live victims' organs (cf. plate 66).
   Possibly Blake knew of Bernard Picard's seven-volume *Ceremonies and Religious Customs of the
   Various Nations of the Known World* (trans. 1733–39).

To Create a World of Generation from the World of Death:
Dividing the Masculine & Feminine; for the comingling
Of Albion's & Luvah's Spectres was Hermaphroditic.   20

Urizen wrathful strode above directing the awful Building:
As a Mighty Temple; delivering Form out of confusion
Jordan sprang beneath its threshold bubbling from beneath
Its pillars: Euphrates ran under its arches: white sails
And silver oars reflect on its pillars, & sound on its ecchoing
Pavements; where walk the Sons of Jerusalem who remain
     Ungenerate
But the revolving Sun and Moon pass thro its porticoes,
Day & night, in sublime majesty & silence they revolve
And shine glorious within; Hand & Koban archd over the Sun
In the hot noon, as he traveld thro his journey; Hyle & Skofield   30
Archd over the Moon at midnight & Los Fixd them there,
With his thunderous Hammer; terrified the Spectres rage & flee
Canaan is his portico; Jordan is a fountain in his porch;
A fountain of milk & wine to relieve the traveller:
Egypt is the eight steps within, Ethiopia supports his pillars;
Lybia & the Lands unknown, are the ascent without;
Within is Asia & Greece, ornamented with exquisite art:
Persia & Media are his halls; his inmost hall is Great Tartary.
China & India & Siberia are his temples for entertainment
Poland & Russia & Sweden, his soft retired chambers.   40
France & Spain & Italy & Denmark & Holland & Germany
Are the temples among his pillars, Britain is Los's Forge;
America North & South are his baths of living waters,

Such is the Ancient World of Urizen in the Satanic Void
Created from the Valley of Middlesex by London's River
From Stone-henge & from London Stone, from Cornwall to
     Cathnes
The Four Zoa's rush around on all sides in dire ruin.
Furious in pride of Selfhood the terrible Spectres of Albion
Rear their dark Rocks among the Stars of God: stupendous
Works! A World of Generation continually Creating; out of   50
The Hermaphroditic Satanic World of rocky destiny,
And formed into Four precious stones, for enterance from
     Beulah.   59

For the Veil of Vala which Albion cast into the Atlantic Deep
To catch the Souls of the Dead: began to Vegetate & Petrify
Around the Earth of Albion, among the Roots of his Tree.
This Los formed into the Gates & mighty Wall, between the Oak
Of Weeping & the Palm of Suffering beneath Albion's Tomb.
Thus in process of time it became the beautiful Mundane Shell.[6]
The Habitation of the Spectres of the Dead & the Place
Of Redemption & of awaking again into Eternity

For Four Universes round the Mundane Egg remain Chaotic   10
One to the North: Urthona: One to the South: Urizen;

6. The hardened, crystalline form of Vala's veil, probably the same as the "sublime Universe" in **23**:21; a continuation of Albion's action in **23**:20–26. See n. 8, p. 165.

One to the East: Luvah: One to the West, Tharmas;
They are the Four Zoas that stood around the Throne Divine
Verulam: London: York & Edinburgh: their English names
But when Luvah assumed the World of Urizen Southward
And Albion was slain upon his Mountains & in his Tent.
All fell towards the Center, sinking downwards in dire ruin
In the South remains a burning Fire: in the East, a Void
In the West, a World of raging Waters; in the North: solid
    Darkness
Unfathomable without end: but in the midst of these   20
Is Built eternally the sublime Universe of Los & Enitharmon

And in the North Gate, in the West of the North, toward Beulah
Cathedron's Looms are builded, and Los's Furnaces in the South
A wondrous golden Building immense with ornaments sublime
Is bright Cathedron's golden Hall, its Courts, Towers &
    Pinnacles.

And one Daughter of Los sat at the fiery Reel & another
Sat at the shining Loom with her Sisters attending round
Terrible their distress & their sorrow cannot be utterd,
And another Daughter of Los sat at the Spinning Wheel
Endless their labour, with bitter food, void of sleep.   30
Tho hungry they labour; they rouze themselves anxious
Hour after hour labouring at the whirling Wheel
Many Wheels & as many lovely Daughters sit weeping
Yet the intoxicating delight that they take in their work
Obliterates every other evil; none pities their tears
Yet they regard not pity & they expect no one to pity
For they labour for life & love, regardless of any one
But the poor Spectres that they work for, always incessantly

They are mockd, by every one that passes by. They regard not,
They labour; & when their Wheels are broken by scorn & malice   40
They mend them sorrowing with many tears & afflictions,
Other Daughters Weave on the Cushion & Pillow, Network fine
That Rahab & Tirzah may exist & live & breathe & love
Ah, that it could be as the Daughters of Beulah wish!

Other Daughters of Los, labouring at Looms less fine
Create the Silk-worm & the Spider & the Catterpiller
To assist in their most grievous work of pity & compassion,
And others Create the wooly Lamb & the downy Fowl
To assist in the work: the Lamb bleats! the Sea-fowl cries
Men understand not the distress & the labour & sorrow   50
That in the Interior Worlds is carried on in fear & trembling,
Weaving the shuddring fears & loves of Albion's Families.
Thunderous rage the Spindles of iron, & the iron Distaff
Maddens in the fury of their hands, Weaving in bitter tears
The Veil of Goats-hair & Purple & Scarlet & fine twined Linen.[7]

---

7. Cf. materials for curtains and priestly robes for the tabernacle (Exodus 26:1, 27:16, 28:6) and the
    veil crafted by Los as a protection from chaos, as elaborated in 59:2–21. A continuation and cor-
    rection of Albion's action in 23:20–26 (cf. 64:1).

The clouds of Albion's Druid Temples rage in the eastern heaven [60]
While Los sat terrified beholding Albion's Spectre who is Luvah
Spreading in bloody veins in torments over Europe & Asia;
Not yet formed but a wretched torment unformed & abyssal
In flaming fire; within the Furnaces the Divine Vision appeard
On Albion's hills: often walking from the Furnaces in clouds
And flames among the Druid Temples & the Starry Wheels
Gatherd Jerusalem's Children in his arms & bore them like
A Shepherd in the night of Albion which overspread all the
    Earth.

"I gave thee liberty and life O lovely Jerusalem   10
And thou hast bound me down upon the Stems of Vegetation.
I gave thee Sheep-walks upon the Spanish Mountains,
    Jerusalem
I gave thee Priam's City and the Isles of Grecia lovely!
I gave thee Hand & Scofield & the Counties of Albion!
They spread forth like a lovely root into the Garden of God:
They were as Adam before me: united into One Man.
They stood in innocence & their skiey tent reachd over Asia
To Nimrod's Tower[8] to Ham & Canaan walking with Mizraim
Upon the Egyptian Nile, with solemn songs to Grecia
And sweet Hesperia even to Great Chaldea & Tesshina   20
Following thee as a Shepherd by the Four Rivers of Eden.
Why wilt thou rend thyself apart, Jerusalem?
And build this Babylon & sacrifice in secret Groves,[9]
Among the Gods of Asia; among the fountains of pitch & nitre?
Therefore thy Mountains are become barren Jerusalem!
Thy Valleys, Plains of burning sand, thy Rivers; waters of death
Thy Villages die of the Famine and thy Cities
Beg bread from house to house, lovely Jerusalem.
Why wilt thou deface thy beauty & the beauty of thy little-ones
To please thy Idols, in the pretended chastities of
    Uncircumcision?   30
Thy Sons are lovelier than Egypt or Assyria; wherefore
Dost thou blacken their beauty by a Secluded place of rest,
And a peculiar Tabernacle to cut the integuments of beauty
Into veils of tears and sorrows O lovely Jerusalem!
They have perswaded thee to this, therefore their end shall
    come
And I will lead thee thro the Wilderness in shadow of my cloud
And in my love I will lead thee, lovely Shadow of Sleeping
    Albion."

This is the Song of the Lamb, sung by Slaves in evening time.

But Jerusalem faintly saw him, closd in the Dungeons of
    Babylon.

---

8. The tower of Babel (Genesis 11) in Nimrod's kingdom (Genesis 10:8–10; cf. *J* 7:19, **22**:3). Babel
   is often identified with Babylon.
9. Both Druids and idolatrous Israelites worshiped in groves, a sin for which the prophets repeatedly
   warn that God will disinherit his people and dry up their land—before leading them to ultimate
   redemption.

Her Form was held by Beulah's Daughters, but all within unseen   40
She sat at the Mills, her hair unbound her feet naked
Cut with the flints: her tears run down, her reason grows like
The Wheel of Hand, incessant turning day & night without
    rest.
Insane she raves upon the winds hoarse, inarticulate:
All night Vala hears. She triumphs in pride of holiness
To see Jerusalem deface her lineaments with bitter blows
Of despair, while the Satanic Holiness triumphd in Vala
In a Religion of Chastity & Uncircumcised Selfishness
Both of the Head & Heart & Loins, closd up in Moral Pride.

But the Divine Lamb stood beside Jerusalem. Oft she saw   50
The lineaments Divine & oft the Voice heard, & oft she said,

"O Lord & Saviour, have the Gods of the Heathen pierced
    thee?
Or hast thou been pierced in the House of thy Friends?
Art thou alive! & livest thou for-evermore? or art thou
Not: but a delusive shadow, a thought that liveth not?
Babel mocks saying, there is no God nor Son of God
That thou O Human Imagination, O Divine Body art all
A delusion. But I know thee O Lord when thou arisest upon
My weary eyes even in this dungeon & this iron mill.
The Stars of Albion cruel rise: thou bindest to sweet influences: 60
For thou also sufferest with me altho I behold thee not;
And altho I sin & blaspheme thy holy name, thou pitiest me;
Because thou knowest I am deluded by the turning mills.
And by these visions of pity & love because of Albion's death."

Thus spake Jerusalem, & thus the Divine Voice replied.

"Mild Shade of Man, pitiest thou these Visions of terror & woe!
Give forth thy pity & love, fear not! lo I am with thee always.[1]
Only believe in me that I have power to raise from death
Thy Brother who Sleepeth in Albion: fear not trembling Shade.

Behold: in the Visions of Elohim Jehovah, behold Joseph &
    Mary
And be comforted O Jerusalem in the Visions of Jehovah
    Elohim."[2]

[61]

She looked & saw Joseph the Carpenter in Nazareth & Mary
His espoused Wife. And Mary said, "If thou put me away from
    thee
Dost thou not murder me?" Joseph spoke in anger & fury. "Should I
Marry a Harlot & an Adulteress?" Mary answered, "Art thou more
    pure

1. Jesus' promise before his ascension (Matthew 28:20), followed by a paraphrase of his assurances
to Martha before raising Lazarus (John 11:40) and his words to the synagogue ruler Jairus before
raising his daughter (Mark 5:36). "Bindest to sweet influences" (line 60); cf. Job 38:31.
2. Jehovah and Elohim are usually presented as separate "Eyes of God." The Divine Voice's adjura-
tion, "be comforted," may allude to "Comfort ye . . . Speak ye comfortably to Jerusalem" from Isaiah 40 (Ostriker), also familiar as the opening of Handel's *Messiah* (1742).

Than thy Maker³ who forgiveth Sins & calls again Her that is Lost?
Tho She hates, he calls her again in love. I love my dear Joseph
But he driveth me away from his presence, yet I hear the voice of
    God
In the voice of my Husband. Tho he is angry for a moment, he
    will not   10
Utterly cast me away. If I were pure, never could I taste the sweets
Of the Forgivess of Sins: if I were holy: I never could behold the
    tears
Of love! of him who loves me in the midst of his anger in furnace
    of fire."

"Ah my Mary:" said Joseph: weeping over & embracing her closely
    in
His arms: "Doth he forgive Jerusalem & not exact Purity from her
    who is
Polluted? I heard his voice in my sleep & his Angel in my dream:

Saying 'Doth Jehovah Forgive a Debt only on condition that it
    shall
Be Payed? Doth he Forgive Pollution only on conditions of Purity?
That Debt is not Forgiven! That Pollution is not Forgiven
Such is the Forgiveness of the Gods, the Moral Virtues of the   20
    Heathen, whose tender Mercies are Cruelty. But Jehovah's
    Salvation
Is without Money & without Price,⁴ in the Continual Forgiveness
    of Sins
In the Perpetual Mutual Sacrifice in Great Eternity! for behold!
There is none that liveth & Sinneth not! And this is the
    Covenant
Of Jehovah: If you Forgive one-another, so shall Jehovah Forgive
    You:⁵
That He Himself may Dwell among You. Fear not then to take
To thee Mary thy Wife, for she is with Child by the Holy Ghost.' "⁶

Then Mary burst forth into a Song! she flowed like a River of
Many Streams in the arms of Joseph & gave forth her
    tears of joy
Like many waters, and Emanating into gardens & palaces upon   30
Euphrates & to forests & floods & animals wild & tame from
Gihon to Hiddekel, & to corn fields & villages & inhabitants
Upon Pison & Arnon & Jordan.⁷ And I heard the voice among

3. Echoing Job 4:17. Mary's embrace of the "fortunate fall" resembles Oothoon's in *Visions* 6/3:17–19.
4. Quoting Isaiah 55:1 on the free gift of mercy; spoken by the angel in Matthew 1:20. Cf. Los's condemnation of Atonement in 39/35:25 ff.
5. Echoing Matthew 6:14, Jesus' explanation of the terms of forgiveness in the Lord's Prayer (Matthew 6:12). The emphasis is on *mutual* forgiveness, for "There is none that liveth & Sinneth not" (cf. 1 Kings 8:46 and Paul's "all have sinned," Romans 3:23).
6. Jerusalem's vision of another woman under accusation of sin (61:3–46) affords one of the poem's crucial insights: it is only after Joseph, as a wronged husband, whole-heartedly accepts Mary's unexplained pregnancy (61:14 ff.) that his earlier dream of the Holy Spirit's involvement (J 61:27; Matthew 1:18–24) takes on meaning. Blake rejects the implication, in the doctrine of the Virgin Birth, that sexual reproduction is not holy (cf. "Everlasting Gospel"). On reworkings of early Christian heresies, see William E. Phipps, "Blake on Joseph's Dilemma," *Theology Today*, 1971.
7. To the four rivers of Paradise are added the Arnon, which flows along the border of Moab into the Dead Sea, and the Jordan. Mary's joyous response, as Wicksteed notes, is a new Magnificat (Luke 1:46–55).

The Reapers Saying. "Am I Jerusalem the lost Adulteress? or am I
Babylon come up to Jerusalem?" And another voice answered
    Saying

"Does the voice of my Lord call me again? Am I pure thro his
    Mercy
And Pity? Am I become lovely as a Virgin in his sight who am
Indeed a Harlot drunken with the Sacrifice of Idols? Does he
Call her pure as he did in the days of her Infancy when She
Was cast out to the loathing of her person?[8] The Chaldean took   40
Me from my Cradle. The Amalekite stole me away upon his
    Camels
Before I had ever beheld with love the Face of Jehovah; or known
That there was a God of Mercy; O Mercy O Divine Humanity!
O Forgiveness & Pity & Compassion! If I were Pure I should never
Have known Thee; If I were Unpolluted I should never have
Glorified thy Holiness, or rejoiced in thy great Salvation."

Mary leaned her side against Jerusalem, Jerusalem recieved
The Infant into her hands in the Visions of Jehovah. Times
    passed on.
Jerusalem fainted over the Cross & Sepulcher. She heard the voice
"Wilt thou make Rome thy Patriarch Druid & the Kings of Europe
    his   50
Horsemen? Man in the Resurrection changes his Sexual Garments
    at Will
Every Harlot was once a Virgin;[9] every Criminal an Infant Love:

62

Repose on me till the morning of the Grave, I am thy life."

Jerusalem replied. "I am an outcast: Albion is dead;
I am left to the trampling foot & the spurning heel!
A Harlot I am calld. I am sold from street to street!
I am defaced with blows & with the dirt of the Prison!
And wilt thou become my Husband O my Lord & Saviour?

8. Echoing Ezekiel 16:3; cf. the prophets' descriptions of Jerusalem as a harlot beloved by God
(Ezekiel 16, 25; Hosea 2).
9. Cf. the final plate of *Gates of Paradise*.

Shall Vala bring thee forth! shall the Chaste be ashamed also?
I see the Maternal Line, I behold the Seed of the Woman!
Cainah & Ada & Zillah & Naamah Wife of Noah.
Shuah's daughter & Tamar & Rahab the Canaanites;   10
Ruth the Moabite & Bathsheba of the daughters of Heth
Naamah the Ammonite, Zibeah the Philistine, & Mary.[1]
These are the Daughters of Vala, Mother of the Body of death
But I thy Magdalen behold thy Spiritual Risen Body
Shall Albion arise? I know he shall arise at the Last Day!
I know that in my flesh I shall see God:[2] but Emanations
Are weak, they know not whence they are, nor whither tend."

Jesus replied. "I am the Resurrection & the Life.[3]
I Die & pass the limits of possibility, as it appears
To individual perception. Luvah must be Created   20
And Vala; for I cannot leave them in the gnawing Grave.
But will prepare a way for my banished-ones to return.
Come now with me into the villages, walk thro all the cities.
Tho thou art taken to prison & judgment, starved in the streets
I will command the cloud to give thee food & the hard rock
To flow with milk & wine, tho thou seest me not a season
Even a long season & a hard journey & a howling wilderness:[4]
Tho Vala's cloud hide thee & Luvah's fires follow thee:
Only believe & trust in me, Lo. I am always with thee."

So spoke the Lamb of God while Luvah's Cloud reddening
    above   30
Burst forth in streams of blood upon the heavens & dark night
Involvd Jerusalem, & the Wheels of Albion's Sons turnd hoarse
Over the Mountains & the fires blaz'd on Druid Altars
And the Sun set in Tyburn's Brook where Victims howl & cry,

But Los beheld the Divine Vision among the flames of
    the Furnaces[5]
Therefore he lived & breathed in hope, but his tears fell incessant
Because his Children were closd from him apart; & Enitharmon
Dividing in fierce pain: also the Vision of God was closd in clouds

1. Jesus' maternal line (cf. "Mother of my Mortal part" in "To Tirzah") descends through twelve foreign, transgressive, or otherwise disreputable foremothers, extrapolated from the five women named in the lineage of his earthly father Joseph: the widowed seductress Tamar (Genesis 38:6–26), the Canaanite harlot Rahab (Joshua 2, 6, as Rachab, mother of Boaz), the Moabite Ruth, and the adulteress Bathsheba (2 Samuel 11:1–5). On that model, the "Seed of the Woman" is traced back to "Cainah," Blake's name for the wife of Adam and Eve's first son, Cain (she is thought to be either his sister or some non-Adamic form of humanity), in the land of Nod (Genesis 4:16–17). Ada and Zillah are the co-wives of Cain's son Lamech (Genesis 4:23). Zillah's daughter Naamah (Genesis 4:22), without biblical authority, is identified as Noah's wife. The Canaanite Shuah's nameless daughter (Genesis 38:1, 38:12) is Judah's wife, but his descendants stem from his daughter-in-law Tamar. The next Naamah is an Ammonite wife of Solomon, mother of the idolatrous King Rehoboam (1 Kings 14:21). Zibeah (Zibiah) of Beersheba is the mother of King Jehoash (2 Kings 12:1), who gave away the Temple treasures to Syria. The male line goes back to Adam through his third son, Seth (Luke 3:23 ff.).
2. Jerusalem quotes Martha (John 11:24) and Job (19:26).
3. Jesus responds with his reassurance to Martha (John 11:25); cf. **50**:11 and **60**:67.
4. Moses, foreseeing the future corruption of the Israelites after his death, sings of God's finding and leading Jacob/Israel "in the waste howling wilderness" (Deuteronomy 32:10–14), making him "suck honey out of the rock," and granting him such gifts as oil, butter, and wine. Jesus' speech ends with the risen Christ's last words to his disciples at the conclusion of Matthew's gospel.
5. See n. 9, p. 216 herein; cf. **60**:5 and **96**:35–37.

Of Albion's Spectres, that Los in despair oft sat, & often ponderd
On Death Eternal in fierce shudders upon the mountains of Albion   40
Walking: & in the vales in howlings fierce, then to his Anvils
Turning, anew began his labours, tho in terrible pains![6]

Jehovah stood among the Druids in the Valley of Annandale |63|
When the Four Zoas of Albion, the Four Living Creatures, the
    Cherubim
Of Albion tremble before the Spectre, in the starry Harness of
    the Plow
Of Nations. And their Names are Urizen & Luvah & Tharmas
    & Urthona.

Luvah slew Tharmas the Angel of the Tongue & Albion
    brought him
To Justice in his own City of Paris, denying the Resurrection.
Then Vala the Wife of Albion, who is the Daughter of Luvah
Took vengeance Twelve-fold among the Chaotic Rocks of
    the Druids
Where the Human Victims howl to the Moon & Thor & Friga [7]
Dance the dance of death contending with Jehovah among the
    Cherubim.   10
The Chariot Wheels filled with Eyes rage along the howling Valley
In the Dividing of Reuben & Benjamin bleeding from Chester's
    River.

The Giants & the Witches & the Ghosts of Albion dance with
Thor & Friga, & the Fairies lead the Moon along the Valley
    of Cherubim
Bleeding in torrents from Mountain to Mountain, a lovely Victim.
And Jehovah stood in the Gates of the Victim, & he appeared
A weeping Infant in the Gates of Birth in the midst of Heaven.
The Cities & Villages of Albion became Rock & Sand
    Unhumanized,
The Druid Sons of Albion & the Heavens a Void around
    unfathomable
No Human Form but Sexual & a little weeping Infant
    pale reflected   20
Multitudinous in the Looking Glass of Enitharmon, on all sides

---

6. The large feet in the design are those of the creature who appears at the top of this plate (p. 288
   herein).
7. Norse deities. "Thor": a warrior whose hammer creates thunder. "Frigga": wife of Odin, a goddess
   of love and sex (like Freya). Likely sources: Henri Mallet's *Northern Antiquities* (1770), Fuseli's
   paintings of Norse subjects. The wheels with eyes (line 11) are from Ezekiel 10:12.

Around in the clouds of the Female, on Albion's Cliffs of the Dead.

Such the appearance in Cheviot: in the Divisions of Reuben

When the Cherubim hid their heads under their wings in deep
    slumbers,
When the Druids demanded Chastity from Woman & all was lost,

"How can the Female be Chaste O thou stupid Druid" Cried Los
"Without the Forgiveness of Sins in the merciful clouds
    of Jehovah
And without the Baptism of Repentance to wash away Calumnies,
    and
The Accusations of Sin that each may be Pure in their Neighbour's
    sight
O when shall Jehovah give us Victims from his Flocks & Herds   30
Instead of Human Victims by the Daughters of Albion & Canaan?"

Then laugh'd Gwendolen & her laughter shook the Nations &
    Familys of
The Dead beneath Beulah from Tyburn to Golgotha, and from
Ireland to Japan. Furious her Lions & Tygers & Wolves sport before
Los on the Thames & Medway. London & Canterbury groan in pain.

Los knew not yet what was done: he thought it was all in Vision
In Visions of the Dreams of Beulah among the Daughters of Albion
Therefore the Murder was put apart in the Looking Glass
    of Enitharmon.

He saw in Vala's hand the Druid Knife of Revenge & the Poison Cup
Of Jealousy, and thought it a Poetic Vision of the Atmospheres   40
Till Canaan rolld apart from Albion across the Rhine: along
    the Danube

And all the Land of Canaan suspended over the Valley of Cheviot
From Bashan to Tyre & from Troy to Gaza of the Amalekite,
And Reuben fled with his head downwards among the Caverns
Of the Mundane Shell which froze on all sides round   64
    Canaan on
The vast Expanse: where the Daughters of Albion Weave the Web
Of Ages & Generations, folding & unfolding it, like a Veil
    of Cherubim.
And sometimes it touches the Earth's summits, & sometimes
    spreads
Abroad into the Indefinite Spectre, who is the Rational Power.

Then All the Daughters of Albion became One before Los:
    even Vala!
And she put forth her hand upon the Looms in dreadful howlings
Till she vegetated into a hungry Stomach & a devouring Tongue.
Her Hand is a Court of Justice, her Feet: two Armies in Battle,
Storms & Pestilence: in her Locks: & in her Loins Earthquake   10
And Fire, & the Ruin of Cities & Nations & Families & Tongues.

She cries: "The Human is but a Worm, & thou O Male; Thou art
Thyself Female, a Male: a breeder of Seed: a Son & Husband: & Lo,
The Human Divine is Woman's Shadow, a Vapor in the summer's
    heat.
Go assume Papal dignity thou Spectre, thou Male Harlot! Arthur
Divide into the Kings of Europe in times remote, O Woman-born
And Woman-nourishd & Woman-educated & Woman-scorn'd!"

"Wherefore art thou living?" said Los, "& Man cannot live in
    thy presence.
Art thou Vala the Wife of Albion O thou lovely Daughter of Luvah?
All Quarrels arise from Reasoning, the secret Murder, and   20
The violent Man-slaughter, these are the Spectre's double Cave,
The Sexual Death living on accusation of Sin & Judgment
To freeze Love & Innocence into the gold & silver of the Merchant
Without Forgiveness of Sin. Love is Itself Eternal Death."

Then the Spectre drew Vala into his bosom magnificent, terrific
Glittering with precious stones & gold, with Garments of blood &
    fire.
He wept in deadly wrath of the Spectre, in self-contradicting agony
Crimson with Wrath & green with Jealousy, dazling with Love
And Jealousy immingled & the purple of the violet darkend deep
Over the Plow of Nations thundring in the hand of Albion's
    Spectre.   30

A dark Hermaphrodite they stood[8] frowning upon London's River
And the Distaff & Spindle in the hands of Vala with the Flax of
Human Miseries turnd fierce with the Lives of Men along
    the Valley
As Reuben fled before the Daughters of Albion Taxing the Nations.

Derby Peak yawnd a horrid Chasm at the Cries of Gwendolen, & at
The stamping feet of Ragan upon the flaming Treddles
    of her Loom
That drop with crimson gore with the Loves of Albion & Canaan
Opening along the Valley of Rephaim, weaving over the Caves of
    Machpelah.[9]

To decide Two Worlds with a great decision: a World of
    Mercy, and   65
A World of Justice: the World of Mercy for Salvation,
To cast Luvah into the Wrath, and Albion into the Pity
In the Two Contraries of Humanity & in the Four Regions.

For in the depths of Albion's bosom in the eastern heaven,
They sound the clarions strong! they chain the howling
    Captives!

---

8. Cf. "Two Horn'd Reasoning Cloven Fiction / In Doubt which is Self contradiction / A dark Hermaphrodite We stood / Rational Truth Root of Evil & Good" (from "The Keys to the Gates," *For the Sexes: The Gates of Paradise*).
9. A family burial place that Abraham purchased in Canaan after Sarah's death (Genesis 23:2 ff., 49:30). "Rephaim": see n. 5, p. 269 herein.

They cast the lots into the helmet; they give the oath of blood in
    Lambeth
They vote the death of Luvah, & they naild him to Albion's Tree
    in Bath:
They staind him with poisonous blue, they inwove him in cruel
    roots
To die a death of Six thousand years bound round with vegetation.[1]   10
The sun was black & the moon rolld a useless globe thro Britain!

Then left the Sons of Urizen the plow & harrow, the loom
The hammer & the chisel, & the rule & compasses; from London
    fleeing
They forg'd the sword on Cheviot, the chariot of war & the battle-ax,
The trumpet fitted to mortal battle, & the flute of summer
    in Annandale.
And all the Arts of Life they changd into the Arts of Death
    in Albion.
The hour-glass contemnd because its simple workmanship
Was like the workmanship of the plowman, & the water wheel.
That raises water into cisterns broken & burnd with fire:
Because its workmanship was like the workmanship of the
    shepherd.   20
And in their stead intricate wheels invented, wheel without wheel:
To perplex youth in their outgoings, & to bind to labours in Albion
Of day & night the myriads of eternity that they may grind
And polish brass & iron hour after hour, laborious task!
Kept ignorant of its use, that they might spend the days of wisdom
In sorrowful drudgery, to obtain a scanty pittance of bread:
In ignorance to view a small portion & think that All,
And call it Demonstration: blind to all the simple rules of life.

"Now: now the battle rages round thy tender limbs O Vala.
Now smile among thy bitter tears: now put on all thy beauty   30
Is not the wound of the sword sweet! & the broken bone
    delightful?
Wilt thou now smile among the scythes when the wounded groan
    in the field
We were carried away in thousands from London; & in tens
Of thousands from Westminster & Marybone in ships closd up:
Chaind hand & foot, compelled to fight under the iron whips
Of our captains; fearing our officers more than the enemy.
Lift up thy blue eyes Vala & put on thy sapphire shoes:
O melancholy Magdalen behold the morning over Malden break:
Gird on thy flaming zone, descend into the sepulcher of
    Canterbury.
Scatter the blood from thy golden brow, the tears from thy silver
    locks: 40
Shake off the waters from thy wings! & the dust from thy white
    garments

---

1. In the six thousand years of fallen human history, Luvah is the archetypal dying vegetation god, now
under torments of Napoleonic-era warfare. "Poisonous blue": the woad of the ancient Britons' war
paint. The subsequent montage includes images of industrialized weapons production (**65**:21–28) and
the capture of sailors by press-gangs (**65**:33–36) in sufferings of the "Spectre sons of Albion" (**65**:56).

Remember all thy feigned terrors on the secret couch of Lambeth's
    Vale
When the sun rose in glowing morn, with arms of mighty hosts
Marching to battle, who was wont to rise with Urizen's harps
Girt as a sower with his seed to scatter life abroad over Albion!
Arise O Vala! bring the bow of Urizen: bring the swift arrows of light.
How rag'd the golden horses of Urizen, compelld to the chariot
    of love!
Compelld to leave the plow to the ox, to snuff up the winds of
    desolation
To trample the corn fields in boastful neighings: this is no gentle
    harp
This is no warbling brook, nor shadow of a mirtle tree: 50
But blood and wounds and dismal cries, and shadows of the oak:
And hearts laid open to the light, by the broad grizly sword:
And bowels hid in hammerd steel rip'd quivering on the ground.
Call forth thy smiles of soft deceit: call forth thy cloudy tears:
We hear thy sighs in trumpets shrill when morn shall blood renew."

So sang the Spectre Sons of Albion round Luvah's Stone of Trial:
Mocking and deriding at the writhings of their Victim on
    Salisbury:[2]
Drinking his Emanation in intoxicating bliss rejoicing in Giant
    dance
For a Spectre has no Emanation but what he imbibes from
    decieving
A Victim! Then he becomes her Priest & she his Tabernacle,   60
And his Oak Grove, till the Victim rend the woven Veil
In the end of his sleep when Jesus calls him from him his grave.

Howling the Victims on the Druid Altars yield their souls
To the stern Warriors: lovely sport the Daughters round their
    Victims;
Drinking their lives in sweet intoxication. Hence arose
    from Bath
Soft deluding odours, in spiral volutions intricately winding
Over Albion's mountains, a feminine indefinite cruel delusion.
Astonishd: terrified & in pain & torment, Sudden they behold
Their own Parent the Emanation of their murderd Enemy
Become their Emanation and their Temple and Tabernacle.   70
They knew not this Vala was their beloved Mother Vala Albion's
    Wife.

Terrified at the sight of the Victim: at his distorted sinews!
The tremblings of Vala vibrate thro' the limbs of Albion's Sons:
While they rejoice over Luvah in mockery & bitter scorn:
Sudden they become like what they behold in howlings & deadly
    pain
Spasms smite their features, sinews & limbs: pale they look on one
    another.
They turn, contorted: their iron necks bend unwilling towards

---

2. Stonehenge is on Salisbury Plain (cf. 66:2), not far from the cathedral city Salisbury.

Frontispiece for *Europe a Prophecy* (1794), Plate 1/i. Copy K, 1821.

This depiction of a mighty creator, or delimiter, in action is not linked to a particular text. The white hair and beard, traditionally associated with God the Father in Christian art, are in Blake's prophetic works attributes of Urizen, who, in a different poem, "formed golden compasses / And began to explore the Abyss" (*Urizen* 20:40). With hair and beard blowing and eyes downcast, he leans out of a red (yellow, in some copies) sunlike disc, too small for his body if he were standing upright, to delineate or measure— with his left hand—the primal form of the material universe. In some copies of *Europe*, the veins on his muscular left arm stand out; in this copy, tears run down his cheeks. On his deathbed, Blake colored a separate print of this image for one of his young followers (see p. 96).

Title page for *Europe*, Plate 2/ii. Copy K, 1821.

This coiled and upreared crested serpent, a manifestation of the fiery rebel Orc in many of Blake's works, reappears along the left border of plate 10, its head in flames. In most copies of the title page, the snake's powerful tail extends out of and back into the picture frame on the left, but here an extra loop keeps most of it in view. In the text, the serpent is associated not with Orc but with the "ancient temple serpent-form'd" (13/10:2) of "Albion's angels." This edifice, believed in Blake's time to have been built by Druids, appears in the background of color plate 16.

Title page for *The Book of Urizen* (1794), plate 1. Copy G, c. 1818.

Sitting doubled over on an open book, with blank tablets of the Ten Commandments like tombstones behind him, Urizen writes on two surfaces simultaneously with two different implements (see p. 114), marking his place in the indecipherable text with the big toe of his right foot. In most copies Urizen writes on stone slabs instead of books. The word "FIRST" was removed from the title in this copy.

Urizen, plate 22. Copy G, c. 1818.

With knees drawn up (as on the title page), eyes closed, and beams streaming from his head, Urizen endures Los's fetters of time, space, and the human body (10:9, 10:27). Urizen's tears, added in this copy, are not mentioned in the text, but his weeping is emphasized in *The Song of Los* (4:17 and 7:42). As with all full-page designs in this work, placement varies from copy to copy; this eleventh page is number 22 in the standard order (see p. 114).

Title page for *Milton a Poem* (1804/1811), plate 1. Copy D, c. 1818.

Inspired by a Bard's Song in Eternity, Milton heroically abandons his safe place among the Elect and re-enters mortal existence, pushing through the syllables of his name and the poem's title, to search for his lost Emanation. On the mound beneath his feet is a restatement of Milton's epic theme in *Paradise Lost* 1.26, as discussed on p. 144.

Title page for *Jerusalem The Emanation of the Giant Albion* (1804/1820), plate 2. Copy E, c. 1821.

The sleeping Jerusalem, with planets, moons, and stars in her wings, is attended by four other winged beings, not counting the bird and others amidst the words of the title. Her metamorphosis complete, she is next seen fully awake on plate 14 (p.225), a design also filled with astronomical objects, as she hovers under a rainbow above a reclining Albion, flanked by mourners. She is later described as "Winged with Six Wings" (86:1), attributes of a seraph. On her relationship to Albion and her transformations in the poem, see p. 205.

Frontispiece for Chapter 4 of *Jerusalem*, "To the Christians," plate 76. Copy E, c. 1821.

Inscriptions in uncolored impressions of this plate identify the two figures as Albion and Jesus. In the posture of a devotee, Albion contemplates Jesus' cruci-fixion on what appears to be an oak tree, associated with Druid rituals and the "Stems of Vegetation" (60:9) on which the Divine Vision is bound. Yet the tree's abundant fruit may be associated with that of the Tree of Life, lost to humanity with the expulsion from Eden and restored with the New Jerusalem (Revelation 22:2). Near the end of the poem, when Albion learns that "every kindness to another is a little Death / In the Divine Image" (96:27–28) and is moved to yield his own life for the sake of his friend, the illusion of mortality is dispelled. For more on the structure of the work, see p. 205.

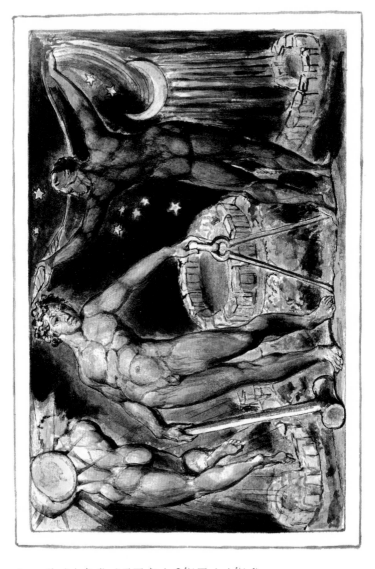

Tailpiece for *Jerusalem*, plate 100. Copy E, c. 1821.

In this concluding design, which Blake set lengthwise on the page, the hammer and tongs are implements of Los, flanked by his fellow laborers: his Spectre rising with the sun on his shoulder, his Emanation, Enitharmon, holding her spindle in her left hand as she draws out red fibers associated with the circulatory system. The trilithons in the background recall "Serpent Temples thro the Earth, from the wide Plain of Salisbury" (80:48), as diagrammed by William Stukeley in *Abury, a Temple of the British Druids* (1743), perhaps implying that Los's great task of rebuilding Jerusalem is yet to be accomplished.

Luvah: their lips tremble: their muscular fibres are crampd
  & smitten
They become like what they behold! Yet immense in strength
  & power,

In awful pomp & gold, in all the precious unhewn stones of Eden |66|
They build a stupendous Building on the Plain of Salisbury;
  with chains
Of rocks round London Stone: of Reasonings: of unhewn
  Demonstrations
In labyrinthine arches (Mighty Urizen the Architect) thro which
The Heavens might revolve & Eternity be bound in their chain.
Labour unparallelld! a wondrous rocky World of cruel destiny
Rocks piled on rocks reaching the stars; stretching from pole to pole.
The Building is Natural Religion & its Altars Natural Morality
A building of eternal death: whose proportions are eternal despair
Here Vala stood turning the iron Spindle of destruction   10
From heaven to earth: howling! invisible! but not invisible
Her Two Covering Cherubs afterwards named Voltaire & Rousseau:
Two frowning Rocks; on each side of the Cove³ & Stone of Torture:
Frozen Sons of the feminine Tabernacle of Bacon, Newton & Locke.
For Luvah is France: the Victim of the Spectres of Albion.
Los beheld in terror: he pour'd his loud storms on the Furnaces:
The Daughters of Albion clothed in garments of needle work
Strip them off from their shoulders and bosoms, they lay aside
Their garments; they sit naked upon the Stone of trial,
The Knife of flint⁴ passes over the howling Victim: his blood   20
Gushes & stains the fair side of the fair Daughters of Albion.
They put aside his curls; they divide his seven locks⁵ upon
His forehead: they bind his forehead with thorns of iron
They put into his hand a reed, they mock Saying: Behold
The King of Canaan whose are seven hundred chariots of iron!
They take off his vesture whole with their Knives of flint:
But they cut asunder his inner garments; searching with
Their cruel fingers for his heart, & there they enter in pomp.
In many tears; & there they erect a temple & an altar;
They pour cold water on his brain in front, to cause.   30
Lids to grow over his eyes in veils of tears: and caverns
To freeze over his nostrils, while they feed his tongue from cups
And dishes of painted clay. Glowing with beauty & cruelty:
They obscure the sun & the moon; no eye can look upon them.

Ah! alas! at the sight of the Victim, & at sight of those who are
  smitten,
All who see become what they behold. Their eyes are coverd
With veils of tears and their nostrils & tongues shrunk up

---

3. Paley cites the antiquarian Stukeley on this "immense" central feature of a Druid temple, "consisting of three stones plac'd with an obtuse angle toward each other." Two, leaning toward each other, remain at Avebury.
4. In Francisco Javier Clavigero's *History of Mexico* (trans. 1787, 2nd ed. 1807), the high priest, "with a cutting knife made of flint, dexterously opened [the sacrificial victim's] breast and tore out his heart, which, while yet palpitating, he offered to the sun" and afterward fed the idol (2:279, Garland rpt. 1979).
5. Samson loses his strength after his "seven locks" are shaved (Judges 16:19).

Their ear bent outwards, as their Victim, so are they in the pangs
Of unconquerable fear! amidst delights of revenge Earth-shaking!
And as their eye & ear shrunk, the heavens shrunk away.   40
The Divine Vision became First a burning flame, then a column
Of fire, then an awful fiery wheel surrounding earth & heaven:
And then a globe of blood wandering distant in an unknown night;
Afar into the unknown night the mountains fled away:
Six months of mortality; a summer: & six months of mortality;
    a winter:
The Human form began to be alterd by the Daughters of Albion
And the perceptions to be dissipated into the Indefinite, Becoming
A mighty Polypus nam'd Albion's Tree: they tie the Veins
And Nerves into two knots: & the Seed into a double knot:[6]
They look forth: the Sun is shrunk; the Heavens are shrunk   50
Away into the far remote: and the Trees & Mountains witherd
Into indefinite cloudy shadows in darkness & separation.
By Invisible Hatreds adjoind, they seem remote and separate
From each other; and yet are a Mighty Polypus in the Deep!
As the Misletoe grows on the Oak, so Albion's Tree on Eternity: Lo!
He who will not comingle in Love must be adjoind by Hate.

They look forth from Stone-henge! from the Cove round London
    Stone
They look on one another: the mountain calls out to the
    mountain:
Plinlimmon shrunk away: Snowdon trembled: the mountains
Of Wales & Scotland beheld the descending War: the routed
    flying: 60
Red run the streams of Albion: Thames is drunk with blood;
As Gwendolen cast the shuttle of war; as Cambel returnd the
    beam.
The Humber & the Severn are drunk with the blood of the slain:
London feels his brain cut round: Edinburgh's heart is
    circumscribed!
York & Lincoln hide among the flocks, because of the griding[7]
    Knife.
Worcester & Hereford: Oxford & Cambridge reel & stagger,
Overwearied with howling: Wales & Scotland alone sustain the
    fight!
The inhabitants are sick to death; they labour to divide into Days
And Nights, the uncertain Periods; and into Weeks & Months. In
    vain
They send the Dove & Raven: & in vain the Serpent over the
    mountains.   70
And in vain the Eagle & Lion over the four-fold wilderness.
They return not; but generate in rocky places desolate.
They return not; but build a habitation separate from Man.[8]

6. The Daughters complete their confinement of Luvah, Albion's Zoa of passion, to the mortal body
by forming the heart, brain, and testicles.
7. Piercing.
8. In Genesis 8, the failure of the raven and the dove to return to Noah's ark means that the flood is
over; here, as the senses shrink under the Daughters' tortures, the departure of the animals—and
the retreat a few lines later of the sun, moon, and stars—confirms humanity's separation from
nature.

The Sun forgets his course like a drunken man; he hesitates,
Upon the Cheselden hills, thinking to sleep on the Severn
In vain; he is hurried afar into an unknown Night
He bleeds in torrents of blood as he rolls thro heaven above
He chokes up the paths of the sky; the Moon is leprous as snow:
Trembling & descending down seeking to rest upon high Mona:[9]
Scattering her leprous snows in flakes of disease over Albion.   80
The Stars flee remote: the heaven is iron, the earth is sulphur.
And all the mountains & hills shrink up like a withering gourd.
As the Senses of Men shrink together under the Knife of flint.
In the hands of Albion's Daughters, among the Druid Temples,
By those who drink their blood & the blood of their Covenant.[1] | 67 |

And the Twelve Daughters of Albion united in Rahab & Tirzah
A Double Female: and they drew out from the Rocky Stones
Fibres of Life to Weave for every Female is a Golden Loom.
The Rocks are opake hardnesses covering all Vegetated things.
And as they Wove & Cut from the Looms in various divisions
Stretching over Europe & Asia from Ireland to Japan
They divided into many lovely Daughters to be counterparts
To those they Wove, for when they Wove a Male, they divided
Into a Female to the Woven Male; in opake hardness   10
They cut the Fibres from the Rocks; groaning in pain they Weave;
Calling the Rocks Atomic Origins of Existence: denying Eternity
By the Atheistical Epicurean Philosophy of Albion's Tree.[2]
Such are the Feminine & Masculine when separated from Man
They call the Rocks Parents of Men, & adore the frowning Chaos
Dancing around in howling pain clothed in the bloody Veil,
Hiding Albion's Sons within the Veil, closing Jerusalem's
Sons without! to feed with their Souls the Spectres of Albion
Ashamed to give Love openly to the piteous & merciful Man
Counting him an imbecile mockery: but the Warrior   20
They adore: & his revenge cherish with the blood of the
    Innocent
They drink up Dan & Gad, to feed with milk Skofeld & Kotope
They strip off Joseph's Coat & dip it in the blood of battle.[3]

Tirzah sits weeping to hear the shrieks of the dying: her Knife
Of flint is in her hand: she passes it over the howling Victim.
The Daughters Weave their Work in loud cries over the Rock
Of Horeb: still eyeing Albion's Cliffs, eagerly siezing & twisting

9. Anglesea, island off the coast of Wales, mentioned in Milton's *Lycidas* 54, just after the "famous *Druids.*"
1. In response to the Israelites' pledge to obey the law, Moses sprinkles blood of sacrificial oxen, saying: "Behold the blood of the covenant" (Exodus 24:8; cf. Zechariah 9:11). At the Last Supper, Jesus declares the cup of wine "my blood of the new testament" (Matthew 26:28), and he is resurrected "through the blood of the everlasting covenant" (Hebrews 13:20; cf. Hebrews 10:29, 12:24). But the Daughters of Albion are like the Whore of Babylon, "drunken with the blood of the saints, and with the blood of the martyrs" (Revelation 17:6; cf. Jeremiah 51:7); see also Jerusalem-Aholibah with the cup of her sister, Samaria-Aholah (Ezekiel 23:32–35).
2. Epicurus, like Democritus before him, taught that all nature derives from atoms colliding in a void; cf. "Mock on Mock on Voltaire Rousseau."
3. After selling Joseph into slavery, Joseph's brothers dip his coat of many colors in goat's blood to make their father think the boy is dead (Genesis 37:31); see also the "vesture dipped in blood" (Revelation 19:13).

The threads of Vala & Jerusalem, running from mountain
    to mountain
Over the whole Earth: loud the Warriors rage in Beth Peor
Beneath the iron whips of their Captains & consecrated banners,   30
Loud the Sun & Moon rage in the conflict: loud the Stars
Shout in the night of battle & their spears grow to their hands
With blood, weaving the deaths of the Mighty into a Tabernacle
For Rahab & Tirzah; till the Great Polypus of Generation covered
    the Earth.[4]

In Verulam[5] the Polypus's Head, winding around his bulk
Thro Rochester, and Chichester, & Exeter & Salisbury.
To Bristol: & his Heart beat strong on Salisbury Plain
Shooting out Fibres round the Earth, thro Gaul & Italy
And Greece, & along the Sea of Rephaim into Judea
To Sodom & Gomorrha: thence to India, China & Japan.   40
The Twelve Daughters in Rahab & Tirzah have circumscribd the
    Brain
Beneath & pierced it thro the midst with a golden pin.
Blood hath staind her fair side beneath her bosom.

"O thou poor Human Form!" said she. "O thou poor child of woe!
Why wilt thou wander away from Tirzah: why me compel to
    bind thee?
If thou dost go away from me I shall consume upon these Rocks.
These fibres of thine eyes that used to beam in distant heavens
Away from me: I have bound down with a hot iron.
These nostrils that expanded with delight in morning skies
I have bent downward with lead melted in my roaring furnaces   50
Of affliction; of love: of sweet despair: of torment unendurable.
My soul is seven furnaces, incessant roars the bellows
Upon my terribly flaming heart, the molten metal runs
In channels thro my fiery limbs: O love: O pity; O fear!
O pain! O the pangs, the bitter pangs of love forsaken
Ephraim was a wilderness of joy where all my wild beasts ran,
The River Kanah wanderd by my sweet Manasseh's side
To see the boy spring into heavens sounding from my sight!
Go Noah[6] fetch the girdle of strong brass, heat it red-hot:
Press it around the loins of this ever expanding cruelty.   60
Shriek not so my only love; I refuse thy joys: I drink
Thy shrieks because Hand & Hyle are cruel & obdurate to me.

O Skofield why art thou cruel? Lo Joseph is thine! to make   **68**
You One: to weave you both in the same mantle of skin
Bind him down Sisters bind him down on Ebal, Mount of cursing:[7]
Malah come forth from Lebanon; & Hoglah from Mount Sinai;
Come circumscribe this tongue of sweets & with a screw of iron
Fasten this ear into the rock: Milcah the task is thine.

4. See n. 3, p. 226 herein.
5. Bacon's home, now a fallen cathedral city; see n. 2, p. 257.
6. A sister of Tirzah, as are Malah, Hoglah, and Milcah (68:4–6). These five (see n. 6, p. 164 herein) bind the five fallen senses to the material world.
7. Identified in Deuteronomy 11:29 and 27:13. The mount of blessing is Gerizim (see n. 4, p. 313 herein and map).

Weep not so Sisters! weep not so! our life depends on this
Or mercy & truth are fled away from Shechem & Mount Gilead[8]
Unless my beloved is bound upon the Stems of Vegetation."

And thus the Warriors cry, in the hot day of Victory, in Songs.   10

"Look: the beautiful Daughter of Albion sits naked upon the Stone
Her panting Victim beside her: her heart is drunk with blood
Tho her brain is not drunk with wine: she goes forth from Albion
In pride of beauty: in cruelty of holiness: in the brightness
Of her tabernacle, & her ark & secret place. The beautiful
     Daughter
Of Albion delights the eyes of the Kings, their hearts & the
Hearts of their Warriors glow hot before Thor & Friga. O Molech!
O Chemosh![9] O Bacchus! O Venus! O Double God of Generation
The Heavens are cut like a mantle around from the Cliffs of Albion
Across Europe; across Africa; in howlings & deadly War.   20
A sheet & veil & curtain of blood is let down from Heaven
Across the hills of Ephraim & down Mount Olivet to
The Valley of the Jebusite: Molech rejoices in heaven
He sees the Twelve Daughters naked upon the Twelve Stones
Themselves condensing to rocks & into the Ribs of a Man.
Lo they shoot forth in tender Nerves across Europe & Asia,
Lo they rest upon the Tribes, where their panting Victims lie.
Molech rushes into the Kings in love to the beautiful Daughters
But they frown & delight in cruelty, refusing all other joy.
Bring your Offerings, your first begotten: pamperd with milk &
     blood   30
Your first born of seven years old! be they Males or Females:
To the beautiful Daughters of Albion: they sport before the Kings
Clothed in the skin of the Victim! blood! human blood: is the life
And delightful food of the Warrior: the well fed Warrior's flesh
Of him who is slain in War: fills the Valleys of Ephraim with
Breeding Women walking in pride & bringing forth under green
     trees
With pleasure, without pain, for their food is blood of the Captive.
Molech rejoices thro the Land from Havilah to Shur:[1] he rejoices
In moral law & its severe penalties: loud Shaddai & Jehovah
Thunder above: when they see the Twelve panting Victims   40
On the Twelve Stones of Power, & the beautiful Daughters of
     Albion.
If you dare rend their Veil with your Spear; you are healed of Love!
From the Hills of Camberwell & Wimbledon: from the Valleys
Of Walton & Esher: from Stone-henge & from Malden's Cove
Jerusalem's Pillars fall in the rendings of fierce War
Over France & Germany: upon the Rhine & Danube
Reuben & Benjamin flee; they hide in the Valley of Rephaim.
Why trembles the Warrior's limbs when he beholds thy beauty

8. Shechem is a city of refuge (Joshua 21:21). Mount Gilead, realm of Tirzah and her sisters in 5:40,
   is where Jacob made a covenant with his father-in-law, Laban (Genesis 31:23 ff.). The land of
   Gilead was famous for its balm (Jeremiah 8:22, 46:11).
9. The Norse and Roman deities are male and female, but the child-devouring Ammonite god Molech and the Moabite Chemosh are both male.
1. Borders of the land where descendants of Ishmael dwell (Genesis 25:18).

Spotted with Victim's blood: by the fires of thy secret tabernacle
And thy ark & holy place: at thy frowns: at thy dire revenge   50
Smitten as Uzzah[2] of old: his armour is softend; his spear
And sword faint in his hand, from Albion across Great Tartary.
O beautiful Daughter of Albion; cruelty is thy delight.
O Virgin of terrible eyes, who dwellest by Valleys of springs
Beneath the Mountains of Lebanon, in the City of Rehob in
      Hamath
Taught to touch the harp: to dance in the Circle of Warriors
Before the Kings of Canaan: to cut the flesh from the Victim
To roast the flesh in fire: to examine the Infant's limbs
In cruelties of holiness: to refuse the joys of love: to bring
The Spies from Egypt, to raise jealousy in the bosoms of the
      Twelve   60
Kings of Canaan: then to let the Spies depart to Meribah Kadesh
To the place of the Amalekite; I am drunk with unsatiated love
I must rush again to War: for the Virgin has frownd & refusd.
Sometimes I curse & sometimes bless thy fascinating beauty.
Once Man was occupied in intellectual pleasures & energies
But now my soul is harrowd with grief & fear & love & desire.
And now I hate & now I love & Intellect is no more:
There is no time for any thing but the torments of love & desire.
The Feminine & Masculine Shadows soft, mild & ever varying
In beauty: are Shadows now no more, but Rocks in Horeb."[3]   70

Then all the Males combined into One Male & every one
Became a ravening eating Cancer growing in the Female,
A Polypus of Roots of Reasoning Doubt Despair & Death.
Going forth & returning from Albion's Rocks to Canaan:
Devouring Jerusalem from every Nation of the Earth.

Envying stood the enormous Form at variance with Itself
In all its Members: in eternal torment of love & jealousy:
Drivn forth by Los time after time from Albion's cliffy shore,
Drawing the free loves of Jerusalem into infernal bondage;
That they might be born in contentions of Chastity & in   10
Deadly Hate between Leah & Rachel. Daughters of Deceit &
      Fraud
Bearing the Images of various Species of Contention
And Jealousy & Abhorrence & Revenge & deadly Murder,
Till they refuse liberty to the male; & not like Beulah
Where every Female delights to give her maiden to her
      husband.
The Female searches sea & land for gratifications to the
Male Genius: who in return clothes her in gems & gold
And feeds her with the food of Eden; hence all her beauty
      beams.

2. A protector of the ark struck dead for touching it when oxen stumbled (2 Samuel 6:6–7, 1 Chronicles 13:9).
3. This densely allusive song is in part a Canaanite reaction to the Exodus. Horeb is another name for Mount Sinai. "Jebusite" (68:23), "Rehob in Hamath" (68:55), and "Spies" (68:60) relate to the first report on the Promised Land (Numbers 13). "Twelve Stones" (68:24, 68:41): commemorate the crossing of the Jordan (Joshua 4). "Meribah" in "Kadesh" (68:61): where Moses struck water from the rock (Exodus 17:6–7; Numbers 20:13, 27:14).

She Creates at her will a little moony night & silence
With Spaces of sweet gardens & a tent of elegant beauty: 20
Closed in by a sandy desart & a night of stars shining,
And a little tender moon & hovering angels on the wing,
And the Male gives a Time & Revolution to her Space
Till the time of love is passed in ever varying delights.
For All Things Exist in the Human Imagination
And thence in Beulah they are stolen by secret amorous theft,
Till they have had Punishment enough to make them commit
      Crimes.
Hence rose the Tabernacle in the Wilderness & all its Offerings,
From Male & Female Loves in Beulah & their Jealousies.
But no one can consummate Female bliss in Los's World without   30
Becoming a Generated Mortal, a Vegetating Death.

And now the Spectres of the Dead awake in Beulah: all
The Jealousies become Murderous: uniting together in Rahab
A Religion of Chastity, forming a Commerce to sell Loves
With Moral Law, an Equal Balance, not going down with
      decision.
Therefore the Male severe & cruel filld with stern Revenge:
Mutual Hate returns & mutual Deceit & mutual Fear.

Hence the Infernal Veil grows in the disobedient Female;
Which Jesus rends & the whole Druid Law removes away
From the Inner Sanctuary; a False Holiness hid within the
      Center,   40
For the Sanctuary of Eden, is in the Camp in the Outline.
In the Circumference: & every Minute Particular is Holy:
Embraces are Cominglings: from the Head even to the Feet
And not a pompous High Priest entering by a Secret Place.

Jerusalem pined in her inmost soul over Wandering Reuben
As she slept in Beulah's Night hid by the Daughters of Beulah.

And this the form of mighty Hand sitting on Albion's cliffs $\boxed{70}$
Before the face of Albion, a mighty threatning Form,

His bosom wide & shoulders huge overspreading wondrous
Bear Three strong sinewy Necks & Three awful & terrible
      Heads
Three Brains in contradictory council brooding incessantly.
Neither daring to put in act its councils, fearing each-other,
Therefore rejecting Ideas as nothing & holding all Wisdom
To consist in the agreements & disagreements of Ideas,
Plotting to devour Albion's Body of Humanity & Love.

Such Form the aggregate of the Twelve Sons of Albion took; &
      such   10
Their appearance when combind: but often by birth-pangs &
      loud groans
They divide to Twelve; the key-bones & the chest dividing in pain
Disclose a hideous orifice; thence issuing the Giant-brood

Arise as the smoke of the furnace, shaking the rocks from sea to
  sea.
And there they combine into Three Forms, named Bacon &
  Newton & Locke.
In the Oak Groves of Albion which overspread all the Earth.

Imputing Sin & Righteousness to Individuals; Rahab
Sat deep within him hid: his Feminine Power unreveal'd
Brooding Abstract Philosophy, to destroy Imagination, the Divine-
-Humanity A Three-fold Wonder: feminine: most beautiful;
  Three-fold   20
Each within other. On her white marble & even Neck, her Heart
Inorb'd and bonified; with locks of shadowing modesty, shining
Over her beautiful Female features, soft flourishing in beauty,
Beams mild, all love and all perfection, that when the lips
Recieve a kiss from Gods or Men, a threefold kiss returns[4]
From the pressd loveliness: so her whole immortal form three-fold
Three-fold embrace returns: consuming lives of Gods & Men
In fires of beauty melting them as gold & silver in the furnace
Her Brain enlabyrinths the whole heaven of her bosom & loins
To put in act what her Heart wills: O who can withstand her
  power?   30
Her name is Vala in Eternity: in Time her name is Rahab.

The Starry Heavens all were fled from the mighty limbs of Albion.

And above Albion's Land was seen the Heavenly Canaan   71

---

4. Cf. "The Crystal Cabinet."

As the Substance is to the Shadow: and above Albion's Twelve
    Sons
Were seen Jerusalem's Sons: and all the Twelve Tribes spreading
Over Albion. As the Soul is to the Body, so Jerusalem's Sons
Are to the Sons of Albion: and Jerusalem is Albion's Emanation.

What is Above is Within, for every-thing in Eternity is translucent!
The Circumference is Within: Without, is formed the Selfish
    Center
And the Circumference still expands going forward to Eternity.
And the Center has Eternal States! these States we now explore.

And these the Names of Albion's Twelve Sons, & of his Twelve
    Daughters
With their Districts. Hand dwelt in Selsey & had Sussex & Surrey   10
And Kent & Middlesex: all their Rivers & their Hills of flocks &
    herds:
Their Villages Towns Cities Sea-Ports Temples sublime Cathedrals;
All were his Friends & their Sons & Daughters intermarry in
    Beulah
For all are Men in Eternity. Rivers Mountains Cities Villages
All are Human & when you enter into their Bosoms you walk
In Heavens & Earths; as in your own Bosom you bear your Heaven
And Earth, & all you behold, tho it appears Without it is Within
In your Imagination of which this World of Mortality is but a
    Shadow.

Hyle dwelt in Winchester comprehending Hants Dorset Devon
    Cornwall,
Their Villages Cities Sea-Ports, their Corn fields & Gardens   20
    spacious,
Palaces, Rivers & Mountains, and between Hand & Hyle arose
Gwendolen & Cambel who is Boadicea: they go abroad & return
Like lovely beams of light from the mingled affections of the
    Brothers.
The Inhabitants of the whole Earth rejoice in their beautiful light.

Coban dwelt in Bath; Somerset Wiltshire Gloucestershire
Obeyd his awful voice. Ignoge is his lovely Emanation;
She adjoind with Gwantoke's Children, soon lovely Cordella arose.
Gwantoke forgave & joyd over South Wales & all its Mountains.

Peachey had North Wales Shropshire Cheshire & the Isle of Man.   30
His Emanation is Mehetabel terrible & lovely upon the Mountains.

Brertun had Yorkshire Durham Westmoreland & his Emanation
Is Ragan, she adjoind to Slade, & produced Gonorill far beaming.

Slade had Lincoln Stafford Derby Nottingham & his lovely
Emanation Gonorill rejoices over hills & rocks & woods & rivers.

Huttn had Warwick Northampton Bedford Buckingham
Leicester & Berkshire; & his Emanation is Gwinefred beautiful.

Skofeld had Ely Rutland Cambridge Huntingdon Norfolk
Suffolk Hartford & Essex; & his Emanation is Gwinevera
Beautiful, she beams towards the east all kinds of precious stones   40
And pearl, with instruments of music in holy Jerusalem.

Kox had Oxford Warwick Wilts: his Emanation is Estrild;
Joind with Cordella she shines southward over the Atlantic.

Kotope had Hereford Stafford Worcester, & his Emanation
Is Sabrina joind with Mehetabel she shines west over America.

Bowen had all Scotland, the Isles, Northumberland & Cumberland
His Emanation is Conwenna, she shines a triple form
Over the north with pearly beams gorgeous & terrible.
Jerusalem & Vala rejoice in Bowen & Conwenna,

But the Four Sons of Jerusalem that never were Generated   50
Are Rintrah and Palamabron and Theotormon and Bromion.
    They
Dwell over the Four Provinces of Ireland in heavenly light
The Four Universities of Scotland, & in Oxford & Cambridge
    & Winchester.

But now Albion is darkened & Jerusalem lies in ruins:
Above the Mountains of Albion, above the head of Los.

And Los shouted with ceaseless shoutings & his tears poured down
His immortal cheeks, rearing his hands to heaven for aid Divine!
But he spoke not to Albion: fearing lest Albion should turn his Back
Against the Divine Vision: & fall over the Precipice of Eternal
    Death.
But he receded before Albion & before Vala, weaving the Veil   60
With the iron shuttle of War among the rooted Oaks of Albion;
Weeping & shouting to the Lord day & night; and his Children
Wept round him as a flock silent Seven Days of Eternity.

And the Thirty-two Counties of the Four Provinces of Ireland   72
Are thus divided: The Four Counties are in the Four Camps
Munster South in Reuben's Gate, Connaut West in Joseph's
    Gate,
Ulster North in Dan's Gate, Leinster East in Judah's Gate.

For Albion in Eternity has Sixteen Gates among his Pillars
But the Four towards the West were Walled up & the Twelve
That front the Four other Points were turned Four Square
By Los for Jerusalem's sake & called the Gates of Jerusalem
Because Twelve Sons of Jerusalem fled successive thro the Gates.
But the Four Sons of Jerusalem who fled not but remaind   10
Are Rintrah & Palamabron & Theotormon & Bromion⁵

---

5. Rintrah and Palamabron are sons of Los and Enitharmon in *Europe*. In *Milton* 26/24:11–12, they are joined by Theotormon and Bromion, the two male characters of *Visions*, as Los's four non-generated sons.

The Four that remain with Los to guard the Western Wall
And these Four remain to guard the Four Walls of Jerusalem
Whose foundations remain in the Thirty-two Counties of Ireland
And in Twelve Counties of Wales, & in the Forty Counties
Of England & in the Thirty-six Counties of Scotland.

And the names of the Thirty-two Counties of Ireland are these
Under Judah & Issachar & Zebulun are Lowth Longford
Eastmeath Westmeath Dublin Kildare Kings County
Queens County Wicklow Catherloh Wexford Kilkenny   20
And those under Reuben & Simeon & Levi are these
Waterford Tipperary Cork Limerick Kerry Clare
And those under Ephraim Manasseh & Benjamin are these
Galway Roscommon Mayo Sligo Leitrim
And those under Dan Asher & Napthali are these
Donnegal Antrim Tyrone Fermanagh Armagh Londonderry
Down Managhan Cavan. These are the Land of Erin.

All these Center in London & in Golgonooza, from whence
They are Created continually East & West & North & South
And from them are Created all the Nations of the Earth   30
Europe & Asia & Africa & America, in fury Fourfold!

And Thirty-two the Nations; to dwell in Jerusalem's Gates.
O Come ye Nations Come ye People Come up to Jerusalem
Return Jerusalem & dwell together as of old: Return
Return; O Albion let Jerusalem overspread all Nations
As in the times of old; O Albion awake! Reuben wanders,
The Nations wait for Jerusalem, they look up for the Bride.

France Spain Italy Germany Poland Russia Sweden Turkey
Arabia Palestine Persia Hindostan China Tartary Siberia
Egypt Lybia Ethiopia Guinea Caffraria Negroland Morocco   40
Congo Zaara Canada Greenland Carolina Mexico
Peru Patagonia Amazonia Brazil. Thirty-two Nations
And under these Thirty-two Classes of Islands in the Ocean
All the Nations Peoples & Tongues throughout all the Earth.

And the Four Gates of Los surround the Universe Within and
Without; & whatever is visible in the Vegetable Earth, the same
Is visible in the Mundane Shell: reversd in mountain & vale
And a Son of Eden was set over each Daughter of Beulah to
   guard

In Albion's Tomb the wondrous Creation; & the Four-fold Gate
Towards Beulah is to the South. Fenelon, Guion, Teresa,   50
Whitefield & Hervey[6] guard that Gate; with all the gentle Souls
Who guide the great Wine-press of Love; Four precious stones
  that Gate:[7]

Such are Cathedron's golden Halls: in the City of Golgonooza.   ⎡73⎤

And Los's Furnaces howl loud; living; self-moving; lamenting
With fury & despair. & they stretch from South to North
Thro all the Four Points: Lo! the Labourers at the Furnaces
Rintrah & Palamabron, Theotormon & Bromion, loud labring
With the innumerable multitudes of Golgonooza, round the
  Anvils
Of Death, But how they came forth from the Furnaces & how
  long
Vast & severe the anguish eer they knew their Father; were
Long to tell & of the iron rollers, golden axle-trees & yokes
Of brass, iron chains & braces & the gold, silver & brass   10
Mingled or separate: for swords; arrows; cannons; mortars
The terrible ball: the wedge: the loud sounding hammer of
  destruction
The sounding flail to thresh: the winnow: to winnow kingdoms
The water wheel & mill of many innumerable wheels resistless
Over the Fourfold Monarchy from Earth to the Mundane Shell.

Perusing Albion's Tomb in the starry characters of Og & Anak:
To Create the lion & wolf the bear: the tyger & ounce:
To Create the wooly lamb & downy fowl & scaly serpent
The summer & winter: day & night: the sun & moon & stars
The tree: the plant: the flower: the rock: the stone: the metal;   20
Of Vegetative Nature; by their hard restricting condensations.

Where Luvah's World of Opakeness grew to a period: It
Became a Limit, a Rocky hardness without form & void[8]
Accumulating without end: here Los who is of the Elohim
Opens the Furnaces of affliction in the Emanation
Fixing The Sexual into an ever-prolific Generation
Naming the Limit of Opakeness Satan & the Limit of
  Contraction
Adam, who is Peleg & Joktan: & Esau & Jacob: & Saul &
  David.[9]

6. These five religious enthusiasts—three Catholics, two Protestants—cultivated an intensely personal relationship with Jesus that sometimes scandalized those around them. François Fénelon
  (1651–1751), Jeanne Marie Guyon (1647–1717), Saint Teresa of Avila (1515–1582), the
  Methodist evangelist Whitefield (see n. 1, p. 274 herein), and the Anglican divine James Hervey
  (1714–1758) all believed, as Paley notes, in "the inner regeneration of the self." Cf. Palmer on
  Blake's interest in "writers on the interior life" (p. 516 herein) and the c.1820 painting (Butlin,
  770) inspired by Hervey's *Meditations among the Tombs* (1746).
7. In reversed writing, beneath a serpent creeping across the bottom of the page: "Women the com-
  forters of Men become the Tormenters and Punishers."
8. This echo of Genesis 1:2 hints that Luvah's descent to a rock-bottom extreme offers a new starting point for creation.
9. The brothers Peleg ("to divide") and Joktan ("to make small"; cf. Paley, citing Damon) are among
  those by whom the nations are "divided in the earth after the flood" (Genesis 10:25 ff.). The brothers Jacob and Esau become enemies, as do the first two kings of Israel, Saul and David.

Voltaire insinuates that these Limits are the cruel work of God,
Mocking the Remover of Limits & the Resurrection of the Dead,   30
Setting up Kings in wrath: in holiness of Natural Religion
Which Los with his mighty Hammer demolishes time on time
In miracles & wonders in the Four-fold Desert of Albion
Permanently Creating to be in Time Reveald & Demolishd
Satan Cain Tubal Nimrod Pharoh Priam Bladud Belin
Arthur Alfred the Norman Conqueror Richard John.[1]

And all the Kings & Nobles of the Earth & all their Glories
These are Created by Rahab & Tirzah in Ulro; but around
These, to preserve them from Eternal Death Los Creates
Adam Noah Abraham Moses Samuel David Ezekiel   40

Dissipating the rocky forms of Death by his thunderous Hammer.
As the Pilgrim passes while the Country permanent remains
So Men pass on! but States remain permanent for ever.

The Spectres of the Dead howl round the porches of Los
In the terrible Family feuds of Albion's cities & villages
To devour the Body of Albion, hungring & thirsting & ravning
The Sons of Los clothe them & feed & provide houses & gardens
And every Human Vegetated Form in its inward recesses
Is a house of pleasantness & a garden of delight Built by the
Sons & Daughters of Los in Bowlahoola & in Cathedron.   50

From London to York & Edinburgh the Furnaces rage terrible
Primrose Hill is the mouth of the Furnace & the Iron Door;

The Four Zoa's clouded rage; Urizen stood by Albion   74
With Rintrah and Palamabron and Theotormon and Bromion.
These Four are Verulam & London & York & Edinburgh
And the Four Zoa's are Urizen & Luvah & Tharmas & Urthona
In opposition deadly, and their Wheels in poisonous
And deadly stupor turn'd against each other, loud & fierce
Entering into the Reasoning Power, forsaking Imagination
They became Spectres; & their Human Bodies were reposed
In Beulah by the Daughters of Beulah with tears & lamentations.

The Spectre is the Reasoning Power in Man; & when separated   10
From Imagination, and closing itself as in steel in a Ratio
Of the Things of Memory, It thence frames Laws & Moralities
To destroy Imagination! the Divine Body, by Martyrdoms & Wars.

Teach me O Holy Spirit the Testimony of Jesus![2] let me
Comprehend wonderous things out of the Divine Law.

1. Kings "spiritually descended from Satan" (Ostriker), drawn from the Bible (including Tubal-cain, Genesis 4:22), from the *Iliad* (Priam, king of Troy), from legendary British history (Bladud supposedly founded Bath in 813 B.C.E. after being cured of leprosy by its waters; Belin or Belinus supposedly conquered Rome with his brother Brennius, established Billingsgate, and built the Tower of London in the fourth century B.C.E), and from more recent history. After line 36, Erdman has recovered a deleted line—"Edward Henry Elizabeth James Charles William George"—and another after line 40— "Pythagoras Socrates Euripedes Virgil Dante Milton."
2. At this low point, the poet interrupts the action with a prayer that becomes a renewed invocation to the muse.

I behold Babylon in the opening Streets of London, I behold
Jerusalem in ruins wandering about from house to house.
This I behold, the shudderings of death attend my steps
I walk up and down in Six Thousand Years: their Events are
    before me,[3]
To tell how Los in grief & anger, whirling round his Hammer on
    present high   20
Drave the Sons & Daughters of Albion from their ancient
    mountains.
They became the Twelve Gods of Asia Opposing the Divine Vision.

The Sons of Albion are Twelve: the Sons of Jerusalem Sixteen
I tell how Albion's Sons by Harmonies of Concords & Discords
Opposed to Melody, and by Lights & Shades, opposed to Outline
And by Abstraction opposed to the Visions of Imagination
By cruel Laws divided Sixteen into Twelve Divisions
How Hyle roofd Los in Albion's Cliffs by the Affections rent
Asunder & opposed to Thought, to draw Jerusalem's Sons
Into the Vortex of his Wheels, therefore Hyle is called Gog.   30
Age after age drawing them away towards Babylon,
Babylon, the Rational Morality deluding to death the little ones
In strong temptations of stolen beauty; I tell how Reuben slept
On London Stone & the Daughters of Albion ran around
    admiring
His awful beauty: with Moral Virtue the fair deciever; offspring
Of Good & Evil, they divided him in love upon the Thames &
    sent
Him over Europe in streams of gore out of Cathedron's Looms,
How Los drave them from Albion & they became Daughters of
    Canaan.
Hence Albion was calld the Canaanite & all his Giant Sons.
Hence is my Theme. O Lord my Saviour open thou the Gates   40
And I will lead forth thy Words, telling how the Daughters
Cut the Fibres of Reuben, how he rolld apart & took Root
In Bashan. Terror-struck Albion's Sons look toward Bashan.
They have divided Simeon he also rolld apart in blood
Over the Nations till he took Root beneath the shining Looms
Of Albion's Daughters in Philistea by the side of Amalek.
They have divided Levi: he hath shot out into Forty eight Roots
Over the Land of Canaan: they have divided Judah
He hath took Root in Hebron, in the Land of Hand & Hyle.
Dan: Napthali: Gad: Asher: Issachar: Zebulun: roll apart   50
From all the Nations of the Earth to dissipate into Non Entity.

I see a Feminine Form arise from the Four terrible Zoas,
Beautiful but terrible struggling to take a form of beauty,
Rooted in Shechem: this is Dinah, the youthful form of Erin.[4]
The Wound I see in South Molton Steet & Stratford place

---

3. The narrator now claims to have the perspective he accords Los in 75:6–7; cf. 13:59.
4. For the grim story of Dinah, daughter of Jacob/Israel, and her lover, Shechem—slaughtered by her
brothers with all the menfolk of his city "when they are sore" after fulfilling their commitment to be
circumcised—see Genesis 34. The powerless, suffering, but redemptive figures of Dinah of Israel and
Erin of Great Britain, in the poet's vision, oppose Rahab and offer a faint hope of Albion's recovery.

Whence Joseph & Benjamin rolld apart away from the Nations.
In vain they rolld apart; they are fixd into the Land of Cabul.

And Rahab Babylon the Great hath destroyed Jerusalem.   75
Bath stood upon the Severn with Merlin & Bladud & Arthur
The Cup of Rahab in his hand; her Poisons Twenty-seven-fold.

And all her Twenty-seven Heavens now hid & now reveal'd
Appear in strong delusive light of Time & Space drawn out
In shadowy pomp by the Eternal Prophet created evermore
For Los in Six Thousand Years walks up & down continually
That not one Moment of Time be lost & every revolution
Of Space he makes permanent in Bowlahoola & Cathedron.

And these the names of the Twenty-seven Heavens & their
    Churches   10
Adam, Seth, Enos, Cainan, Mahalaleel, Jared, Enoch,
Methuselah, Lamech; these are the Giants mighty,
    Hermaphroditic.
Noah, Shem, Arphaxad, Cainan the Second, Salah, Heber,
Peleg, Reu, Serug, Nahor, Terah: these are the Female Males:
A Male within a Female hid as in an Ark & Curtains.
Abraham, Moses, Solomon, Paul, Constantine, Charlemaine,
Luther, these Seven are the Male Females: the Dragon Forms
The Female hid within a Male: thus Rahab is reveald
Mystery Babylon the Great; the Abomination of Desolation
Religion hid in War; a Dragon red & hidden Harlot.[5]   20
But Jesus breaking thro' the Central Zones of Death & Hell
Opens Eternity in Time & Space; triumphant in Mercy.

Thus are the Heavens formd by Los within the Mundane
    Shell
And where Luther ends Adam begins again in Eternal Circle
To awake the Prisoners of Death; to bring Albion again
With Luvah into light eternal, in his eternal day.

But now the Starry Heavens are fled from the mighty limbs of
    Albion.[6]

5. Within time and space, Los can reveal Rahab only fitfully and uncertainly (75:4–6) in her twenty-
   seven heavens—an ominous threefold multiple of three, split asymmetrically into gender-confused
   groupings of nine gigantic antediluvian "Hermaphroditic" churches, the long-lived early descendants of Adam (Genesis 5:1–25); eleven "Female Males" continuing the line from Lamech's son
   Noah to Abraham's father, Terah (following Luke 3:34–36 instead of Genesis 11:10–26, to include
   the second Cainan, as Damon notes in his heroic struggle to explicate the "Churches" in his *Dictionary*); and seven "Male Females," marking stages in the evolution of the Judeo-Christian faith
   from Abraham's covenant to Luther's Reformation, and looping back to Adam in an "Eternal Circle" of repetition (J 75:24) under the unholy trinity of "MYSTERY, BABYLON THE GREAT, THE
   MOTHER OF HARLOTS AND ABOMINATIONS OF THE EARTH" (Revelation 17:5), the
   "Abomination of Desolation" (Daniel 9:27; cf. J 10:15), and the "great red dragon" (Revelation
   12:3). Cf. *Milton* 39/35:63.
6. This line is quoted in the Preface to Chapter 2 (27) and repeated at 70:32. In the concluding
   design for Chapter 1 (25), and in Chapter 2 (34/30:20), Albion's limbs still contain the starry
   heavens.

To the Christians. 77

Devils are	I give you the end of a golden string,
False Religions	Only wind it into a ball:
"Saul Saul"	It will lead you in at Heaven's gate,
"Why persecutest thou me?"[7]	Built in Jerusalem's wall.

We are told to abstain from fleshly desires that we may lose no time from the Work of the Lord.[8] Every moment lost, is a moment that cannot be redeemed; every pleasure that intermingles with the duty of our station is a folly unredeemable & is planted like the seed of a wild flower among our wheat. All the tortures of repentance are tortures of self-reproach on account of our leaving the Divine Harvest to the Enemy, the struggles of intanglement with incoherent roots. I know of no other Christianity and of no other Gospel than the liberty both of body & mind to exercise the Divine Arts of Imagination - Imagination the real & eternal World of which this Vegetable Universe is but a faint shadow & in which we shall live in our Eternal or Imaginative Bodies, when these Vegetable Mortal Bodies are no more. The Apostles knew of no other Gospel. What were all their spiritual gifts? What is the Divine Spirit? Is the Holy Ghost any other than an Intellectual Fountain? What is the Harvest of the Gospel & its Labours? What is that Talent which it is a curse to hide? What are the Treasures of Heaven which we are to lay up for ourselves, are they any other than Mental Studies & Performances? What are all the Gifts of the Gospel; are they not all Mental Gifts? Is God a Spirit who must be worshipped in Spirit & in Truth and are not the Gifts of the Spirit Every-thing to Man? O ye Religious discountenance every one among you who shall pretend to despise Art & Science! I call upon you in the Name of Jesus! What is the Life of Man but Art & Science? is it Meat & Drink? is not the Body more than Raiment? What is Mortality but the things relating to the Body, which Dies? What is Immortality but the things relating to the Spirit, which Lives Eternally! What is the Joy of Heaven but Improvement in the things of the Spirit? What are the Pains of Hell but Ignorance, Bodily Lust, Idleness & devastation of the things of the Spirit? Answer this to yourselves, & expel from among you those who pretend to despise the labours of Art & Science, which alone are the labours of the Gospel: Is not this plain & manifest to the thought? Can you think at all, & not pronounce heartily! That to Labour in Knowledge is to Build up Jerusalem: and to Despise Knowledge, is to Despise Jerusalem & her Builders. And remember: He who despises & mocks a Mental Gift in

---

7. Jesus' question that leads to the anti-Christian Pharisee Saul's becoming the apostle Paul (Acts 9:4); quotation marks, except for the last, are by Blake himself. At the right margin, a striding figure grasps the end of a string leading oven "Devils." For this chapter's frontispiece, see color plate 15.

8. Despite "We are told," the strenuous work ethic of this paragraph is not specifically biblical, though the passage abounds in New Testament allusions: "abstain from fleshly lusts" (1 Peter 2:11); "work of the Lord" (1 Corinthians 15:58), "redeeming the time" (Ephesians 5:16), wheat and tares (Matthew 13:24–30, 13:36–43); "any other gospel" (Galatians 1:6–12); Christian "liberty" (Romans 8:21, 2 Corinthians 3:17, Galatians 5:1, James 1:25); "spiritual gifts" (1 Corinthians 12:1, 12:4–11; 1 Timothy 4:14); harvest and laborers (Matthew 9:37–38; John 4:35–38; cf. Joel 3:13, Revelation 14:15); talents (Matthew 25:14–30; cf. Milton's "Talent which is death to hide," Sonnet 19, line 3 [Paley] and Blake's own resolution not to "bury [his] Talents in the Earth" [letter to Butts, April 25, 1803]); "treasures in heaven" (Matthew 6:25); "God is a Spirit, . . . worship him in spirit and in truth" (John 4:24); "body [more] than raiment" (Matthew 6:25); "laboured . . . in the gospel" (Philippians 4:3; cf. Colossians 1:29, 1 Thessalonians 3:2); and "as much as lieth in you" (Romans 12:18). Cf. "The worship of God is: Honouring his gifts in other men" (*Marriage* 22–23, reaffirmed by Los in *Jerusalem* 91:6–9.

another; calling it pride & selfishness & sin; mocks Jesus the giver of every
Mental Gift, which always appear to the ignorance-loving Hypocrite, as
Sins. But that which is a Sin in the sight of cruel Man, is not so in the sight
of our kind God. Let every Christian as much as in him lies engage himself
openly & publicly before all the World in some Mental pursuit for the
Building up of Jerusalem.

> I stood among my valleys of the south
> And saw a flame of fire, even as a Wheel
> Of fire⁹ surrounding all the heavens: it went
> From west to east against the current of
> Creation, and devourd all things in its loud   5
> Fury & thundering course round heaven & earth
> By it the Sun was rolld into an orb:
> By it the Moon faded into a globe,
> Travelling thro the night: for from its dire
> And restless fury, Man himself shrunk up   10
> Into a little root a fathom long.
> And I asked a Watcher & a Holy-One¹
> Its Name? He answerd, "It is the Wheel of Religion."
> I wept & said, "Is this the law of Jesus,
> This terrible devouring sword turning every way?"²   15
> He answerd; "Jesus died because he strove
> Against the current of this Wheel: its Name
> Is Caiaphas, the dark Preacher of Death
> Of sin, of sorrow, & of punishment;
> Opposing Nature! It is Natural Religion.³   20
> But Jesus is the bright Preacher of Life
> Creating Nature from this fiery Law,
> By self-denial & forgiveness of Sin:
> Go therefore, cast out devils in Christ's name
> Heal thou the sick of spiritual disease   25
> Pity the evil, for thou art not sent
> To smite with terror & with punishments
> Those that are sick, like to the Pharisees
> Crucifying & encompassing sea & land
> For proselytes to tyranny & wrath.   30
> But to the Publicans & Harlots go!
> Teach them True Happiness, but let no curse
> Go forth out of thy mouth to blight their peace
> For Hell is opend to Heaven; thine eyes beheld
> The dungeons burst & the Prisoners set free."⁴   35

9. Cf. the hellish "wheel of fire" in *King Lear* IV.vii.46.
1. Angelic being (Daniel 4:13). "Little root" (cf. *J* 17:32): associated with Reuben, the natural man (11:22, 15:25, 31/45:43 ff.).
2. Wielded by the cherubim who guard the tree of life in Genesis 3:24 (cf. *Marriage* 14; 41/37: 8; *J* 14:2).
3. Christians committed to a legalistic religious establishment practice a form of Natural Religion, roundly condemned in "To the Deists." "Caiaphas" (line 18): chief priest (Matthew 26:57).
4. Lines 24–35 draw on Jesus' ordination of his disciples (Mark 3:14–15), his rebuking Pharisees who "compass sea and land" to make miserable proselytes (Matthew 23:15), his associating with (and approving of John the Baptist's ministry to) "publicans and harlots" (Matthew 21:31–32; cf. Matthew 9:11, 11:19), his commandment to "bless them that curse you" (Matthew 5:44; cf. Romans 12:14), his proclamation of liberty (Luke 4:18 ff.), and the deliverance from prison of Peter (Acts 12:6–11) and Paul (Acts 16:11 ff.).

England! awake! awake! awake!⁵
  Jerusalem thy Sister calls!
Why wilt thou sleep the sleep of
    death?
    And close her from thy ancient
    walls.

Thy hills & valleys felt her feet   40
  Gently upon their bosoms move:
Thy gates beheld sweet Zion's
    ways;
Then was a time of joy and love.

And now the time returns again:
  Our souls exult & London's towers
Receive the Lamb of God to dwell
  In England's green & pleasant bowers.

Jerusalem C.4   78

    The Spectres of Albion's Twelve Sons revolve mightily
Over the Tomb & over the Body: ravning to devour
The Sleeping Humanity. Los with his mace of iron
Walks round: loud his threats, loud his blows fall
On the rocky Spectres, as the Potter breaks the potsherds;⁶
Dashing in pieces Self-righteousnesses: driving them from Albion's
Cliffs: dividing them into Male & Female forms in his Furnaces
And on his Anvils: lest they destroy the Feminine Affections.
They are broken. Loud howl the Spectres in his iron Furnace.

5. Jerusalem's summons to England to "awake" recalls that of the Holy Word to Earth in "Introduction" to *Experience*. This three-stanza lyric, like the final sentence of the prose preface,
   recalls the prefatory hymn of *Milton*, but after looking back to a "time of joy and love" (cf. Ezekiel
   16:8; *J* 20:41) when Jerusalem and England were united, the poem celebrates the return of that
   time in a new age, in the present tense (lines 10 ff.): the restoration of the Lamb is at hand. For
   ideas on the bird-man of the chapter headpiece, see Judith Ott, *Blake Quarterly* 10 (1976),
   48–51.
6. The potter's metaphoric shattering of vessels appears in Psalm 2:9 (cf. Revelation 2:27), Isaiah
   30:14, and Jeremiah 19:10 ff.). Los, without biblical precedent, uses his metallurgical furnaces to
   melt down and reshape the potsherds into new vessels (cf. **28**:22, **53**:28).

While Los laments at his dire labours, viewing Jerusalem,   10
Sitting before his Furnaces clothed in sackcloth of Hair;
Albion's Twelve Sons surround the Forty-two Gates of Erin,
In terrible armour, raging against the Lamb & against Jerusalem,
Surrounding them with armies to destroy the Lamb of God.
They took their Mother Vala, and they crown'd her with gold:
They named her Rahab, & gave her power of the Earth
The Concave Earth round Golgonooza in Entuthon Benython,
Even to the stars exalting her Throne, to build beyond the Throne[7]
Of God and the Lamb, to destroy the Lamb & usurp the Throne
     of God
Drawing their Ulro Voidness round the Four-fold Humanity.   20

Naked Jerusalem lay before the Gates upon Mount Zion
The Hill of Giants, all her foundations levelld with the dust:

Her Twelve Gates thrown down: her children carried into captivity[8]
Herself in chains: this from within was seen in a dismal night
Outside, unknown before in Beulah, & the twelve gates were fill'd
With blood; from Japan eastward to the Giants' causeway,[9] west
In Erin's Continent: and Jerusalem wept upon Euphrates' banks
Disorganizd; an evanescent shade, scarce seen or heard among
Her children's Druid Temples dropping with blood, wandered
     weeping!
And thus her voice went forth in the darkness of Philisthea.   30

"My brother & my father are no more! God hath forsaken me
The arrows of the Almighty[1] pour upon me & my children
I have sinned and am an outcast from the Divine Presence.

My tents are fall'n! my pillars are in ruins! my children dashd   79
Upon Egypt's iron floors, & the marble pavements of Assyria;
I melt my soul in reasonings among the towers of Heshbon;[2]
Mount Zion is become a cruel rock & no more dew
Nor rain; no more the spring of the rock[3] appears; but cold
Hard & obdurate are the furrows of the mountain of wine & oil;
The mountain of blessing is itself a curse & an astonishment;[4]

---

7. Alluding to Lucifer's attempt to "exalt [his] throne above the stars of God" (Isaiah 14:13); cf. allusion to the Tower of Babel in **90**:50.
8. The period of exile in Babylonia after Nebuchadnezzar's destruction of the temple (1 Kings 24–25; Jeremiah 39, 52; Psalm 137), also encompassing Israel's earlier enslavement in Egypt and captivity in Assyria (**79**:2).
9. Contiguous lava-formed hexagonal basalt pillars that extend almost three hundred feet into the Irish sea on the northeastern coast of Ireland; legendarily, a bridge built by the giant Fionn mac Cumhail (or Finn MacCool) to prepare for a fight with his Scottish rival Benandonner, who lived on Staffa in Fingal's Cave (see map), made of similar columns (memorably described by Keats, July 26, 1818; cf. William Hamilton Drummond's topographical poem, *The Giants' Causeway* [1811]).
1. Echoing Job 6:4. Jerusalem's "father" and "brother" are both Albion, as Vala's "Father" and "beloved" are both Luvah (**80**:16–31). Jerusalem's complaint that God has forsaken her may allude to Jesus' dying words (Matthew 27:46; cf. Psalm 22:1).
2. Moabite city taken by the Amorite king Sihon (Numbers 21:26–30) and given to Reuben (Numbers 32:37) cf. **32**:10.
3. Refers to Moses' miracle (Numbers 20:11; Deuteronomy 32:13–14; cf. Jesus' words to Jerusalem at **62**:25–26).
4. The "mount of blessing" is Gerizim, as opposed to Ebal, mount of cursing (Deuteronomy 11:26–29, Joshua 8:33–34; cf. **68**:3); Jerusalem and the cities of Judah are made "an astonishment, a hissing, and a curse" (Jeremiah 25:18).

The hills of Judea are fallen with me into the deepest hell
Away from the Nations of the Earth, & from the Cities of the
    Nations;
I walk to Ephraim. I seek for Shiloh: I walk like a lost sheep   10
Among precipices of despair: in Goshen I seek for light
In vain; and in Gilead⁵ for a physician and a comforter.
Goshen hath followd Philistea: Gilead hath joind with Og!
They are become narrow places in a little and dark land:
How distant far from Albion! his hills & his valleys no more
Recieve the feet of Jerusalem: they have cast me quite away:
And Albion is himself shrunk to a narrow rock in the midst of
    the sea!
The plains of Sussex & Surrey, their hills of flocks & herds
No more seek to Jerusalem nor to the sound of my Holy-ones.
The Fifty-two Counties of England are hardend against me.   20
As if I was not their Mother, they despise me & cast me out.
London coverd the whole Earth, England encompassd the
    Nations:
And all the Nations of the Earth were seen in the Cities of
    Albion:
My pillars reachd from sea to sea: London beheld me come
From my east & from my west; he blessed me and gave
His children to my breasts, his sons & daughters to my knees
His aged parents sought me out in every city & village:
They discernd my countenance with joy! they shewd me to their
    sons
Saying 'Lo Jerusalem is here! she sitteth in our secret chambers
Levi and Judah & Issachar: Ephram, Manasseh, Gad and Dan   30
Are seen in our hills & valleys: they keep our flocks & herds:
They watch them in the night: and the Lamb of God appears
    among us.'
The river Severn stayd his course at my command:
Thames poured his waters into my basons and baths;
Medway: mingled with Kishon: Thames recievd the heavenly
    Jordan.⁶
Albion gave me to the whole Earth to walk up & down; to pour
Joy upon every mountain; to teach songs to the shepherd &
    plowman.
I taught the ships of the sea to sing the songs of Zion.
Italy saw me, in sublime astonishment: France was wholly mine:
As my garden & as my secret bath; Spain was my heavenly couch: 40
I slept in his golden hills: the Lamb of God met me there,
There we walked as in our secret chamber among our little ones.
They looked upon our loves with joy: they beheld our secret joys:
With holy raptures of adoration rapd⁷ sublime in the Visions of God:
Germany; Poland & the North wooed my footsteps; they found
My gates in all their mountains & my curtains in all their vales

5. Land of healing balm (Jeremiah 8:22, 51:8). Mount Gilead, however, is occupied by Tirzah and
    her sisters (*J* 5:40, 68:8).
6. A concise example of the fusion of British and biblical landscapes throughout this work. Kishon,
    near Carmel, miraculously swept away the Canaanite Sisera's forces (Judges 5:12); its union with
    the Medway recalls Spenser's *Faerie Queene* 4.9. On the arrested flow of the Severn in Wales, cf.
    Joshua 3:13–17.
7. Rapt, carried away, enraptured.

The furniture of their houses was the furniture of my chamber
Turkey & Grecia saw my instruments of music, they arose
They siezd the harp: the flute: the mellow horn of Jerusalem's joy.
They sounded thanksgivings in my courts; Egypt & Lybia heard.   50
The swarthy sons of Ethiopia stood round the Lamb of God
Enquiring for Jerusalem: he led them up my steps to my altar:
And thou America! I once beheld thee but now behold no more
Thy golden mountains where my Cherubim & Seraphim rejoicd
Together among my little-ones. But now, my Altars run with blood!
My fires are corrupt! my incense is a cloudy pestilence
Of seven diseases! Once a continual cloud of salvation rose
From all my myriads; once the Four-fold World rejoicd among
The pillars of Jerusalem, between my winged Cherubim:
But now I am closd out from them in the narrow passages   60
Of the valleys of destruction into a dark land of pitch & bitumen.
From Albion's Tomb afar and from the four-fold wonders of God
Shrunk to a narrow doleful form in the dark land of Cabul;[8]
There is Reuben & Gad & Joseph & Judah & Levi, closd up
In narrow vales; I walk & count the bones of my beloveds
Along the Valley of Destruction, among these Druid Temples
Which overspread all the Earth in patriarchal pomp & cruel
     pride.
Tell me O Vala thy purposes; tell me wherefore thy shuttles
Drop with the gore of the slain; why Euphrates is red with blood
Wherefore in dreadful majesty & beauty outside appears   70
Thy Masculine from thy Feminine hardening against the heavens
To devour the Human! Why dost thou weep upon the wind among
These cruel Druid Temples; O Vala! Humanity is far above
Sexual organization; & the Visions of the Night of Beulah
Where Sexes wander in dreams of bliss among the Emanations
Where the Masculine & Feminine are nurs'd into Youth & Maiden
By the tears & smiles of Beulah's Daughters till the time of Sleep
     is past.
Wherefore then do you realize these nets of beauty & delusion
In open day to draw the souls of the Dead into the light,
Till Albion is shut out from every Nation under Heaven?[9]   80

Encompassd by the frozen Net and by the rooted Tree,   ┃80┃
I walk weeping in pangs of a Mother's torment for her Children:
I walk in affliction: I am a worm, and no living soul![1]
A worm going to eternal torment! raisd up in a night
To an eternal night of pain. Lost ! lost! lost ! for ever!"

Beside her Vala howld upon the winds in pride of beauty
Lamenting among the timbrels of the Warriors: among the
     Captives
In cruel holiness, and her lamenting songs were from Arnon

---

8. The collective name of Solomon's unappreciated gift of twenty Galilean cities to King Hiram of
   Tyre (1 Kings 9:10–14).
9. At Pentacost, when the spirit-filled disciples speak in tongues, their words are understood in the
   languages of "every nation under heaven" (Acts 2:5).
1. Cf. "I am a worm, and no man" (Psalm 22:6), the eternally tormented worm (Isaiah 66:24, Mark
   9:48), and the worm that destroys the sheltering vine that "came up in a night, and perished in a
   night" (Jonah 4:7–10).

And Jordan to Euphrates. Jerusalem followd trembling,
Her children in captivity, listening to Vala's lamentation   10
In the thick cloud & darkness, & the voice went forth from
The cloud. "O rent in sunder from Jerusalem the Harlot daughter!
In an eternal condemnation in fierce burning flames
Of torment unendurable: and if once a Delusion be found
Woman must perish & the Heavens of Heavens remain no more.

My Father gave to me command to murder Albion
In unreviving Death; my Love, my Luvah orderd me in night
To murder Albion the King of Men. He fought in battles fierce,
He conquerd Luvah my beloved: he took me and my Father,
He slew them: I revived them to life in my warm bosom.   20
He saw them issue from my bosom, dark in Jealousy
He burnd before me: Luvah framd the Knife & Luvah gave
The Knife into his daughter's hand! such thing was never known
Before in Albion's land, that one should die a death never to be
    reviv'd:
For in our battles we the Slain men view with pity and love:
We soon revive them in the secret of our tabernacles
But I Vala, Luvah's daughter, keep his body embalmd in moral
    laws
With spices of sweet odours of lovely jealous stupefaction:
Within my bosom, lest he arise to life & slay my Luvah.
Pity me then O Lamb of God! O Jesus pity me!   30
Come into Luvah's Tents, and seek not to revive the Dead!"[2]

So sang she! and the Spindle turnd furious as she sang:
The Children of Jerusalem the Souls of those who sleep
Were caught into the flax of her Distaff: & in her Cloud
To weave Jerusalem a body according to her will
A Dragon form on Zion Hill's most ancient promontory.

The Spindle turnd in blood & fire: loud sound the trumpets
Of war: the cymbals play loud before the Captains
With Cambel & Gwendolen in dance and solemn song
The Cloud of Rahab vibrating with the Daughters of Albion.   40
Los saw terrified, melted with pity & divided in wrath
He sent them over the narrow seas in pity and love
Among the Four Forests of Albion which overspread all the
    Earth
They go forth & return swift as a flash of lightning.
Among the tribes of warriors; among the Stones of power!
Against Jerusalem they rage thro all the Nations of Europe
Thro Italy & Grecia, to Lebanon & Persia & India.

The Serpent Temples thro the Earth, from the wide Plain
    of Salisbury

2. The ambiguity of Vala's pronoun references and her double relationship to Luvah, as both daughter and beloved, make her brief song especially hard to follow. The gist, in quasi-chronological
order: Albion slew Luvah and Vala (lines19–20); Vala revived herself and Luvah in her warm bosom
(line 20); Albion became jealous (lines 21–22); Luvah ordered Vala to kill Albion (lines:16, 22–23);
Vala now keeps Albion's body embalmed in moral laws to prevent his rising and (again) slaying
Luvah in return (27–29).

Resound with cries of Victims, shouts & songs & dying groans
And flames of dusky fire, to Amalek, Canaan and Moab.   50
And Rahab like a dismal and indefinite hovering Cloud
Refusd to take a definite form; she hoverd over all the Earth
Calling the definite, sin: defacing every definite form;
Invisible, or Visible, stretch'd out in length or spread in breadth:
Over the Temples drinking groans of victims weeping in pity,
And joying in the pity, howling over Jerusalem's walls.

Hand slept on Skiddaw's top:[3] drawn by the love of beautiful
Cambel; his bright beaming Counterpart divided from him
And her delusive light beamd fierce above the Mountain,
Soft! invisible; drinking his sighs in sweet intoxication: 60
Drawing out fibre by fibre; returning to Albion's Tree
At night: and in the morning to Skiddaw; she sent him over
Mountainous Wales into the Loom of Cathedron fibre by fibre:
He ran in tender nerves across Europe to Jerusalem's Shade,
To weave Jerusalem a Body repugnant to the Lamb.

Hyle on East Moor[4] in rocky Derbyshire rav'd to the Moon
For Gwendolen: she took up in bitter tears his anguishd heart,
That apparent to all in Eternity glows like the Sun in the breast:
She hid it in his ribs & back: she hid his tongue with teeth
In terrible convulsions pitying & gratified drunk with pity   70
Glowing with loveliness before him, becoming apparent
According to his changes: she roll'd his kidneys round
Into two irregular forms: and looking on Albion's dread Tree,
She wove two vessels of seed, beautiful as Skiddaw's snow;
Giving them bends of self interest & selfish natural virtue:
She hid them in his loins;[5] raving he ran among the rocks,
Compelld into a shape of Moral Virtue against the Lamb.
The invisible lovely one giving him a form according to
His Law, a form against the Lamb of God opposd to Mercy
And playing in the thunderous Loom in sweet intoxication   80
Filling cups of silver & crystal with shrieks & cries, with groans
And dolorous sobs; the wine of lovers in the Wine-press of Luvah.

"O sister Cambel" said Gwendolen; as their long beaming light
Mingled above the Mountain "what shall we do to keep
These awful forms in our soft bands: distracted with trembling

I have mockd those who refused cruelty & I have admired   [81]
The cruel Warrior. I have refused to give love to Merlin the
    piteous.
He brings to me the Images of his Love & I reject in chastity
And turn them out into the streets for Harlots to be food
To the stern Warrior. I am become perfect in beauty over my
    Warrior
For Men are caught by Love: Woman is caught by Pride

---

3. Mountain in England's Lake District (see map).
4. A high point in the Peak District of Derbyshire.
5. Cf.Tirzah's similar actions to limit sensory experience to the finite organs of the body, ending with
   the genitals (*Milton* 21/19:55–22/20:6).

That Love may only be obtain in the passages of Death.
Let us look: let us examine! is the Cruel become an Infant
Or is he still a cruel Warrior? look Sisters, look! O piteous
I have destroyd Wandring Reuben who strove to bind my Will   10
I have stripd off Joseph's beautiful integument for my Beloved,
The Cruel-one of Albion: to clothe him in gems of my Zone.[6]
I have named him Jehovah of Hosts. Humanity is become
A weeping Infant in ruind lovely Jerusalem's folding Cloud.

In heaven Love begets Love: But Fear is the Parent of Earthly Love!
And he who will not bend to Love must be subdued by Fear.[7]

I have heard Jerusalem's groans; from Vala's cries &   82
    lamentations
I gather our eternal fate: Outcasts from life and love:
Unless we find a way to bind these awful Forms to our
Embrace we shall perish annihilate, discoverd our Delusions.
Look I have wrought without delusion: Look! I have wept!

6. Poetic diction for a lowslung belt or girdle; metaphorically the pubis; cf. Vala's "flaming zone," **65**:39 and Quarles's *Emblems*: "Shall these coarse hands untie / The sacred Zone of thy Virgini-tie?"). "Joseph's beautiful integument": cf. his coat of many colors (Genesis 37).
7. Set below the design, interrupting the "I have . . ." pattern of Gwendolen's narrative; possibly, then, a two-line caption or motto. The design itself, depicting her action in **82**:17–21, contains a backward-written motto of its own: "In Heaven the only Art of Living / Is Forgetting & Forgiving / Especially to the Female / But if you on Earth Forgive / You shall not find where to Live."

And given soft milk mingled together with the spirits of flocks
Of lambs and doves, mingled together in cups and dishes
Of painted clay; the mighty Hyle is become a weeping infant;
Soon shall the Spectres of the Dead follow my weaving threads."

The Twelve Daughters of Albion attentive listen in secret shades   10
On Cambridge and Oxford beaming soft uniting with Rahab's
    cloud
While Gwendolen spoke to Cambel turning soft the spinning reel:
Or throwing the wingd shuttle; or drawing the cords with softest
    songs
The golden cords of the Looms animate beneath their touches soft,
Along the Island white, among the Druid Temples, while
    Gwendolen
Spoke to the Daughters of Albion standing on Skiddaw's top.

So saying she took a Falshood & hid it in her left hand:[8]
To entice her Sisters away to Babylon on Euphrates.
And thus she closed her left hand and utterd her Falshood:
Forgetting that Falshood is prophetic, she hid her hand behind
    her,   20
Upon her back behind her loins & thus utterd her Deceit.

"I heard Enitharmon say to Los! 'Let the Daughters of Albion
Be scatterd abroad and let the name of Albion be forgotten:
Divide them into three; name them Amalek Canaan & Moab.
Let Albion remain a desolation without an inhabitant:
And let the Looms of Enitharmon & the Furnaces of Los
Create Jerusalem & Babylon & Egypt & Moab & Amalek,
And Helle & Hesperia & Hindostan & China & Japan.
But hide America, for a Curse, an Altar of Victims & a Holy
    Place.'
See Sisters Canaan is pleasant, Egypt is as the Garden of Eden: 30
Babylon is our chief desire, Moab our bath in summer:
Let us lead the stems of this Tree let us plant it before Jerusalem
To judge the Friend of Sinners to death without the Veil:
To cut her off from America, to close up her secret Ark!
And the fury of Man exhaust in War, Woman permanent remain.
See how the fires of our loins point eastward to Babylon.
Look, Hyle is become an infant Love; look: behold! see him lie!
Upon my bosom; look! here is the lovely wayward form
That gave me sweet delight by his torments beneath my Veil;
By the fruit of Albion's Tree I have fed him with sweet milk   40
By contentions of the mighty for Sacrifice of Captives:
Humanity the Great Delusion: is changd to War & Sacrifice;
I have naild his hands on Beth Rabbim[9] & his hands on
    Heshbon's Wall,

8. Shown in the design for J 81; cf. the self-deceived idol-worshiper's inability to ask, "Is there not a
   lie in my right hand?" (Isaiah 44:20) and the "right hand of falsehood" of David's enemies (Psalm
   144:8). Gwendolen claims to have overheard Enitharmon plotting with Los (82: 22–29).
9. A mistake for Bath-Rabbim (Damon): the beloved's eyes are "like the fishpools in Heshbon, by the
   gate of Bath-rabbim" (Song of Solomon 7:4; cf. 89:25–26; on Heshbon alone, see 32:10, 79:3).
   Blake may have intended to write "feet" instead of the second "hands" in this line.

O that I could live in his sight; O that I could bind him to my
    arm."
So saying: She drew aside her Veil from Mam-Tor to Dovedale
Discovering her own perfect beauty to the Daughters of Albion
And Hyle a winding Worm beneath
                              & not a weeping Infant.[1]

Trembling & pitying she screamd & fled upon the wind:
Hyle was a winding Worm and herself perfect in beauty;   50
The desarts tremble at his wrath; they shrink themselves in fear.

Cambel trembled with jealousy: she trembled! she envied!
The envy ran thro Cathedron's Looms into the Heart
Of mild Jerusalem, to destroy the Lamb of God. Jerusalem
Languishd upon Mount Olivet, East of mild Zion's Hill.

Los saw the envious blight above his Seventh Furnace
On London's Tower on the Thames: he drew Cambel in wrath
Into his thundering Bellows, heaving it for a loud blast!
And with the blast of his Furnace upon fishy Billingsgate.[2]
Beneath Albion's fatal Tree,[3] before the Gate of Los;   60
Shewd her the fibres of her beloved to ameliorate
The envy; loud she labourd in the Furnace of fire,
To form the mighty form of Hand according to her will.
In the Furnaces of Los & in the Wine-press treading day &
    night
Naked among the human clusters: bringing wine of anguish
To feed the afflicted in the Furnaces;[4] she minded not
The raging flames, tho she returnd
                              instead of beauty
Deformity: she gave her beauty to another: bearing abroad
Her struggling torment in her iron arms: and like a chain,   70
Binding his wrists & ankles with the iron arms of love.

Gwendolen saw the Infant in her sister's arms: she howld
Over the forests with bitter tears, and over the winding Worm
Repentant: and she also in the eddying wind of Los's Bellows
Began her dolorous task of love in the Wine-press of Luvah
To form the Worm into a form of love by tears & pain.
The Sisters saw! trembling ran thro their Looms! softening mild
Towards London: then they saw the Furnaces opend, & in tears
Began to give their souls away in the Furnaces of affliction.

1. Gaps in lines 47–48 and 67–68 are caused by deletions. The area "from Mam-Tor to Dovedale,"
   one side of a double peak and a narrow wooded valley in Derbyshire, is Gwendolen's naked torso
   (Damon).
2. Ancient water gate on the Thames, east of London Bridge; the site of a fish market synonymous
   with foul, abusive language. Los's Seventh Furnace, the ultimate stage of his refining, recasting,
   and renewing activities conducted near the Tower of London, east of Billingsgate along the
   Thames, is where Eno opened a moment of time and an atom of space (48:30–44) and God's finger prepared a place for Jerusalem (48:45).
3. Usually identified with the Tyburn gallows, further west (see map).
4. Cambel's surprisingly positive work in the furnace is a false dawn that nevertheless hints that Los's
   labors are not in vain.

Los saw & was comforted at his Furnaces uttering thus his
   voice.   80
"I know I am Urthona keeper of the Gates of Heaven.
And that I can at will expatiate in the Gardens of bliss;
But pangs of love draw me down to my loins which are
Become a fountain of veiny pipes:[5] O Albion! my brother!

Corruptibility appears upon thy limbs, and never more   **83**
Can I arise and leave thy side, but labour here incessant
Till thy awaking! yet alas I shall forget Eternity!
Against the Patriarchal pomp and cruelty, labouring incessant
I shall become an Infant horror. Enion! Tharmas![6] friends
Absorb me not in such dire grief: O Albion, my brother!
Jerusalem hungers in the desert; affection to her children!
The scorn'd and contemnd youthful girl, where shall she fly?
Sussex shuts up her Villages. Hants, Devon & Wilts
Surrounded with masses of stone in orderd forms. Determine
   then   10
A form for Vala and a form for Luvah, here on the Thames
Where the Victim nightly howls beneath the Druid's knife;
A Form of Vegetation, nail them down on the stems of Mystery;
O when shall the Saxon return with the English his redeemed
   brother!
O when shall the Lamb of God descend among the Reprobate!
I woo to Amalek to protect my fugitives; Amalek trembles:
I call to Canaan & Moab in my night watches, they mourn:
They listen not to my cry, they rejoice among their warriors
Woden and Thor and Friga wholly consume my Saxons:[7]
On their enormous Altars built in the terrible north: 20
From Ireland's rocks to Scandinavia Persia and Tartary:
From the Atlantic Sea to the universal Erythrean.[8]
Found ye London! enormous City! weeps thy River?
Upon his parent bosom lay thy little ones O Land
Forsaken. Surrey and Sussex are Enitharmon's Chamber.
Where I will build her a Couch of repose & my pillars
Shall surround her in beautiful labyrinths: Oothoon?
Where hides my child? in Oxford hidest thou with Antamon?
In graceful hidings of error: in merciful deceit
Lest Hand the terrible destroy his Affection, thou hidest her: 30
In chaste appearances for sweet deceits of love & modesty
Immingled, interwoven, glistening to the sickening sight.
Let Cambel and her Sisters sit within the Mundane Shell:
Forming the fluctuating Globe according to their will.
According as they weave the little embryon nerves & veins,

5. Los has the ability to reenter Eden but remains in the world of Generation for the sake of others. The empathetic love pangs of his "veiny pipes" are in his genitals (cf. the "vegetating blood in veiny pipes" in the heart of the humanized London, 38/34:36).
6. Parents of Los and Enitharmon in *The Four Zoas*, a relationship not hinted at in *Jerusalem*.
7. The chief Norse god, also called Odin (*Song of Los* 3:30; (**27**/25:53). Perhaps included with Thor and Friga (=Freya; cf. *J* **63**:9, **68**:17) because their three names survive in English as Wednesday, Thursday, and Friday. The Saxons, one element in British stock (**43**/38:51, **92**:1), have been separated from their kin in the German state of Saxony (**83**:14). Blake thought that inhabitants of Sussex looked like "genuine Saxons handsomer than the people about London" (p. 476 herein).
8. In this context not just the Red Sea but, according to Bryant's *New System*, the entire Indian Ocean (Damon).

The Eye, the little Nostrils, & the delicate Tongue & Ears
Of labyrinthine intricacy: so shall they fold the World
That whatever is seen upon the Mundane Shell, the same
Be seen upon the Fluctuating Earth woven by the Sisters.
And sometimes the Earth shall roll in the Abyss & sometimes   40
Stand in the Center & sometimes stretch flat in the Expanse,
According to the will of the lovely Daughters of Albion.
Sometimes it shall assimilate with mighty Golgonooza:
Touching its summits: & sometimes divided roll apart
As a beautiful Veil, so these Females shall fold & unfold
According to their will the outside surface of the Earth
An outside shadowy Surface superadded to the real Surface;
Which is unchangeable for ever & ever Amen: so be it!
Separate Albion's Sons gently from their Emanations
Weaving bowers of delight on the current of infant Thames   50
Where the old Parent still retains his youth as I alas!
Retain my youth eight thousand and five hundred years,[9]
The labourer of ages in the Valleys of Despair;
The land is markd for desolation & unless we plant
The seeds of Cities & of Villages in the Human bosom
Albion must be a rock of blood: mark ye the points
Where Cities shall remain & where Villages for the rest:
It must lie in confusion till Albion's time of awaking.
Place the Tribes of Llewellyn[1] in America for a hiding place!
Till sweet Jerusalem emanates again into Eternity   60
The night falls thick: I go upon my watch: be attentive:
The Sons of Albion go forth; I follow from my Furnaces:
That they return no more: that a place be prepard on Euphrates.
Listen to your Watchman's[2] voice: sleep not before the Furnaces
Eternal Death stands at the door, O God pity our labours."

So Los spoke to the Daughters of Beulah while his Emanation
Like a faint rainbow waved before him in the awful gloom
Of London, City on the Thames from Surrey Hills to Highgate:
Swift turn the silver spindles, & the golden weights play soft
And lulling harmonies beneath the Looms, from Caithness in
     the north   70
To Lizard-point & Dover in the south: his Emanation
Joy'd in the many weaving threads in bright Cathedron's Dome
Weaving the Web of life for Jerusalem; the Web of life
Down flowing into Entuthon's Vales glistens with soft affections.

While Los arose upon his Watch, and down from Golgonooza
Putting on his golden sandals to walk from mountain to mountain
He takes his way, girding himself with gold & in his hand
Holding his iron mace: The Spectre remains attentive
Alternate they watch on night; alternate labour in day
Before the Furnaces labouring, while Los all night watches   80
The stars rising & setting, & the meteors & terrors of night.

9. Here and in the period of Albion's death (48:36) Blake lengthens the traditional six-thousand-year
   span of human history by an extra two and a half millennia.
1. A common name in Wales.
2. Cf. the watchmen who warn or protect Israel/Jerusalem in biblical prophecy (Isaiah 21:6, 21:11;
   62:6; Jeremiah 6:17; Ezekiel 3:17, Micah 7:4).

With him went down the Dogs of Leutha at his feet
They lap the water of the trembling Thames then follow swift
And thus he heard the voice of Albion's daughters on Euphrates,

"Our Father Albion's land: O it was a lovely land! & the Daughters
    of Beulah
Walked up and down in its green mountains: but Hand is fled
Away: & mighty Hyle; & after them Jerusalem is gone, Awake

Highgate's heights & Hampstead's, to Poplar Hackney & Bow: 84
To Islington & Paddington & the Brook of Albion's River,
We builded Jerusalem as a City & a Temple: from Lambeth
We began our Foundations; lovely Lambeth! O lovely Hills
Of Camberwell, we shall behold you no more in glory & pride,
For Jerusalem lies in ruins & the Furnaces of Los are builded
    there.
You are now shrunk up to a narrow Rock in the midst of the Sea
But here we build Babylon on Euphrates, compelld to build
And to inhabit, our Little-ones to clothe in armour of the gold
Of Jerusalem's Cherubims & to forge them swords of her Altars.   10
I see London blind & age-bent begging thro the Streets
Of Babylon, led by a child,[3] his tears run down his beard.
The voice of Wandering Reuben ecchoes from street to street
In all the Cities of the Nations Paris Madrid Amsterdam
The Corner of Broad Street weeps; Poland Street languishes
To Great Queen Street & Lincoln's Inn all is distress & woe.[4]

The night falls thick, Hand comes from Albion in his strength.
He combines into a Mighty-one the Double Molech & Chemosh
Marching thro Egypt in his fury; the East is pale at his course.
The Nations of India, the Wild Tartar that never knew Man   20
Starts from his lofty places & casts down his tents & flees away
But we woo him all the night in songs. O Los come forth O Los
Divide us from these terrors & give us power them to subdue
Arise upon thy Watches let us see thy Globe of fire[5]
On Albion's Rocks & let thy voice be heard upon Euphrates."

Thus sang the Daughters in lamentation, uniting into One
With Rahab as she turned the iron Spindle of destruction.
Terrified at the Sons of Albion they took the Falshood which
Gwendolen hid in her left hand. It grew & grew till it

Became a Space & an Allegory around the Winding Worm.   85
They namd it Canaan & built for it a tender Moon.
Los smild with joy thinking on Enitharmon & he brought
Reuben from his twelvefold wandrings & led him into it,
Planting the Seeds of the Twelve Tribes & Moses & David

3. The design for this plate (not included in this edition) is anticipated in the headpiece for "London"; but in *Jerusalem* the figures move from right to left in front of side-by-side facades of (Gothic) Westminster Abbey and (Neoclassical) St. Paul's (cf. the contrasting architecture shown on J 57).
4. Blake's birthplace (Broad Street), his second home with Catherine (Poland Street), and his quarters as an apprentice in Basire's home (Great Queen Street, near Lincoln's Inn Fields). Cf. other important addresses in 38/34:40, 38/34:42, and 74:55 (see map). Four lines have been deleted.
5. Used by Los for illumination (see also 85:18; cf. frontispiece) to "search the interiors of Albion's / Bosom (31/45:3–4).

And gave a Time & Revolution to the Space, Six Thousand Years.
He calld it Divine Analogy, for in Beulah the Feminine
Emanations Create Space, the Masculine Create Time, & plant
The Seeds of beauty in the Space: listning to their lamentation
Los walks upon his ancient Mountains in the deadly darkness   10
Among his Furnaces directing his laborious Myriads watchful
Looking to the East: & his voice is heard over the whole Earth
As he watches the Furnaces by night, & directs the labourers.

And thus Los replies upon his Watch: the Valleys listen silent:
The Stars stand still to hear: Jerusalem & Vala cease to mourn!
His voice is heard from Albion: the Alps & Appenines
Listen: Hermon & Lebanon bow their crowned heads
Babel & Shinar look toward the Western Gate, they sit down
Silent at his voice: they view the red Globe of fire in Los's hand
As he walks from Furnace to Furnace directing the Labourers   20
And this is the Song of Los, the Song that he sings on his Watch

"O lovely mild Jerusalem! O Shiloh of Mount Ephraim![6]
I see thy Gates of precious stones! thy Walls of gold & silver
Thou art the soft reflected Image of the Sleeping Man
Who, stretchd on Albion's rocks, reposes amidst his
    Twenty-eight
Cities: where Beulah lovely terminates, in the hills & valleys of
    Albion
Cities not yet embodied in Time and Space: plant ye
The Seeds O Sisters in the bosom of Time & Space's womb
To spring up for Jerusalem: lovely Shadow of Sleeping Albion
Why wilt thou rend thyself apart & build an Earthly Kingdom   30
To reign in pride & to opress & to mix the Cup of Delusion
O thou that dwellest with Babylon! Come forth O lovely-one

I see thy Form O lovely mild Jerusalem, Wingd with Six Wings[7] |86|
In the opacous Bosom of the Sleeper, lovely Three-fold
In Head & Heart & Reins three Universes of love & beauty
Thy forehead bright: Holiness to the Lord[8] with Gates of pearl
Reflects Eternity beneath thy azure wings of feathery down
Ribbd delicate & clothd with featherd gold & azure & purple
From thy white shoulders shadowing, purity in holiness!
Thence featherd with soft crimson of the ruby bright as fire
Spreading into the azure Wings which like a canopy
Bends over thy immortal Head in which Eternity dwells.   10
Albion beloved Land; I see thy mountains & thy hills
And valleys & thy pleasant Cities Holiness to the Lord
I see the Spectres of thy Dead O Emanation of Albion.

---

6. A city in the mountainous territory of the half-tribe of Ephraim, where the ark of the covenant
   resided for a time (Joshua 18:9, Judges 18:31, 1 Samuel 1:1–3).
7. This vision of Jerusalem as a six-winged seraph (cf. Isaiah 6:2) is anticipated in her butterfly or
   moth form; cf. title page (color plate 13) and tailpiece to plate 14. Her downy feathers and brilliant colors (86:5–9) owe something to both Milton's seraph Raphael (PL 5:277 ff.) and Aaron's
   breastplate (Exodus 28).
8. Words engraved on Aaron's mitre (Exodus 28:36; 39:30); but see also the prophecy against Tyre
   (Isaiah 23:18).

Thy Bosom white, translucent coverd with immortal gems,
A sublime ornament not obscuring the outlines of beauty,
Terrible to behold, for thy extreme beauty & perfection
Twelve-fold, here all the Tribes of Israel I behold
Upon the Holy Land: I see the River of Life & Tree of Life
I see the New Jerusalem descending out of Heaven[9]
Between thy Wings of gold & silver featherd immortal   20
Clear as the rainbow, as the cloud of the Sun's tabernacle

Thy Reins[1] coverd with Wings translucent sometimes covering
And sometimes spread abroad reveal the flames of holiness
Which like a robe covers: & like a Veil of Seraphim
In flaming fire unceasing burns from Eternity to Eternity.
Twelvefold I there behold Israel in her Tents
A Pillar of a Cloud by day: a Pillar of fire by night[2]
Guides them: there I behold Moab & Ammon & Amalek
There Bells of silver round thy knees living articulate
Comforting sounds of love & harmony & on thy feet   30
Sandals of gold & pearl, & Egypt & Assyria before me
The Isles of Javan, Philistea, Tyre and Lebanon."[3]

Thus Los sings upon his Watch walking from Furnace to
    Furnace.
He siezes his Hammer every hour, flames surround him as
He beats: seas roll beneath his feet, tempests muster
Around his head, the thick hail stones stand ready to obey
His voice in the black cloud, his Sons labour in thunders
At his Furnaces; his Daughters at their Looms sing woes,
His Emanation separates in milky fibres agonizing
Among the golden Looms of Cathedron sending Fibres of
    love   40
From Golgonooza with sweet visions for Jerusalem, wanderer.

Nor can any consummate bliss without being Generated
On Earth; of those whose Emanations weave the loves
Of Beulah for Jerusalem & Shiloh, in immortal Golgonooza
Concentering in the majestic form of Erin in eternal tears
Viewing the Winding Worm on the Desarts of Great Tartary
Viewing Los in his shudderings, pouring balm on his sorrows.
So dread is Los's fury that none dare him to approach
Without becoming his Children in the Furnaces of affliction.

And Enitharmon like a faint rainbow waved before him   50
Filling with Fibres from his loins which reddend with desire
Into a Globe of blood beneath his bosom[4] trembling in darkness

9. "Gates of pearl" (86:4), "River of Life & Tree of Life," and the descent of the New Jerusalem are all in Revelation 21.
1. Kidneys; along with the heart, the seat of affections (Psalm 7:9, Jeremiah 11:20, Revelation 2:23); here equivalent to the loins. Cf. 86:3; M 5:6.
2. As in 5:48, alluding to God's guiding Israel in the wilderness (Exodus 13:21–22).
3. Javan is the son of Noah's son Japeth, whose descendants divided "the isles of the Gentiles" (Genesis 10:2, 10:5). The other place names are on the mainland.
4. Cf. Urizen 18; but this time the globe containing Enitharmon will emerge from Los's loins instead of his breast.

Of Albion's clouds. He fed it with his tears & bitter groans
Hiding his Spectre in invisibility from the timorous Shade
Till it became a separated cloud of beauty grace & love
Among the darkness of his Furnaces dividing asunder till
She separated stood before him a lovely Female weeping.
Even Enitharmon separated outside, & his Loins closed
And heal'd after the separation: his pains he soon forgot:
Lured by her beauty outside of himself in shadowy grief.   60
Two Wills they had; Two Intellects: & not as in times of old.

Silent they wanderd hand in hand like two Infants wandring
From Enion in the deserts, terrified at each other's beauty
Envying each other yet desiring, in all devouring Love

Repelling weeping Enion blind & age-bent into the fourfold   87
Desarts. Los first broke silence & began to utter his love

"O lovely Enitharmon: I behold thy graceful forms
Moving beside me till intoxicated with the woven labyrinth
Of beauty & perfection my wild fibres shoot in veins
Of blood thro all my nervous limbs. Soon overgrown in roots
I shall be closed from thy sight. Sieze therefore in thy hand
The small fibres as they shoot around me draw out in pity
And let them run on the winds of thy bosom: I will fix them
With pulsations, we will divide them into Sons & Daughters   10
To live in thy Bosom's translucence as in an eternal morning."

Enitharmon answerd, "No! I will sieze thy Fibres & weave
Them; not as thou wilt but as I will, for I will Create
A round Womb beneath my bosom lest I also be overwoven
With Love; be thou assured I never will be thy slave.
Let Man's delight be Love; but Woman's delight be Pride.
In Eden our loves were the same here they are opposite
I have Loves of my own I will weave them in Albion's Spectre.
Cast thou in Jerusalem's shadows thy Loves! silk of liquid
Rubies Jacinths Crysolites:[5] issuing from thy Furnaces, While   20
Jerusalem divides thy care: while thou carest for Jerusalem
Know that I never will be thine: also thou hidest Vala.
From her these fibres shoot to shut me in a Grave.
You are Albion's Victim, he has set his Daughter in your path."

Los answerd sighing like the Bellows of his Furnaces   88

"I care not! the swing of my Hammer shall measure the starry
   round
When in Eternity Man converses with Man they enter
Into each other's Bosom (which are Universes of delight)
In mutual interchange, and first their Emanations meet
Surrounded by their Children; if they embrace & comingle

---

5. Evoking the somewhat different jewels of Jerusalem's foundations (Isaiah 54:11–12, Revelation
21:19–21); cf. 9:23–25 and Aaron's breastplate (Exodus 28:17–21); also the "covering" of the
cherub (Ezekiel 28:13).

The Human Four-fold Forms mingle also in thunders of
    Intellect
But if the Emanations mingle not; with storms & agitations
Of earthquakes & consuming fires they roll apart in fear.
For Man cannot unite with Man but by their Emanations   10
Which stand both Male & Female at the Gates of each
    Humanity.
How then can I ever again be united as Man with Man
While thou my Emanation refusest my Fibres of dominion.
When Souls mingle & join thro all the Fibres of Brotherhood
Can there be any secret joy on Earth greater than this?"

Enitharmon answerd: "This is Woman's World, nor need
    she any
Spectre to defend her from Man. I will Create secret places
And the masculine names of the places Merlin & Arthur.
A triple Female Tabernacle for Moral Law I weave
That he who loves Jesus may loathe terrified Female love   20
Till God himself become a Male subservient to the Female."

She spoke in scorn & jealousy alternate torments; and
So speaking she sat down on Sussex shore[6] singing lulling
Cadences & playing in sweet intoxication among the
    glistening
Fibres of Los: sending them over the Ocean eastward into
The realms of dark death; O perverse to thyself, contrarious
To thy own purposes; for when she began to weave
Shooting out in sweet pleasure her bosom in milky Love
Flowd into the aching fibres of Los, yet contending against
    him
In pride sending his Fibres over to her objects of jealousy   30
In the little lovely Allegoric Night of Albion's Daughters
Which stretchd abroad expanding east & west & north &
    south
Thro' all the World of Erin & of Los & all their Children.

A sullen smile broke from the Spectre in mockery & scorn
Knowing himself the author of their divisions & shrinkings,
    gratified
At their contentions, he wiped his tears he washd his visage.

"The Man who respects Woman shall be despised by Woman
And deadly cunning & mean abjectness only, shall enjoy them.
For I will make their places of joy & love, excrementitious.
Continually building, continually destroying in Family feuds   40
While you are under the dominion of a jealous Female
Unpermanent for ever because of love & jealousy.
You shall want all the Minute Particulars of Life."

Thus joyd the Spectre in the dusky fires of Los's Forge, eyeing
Enitharmon who at her shining Looms sings lulling cadences

---

6. Location of Felpham, the Blakes' home near Hayley (see map and Chronology).

While Los stood at his Anvil in wrath the victim of their love
And hate: dividing the Space of Love with brazen Compasses
In Golgonooza & in Udan-Adan & in Entuthon of Urizen.

The blow of his Hammer is Justice, the swing of his Hammer
  Mercy,
The force of Los's Hammer is eternal Forgiveness; but   50
His rage or his mildness were vain. She scatterd his love on
  the wind
Eastward into her own Center, creating the Female Womb
In mild Jerusalem around the Lamb of God. Loud howl
The Furnaces of Los! loud roll the Wheels of Enitharmon
The Four Zoa's in all their faded majesty burst out in fury
And fire. Jerusalem took the Cup which foamd in Vala's hand
Like the red Sun upon the mountains in the bloody day
Upon the Hermaphroditic Wine-presses of Love & Wrath.

Tho divided by the Cross & Nails & Thorns & Spear   89
In cruelties of Rahab & Tirzah permanent endure
A terrible indefinite Hermaphroditic form
A Wine-press of Love & Wrath double Hermaphroditic
Twelvefold in Allegoric pomp in selfish holiness
The Pharisaion, the Grammateis, the Presbuterion.
The Archiereus, the Iereus, the Saddusaion,[7] double
Each withoutside of the other, covering eastern heaven.

Thus was the Covering Cherub reveald majestic image
Of Selfhood, Body put off, the Antichrist accursed   10
Coverd with precious stones, a Human Dragon terrible
And bright, stretchd over Europe & Asia gorgeous
In three nights he devourd the rejected corse of death.[8]

His Head dark, deadly, in its Brain incloses a reflexion

---

7. Institutions of the Pharisees, scribes, elders, high priest, priests, and Sadducees—all invented names, except for "Presbuterion" (the original Greek translated *elders* in Luke 22:66 [Stevenson]).
8. This climactic revelation of absolute evil (see "consolidation of error," in Frye, *Fearful Symmetry*) clarifies, under a series of related names, all that has prevented Albion from recognizing and acknowledging his own divinity. "Covering Cherub": a false ideal of unapproachable holiness, blocks humanity's return to Eden (cf. n. 7, p. 195 herein). The shrunken, sexually repressed, self-defensive, inverted, hyperrational "Selfhood," by suppressing and devaluing the human imagination, blocks fellowship with humanity as a whole. "Body put off": the "natural body" distinct from the resurrected "spiritual body" (1 Corinthians 15:44), the "old man" that must be "put off" before the "new man" can be "put on" (Colossians 3:9–10, Ephesians 4:22; cf. Colossians 2:11); see also "The Eternal Body" in Tristanne J. Connolly's *William Blake and the Body* (2002). According to Swedenborg, the delights of love "are perceived but in a faint obscure Manner by Man, so long as he liveth in the natural Body, because that Body absorbs and deadens them; but . . . when the material Body is put off, . . . the Delights of Love and the Pleasantnesses of Thought are then rendered fully sensible and perceivable" (*True Christian Religion*, 569). In Blake, this "improvement of sensory enjoyment" (*Marriage*) can occur in this life whenever the Covering Cherub is challenged and overcome. "Antichrist": the ultimate enemy of Jesus who appears at the end of time (1 John 2:18, 4:3; 2 John 1:7; cf. 2 Thessalonians 2:3 ff.), is here identified with the Covering Cherub by his covering of precious stones (Ezekiel 28:13). "Human Dragon": the "great red dragon" of Revelation (12:3–13, 20:2; cf. Isaiah 27:1), the implicit prototype of the Druidical serpent-temples of blood sacrifice that have spread over the earth (J 42:76, 80:48, 80:88, 89:42). He devours Jesus' merely material "vegetated" corpse in the three days between the crucifixion and the resurrection (cf. "Everlasting Gospel" 93). For related images, see the disease-formed "Body of Death" prepared to "devour the body of Albion" (9:9–10), the Spectres who "devour the Dead" (11:6), and the Sons of Albion, "ravning to devour / The Sleeping Humanity" (78:2–3).

Of Eden all perverted; Egypt on the Gihon[9] many tongued
And many mouthd: Ethiopia, Lybia, the Sea of Rephaim
Minute Particulars in slavery I behold among the brick-kilns
Disorganizd, & there is Pharoh in his iron Court:
And the Dragon of the River & the Furnaces of iron.
Outwoven from Thames & Tweed & Severn awful streams   20
Twelve ridges of Stone frown over all the Earth in tyrant pride
Frown over each River stupendous Works of Albion's Druid Sons
And Albion's Forests of Oaks coverd the Earth from Pole to Pole.

His Bosom wide reflects Moab & Ammon on the River
Pison, since calld Arnon, there is Heshbon[1] beautiful
The flocks of Rabbath on the Arnon & the Fish-pools of Heshbon
Whose currents flow into the Dead Sea by Sodom & Gomorra.
Above his Head high arching Wings black filld with Eyes
Spring upon iron sinews from the Scapulae & Os Humeri.[2]
There Israel in bondage to his Generalizing Gods   30
Molech & Chemosh, & in his left breast is Philistea
In Druid Temples over the whole Earth with Victims' Sacrifice,
From Gaza to Damascus Tyre & Sidon & the Gods
Of Javan thro the Isles of Grecia & all Europe's Kings
Where Hiddekel pursues his course among the rocks.
Two Wings spring from his ribs of brass, starry, black as night
But translucent their blackness as the dazling of gems.

His Loins inclose Babylon on Euphrates beautiful
And Rome in sweet Hesperia, there Israel scatterd abroad
In martyrdoms & slavery I behold: ah vision of sorrow!   40
Inclosed by eyeless Wings, glowing with fire as the iron
Heated in the Smith's forge, but cold the wind of their dread
    fury.

But in the midst of a devouring Stomach, Jerusalem
Hidden within the Covering Cherub as in a Tabernacle
Of threefold workmanship in allegoric delusion & woe
There the Seven Kings of Canaan & Five Baalim[3] of Philistea
Sihon & Og the Anakim & Emim Nephilim & Gibborim[4]
From Babylon to Rome & the Wings spread from Japan
Where the Red Sea terminates, the World of Generation &
    Death,
To Ireland's farthest rocks where Giants builded their Causeway   50
Into the Sea of Rephaim,[5] but the Sea oerwhelmd them all.

9. One of the four rivers of Eden (Genesis 2:10–14); cf. J 61:32–33. In the Covering Cherub's perverted reflection of Eden they flow, with the rivers of Britain (line 20), in Druid, pagan, and enemy
   territory.
1. See n. 9, p. 319 herein.
2. Shoulderblades and upper armbones essential to the physical mechanics of flying, probably covered in Royal Academy anatomy lessons.
3. Plural of *Baal* ("lord" or "owner"; Semitic). Both singular and plural forms appear repeatedly as
   deities and idols (e.g., Judges 2:11–12; 1 Samuel 12:10; 1 Kings 16:32).
4. Giant enemies of the Israelites. For Sihon and Og, see n. 8, p. 270 herein. For Anakim, see
   Deuteronomy Numbers 1:28 and 13:33. For Emim, see Deuteronomy 2:11. For Nephilim (trans.
   "giants") and Gibborim (trans. "mighty men)," see Genesis 6:4.
5. Translated as "giants" in Joshua 18:16. On the Causeway, see n. 9, p. 313 herein.

A Double Female now appeard within the Tabernacle,
Religion hid in War, a Dragon red & hidden Harlot[6]
Each within other, but without a Warlike Mighty-one
Of dreadful power sitting upon Horeb[7] pondering dire
And mighty preparations mustering multitudes innumerable
Of warlike sons among the sands of Midian & Aram.
For multitudes of those who sleep in Alla descend,
Lured by his warlike symphonies of tabret pipe & harp,
Burst the bottoms of the Graves & Funeral Arks of Beulah,   60
Wandering in that unknown Night beyond the silent Grave
They become One with the Antichrist & are absorbd in him.

The Feminine separates from the Masculine & both from Man,   90
Ceasing to be His Emanations, Life to Themselves assuming:
And while they circumscribe his Brain, & while they circumscribe
His Heart, & while they circumscribe his Loins! a Veil & Net
Of Veins of red Blood grows around them like a scarlet robe.[8]
Covering them from the sight of Man like the woven Veil of Sleep
Such as the Flowers of Beulah weave to be their Funeral Mantles
But dark: opake: tender to touch, & painful: & agonizing
To the embrace of love, & to the mingling of soft fibres
Of tender affection, that no more the Masculine mingles   10
With the Feminine, but the Sublime is shut out from the Pathos
In howling torment, to build stone walls of separation, compelling
The Pathos to weave curtains of hiding secresy from the torment.

Bowen & Conwenna stood on Skiddaw cutting the Fibres
Of Benjamin from Chester's River: loud the River; loud the Mersey
And the Ribble thunder into the Irish sea, as the Twelve Sons
Of Albion drank & imbibed the Life & eternal Form of Luvah.
Cheshire & Lancashire & Westmoreland groan in anguish
As they cut the fibres from the Rivers he[9] sears them with hot
Iron of his Forge & fixes them into Bones of chalk & Rock.   20
Conwenna sat above: with solemn cadences she drew
Fibres of life out from the Bones into her golden Loom
Hand had his Furnace on Highgate's heights & it reachd
To Brockley Hills across the Thames! he with double Boadicea[1]
In cruel pride cut Reuben apart from the Hills of Surrey
Comingling with Luvah & with the Sepulcher of Luvah
For the Male is a Furnace of beryll; the Female is a golden Loom.

Los cries; "No Individual ought to appropriate to Himself
Or to his Emanation any of the Universal Characteristics

6. The fully revealed evil of Rahab (repeating 75:20) replaces Jerusalem (89:43) in the Holy of Holies,
   the mercy seat of the ark.
7. The false traditional idea of the true God as Jehovah the Lawgiver on Horeb (Sinai).
8. Placenta, hymen, circulatory system, mortal body (cf. 21:50, 23:20–23). "Man" is humanity, Albion.
   In parts of *The Four Zoas* not included in this edition, the dying fertility god Luvah wears "robes of
   blood" over millennia until Jesus takes them on and, in one act of self-giving, ends the cycle. On
   this garment imagery, see Paley in *Blake's Sublime Allegory* (1973), ed. Curran and Wittreich.
9. This pronoun makes sense only if it refers to Bowen, the first of Albion's sons to become a blacksmith, though still in opposition to Los.
1. British warrior queen (d. 60/61 C.E.) who led an uprising against the Roman occupation, as
   reported by Tacitus. Cambel, Hand's usual consort, is identified with Boadicea in 71:23; hence she
   is "double."

Of David or of Eve, of the Woman, or of the Lord,   30
Of Reuben or of Benjamin, of Joseph or Judah or Levi.
Those who dare appropriate to themselves Universal Attributes
Are the Blasphemous Selfhoods & must be broken asunder.
A Vegetated Christ & a Virgin Eve are the Hermaphroditic
Blasphemy, by his Maternal Birth he is that Evil-One
And his Maternal Humanity must be put off Eternally
Lest the Sexual Generation swallow up Regeneration
Come Lord Jesus take on thee the Satanic Body of Holiness."[2]

So Los cried in the Valleys of Middlesex in the Spirit of
    Prophecy
While in Selfhood Hand & Hyle & Bowen & Skofeld appropriate   40
The Divine Names: seeking to Vegetate the Divine Vision
In a corporeal & ever dying Vegetation & Corruption
Mingling with Luvah in One, they become One Great Satan.

Loud scream the Daughters of Albion beneath the Tongs &
    Hammer
Dolorous are their lamentations in the burning Forge.
They drink Reuben & Benjamin as the iron drinks the fire
They are red hot with cruelty: raving along the Banks of Thames
And on Tyburn's Brook among the howling Victims in loveliness
While Hand & Hyle condense the Little-ones & erect them into
A mighty Temple even to the stars: but they Vegetate   50
Beneath Los's Hammer, that Life may not be blotted out.

For Los said: "When the Individual appropriates Universality
He divides into Male & Female: & when the Male & Female
Appropriate Individuality, they become an Eternal Death.
Hermaphroditic worshippers of a God of cruelty & law!
Your Slaves & Captives: you compell to worship a God of Mercy.
These are the Demonstrations of Los, & the blows of my mighty
    Hammer."

So Los spoke. And the Giants of Albion terrified & ashamed
With Los's thunderous Words, began to build trembling rocking
    Stones[3]
For his Words roll in thunders & lightnings among the Temples   60
Terrified rocking to & fro upon the earth, & sometimes
Resting in a Circle in Malden or in Strathness or Dura,
Plotting to devour Albion & Los the friend of Albion
Denying in private; mocking God & Eternal Life: & in Public
Collusion, calling themselves Deists, Worshipping the Maternal
Humanity: calling it Nature, and Natural Religion.

---

2. Cf. the "Satanic Holiness" of Vala's religion of chastity, selfishness, and moral pride (60:47–49);
also the "Holiness" of the "Abomination of Desolation" (10:7–16). Los, resisting individuals' appropriation of universal biblical types, prays to Jesus (cf. Revelation 22:21) to transform this body of
error. Paley cites Swedenborg: "The Lord Successively put off the humanity taken from the Mother,
and put on the Humanity from the divinity in Himself, which is the Divine Humanity and the Son
of God."
3. The giants redouble their commitment to Natural Religion under the modern name of Deists (line
65). The geological marvel of "rocking Stones," upright megaliths balanced on smaller stones, is
legendarily attributed to Druids.

But still the thunder of Los peals loud & thus the thunders cry
"These beautiful Witchcrafts of Albion are gratifyd by Cruelty.

It is easier to forgive an Enemy than to forgive a Friend: 91
The man who permits you to injure him deserves your vengeance:
He also will recieve it: go Spectre! obey my most secret desire!
Which thou knowest without my speaking: Go to these Fiends of
    Righteousness
Tell them to obey their Humanities, & not pretend Holiness;
When they are murderers: as far as my Hammer & Anvil permit
Go, tell them that the Worship of God is honouring his gifts
In other men: & loving the greatest men best, each according
To his Genius; which is the Holy Ghost in Man; there is no other
God, than that God who is the intellectual fountain of Humanity:[4]   10
He who envies or calumniates: which is murder & cruelty,
Murders the Holy-one! Go tell them this & overthrow their cup,
Their bread, their altar-table, their incense & their oath:
Their marriage & their baptism, their burial & consecration:
I have tried to make friends by corporeal gifts but have only
Made enemies: I never made friends but by spiritual gifts;
By severe contentions of friendship & the burning fire of thought.
He who would see the Divinity must see him in his Children,
One first, in friendship & love; then a Divine Family, & in the
    midst
Jesus will appear;[5] so he who wishes to see a Vision; a perfect
    Whole   20
Must see it in its Minute Particulars; Organized & not as thou
O Fiend of Righteousness pretendest; thine is a Disorganized
And snowy cloud; brooder of tempests & destructive War
You smile with pomp & rigor: you talk of benevolence & virtue!
I act with benevolence & virtue & get murderd time after time:
You accumulate Particulars, & murder by analyzing, that you
May take the aggregate; & you call the aggregate Moral Law:
And you call that Swelld & bloated Form; a Minute Particular,
But General Forms have their vitality in Particulars: & every
Particular is a Man; a Divine Member of the Divine Jesus."   30

So Los cried at his Anvil in the horrible darkness weeping!

The Spectre builded stupendous Works, taking the Starry
    Heavens
Like to a curtain & folding them according to his will
Repeating the Smaragdine Table of Hermes[6] to draw Los down
Into the Indefinite, refusing to believe without demonstration.
Los reads the Stars of Albion! the Spectre reads the Voids
Between the Stars; among the arches of Albion's Tomb sublime
Rolling the Sea in rocky paths! forming Leviathan

---

4. These words of Los (lines: 7–10), as Wittreich notes (*Angel of Apocalypse* 250), are practically identical with those of a Devil in *Marriage* 22–23.
5. Los's interpretation of "where two or three are gathered together in my name, there am I in the
   midst of them" (Matthew 18:20).
6. Basic text of alchemy attributed to the legendary Egyptian Hermes Trismegistus (thrice-greatest);
   cf. *Song of Los* 3:18. "Smaragdine": emerald.

And Behemoth;[7] the War by Sea enormous & the War
By Land astounding: erecting pillars in the deepest Hell.   40
To reach the heavenly arches; Los beheld undaunted furious
His heavd Hammer; he swung it round & at one blow,
In unpitying ruin driving down the pyramids of pride
Smiting the Spectre on his Anvil & the integuments of his Eye
And Ear unbinding in dire pain, with many blows,
Of strict severity self-subduing, & with many tears labouring.

Then he sent forth the Spectre; all his pyramids were grains
Of sand & his pillars: dust on the fly's wing: & his starry
Heavens; a moth of gold & silver mocking his anxious grasp
Thus Los alterd his Spectre & every Ratio of his Reason   50
He alterd time after time, with dire pain & many tears
Till he had completely divided him into a separate space.

Terrified Los sat to behold trembling & weeping & howling
"I care not whether a Man is Good or Evil; all that I care
Is whether he is a Wise Man or a Fool, Go! put off Holiness
And put on Intellect: or my thundrous Hammer shall drive thee
To wrath which thou condemnest: till thou obey my voice."

So Los terrified cries; trembling & weeping & howling!
   Beholding

"What do I see! The Briton Saxon Roman Norman
   amalgamating[8]   92
In my Furnaces into One Nation the English: & taking refuge
In the Loins of Albion. The Canaanite united with the fugitive
Hebrew, whom she[9] divided into Twelve & sold into Egypt
Then scatterd the Egyptian & Hebrew to the four Winds:
This sinful Nation Created in our Furnaces & Looms is Albion."

So Los spoke. Enitharmon answerd in great terror in Lambeth's Vale

"The Poet's Song draws to its period & Enitharmon is no more.
For if he be that Albion I can never weave him in my Looms
But when he touches the first fibrous thread, like filmy dew   10

My Looms will be no more & I annihilate vanish for ever
Then thou wilt Create another Female according to thy Will."

Los answerd swift as the shuttle of gold. "Sexes must vanish &
   cease
To be when Albion arises from his dread repose O lovely
   Enitharmon:
When all their Crimes, their Punishments their Accusations of Sin:
All their Jealousies Revenges, Murders, hidings of Cruelty in Deceit

7. Great beasts of sea and land (Job 40:15, 41:1). On the association of these monsters with Britain's
   actions under Nelson and Pitt, see *Descriptive Catalogue*.
8. The melting of Britain's historic ethnic constituencies into one nation also encompasses a
   Canaanite-Hebrew union.
9. The antecedent must be "Canaanite," but Israel's own sons generated the twelve tribes and sold
   Joseph into Egyptian slavery.

Appear only in the Outward Spheres of Visionary Space and Time,
In the shadows of Possibility by Mutual Forgiveness forevermore
And in the Vision & in the Prophecy, that we may Foresee & Avoid
The terrors of Creation & Redemption & Judgment, Beholding
   them   20
Displayd in the Emanative Visions of Canaan in Jerusalem & in
   Shiloh
And in the Shadows of Remembrance & in the Chaos of the
   Spectre—
Amalek, Edom, Egypt, Moab, Ammon, Ashur, Philistea, around
   Jerusalem
Where the Druids reard their Rocky Circles to make permanent
   Remembrance
Of Sin, & the Tree of Good & Evil sprang from the Rocky Circle &
   Snake
Of the Druid, along the Valley of Rephaim from Camberwell to
   Golgotha
And framed the Mundane Shell Cavernous in Length Bredth &
   Highth."

Enitharmon heard. She raisd her head like the mild Moon.[1]   93

"O Rintrah! O Palamabron! What are your dire & awful purposes
Enitharmon's name is nothing before you: you forget all my Love!
The Mother's love of obedience is forgotten & you seek a Love
Of the pride of dominion that wilt Divorce Ocalythron & Elynittria[2]
Upon East Moor in Derbyshire & along the Valleys of Cheviot.

Could you Love me Rintrah, if you Pride not in my Love?
As Reuben found Mandrakes in the field & gave them to his Mother
Pride meets with Pride upon the Mountains in the stormy day
In that terrible Day of Rintrah's Plow & of Satan's driving the
   Team.[3]   10

1. Depicted in the bottom design (not included in this edition). Inscriptions on the top design—
presumably Albion's son Hand (see headnote, p. 207 herein), based on the typographical pointing-
finger signature of the three Hunt brothers—refer to the accusers of Socrates and Jesus: "Anytus
Melitus & Lycon thought Socrates a very Pernicious Man / So Caiphas thought Jesus"; cf. "The
Everlasting Gospel" and "Public Address."
2. Emanations of Rintrah and Palamabron (*Europe* 11/8:3–7).
3. Cf. *Milton* 7:6 ff. (where Satan usurps Palamabron's harrow, not Rintrah's plow). For Reuben's
mandrakes, see 11:22.

Ah! then I heard my little ones weeping along the Valley:
Ah! then I saw my beloved ones fleeing from my Tent
Merlin was like thee Rintrah among the Giants of Albion
Judah was like Palamabron: O Simeon! O Levi! ye fled away
How can I hear my little ones weeping along the Valley
Or how upon the distant Hills see my beloveds' Tents."

Then Los again took up his speech as Enitharmon ceast.

"Fear not my Sons this Waking Death, he is become One with
   me.[4]
Behold him here! We shall not Die! we shall be united in Jesus.
Will you suffer this Satan, this Body of Doubt that Seems but Is
   Not,   20
To occupy the very threshold of Eternal Life? If Bacon, Newton,
   Locke
Deny a Conscience in Man & the Communion of Saints & Angels,
Contemning the Divine Vision & Fruition, Worshiping the Deus
Of the Heathen, The God of This World & the Goddess Nature
Mystery Babylon the Great, The Druid Dragon & hidden Harlot,
Is it not that Signal of the Morning which was told us in the
   Beginning?"
Thus they converse upon Mam-Tor. The Graves thunder under
   their feet.

Albion cold lays on his Rock: storms & snows beat round him. [94]
Beneath the Furnaces & the starry Wheels & the Immortal Tomb
Howling winds cover him: roaring seas dash furious against him
In the deep darkness broad lightnings glare, long thunders roll.

The weeds of Death inwrap his hands & feet blown incessant
And washd incessant by the for-ever restless sea-waves foaming
   abroad
Upon the white Rock.[5] England a Female Shadow, as deadly
   damps
Of the Mines of Cornwall & Derbyshire, lays upon his bosom
   heavy,
Moved by the wind in volumes of thick cloud returning folding
   round
His loins & bosom unremovable by swelling storms & loud rending 10
Of enraged thunders. Around them the Starry Wheels of their
   Giant Sons
Revolve: & over them the Furnaces of Los & the Immortal Tomb
   around
Erin sitting in the Tomb, to watch them unceasing night and day.
And the Body of Albion was closed apart from all Nations.

Over them the famishd Eagle screams on boney Wings and around
Them howls the Wolf of famine; deep heaves the Ocean black
   thundering

---

4. Echoing *Milton* 25/23:33; here probably referring to Albion.
5. The white cliffs of Dover. See also the enwrapping weeds and billowing waves of Jonah 2.

Around the wormy Garments of Albion: then pausing in deathlike
   silence.

Time was Finished! The Breath Divine Breathed over Albion
Beneath the Furnaces & starry Wheels and in the Immortal Tomb
And England who is Brittannia awoke from Death on Albion's
   bosom.[6]   20
She awoke pale & cold she fainted seven times on the Body of
   Albion.

"O pitious Sleep O pitious Dream! O God O God awake I have slain
In Dreams of Chastity & Moral Law I have Murdered Albion! Ah!
In Stone-henge & on London Stone & in the Oak Groves of Malden
I have Slain him in my Sleep with the Knife of the Druid O England
O all ye Nations of the Earth behold ye the Jealous Wife,
The Eagle & the Wolf & Monkey & Owl & the King & Priest were
   there."

Her voice pierc'd Albion's clay cold ear; he moved upon the Rock.   95
The Breath Divine went forth upon the morning hills. Albion
   mov'd
Upon the Rock; he opend his eyelids in pain; in pain he mov'd
His stony members, he saw England. Ah! shall the Dead live again.

The Breath Divine went forth over the morning hills. Albion rose
In anger: the wrath of God breaking bright flaming on all sides
   around
His awful limbs; into the Heavens he walked clothed in flames
Loud thundring, with broad flashes of flaming lightning & pillars
Of fire, speaking the Words of Eternity in Human Forms, in direful
Revolutions of Action & Passion, thro the Four Elements on all
   sides   10
Surrounding his awful Members. Thou[7] seest the Sun in heavy
   clouds
Struggling to rise above the Mountains, in his burning hand
He takes his Bow, then chooses out his arrows of flaming gold
Murmuring the Bowstring breathes with ardor! clouds roll
   round the
Horns of the wide Bow, loud sounding winds sport on the
   mountain brows
Compelling Urizen to his Furrow; & Tharmas to his Sheepfold;
And Luvah to his Loom: Urthona he beheld mighty labouring at
His Anvil, in the Great Spectre Los[8] unwearied labouring &
   weeping
Therefore the Sons of Eden praise Urthona's Spectre in songs
Because he kept the Divine Vision in time of trouble.[9]   20

As the Sun & Moon lead forward the Visions of Heaven & Earth
England who is Brittannia enterd Albion's bosom rejoicing.

---

6. First mentioned in 36/32:28 when she "divided into Jerusalem & Vala"; her memories, however,
   are strictly Vala's (and the constituent Daughters').
7. The reader.
8. Los has so completely subdued his Spectre that the two are virtually indistinguishable.
9. Reprise of 30:15.

Rejoicing in his indignation! adoring his wrathful rebuke.
She who adores not your frowns will only loathe your smiles.[1]

As the Sun & Moon lead forward the Visions of Heaven & Earth   96
England who is Brittannia entered Albion's bosom rejoicing

Then Jesus appeared standing by Albion as the Good Shepherd[2]
By the lost Sheep that he hath found & Albion knew that it
Was the Lord the Universal Humanity, & Albion saw his Form
A Man, & they conversed as Man with Man, in Ages of Eternity
And the Divine Appearance was the likeness & similitude of Los.

Albion said, "O Lord what can I do: my Selfhood cruel
Marches against thee deceitful from Sinai & from Edom
Into the Wilderness of Judah to meet thee in his pride.   10
I behold the Visions of my deadly Sleep of Six Thousand Years
Dazling around thy skirts like a Serpent of precious stones & gold.
I know it is my Self; O my Divine Creator & Redeemer."

Jesus replied "Fear not Albion, unless I die thou canst not live
But if I die I shall arise again & thou with me[3]
This is Friendship & Brotherhood, without it Man Is Not."

So Jesus spoke: the Covering Cherub coming on in darkness
Overshadowd them & Jesus said "Thus do Men in Eternity
One for another to put off by forgiveness, every sin."

Albion replyd. "Cannot Man exist without Mysterious   20
Offering of Self for Another, is this Friendship & Brotherhood?
I see thee in the likeness and similitude of Los my Friend."

Jesus said. "Wouldest thou love one who never died
For thee or ever die for one who had not died for thee,
And if God dieth not for Man & giveth not himself
Eternally for Man, Man could not exist, for Man is Love:
As God is Love: every kindness to another is a little Death
In the Divine Image nor can Man exist but by Brotherhood."[4]

So saying, the Cloud overshadowing divided them asunder.
Albion stood in terror: not for himself but for his Friend   30
Divine, & Self was lost in the contemplation of faith[5]
And wonder at the Divine Mercy & at Los's sublime honour.

"Do I sleep amidst danger to Friends! O my Cities & Counties
Do you sleep! rouze up: rouze up. Eternal Death is abroad."

---

1. Apparently a gratuitous authorial aside punctuating reiterated lines (J **95**:21–22 and **96**:1–2).
2. Jesus' epithet for himself (John 10:11 ff.); cf. parable of the lost sheep (Matthew 18:12 ff.) and "The Little Black Boy" tailpiece (Songs **10**).
3. Alluding to John 14:19–20 and Romans 6:3–11.
4. Amalgamating echoes of John 15:13 ("Greater love hath no man than this, that a may lay down his life for his friends"), 1 John 3:16 ("because he laid down his life for us: and we ought to lay down our lives for the brethren"), and 1 John 4:8–12 ("God is love. . . . If we love one another, God dwelleth in us, and his love is perfected in us").
5. See the frontispiece to this chapter (color plate 15); for helpful commentary, see Paley, *Continuing City*, 113ff.

So Albion spoke & threw himself into the Furnaces of affliction.
All was a Vision, all a Dream: the Furnaces became
Fountains of Living Waters flowing from the Humanity Divine
And all the Cities of Albion rose from their Slumbers, and All
The Sons & Daughters of Albion on soft clouds Waking from
   Sleep.
Soon all around remote the Heavens burnt with flaming fires   40
And Urizen & Luvah & Tharmas & Urthona arose into
Albion's Bosom: Then Albion stood before Jesus in the Clouds
Of Heaven Fourfold among the Visions of God in Eternity.

"Awake! Awake Jerusalem! O lovely Emanation of Albion   97
Awake and overspread all Nations as in Ancient Time
For lo: the Night of Death is past and the Eternal Day
Appears upon our Hills! Awake Jerusalem, and come away."

So spake the Vision of Albion & in him so spake in my hearing
The Universal Father. Then Albion stretchd his hand into
   Infinitude,
And took his Bow, Fourfold the Vision for bright beaming Urizen
Layd his hand on the South & took a breathing Bow of carved
   Gold
Luvah his hand stretch'd to the East & bore a Silver Bow bright
   shining
Tharmas Westward a Bow of Brass pure flaming richly wrought   10
Urthona Northward in thick storms a Bow of Iron terrible
   thundering.

And the Bow is a Male & Female & the Quiver of the Arrows of
   Love
Are the Children of this Bow: a Bow of Mercy & Loving-kindness:
   laying
Open the hidden Heart in Wars of mutual Benevolence Wars of
   Love.
And the Hand of Man grasps firm between the Male & Female
   Loves
And he Clothed himself in Bow & Arrows in awful state Fourfold
In the midst of his Twenty-eight Cities each with his Bow
   breathing.

Then each an Arrow flaming from his Quiver fitted carefully   98
They drew fourfold the unreprovable String, bending thro the
   wide Heavens
The horned Bow Fourfold, loud sounding flew the flaming Arrow
   fourfold,

Murmuring the Bow-string breathes with ardor. Clouds roll
   round the horns
Of the wide Bow, loud sounding Winds sport on the Mountain's
   brows:
The Druid Spectre was Annihilate, loud thundring rejoicing
   terrific vanishing

Fourfold Annihilation & at the clangor of the Arrows of Intellect
The innumerable Chariots of the Almighty appeard in Heaven.
And Bacon & Newton & Locke, & Milton & Shakspear &
    Chaucer
A Sun of blood red wrath surrounding heaven on all sides around   10
Glorious incomprehensible by Mortal Man & each Chariot was
    Sexual Threefold,

And every Man stood Fourfold. Each Four Faces had, One to the
    West
One toward the East One to the South One to the North, the
    Horses Fourfold
And the dim Chaos brightend beneath, above, around! Eyed as the
    Peacock
According to the Human Nerves of Sensation, the Four Rivers of
    the Water of Life.

South stood the Nerves of the Eye, East in Rivers of bliss the
    Nerves of the
Expansive Nostrils, West flowd the Parent Sense the Tongue, North
    stood

The labyrinthine Ear, Circumscribing & Circumcising the
  excrementitious
Husk & Covering, into Vacuum evaporating revealing the
  lineaments of Man,
Driving outward the Body of Death in an Eternal Death &
  Resurrection   20
Awaking it to Life among the Flowers of Beulah rejoicing in Unity
In the Four Senses in the Outline the Circumference & Form for
  ever
In Forgiveness of Sins which is Self Annihilation; it is the Covenant
  of Jehovah.

The Four Living Creatures, Chariots of Humanity Divine
  Incomprehensible
In beautiful Paradises expand. These are the Four Rivers of Paradise
And the Four Faces of Humanity fronting the Four Cardinal Points
Of Heaven going forward forward irresistible from Eternity to
  Eternity.

And they conversed together in Visionary forms dramatic which
  bright
Redounded from their Tongues in thunderous majesty, in Visions
In new Expanses, creating exemplars of Memory and of Intellect,   30
Creating Space, Creating Time according to the wonders Divine
Of Human Imagination, throughout all the Three Regions
  immense
Of Childhood, Manhood & Old Age, & the all tremendous
  unfathomable NonEns
Of Death was seen in regenerations terrific or complacent varying
According to the subject of discourse & every Word & every
  Character
Was Human according to the Expansion or Contraction, the
  Translucence or
Opakeness of Nervous fibres. Such was the variation of Time &
  Space
Which vary according as the Organs of Perception vary & they
  walked
To & fro in Eternity as One Man reflecting each in each &
  clearly seen
And seeing: according to fitness & order. And I heard Jehovah
  speak   40
Terrific from his Holy Place & saw the Words of the Mutual
  Covenant Divine
On Chariots of gold & jewels with Living Creatures starry &
  flaming
With every Colour. Lion. Tyger. Horse. Elephant. Eagle. Dove.
  Fly. Worm.
And the all wondrous Serpent clothed in gems & rich array
  Humanize
In the Forgiveness of Sins according to the Covenant of Jehovah.
  They Cry

"Where is the Covenant of Priam, the Moral Virtues of the
  Heathen;

Where is the Tree of Good & Evil that rooted beneath the cruel
    heel
Of Albion's Spectre the Patriarch Druid! where are all his
    Human Sacrifice
For Sin in War & in the Druid Temples of the Accuser of Sin:
    beneath
The Oak Groves of Albion that coverd the whole Earth beneath
    his Spectre?   50
Where are the Kingdoms of the World & all their glory[6] that
    grew on Desolation
The Fruit of Albion's Poverty Tree when the Triple Headed
    Gog-Magog[7] Giant
Of Albion Taxed the Nations into Desolation & then gave the
    Spectrous Oath."

Such is the Cry from all the Earth from the Living Creatures of
    the Earth
And from the great City of Golgonooza in the Shadowy
    Generation—

And from the Thirty-two Nations of the Earth among the Living
    Creatures

All Human Forms identified even Tree Metal Earth & Stone,
    all $\boxed{99}$
Human Forms identified, living going forth & returning wearied
Into the Planetary lives of Years Months Days & Hours reposing
And then Awaking into his Bosom in the Life of Immortality.

And I heard the Name of their Emanations they are named
    Jerusalem.

The End of The Song
of Jerusalem[8]

FOR THE SEXES: THE GATES
OF PARADISE (1820)

We present only the final textual portion of Blake's revised and expanded edition
(c. 1820) of this emblem book, first issued as *For Children: The Gates of Paradise*
(1793). Although *For Children* and *For the Sexes* are the first words on the title
pages of their respective editions, these introductory phrases appear in smaller
lettering above the main title, *The Gates of Paradise*, alluding to Michelangelo's
name for Ghiberti's Baptistry doors in Florence. Numbered lines in "The Keys
of the Gates" refer to emblematic designs (not included in this edition) which,
with their captions, are an integral portion of the work's full meaning; the verse
"keys" unlock the deeper significance of the cryptic emblems. The textual part

6. Rejected by Jesus in response to the devil's final temptation (Matthew 4:8–10).
7. According to Geoffrey of Monmouth, the last giant overcome by the Trojan settlers of Britain was
   Gogmagog, apparently a hybrid of two mysterious names in Revelation 20:8 (cf. Ezekiel 38–39);
   represented as giant statues at the entrance to London's Guildhall.
8. For the visual conclusion, *J* 100, see color plate 16.

alone, however—consisting of an untitled prologue and three pages of aphoristic verse that Blake added when he reissued *The Gates of Paradise* under the supratitle *For the Sexes*—distills themes developed in *Jerusalem*, "The Everlasting Gospel," *The Ghost of Abel*, and *[Yah] & and His Two Sons*. In all these writings, the master key that opens paradise is "Mutual Forgiveness." Most studies of the work deal with the emblems, but see Frye's 1966 essay, "The Keys to the Gates," *The Stubborn Structure* (1970), 175–99, and George Wingfield Digby, *Symbol and Image in Blake* (1957). *The Gates*, omitted from the Blake Trust series edited by David Bindman (1991–95), appears in facsimile in a Blake Trust/Trianon Press edition by Geoffrey Keynes (1968). Both versions are reproduced, with designs and commentary, in Erdman, *The Illuminated Blake* (1974; 1992), and both the Erdman and the Bentley editions reproduce all the emblems and their captions. The source of our text is the Blake Archive's transcription of Copy D (Pierpont Morgan Library), printed about 1825.

For the Sexes   2/ii

The Gates of Paradise

Mutual Forgiveness of each Vice
Such are the Gates of Paradise.
Against the Accuser's chief desire[1]
Who walkd among the Stones of Fire[2]
Jehovah's Finger Wrote the Law   5
Then Wept! then rose in Zeal & Awe,
And the Dead Corpse from Sinai's heat
Buried beneath his Mercy Seat.[3]
O Christians Christians! tell me Why
You rear it on your Altars high.   10

The Keys of the Gates   19/17

The Catterpiller on the Leaf
Reminds thee of thy Mother's Grief.

1 My Eternal Man set in Repose
The Female from his darkness rose;[4]
And She found me beneath a Tree   5
A Mandrake & in her Veil hid me.
Serpent Reasonings us entice
Of Good & Evil: Virtue & Vice.
2 Doubt Self Jealous Watry folly
3 Struggling thro Earth's Melancholy   10
4 Naked in Air in Shame & Fear
5 Blind in Fire with shield & spear.
Two Hornd Reasoning Cloven Fiction,
In Doubt which is Self contradiction,
A dark Hermaphrodite We stood,   15

1. The chief desire of Satan, the Accuser (Revelation 12:10), is to charge humanity with sin.
2. See Ezekiel 28:14–15; *Jerusalem* 49:73; and *Milton* 41/37: 8 and 42/38:6.
3. God writes the law with his finger (Exodus 31:18), but the law is rendered defunct by Jesus' absorption of its consequences. Protestants symbolized their rejection of Catholic theology by replacing the crucifix with the empty cross; here all Christians err in worshiping the dead body of law.
4. As with the story of Albion and his emanation in *Jerusalem*, humanity falls into the sleep of the finite material world and separates into male and female.

Rational Truth Root of Evil & Good.
Round me flew the Flaming Sword
Round her snowy Whirlwinds roard
Freezing her Veil the Mundane Shell.
6 I rent the Veil where the Dead dwell.   20
When weary Man enters his Cave
He meets his Saviour in the Grave   20/18
Some find a Female Garment there
And some a Male, woven with care
Lest the Sexual Garments sweet   25
Should grow a devouring Winding sheet.
7 One Dies! Alas! the Living & Dead
One is slain & One is fled.
8 In Vain-glory hatcht & nurst
By double Spectres, Self Accurst.   30
My Son! my Son! thou treatest me
But as I have instructed thee.
9 On the shadows of the Moon
Climbing thro Night's highest noon
10 In Time's Ocean falling drownd;   35
In Aged Ignorance profound
11 Holy & cold I clipd the Wings
Of all Sublunary Things,
12 And in depths of my Dungeons
Closed the Father & the Sons.   40
13 But when once I did descry
The Immortal Man[5] that cannot Die
14 Thro evening shades I haste away
To close the Labours of my Day.
15 The Door of Death I open found   45
And the Worm Weaving in the Ground.
16 Thou'rt my Mother from the Womb
Wife, Sister, Daughter to the Tomb
Weaving to Dreams the Sexual strife
And weeping over the Web of Life.   50

To The Accuser who is   21/19
The God of This World[6]

Truly My Satan thou art but a Dunce
And dost not know the Garment from the Man.
Every Harlot was a Virgin once
Nor canst thou ever change Kate into Nan.[7]

Tho thou art Worshipd by the Names Divine   5
Of Jesus & Jehovah, thou art still
The Son of Morn[8] in weary Night's decline,
The lost Traveller's Dream under the Hill.

5. The "Keys," as a first-person narrative woven around the emblems, follows one human being from
   birth to death, which is envisioned as a liberation of the "Immortal Man," even though this section ends with the triumph of the worm over the body.
6. Cf. 2 Corinthians 4:4, traditionally interpreted as a reference to Satan. Cf. "prince of this world,"
   John 12:31, 14:30, and 16:11.
7. Cf. the distinction between "States" and "Individuals" in *Milton* 35/32:30–31.
8. Lucifer (Isaiah 14:12). The Traveller and his Dream are depicted in the design (p. 344 herein).

THE GHOST OF ABEL (1822)

In this two-page visionary drama addressing Byron as a prophet "in the Wilderness," Blake implicitly recognizes Byron's *Cain, A Mystery* (1821), condemned as blasphemous in its time, as a prophecy. In the spirit of Blake's Devil in *The Marriage of Heaven and Hell,* Byron's Cain challenges the moral system of the deity who cast his parents out of paradise. But just as Blake explores and alters Milton's theodicy in *Milton a Poem,* he also subjects Byron's inquiry into the origin of evil to rigorous scrutiny in *The Ghost of Abel.* Mere rebellion against a false God is not enough to reverse the fall of man. As the playlet opens, Blake's grief-stricken Adam and Eve, urged by their dead son's ghost to believe in a vengeful God, are on the brink of an even deeper fall from their full and true humanity. But when they choose to trust imaginative or "Spiritual Vision," or the "Mind's Eye," rather than merely natural perception, they recognize Abel's cry for vengeance and the God who authorizes it (here called Satan and Elohim) as evil delusions, whereupon their eyes are opened to the true God of self-sacrifice and forgiveness (here called Jehovah). For commentary, see Leslie Tannenbaum in *Blake in His Time* (1978), ed. Robert N. Essick and Donald Pearce; Martin Bidney, *Blake Studies* 8 (1979), 145–65; Kerry Ellen McKeever, *Studies in Romanticism* 34 (1995), 615–36; Essick and Viscomi's notes to the Blake Trust edition, *Milton . . . and the Final Illuminated Works* (1993); and Paley, *The Traveller in the Evening* (2004). To make the dialogue easier to follow, we have modified our base text—the Blake Archive transcription of Copy A (Library of Congress)—by italicizing the stage directions, slightly streamlining and regularizing the layout, and sparingly adding or altering punctuation.

The Ghost of Abel   1

A Revelation In the Visions of Jehovah

Seen by William Blake

To LORD BYRON in the Wilderness

What doest thou here Elijah?[1]

---

1. God's question to Elijah (1 Kings 19:9, 19:13) after the prophet has defeated and slain 450 prophets of Baal and fled into the wilderness to escape Jezebel's threat on his life. Elijah twice replies that he is the only prophet left who keeps God's covenant.

Can a Poet doubt the Visions of Jehovah? Nature has no Outline: but Imagination has, Nature has no Tune:[2] but Imagination has! Nature has no Supernatural & dissolves: Imagination is Eternity.

> *Scene. A rocky Country. Eve fainted over the dead body of Abel*[3]   5
> *which lays near a Grave. Adam kneels by her. Jehovah stands*
> *above.*

Jehovah—	Adam!
Adam—	I will not hear thee more thou Spiritual Voice. Is this Death?
Jehovah—	Adam? 10
Adam—	It is in vain: I will not hear thee Henceforth! Is this thy Promise that the Woman's Seed Should bruise the Serpent's head:[4] Is this the Serpent? Ah! Seven times O Eve thou hast fainted over the Dead Ah! Ah!

> *Eve revives*   15

Eve—	Is this the Promise of Jehovah! O it is all a vain delusion Death & this Life & this Jehovah!
Jehovah—	Woman! lift thine eyes

> *A Voice is heard coming on*

Voice—	O Earth cover not thou my Blood! cover not thou my Blood[5] 20

> *Enter the Ghost of Abel*

Eve—	Thou Visionary Phantasm thou art not the real Abel.
Abel—	Among the Elohim[6] a Human Victim I wander I am their House,
	Prince of the Air & our dimensions compass Zenith & Nadir
	Vain is thy Covenant O Jehovah I am the Accuser & Avenger[7] 25
	Of Blood O Earth Cover not thou the Blood of Abel.

Jehovah—	What Vengeance dost thou require
Abel—	Life for Life! Life for Life![8]
Jehovah—	He who shall take Cain's life must also Die O Abel

---

2. Cf. the association of outline (as opposed to light and shade) and of melody (as opposed to harmony) with imagination in *Jerusalem* 74:24–26; see also the "bounding line" in *Descriptive Catalogue* (p. 431 herein).

3. The subject of a watercolor, *The Body of Abel Found by Adam and Eve* (c. 1805–9; Butlin 664); this is Adam and Eve's first encounter with death, the threatened result of their eating the forbidden fruit (Genesis 2:17).

4. Genesis 3:15; traditionally taken by Christians as a prophecy of Jesus' victory over Satan.

5. Alluding to Genesis 4:10, but the quotation is derived from Job 16:18.

6. Plural form of "God," alternating in Genesis with the ineffable name translated "Jehovah," represented by "the Lord." In Blake's time scholars had just begun to propose that texts with these different names derived from different sources.

7. Abel's ghost, in identifying himself with the "Prince of the Air" (an epithet for Satan, cf. Ephesians 2:2) and "the Accuser & Avenger," reveals himself to be evil; as Eve has correctly perceived, he is not "the real Abel."

8. The foundational concept of the whole law of retaliatory justice: "And if any mischief follow, then thou shalt give life for life, eye for eye, tooth for tooth, hand for hand, foot for foot, burning for burning, wound for wound, stripe for stripe" (Exodus 21:23–25). On Blake's possible reference to Byron's use of the phrase, see Angus Whitehead, *Notes and Queries* 53 (2006).

	And who is he? Adam wilt thou, or Eve thou, do this[9] 35
Adam—	It is all a Vain delusion of the all creative Imagination.

Eve come away & let us not believe these vain delusions
Abel is dead & Cain slew him! We shall also Die a Death
And then! what then! be as poor Abel a Thought: or as
This! O what shall I call thee Form Divine: Father of
    Mercies   35
That appearest to my Spiritual Vision: Eve seest thou also.

Eve—
  I see him plainly with my Mind's Eye, I see also Abel living:
Tho terribly afflicted as We also are, yet Jehovah sees him
Alive & not Dead: were it not better to believe Vision
With all our might & strength tho we are fallen & lost.   2

Adam—
  Eve thou hast spoken truly. Let us kneel before his feet.
    They Kneel before Jehovah

Abel—
  Are these the Sacrifices of Eternity O Jehovah, a Broken
    Spirit   5
And a Contrite Heart.[1] O I cannot Forgive! the Accuser hath
Enterd into Me as into his House & I loathe thy Tabernacles
As thou hast said so is it come to pass; My desire is unto
    Cain
And He doth rule over Me:[2] therefore My Soul in fumes
    of Blood
Cries for Vengeance: Sacrifice on Sacrifice Blood on
    Blood.   10

Jehovah—
  Lo I have given you a Lamb for an Atonement instead
Of the Transgresor, or no Flesh or Spirit could ever Live.

Abel—
  Compelled I cry O Earth cover not the Blood of Abel.
    Abel sinks down into the Grave, from which arises Satan
    Armed in glittering scales with a Crown & a Spear   15

Satan—
  I will have Human Blood & not the blood of Bulls or Goats
And no Atonement[3] O Jehovah the Elohim live on Sacrifice
Of Men; hence I am God of Men: Thou Human O Jehovah.
By the Rock & Oak of the Druid creeping Misletoe &
    Thorn
Cain's City built with Human Blood, not Blood of Bulls &
    Goats   20
Thou shalt Thyself be Sacrificed to Me thy God on
    Calvary.

Jehovah—
  Such is My Will: *Thunders*
                that Thou Thyself go to Eternal Death
In Self Annihilation even till Satan Self-subdud Put off
    Satan

---

9. I.e., if life-for-life retribution is to be exacted, then either Adam or Eve must kill this one remaining son; after that, the life of Cain's killer must be taken by the last person left on earth.
1. Close paraphrase of Psalm 51:17. Cf. "broken heart" and "contrite spirit" in Psalm 34:18.
2. A twist on both Eve's fallen relationship to Adam (Genesis 3:16) and the warning to Cain of the consequences of his jealous anger toward Abel.
3. Cf. biblical contexts for "I delight not in the blood of bullocks, or of lambs, or of he goats" (Isaiah 1:11; cf. Psalm 50:13) and "For it is not possible that the blood of bulls and of goats should take away sins" (Hebrews 10:4). Satan, speaking as the deity of the Druidic religion of human sacrifice, demands the blood of the "Human" Jehovah on Calvary.

Into the Bottomless Abyss whose torment arises for
    ever & ever[4]   25

On each side a Chorus of Angels entering Sing the following

The Elohim of the Heathen Swore Vengeance for Sin! Then
    Thou stoodst
Forth O Elohim Jehovah! in the midst of the darkness of the Oath!
    All Clothed
In Thy Covenant of the Forgiveness of Sins: Death O Holy! Is this
    Brotherhood
The Elohim saw their Oath Eternal Fire; they rolled apart trembling
    over The   30
Mercy Seat: each in his station fixt in the Firmament by Peace
    Brotherhood and Love.

The Curtain falls

The Voice of Abel's Blood

1822 W Blakes Original Stereotype was 1788[5]

ON HOMER'S POETRY /
ON VIRGIL (1822)

This single illuminated leaf, printed along with *The Ghost of Abel* about 1822
(Viscomi, 336), contains two distinct but related tractates on the Greek and
Latin classics, revolving around the relation of form and content. Both pieces,
as responses to specific texts, are reminiscent of Blake's marginalia, except that
they have been whittled down to a one-page grouping of complementary sets of
aphorisms, with broad implications for interpretation of visual and literary arts
in general. *On Homer's Poetry*, with its title centered at the top, is positioned as
the dominant work, while *On Virgil*, with its side-set title midway down the page,
looks like a subsection or corollary to the lead article. The inscription over
On Virgil, which editors traditionally have printed as the last sentence in *On
Homer's Poetry*, could equally well be considered the epigraph for *On Virgil*. *On
Homer's Poetry* challenges Aristotle's foundational statements on unity and character; *On Virgil* zeroes in on a single line of the *Aeneid* as a peg for accusing the
ancients of preferring war and empire to art. The upshot, for both pieces, is a
proclamation of the superiority of Christian or Gothic art to the Classics. For
commentary, see Essick and Viscomi, eds. *Milton a Poem and the Final Illuminated Works* (Blake Trust, 1993), 265–67. Our text, slightly repunctuated, is
based on a collation of the Blake Archive's transcriptions of Copies B and F, both
produced with all other copies in the same printing session.

---

4. Cf. the bottomless pit of eternal torment in Revelation 20:10. "Self Annihilation": see *Milton*
   48/41:2. For theological commentary, see Altizer, *The New Apocalypse* (1967).
5. The presumed date of *All Religions Are One* and *There Is No Natural Religion*, Blake's first works
   in illuminated printing. In 1819 Blake's friend Cumberland had asked his sons to tell the poet that
   someone else (probably the Scots engraver William Home Lizars [1788–1859], misidentifed by
   Cumberland as "Sivewright," Lizars's patron) had claimed "As his own invention Blakes Method"
   (Viscomi, *Blake and the Art of the Book* 337; *Blake Records* 2004, 344); another claimant to the
   invention is William Ged (Essick and Viscomi 263).

On Homer's Poetry

Every Poem must necessarily be a perfect Unity, but why Homer's is peculiarly so, I cannot tell; he has told the story of Bellerophon & omitted the Judgment of Paris which is not only a part, but a principal part of Homer's subject.[1]

But when a Work has Unity it is as much in a Part as in the Whole. The Torso is as much a Unity as the Laocoon.[2] As Unity is the cloke of folly so Goodness is the cloke of knavery. Those who will have Unity exclusively in Homer come out with a Moral like a sting in the tail: Aristotle says Characters are either Good or Bad:[3] now Goodness or Badness has nothing to do with Character. An Apple tree a Pear tree a Horse a Lion are Characters but a Good Apple tree or a Bad, is an Apple tree still: a Horse is not more a Lion for being a Bad Horse, that is its Character: its Goodness or Badness is another consideration.

It is the same with the Moral of a whole Poem as with the Moral Goodness of its parts. Unity & Morality are secondary considerations & belong to Philosophy & not to Poetry, to Exception & not to Rule, to Accident & not to Substance. The Ancients call'd it eating of the tree of good & evil.

The Classics, it is the Classics!
& not Goths nor Monks, that
Desolate Europe with Wars.

On Virgil

Sacred Truth has pronounced that Greece & Rome as Babylon & Egypt: so far from being parents of Arts & Sciences as they pretend: were destroyers

1. To illustrate the principle of unity of plot, according to which no part can be displaced or removed without damaging the whole, Aristotle cites Homer's omission of nonessential parts of Odysseus' story in the *Odyssey* (*Poetics* VIII). In Blake's counterexample of the *Iliad*, the action stops while the minor character Glaucus, grandson of Bellerophon, recounts the family saga to his opponent Diomedes (Book VI), yet Homer omits the first link in the chain of events leading to the Trojan War, Paris's selection of Aphrodite as the most beautiful goddess (subject of Blake's 1811 watercolor, Butlin 675), which led to her awarding Paris the most beautiful woman, Menalaus' wife Helen, and prompted her jealous rivals Athena and Hera to back the Greeks' effort to get her back. See Hazard Adams, "Must a Poem Be a Perfect Unity?" *Blake: Quarterly* 21, no. 2 (1987), 74–77 (but for "Tydeus" read "Glaucus").
2. Sketching plaster casts of these famous works from antiquity was part of every artist's training: both the Torso, a magnificent fragment of a muscular male, probably Hercules, and the Laocoon group, a Trojan priest and his two sons struggling with serpents (see יה *[Yah] & His Two Sons*), are in the Vatican Museum. In 1800 Napoleon claimed the Laocoon and other famous classical sculptures as spoils of war and brought them to Paris; after the British victory at Waterloo (1814), the plunder was returned to the Vatican, receiving much cultural attention.
3. The "first and most important" requirement of a character is that it "should be good" (*Poetics* XV); characters in tragedy should be between the extremes of good and bad (*Poetics* XIII).

of all Art. Homer Virgil & Ovid confirm this opinion & make us reverence The Word of God, the only light of antiquity that remains unperverted by War.[4] Virgil in the Eneid Book VI. line 848 says Let others study Art; Rome has somewhat better to do, namely War & Dominion.[5]

Rome & Greece swept Art into their maw & destroyd it. A Warlike State never can produce Art. It will Rob & Plunder & accumulate into one place, & Translate & Copy & Buy & Sell & Criticise, but not Make. Grecian is Mathematic Form. Gothic is Living Form.

Mathematic Form is Eternal in the Reasoning Memory. Living Form is Eternal Existence.

יה[YAH] & HIS TWO SONS SATAN & ADAM [THE LAOCOON] (1826)

Blake's final work in illuminated printing, a single broadsheet (c. 1826–27), is even more resistant than its predecessors to publication in the sequential lines of conventional typography. Its textual portion, an unruly array of lightly etched aphorisms, labels, mottoes, and expostulations in English, Hebrew, and Greek, crowds in on and loops around its visual portion, a highly finished engraving of *The Laocoon*, a famous Greco-Roman sculpture. The argumentative inscriptions, in various sizes and styles of lettering, operate as graffiti or marginalia, undermining the authority of the classical work to redefine it as a copy of a much greater Hebrew original and make it an emblem of derivative art, false religion, and such enemies of the creative imagination as empire, money, and morality. *The Laocoon* (pronounced Lay-OCK-uh-wan) itself is based on an episode in Virgil's *Aeneid* 2 (41–43, 201–33) in which a Trojan priest of that name is caught up with his two sons in the deadly coils of two hissing and biting serpents sent to punish him for trying to warn Troy against the Trojan horse. But in Blake's hands these personages become God and his "sons" Satan and Adam (the limits of opacity and contradiction in *Milton* 13:20 and *Jerusalem* 35:11), entangled in the suffocating intertwined constrictions of Good and Evil. Blake reportedly gave his young friend Samuel Palmer this print in response to questions about his beliefs, saying, "You will find my creed there" (*Blake Records* 2, 726); and indeed the thematic concerns of יה *[Yah] and His Two Sons* intersect with those of "The Everlasting Gospel" (c. 1818), *For the Sexes: The Gates of Paradise* (1820), *On Homer's Poetry/On Virgil* (1822), the *Illustrations of the Book of Job* (1825; not included in this edition), and the annotations to Thornton (1827).

The complex history of *The Laocoon*, attributed by Pliny to three Rhodian sculptors, is beyond our scope: it was excavated in Michelangelo's time, hailed as a masterpiece, widely reproduced in prints and plaster casts and made a standard part of the art-school curriculum, notoriously seized by Napoleon as a spoil of war in 1800, and then returned to the Vatican Museum after his 1814 defeat (see *On Homer's Poetry/On Virgil* notes). Of Blake's several alterations to the appearance of the sculptural group as he knew it in the Royal Academy's cast, the most subtle is his angling of the base with respect to the longer supporting block (the plinth), as if signaling that he was twisting the piece to serve his own purposes: the Greeks had wrested away and perverted the art of the Hebrews.

---

4. A notable change from Blake's position in his annotations to Watson (p. 456 herein).
5. Cited also in יה *[Yah] & His Two Sons.*

To accept the conventional title, "The Laocoön," for Blake's print is to obscure the artist's purposeful omission of any sort of reference to the story Virgil told.

The print's central image, as Rosamund Paice explains (*Blake: An Illustrated Quarterly* 37 [2003], 44–62), may date from 1815, when Blake was working on an engraving (1816) of this subject for Abraham Rees's *Cyclopaedia* (1802–20). For commentary, in addition to Paice, see Irene Tayler, *Blake Newsletter* 10:3 (Winter 1976–77), 72–81; David E. James, *PMLA* 98 (1983), 225–36; David Sten Herrstrom, *Bucknell Review* 30:1 (1986), 37–71; Wright, *Blake, Nationalism, and the Politics of Alienation* (2004); and (the main sources for our notes) Essick and Viscomi, eds. *Milton . . . and the Final Illuminated Works* (Blake Trust, 1993) and Paley, *The Traveller in the Evening* (2004). Our reading text, recast in conventional lines and lightly repunctuated, is derived from the Blake Archive's transcription of Copy B (Essick)—one of only two known imprints of the work—collated with facsimiles.

יה [Yah] & his two Sons Satan & Adam

[Full title (below the engraving of the *Laocoon* group)]

יה' & his two Sons Satan & Adam as they were copied from the Cherubim[2] of Solomon's Temple by three Rhodians[3] & applied to Natural Fact, or History of Ilium

[Emphasized in a burnished space on the base, or plinth, of the sculpture]
Drawn & Engraved by William Blake.
[Epigraph lightly scratched above title, an afterthought?]
If Morality was Christianity Socrates was the Saviour[4]

[Motto below title]
Art Degraded Imagination Denied War Governed the Nations

[Names for the central father figure (Yah)]

The Angel of the Divine Presence

מלאך יהוה [Angel of Yahweh]

ΟΦΙουΧος [Ophiucus][5]

---

1. The first syllable (Hebrew *Yod-He*, reading right to left) of the Tetragrammatron, God's ineffable name (usually transliterated YHWH, "Yahweh"), the I AM of Exodus 3:14. Too holy to be pronounced, the name is replaced in Scripture readings with "Adonai" (the Lord). In English, "Jehovah" (Exodus 6:3) is a transliteration of an artificial word combining the four consonants of YHWH and three vowels of Adonai.
2. In the Bible cherubim appear in pairs, not threes (as in this sculptural grouping): one ten-cubit-high pair in gold-covered olive wood, with a wall-to-wall wingspread, was made for Solomon's temple, to stand inside the "oracle," or Holy of Holies (1 Kings 6:23 ff.), the repository of the Ark of the Covenant and the Mercy Seat; the other pair, of pure gold, was made for the tabernacle in the wilderness, to cover the Mercy Seat (Exodus 25:18 ff.; 37:7 ff.). Cf. "wonderful originals" in *Descriptive Catalogue* No. 2.
3. Hagesander, Polydorus, and Athenodorus (Pliny the Elder, *Natural History* 36.37).
4. See marginalia to Thornton (n. 2, p. 468 herein).
5. Serpent holder (Greek); refers to a constellation in the north sky, a giant wrestling with a serpent. In *Milton* 41/37:50, it is the astral sign ruling the Canaanite king Sihon; cf. Milton's comparison of Satan to a comet: "That fires the length of Ophiucus huge / In th' Artick Sky, and from his horrid hair / Shakes Pestilence and War" (*Paradise Lost* 2:710–11). The Angel (messenger; Hebrew) of the Divine Presence, though not directly biblical, is drawn from Isaiah 63:9, "the angel of his presence," referring in turn to Exodus 23:20 (cf. Exodus 3:2). Exactly the same inscription appears in the border of the second design in Blake's first engraved series, *Illustrations of the Book of Job* (1825), and the serpent imagery appears in design five. In the biblical watercolor series, this lesser, fallen manifestation of the divine brings Eve to Adam and clothes the couple with animal skins after the fall (Butlin, 436).

[Labels for the serpents]

Evil [Head attacking the younger son (presumably Adam) on Yah's right (viewer's left)]
Good [Head attacking Yah's left side near the older son (presumably Satan), on the viewer's right]

[Comments nearest the main figures, Yah, Adam, and Satan]

[Yah] Hebrew art is called Sin by the Deist Science
All that we See is Vision from Generated Organs gone as soon as come Permanent in The Imagination, Considered as Nothing by the Natural Man

The Gods of Priam are the Cherubim of Moses & Solomon The Hosts of Heaven
Without Unceasing Practise nothing can be done Practise is Art If you leave off you are Lost

[Adam] Good & Evil are Riches & Poverty a Tree of Misery propagating Generation & Death

[Satan] Satan's Wife the Goddess Nature is War & Misery & Heroism a Miser / לילית [Lilith][6]

[Leading statements at the top of the page]

Where any view of Money exists Art cannot be carried on, but War only by pretences to the Two Impossibilities Chastity & Abstinence Gods of the Heathen Read Matthew C X. 9 & 10v
He repented that he had made Adam (of the Female, the Adamah) & it grieved him at his heart.[7]

[Other comments on the horizontal plane]

Art can never exist without Naked Beauty displayed
The Gods of Greece & Egypt were Mathematical Diagrams See Plato's Works
Divine Union Deriding And Denying Immediate Communion with God
The Spoilers say Where are his Works that he did in the Wilderness
Lo what are these / Whence came they
These are not the Works Of Egypt nor Babylon Whose Gods are the Powers / Of this World. Goddess, Nature. Who first spoil & then destroy Imaginative Art / For their Glory is War and Dominion Empire against Art See Virgil's Eneid. Lib. VI.v [8]
For every Pleasure Money Is Useless

There are States in which all Visionary Men are accounted Mad Men / such are Greece & Rome Such is Empire or Tax See Luke Ch 2.v l

---

6. Translated "screech owl" in Isaiah 34:14; in Jewish legend, Adam's first wife, a demonness. Here, as Satan's wife, she rules nature and is identified with war and its consequences. She is a "Miser," in Blake's etymological wordplay, who causes "Misery."
7. Quoting Genesis 6:6, but Blake reads "on the earth" as "from the earth" and replaces "earth" with a transliteration of the feminine noun in Hebrew.
8. Quoted (and footnoted) in *On Homer's Poetry*. The "Works . . . in the Wilderness" are itemized in Psalm 78:11–20.

[Vertical interjection among horizontal inscriptions]

What can be Created Can be Destroyed / Adam is only The Natural Man & not the Soul or Imagination

[Along left side, near Adam, beginning with the leading statement (in larger lettering)]

The Eternal Body of Man is The Imagination,

that is   God himself   }   ישע[9] Jesus we are his Members
       The Divine Body }

It manifests itself in his Works of Art (In Eternity All is Vision)
The True Christian Charity not dependent on Money (the life's blood of Poor Families) that is on Caesar or Empire or Natural Religion / Money, which is The Great Satan or Reason the Root of Good & Evil In The Accusation of Sin

[near left margin]

Spiritual War
Israel deliverd from Egypt is Art deliverd from Nature & Imitation

A Poet a Painter a Musician an Architect: the Man Or Woman who is not one of these is not a Christian
You must leave Fathers & Mothers & Houses & Lands if they stand in the way of Art
Prayer is the Study of / Art Praise is the Practise of Art / Fasting &c. all relate to Art
The outward Ceremony is Antichrist

[Along right side, beginning with statement in larger lettering near top of page, continuing from the right margin and moving toward Satan]

The Old & New Testaments are the Great Code of Art Art is the Tree of Life GOD is Jesus / The whole Business of Man is the Arts and All things Common

Jesus & his Apostles & Disciples were all Artists Their Works were destroyd by the Seven Angels of the Seven Churches in Asia Antichrist Science The unproductive Man is not a Christian much less the Destroyer

Christianity is Art & not Money / Money is its Curse
What we call Antique Gems are the Gems of Aaron's Breast Plate[1]

Is not every Vice possible to Man described in the Bible openly
All is not Sin that Satan calls so all the Loves & Graces of Eternity

9. Consonants for "Yeshua" (Joshua), the name rendered Ιησους (Jesus) in the New Testament.
1. Blake engraved a plate for Rees's article on gem engraving, which traces the Greco-Roman art to the carving of the twelve tribes' names "like engravings in a signet" on the gems of Aaron's breastplate (Exodus 28:21), another example of a stolen Hebrew original (Essick and Viscomi, eds., *Milton . . . and the Final Illuminated Works*, p. 276).

OTHER WRITINGS

FROM POETICAL SKETCHES (1783)†

TO SPRING¹

O thou, with dewy locks, who lookest down
Thro' the clear windows of the morning; turn
Thine angel eyes upon our western isle,
Which in full choir hails thy approach, O Spring!

The hills tell each other, and the list'ning   5
Vallies hear; all our longing eyes are turned
Up to thy bright pavillions: issue forth,
And let thy holy feet² visit our clime.

Come o'er the eastern hills, and let our winds
Kiss thy perfumed garments;³ let us taste   10
Thy morn and evening breath; scatter thy pearls
Upon our love-sick land⁴ that mourns for thee.

O deck her forth with thy fair fingers; pour
Thy soft kisses on her bosom; and put
Thy golden crown upon her languish'd head,⁵   15
Whose modest tresses were bound up for thee!

TO SUMMER

O thou, who passest thro' our vallies in
Thy strength, curb thy fierce steeds, allay the heat
That flames from their large nostrils! thou, O Summer,

---

† In 1783, the Reverend A. S. Mathew and his wife, Harriet, whose literary salon Blake attended, joined another friend, the sculptor John Flaxman, in having Blake's first volume of poems printed at their expense, for the author to sell or circulate as he saw fit. The book appeared in letterpress, without illuminations, in a small edition, attributed simply to "W.B."; for a facsimile, see Bentley's *William Blake's Works in Conventional Typography* (1984). Twenty-two copies are extant, a few with typographical errors corrected in Blake's hand. Apparently Blake never offered the *Sketches* for sale.

According to an unsigned prefatory note, Blake composed these poems between his twelfth and twentieth years (1769–77), a period roughly corresponding to his apprenticeship as an engraver. This selection, with typographical errors corrected and punctuation very slightly modified from the eighteenth-century conventions of the original, centers on short poems that anticipate some of Blake's later themes and techniques. The full collection includes experiments in such popular late-eighteenth-century genres and subjects as the historical or legendary verse drama, the ballad, and the "Ossianic" prose-poem (see headnote to *Visions*). For detailed commentary, see Margaret Ruth Lowery, *Windows of the Morning* (1940); Michael J. Tolley, "Blake's Songs of Spring," in Paley and Phillips (1973); Robert F. Gleckner, *Blake's Prelude* (1982); Mark L. Greenberg, ed. *Speak Silence: Rhetoric and Culture in Blake's Poetical Sketches* (1996); and Susan J. Wolfson's chapter on this work in her *Formal Charges* (1997).

1. Pope's first volume of poetry (*Pastorals*, 1709), written at age sixteen, was organized according to the four seasons; the most famous eighteenth-century seasonal cycle was James Thompson's *The Seasons* (1716–30). Imagery of the personified Spring's approach recalls Psalm 65:9–13; the Song of Solomon 2:8, 3:6; and Horace, *Odes* 1.4.
2. Cf. "Song: 'Fresh from the dewy hill' " (lines 7, 16), anticipating "those feet" in the prefatory lyric for *Milton*.
3. Worn by a Middle Eastern bridegroom (Song of Solomon 3:6).
4. I.e., England, the bride.
5. Derives from Milton's *Comus* 744 and *Samson Agonistes* 119.

Oft pitched'st here thy golden tent, and oft
Beneath our oaks hast slept, while we beheld   5
With joy, thy ruddy limbs and flourishing hair.[6]

Beneath our thickest shades we oft have heard
Thy voice, when noon upon his fervid car
Rode o'er the deep of heaven; beside our springs
Sit down, and in our mossy vallies, on   10
Some bank beside a river clear, throw thy
Silk draperies off, and rush into the stream:
Our vallies love the Summer in his pride.

Our bards are fam'd who strike the silver wire:
Our youth are bolder than the southern swains: 15
Our maidens fairer in the sprightly dance:
We lack not songs, nor instruments of joy,
Nor echoes sweet, nor waters clear as heaven,
Nor laurel wreaths against the sultry heat.

TO AUTUMN

O Autumn, laden with fruit, and stained
With the blood of the grape, pass not, but sit
Beneath my shady roof, there thou may'st rest,
And tune thy jolly voice to my fresh pipe;
And all the daughters of the year shall dance!   5
Sing now the lusty song of fruits and flowers.

"The narrow bud opens her beauties to
The sun, and love runs in her thrilling veins;
Blossoms hang round the brows of morning, and
Flourish down the bright cheek of modest eve,   10
Till clust'ring Summer breaks forth into singing,
And feather'd clouds strew flowers round her head.

The spirits of the air live on the smells
Of fruit; and joy, with pinions light, roves round
The gardens, or sits singing in the trees."   15
Thus sang the jolly Autumn as he sat,
Then rose, girded himself, and o'er the bleak
Hills fled from our sight; but left his golden load.

TO WINTER[7]

O Winter! bar thine adamantine doors:
The north is thine; there hast thou built thy dark

6. Cf. "ruddy limbs & flaming hair" in "Abstinence sows sand all over," p. 389.
7. The chilling atmosphere recalls that of William Collins's *Ode to Fear* and Thomson's *Winter*, the poem that made the Icelandic volcano Mount Hecla (line 16) famous in Europe (Lowery 152–155); there is another Mount Hecla in the Outer Hebrides. All four of the seasonal personifications anticipate Blake's forging of myths uniting human perceptions and natural phenomena.

Deep-founded habitation. Shake not thy roofs,
Nor bend thy pillars with thine iron car.

He hears me not, but o'er the yawning deep 5
Rides heavy; his storms are unchain'd; sheathed
In ribbed steel, I dare not lift mine eyes;
For he hath rear'd his sceptre o'er the world.

Lo! now the direful monster, whose skin clings
To his strong bones, strides o'er the groaning rocks: 10
He withers all in silence, and his hand
Unclothes the earth, and freezes up frail life.

He takes his seat upon the cliffs, the mariner
Cries in vain. Poor little wretch! that deal'st
With storms; till heaven smiles, and the monster 15
Is driv'n yelling to his caves beneath mount Hecla.

TO THE EVENING STAR[8]

Thou fair-hair'd angel of the evening,
Now, while the sun rests on the mountains, light
Thy bright torch of love;[9] thy radiant crown
Put on, and smile upon our evening bed!
Smile on our loves; and, while thou drawest the 5
Blue curtains of the sky, scatter thy silver dew
On every flower that shuts its sweet eyes
In timely sleep. Let thy west wind sleep on
The lake; speak silence with thy glimmering eyes,
And wash the dusk with silver. Soon, full soon, 10
Dost thou withdraw; then the wolf rages wide,
And the lion glares thro' the dun forest:
The fleeces of our flocks are cover'd with
Thy sacred dew: protect them with thine influence.

SONG[1]

How sweet I roam'd from field to field,
And tasted all the summer's pride,
'Till I the prince of love beheld,
Who in the sunny beams did glide!

He shew'd me lilies for my hair, 5
And blushing roses for my brow;
He led me through his gardens far,
Where all his golden pleasures grow,

8. The planet Venus, the love goddess who is being implored to bless the lovers' bed.
9. Recalls Psyche's signal to Cupid.
1. According to Blake's friend Thomas Malkin (see the chronology, 1806), Blake wrote this poem
   before he was fourteen years old.

With sweet May dews my wings were wet,
And Phoebus fir'd my vocal rage;   10
He caught me in his silken net,
And shut me in his golden cage.[2]

He loves to sit and hear me sing,
Then, laughing, sports and plays with me;
Then stretches out my golden wing,   15
And mocks my loss of liberty.

SONG

Love and harmony combine,
And around our souls intwine,
While thy branches mix with mine,
And our roots together join.[3]

Joys upon our branches sit,   5
Chirping loud, and singing sweet;
Like gentle streams beneath our feet
Innocence and virtue meet.

Thou the golden fruit dost bear,
I am clad in flowers fair;   10
Thy sweet boughs perfume the air,
And the turtle buildeth there.[4]

There she sits and feeds her young,
Sweet I hear her mournful song;
And thy lovely leaves among,   15
There is love: I hear his[5] tongue.

There his charming nest doth lay,
There he sleeps the night away;
There he sports along the day,
And doth among our branches play.   20

MAD SONG[6]

The wild winds weep,
And the night is a-cold;

---

2. Cf. "Wives are as birds in golden cages kept" (Davies, *A Contention betwixt a Wife, a Widow, and a Maid* [1608]), noted in Bloom, *The Visionary Company* (1961). See also "Matrimony's Golden Cage," in Quid's song "Hail Matrimony," *An Island in the Moon.* The sun-god Phoebus Apollo is here a teasing love god.
3. Sometimes pronounced "jine" in the eighteenth century.
4. The turtledove, both a lovebird and a sign of spring, appears in a famous line of the biblical love poem, the Song of Solomon (2:12): "The voice of the turtle is heard in our land."
5. Printed as "her" but corrected by hand to refer to "love" or a male bird, described in the next stanza.
6. Cf. the mad songs in *King Lear*, Act 3.

Come hither, Sleep,
And my griefs infold:[7]
But lo! the morning peeps   5
Over the eastern steeps,
And the rustling birds[8] of dawn
The earth do scorn.

Lo! to the vault
Of paved heaven,   10
With sorrow fraught
My notes are driven:
They strike the ear of night,
Make weep the eyes of day;
They make mad the roaring winds,   15
And with tempests play.

Like a fiend in a cloud[9]
With howling woe,
After night I do croud,
And with night will go;   20
I turn my back to the east,
From whence comforts have increas'd;
For light doth seize my brain
With frantic pain.

TO THE MUSES

Whether on Ida's shady brow,[1]
Or in the chambers of the East,
The chambers of the sun, that now
From antient melody have ceas'd;

Whether in Heav'n ye wander fair,   5
Or the green corners of the earth,
Or the blue regions of the air,
Where the melodious winds have birth;

Whether on chrystal rocks ye rove,
Beneath the bosom of the sea   10
Wand'ring in many a coral grove,
Fair Nine, forsaking Poetry!

---

7. Hand-corrected from "unfold."
8. Corrected from "beds."
9. Occurs again in "Infant Sorrow" (line 4).
1. Either Mount Ida on Crete, where Saturn ruled and Zeus was reared, or another Mount Ida near
   Troy, where the Judgment of Paris took place and the gods watched the Trojan War. The theme
   of the Westering of Culture from Greece to Britain, following the spirit of freedom, was set forth
   in Thomas Gray's "The Progress of Poesy" (1754) 2.3:12–17; Blake was later to depict the
   Muses' flight from "tyrant Power" in his 1799 illustrations of Gray (Butlin, 335:48; see the
   chronology).

How have you left the antient love
That bards of old enjoy'd in you!
The languid strings do scarcely move!   15
The sound is forc'd, the notes are few![2]

[AN ISLAND IN THE MOON] (1785)[†]

[Chapter 1]

In the Moon,[1] is a certain Island near by a mighty continent, which small island seems to have some affinity to England, & what is more extraordinary the people are so much alike & their language so much the same that you would think you was among your friends. In this Island dwells three Philosophers: Suction the Epicurean, Quid[2] the Cynic, & Sipsop the

---

2. The Celtic and classical traditions of poetry are imagined once to have been united. Now the derivative neoclassical poets among Blake's contemporaries, deserted by the muses, manage only a few feeble forced notes. Blake renews the bardic tradition in "The Voice of the Ancient Bard," the "Introduction" to *Songs of Experience*, and later works in which the ideal poet is the British bard rather than the Greek lyrist.

† This early venture into satiric fiction (c. 1785)—a form that came into its own, in the Romantic era, with Thomas Love Peacock—survives in an untitled manuscript that lacks one or more leaves near the end; the final portion, which fills only half of a new leaf, seems to break off without a conclusion. Nevertheless, *An Island in the Moon* (a title derived from the manuscript's first sentence) succeeds brilliantly as a send-up of artsy pseudo-intellectuals, rendered in the endearingly silly British music-hall style preserved and internationally popularized by Monty Python. Occasionally the outside world breaks in through voices of street vendors or fleeting references to poverty, disease, or pain; and the shallowness and emptiness of coterie life can be sensed in the characters' constant drifting from house to house, their loony non-sequitur arguments that go nowhere, their isolation amid unending chatter. Yet these bored, disengaged Moon people are the first to sing "Holy Thursday," "Nurse's Song," and "The Little Boy Lost" (cf. *Songs of Innocence*), conversation-stopping songs with such power of innocence that "nobody could sing any longer." But the moment quickly passes, and the next song is about a rough children's game of cricket, involving a dirty ball and a black eye.

  In this worldly wise sketch, which takes as its comic premise the surprising similarity between party talk on a lunar Island and that of a London drawing room, three anchor commentators, nominal disciples of the classical philosophers Epicurus (whose highest good is pleasure), the Cynics (who scoff at everything), and Pythagoras (for whom mathematics and mysticism are one), provide a thin thread of continuity. Most critics think Blake's heart lies closest to Quid the Cynic, intellectual descendant of Diogenes the Cynic, the scourge and scandal of Athens (celebrated in *Marriage* 13). As is usual in satire, *An Island* responds to the fashions and foibles of its time, and most of its fifteen characters have been conjecturally identified with Blake's contemporaries, especially those associated with the salon of his patroness Harriett Mathew (see the chronology and the dagger note to *Poetical Sketches*). Our identifications of selected luminaries are culled from Erdman's *Prophet against Empire* (3rd ed., 1977), Martha W. England's contribution to *Blake's Visionary Forms Dramatic* (1970), G. M. Harper's *The Neoplatonism of William Blake* (1961), and, especially, Michael Phillips's comprehensive annotations in his William Blake, *An Island in the Moon, A Facsimile of the Manuscript* (1987); see also K. E. Smith, *An Analysis of Blake's Early Works* (1999) and chapter 5 in Nick Rawlinson, *William Blake's Comic Vision* (2003). The boisterous good humor and sheer theatricality of the work is evident in a 1983 Cornell University performance organized and placed online by Joseph Viscomi (www.ibiblio.org/jsviscom/island).

  The 1782–85 period of composition is inferred from references to current events and from Phillips's examination of various inks in layers of the manuscript. We have lightly repunctuated the text, a collation of the Erdman edition with Phillips's transcription, corrected a few obvious slips of the pen, and altered the layout to make the fast-paced dialogue easier to follow.

1. Vincent Lunardi's September 1784 balloon ascent near London stimulated moon/balloon, Lunardi/lunatic wordplay and such ephemera as *The air-balloon; or, the sages adventures in a flight to the moon*. Cf. Hogarth, *Some of the Principal Inhabitants of the MOON as they Were Perfectly Discovered by a Telescope* (1724); Cyrano de Bergerac, *A Voyage to the Moon*, trans. Derrick (1754); Aphra Behn, *The Emperor of the Moon* (1757).

2. What, this, something, essence (Latin). Also slang for the British pound sterling.

Pythagorean. I call them by the names of these sects tho the sects are not ever mentiond there as being quite out of date however the things still remain, and the vanities are the same. The three Philosophers sat together thinking of nothing. In comes -

Etruscan Column the Antiquarian[3] & after an abundance of Enquiries to no purpose sat himself down & described something that nobody listend to. So they were employd when Mrs Gimblet came in. The corners of her mouth seemd I dont know how, but very odd as if she hoped you had not an ill opinion of her. To be sure we are all poor creatures. Well she seated & seemd to listen with great attention while the Antiquarian seemd to be talking of virtuous cats,[4] but it was not so. She was thinking of the shape of her eyes & mouth & he was thinking of his eternal fame. The three Philosophers at this time were each endeavouring to conceal his laughter, (not at them but) at his own imaginations. This was the situation of this improving company, when in a great hurry, Inflammable Gass the Wind finder[5] enterd. They seemd to rise & salute each other.

Etruscan Column & Inflammable Gass fixd their eyes on each other, their tongues went in question & answer, but their thoughts were otherwise employd.

I dont like his eyes said Etruscan Column. He's a foolish puppy said Inflammable Gass, smiling on him. The 3 Philosophers, the Cynic smiling the Epicurean seeming studying the flame of the candle & the Pythagorean playing with the cat, listend with open mouths to the edifying discourses.

Sir said the Antiquarian I have seen these works & I do affirm that they are no such thing. They seem to me to be the most wretched paltry flimsy Stuff that ever

—What d'ye say What dye say said Inflammable Gass, why why I wish I could see you write so.

Sir said the Antiquarian, according to my opinion the author is an errant[6] blockhead.

—Your reason Your reason said Inflammable Gass—why why I think it very abominable to call a man a blockhead that you know nothing of.

—Reason Sir said the Antiquarian I'll give you an example for your reason. As I was walking along the street I saw a vast number of swallows on the rails of an old Gothic square. They seemd to be going on their passage, as Pliny[7] says. As I was looking up, a little outré fellow pulling me by the

3. Under Basire, Blake made engravings for the Society of Antiquaries, which elected the Reverend John Brand (1744–1806) secretary in 1784.
4. The stage comedian Samuel Foote spoofed the Antiquaries' discussion of Dick Whittington's (?1358–1423) cat, who saved London from a plague of rats.
5. Proposed models include theologian and chemist Joseph Priestley (1733–1804), member of the Lunar Society in Birmingham, whose discovery of oxygen (1774) intensified popular interest in "airs," or gases; chemist and physicist Henry Cavendish (1731–1810), who discovered "inflammable air" or hydrogen (1766); William Nicolson (1753–1815), author of An Introduction to Natural Philosophy (1782), for which Blake etched a title vignette; the Prussian illusionist Gustavus Katterfelto (d. 1799), who performed three "scientific" stage shows daily (1783–84); and Dr. George Fordyce (1736–1802), who supplied hydrogen for Lunardi's balloon. Joseph Wright of Derby painted many scenes of scientific experimentation such as Experiment on a Bird in the Air Pump (1768).
6. Variant of "arrant" (unmitigated, notorious), here punning on "error." (Primary meaning: wandering.) The writer whose works they are debating turns out to be Voltaire.
7. Pliny the Elder (23–79 c.e.) mentions the migration of swallows in Natural History (10:24); cited in Thomas Pennant, British Zoology (1768–70), 1:220.

sleeve cries pray Sir who do all they belong to. I turnd my self about with great contempt. Said I, Go along you fool.

—Fool said he who do you call fool I only askd you a civil question

—I had a great mind to have thrashd the fellow only he was bigger than I—here Etruscan column left off—

Inflammable Gass, recollecting himself. Indeed I do not think the man was a fool for he seems to me to have been desirous of enquiring into the works of nature.

—Ha Ha Ha, said the Pythagorean.

It was reechod by Inflammable Gass to overthrow the argument—

Etruscan Column then starting up & clenching both his fists was prepared to give a formal answer to the company But Obtuse Angle,[8] entering the room having made a gentle bow, proceeded to empty his pockets of a vast number of papers, turned about & sat down wiped his face with his pocket handkerchief & shutting his eyes began to scratch his head.

—Well gentlemen said he what is the cause of strife. The Cynic answerd, they are only quarreling about Voltaire.

—Yes said the Epicurean & having a bit of fun with him.

And said the Pythagorean endeavoring to incorporate their souls with their bodies.

Obtuse Angle giving a grin said Voltaire understood nothing of the Mathematics and a man must be a fool i'faith not to understand the Mathematics.

Inflammable Gass turning round hastily in his chair said Mathematics, he found out a number of Queries[9] in Philosophy.

Obtuse Angle shutting his eyes & saying that he always understood better when he shut his eyes said In the first place it is of no use for a man to make Queries but to solve them, for a man may be a fool & make Queries but a man must have good sound sense to solve them. A query & an answer are as different as a strait line & a crooked one. Secondly

I, I, I, aye Secondly, Voltaire's a fool, says the Epicurean.

—Pooh says the Mathematician scratching his head with double violence, it is not worth Quarreling about.

—The Antiquarian here got up—& hemming twice to shew the strength of his Lungs, said but my Good Sir, Voltaire was immersed in matter, & seems to have understood very little but what he saw before his eyes, like the Animal upon the Pythagoreans lap always playing with its own tail.

Ha Ha Ha said Inflammable Gass he was the Glory of France—I have got a bottle of air that would spread a Plague.

Here the Antiquarian shruggd up his shoulders & was silent while Inflammable Gass talkd for half an hour.

When Steelyard[1] the lawgiver coming in stalking—with an act of parliament in his hand said that it was a shameful thing that acts of parliament

---

8. Possibly Thomas Taylor "the Platonist" (1758–1835), with whom Blake studied geometry. Blake depicts geometrical diagrams in his title page engraving for John Bonnycastle's *An Introduction to Mensuration* (1782).
9. Voltaire's *The Ignorant Philosopher* (trans. 1767, 1779) is organized as a series of questions. But the best-known "Queries" are those Newton appended to his most accessible work, *Opticks* (1704; expanded 1718), one of which is discussed in Voltaire's *The Metaphysics of Sir Isaac Newton* (trans. 1747).
1. A set of scales. For more on this character, see Chapter 8.

should be in a free state, it had so engrossed his mind that he did not salute the company. Mrs Gimblet drew her mouth downwards.

Chap 2d

Tilly Lally the Siptippidist, Aradobo the dean of Morocco, Miss Gittipin, Mrs Nannicantipot, Mrs Sigtagatist, Gibble Gabble the wife of Inflammable Gass—& Little Scopprell enterd the room.

(If I have not presented you with every character in the piece call me ass.)

Chap 3d

In the Moon as Phebus stood over his oriental Gardening—O ay come Ill sing you a song said the Cynic.

    The trumpeter shit in his hat said the Epicurean
    & clapt it on his head said the Pythagorean.

    Ill begin again said the Cynic
        Little Phebus came strutting in
        With his fat belly & his round chin
        What is it you would please to have
        Ho Ho
        I wont let it go at only so & so

Mrs Gimblet lookd as if they meant her. Tilly Lally laught like a Cherry clapper.

    Aradobo askd who was Phebus Sir.

    Obtuse Angle answerd, quickly, He was the God of Physic, Painting Perspective Geometry Geography Astronomy, Cookery, Chymistry, Mechanics, Tactics Pathology Phraseology Theology Mythology Astrology Osteology, Somatology.[2] In short every art & science adorn'd him as beads round his neck. Here Aradobo lookd Astonishd & askd if he understood Engraving.

    —Obtuse Angle Answerd indeed he did.

    —Well said the other he was as great as Chatterton.[3]

Tilly Lally turnd round to Obtuse Angle & askd who it was that was as great as Chatterton.

    Hay, how should I know Answerd Obtuse Angle. Who was It Aradobo.

    Why sir said he the Gentleman that the song was about.

    Ah said Tilly Lally I did not hear it, what was it Obtuse Angle.

    Pooh said he Nonsense.

    Mhm said Tilly Lally

    —It was Phebus said the Epicurean

    Ah that was the Gentleman said Aradobo.

    Pray Sir said Tilly Lally who was Phebus.

    Obtuse Angle answer the heathens in the old ages usd to have Gods that they worshipd & they usd to sacrifice to them you have read about that in the bible.

2. Extrapolated from attributes of the moon goddess Phoebe's twin brother Phoebus Apollo, god of the sun, poetry, music, and medicine (or "physic"; also: purgative, laxative). Jonathan Richardson, *Theory of Painting* (1715), recommends Osteology, the study of bones, among other disciplines, to painters.
3. At age fifteen, Thomas Chatterton (1752–1770) of Bristol began publishing (faked) fifteenth-century manuscripts. His death in a garret from arsenic and laudanum poisoning at age seventeen, a few months after moving to London to support himself by his pen, fueled the myth of the starving, unappreciated artist. Debate on the authenticity of his posthumously published poems by the monk "Rowley" (Blake owned a 1778 edition) raged into the 1780s. Chapters 5 and 7 return to this subject.

Ah said Aradobo I thought I had read of Phebus in the Bible.

—Aradobo you should always think before you speak said Obtuse Angle

—Ha Ha Ha he means Pharaoh said Tilly Lally

—I am ashamd of you making use of the names in the Bible said M^rs. Sigtagatist.

Ill tell you what Mrs Sinagain[4] I dont think theres any harm in it, said Tilly Lally

—No said Inflammable Gass. I have got a camera obscura[5] at home. What was it you was talking about.

Law said Tilly Lally what has that to do with Pharaoh

—Pho nonsense hang Pharoh & all his host said the Pythagorean. Sing away Quid— Then the Cynic sung

> Honour & Genius is all I ask
> And I ask the Gods no more[6]
> No more No more No more No more the three Philosophers
>   bear Chorus

Here Aradobo suckd his under lip.

Chap 4

Hang names said the Pythagorean whats Pharoh better than Phebus or Phebus than Pharoh.

Hang them both said the Cynic.

Dont be prophane said Mrs Sigtagatist.

Why said Mrs Nannicantipot I dont think its prophane to say hang Pharoh.

Ah said M^rs. Sinagain, I'm sure you ought to hold your tongue, for you never say any thing about the scriptures, & you hinder your husband from going to church.

—Ha Ha said Inflammable Gass what dont you like to go to church.

No said Mrs Nannicantipot I think a person may be as good at home.

If I had not a place of profit that forces me to go to church said Inflammable Gass Id see the parsons all hangd a parcel of lying—

O said Mrs Sigtagatist if it was not for churches & chapels I should not have livd so long—there was I up in a Morning at four o clock when I was a Girl. I would run like the dickins till I was all in a heat. I would stand till I was ready to sink into the earth. Ah Mr Huffcap[7] would kick the bottom of the Pulpit out, with Passion, would tear off the sleeve of his Gown, & set his wig on fire & throw it at the people. Hed cry & stamp & kick & sweat and all for the good of their souls.

4. A sarcastic alternative name for Mrs. Sigtagatist, repeated in Chapter 4.
5. Dark room (Latin): a box in which light enters a pinhole at one end, projecting an inverted image of exterior objects onto the opposite side; used in ancient China, Greece, and Arabia to view eclipses of the sun. Described by Leonardo and, with improvements of a lens and a mirror, used by sixteenth- to eighteenth-century artists and amateurs as an aid to perspective drawing. Some eighteenth-century science shows featured a camera obscura "microscope" that projected enlarged images of live insects, held between two glass "sliders," onto a screen, as in Chapter 10.
6. In James Harris's *Daphnis and Amaryllis* (1766), set to music by Handel, Phillis sings of the Nymphs' perfect year-around contentment with only "A bleating flock, an humble cot" and "simple food": "We ask the Gods no more." Scopprel returns to this refrain in Chapter 9.
7. Conjecturally based on the charismatic (and cross-eyed) Methodist evangelist George Whitefield (1714–1770), called "Squintum" in the epilogue to Foote's *The Minor* (1760).

—Im sure he must be a wicked villain said Mrs Nannicantipot a passionate wretch. If I was a man Id wait at the bottom of the pulpit stairs & knock him down & run away.

—You would You Ignorant jade I wish I could see you hit any of the ministers. You deserve to have your ears boxed you do.

—Im sure this is not religion answers the other.

—Then Mr Inflammable Gass ran & shovd his head into the fire & set his hair all in a flame & ran about the room— No No he did not I was only making a fool of you.

Chap 5

Obtuse Angle Scopprell Aradobo & Tilly Lally are all met in Obtuse Angles study—

Pray said Aradobo is Chatterton a Mathematician.

No said Obtuse Angle how can you be so foolish as to think he was.

Oh I did not think he was I only askd said Aradobo.

How could you think he was not, & ask if he was said Obtuse Angle.

—Oh no Sir I did think he was before you told me but afterwards I thought he was not.

Obtuse Angle said in the first place you thought he was & then afterwards when I said he was not you thought he was not. Why I know that.

—Oh no sir I thought that he was not but I askd to know whether he was.

—How can that be said Obtuse Angle how could you ask & think that he was not

—Why said he. It came into my head that he was not.

—Why then said Obtuse Angle you said that he was.

Did I say so Law I did not think I said that.

—Did not he said Obtuse Angle

Yes said Scopprell.

But I meant said Aradobo I I I cant think Law Sir I wish youd tell me, how it is.

Then Obtuse Angle put his chin in his hand & said when ever you think you must always think for yourself

—How Sir said Aradobo, whenever I think I must think myself—I think I do—in the first place said he with a grin.

—Poo Poo said Obtuse Angle dont be a fool—

Then Tilly Lally took up a Quadrant & askd. Is not this a sun dial.

Yes said Scopprell but its broke—at this moment the three Philosophers enterd and lowring darkness hoverd oer the assembly.

Come said the Epicurean lets have some rum & water & hang the mathematics. Come Aradobo say some thing.

Then Aradobo began In the first place I think I think in the first place that Chatterton was clever at Fissic Follogy, Pistinology, Aridology, Arography, Transmography Phizography, Hogamy HAtomy, & hall that but in the first place he eat wery little wickly. That is he slept very little which he brought into a consumsion, & what was that that he took Fissic or somethink & so died.

So all the people in the book enterd into the room & they could not talk any more to the present purpose.

Chap 6

They all went home & left the Philosophers. Then Suction Askd if Pindar was not a better Poet, than Ghiotto was a Painter

Plutarch has not the life of Ghiotto said Sipsop.[8]

No said Quid. To be sure he was an Italian.

Well said Suction that is not any proof.

Plutarch was a nasty ignorant puppy said Quid. I hate your sneaking rascals. Theres Aradobo in ten or twelve years will be a far superior genius.

Ah, said the Pythagorean. Aradobo will make a very clever fellow.

Why said Quid I think that any natural fool would make a clever fellow if he was properly brought up.

—Ah hang your reasoning said the Epicurean I hate reasoning I do every thing by my feelings—

Ah said Sipsop, I only wish Jack Tearguts[9] had had the cutting of Plutarch. He understands anatomy better than any of the Ancients. He'll plunge his knife up to the hilt in a single drive and thrust his fist in, and all in the space of a Quarter of an hour. He does not mind their crying—tho they cry ever so he'll Swear at them & keep them down with his fist & tell them that he'll scrape their bones if they dont lay still & be quiet—What the devil should the people in the hospital that have it done for nothing, make such a piece of work for.

Hang that said Suction let us have a Song.

Then the Cynic sang

When old corruption[1] first begun
Adornd in yellow vest
He committed on flesh a whoredom
O what a wicked beast

2

From them a callow babe did spring
And old corruption smild
To think his race should never end
For now he had a child

3

He calld him Surgery & fed
The babe with his own milk
For flesh & he could neer agree
She would not let him suck

4

And this he always kept in mind
And formd a crooked knife

8. Plutarch's *Lives* (99–107 c.e.) of eminent Greeks and Romans does not include Pindar (518–438 b.c.e.). Giotto's exclusion is of course based on his lifespan (1267–1337), not his nationality.
9. Blake crossed out "Hunter" to write "Tearguts." The great surgeon John Hunter (1728–1793) had recently delivered lectures on muscular motion (1776–82), based on experiments with live animals; his Hunterian Museum (now in the Royal College of Surgeons) exhibited body parts and other organic specimens.
1. In Christian tradition, original sin; also radical 1780s slang for the social-political-economic establishment (Paine, Godwin, Cobbett). The strange genealogies anticipate those of "The Mental Traveller."

And ran about with bloody hands
To seek his mothers life

5

And as he ran to seek his mother
He met with a dead woman
He fell in love & married her
A deed which is not common

6

She soon grew pregnant & brought forth
Scurvy & spotted fever
The father grind & skipt about
And said I'm made for ever

7

For now I have procurd these imps
Ill try experiments
With that he tied poor scurvy down
& stopt up all its vents

8

And when the child began to swell
He shouted out aloud
Ive found the dropsy out & soon
Shall do the world more good

9

He took up fever by the neck
And cut out all its spots
And thro the holes which he had made
He first discoverd guts

Ah said Sipsop you think we are rascals & we think you are rascals. I do as I chuse what is it to any body what I do I am always unhappy too. When I think of Surgery—I dont know I do it because I like it. My father does what he likes & so do I. I think some how Ill leave it off there was a woman having her cancer cut & she shriekd so, that I was quite sick.

Chap 7

Good night said Sipsop, Good night said the other two. Then Quid & Suction were left alone. Then said Quid I think that Homer is bombast & Shakespeare is too wild & Milton has no feelings. They might be easily outdone. Chatterton never writ those poems. A parcel of fools going to Bristol—if I was to go Id find it out in a minute, but Ive found it out already.

—If I dont knock them all up next year in the Exhibition[2] Ill be hangd said Suction. Hang Philosophy I would not give a farthing for it. Do all by your feelings and never think at all about it. Im hangd if I dont get up to morrow morning by four o clock & work Sir Joshua[3]

2. In 1784, Blake had two works in the Royal Academy's annual spring exhibition; in 1785, four.
3. The prolific painter Sir Joshua Reynolds (1723–1793) was said to have been shaved, powdered, and at work by 9:00 A.M. (*Oxford Dictionary of National Biography*). For Blake's fiercest attack on Reynolds, see annotations to *Discourses on Art* (p. 461 herein).

—Before ten years are at an end said Quid how I will work these poor milk sop devils, an ignorant pack of wretches.

So they went to bed.

Chap 8

Steelyard the Lawgiver, sitting at his table taking extracts from Herveys Meditations among the tombs & Youngs Night thoughts.[4] He is not able to hurt me (said he) more than making me Constable or taking away the parish business. Hah!

My crop of corn is but a field of tares[5]

Says Jerome happiness is not for us poor crawling reptiles of the earth. Talk of happiness & happiness its no such thing—every person has a something

Hear then the pride & knowledge of a Sailor
His sprit sail fore sail main sail & his mizen
A poor frail man god wot I know none frailer
I know no greater sinner than John Taylor[6]

If I had only myself to care for I'd soon make Double Elephant look foolish, & Filligree[7] work I hope shall live to see—

The wreck of matter & the crush of worlds
as Younge says[8]

Obtuse Angle enterd the Room. What news Mr Steelyard

—I am Reading Theron & Aspasio,[9] said he.

Obtuse Angle took up the books one by one. I dont find it here said he.

Oh no said the other it was the meditations.

Obtuse Angle took up the book & read till the other was quite tir'd out

Then Scopprell & Miss Gittipin coming in, Scopprell took up a book & read the following passage.

An Easy of Huming Understanding by John Lookye Gent[1]

John Locke said Obtuse Angle.

O ay Lock said Scopprell.

Now here said Miss Gittipin I never saw such company in my life. You are always talking of your books I like to be where we talk.—you had better take a walk, that we may have some pleasure. I am sure I never see any pleasure. Theres Double Elephants Girls they have their own way, & theres Miss Filligree work she goes out in her coaches & her footman & her maids

---

4. Steelyard's interest in these gloomy works (James Hervey, *Meditations Among the Tombs*, 1746; Edward Young, *The Complaint and the Consolation; or, Night Thoughts on Life Death and Immortality*, 1742–45) may point to John Flaxman as the model. Flaxman's brief service as rate collector was his "parish business." Blake later designed 537 watercolor illustrations of Young (1795–97) and an *Epitome* of Hervey's *Meditations* (c. 1820); Butlin, 770.

5. The first line of a poem by eighteen-year-old Chidiock Tichborne (d. 1586) on the eve of his execution (by hanging, drawing, and quartering) for plotting to assassinate Queen Elizabeth.

6. This poem, which follows an unidentified quotation from St. Jerome, is paraphrased from the opening lines of *Urania* (1630) by the self-styled Water Poet John Taylor (1583–1653), sailor and pamphleteer.

7. Steelyard's competitors are named for huge and tiny formats: "Double Elephant": largest size of paper (twenty-six and a half by thirty-nine inches). Filigree work involves coiling thin strips of paper or metal into delicate ornaments. A few lines later, the daughters of these artists turn out to be the envy of Miss Gittipin.

8. Not by Young; from Joseph Addison's *Cato* (1713), 5.1.28.

9. Another work by Hervey (1775).

1. Scopprell's mispronunciation links John Locke's (1632–1704) *Essay on Human Understanding* (1690) with the name of a later rationalist-empiricist philosopher, David Hume (1711–1776).

& Stormonts & Balloon hats & a pair of Gloves every day & the sorrows of Werter & Robinsons & the Queen of Frances Puss colour[2] & my Cousin Gibble Gabble says that I am like nobody else I might as well be in a nunnery.

There they go in Post chaises & Stages to Vauxhall & Ranelagh[3] And I hardly know what a coach is, except when I go to Mr Jacko's he knows what riding is & his wife is the most agreeable woman you hardly know she has a tongue in her head and he is the funniest fellow, & I do believe he'll go in partnership with his master,[4] & they have black servants lodge at their house. I never saw such a place in my life. He says he has Six & twenty rooms in his house, and I believe it & he is not such a liar as Quid thinks he is.

Poo Poo hold your tongue hold your tongue, said the Lawgiver. This quite provokd Miss Gittipin to interrupt her in her favourite topic & she proceeded to use every Provoking speech that ever she could, & he bore it more like a Saint than a Lawgiver and with great Solemnity he addressd the company in these words.

They call women the weakest vessel but I think they are the strongest. A girl has always more tongue than a boy. I have seen a little brat no higher than a nettle & she had as much tongue as a city clark but a boy would be such a fool not have any thing to say and if any body askd him a question he would put his head into a hole & hide it. I am sure I take but little pleasure you have as much pleasure as I have. There I stand & bear every fools insult. If I had only myself to care for, I'd wring off their noses.

To this Scopprell answerd. I think the Ladies discourses Mr Steelyard are some of them more improving than any book. That is the way I have got some of my knowledge.

Then said Miss Gittipin, Mr Scopprell do you know the song of Phebe and Jellicoe

—no Miss said Scopprell—then she repeated these verses while Steelyard walkd about the room.

> Phebe drest like beauties Queen
> Jellicoe in faint peagreen
> Sitting all beneath a grot
> Where the little lambkins trot
>
> Maidens dancing loves a sporting
> All the country folks a courting
> Susan Johnny Bet & Joe
> Lightly tripping on a row

2. The coveted fashions are Stormonts (roller-printed fabric designs, patented 1783, named after a government minister; see www.manchestergalleries.org/costume); balloon bonnets (celebrating Lunardi's balloon ascent); Sorrows of Werther hats (honoring Goethe's novel of 1774, trans. 1780); Robinson vests, hats, and chemises (named for the writer, actress, and trend-setter Mary "Perdita" Robinson, the Prince of Wales's ex-mistress); and puce ("flea" color, Marie Antoinette's favorite).
3. Pleasure gardens; see map.
4. Mr. Jacko, conjecturally based on the wealthy miniaturist Richard Cosway, Blake's drawing master at Pars's school, is named for a monkey in Astley's circus (1785). His wife, Maria, was also a painter; his "master" was the Prince of Wales; his servant was Ottobah Cugano, author of an anti-slavery tract (1787; see Keri Davies, Blake Quarterly 3 [2006], 106).

Happy people who can be
In happiness compard with ye
The Pilgrim with his crook & hat
Sees your happiness compleat

A charming Song indeed miss said Scopprell. Here they recievd a summons for a merry making at the Philosophers house.

Chap 9

I say this evening we'll all get drunk. I say dash, an Anthem an Anthem, said Suction.

Lo the Bat with Leathern wing[5]
Winking & blinking
Winking & blinking
Winking & blinking
Like Doctor Johnson

Quid——   O ho Said Doctor Johnson
To Scipio Africanus
If you dont own me a Philosopher
Ill kick your Roman Anus

Suction——   A ha To Doctor Johnson
Said Scipio Africanus
Lift up my Roman Petticoatt
And kiss my Roman Anus[6]

And the Cellar goes down with a Step   (Grand Chorus
Ho Ho Ho Ho Ho Ho Ho Hooooo my poooooor siiides I I should die if I was to live here said Scopprell Ho Ho Ho Ho Ho

1st Vo	Want Matches
2d Vo	Yes Yes Yes
1 Vo	Want Matches
2d Vo	No——
1st Vo	Want Matches
2d Vo	Yes Yes Yes
1st Vo	Want Matches
2d Vo	No——

Here was Great confusion & disorder. Aradobo said that the boys in the street sing something very pritty & funny about Matches. Then Mrs Nannicantipot sung

I cry my matches as far as Guild hall
God bless the duke & his aldermen all

Then sung Scopprell

---

5. From William Collins, "To Evening" (1747).
6. Johnson, who had died on December 13, 1784, had poor eyesight. His encounter with Scipio Africanus (236–184 B.C.E.), conqueror of Hannibal's Carthage, takes off from Lucian's (120–80) widely imitated *Dialogues of the Dead*. Fenelon's work of the same name (1718) includes two dialogues between Scipio and Hannibal.

        I ask the Gods no more
           no more no more
Then Said Suction come Mr Lawgiver your song and the Lawgiver sung
    As I walkd forth one may morning
    To see the fields so pleasant & so gay
    O there did I spy a young maiden sweet
    Among the Violets that smell so sweet
             Smell so sweet
             Smell so sweet
    Among the Violets that smell so sweet

Hang your Violets heres your Rum & water. O ay said Tilly Lally. Joe Bradley & I was going along one day in the Sugar house. Joe Bradley saw, for he had but one eye, saw a treacle Jar. So he goes of his blind side & dips his hand up to the shoulder in treacle. here lick lick lick said he. Ha Ha Ha Ha Ha For he had but one eye Ha Ha Ha Ho. Then sung Scopprell
    And I ask the Gods no more
          no more no more
          no more no more

Miss Gittipin said he you sing like a harpsichord. Let your bounty descend to our fair ears and favour us with a fine song.
    Then she sung
          This frog he would a wooing ride
          Kitty alone Kitty alone
          This frog he would a wooing ride
          Kitty alone & I

          Sing cock I cary Kitty alone
          Kitty alone Kitty alone
          Cock I cary Kitty alone
          Kitty alone & I
Charming truly elegant said Scopprell
          And I ask the gods no more
Hang your Serious Songs, said Sipsop & he sung as follows
          Fa ra so bo ro
          Fa ra bo ra
          Sa ba ra ra ba rare roro
          Sa ra ra ra bo ro ro ro
          Radara Sarapodo no flo ro
Hang Italian songs lets have English said Quid. English Genius for ever here I go
          Hail Matrimony made of Love[7]
          To thy wide gates how great a drove
          On purpose to be yok'd do come
          Widows & maids & Youths also
          That lightly trip on beauty's toe
          Or sit on beauty's bum

          Hail fingerfooted lovely Creatures
          The females of our human Natures
          Formed to suckle all Mankind

---

7. Cf. "Hail wedded love" (cf. Milton, *Paradise Lost* 4:750).

Tis you that come in time of need
Without you we shoud never Breed
Or any Comfort find

For if a Damsel's blind or lame
Or Nature's hand has crooked her frame
Or if she's deaf or is wall eyed
Yet if her heart is well inclined
Some tender lover she shall find
That panteth for a Bride

The universal Poultice this
To cure whatever is amiss
In damsel or in Widow gay
It makes them smile it makes them skip
Like Birds just cured of the pip
They chirp & hop away

Then come ye Maidens come ye Swains
Come & be eased of all your pains
In Matrimony's Golden cage[8]—

Go & be hanged said Scopprel how can you have the face to make game
of Matrimony—Then Quid calld upon Obtuse Angle for a Song & he wiping his face & looking on the corner of the cieling Sang

To be or not to be
Of great capacity
Like Sir Isaac Newton
Or Locke or Doctor South
Or Sherlock upon death
Id rather be Sutton[9]

For he did build a house
For aged men & youth
With walls of brick & stone
He furnishd it within
With whatever he could win
And all his own

He drew out of the Stocks
His money in a box
And sent his servant
To Green the Bricklayer
And to the Carpenter
He was so fervent

The chimneys were three score
The windows many more
And for convenience

8. Recalls the one in "How sweet I roamd" (*Poetical Sketches*).
9. Thomas Sutton, wealthy merchant and moneylender, founded the London Charterhouse in 1611,
   at that time by far the largest charitable institution in British history.

He sinks & gutters made
And all the way he pavd
To hinder pestilence

Was not this a good man
Whose life was but a span
Whose name was Sutton
As Locke or Doctor South
Or Sherlock upon Death[1]
Or Sir Isaac Newton

The Lawgiver was very attentive & begd to have it sung over again & again till the company were tired & insisted on the Lawgiver singing a song himself which he readily complied with

This city & this country has brought forth many mayors
To sit in state & give forth laws out of their old oak chairs
With face as brown as any nut with drinking of strong ale
Good English hospitality O then it did not fail

With scarlet gowns & broad gold lace would make a yeoman
    sweat
With stockings rolld above their knees & shoes as black as jet
With eating beef & drinking beer O they were stout & hale
Good English hospitality O then it did not fail

Thus sitting at the table wide the Mayor & Aldermen
Were fit to give law to the city each eat as much as ten
The hungry poor enterd the hall to eat good beef & ale
Good English hospitality O then it did not fail[2]

Here they gave a shout & the company broke up.

Chap 10

Thus these happy Islanders spent their time but felicity does not last long, for being met at the house of Inflammable Gass the windfinder, the following affairs happend.

Come Flammable said Gibble Gabble & lets enjoy ourselves bring the Puppets.

Hay Hay, said he, you sho, why ya ya, how can you be so foolish.—Ha Ha Ha she calls the experiments puppets Then he went up stairs & loaded the maid with glasses, & brass tubes, & magic pictures.

Here ladies & gentlemen said he Ill shew you a louse or a flea or a butterfly or a cock chafer the blade bone of a tittle back. No no heres a bottle of wind that I took up in the bog house, o dear o dear the waters got into the sliders. Look here Gibble Gabble—lend me your handkerchief Tilly Lally. Tilly Lally took out his handkerchief which smeard the glass worse than ever.

1. Referring to religious controversialists William Sherlock (1639–1707), author of *A Practical Discourse concerning Death* (1689), and Robert South (1634–1716), clergymen who attacked each other in many of their books.
2. In spirit this song recalls Fielding's "The Roast Beef of Old England" in *Grub Street Opera* (1731); cf. Hogarth's *Beer Street* (1750–51).

Then he screwd it on then he took the sliders & then he set up the glasses for the Ladies to view the pictures. Thus he was employd & quite out of breath.

While Tilly Lally & Scopprell were pumping at the air pump Smack went the glass.

—Hang said Tilly Lally.

Inflammable Gass turnd short round & threw down the table & Glasses & Pictures, & broke the bottles of wind & let out the Pestilence He saw the Pestilence fly out of the bottle & cried out while he ran out of the room, come out come out we are putrified, we are corrupted, our lungs are destroyd with the Flogiston[3] this will spread a plague all thro' the Island. He was down stairs the very first on the back of him came all the others in a heap

So they need not bidding go.

Chap 11

Another merry meeting at the house of Steelyard the Lawgiver. After Supper Steelyard & Obtuse Angle had pumpd Inflammable Gass quite dry. They playd at forfeits & tryd every method to get good humour. Said Miss Gittipin pray Mr Obtuse Angle sing us a song. Then he sung

> Upon a holy thursday their innocent faces clean
> The children walking two & two in grey & blue & green
> Grey headed beadles walkd before with wands as white as snow
> Till into the high dome of Pauls they like thames waters flow
>
> O what a multitude they seemd, these flowers of London town
> Seated in companies they sit with radiance all their own
> The hum of multitudes were there but multitudes of lambs
> Thousands of little girls & boys raising their innocent hands
>
> Then like a mighty wind they raise to heavn the voice of song
> Or like harmonious thunderings the seats of heavn among
> Beneath them sit the revrend men the guardians of the poor
> Then cherish pity lest you drive an angel from your door

After this they all sat silent for a quarter of an hour, & Mrs Nannicantipot said it puts me in Mind of my mothers song

> When the tongues of children are heard on the green
> And laughing is heard on the hill
> My heart is at rest within my breast
> And every thing else is still
>
> Then come home my children the sun is gone down
> And the dews of night arise
> Come Come leave off play & let us away
> Till the morning appears in the skies
>
> No No let us play for it is yet day
> And we cannot go to sleep

3. Phlogiston, hypothetically the odorless, colorless, weightless substance of fire; disproved by Lavoisier but defended by Priestley. Inflammable Gass's bottle of wind from the boghouse (privy) is methane.

Besides in the Sky the little birds fly
And the meadows are coverd with Sheep

Well Well go & play till the light fades away
And then go home to bed
The little ones leaped & shouted & laughd
And all the hills ecchoed

Then sung Quid[4]

O father father where are you going
O do not walk so fast
O speak father speak to your little boy
Or else I shall be lost

The night it was dark & no father was there
And the child was wet with dew
The mire was deep & the child did weep
And away the vapour flew

Here nobody could sing any longer, till Tilly Lally pluckd up a spirit & he sung.

O I say you Joe
Throw us the ball
Ive a good mind to go
And leave you all
I never saw saw such a bowler
To bowl the ball in a turd[5]
And to clean it with my handkercher
Without saying a word

That Bills a foolish fellow
He has given me a black eye
He does not know how to handle a bat
Any more than a dog or a cat
He has knockd down the wicket
And broke the stumps
And runs without shoes to save his pumps

Here a laugh began and Miss Gittipin sung
Leave O leave [me] to my sorrows
Here Ill sit & fade away
Till Im nothing but a spirit
And I lose this form of clay

Then if chance along this forest
Any walk in pathless ways
Thro the gloom he'll see my shadow
Hear my voice upon the Breeze

4. Blake first wrote "Miss Gittipin," then "Tilly Lally," then "Quid" (crossed out, then restored).
Phillips notes that Blake's father had recently died. This song is the third in the group that became
"Holy Thursday," "Nurse's Song," and "The Little Boy Lost" in *Songs of Innocence* (1789).
5. Blake replaced this word with the euphemism "tansey," a strong-smelling yellow flower used in
cookery for its color, but he neglected to change the rhyme.

The Lawgiver all the while sat delighted to see them in such a serious humour. Mr Scopprell, said he, You must be acquainted with a great many songs. O dear sir Ho Ho Ho I am no singer I must beg of one of these tender hearted ladies to sing for me—they all declined & he was forced to sing himself

> Theres Doctor Clash And Signior Falalasole
> O they sweep in the cash
> Into their purse hole
> Fa me la sol La me fa sol
>
> Great A little A Bouncing B[6]
> Play away Play away
> Your out of the key
> Fa me la sol La me fa sol
>
> Musicians should have
> A pair of very good ears
> And Long fingers & thumbs
> And not like clumsy bears
> Fa me la sol La me fa sol
>
> Gentlemen Gentlemen
> Rap Rap Rap
> Fiddle Fiddle Fiddle
> Clap Clap Clap
> Fa me la sol La me fa sol

Hm said the Lawgiver, funny enough. Lets have Handels waterpiece.[7] Then Sipsop sung

> A crowned king,
> On a white horse sitting
> With his trumpets sounding
> And Banners flying
> Thro the clouds of smoke he makes his way
> And the shout of his thousands fills his heart with rejoicing & victory
> And the shout of his thousands fills his heart with rejoicing & victory
> Victory Victory—twas William the prince of Orange

[Here a leaf or more is missing]
. . . them Illuminating the Manuscript[8]
   —Ay said she that would be excellent.
   Then said he I would have all the writing Engraved instead of Printed &

6. An alphabetical nursery rhyme published in Joseph Ritson, *Gammer Gurton's Garland* (1783).
7. Handel's (1685–1759) *Water Music*, an orchestral piece, was not played during the five-concert Handel festival of 1784. But the festival opened with the Coronation Anthem "Zadok the Priest" (1727), possibly inspiring Sipsop's song about William of Orange (1650–1702), leader of the 1688 Glorious Revolution to depose Catholic James II and establish the Protestant reign of William and Mary.
8. The beginning of this sentence is lost. Quid's description of "Illuminated" work fits Cumberland's experiments of this period better than Blake's work of 1788. The woman in this scene is either Mrs. Nannicantipot or, less likely, Miss Gittipin.

at every other leaf a high finishd print all in three Volumes folio, & sell them a hundred pounds a piece. They would Print off two thousand.

Then said she whoever will not have them will be ignorant fools & will not deserve to live.

Dont you think I have something of the Goats face says he. Very like a Goats face—she answerd

—I think your face said he is like that noble beast the Tyger

—Oh I was at Mrs Sicknakers & I was speaking of my abilities but their nasty hearts poor devils are eat up with envy

—They envy me my abilities & all the Women envy your abilities my dear they hate people who are of higher abilities than their nasty filthy Selves but do you outface them & then Strangers will see you have an opinion

—now I think we should do as much good as we can when we are at Mr Femality's⁹ do you snap & take me up—and I will fall into such a passion Ill hollow and stamp & frighten all the People there & show them what truth is

—at this Instant Obtuse Angle came in Oh I am glad you are come said quid

TO THE PUBLIC [PROSPECTUS] (1793)†

October 10, 1793.

The Labours of the Artist, the Poet, the Musician, have been proverbially attended by poverty and obscurity; this was never the fault of the Public, but was owing to a neglect of means to propagate such works as have wholly absorbed the Man of Genius. Even Milton and Shakespeare could not publish their own works.

This difficulty has been obviated by the Author of the following productions now presented to the Public; who has invented a method of Printing both Letter-press and Engraving in a style more ornamental, uniform, and grand, than any before discovered, while it produces works at less than one fourth of the expense.

If a method of Printing which combines the Painter and the Poet is a phenomenon worthy of public attention, provided that it exceeds in elegance all former methods, the Author is sure of his reward.

---

9. Probably based on the French transvestite spy the Chevalier D'Eon, member of British occultist circles by 1785; see Marsha Keith Schuchard, *Studies in Eighteenth-Century Culture* 22 (1992): 51–71.

† This advertising circular, known only from a transcript in Gilchrist's *Life* (2:263–64)—the source of our text—is described there as a "Prospectus . . . issued . . . in engraved writing printed in blue on a single leaf." Advertised items 1 and 2 (Essick, *Separate Plates* V and IV) are conventional intaglio engravings; the two series for which they were intended as samples never materialized. Items 3–8 constitute the artist's first known public announcement of works in illuminated printing; in both this 1793 list and the price list in Blake's 1818 letter to Dawson Turner (p. 491 herein), *Songs of Experience* appears as a separate volume, but almost all extant copies are part of *Songs of Innocence and of Experience* (first issued 1794). Item 9 is now lost. Item 10, *The Gates of Paradise*, which bears a supratitle *For Children*, is an eighteen-plate book of small engraved emblems with captions; revised about 1820 under a new heading, *For the Sexes*, with amplified inscriptions and new pages of verse commentary (see p. 341 herein).

Mr. Blake's powers of invention very early engaged the attention of many persons of eminence and fortune; by whose means he has been regularly enabled to bring before the Public works (he is not afraid to say) of equal magnitude and consequence with the productions of any age or country: among which are two large highly finished engravings (and two more are nearly ready) which will commence a Series of subjects from the Bible, and another from the History of England.

The following are the Subjects of the several Works now published and on Sale at Mr. Blake's, No. 13, Hercules Buildings, Lambeth.

1. Job, a Historical Engraving. Size 1 ft. 7½ in. by 1 ft. 2 in.: price 12s.

2. Edward and Elinor, a Historical Engraving. Size 1 ft. 6½ in. by 1 ft.: price 10s. 6d.

3. America, a Prophecy, in Illuminated Printing. Folio, with 18 designs: price 10s. 6d.

4. Visions of the Daughters of Albion, in Illuminated Printing. Folio, with 8 designs, price 7s. 6d.

5. The Book of Thel, a Poem in Illuminated Printing. Quarto, with 6 designs, price 3s.

6. The Marriage of Heaven and Hell, in Illuminated Printing. Quarto, with 14 designs, price 7s. 6d.

7. Songs of Innocence, in Illuminated Printing. Octavo, with 25 designs, price 5s.

8. Songs of Experience, in Illuminated Printing. Octavo, with 25 designs, price 5s.

9. The History of England, a small book of Engravings. Price 3s.

10. The Gates of Paradise, a small book of Engravings. Price 3s.

The Illuminated Books are Printed in Colours, and on the most beautiful wove paper that could be procured.

No Subscriptions for the numerous great works now in hand are asked, for none are wanted; but the Author will produce his works, and offer them to sale at a fair price.

FROM THE NOTEBOOK (1787–1818)†

London

(Drafts, c. 1792)

I wander thro each dirty street   N109
Near where the dirty Thames does flow
    mark
And ~~see~~ in every face I meet
Marks of weakness marks of woe

In every cry of every man
    every infants cry of fear
In ~~every voice of every child~~
In every voice in every ban
    mind   manacles I hear
The ~~german~~ forgd ~~links I hear~~

How
~~But most~~ the chimney sweepers cry
Every blackning church appalls
~~Blackens oer the churches walls~~
And the hapless soldiers sigh
Runs in blood down palace walls

But most the midnight harlots curse
From every dismal street I hear
Weaves around the marriage hearse
And blasts the new born infants tear

        thro wintry
But most ~~from every~~ streets I hear
How the midnight harlots curse

† A fascinating workbook of sketches and drafts, sometimes called "The Rossetti Manuscript" because Dante Gabriel Rossetti purchased it in 1847; see the superb facsimile edited by David V. Erdman and Donald K. Moore (1973; rev. 1977) and the British Library's interactive images of the whole book (www.bl.uk/onlinegallery/ttp//ttpbooks.html). In 1787, after the death of his brother and drawing pupil Robert, Blake took over Robert's sketchbook and used it for his own private memoranda, angry epigrams, drawings, and drafts of poetry and prose until he filled almost every space, about 1818. Among the Notebook's contents are many brilliant though never-published lyrics, sketches for *The Gates of Paradise*, drafts for all but three poems in *Songs of Experience* (1794), and important unfinished works published by later editors as "The Everlasting Gospel," "Public Address," and "Vision of the Last Judgment." Our selections begin with three working drafts, transcribed with minor simplifications and corrections from the Erdman-Moore edition of the Notebook: "London" and "The Tyger" show inspired improvements in diction and organization; "Infant Sorrow," as a work in progress, links the short lyrics of *Experience* with the experimental ballads of "The 'Auguries' Manuscript" (Pickering Manuscript). In these three poems, Blake's long diagonal and vertical cancellations do not always indicate deletions but often show merely that a passage has reached a satisfactory state of revision. See Michael Phillips (2000) for analysis.

    In our selection of the most arresting poems in the Notebook, we attempt to present each work at an optimum stage of realization by eliminating early drafts and, occasionally, what we consider to be uninspired afterthoughts. We also omit most of Blake's doggerel complaints against friends, acquaintances, rivals, and pet antipathies. Despite these omissions, which favor aesthetic above biographical values, our selections should convey a fair self-portrait of Blake the man—a disputatious but hardworking and hopeful craftsman who tempered righteous indignation with humor, fantasy, and insouciant irreverence.

    The texts of the selections are based on Erdman's edition, compared with the Erdman-Moore facsimile. They are arranged loosely by theme, without added punctuation. Untitled poems are separated by ornamental rules.

Blasts the new born infants tear
And ~~hangs~~ smites with plagues the marriage hearse

But most the shrieks of youth I hear
But most thro midnight &c I hear
How the youthful

The Tyger[1]

(Drafts, c. 1792)

Tyger Tyger burning bright   N109
In the forests of the night
What immortal hand or eye
~~Could~~ Dare frame thy fearful symmetry

In what distant deeps or skies Burnt in
~~Burnt the~~ The cruel fire of thine eyes
On what wings dare he aspire
What the hand dare sieze the fire

And what shoulder & what art
Could twist the sinews of thy heart
And when thy heart began to beat
What dread hand & what dread feet

~~Could fetch it from the furnace deep~~
~~And in thy horrid ribs dare steep~~
~~In the well of sanguine woe~~

~~In what clay & in what mould~~
~~Were thy eyes of fury rolld~~

~~What~~ Where the hammer ~~what~~ where the chain
In what furnace was thy brain
What the anvil what ~~the arm arm grasp clasp~~ dread grasp
~~Could~~ Dare its deadly terrors ~~clasp grasp~~ clasp

Tyger Tyger burning bright
In thee forests of the night
What immortal hand & eye
Dare ~~form~~ frame thy fearful symmetry

---

1. For an enlarged image of the page containing "London" (upper left) and "The Tyger" (bottom right),
   see www.bl.uk/onlinegallery/themes/englishlit/williamblakelge.html.

(Trial stanzas)

Burnt in distant deeps ~~or~~ skies
The ~~cruel~~ fire ~~of~~ thine eyes,
Could heart descend or wings aspire
What the hand dare sieze the fire

5   dare   he ~~smile laugh~~
3   And ~~did he laugh~~ his work to see
                ankle
    ~~What the shoulder what the knee~~

    Dare
4   ~~Did~~ he who made the lamb make thee
1   When the stars drew down their spears
2   And waterd heaven with their tears

(Second full draft)

Tyger Tyger burning bright.
In the forests of the night
What Immortal hand & eye
Dare frame thy fearful symmetry

And what shoulder & what art
Could twist the sinews of thy heart
And when thy heart began to beat
What dread hand & what dread feet

When the stars threw down their spears
And waterd heaven with their tears
Did he smile his work to see
Did he who made the lamb make thee

Tyger Tyger burning bright
In the forests of the night
What immortal hand & eye
Dare frame thy fearful symmetry

Infant Sorrow

(Drafts, of uncertain date)

My mother groand my father wept
Into the dangerous world I leapt
Helpless naked piping loud
Like a fiend hid in a cloud

Struggling in my fathers hands
Striving against my swaddling bands
Bound & weary I thought best
To sulk upon my mothers breast

soothd
And I ~~smild~~ day after day
Till upon the ground I stray
smild
And I ~~grew~~ night after night
Seeking only for delight

~~But upon the nettly ground~~
~~No delight was to be found~~
And I saw before me shine
Clusters of the wandring vine
And many a lovely flower & tree
~~And beyond a mirtle tree~~
their
Stretchd ~~its~~ blossoms out to me

My father then
~~But many a~~
~~But a Priest~~ with holy look
their
In ~~his~~ hands a holy book
my
Pronouncd curses on ~~his~~ head
And bound me in a mirtle shade
~~Who the fruit or blossoms shed~~
I beheld the Priests by night
They   the blossoms
~~He embraced my mirtle bright~~
He
~~I beheld the Priests by day~~
Underneath the   they
~~Where beneath my vines he~~ lay
to
~~Like a serpents in the night~~
They   blossoms
~~He embraced my mirtle bright~~
to holy men by
Like ~~a serpent in the~~ day
the   they
Underneath ~~my~~ vines ~~he~~ lay

their
So I smote them & ~~his~~ gore
Staind the roots my mirtle bore
But the time of youth is fled
And grey hairs are on my head

(Marked for insertion after second stanza)

———

When I saw that rage was vain
lk
And to su~~ek~~ would nothing gain
Turning many a trick or wile
~~I began to so Seeking many an artful wile~~
I began to soothe & smile

Motto to the Songs of Innocence
& of Experience

The Good are attracted by Mens perceptions   N101
And Think not for themselves
Till Experience teaches them to catch
And to cage the Fairies & Elves

And then the Knave begins to snarl   5
And the Hypocrite to howl
And all his good Friends shew their private ends
And the Eagle is known from the Owl

A cradle song[2]

Sleep Sleep beauty bright   N114
Dreaming oer the joys of night
Sleep Sleep; in thy sleep
Little sorrows sit & weep

Sweet Babe in thy face   5
Soft desires I can trace
Secret joys & secret smiles
Little pretty infant wiles.

As thy softest limbs I feel
Smiles as of the morning steal   10
Oer thy cheek & oer thy breast
Where thy little heart does rest

O the cunning wiles that creep
In thy little heart asleep
When thy little heart does wake   15
Then the dreadful lightnings break

From thy cheek & from thy eye
Oer the youthful harvests nigh
Infant wiles & infant smiles
Heaven & Earth of peace beguiles   20

I heard an Angel singing   N114
When the day was springing
Mercy Pity Peace
Is the worlds release

Thus he sung all day   5
Over the new mown hay
Till the sun went down
And haycocks looked brown

2. An *Experience* contrary to the song of the same name in *Innocence*; never etched.

I heard a Devil curse
Over the heath & the furze   10
Mercy could be no more
If there was nobody poor

And pity no more could be
If all were as happy as we
At his curse the sun went down   15
And the heavens gave a frown

Down pourd the heavy rain
Over the new reapd grain
And Miseries increase
Is Mercy Pity Peace   20

An ancient Proverb

Remove away that blackning church   N107
Remove away that marriage hearse
Remove away that man of blood
Youll quite remove the ancient curse

Why should I care for the men of thames   N113
Or the cheating waves of charterd streams
Or shrink at the little blasts of fear
That the hireling blows into my ear

Tho born on the cheating banks of Thames   5
Tho his waters bathed my infant limbs
The Ohio shall wash his stains from me
I was born a slave but I go to be free

How to know Love from Deceit

Love to faults is always blind   N106-7
Always is to joy inclind
Lawless wingd & unconfind
And breaks all chains from every mind

Deceit to secresy confind   5
Lawful cautious & refind
To every thing but interest blind
And forges fetters for the mind

O lapwing thou fliest around the heath[3]   N113
Nor seest the net that is spread beneath

---

3. The first of five poems marked "To go on one plate." The others are "An answer to the parson," (p. 386
   herein) ["Thou hast a lap full of seed"], ["If you trap the moment before its ripe"], and "Riches," (p. 394).

Why dost thou not fly among the corn fields
They cannot spread nets where a harvest yields

Thou hast a lap full of seed
And this is a fine country
Why dost thou not cast thy seed
And live in it merrily

Shall I cast it on the sand   5
And turn it into fruitful land
For on no other ground
Can I sow my seed
Without tearing up
Some stinking weed   10

The sword sung on the barren heath   N105
The sickle in the fruitful field
The sword he sung a song of death
But could not make the sickle yield

If you trap the moment before its ripe   N105
The tears of repentance youll certainly wipe
But if once you let the ripe moment go
You can never wipe off the tears of woe

Eternity

He who binds to himself a joy   N105
Does the winged life destroy
But he who kisses the joy as it flies
Lives in eternity's sun rise

The Angel that presided oer my birth   N32
Said Little creature formd of Joy & Mirth
Go love without the help of any Thing on Earth

Morning

To find the western path   N8
Right thro the gates of Wrath
I urge my Way
Sweet Mercy lead me on
With soft repentant moan
I see the break of day

The war of swords & spears
Melted by dewy tears

Exhales on high
The Sun is freed from fears
And with soft grateful tears
Ascends the Sky

—————————

Great things are done when Men & Mountains meet   N43
This is not Done by Jostling in the Street

An answer to the parson

Why of the sheep do you not learn peace   N103
Because I dont want you to shear my fleece

To God

If you have formd a Circle to go into   N73
Go into it yourself & see how you would do

To Nobodaddy

Why art thou silent & invisible   N109
Father of Jealousy
Why dost thou hide thyself in clouds
From every searching Eye

Why darkness & obscurity   5
In all thy words & laws
That none dare eat the fruit but from
The wily serpents jaws
Or is it because Secresy gains females loud applause

—————————

Let the Brothels of Paris be opened   N99
With many an alluring dance
To awake the Physicians thro the city
Said the beautiful Queen of France

Then old Nobodaddy aloft   5
Farted & belchd & coughd
And said I love hanging & drawing & quartering
Every bit as well as war & slaughtering

Then he swore a great & solemn Oath
To kill the people I am loth   10
But If they rebel they must go to hell
They shall have a Priest & a passing bell

The King awoke on his couch of gold
As soon as he heard these tidings told

Arise & come both fife & drum   15
And the ~~Famine~~ shall eat both crust & crumb

The Queen of France just touchd this Globe
And the Pestilence darted from her robe
But our good Queen quite grows to the ground
And a great many suckers grow all around   20

When Klopstock[4] England defied   N1
Uprose terrible Blake in his pride
For old Nobodaddy aloft
Farted & Belchd & coughd
Then swore a great oath that made heavn quake   5
And calld aloud to English Blake
Blake was giving his body ease
At Lambeth beneath the poplar trees
From his seat then started he
And turnd himself round three times three   10
The Moon at that sight blushd scarlet red
The stars threw down their cups & fled
And all the devils that were in hell
Answered with a ninefold yell
Klopstock felt the intripled turn   15
And all his bowels began to churn
And his bowels turned round three times three
And lockd in his soul with a ninefold key
That from his body it neer could be parted
Till to the last trumpet it was farted   20

Then again old nobodaddy swore
He neer had seen such a thing before
Since Noah was shut in the ark
Since Eve first chose her hell fire spark
Since twas the fashion to go naked   25
Since the old anything was created
And in pity he begd him to turn again
And ease poor Klopstocks nine fold pain
From pity then he redend round
And the ninefold Spell unwound   30
If Blake could do this when he rose up from shite
What might he not do if he sat down to write

The Hebrew Nation did not write it   N39
Avarice & Chastity did Shite it

---

4. Friedrich Gottlieb Klopstock (1724–1803), author of a four-volume epic in hexameters, *The Messiah* (1748–73; partially trans. 1763), was celebrated as the "German Milton." On Blake's outhouse and other features of his home in Lambeth, see Michael Phillips, *History Today* 50, no. 11 (November 2000), 18–25.

If it is True What the Prophets write   N33
That the heathen Gods are all stocks & stones[5]
Shall we for the sake of being Polite
Feed them with the juice of our marrow bones
And if Bezaleel & Aholiab[6] drew   5
What the Finger of God pointed to their View
Shall we suffer the Roman & Grecian Rods
To compell us to worship them as Gods
They stole them from the Temple of the Lord[7]
And Worshippd them that they might make
    Inspired Art Abhorrd   10
The Wood & Stone were calld The Holy Things—
And their Sublime Intent given to their Kings
All the Atonements of Jehovah spurnd
And Criminals to Sacrifices Turnd

I saw a chapel all of gold   N115
That none did dare to enter in
And many weeping stood without
Weeping mourning worshipping

I saw a serpent rise between   5
The white pillars of the door
And he forcd & forcd & forcd
Down the golden hinges tore

And along the pavement sweet
Set with pearls & rubies bright   10
All his slimy length he drew
Till upon the altar white

Vomiting his poison out
On the bread & on the wine
So I turnd into a sty   15
And laid me down among the swine

Merlins prophecy

The harvest shall flourish in wintry Weather   N106
When two virginities meet together

The King & the Priest must be tied in a tether
Before two virgins can meet together

---

5. On consorting with "stocks and stones" as a metaphor for idolatry, see Jeremiah 3:9.
6. Inspired artisans whom Moses appointed to make furnishings and precious objects for the tabernacle (Exodus 36:1–2). Bezaleel made the wooden ark of the covenant (Exodus 37:1), the gold cherubim, lamps, and candlesticks (Exodus 37) and the brazen altar (2 Chronicles 1:5). Aholiab, an engraver and embroiderer (Exodus 38:23), made the curtains, hangings, and the vestments and breastplate of Aaron.
7. For more on the claim that Greek and Roman was stolen from Hebrew originals, see "Descriptive Catalogue," p. 425 herein.

Soft Snow

I walked abroad in a snowy day   N107
I askd the soft snow with me to play
She playd & she melted in all her prime
And the winter calld it a dreadful crime

Abstinence sows sand all over   N105
The ruddy limbs & flaming hair
But Desire Gratified
Plants fruits of life & beauty there

What is it men in women do require   N103
The lineaments of Gratified Desire
What is it women do in men require
The lineaments of Gratified Desire

In a wife I would desire   N105
What in whores is always found
The lineaments of Gratified desire

When a Man has Married a Wife
          he finds out whether   N14
Her knees & elbows are only
          glued together

A Woman Scaly & a Man all Hairy   N93
Is such a Match as he who dares
Will find the Womans Scales Scrape off the Mans Hairs

Her whole Life is an Epigram smack smooth &
          nobly pend   N100
Platted quite neat to catch applause with a sliding
          noose at the end

An old maid early eer I knew   N100
Ought but the love that on me grew
And now Im coverd oer & oer
And wish that I had been a Whore

O I cannot cannot find   5
The undaunted courage of a Virgin Mind
For Early I in love was crost
Before my flower of love was lost

The Fairy

Come hither my sparrows   N105
My little arrows
If a tear or a smile
Will a man beguile
If an amorous delay   5
Clouds a sunshiny day
If the step of a foot
Smites the heart to its root
Tis the marriage ring
Makes each fairy a king   10

So a fairy sung
From the leaves I sprung
He leapd from the spray
To flee away
But in my hat caught   15
He soon shall be taught
Let him laugh let him cry
Hes my butterfly
For I've pulld out the Sting
Of the marriage ring

———————

Never pain to tell thy Love   N115
Love that never told can be
For the gentle wind does move
Silently invisibly

I told my love I told my love   5
I told her all my heart
Trembling cold in ghastly fears
Ah she doth depart

Soon as she was gone from me
A traveller came by   10
Silently invisibly
O was no deny

———————

I asked a thief to steal me a peach   N114
He turned up his eyes
I ask'd a lithe lady to lie her down
Holy & meek she cries—

As soon as I went   5
An angel came.
He wink'd at the thief
And smild at the dame—
And without one word spoke
Had a peach from the tree   10

And betwixt earnest and joke
Enjoy'd the lady.[8]

———————

My Spectre around me night & day   N14-13
Like a Wild beast guards my way
My Emanation far within
Weeps incessantly for my Sin

A Fathomless & boundless deep   5
There we wander there we weep
On the hungry craving wind
My Spectre follows thee behind

He scents thy footsteps in the snow
Wheresoever thou dost go   10
Thro the wintry hail & rain
When wilt thou return again

Dost thou not in Pride & scorn
Fill with tempests all my morn
And with jealousies & fears   15
Fill my pleasant nights with tears

Seven of my sweet loves thy knife
Has bereaved of their life
Their marble tombs I built with tears
And with cold & shuddering fears   20

Seven more loves weep night & day
Round the tombs where my loves lay
And seven more loves attend each night
Around my couch with torches bright

And seven more Loves in my bed   25
Crown with wine my mournful head
Pitying & forgiving all
Thy transgressions great & small

When wilt thou return & view
My loves & them to life renew   30
When wilt thou return & live
When wilt thou pity as I forgive

Never Never I return
Still for Victory I burn
Living thee alone Ill have   35
And when dead Ill be thy Grave

————————

8. Blake later softened the impertinence of this poem by changing "spoke" (line 9) to "said" and
   replacing line 11 with "And still as a maid." He also made a stanza break after "dame" when he
   wrote out a fair copy of his revision, signed "W Blake Lambeth 1796."

Thro the Heavn & Earth & Hell
Thou shalt never never quell
I will fly & thou pursue
Night & Morn the flight renew   40

Till I turn from Female Love
And root up the Infernal Grove
I shall never worthy be
To Step into Eternity

And to end thy cruel mocks   45
Annihilate thee on the rocks
And another form create
To be subservient to my Fate

Let us agree to give up Love
And root up the infernal grove   50
Then shall we return & see
The worlds of happy Eternity

& Throughout all Eternity
I forgive you you forgive me
As our dear Redeemer said   55
This the Wine & this the Bread

[Related Stanzas]

Oer my Sins Thou sit & moan   N12
Hast thou no Sins of thy own
Oer my Sins thou sit & weep
And lull thy own Sins fast asleep

What Transgressions I commit   5
Are for thy Transgressions fit
They thy Harlots thou their Slave
And my Bed becomes their Grave

Poor pale pitiable form
That I follow in a Storm   10
Iron tears & groans of lead
Bind around my akeing head

And let us go to the highest downs
With many pleasing wiles
The Woman that does not love your Frowns   15
Will never embrace your smiles

———————

You dont believe I wont attempt to make ye   N21
You are asleep I wont attempt to wake ye
Sleep on Sleep on while in your pleasant dreams
Of Reason you may drink of Lifes clear streams
Reason and Newton they are quite two things   5

For so the Swallow & the Sparrow sings
Reason says Miracle. Newton says Doubt
Aye thats the way to make all Nature out
Doubt Doubt & dont believe without experiment
That is the very thing that Jesus meant   10
When he said Only Believe Believe & try
Try Try & never mind the Reason why

———————

Mock on Mock on Voltaire Rousseau   N9
Mock on Mock on! tis all in vain!
You throw the sand against the wind
And the wind blows it back again

And every sand becomes a Gem   5
Reflected in the beams divine
Blown back they blind the mocking Eye
But still in Israels paths they shine

The Atoms of Democritus
And Newtons Particles of light   10
Are sands upon the Red sea shore
Where Israels tents do shine so bright

———————

The only Man that eer I knew   N50
Who did not make me almost spew
Was Fuseli he was both Turk & Jew
And so dear Christian Friends how do you do

———————

The Caverns of the Grave Ive seen   N87
And these I shewd to Englands Queen[9]
But now the Caves of Hell I view
Who shall I dare to shew them to
What mighty Soul in Beautys form   5
Shall dauntless View the Infernal Storm
Egremonts Countess[1] can controll
The flames of Hell that round me roll
If she refuse I still go on
Till the Heavens & Earth are gone   10
Still admird by Noble minds
Followd by Envy on the winds
Reengravd Time after Time
Ever in their Youthful prime
My Designs unchangd remain   15
Time may rage but rage in vain
For above Times troubled Fountains
On the Great Atlantic Mountains

9. Designs for Robert Blair's *The Grave* (1808), dedicated to Queen Charlotte.
1. Elizabeth Ilive (d. 1822) married Blake's patron the third earl of Egremont (1751–1837) in 1801,
   after bearing the fifth of their six children, a fact probably unknown to Blake when he painted a
   panorama of characters in Spenser's *Faerie Queene* for Petworth House, Egremont's home in Sussex.

In my Golden House on high
There they Shine Eternally   20

Riches

The countless gold of a merry heart   N103
The rubies & pearls of a loving eye
The indolent never can bring to the mart
Nor the secret hoard up in his treasury

———————

Since all the Riches of this World   N73
May be gifts from the Devil & Earthly Kings
I should suspect that I worshipd the Devil
If I thankd my God for Worldly things

———————

I rose up at the dawn of day   N89
Get thee away get thee away
Prayst thou for Riches away away
This is the Throne of Mammon grey

Said I this sure is very odd   5
I took it to be the Throne of God
For every Thing besides I have
It is only for Riches that I can crave

I have Mental Joy & Mental Health
And Mental Friends & Mental wealth   10
Ive a Wife I love & that loves me
Ive all But Riches Bodily

I am in Gods presence night & day
And he never turns his face away
The accuser of sins by my side does stand   15
And he holds my money bag in his hand

For my worldly things God makes him pay
And hed pay for more if to him I would pray
And so you may do the worst you can do
Be assurd Mr Devil I wont pray to you   20

Then If for Riches I must not Pray
God knows I little of Prayers need say
So as a Church is known by its Steeple
If I pray it must be for other People

He says if I do not worship him for a God   25
I shall eat coarser food & go worse shod
So as I dont value such things as these
You must do Mr Devil just as God please

Blakes apology for his Catalogue

Having given great offence by writing in Prose   N65
Ill write in Verse as Soft as Bartolloze²
Some blush at what others can see no crime in
But nobody sees any harm in Rhyming
Dryden in Rhyme cries Milton only plannd   5
Every Fool shook his bells throughout the land
Tom Cooke cut Hogarth down with his clean graving
Thousands of Connoisseurs with joy ran raving
Thus Hayley on his toilette seeing the Sope
Cries Homer is very much improvd by Pope   10
Some say Ive given great Provision to my foes
And that now I lead my false friends by the nose
Flaxman & Stothard smelling a sweet savour
Cry Blakified drawing spoils painter & Engraver
While I looking up to my Umbrella   15
Resolvd to be a very contrary fellow
Cry looking quite from Skumference to Center
No one can finish so high as the original Inventor
Thus Poor Schiavonetti died of the Cromek
A thing thats tied around the Examiners neck   20
This is my sweet apology to my friends
That I may put them in mind of their latter Ends

[THE "AUGURIES" (PICKERING) MANUSCRIPT] (c. 1805)†

The Smile

There is a Smile of Love
And there is a Smile of Deceit
And there is a Smile of Smiles
In which these two Smiles meet

And there is a Frown of Hate   5
And there is a Frown of disdain

---

2. Francesco Bartolozzi (1727–1815), Italian engraver whose "soft" stipple or dotted engraving style
   was much in demand, unlike the old-fashioned "hard" linear style Blake had learned from Basire.
   The "Prose" (line 1) is Blake's *Descriptive Catalogue* (1809), ridiculed by Robert Hunt in *The
   Examiner* (see line 20 and p. 497 herein). Most of the rest of the names are paired examples of
   original and derivative artists: Dryden set *Paradise Lost* in rhyme; Cooke (Cook) reengraved Hogarth's works as *Hogarth Restored* (1806); Pope translated Homer into English "heroic" couplets;
   Robert Cromek, entrepreneur behind the edition of Blair's *Grave* that Blake illustrated and
   expected to engrave, replaced Blake with Luigi (Louis) Schiavonetti (1765–1810), who had worked
   under Bartolozzi for a time.
† Probably about 1805, Blake assembled a neatly handwritten collection of ten notable poems, including "Auguries of Innocence" and "The Mental Traveller," in an untitled twenty-two-page booklet.
   These are not working drafts (two poems, "The Golden Net" and "The Grey Monk," were started in
   the Notebook) but the polished work of an artist able to crystallize sweeping cosmic myths, profound
   theological speculations, bold sociopolitical critiques, and disturbing psychosexual insights into
   brief masterpieces of stunning originality. The booklet, long known as "The Pickering Manuscript"

And there is a Frown of Frowns
Which you strive to forget in vain

For it sticks in the Hearts deep Core
And it sticks in the deep Back bone   10
And no Smile that ever was smild
But only one Smile alone

That betwixt the Cradle & Grave
It only once Smild can be
But when it once is Smild   15
Theres an end to all Misery

The Golden Net

Three Virgins at the break of day
Whither young Man whither away
Alas for woe! alas for woe!
They cry & tears for ever flow
The one was Clothd in flames of fire   5
The other Clothd in iron wire
The other Clothd in tears & sighs
Dazling bright before my Eyes
They bore a Net of Golden twine
To hang upon the Branches fine   10
Pitying I wept to see the woe
That Love & Beauty undergo
To be consumd in burning Fires
And in ungratified Desires
And in tears clothd Night & day   15
Melted all my Soul away
When they saw my Tears a Smile
That did Heaven itself beguile
Bore the Golden Net aloft
As on downy Pinions soft   20
Over the Morning of my Day
Underneath the Net I stray
Now intreating Burning Fire
Now intreating Iron Wire
Now intreating Tears & Sighs   25
O when will the morning rise

---

after an early owner, has also been called "The Ballads Manuscript" because, as Bentley discovered (*Studies in Bibliography* 19 [1966]), it was written on paper salvaged from *Designs to a Series of Ballads* (1802), a collaborative project with Blake's Felpham patron William Hayley (see the chronology). Our own title, "The 'Auguries' Manuscript," named for the booklet's longest poem, recognizes the portentousness of the entire collection in broaching themes and images that recur in Blake's later writings.

For commentary on the whole series, see Hazard Adams, *William Blake: A Reading of the Shorter Poems* (1963); on the sexual themes, see Catherine L. McClenahan in *Spirits of Fire: English Romantic Writers and Contemporary Historical Methods* (1990), ed. G. A. Rosso and Daniel P. Watkins; and John Sutherland, *PMLA* 87, no. 3 (1972), 424–31. Our text is derived from the facsimile of the manuscript published by the Pierpont Morgan Library, New York, with an introduction by Charles Ryskamp (1972), collated with Erdman's, Bentley's, and Ostriker's texts.

The Mental Traveller[1]

I traveld thro' a Land of Men
A Land of Men & Women too
And heard & saw such dreadful things
As cold Earth wanderers never knew

For there the Babe is born in joy   5
That was begotten in dire woe
Just as we Reap in joy the fruit
Which we in bitter tears did sow

And if the Babe is born a Boy
He's given to a Woman Old   10
Who nails him down upon a rock
Catches his Shrieks in Cups of gold

She binds iron thorns around his head
She pierces both his hands & feet
She cuts his heart out at his side   15
To make it feel both cold & heat

Her fingers number every Nerve
Just as a Miser counts his gold
She lives upon his shrieks & cries
And She grows young as he grows old   20

Till he becomes a bleeding youth
And she becomes a Virgin bright
Then he rends up his Manacles
And binds her down for his delight

He plants himself in all her Nerves   25
Just as a Husbandman his mould
And she becomes his dwelling place
And Garden fruitful Seventy fold

An aged Shadow soon he fades
Wandring round an Earthly Cot[2]   30
Full filled all with gems & gold
Which he by industry had got

And these are the gems of the Human Soul
The rubies & pearls of a lovesick eye
The countless gold of the akeing heart   35
The martyrs groan & the lovers sigh

1. For commentaries, see John H. Sutherland, *ELH* 22, no. 2 (1955), 136–47; Martin K. Nurmi, *Studies in Romanticism* 3 (1964), 109–17; Gerald E. Enscoe, *Papers on Language and Literature* 4 (1968), 400–13; and Izak Bouwer and Paul McNally, *Blake: An Illustrated Quarterly* 12 (1978), 184–92. The poem figures prominently in Joyce Cary's *The Horse's Mouth* (see Annette S. Levitt in *William Blake and the Moderns* [1982], ed. Robert J. Bertholf and Levitt).
2. Cottage.

They are his meat they are his drink
He feeds the Beggar & the Poor
And the wayfaring Traveller
For ever open is his door   40

His grief is their eternal joy
They make the roofs & walls to ring
Till from the fire on the hearth
A little Female Babe does spring

And she is all of solid fire   45
And gems & gold that none his hand
Dares stretch to touch her Baby form
Or wrap her in his swaddling-band

But She comes to the Man she loves
If young or old or rich or poor   50
They soon drive out the aged Host
A Beggar at anothers door

He wanders weeping far away
Untill some other take him in
Oft blind & age-bent sore distrest   55
Untill he can a Maiden win

And to Allay his freezing Age
The Poor Man takes her in his arms
The Cottage fades before his Sight
The Garden & its lovely Charms   60

The Guests are scatterd thro' the land
For the Eye altering alters all
The Senses roll themselves in fear
And the flat Earth becomes a Ball

The Stars Sun Moon all shrink away   65
A desart vast without a bound
And nothing left to eat or drink
And a dark desart all around

The honey of her Infant lips
The bread & wine of her sweet smile   70
The wild game of her roving Eye
Does him to Infancy beguile

For as he eats & drinks he grows
Younger & younger every day
And on the desart wild they both   75
Wander in terror & dismay

Like the wild Stag she flees away
Her fear plants many a thicket wild
While he pursues her night & day
By various arts of Love beguild   80

By various arts of Love & Hate
Till the wide desert planted oer
With Labyrinths of wayward Love
Where roams the Lion Wolf & Boar

Till he becomes a wayward Babe   85
And she a weeping Woman Old
Then many a Lover wanders here
The Sun & Stars are nearer rolld

The trees bring forth sweet Extacy
To all who in the desert roam   90
Till many a City there is Built
And many a pleasant Shepherds home

But when they find the frowning Babe
Terror strikes thro the region wide
They cry the Babe the Babe is Born   95
And flee away on Every side

For who dare touch the frowning form
His arm is witherd to its root
Lions Boars Wolves all howling flee
And every Tree does shed its fruit   100

And none can touch that frowning form
Except it be a Woman Old
She nails him down upon the Rock
And all is done as I have told

The Land of Dreams

Awake awake my little Boy
Thou wast thy Mothers only joy
Why dost thou weep in thy gentle sleep
Awake thy Father does thee keep

O what Land is the Land of Dreams   5
What are its Mountains & what are its Streams
O Father I saw my Mother there
Among the Lillies by waters fair

Among the Lambs clothed in white
She walkd with her Thomas in sweet delight   10
I wept for joy like a dove I mourn
O when shall I again return

Dear Child I also by pleasant Streams
Have wanderd all Night in the Land of Dreams
But tho calm & warm the Waters wide   15
I could not get to the other side

Father O Father what do we here
In this Land of unbelief & fear
The Land of Dreams is better far
Above the light of the Morning Star   20

Mary

Sweet Mary the first time she ever was there
Came into the Ball room among the Fair
The young Men & Maidens around her throng
And these are the words upon every tongue

An Angel is here from the heavenly Climes   5
Or again does return the Golden times
Her eyes outshine every brilliant ray
She opens her lips tis the Month of May

Mary moves in soft beauty & conscious delight
To augment with sweet smiles all the joys of the Night 10
Nor once blushes to own to the rest of the Fair
That sweet Love & Beauty are worthy our care

In the Morning the Villagers rose with delight
And repeated with pleasure the joys of the night
And Mary arose among Friends to be free   15
But no Friend from henceforward thou Mary shalt see

Some said she was proud some calld her a whore
And some when she passed by shut to the door
A damp cold came oer her her blushes all fled
Her lillies & roses are blighted & shed   20

O why was I born with a different Face[3]
Why was I not born like this Envious Race
Why did Heaven adorn me with bountiful hand
And then set me down in an envious Land

To be weak as a Lamb & smooth as a Dove   25
And not to raise Envy is calld Christian Love
But if you raise Envy your Merits to blame
For planting such spite in the weak & the tame

I will humble my Beauty I will not dress fine
I will keep from the Ball & my Eyes shall not shine   30
And if any Girls Lover forsakes her for me
I'll refuse him my hand & from Envy be free

She went out in Morning attird plain & neat
Proud Marys gone Mad said the Child in the Street
She went out in Morning in plain neat attire   35
And came home in Evening bespatterd with mire

---

3. For a variation on this quatrain, see Blake's letter to Butts, August 16, 1803.

She trembled & wept sitting on the Bed side
She forgot it was Night & she trembled & cried
She forgot it was Night she forgot it was Morn
Her soft Memory imprinted with Faces of Scorn   40

With Faces of Scorn & with Eyes of disdain
Like foul Fiends inhabiting Marys mild Brain
She remembers no Face like the Human Divine
All Faces have Envy sweet Mary but thine

And thine is a Face of sweet Love in Despair   45
And thine is a Face of mild sorrow & care
And thine is a Face of wild terror & fear
That shall never be quiet till laid on its bier

The Crystal Cabinet[4]

The Maiden caught me in the Wild
Where I was dancing merrily
She put me into her Cabinet
And Lockd me up with a golden Key

This Cabinet is formd of Gold   5
And Pearl & Crystal shining bright
And within it opens into a World
And a little lovely Moony Night

Another England there I saw
Another London with its Tower   10
Another Thames & other Hills
And another pleasant Surrey Bower

Another Maiden like herself
Translucent lovely shining clear
Threefold each in the other closd   15
O what a pleasant trembling fear

O what a smile a threefold Smile
Filld me that like a flame I burnd
I bent to Kiss the lovely Maid
And found a Threefold Kiss returnd   20

I strove to sieze the inmost Form
With ardor fierce & hands of flame
But burst the Crystal Cabinet
And like a Weeping Babe became

A weeping Babe upon the wild   25
And Weeping Woman pale reclind

---

4. For commentary, see Thomas A. Vogler in *Enlightenment Allegory: Theory, Practice, and Context of Allegory in the Late Seventeenth and Eighteenth Centuries* (1993), ed. Kevin L. Cope.

And in the outward air again
I filld with woes the passing Wind

The Grey Monk[5]

I die I die the Mother said
My Children die for lack of Bread
What more has the merciless Tyrant said
The Monk sat down on the Stony Bed

The blood red ran from the Grey Monks side   5
His hands & feet were wounded wide
His Body bent his arms & knees
Like to the roots of ancient trees

His eye was dry no tear could flow
A hollow groan first spoke his woe   10
He trembled & shudderd upon the Bed
At length with a feeble cry he said

When God commanded this hand to write
In the studious hours of deep midnight
He told me the writing I wrote should prove   15
The Bane of all that on Earth I lovd

My Brother starvd between two Walls
His Childrens Cry my Soul appalls
I mockd at the wrack & griding chain
My bent body mocks their torturing pain   20

Thy Father drew his sword in the North
With his thousands strong he marched forth
Thy Brother has armd himself in Steel
To avenge the wrongs thy Children feel

But vain the Sword & vain the Bow   25
They never can work Wars overthrow
The Hermits Prayer & the Widows tear
Alone can free the World from fear

For a Tear is an Intellectual Thing
And a Sigh is the Sword of an Angel King   30
And the bitter groan of the Martyrs woe
Is an Arrow from the Almighties Bow

The hand of Vengeance found the Bed
To which the Purple Tyrant fled
The iron hand crushd the Tyrants head   35
And became a Tyrant in his stead

---

5. Without changing a word, Blake reset stanzas 2 and 8 as stanzas 4 and 6 of "I saw a Monk of Charlemaine" in "To the Deists," Preface to *Jersualem*, Chapter 3 (**53**).

Auguries of Innocence

To see a World in a Grain of Sand
And a Heaven in a Wild Flower
Hold Infinity in the palm of your hand
And Eternity in an hour
A Robin Red breast in a Cage[6]   5
Puts all Heaven in a Rage
A Dove house filld with doves & Pigeons
Shudders Hell thro all its regions
A dog starvd at his Masters Gate
Predicts the ruin of the State   10
A Horse misusd upon the Road
Calls to Heaven for Human blood
Each outcry of the hunted Hare
A fibre from the Brain does tear
A Skylark wounded in the wing   15
A Cherubim does cease to sing
The Game Cock clipd & armd for fight
Does the Rising Sun affright
Every Wolfs & Lions howl
Raises from Hell a Human Soul   20
The wild deer wandring here & there
Keeps the Human Soul from Care
The Lamb misusd breeds Public strife
And yet forgives the Butchers Knife
The Bat that flits at close of Eve   25
Has left the Brain that wont Believe
The Owl that calls upon the Night
Speaks the Unbelievers fright
He who shall hurt the little Wren
Shall never be belovd by Men   30
He who the Ox to wrath has movd
Shall never be by Woman lovd
The wanton Boy that kills the Fly
Shall feel the Spiders enmity
He who torments the Chafers sprite   35
Weaves a Bower in endless Night
The Catterpiller on the Leaf
Repeats to thee thy Mothers grief
Kill not the Moth nor Butterfly
For the Last Judgment draweth nigh   40
He who shall train the Horse to War
Shall never pass the Polar Bar
The Beggers Dog & Widows Cat
Feed them & thou wilt grow fat
The Gnat that sings his Summers song   45
Poison gets from Slanders tongue
The poison of the Snake & Newt
Is the sweat of Envys Foot

6. On the stanzas on cruelty to animals, brought together in Erdman's editorial arrangement, see David Perkins, *Blake: An Illustrated Quarterly* 33 (1999), 4–11 and his *Romanticism and Animal Rights* (2003).

The Poison of the Honey Bee
Is the Artists jealousy   50
The Princes Robes & Beggars Rags
Are Toadstools on the Misers Bags
A truth thats told with bad intent
Beats all the Lies you can invent
It is right it should be so   55
Man was made for Joy & Woe
And when this we rightly know
Thro the World we safely go
Joy & Woe are woven fine
A Clothing for the soul divine   60
Under every grief & pine
Runs a joy with silken twine
The Babe is more than Swadling Bands
Throughout all these Human Lands
Tools were made & Born were hands   65
Every Farmer Understands
Every Tear from Every Eye
Becomes a Babe in Eternity
This is caught by Females bright
And returnd to its own delight   70
The Bleat the Bark Bellow & Roar
Are Waves that Beat on Heavens Shore
The Babe that weeps the Rod beneath
Writes Revenge in realms of Death
The Beggars Rags fluttering in Air   75
Does to Rags the Heavens tear
The Soldier armd with Sword & Gun
Palsied strikes the Summers Sun
The poor Mans Farthing is worth more
Than all the Gold on Africs Shore.   80
One Mite wrung from the Labrers hands
Shall buy & sell the Misers Lands
Or if protected from on high
Does that whole Nation sell & buy
He who mocks the Infants Faith   85
Shall be mock'd in Age & Death
He who shall teach the Child to Doubt
The rotting Grave shall neer get out
He who respects the Infants faith
Triumphs over Hell & Death   90
The Childs Toys & the Old Mans Reasons
Are the Fruits of the Two seasons
The Questioner who sits so sly
Shall never know how to Reply
He who replies to words of Doubt   95
Doth put the Light of Knowledge out
The Strongest Poison ever known
Came from Caesars Laurel Crown
Nought can Deform the Human Race
Like to the Armours iron brace   100
When Gold & Gems adorn the Plow

To peaceful Arts shall Envy Bow
A Riddle or the Crickets Cry
Is to Doubt a fit Reply
The Emmets Inch & Eagles Mile   105
Make Lame Philosophy to smile
He who Doubts from what he sees
Will neer Believe do what you Please
If the Sun & Moon should Doubt
Theyd immediately Go out   110
To be in a Passion you Good may do
But no Good if a Passion is in you
The Whore & Gambler by the State
Licencd build that Nations Fate
The Harlots cry from Street to Street   115
Shall weave Old Englands winding Sheet
The Winners Shout the Losers Curse
Dance before dead Englands Hearse
Every Night & every Morn
Some to Misery are Born   120
Every Morn & every Night
Some are Born to sweet delight
Some are Born to sweet delight
Some are Born to Endless Night
We are led to Believe a Lie   125
When we see not Thro the Eye
Which was Born in a Night to perish in a Night[7]
When the Soul Slept in Beams of Light
God Appears & God is Light
To those poor Souls who dwell in Night   130
But does a Human Form Display
To those who Dwell in Realms of day

Long John Brown & Little Mary Bell

Little Mary Bell had a Fairy in a Nut
Long John Brown had the Devil in his Gut
Long John Brown lovd Little Mary Bell
And the Fairy drew the Devil into the Nut-shell

Her Fairy skipd out & her Fairy skipd in   5
He laughd at the Devil saying Love is a Sin
The devil he raged & the Devil he was wroth
And the devil enterd into the Young Mans broth

He was soon in the Gut of the loving Young Swain
For John eat & drank to drive away Loves pain   10
But all he could do he grew thinner & thinner
Tho he eat & drank as much as ten Men for his dinner

---

7. Cf. Jonah 4:10: "Thou hast had pity on the gourd . . . which came up in a night, and perished in a night." Lines 125–128 reappear, slightly altered, in "The Everlasting Gospel" [k] 103–106.

Some said he had a Wolf in his stomach day & night
Some said he had the Devil & they guessd right
The fairy skipd about in his glory Joy & Pride   15
And he laughd at the Devil till poor John Brown died

Then the Fairy skipd out of the old Nut shell
And woe & alack for Pretty Mary Bell
For the Devil crept in when The Fairy skipd out
And there goes Miss Bell with her fusty old Nut   20

William Bond

I wonder whether the Girls are mad
And I wonder whether they mean to kill
And I wonder if William Bond will die
For assuredly he is very ill

He went to Church in a May morning   5
Attended by Fairies one two & three
But the Angels Of Providence drove them away
And he returnd home in Misery

He went not out to the Field nor Fold
He went not out to the Village nor Town   10
But he came home in a black black cloud
And took to his Bed & there lay down

And an Angel of Providence at his Feet
And an Angel of Providence at his Head
And in the midst a Black Black Cloud   15
And in the midst the Sick Man on his Bed

And on his Right hand was Mary Green
And on his Left hand was his Sister Jane
And their tears fell thro the black black Cloud
To drive away the sick mans pain   20

O William if thou dost another Love
Dost another Love better than poor Mary
Go & take that other to be thy Wife
And Mary Green shall her Servant be

Yes Mary I do another Love   25
Another I Love far better than thee
And Another I will have for my Wife
Then what have I to do with thee

For thou art Melancholy Pale
And on thy Head is the cold Moons shine   30
But she is ruddy & bright as Day
And the Sun beams dazzle from her eyne

Mary trembled & Mary chilld
And Mary fell down on the right hand floor
That William Bond & his Sister Jane   35
Scarce could recover Mary more

When Mary woke & found her Laid
On the Right hand of her William dear
On the Right hand of his loved Bed
And saw her William Bond so near   40

The Fairies that fled from William Bond
Danced around her Shining Head
They danced over the Pillow white
And the Angels of Providence left the Bed

I thought Love livd in the hot sun Shine   45
But O he lives in the Moony light
I thought to find Love in the heat of day
But sweet Love is the Comforter of Night

Seek Love in the Pity of others Woe
In the gentle relief of anothers care   50
In the darkness of night & the winters snow
In the naked & outcast Seek Love There

FROM VALA/THE FOUR ZOAS (C. 1797–1805)[†]

The Four Zoa's $\boxed{1}$

The torments of Love & Jealousy in
The Death and Judgement
of Albion the Ancient Man

by William Blake 1797

Rest before Labour[1] $\boxed{2}$

VALA

Night the First[2] $\boxed{3}$

The Song of the Aged Mother which shook the heavens
    with wrath
Hearing the march of long resounding strong heroic Verse
Marshalld in order for the day of Intellectual Battle

---

† Blake's original title for his first epic-scale work, carefully inked in 1797 on fine atlas-size paper
left over from his work on engravings for Edward Young's *Night Thoughts* (1796–97), was *Vala, or
The Death and Judgement of the Ancient Man, A Dream of Nine Nights.* After taking the manuscript
with him to Felpham and back (1800–3) and repeatedly reworking the inked text and associated
drawings, supplemented by pages salvaged from proof sheets of the *Night Thoughts* engravings, he
revised the title, presented here in Erdman's simplified lineation: "The Four Zoa's / ~~VALA~~ / ~~or~~ / The

Four Mighty Ones are in every Man: a Perfect Unity
Cannot Exist but from the Universal Brotherhood of Eden   5
The Universal Man. To Whom be Glory Evermore Amen[3]

What are the Natures of those Living Creatures the
    Heavenly Father only
Knoweth No Individual Knoweth nor Can know in all Eternity

Los was the fourth immortal starry one, & in the Earth
Of a bright Universe, Empery attended day & night   10
Days & nights of revolving joy, Urthona was his name
In Eden; in the Auricular Nerves of Human life   4
Which is the Earth of Eden, he his Emanations propagated
Fairies of Albion afterwards Gods of the Heathen, Daughter of
    Beulah Sing
His fall into Division & his Resurrection to Unity

---

torments of Love & Jealousy in / The Death and / Judgement / of ^Albion^ the / Ancient Man / ~~A DREAM~~ / ~~of Nine Nights~~." Blake adapted some of his material for *Milton* and *Jerusalem* but never fully abandoned, or "finished," the *Vala/Four Zoas* manuscript. And so it remains perpetually a work in progress, a thing of loose ends and blind alleys, fascinating in its brilliance, beauty, power, and open-endedness, irreducible to a text both readable and fully accurate.

To distinguish the basic plot, or plots, emerging from this multilayered manuscript, it is necessary to oversimplify attributes of the complex and constantly fluctuating leading actors. In *Vala*, Universal Man (heaven and earth, divine and human, male and female) lapses into finitude, the world of time and space, because he cannot resist the beautiful Vala, who is objectified as the deceptive goddess of nature and physical desire. In The *Four Zoas*, the Man, renamed "Albion" as the personification of Britain, falls into disarray because he cannot reconcile and unite his four warring primary attributes, called "Zoas"—Blake's English plural for a word (already plural in Greek) translated "beasts" in Revelation 4:6; (from the Hebrew) "living creatures" in Ezekiel 1:5, 19–23. Humanity (Albion) should be composed of wisdom (Urizen), love (Luvah), imagination (Urthona), and strength (Tharmas), but in the fallen state he is torn apart by hypocritical morality and hyperrationality (Urizen), lust and rage (Orc), confused fantasy (Los), and chaotic weakness (Tharmas).These figures in turn are divided from their Emanations Ahania (intellectual pleasure), Vala (fulfilled desire), Enitharmon (creative inspiration and productivity), and Enion (maternal instinct). In late revisions, Blake further strains the epic framework by introducing Jesus as fallen humanity's protector during the chaotic eons of oblivion and as the saving personification of humanity's fully realized divine potential. For commentary, see Brian Wilkie and Mary Lynn Johnson, *Blake's* Four Zoas: *The Design of a Dream* (1978); Helen T. McNeil, in *Blake's Visionary Forms Dramatic* (1970), ed. Erdman and Grant; and Grant's investigation of the major pictures in *Blake's Sublime Allegory* (1973), ed. Curran and Wittreich, along with such theoretically advanced studies as Donald Ault, *Narrative Unbound: Re-Visioning . . . The Four Zoas* (1987); G. A. Rosso, *Blake's Prophetic Workshop* (1993); Andrew Lincoln, *Spiritual History: A Reading* (1995); John B. Pierce, *Flexible Design: Revisionary Poetics in Blake's* Vala or The Four Zoas (1998); Peter Otto, *Blake's Critique of Transcendence* (2000).

The text of these selections is based on Erdman, *Complete Poetry and Prose* (1988) compared with Bentley, *Writings* (1978) and with indispensable facsimile editions by G. E. Bentley Jr. (full scale, 1963) and by Cettina Tramontano Magno and David V. Erdman (reduced but sharper images, 1987). See also H. M. Margoliouth, *Vala: Blake's Numbered Text* (1956), an attempt to recover the earliest stage of the work from erasures and overwriting, and, for full annotations, see the Penguin edition of Blake's *Complete Poems* by Alicia Ostriker (1977) and the Longman edition by W. H. Stevenson (3rd ed. 2007). Where Blake has crossed out inked words, but then erased his penciled insertions, we have reinstituted his earlier wording. We have also silently corrected obvious slips of the pen (such as omitted letters), removed or altered medial periods, and broadened spaces between words to separate unpunctuated run-on clauses. Page numbers (in boldface) refer to inked numbers (not Blake's) on the manuscript; when page numbers are doubled (21/19) the first numeral refers to the corrected order in the Magno-Erdman facsimile.

1. The roughly scrawled motto is in pencil. A carefully inked Greek epigraph on the third page comes from Ephesians 6:12: "For we wrestle not against flesh and blood, but against principalities, against powers, against the rulers of the darkness of this world, against spiritual wickedness in high places," a passage that radical Protestants understood as sanction to resist the established authority of church and state. Blake taught himself Greek, with Hayley's help, in Felpham (1800–03).
2. Modeled on the organization of Young's *Night Thoughts* into nine "Nights."
3. In the margin of lines 4–6 Blake cites John 17:21–23 (Jesus' prayer for his disciples: "That all may be one; as thou, Father, art in me, and I in thee, that they also may be one in us. . . . I in them, and thou in me, that they may be made perfect in one") and John 1:14 ("And the Word was made flesh, and dwelt among us") and repeats part of the latter text in Greek. (For the "Four Mighty Ones," the Zoas, see the dagger footnote.)

His fall into the Generation of Decay & Death & his Regeneration
  by the Resurrection from the dead   5

*   *   *

Then those in Great Eternity met in the Council of God   19/21
As one Man for contracting their Exalted Senses
They behold Multitude or Expanding they behold as one
As One Man all the Universal family & that one Man
They call Jesus the Christ & they in him & he in them   5
Live in Perfect harmony in Eden the land of life
Consulting as One Man above the Mountain of Snowdon Sublime

For messengers from Beulah come in tears & darkning clouds
Saying Shiloh is in ruins our brother is sick Albion He
Whom thou lovest is sick he wanders from his house of
  Eternity   10
The daughters of Beulah terrified have closd the Gate of the
  Tongue
Luvah & Urizen contend in war around the holy tent

*   *   *

So spoke the Messengers of Beulah. Silently removing   21/19

*   *   *

The Family Divine drew up the Universal tent
Above High Snowdon & closd the Messengers in clouds around
Till the time of the End. Then they Elected Seven, called the
  Seven
Eyes of God & the Seven lamps of the Almighty[4]   5
The Seven are one within the other the Seventh is named Jesus

*   *   *

From Night the [Second]

*   *   *

Then rose the Builders; First the Architect divine his plan   30
Unfolds, The wondrous scaffold reard all round the infinite
Quadrangular the building rose the heavens squared by a line   10
Trigon & cubes[5] divide the elements in finite bonds

*   *   *

But infinitely beautiful the wondrous work arose   32
In sorrow & care, a Golden World whose porches round the
  heavens
And pillard halls & rooms recievd the eternal wandering stars
A wondrous golden Building; many a window many a door   10

---

4. The Seven Eyes—stages in humanity's evolving conception of the divine from a baby-eating idol
   to a self-sacrificing Savior—are named in *Milton* 14/13:17 ff.
5. From this point on, the mathematical imagery of Urizen's Golden World is reminiscent of the Creator's "Solids, Cubes, Cylinders, Cones, Pyramides, Prismas, Dodechædrons" in Guillaume Du
   Bartas's *His Divine Weeks and Works* (1621), trans. Joshua Sylvester. Blake studied geometry with
   Thomas Taylor the Platonist (James King, *Studies in Romanticism* 11 [1972], 153–57).

And many a division let in & out into the vast unknown
Circled in infinite orb immoveable, within its walls & cielings
The heavens were closd and spirits mournd their bondage
   night and day
And the Divine Vision appeard in Luvahs robes of blood
Thus was the Mundane Shell builded by Urizens strong power   15

※   ※   ※

Thus were the stars of heaven created like a golden chain | 33 |
To bind the Body of Man to heaven from falling into the Abyss
Each took his station, & his course began with sorrow & care

In sevens & tens & fifties, hundreds, thousands, numberd all
According to their various powers. Subordinate to Urizen   20
And to his sons in their degrees & to his beauteous daughters
Travelling in silent majesty along their orderd ways
In right lined paths outmeasurd by proportions of number weight
And measure,[6] mathematic motion wondrous, along the deep
In fiery pyramid, or Cube, or unornamented pillar   25
Of fire far shining, travelling along even to its destind end
Then falling down, a terrible space recovring in winter dire
Its wasted strength, it back returns upon a nether course
Till fired with ardour fresh recruited in its humble season
It rises up on high all summer till its wearied course   30
Turns into autumn, such the period of many worlds.
Others triangular right angled course maintain, others obtuse
Acute Scalene, in simple paths, but others move
In intricate ways biquadrate, Trapeziums Rhombs Rhomboids
Paralellograms, triple & quadruple, polygonic   35
In their amazing hard subdued course in the vast deep

※   ※   ※

Thus Enion wails from the dark deep, the golden heavens tremble   100

I am made to sow the thistle for wheat; the nettle for a nourishing
   dainty | 35 |
I have planted a false oath in the earth, it has brought forth
   a poison tree
I have chosen the serpent for a councellor & the dog
For a schoolmaster to my children
I have blotted out from light & living the dove & nightingale   5
And I have caused the earth worm to beg from door to door
I have taught the thief a secret path into the house of the just
I have taught pale artifice to spread his nets upon the morning
My heavens are brass my earth is iron my moon a clod of clay
My sun a pestilence burning at noon & a vapour of death in night 10

What is the price of Experience do men buy it for a song
Or wisdom for a dance in the street? No it is bought with the price

6. Cf. *Marriage* 7, Proverb 14, and n. 2, p. 72 herein. The entire passage alludes to Young's praise of
   the orderly heavens in *Night Thoughts* 9:1081, satirically represented in Blake's watercolor design
   (Butlin 330:473).

Of all that a man hath his house his wife his children
Wisdom is sold in the desolate market where none come to buy
And in the witherd field where the farmer plows for bread in vain   15

It is an easy thing to triumph in the summers sun
And in the vintage & to sing on the waggon loaded with corn
It is an easy thing to talk of patience to the afflicted
To speak the laws of prudence to the houseless wanderer
To listen to the hungry ravens cry in wintry season $\boxed{36}$
When the red blood is filld with wine & with the marrow of lambs

It is an easy thing to laugh at wrathful elements
To hear the dog howl at the wintry door, the ox in the slaughter
    house moan
To see a god on every wind & a blessing on every blast   5
To hear sounds of love in the thunder storm that destroys our
    enemies house
To rejoice in the blight that covers his field, & the sickness that
    cuts off his children
While our olive & vine sing & laugh round our door & our children
    bring fruits & flowers

Then the groan & the dolor are quite forgotten & the slave grinding
    at the mill
And the captive in chains & the poor in the prison, & the soldier in
    the field   10
When the shatterd bone hath laid him groaning among the happier
    dead

It is an easy thing to rejoice in the tents of prosperity
Thus could I sing & thus rejoice, but it is not so with me!

*   *   *

From Night the Fifth

*   *   *

The groans of Enitharmon shake the skies the labring Earth
Till from her heart rending his way a terrible Child sprang forth $\boxed{58}$
In thunder smoke & sullen flames & howlings & fury & blood

Soon as his burning Eyes were opend on the Abyss
The horrid trumpets of the deep bellowd with bitter blasts   20
The Enormous Demons woke & howld around the new born king
Crying Luvah King of Love thou art the King of rage & death

*   *   *

But when fourteen summers & winters had revolved over[7] $\boxed{60}$
Their solemn habitation Los beheld the ruddy boy
Embracing his bright mother & beheld malignant fires

---

7. This episode (60:6–63:9) on Oedipal conflict elaborates on *Urizen* Chapter 7 (20:6–25). For corresponding images, see *Urizen* **21** (front cover) and *America* 3/1.

In his young eyes discerning plain that Orc plotted his death
Grief rose upon his ruddy brows, a tightening girdle grew   10
Around his bosom like a bloody cord. in secret sobs
He burst it, but next morn another girdle succeeds
Around his bosom. Every day he viewd the fiery youth
With silent fear & his immortal cheeks grew deadly pale
Till many a morn & many a night passd over in dire woe   15
Forming a girdle in the day & bursting it at night
The girdle was formd by day by night was burst in twain
Falling down on the rock an iron chain link by link lockd

Enitharmon beheld the bloody chain of nights & days
Depending from the bosom of Los & how with griding pain   20
He went each morning to his labours, with the spectre dark
Calld it the chain of Jealousy. Now Los began to speak
His woes aloud to Enitharmon, since he could not hide
His uncouth plague. He siezd the boy in his immortal hands
While Enitharmon followd him weeping in dismal woe   25
Up to the iron mountains top & there the Jealous chain
Fell from his bosom on the mountain. The Spectre dark
Held the fierce boy Los naild him down binding around his limbs
The accursed chain O how bright Enitharmon howld & cried
Over her son. Obdurate Los bound down her loved Joy   30

                              *   *   *

But when returnd to Golgonooza Los & Enitharmon | 62 |
Felt all the sorrow Parents feel. they wept toward one another   10
And Los repented that he had chaind Orc upon the mountain
And Enitharmons tears prevaild parental love returnd
Tho terrible his dread of that infernal chain They rose
At midnight hasting to their much beloved care
Nine days they traveld thro the Gloom of Entuthon Benithon   15
Los taking Enitharmon by the hand led her along
The dismal vales & up to the iron mountains top where Orc
Howld in the furious wind he thought to give to Enitharmon
Her son in tenfold joy & to compensate for her tears
Even if his own death resulted so much pity him paind   20

But when they came to the dark rock & to the spectrous cave
Lo the young limbs had strucken root into the rock & strong
Fibres had from the Chain of Jealousy inwove themselves
In a swift vegetation round the rock & round the Cave
And over the immortal limbs of the terrible fiery boy   25
In vain they strove now to unchain. In vain with bitter tears
To melt the chain of Jealousy not Enitharmons death
Nor the Consummation of Los could ever melt the chain
Nor unroot the infernal fibres from their rocky bed
Nor all Urthonas strength nor all the power of Luvahs Bulls   30
Tho they each morning drag the unwilling Sun out of the deep
Could uproot the infernal chain, for it had taken root
Into the iron rock & grew a chain beneath the Earth | 63 |
Even to the Center wrapping round the Center & the limbs
Of Orc entering with fibres became one with him a living Chain

Sustained by the Demons life. Despair & Terror & Woe & Rage
Inwrap the Parents in cold clouds as they bend howling over   5
The terrible boy till fainting by his side the Parents fell

Not long they lay Urthonas spectre found herbs of the pit
Rubbing their temples he reviv'd them. all their lamentations
I write not here but all their after life was lamentation

When satiated with grief they returnd back to Golgonooza
Enitharmon on the road of Dranthon felt the inmost gate   10
Of her bright heart burst open & again close with a deadly pain

*   *   *

The Woes of Urizen shut up in the deep dens of Urthona

Ah how shall Urizen the King submit to this dark mansion
Ah how is this! Once on the heights I stretchd my throne
   sublime   25
The mountains of Urizen once of silver where the sons of
   wisdom dwelt
And on whose tops the Virgins sang are rocks of Desolation

My fountains once the haunt of Swans now breed the scaly
   tortoise
The houses of my harpers are become a haunt of crows
The gardens of wisdom are become a field of horrid graves   30
And on the bones I drop my tears & water them in vain

Once how I walked from my palace in gardens of delight $\boxed{64}$
The sons of wisdom stood around the harpers followd with
   harps
Nine virgins clothd in light composd the song to their immortal
   voices
And at my banquets of new wine my head was crownd with joy

Then in my ivory pavilions I slumberd in the noon   5
And walked in the silent night among sweet smelling flowers
Till on my silver bed I slept & sweet dreams round me hoverd
But now my land is darkend & my wise men are departed

My songs are turned to cries of Lamentation
Heard on my Mountains & deep sighs under my palace roofs   10
Because the Steeds of Urizen once swifter than the light
Were kept back from my Lord & from his chariot of mercies[8]

O did I keep the horses of the day in silver pastures
O I refusd the Lord of day the horses of his prince

8. The various Zoas give overlapping and sometimes contradictory accounts of the fall. Urizen's version is based on a combination of the myths of Lucifer and of Phaeton. "My Lord": probably the
Divine Humanity, the true God. Urizen, the light of the mind, obeys the command in 64:22 (recalling Genesis 1:3, "Let there be light"), but like Satan in *Paradise Lost* 5:603–15, he refuses further
service.

O did I close my treasuries with roofs of solid stone   15
And darken all my Palace walls with envyings & hate

O Fool to think that I could hide from his all piercing eyes
The gold & silver & costly stones his holy workmanship
O Fool could I forget the light that filled my bright spheres
Was a reflection of his face who calld me from the deep   20

I well remember for I heard the mild & holy voice
Saying O light spring up & shine & I sprang up from the deep
He gave to me a silver scepter & crownd me with a golden crown
& said Go forth & guide my Son who wanders on the ocean

I went not forth. I hid myself in black clouds of my wrath   25
I calld the stars around my feet in the night of councils dark
The stars threw down their spears & fled naked away[9]
We fell. I siezd thee dark Urthona In my left hand falling

I siezd thee beauteous Luvah[1] thou art faded like a flower
And like a lilly is thy wife Vala witherd by winds   30
When thou didst bear the golden cup at the immortal tables
Thy children smote their fiery wings crownd with the gold
     of heaven

Thy pure feet stepd on the steps divine, too pure for other feet | 65 |
And thy fair locks shadowd thine eyes from the divine effulgence
Then thou didst keep with Strong Urthona the living gates
     of heaven
But now thou art bound down with him even to the gates of hell

Because thou gavest Urizen the wine of the Almighty   5
For steeds of Light that they might run in thy golden chariot of
     pride
I gave to thee the Steeds I pourd the stolen wine
And drunken with the immortal draught fell from my throne
     sublime

I will arise Explore these dens & find that deep pulsation
That shakes my caverns with strong shudders. perhaps this is
     the night   10
Of Prophecy & Luvah hath burst his way from Enitharmon
When Thought is closd in Caves. Then love shall shew its root
     in deepest Hell

End of the Fifth Night

*   *   *

---

9. Echoes "The Tyger," line 17.
1. The Zoa of love in Eternity, now the rage- and lust-filled Orc, is associated with wine through his
   similarities with Ganymede, cupbearer for Zeus, Dionysus, orgiastic god of wine and vegetation,
   and the Edomite who treads in the winepress in Isaiah 63:2–4. Luvah's role as a dying god, in the
   annual seasonal cycle, is ended by Jesus' entering into his sufferings in a section of Night the Ninth
   not included in this edition.

From Night the Seventh

And Urizen Read in his book of brass in sounding tones   80

Listen O Daughters to my voice Listen to the Words of Wisdom
So shall ye govern over all let Moral Duty tune your tongue
But be your hearts harder than the nether millstone

* * *

Compell the poor to live upon a Crust of bread by soft mild arts
Smile when they frown frown when they smile & when a man
    looks pale   10
With labour & abstinence say he looks healthy & happy
And when his children Sicken let them die there are enough
Born even too many & our Earth will be overrun[2]
Without these arts If you would make the poor live with temper
With pomp give every crust of bread you give with gracious
    cunning   15
Magnify small gifts reduce the man to want a gift & then give
    with pomp
Say he smiles if you hear him sigh If pale say he is ruddy
Preach temperance say he is overgorgd & drowns his wit
In strong drink tho you know that bread & water are all
He can afford Flatter his wife pity his children till we can   20
Reduce all to our will as spaniels are taught with art

* * *

Then left the Sons of Urizen the plow & harrow the loom   92
The hammer & the Chisel & the rule & compasses
They forgd the sword the chariot of war the battle ax
The trumpet fitted to the battle & the flute of summer   20
And all the arts of life they changd into the arts of death
The hour glass contemnd because its simple workmanship
Was as the workmanship of the plowman & the water wheel
That raises water into Cisterns broken & burnd in fire
Because its workmanship was like the workmanship of the
    Shepherd   25
And in their stead intricate wheels invented Wheel without
    wheel[3]
To perplex youth in their outgoings & to bind to labours
Of day & night the myriads of Eternity, that they might file
And polish brass & iron hour after hour laborious workmanship
Kept ignorant of the use that they might spend the days
    of wisdom   30
In sorrowful drudgery to obtain a scanty pittance of bread
In ignorance to view a small portion & think that All
And call it Demonstration blind to all the simple rules of life

* * *

2. Perhaps referring to Thomas Malthus, *Essays on the Principles of Population* (1798), though this attitude toward the poor was current before Malthus.
3. The cogwheel, an inversion of the wheels within wheels in the vision of the four "living creatures" (Ezekiel 1), is a synecdoche for the Industrial Revolution and the alienating drudgery of factory labor, especially in the manufacture of weapons.

But then the Spectre enterd Los's bosom Every sigh & groan   95/87
Of Enitharmon bore Urthonas Spectre on its wings
Obdurate Los felt Pity Enitharmon told the tale
Of Urthona. Los embracd the Spectre first as a brother
Then as another Self; astonishd humanizing & in tears   30
In Self abasement Giving up his Domineering lust

           *   *   *

They Builded Golgonooza Los labouring builded pillars high   87
And Domes terrific in the nether heavens for beneath
Was opend new heavens & a new Earth beneath & within
Threefold within the brain within the heart within the loins
A Threefold Atmosphere Sublime continuous from Urthonas
    world   10
But yet having a Limit Twofold named Satan & Adam
But Los stood on the Limit of Translucence weeping &
    trembling

           *   *   *

And first he drew a line upon the walls of shining heaven   98/90
And Enitharmon tincturd it with beams of blushing love[4]
It remaind permanent a lovely form inspird divinely human
Dividing into just proportions Los unwearied labourd
The immortal lines upon the heavens till with sighs of love
Sweet Enitharmon mild Entrancd breathd forth upon the wind   40
The spectrous dead Weeping the Spectres viewd the immortal
    works
Of Los Assimilating to those forms Embodied & Lovely
In youth & beauty in the arms of Enitharmon mild reposing

           *   *   *

Startled was Los he found his Enemy Urizen now
In his hands, he wonderd that he felt love & not hate   65
His whole soul loved him he beheld him an infant
Lovely breathd from Enitharmon he trembled within himself

End of The Seventh Night

From Night the Eighth

           *   *   *

Los took the Body from the Cross Jerusalem weeping over   106
They bore it to the Sepulcher which Los had hewn in the rock   15
Of Eternity for himself he hewed it despairing of Life Eternal[5]

           *   *   *

---

4. Often taken as a mythic account of the cooperative artistic labors of William and Catherine Blake,
   since Catherine worked at Blake's side and sometimes colored the illuminated books. The world
   they are creating is an imaginative, regenerative perception of mundane reality.
5. Los plays the part of Joseph of Arimathea (Matthew 27:60); Vala, the role of Mary Magdalene (not
   included here, but see *Jerusalem* 65:37 ff.).

From Night the Ninth

Being / The Last Judgment

And Los & Enitharmon builded Jerusalem weeping   117
Over the Sepulcher & over the Crucified body
Which to their Phantom Eyes appear'd still in the Sepulcher
But Jesus stood beside them in the Spirit Separating
Their Spirit from their body. Terrified at Non Existence   5
For such they deemd the death of the body. Los his
   vegetable hands
Outstretchd his right hand branching out in fibrous Strength
Siezd the Sun. His left hand like dark roots coverd the Moon
And tore them down cracking the heavens across from immense
   to immense
Then fell the fires of Eternity with loud & shrill   10

Sound of Loud Trumpet thundering along from heaven to heaven
A mighty sound articulate Awake ye dead & come
To judgment from the four winds Awake & Come away
Folding like scrolls of the Enormous volume of Heaven & Earth

❋   ❋   ❋

In the fierce flames the limbs of Mystery lay consuming with
    howling | 119 |
And deep despair. Rattling go up the flames around the
    Synagogue
Of Satan Loud the Serpent Orc ragd thro his twenty Seven
Folds. The tree of Mystery went up in folding flames
Blood issud out in mighty volumes pouring in whirlpools fierce   5
From out the flood gates of the Sky The Gates are burst down pour
The torrents black upon the Earth the blood pours down incessant
Kings in their palaces lie drownd Shepherds their flocks their tents
Roll down the mountains in black torrents Cities Villages
High spires & Castles drownd in the black deluge Shoal on Shoal   10
Float the dead carcases of Men & Beasts driven to & fro on waves
Of foaming blood beneath the black incessant Sky till all
Mysterys tyrants are cut off & not one left on Earth

And when all Tyranny was cut off from the face of Earth
Around the Dragon form of Urizen & round his stony form   15
The flames rolling intense thro the wide Universe
Began to Enter the Holy City Entring the dismal clouds
In furrowd lightnings break their way the wild flames licking up
The Bloody Deluge living flames winged with intellect
And Reason round the Earth they march in order flame by flame   20
From the clotted gore & from the hollow den
Start forth the trembling Millions into flames of mental fire
Bathing their Limbs in the bright visions of Eternity

❋   ❋   ❋

Urizen wept in the dark deep anxious his Scaly form | 121 |
To reassume the human & he wept in the dark deep

Saying O that I had never drank the wine nor eat the bread
Of dark mortality nor cast my view into futurity nor turnd
My back darkning the present clouding with a cloud   5
And building arches high & cities turrets & towers & domes
Whose smoke destroyd the pleasant gardens & whose running
    Kennels
Chokd the bright rivers burdning with my Ships the angry deep
Thro Chaos seeking for delight & in spaces remote
Seeking the Eternal which is always present to the wise   10
Seeking for pleasure which unsought falls round the infants path
And on the fleeces of mild flocks who neither care nor labour
But I the labourer of ages whose unwearied hands
Are thus deformd with hardness with the sword & with the spear
And with the Chisel & the mallet I whose labours vast   15
Order the nations separating family by family
Alone enjoy not I alone in misery supreme

Ungratified give all my joy unto this Luvah & Vala
Then Go O dark futurity I will cast thee forth from these
Heavens of my brain nor will I look upon futurity more   20
I cast futurity away & turn my back upon that void
Which I have made for lo futurity is in this moment
Let Orc consume let Tharmas rage let dark Urthona give
All strength to Los & Enitharmon & let Los self-cursd
Rend down this fabric as a wall ruind & family extinct   25
Rage Orc Rage Tharmas Urizen no longer curbs your rage

So Urizen spoke he shook his snows from off his Shoulders &
     arose
As on a Pyramid of mist his white robes scattering
The fleecy white renewd he shook his aged mantles off
Into the fires Then glorious bright Exulting in his joy   30
He sounding rose into the heavens in naked majesty
In radiant Youth. * * *

                         *   *   *

He ceasd for rivn link from link the bursting Universe explodes   **122**
All things reversd flew from their centers rattling bones
To bones join, shaking convulsd the shivering clay breathes
Each speck of dust to the Earths center nestles round & round
In pangs of an Eternal Birth in torment & awe & fear   30
All spirits deceasd let loose from reptile prisons come in shoals
Wild furies from the tygers brain & from the lions Eyes
And from the ox & ass come moping terrors. from the Eagle
And raven numerous as the leaves of Autumn every species
Flock to the trumpet muttring over the sides of the grave &
     crying   35
In the fierce wind round heaving rocks & mountains filld with
     groans
On rifted rocks suspended in the air by inward fires
Many a woful company & many on clouds & waters
Fathers & friends Mothers & Infants Kings & Warriors
Priests & chaind Captives met together in a horrible fear   40
And every one of the dead appears as he had livd before

And all the marks remain of the Slaves scourge & tyrants Crown   **123**
And of the Priests oergorged Abdomen & of the merchants thin
Sinewy deception & of the warriors outbraving & thoughtlessness
In lineaments too extended & in bones too strait & long

They shew their wounds they accuse they sieze the opressor
     howlings began   5
On the golden palace Songs & joy on the desart the Cold babe
Stands in the furious air he cries the children of six
     thousand years
Who died in infancy rage furious a mighty multitude rage furious
Naked & pale standing on the expecting air to be deliverd
Rend limb from limb the Warrior & the tyrant reuniting in pain   10

                         *   *   *

They see him whom they have piercd they wail because of him   20
They magnify themselves no more against Jerusalem Nor
Against her little ones the innocent accused before the Judges
Shines with immortal Glory trembling the judge springs from
    his throne
Hiding his face in the dust beneath the prisoners feet & saying
Brother of Jesus what have I done intreat thy lord for me   25

Perhaps I may be forgiven While he speaks the flames roll on
And after the flames appears the Cloud of the Son of Man
Descending from Jerusalem with power and great Glory
All nations look up to the Cloud & behold him who was Crucified

The Prisoner answers you scourgd my father to death before
    my face   30
While I stood bound with cords & heavy chains. Your hipocrisy
Shall now avail you nought.[6] So speaking he dashd him with
    his foot

The Cloud is Blood dazling upon the heavens & in the cloud
Above upon its volumes is beheld a throne & a pavement[7]
Of precious stones, surrounded by twenty four venerable
    patriarchs   35
And these again surrounded by four Wonders of the Almighty
Incomprehensible, pervading all amidst & round about
Fourfold each in the other reflected they are named Life's[8]
    in Eternity.
Four Starry Universes going forward from Eternity to Eternity
And the Falln Man who was arisen upon the Rock of Ages   40
Beheld the Vision of God & he arose up from the Rock   124
And Urizen arose up with him walking thro the flames
To meet the Lord coming to Judgment but the flames repelld
    them
Still to the Rock in vain they strove to Enter the Consummation
Together for the Redeemd Man could not enter the
    Consummation   45

           *   *   *

The Sun has left his blackness & has found a fresher morning   138
And the mild moon rejoices in the clear & cloudless night
And Man walks forth from midst of the fires the evil is all consumd
His eyes behold the Angelic spheres arising night & day
The stars consumd like a lamp blown out & in their stead behold
The Expanding Eyes of Man behold the depths of wondrous worlds   25
One Earth one sea beneath nor Erring Globes wander but Stars
Of fire rise up nightly from the Ocean & one Sun
Each morning like a New born Man issues with songs & Joy
Calling the Plowman to his Labour & the Shepherd to his rest

6. The Prisoner's three-line reply, added in the margin, interrupts the apocalyptic series of reconciliations with a realistic expression of the all-too-human desire for vengeance.
7. The throne and its surroundings are from Revelation 4:2 ff; the cloud(s), power, and "great Glory"
(line 23) are from Matthew 24:30.
8. Another translation of *zoa*.

He walks upon the Eternal Mountains raising his heavenly voice   30
Conversing with the Animal forms of wisdom night & day
That risen from the Sea of fire renewd walk oer the Earth

For Tharmas brought his flocks upon the hills & in the Vales
Around the Eternal Mans bright tent the little Children play
Among the wooly flocks The hammer of Urthona sounds   35
In the deep caves beneath his limbs renewd his Lions roar
Around the Furnaces & in Evening sport upon the plains
They raise their faces from the Earth conversing with the Man

How is it we have walkd thro fires & yet are not consumd
How is it that all things are changd even as in ancient times   40
The Sun arises from his dewy bed & the fresh airs | 139 |
Play in his smiling beams giving the seeds of life to grow
And the fresh Earth beams forth ten thousand thousand springs
   of life
Urthona is arisen in his strength no longer now
Divided from Enitharmon no longer the Spectre Los   5
Where is the Spectre of Prophecy where the delusive Phantom
Departed & Urthona rises from the ruinous walls
In all his ancient strength to form the golden armour of science
For intellectual War The war of swords departed now
The dark Religions are departed & sweet Science reigns   10

End of The Dream

FROM EXHIBITION OF PAINTINGS IN FRESCO [ADVERTISEMENT] (1809)[†]

Poetical and Historical Inventions,

By Wm. BLAKE

THE ANCIENT BRITONS—Three Ancient Britons
overthrowing the Army of armed Romans; the Figures
full as large as Life—From the Welch Triades.[1]

In the last Battle that Arthur fought, the most Beautiful was one
That return'd, and the most Strong another: with them also return'd
The most Ugly, and no other beside return'd from the bloody Field.

[†] A commercially printed flyer advertising Blake's 1809 exhibition.
1. Blake probably embellished a manuscript translation of this triad (a Welsh folk form based on groups of three) given him by the commissioner and owner of this now-lost painting, William Owen (later Owen Pughe), who published these lines in Welsh in *Myvyrian Archialogy* (1801–7); see Damon's *Dictionary* 443 and Bentley's *Blake Records* (2004) 308. The only published translation at the time was a three-line passage in Edward Jones, *The Bardic Museum* (1802), 2:25 (Bentley, *Writings* 2:820.n), which identifies the survivors by name but omits mention of the Roman warriors. Blake's younger acquaintance Seymour Kirkup, writing to Rossetti in 1866, refers to a later translation: "The three men who escaped from the battle of Camlan, Mor[vran] son of Tegid, who being so ugly, every one thought he was [the] devil from hell, & fled before him; Sandde, Angel aspect, who having so fine a shape, so beautiful, & so lovely, that no one raised an arm against him, thinking he was an angel [from heaven]; & Glewlwyd with the Mighty

The most Beautiful, the Roman Warriors trembled before and worshipped: The most Strong, they melted before him and dissolved in his presence: The most Ugly they fled with outcries and contortion of their Limbs.

*   *   *

"Fit Audience find tho' few" MILTON.

*   *   *

The Invention of a portable Fresco.

A Wall [of] Canvas or Wood, or any other portable thing, of dimensions ever so large, or ever so small, which may be removed with the same convenience as so many easel Pictures; is worthy the consideration of the Rich and those who have the direction of public Works. If the Frescos of APELLES, of PROTOGENES, of RAPHAEL, or MICHAEL ANGELO could have been removed, we might, perhaps, have them now in England.[2] I could divide Westminster Hall, or the walls of any other great Building, into compartments and ornament them with Frescos, which would be removable at pleasure.

Oil will not drink or absorb Colour enough to stand the test of very little Time and of the Air; it grows yellow, and at length brown. It was never generally used till after VANDYKE's time. All the little old Pictures, called cabinet Pictures, are in Fresco, and not in Oil.

Fresco Painting is properly Miniature, or Enamel Painting; every thing in Fresco is as high finished as Miniature or Enamel, although in Works larger than Life.[3] The Art has been lost: I have recovered it. How this was done, will be told, together with the whole Process, in a Work on Art, now in the Press.[4] The ignorant Insults of Individuals will not hinder me from doing my duty to my Art. Fresco Painting, as it is now practised, is like most other things, the contrary of what it pretends to be.

The execution of my Designs, being all in Water-colours, (that is in Fresco) are regularly refused to be exhibited by the *Royal Academy*, and the *British Institution* has, this year, followed its example, and has effectually excluded me by this Resolution;[5] I therefore invite those Noblemen and Gentleman, who are its Subscribers, to inspect what they have excluded; and those who have been told that my Works are but an unscientific and irregular Eccentricity, a Madman's Scrawls, I demand of them to do me the justice to examine before they decide.

Grasp, for so la[rge] was his size & mighty his strength, that no one could stand before him, & every one fled at his approach" (William Probert, *The Ancient Laws of Cambria* [1823], 403; *Blake Records* [2004], 291). The Romans are included in the version of the Triad that appears in the tale of Culwch and Olwen, first translated (as part of *The Mabinogion*) by Lady Charlotte Guest in 1849.

2. A brazen appeal to the imperialistic spirit of acquisition, at a time when Napoleon was filling the Louvre (renamed Museé Napoleon) with art treasures from the countries he conquered.

3. In insisting that his reinvented fresco—watercolor on a ground of whiting and carpenter's glue affixed to a moveable surface—dries to a hard enamel-like finish, Blake claims for watercolor the durability, portability, and depth of color that had made oil painting, by the eighteenth century, the most prestigious medium for an artist.

4. No such work is known; the reference may be to the *Descriptive Catalogue* (also commercially printed) which though not a formal treatise contains numerous asides on his theories and processes.

5. The Royal Academy had in fact accepted two watercolors (Numbers I and II, *Descriptive Catalogue*) only the year before; for Blake's intermittent 1780–1808 exhibition record, see the chronology. But both the academy and the new British Institution (founded 1805) apparently rejected his experimental frescoes, or "temperas" in 1809 (the very year that John Linnell, later Blake's dear friend, won the British Institution's fifty-guinea prize for a dark landscape in the Dutch manner).

There cannot be more than two or three great Painters or Poets in any Age or Country; and these, in a corrupt state of Society, are easily excluded, but not so easily obstructed. They have excluded Water-colours; it is therefore become necessary that I should exhibit to the Public, in an Exhibition of my own, my Designs, Painted in Water-colours. If Italy is enriched and made great by RAPHAEL, if MICHAEL ANGELO is its supreme glory, if Art is the glory of a Nation, if Genius and Inspiration are the great Origin and Bond of Society, the distinction my Works have obtained from those who best understand such things, calls for my Exhibition as the greatest of Duties to my Country.[6]

[May 15, 1809]   *WILLIAM BLAKE*.

FROM A DESCRIPTIVE CATALOGUE
OF PICTURES (1809)[†]

Poetical and Historical Inventions,

Painted by William Blake in Water Colours,
Being the Ancient Method of Fresco Painting Restored:
And Drawings for Public Inspection
And For Sale by Private Contract

*   *   *

PREFACE.

The eye that can prefer the Colouring of Titian and Rubens to that of Michael Angelo and Rafael, ought to be modest and to doubt its own powers. Connoisseurs talk as if Rafael and Michael Angelo had never seen the

---

6. Cf. "England expects that every man should do his duty, in Arts, as well as in Arms" (E 549), alluding to Nelson's words at Trafalgar (1805).

† The aggrieved and combative tone of Blake's *Catalogue* for his 1809 exhibition in his brother's shop is, in large part, a reaction to Robert Hunt's contemptuous notice of Blake's designs for Blair's *Grave* in *The Examiner* (p. 497 herein) and to a series of slights by Cromek (on this complex quarrel, see note to *Public Address*, p. 439 herein). Although no one else put ideas on art, philosophy, and mythological history together in quite this way, a few of Blake's contemporaries—Henry Fuseli, for example—shared one or another of his provocative opinions. And at least three viewers of the exhibition met his high Miltonic standard of a "fit audience" (quoted in his Advertisement, p. 422 herein): Charles Lamb, who vividly recalled the major pictures (letter of March 15, 1824) but never published his opinion; Henry Crabb Robinson, who purchased six copies of the *Catalogue* to give to friends and praised much of what he read and saw in an essay translated into German for *Vaterlandisches Museum* (January 1811); and the artist Seymour Kirkup, whose appreciative accounts of the grandest and most controversial painting in the show, *The Ancient Britons* (now lost), fifty-five years later, provide eyewitness testimony to its quality. Unfortunately, however, Hunt's hostile review, dismissing Blake as a lunatic, was the only one to appear in an English journal.
The *Catalogue* ranges from commentary on the paintings to explanations of techniques to diatribes on the history of art and contemporary institutions, connoisseurs, and artists. Our selections center on aesthetic, ethical, and theological concerns that recur in Blake's writings; we omit remarks on the state of British art and the work of earlier artists that would require heavy footnoting. Because the brilliance of Blake's observations on his panoramic cavalcade of the *Canterbury Pilgrims* (Butlin 653) cannot be appreciated apart from a large-scale reproduction of the work, we omit most of his exposition of that piece; for commentary, see Gourlay's contribution to *Prophetic Character* (2003), 97–147, which cites valuable previous studies. Of the sixteen pictures exhibited, seven belonged to Blake's patron Thomas Butts and were lent for the occasion; the remaining eleven were offered for sale, apparently without attracting buyers (the whereabouts of five are now unknown).

colouring of Titian or Correggio: They ought to know that Correggio was born two years before Michael Angelo, and Titian but four years after.[1] Both Rafael and Michael Angelo knew the Venetian, and contemned and rejected all he did with the utmost disdain, as that which is fabricated for the purpose to destroy art.

Mr. B. appeals to the Public, from the judgment of those narrow blinking eyes, that have too long governed art in a dark corner. The eyes of stupid cunning never will be pleased with the work any more than with the look of self-devoting genius. The quarrel of the Florentine with the Venetian is not because he does not understand Drawing, but because he does not understand Colouring. How should he? he who does not know how to draw a hand or a foot, know how to colour it.

Colouring does not depend on where the Colours are put, but on where the lights and darks are put, and all depends on Form or Outline. On where that is put; where that is wrong, the Colouring never can be right; and it is always wrong in Titian and Correggio, Rubens and Rembrandt. Till we get rid of Titian and Correggio, Rubens and Rembrandt, We never shall equal Rafael and Albert Durer, Michael Angelo, and Julio Romano.

NUMBER I.

The spiritual form of Nelson guiding Leviathan, in whose wreathings are infolded the Nations of the Earth.

*   *   *

NUMBER II, ITS COMPANION[2]

The spiritual form of Pitt, guiding Behemoth; he is that Angel who, pleased to perform the Almighty's orders, rides on the whirlwind, directing the storms of war: He is ordering the Reaper to reap the Vine of the Earth, and the Plowman to plow up the Cities and Towers.

This Picture also is a proof of the power of colours unsullied with oil or with any cloggy vehicle. Oil has falsely been supposed to give strength to colours: but a little consideration must shew the fallacy of this opinion. Oil will not drink or absorb colour enough to stand the test of very little time and of the

---

For discussions of the paintings, see Butlin's section on "Blake's Exhibition" in *Paintings and Drawings*, Numbers 649–66. For facsimiles and excellent notes not only on the *Catalogue* but also on all of Blake's conventionally printed writings, see G. E. Bentley Jr., ed. *William Blake's Works in Conventional Typography* (1984). For information on the spirit of the exhibition and facts on how the pictures must have been hung, based on rediscovered floor plans of James Blake's shop, see Troy R. C. Patenaude, *British Art Journal* 4, no. 1 (2003), 52–63; see also the section on temperas in *William Blake: The Painter at Work* (2003), ed. Joyce H. Townsend (Tate Gallery).

1. Blake is wrong about the birth dates: Michaelangelo (1475–1564), Raphael (1483–1520), Titian (c. 1485/88–1576), Correggio (1494–1534).
2. Numbers I and II, now in the Tate Gallery, London (Butlin 649, 651; updated in his Tate catalog, *William Blake*, 1990). Exhibited in 1808 at the Royal Academy and in 1812 at the Water Colour Society. Blake's panegyrical tone notwithstanding, these "grand Apotheoses" (*Exhibition* advertisement) of recently deceased military and political leaders (Nelson in 1805, Pitt in 1806) are apocalyptic visions of the horrors of war.

air. It deadens every colour it is mixed with, at its first mixture, and in a little time becomes a yellow mask over all that it touches. Let the works of modern Artists since Rubens' time witness the villany of some one at that time, who first brought oil Painting into general opinion and practice: since which we have never had a Picture painted, that could shew itself by the side of an earlier production. Whether Rubens or Vandyke, or both, were guilty of this villany, is to be enquired in another work on Painting, and who first forged the silly story and known falshood, about John of Bruges inventing oil colours: in the mean time let it be observed, that before Vandyke's time, and in his time all the genuine Pictures are on Plaster or Whiting grounds and none since.

The two Pictures of Nelson and Pitt are compositions of a mythological cast, similar to those Apotheoses of Persian, Hindoo, and Egyptian Antiquity, which are still preserved on rude monuments, being copies from some stupendous originals now lost or perhaps buried till some happier age. The Artist having been taken in vision into the ancient republics, monarchies, and patriarchates of Asia, has seen those wonderful originals called in the Sacred Scriptures the Cherubim, which were sculptured and painted on walls of Temples, Towers, Cities, Palaces, and erected in the highly cultivated states of Egypt, Moab, Edom, Aram, among the Rivers of Paradise, being originals from which the Greeks and Hetrurians copied Hercules, Farnese, Venus of Medicis, Apollo Belvidere, and all the grand works of ancient art. They were executed in a very superior style to those justly admired copies, being with their accompaniments terrific and grand in the highest degree. The Artist has endeavoured to emulate the grandeur of those seen in his vision, and to apply it to modern Heroes, on a smaller scale.

No man can believe that either Homer's Mythology, or Ovid's, were the production of Greece, or of Latium; neither will any one believe, that the Greek statues, as they are called, were the invention of Greek Artists; perhaps the Torso is the only original work remaining; all the rest are evidently copies, though fine ones, from greater works of the Asiatic Patriarchs. The Greek Muses are daughters of Mnemosyne, or Memory, and not of Inspiration or Imagination, therefore not authors of such sublime conceptions. Those wonderful originals seen in my visions, were some of them one hundred feet in height; some were painted as pictures, and some carved as basso relievos, and some as groupes of statues, all containing mythological and recondite meaning, where more is meant than meets the eye. The Artist wishes it was now the fashion to make such monuments, and then he should not doubt of having a national commission to execute these two Pictures on a scale that is suitable to the grandeur of the nation, who is the parent of his heroes, in high finished fresco, where the colours would be as pure and as permanent as precious stones though the figures were one hundred feet in height.

※   ※   ※

NUMBER III.[3]

*Sir Jeffery Chaucer and the nine and twenty Pilgrims
on their journey to Canterbury.*

*   *   *

The characters of Chaucer's Pilgrims are the characters which compose all ages and nations: as one age falls, another rises, different to mortal sight, but to immortals only the same; for we see the same characters repeated again and again, in animals, vegetables, minerals, and in men; nothing new occurs in identical existence; Accident ever varies, Substance can never suffer change nor decay.

Of Chaucer's characters, as described in his Canterbury Tales, some of the names or titles are altered by time, but the characters themselves for ever remain unaltered, and consequently they are the physiognomies or lineaments of universal human life, beyond which Nature never steps. Names alter, things never alter. I have known multitudes of those who would have been monks in the age of monkery, who in this deistical age are deists. As Newton numbered the stars, and as Linneus numbered the plants, so Chaucer numbered the classes of men.

*   *   *

Visions of these eternal principles or characters of human life appear to poets, in all ages; the Grecian gods were the ancient Cherubim of Phoenicia; but the Greeks, and since them the Moderns, have neglected to subdue the gods of Priam. These Gods are visions of the eternal attributes, or divine names, which, when erected into gods, become destructive to humanity. They ought to be the servants, and not the masters of man, or of society. They ought to be made to sacrifice to Man, and not man compelled to sacrifice to them; for when separated from man or humanity, who is Jesus the Saviour, the vine of eternity, they are thieves and rebels, they are destroyers.

*   *   *

Such are the characters that compose this Picture, which was painted in self-defence against the insolent and envious imputation of unfitness for finished and scientific art; and this imputation, most artfully and industriously endeavoured to be propagated among the public by ignorant hirelings. The painter courts comparison with his competitors, who, having received fourteen hundred guineas and more from the profits of his designs, in that well-known work, Designs for Blair's Grave, have left him to shift for himself, while others, more obedient to an employer's opinions and directions, are employed, at a great expence, to produce works, in succession to his, by which they acquired public patronage. This has hitherto been his lot—to get patronage for others and then to be left and neglected, and his work, which gained that patronage, cried down as eccentricity and madness; as unfinished and neglected by the artist's violent temper, he is sure the works now exhibited, will give the lie to such aspersions.

*   *   *

3. Tempera now in Pollok House, Glasgow (Butlin, 653).

NUMBER IV.[4]

The Bard, from Gray.

* * *

The connoisseurs and artists who have made objections to Mr. B.'s mode of representing spirits with real bodies, would do well to consider that the Venus, the Minerva, the Jupiter, the Apollo, which they admire in Greek statues, are all of them representations of spiritual existences of Gods immortal, to the mortal perishing organ of sight; and yet they are embodied and organized in solid marble. Mr. B. requires the same latitude and all is well. The Prophets describe what they saw in Vision as real and existing men whom they saw with their imaginative and immortal organs; the Apostles the same; the clearer the organ the more distinct the object. A Spirit and a Vision are not, as the modern philosophy supposes, a cloudy vapour or a nothing: they are organized and minutely articulated beyond all that the mortal and perishing nature can produce. He who does not imagine in stronger and better lineaments, and in stronger and better light than his perishing mortal eye can see does not imagine at all. The painter of this work asserts that all his imaginations appear to him infinitely more perfect and more minutely organized than any thing seen by his mortal eye. Spirits are organized men: Moderns wish to draw figures without lines, and with great and heavy shadows; are not shadows more unmeaning than lines, and more heavy? O who can doubt this!

NUMBER V.[5]

The Ancient Britons

In the last Battle of King Arthur only Three Britons escaped, these were the Strongest Man, the Beautifullest Man, and the Ugliest Man; these three marched through the field unsubdued, as Gods, and the Sun of Britain set, but shall arise again with tenfold splendor when Arthur shall awake from sleep, and resume his dominion over earth and ocean.

The three general classes of men who are represented by the most Beautiful, the most Strong, and the most Ugly, could not be represented by any historical facts but those of our own country, the Ancient Britons; without violating costume. The Britons (say historians) were naked civilized men, learned, studious, abstruse in thought and contemplation; naked, simple, plain, in their acts and manners; wiser than after-ages. They were overwhelmed by brutal arms all but a small remnant; Strength, Beauty, and Ugliness escaped the wreck, and remain for ever unsubdued, age after age.

---

4. Tempera now in the Tate Gallery (Butlin, 655). For Blake's watercolor illustrations of Gray's *The Bard*, part of a series of 116 designs for Gray commissioned by Flaxman; see Irene Tayler, *Blake's Illustrations to the Poems of Gray* (1971), the Blake Trust facsimile edited by Keynes (1971), and the online Blake Archive edition; the series is also available in an affordable facsimile by Dover Publications (2000).
5. Blake's largest tempera, now lost (Butlin, 657); commissioned by the antiquarian and translator William Owen, later Owen Pughe (Bentley, *Blake Records* [2004], 291. Estimated by Kirkup, from-memory, at fourteen by ten feet (*Blake Records*, 295); but according to Patenaude (see dagger note), James Blake's shop had no wall quite that large.

The British Antiquities are now in the Artist's hands; all his visionary contemplations, relating to his own country and its ancient glory, when it was as it again shall be, the source of learning and inspiration. Arthur was a name for the constellation Arcturus, or Bootes, the Keeper of the North Pole. And all the fables of Arthur and his round table; of the warlike naked Britons; of Merlin; of Arthur's conquest of the whole world; of his death, or sleep, and promise to return again; of the Druid monuments, or temples; of the pavement of Watlingstreet; of London stone; of the caverns in Cornwall, Wales, Derbyshire, and Scotland; of the Giants of Ireland and Britain; of the elemental beings, called by us by the general name of Fairies; and of these three who escaped, namely, Beauty, Strength, and Ugliness, Mr. B. has in his hands poems of the highest antiquity. Adam was a Druid, and Noah; also Abraham was called to succeed the Druidical age, which began to turn allegoric and mental signification into corporeal command, whereby human sacrifice would have depopulated the earth. All these things are written in Eden. The artist is an inhabitant of that happy country, and if every thing goes on as it has begun, the world of vegetation and generation may expect to be opened again to Heaven, through Eden, as it was in the beginning.

The Strong man represents the human sublime. The Beautiful man represents the human pathetic, which was in the wars of Eden divided into male and female. The Ugly man represents the human reason. They were originally one man, who was fourfold; he was self-divided, and his real humanity slain on the stems of generation, and the form of the fourth was like the Son of God. How he became divided is a subject of great sublimity and pathos. The Artist has written it under inspiration, and will, if God please, publish it; it is voluminous, and contains the ancient history of Britain, and the world of Satan and of Adam.

In the mean time he has painted this Picture, which supposes that in the reign of that British Prince, who lived in the fifth century, there were remains of those naked Heroes, in the Welch Mountains; they are there now, Gray saw them in the person of his bard on Snowdon; there they dwell in naked simplicity; happy is he who can see and converse with them above the shadows of generation and death. The giant Albion, was Patriarch of the Atlantic, he is the Atlas of the Greeks, one of those the Greeks called Titans. The stories of Arthur are the acts of Albion, applied to a Prince of the fifth century, who conquered Europe, and held the Empire of the world in the dark age, which the Romans never again recovered. In this Picture, believing with Milton, the ancient British History, Mr. B. has done, as all the ancients did, and as all the moderns, who are worthy of fame, given the historical fact in its poetical vigour; so as it always happens, and not in that dull way that some Historians pretend, who being weakly organized themselves, cannot see either miracle or prodigy; all is to them a dull round of probabilities and possibilities; but the history of all times and places, is nothing else but improbabilities and impossibilities; what we should say, was impossible if we did not see it always before our eyes.

The antiquities of every Nation under Heaven, is no less sacred than that of the Jews. They are the same thing as Jacob Bryant, and all antiquaries have proved. How other antiquities came to be neglected and disbelieved, while those of the Jews are collected and arranged, is an enquiry, worthy of both the Antiquarian and the Divine. All had originally one language, and one religion, this was the religion of Jesus, the everlasting Gospel.[6] Antiquity preaches the Gospel of Jesus. The reasoning historian, turner and twister of causes and consequences, such as Hume, Gibbon and Voltaire; cannot with all their artifice, turn or twist one fact or disarrange self evident action and reality. Reasons and opinions concerning acts, are not history. Acts themselves alone are history, and these are neither the exclusive property of Hume, Gibbon nor Voltaire, Echard, Rapin, Plutarch, nor Herodotus. Tell me the Acts, O historian, and leave me to reason upon them as I please; away with your reasoning and your rubbish. All that is not action is not worth reading. Tell me the What; I do not want you to tell me the Why, and the How; I can find that out myself, as well as you can, and I will not be fooled by you into opinions, that you please to impose, to disbelieve what you think improbable or impossible. His opinions, who does not see spiritual agency, is not worth any man's reading; he who rejects a fact because it is improbable, must reject all History and retain doubts only.

It has been said to the Artist, take the Apollo for the model of your beautiful Man and the Hercules for your strong Man, and the Dancing Fawn for your Ugly Man. Now he comes to his trial. He knows that what he does is not inferior to the grandest Antiques. Superior they cannot be, for human power cannot go beyond either what he does, or what they have done, it is the gift of God, it is inspiration and vision. * * * Milton, Shakspeare, Michael Angelo, Rafael, the finest specimens of Ancient Sculpture and Painting, and Architecture, Gothic, Grecian, Hindoo and Egyptian, are the extent of the human mind. The human mind cannot go beyond the gift of God, the Holy Ghost. To suppose that Art can go beyond the finest specimens of Art that are now in the world, is not knowing what Art is; it is being blind to the gifts of the spirit.

It will be necessary for the Painter to say something concerning his ideas of Beauty, Strength and Ugliness.

The Beauty that is annexed and appended to folly, is a lamentable accident and error of the mortal and perishing life; it does but seldom happen; but with this unnatural mixture the sublime Artist can have nothing to do; it is fit for the burlesque. The Beauty proper for sublime art, is lineaments, or forms and features that are capable of being the receptacles of intellect; accordingly the Painter has given in his beautiful man, his own idea of intellectual Beauty. The face and limbs that deviates or alters least, from infancy to old age, is the face and limbs of greatest Beauty and perfection.

The Ugly likewise, when accompanied and annexed to imbecility and disease, is a subject for burlesque and not for historical grandeur; the Artist has imagined his Ugly man; one approaching to the beast in features and form, his forehead small, without frontals; his jaws large; his nose high on

6. Here Blake reaffirms his endorsement of Jacob Bryant's ideas on the common origin of all myths; cf. *All Religions Are One* and the preface "To the Jews" of *Jerusalem*. Blake's idea of the "religion of Jesus, the everlasting Gospel" was mutual forgiveness; cf. "The Everlasting Gospel" and "The Keys to the Gates."

the ridge, and narrow; his chest and the stamina of his make, comparatively little, and his joints and his extremities large; his eyes with scarce any whites, narrow and cunning, and every thing tending toward what is truly Ugly; the incapability of intellect.

The Artist has considered his strong Man as a receptacle of Wisdom, a sublime energizer; his features and limbs do not spindle out into length, without strength, nor are they too large and unwieldy for his brain and bosom. Strength consists in accumulation of power to the principal seat, and from thence a regular gradation and subordination; strength is compactness, not extent nor bulk.

The strong Man acts from conscious superiority, and marches on in fearless dependance on the divine decrees, raging with the inspirations of a prophetic mind. The Beautiful Man acts from duty, and anxious solicitude for the fates of those for whom he combats. The Ugly Man acts from love of carnage, and delight in the savage barbarities of war, rushing with sportive precipitation into the very teeth of the affrighted enemy.

*   *   *

The flush of health in flesh, exposed to the open air, nourished by the spirits of forests and floods, in that ancient happy period, which history has recorded, cannot be like the sickly daubs of Titian or Rubens. Where will the copier of nature, as it now is, find a civilized man, who has been accustomed to go naked. Imagination only, can furnish us with colouring appropriate, such as is found in the Frescos of Rafael and Michael Angelo: the disposition of forms always directs colouring in works of true art. As to a modern Man stripped from his load of cloathing, he is like a dead corpse. Hence Rubens, Titian, Correggio, and all of that class, are like leather and chalk; their men are like leather, and their women like chalk, for the disposition of their forms will not admit of grand colouring; in Mr. B.'s Britons, the blood is seen to circulate in their limbs; he defies competition in colouring.[7]

*   *   *

NUMBER IX.[8]

Satan calling up his Legions, from Milton's Paradise Lost; a composition for a more perfect Picture,[9] *afterward executed for a Lady of high rank. An experiment Picture.*

This Picture was likewise painted at intervals, for experiment on colours, without any oily vehicle; it may be worthy of attention, not only on account of its composition, but of the great labour which has been bestowed on it, that is, three or four times as much as would have finished a more perfect

7. The next three frescoes are lost: Numbers VI, *A Spirit Vaulting from a Cloud*; VII, *The Goats*; and VIII, *The Spiritual Preceptor*, on a subject "taken from the visions of Emanuel Swedenborg," *Universal Theology*, No. 623, (incorporated into *True Christian Religion*, 1781).
8. A tempera (Butlin, 661), now in poor condition, in the Victoria and Albert Museum, London.
9. Commissioned by the third earl of Egremont; this version remains at Petworth House, Sussex (Butlin, 662).

Picture; the labor has destroyed the lineaments, it was with difficulty brought back again to a certain effect, which it had at first, when all the lineaments were perfect.

These Pictures, among numerous others painted for experiment, were the result of temptations and perturbations, labouring to destroy Imaginative power, by means of that infernal machine, called Chiaro Oscuro, in the hands of Venetian and Flemish Demons; whose enmity to the Painter himself, and to all Artists who study in the Florentine and Roman Schools, may be removed by an exhibition and exposure of their vile tricks. They cause that every thing in art shall become a Machine. They cause that the execution shall be all blocked up with brown shadows. They put the original Artist in fear and doubt of his own original conception. The spirit of Titian was particularly active, in raising doubts concerning the possibility of executing without a model, and when once he had raised the doubt, it became easy for him to snatch away the vision time after time, for when the Artist took his pencil, to execute his ideas, his power of imagination weakened so much, and darkened, that memory of nature and of Pictures of the various Schools possessed his mind, instead of appropriate execution, resulting from the inventions; like walking in another man's style, or speaking or looking in another man's style and manner, unappropriate and repugnant to your own individual character; tormenting the true Artist, till he leaves the Florentine, and adopts the Venetian practice, or does as Mr. B. has done, has the courage to suffer poverty and disgrace, till he ultimately conquers.[1]

✻   ✻   ✻

NUMBER XV.[2]

Ruth.—A Drawing.

✻   ✻   ✻

The great and golden rule of art, as well as of life, is this: That the more distinct, sharp, and wirey the bounding line, the more perfect the work of art; and the less keen and sharp, the greater is the evidence of weak imitation, plagiarism, and bungling. Great inventors, in all ages, knew this: Protogenes and Apelles knew each other by this line. Rafael and Michael Angelo, and Albert Durer, are known by this and this alone. The want of this determinate and bounding form evidences the want of idea in the artist's mind, and the pretence of the plagiary in all its branches. How do we distinguish the oak from the beech, the horse from the ox, but by the bounding outline? How do we distinguish one face or countenance from another, but by the bounding line and its infinite inflexions and movements? What is it that builds a house and plants a garden, but the

---

1. Blake lists the next five works (some titles are altered in Butlin) with little or no comment: X, *The Brahmins*, depicting "Mr. Wilkin translating the Geeta" (Charles Wilkins, trans. *Bhagvat Geeta* [1785]) a watercolor, now lost; XI, *The Body of Abel Found by Adam and Eve*, a watercolor, Fogg Museum, Harvard University (Butlin, 664); XII, *Soldiers Casting Lots for Christ's Garment*, a watercolor for Butts (as are the next two) Fitzwilliam Museum, Cambridge University (Butlin 495); XIII, *Jacob's Dream*, British Museum (Butlin, 438); XIV, *The Angels Hovering over the Body of Jesus in the Sepulchre*, Victoria and Albert Museum (Butlin 500).
2. A biblical watercolor for Butts, now in the Southampton Art Gallery (Butlin, 456).

definite and determinate? What is it that distinguishes honesty from knavery, but the hard and wirey line of rectitude and certainty in the actions and intentions. Leave out this line and you leave out life itself; all is chaos again, and the line of the almighty must be drawn out upon it before man or beast can exist. Talk no more then of Correggio, or Rembrandt, or any other of those plagiaries of Venice or Flanders. They were but the lame imitators of lines drawn by their predecessors, and their works prove themselves contemptible dis-arranged imitations and blundering misapplied copies.

NUMBER XVI.

The Penance of Jane Shore in St. Paul's Church.—A Drawing.

This Drawing was done above Thirty Years ago, and proves to the Author, and he thinks will prove to any discerning eye, that the productions of our youth and of our maturer age are equal in all essential points.[3] If a man is master of his profession, he cannot be ignorant that he is so; and if he is not employed by those who pretend to encourage art, he will employ himself, and laugh in secret at the pretences of the ignorant, while he has every night dropped into his shoe, as soon as he puts it off, and puts out the candle, and gets into bed, a reward for the labours of the day,[4] such as the world cannot give, and patience and time await to give him all that the world can give.

FINIS.

FROM [A VISION OF THE LAST JUDGMENT] (1810)[†]

For the Year 1810

Additions to Blake's Catalogue of Pictures &c

[N70/E554] The Last Judgment when all those are Cast away who trouble Religion with Questions concerning Good & Evil or Eating of the Tree of those Knowledges or Reasonings which hinder the Vision of God, turning all into a Consuming fire, When Imaginative Art & Science & all Intellectual Gifts,

---

3. If Blake really included in his only major exhibition what he describes in the *Catalogue* as a production of his "youth," "done above Thirty Years ago," he must be referring to a sketchy watercolor drawn c. 1779 (Butlin, 67), the year he entered the Royal Academy, or earlier. The more skillful watercolor of 1793 (Butlin, 69), now in the Tate Gallery, does not support Blake's ironic polemic on the consistency of early and late works.

4. The reference to a reward "dropped in his shoe" seems to blend the folk tale of "The Shoemaker and the Elves" with Dutch lore of gifts left in children's wooden shoes by Saint Nicholas.

† This draft for a postscript to the *Descriptive Catalogue* on a large tempera (now lost), *A Vision of the Last Judgment*, is intermingled with drafts for "A Public Address to the Chalcographic Society" in scattered pages of Blake's Notebook. Although the tempera Blake hoped to exhibit in 1810 has not been traced, most of the figures he describes can be seen in a pen-and-wash drawing of the same period (Butlin, 645), now in the Rosenwald Collection, National Gallery of Art. The lost painting is almost certainly the one that Cumberland's sons saw in 1815 ("he has been labouring at it till it is nearly as black as your Hat" [*Blake Records* 2004, 320]) and is probably the one with

all the Gifts of the Holy Ghost, are lookd upon as of no use & only Contention remains to Man, then the Last Judgment begins & its Vision is seen by the Imaginative Eye of Every one according to the situation he holds.

[N68] The Last Judgment is not Fable or Allegory but Vision. Fable or Allegory are a totally distinct & inferior kind of Poetry. Vision or Imagination is a Representation of what Eternally Exists, Really & Unchangeably. Fable or Allegory is Formd by the Daughters of Memory. Imagination is Surrounded by the daughters of Inspiration who in the aggregate are calld Jerusalem. Fable is Allegory but what Critics call The Fable[1] is Vision itself. The Hebrew Bible & the Gospel of Jesus are not Allegory but Eternal Vision or Imagination of All that Exists. Note here that Fable or Allegory is Seldom without some Vision: Pilgrims Progress is full of it, the Greek Poets the same, but Allegory & Vision ought to be known as Two Distinct Things & so calld for the Sake of Eternal Life. Plato has made Socrates say that Poets & Prophets do not Know or Understand what they write or Utter.[2] This is a most Pernicious Falshood. If they do not, pray is an inferior Kind to be calld Knowing? Plato confutes himself.

[N68] The Last Judgment is one of these Stupendous Visions. I have represented it as I saw it. To different People it appears differently as [N69]every thing else does for tho on Earth things seem Permanent they are less permanent than a Shadow as we all know too well.

The Nature of Visionary Fancy or Imagination is very little Known & the Eternal nature & permanence of its ever Existent Images is considerd as less permanent than the things of Vegetative & Generative Nature. Yet the Oak dies as well as the Lettuce but Its Eternal Image & Individuality never dies, but renews by its seed, just so the Imaginative Image returns by the seed of Contemplative Thought. The Writings of the Prophets illustrate these conceptions of the Visionary Fancy by their various sublime & Divine Images as seen in the Worlds of Vision.

✻   ✻   ✻

[N71] They [the Learned][3] ✻ ✻ ✻ Assert that Jupiter usurped the Throne of his Father Saturn & brought on an Iron Age & Begat on Mnemosyne or Memory The Greek Muses which are not Inspiration as the Bible is. Real-

---

"upwards of one thousand figures, many of them wonderfully conceived and grandly drawn," seen by J. T. Smith in 1827 (p. 502 herein). According to W. M. Rossetti, it measured seven by five feet (152.4 by 213. 4 cm) (Butlin 648). For more on Blake's half dozen or more treatments of this subject between 1806 and 1827, see Butlin 639–648. Our selections from Blake's essay omit his detailed remarks on the figures to focus on concerns also addressed in his other writings. The text, slightly rearranged, is from the Erdman edition, compared with the Erdman-Moore facsimile edition of the Notebook and the Bentley and Keynes texts. Numbers in brackets refer to page numbers in the Notebook, followed (when appropriate) by the page number in the Erdman edition (E). We have normalized most run-on sentences and restored a few deleted passages needed for continuity, but much of the text remains in the raw, unpunctuated state of the Notebook.

1. In classical literary criticism, *fable* is a synonym for *plot*, the "combination of the incidents, or things done in the story" (Aristotle, *The Art of Poetry*, VI). Blake ascribes the world's great stories, the myths of all cultures, to vision or imagination, and he equates fable in a narrower sense with point-for-point allegorical correspondences, which he ascribes to the lower faculty of memory (Mnemosyne, in Greek myth, is the mother of the muses). But cf. his definition of the "Most Sublime Poetry" as "Allegory address'd to the Intellectual powers" (p. 484 herein).
2. In Plato's *Apology of Socrates*, the dying philosopher says that poets and prophets "say many and beautiful things, but they understand nothing of what they say" (cited by Bentley, *Writings*, from Kathleen Raine, *Blake and Tradition* [1968]); similarly, in Plato's *Ion*, Socrates says that "God takes away the minds of poets, . . . diviners and holy prophets" and speaks through their utterances while they are in a "state of unconsciousness."
3. The reference is unclear because the paper is cut off at the top.

ity was Forgot & the Vanities of Time & Space only Rememberd & calld Reality. Such is the Mighty difference between Allegoric Fable & Spiritual Mystery. Let it here be Noted that the Greek Fables originated in Spiritual Mystery[N72] and Real Visions Which are lost & clouded in Fable & Alegory while the Hebrew Bible & the Greek Gospel are Genuine Preservd by the Saviours Mercy. The Nature of my Work is Visionary or Imaginative: it is an Endeavour to Restore what the Ancients calld the Golden Age.

[N69] This world of Imagination is the World of Eternity it is the Divine bosom into which we shall all go after the death of the Vegetated body. This World of Imagination is Infinite & Eternal whereas the world of Generation or Vegetation is Finite & Temporal. There Exist in that Eternal World the Permanent Realities of Every Thing which we see reflected in this Vegetable Glass of Nature.

All Things are comprehended in their Eternal Forms in the Divine [N70] body of the Saviour the True Vine of Eternity The Human Imagination who appeard to Me as Coming to Judgment among his Saints & throwing off the Temporal that the Eternal might be Establishd. Around him were seen the Images of Existences according to a certain order suited to my Imaginative Eye.

*   *   *

[N79/E556] In Eternity one Thing never Changes into another Thing. Each Identity is Eternal, consequently Apuleius's Golden Ass & Ovids Metamorphosis & others of the like kind are Fable yet they contain Vision in a Sublime degree being derived from real Vision in More Ancient Writings. Lots Wife being Changed into Pillar of Salt alludes to the Mortal Body being renderd a Permanent Statue but not Changed or Transformed into Another Identity while it retains its own Individuality. A Man can never become Ass nor Horse. Some are born with shapes of Men who may be both but Eternal Identity is one thing & Corporeal Vegetation is another thing. Changing Water into Wine by Jesus & into Blood by Moses relates to Vegetable Nature also.

*   *   *

[N76/E556] It ought to be understood that the Persons Moses & Abraham are not here meant but the States Signified by those Names, the Individuals being representatives or Visions of those States as they were reveald to Mortal Man in the Series of Divine Revelations as they are written in the Bible. These various States I have seen in my Imagination. When distant they appear as One Man but as you approach they appear Multitudes of Nations.

*   *   *

[N77/E557] The Ladies will be pleasd to see that I have represented the Furies by Three Men & not by three Women. It is not because I think the Ancients wrong but they will be pleasd to remember that mine is Vision & not Fable. The Spectator may suppose them Clergymen in the Pulpit Scourging Sin instead of Forgiving it.

*   *   *

[N80/E556] Man Passes on but States remain for Ever. He passes thro them like a traveller who may as well suppose that the places he has passed thro exist no more as a Man may suppose that the States he has passd thro exist no more. Every Thing is Eternal.

* * *

[N81/E558] An Aged patriarch is awakd by his aged wife. He is Albion[4] our Ancestor patriarch of the Atlantic Continent whose History Preceded that of the Hebrews & in whose Sleep or Chaos Creation began. The Aged Woman is Brittannia the Wife of Albion, Jerusalem is their Daughter.

* * *

[N82/E560] If the Spectator could Enter into these Images in his Imagination approaching them on the Fiery Chariot of his Contemplative Thought, if he could Enter into Noahs Rainbow or into his bosom or could make a Friend & Companion of one of these Images of wonder which always intreats him to leave mortal things as he must know, then would he arise from his Grave then would he meet the Lord in the Air[5] & then he would be happy. General Knowledge is Remote Knowledge. It is in Particulars that Wisdom consists & Happiness too. Both in Art & in Life General Masses are as Much Art as a Pasteboard Man is Human. Every Man has Eyes Nose & Mouth; this Every Idiot knows but he who enters into & discriminates most minutely the Manners & Intentions [N83] the Characters in all their branches is the alone Wise or Sensible Man & on this discrimination All Art is founded. I intreat then that the Spectator will attend to the Hands & Feet to the Lineaments of the Countenances they are all descriptive of Character & not a line is drawn without intention & that most discriminate & particular as Poetry admits not a Letter that is Insignificant so Painting admits not a Grain of Sand or a Blade of Grass Insignificant much less an Insignificant Blur or Mark.

* * *

[N84/E561] A Last Judgment is Necessary because Fools flourish.

Nations Flourish under Wise Rulers & are depressd under foolish Rulers. It is the same with Individuals as Nations: works of Art can only be producd in Perfection where the Man is either in Affluence or is Above the Care of it * * * Some People & not a few Artists have asserted that the Painter of this Picture would not have done so well if he had been properly Encouragd. Let those who think so reflect on the State of Nations under Poverty & their incapability of Art. Tho Art is Above Either the Argument is better for Affluence than Poverty & tho he would not have been a greater Artist yet he would have produced Greater works of Art in proportion to his means. A Last Judgment is not for the purpose of making Bad Men better but for the Purpose of hindering them from opressing the Good with Poverty & Pain by means of Such Vile Arguments & Insinuations.

* * *

---

4. The two much-revised sentences identifying the "Aged patriarch" as Albion are squeezed between lines and down the right margin; at one point Blake wrote "his Emanation or Wife is Jerusalem."
5. A sign of the end of time, sometimes called the "rapture" (1 Thessalonians 4:16–17). The claim at the end of the paragraph that no detail is insignificant accords with Blake's emphasis on "Minute Particulars" throughout *Jerusalem* (38:23, 38:61, 45:8, 45:44, 55:51, 88:43, 89:17, 91:21).

[N84/E562] All Life consists of these Two: Throwing off Error & Knaves from our company continually & recieving Truth or Wise Men into our Company Continually. He who is out of the Church & opposes it is no less an Agent of Religion than he who is in it. To be an Error & to be Cast out is a part of Gods Design. No man can Embrace True Art till he has Explord & Cast out False Art, such is the Nature of Mortal Things, or he will be himself Cast out by those who have Already Embraced True Art. Thus My Picture is a History of Art & Science the Foundation of Society Which is Humanity itself. What are all the Gifts of the Spirit[6] but Mental Gifts? Whenever any Individual Rejects Error & Embraces Truth a Last Judgment passes upon that Individual.

*   *   *

[N85/E562] The Temple stands on the Mount of God from it flows on each side the River of Life on whose banks Grows the tree of Life among whose branches temples & Pinnacles tents & pavilions Gardens & Groves Display Paradise with its Inhabitants walking up & down in Conversations concerning Mental Delights.[7] Here they are no longer talking of what is Good & Evil or of what is Right or Wrong & puzzling themselves in Satans Labyrinth But are Conversing with Eternal Realities as they Exist in the Human Imagination. We are in a World of Generation & death & this world we must cast off if we would be Painters Such as Rafal Mich Angelo & the Ancient Sculptors. If we do not cast off this world we shall be only Venetian Painters who will be cast off & Lost from Art.

*   *   *

[N85/E562] In Eternity Woman is the Emanation of Man she has No Will of her own. There is no such thing in eternity as a Female Will.

*   *   *

[N91/E563] The Greeks represent Chronos or Time as a very Aged Man. This is Fable but the Real Vision of Time is in Eternal Youth. I have however somewhat accomodated my Figure of Time to the Common opinion as I myself am also infected with it & my Vision is also infected & I see Time Aged, alas too much so.

Allegories are things that Relate to Moral Virtues. Moral Virtues do not Exist they are Allegories & dissimulations. But Time & Space are Real Beings a Male & a Female. Time is a Man, Space is a Woman & her Masculine Portion is Death.

*   *   *

Many suppose that before the Creation All was Solitude & Chaos. This is the most pernicious Idea that can enter the Mind as it takes away all sublimity from the Bible & Limits All Existence to Creation & to Chaos, To the Time & Space fixed by the Corporeal Vegetative Eye, & leaves the Man who entertains such an Idea the habitation of Unbelieving Demons. Eternity Exists and All things in Eternity Independent of Creation which was an act of Mercy. * * * [N92] By this it will be seen that I do not consider either the

6. Cf. I Corinthians 12:1–11.
7. This section of the painting sounds much like Blake's c. 1805 watercolor for Butts, *The River of Life* (Butlin 525).

Just or the Wicked to be in a Supreme State but to be every one of them States of the Sleep which the Soul may fall into in its Deadly Dreams of Good & Evil when it leaves Paradise following the Serpent.

[N86/E563] The Combats of Good & Evil is Eating of the Tree of Knowledge. The Combats of Truth & Error is Eating of the Tree of Life. * * * Good & Evil are Qualities in Every Man whether a Good or Evil Man. These are Enemies & destroy one another by every Means in their power both of deceit & of open Violence. The Deist & the Christian are but the Results of these Opposing Natures. Many are Deists who would in certain Circumstances have been Christians in outward appearance. Voltaire was one of this number: he was as intolerant as an Inquisitor. Manners make the Man not Habits. It is the same in Art. By their Works ye [N90] shall know them. The Knave who is Converted to Deism & the Knave who is Converted to Christianity is still a Knave but he himself will not know it tho Every body else does. Christ comes as he came at first to deliver those who were bound under the Knave not to deliver the Knave. He Comes to Deliver Man the Accused & not Satan the Accuser. We do not find any where that Satan is Accused of Sin he is only accused of Unbelief & thereby drawing Man into Sin that he may accuse him. Such is the Last Judgment a Deliverance from Satans Accusation. Satan thinks that Sin is displeasing to God he ought to know that Nothing is displeasing to God but Unbelief & Eating of the Tree of Knowledge of Good & Evil.

[N87] Men are admitted into Heaven not because they have curbed & governd their Passions or have No Passions but because they have Cultivated their Understandings. The Treasures of Heaven are not Negations of Passion but Realities of Intellect from which All the Passions Emanate Uncurbed in their Eternal Glory. The Fool shall not enter into Heaven let him be ever so Holy. Holiness is not The Price of Enterance into Heaven. Those who are cast out Are All Those who having no Passions of their own because No Intellect Have spent their lives in Curbing & Governing other Peoples by the Various arts of Poverty & Cruelty of all kinds. Wo Wo Wo to you Hypocrites.[8] Even Murder, the Courts of Justice more merciful than the Church are compelld to allow, is not done in Passion but in Cool Blooded Design & Intention.

The Modern Church Crucifies Christ with the Head Downwards

[N92/E564] Many Persons such as Paine & Voltaire with some of the Ancient Greeks say we will not Converse concerning Good & Evil, we will live in Paradise & Liberty. You may do so in Spirit but not in the Mortal Body as you pretend till after the Last Judgment for in Paradise they have no Corporeal & Mortal Body; that originated with the Fall & was calld Death & cannot be removed but by a Last judgment. While we are in the world of Mortality we Must Suffer. The Whole Creation Groans to be deliverd. There will always be as many Hypocrites born as Honest Men & they will always have superior Power in Mortal Things. You cannot have Liberty in this World without what you call Moral Virtue & you cannot have Moral Virtue without the Slavery of that half of the Human Race who hate what you call Moral Virtue.

The Nature of Hatred & Envy & of All the Mischiefs in the World are here depicted. No one Envies or Hates one of his Own Party. Even the devils love

---

8. Cf. Matthew 23:13ff.

one another in their Way. They torment one another for other reasons than Hate or Envy. These are only employd against the Just. Neither can Seth Envy Noah or Elijah Envy Abraham but they may both of them Envy the Success [N93] of Satan or of Og or Molech. The Horse never Envies the Peacock nor the Sheep the Goat but they Envy a Rival in Life & Existence whose ways & means exceed their own let him be of what Class of Animals he will. A Dog will envy a Cat who is pamperd at the expense of his comfort as I have often seen. The Bible never tells us that Devils torment one another thro Envy it is thro this that they torment the Just. But for what do they torment one another? I answer For the Coercive Laws of Hell, Moral Hypocrisy. They torment a Hypocrite when he is discovered, they Punish a Failure in the tormentor who has sufferd the Subject of his torture to Escape. In Hell all is Self Righteousness there is no such thing there as Forgiveness of Sin. He who does Forgive Sin is Crucified as an Abettor of Criminals, & he who performs Works of Mercy in Any shape whatever is punishd & if possible destroyd not thro Envy or Hatred or Malice but thro Self Righteousness that thinks it does God service which God is Satan. They do not Envy one another, They contemn & despise one another.

Forgiveness of Sin is only at the Judgment Seat of Jesus the Saviour, where the Accuser is cast out not because he Sins but because he torments the Just & makes them do what he condemns as Sin & what he knows is opposite to their own Identity.

It is not because Angels are Holier than Men or Devils that makes them Angels but because they do not Expect Holiness from one another but from God only.

The Player is a liar when he Says Angels are happier than [N94] Men because they are better.[9] Angels are happier than Men & Devils because they are not always Prying after Good & Evil in One Another & eating the Tree of Knowledge for Satans Gratification.

Thinking as I do that the Creator of this World is a very Cruel Being & being a Worshipper of Christ I cannot help saying the Son O how unlike the Father. First God Almighty comes with a Thump on the Head Then Jesus Christ comes with a balm to heal it.

The Last Judgment is an Overwhelming of Bad Art & Science. Mental Things are alone Real. What is Calld Corporeal Nobody Knows of its Dwelling Place. It is in Fallacy & its Existence an Imposture. Where is the Existence Out of Mind or Thought, Where is it but in the Mind of a Fool. Some People flatter themselves that there will be No Last Judgment & [N95] that Bad Art will be adopted & mixed with Good Art, That Error or Experiment will make a Part of Truth, & they Boast that it is its Foundation. These People flatter themselves. I will not Flatter them. Error is Created, Truth is Eternal. Error or Creation will be Burned Up & then & not till then Truth or Eternity will appear. It is Burnt up the Moment Men cease to behold it. I assert for My self that I do not behold the Outward Creation & that to me it is hindrance & not Action, it is as the Dirt upon my feet No part of Me. What, it will be Questiond, When the Sun rises do you not see a round Disk

---

9. From Nicholas Rowe, *The Fair Penitent* (1703, iii.i), frequently performed in London in Blake's time and excerpted in "beauties" of the English stage. Blake probably knew the text as altered in Edward Bysshe, *The Art of English Poetry* (excerpted under "Happiness"): "To be good is to be happy: Angels / Are happier than Men because they're better." On Blake's use of a one-volume edition of Bysshe (probably 1710), see Bentley's edition, 2.963n.

of fire somewhat like a Guinea? O no no I see an Innumerable company of the Heavenly host crying Holy Holy Holy is the Lord God Almighty.[1] I question not my Corporeal or Vegetative Eye any more than I would Question a Window concerning a Sight. I look thro it & not with it.

FROM A PUBLIC ADDRESS TO THE CHALCOGRAPHIC SOCIETY (1809–10)†

[N11/E571] If Men of weak Capacities have alone the Power of Execution in Art Mr B has now put to the test. If to Invent & to Draw well hinders the Executive Power in Art & his Strokes are still to be Condemnd because they are unlike those of Artists who are Unacquainted with Drawing is now to be Decided by The Public. Mr B s Inventive Powers & his Scientific Knowledge of Drawing is on all hands acknowledgd.[1] It only remains to be Certified whether Physiognomic Strength & Power is to give Place to Imbecillity. In a work of Art it is not fine tints that are required but Fine Forms. Fine Tints without Fine Forms are always the Subterfuge of the Blockhead. * * *

> Rafael Sublime Majestic Graceful Wise
> His Executive Power must I despise
> Rubens Low Vulgar Stupid Ignorant
> His power of Execution I must grant
> Learn the Laborious stumble of a Fool

---

1. Cf. Revelation 4:8; Luke 2:13.
† In 1809–10 Blake squeezed onto scattered pages of his already-full Notebook a spirited defense of his principles and accomplishments in art, imagined as an address to "The Chalcographic [engraving] Society." The defensive oration on the merits of his engraving *The Canterbury Pilgrims* had as its immediate impetus a cluster of events that Blake experienced as a coordinated attack: (1) The engraver-entrepreneur Robert H. Cromek, after commissioning Blake to prepare twenty designs (for £21) for an illustrated edition of Blair's *Grave*, to be engraved by Blake, rejected Blake's unconventional sample engraving (white-line on black) and awarded the promised commission to Luigi (Louis) Schiavonetti (1765–1810), probably paying him more than £500. (2) Cromek also commissioned Blake's old friend Thomas Stothard to execute a wide-format painting and engraving of the Canterbury Pilgrims on horseback, which Stothard completed before Blake issued his own treatment of the same subject. (3) The journalist Robert Hunt ridiculed Blake in two articles, one on his designs for Blair's *Grave*, the other on his 1809 exhibition (the work of an "unfortunate lunatic," see p. 497 herein). Blake struck back furiously against these and any and all other possibly allied combatants, hectoring his imagined audience of fellow engravers on the superiority of his print to Stothard's, the incompetence of other artists (including former friends), the malign influence of the coloristic Dutch and Venetian schools that had eclipsed the clear linearity of the Roman and Florentine schools, and the ruinous political, commercial, and cultural forces that had plunged British art into its present deplorable state. The essential book on these ideas in relation to "English-school discourse" is Morris Eaves, *The Counter-Arts Conspiracy* (1992). On the Chalcographic Society, see Dennis M. Read, *Philological Quarterly* 60 (1981), 69–86, and John Gage, *Print Quarterly* 6 (1989), 123–39. On the Blake-Cromek relationship, see Read, *Modern Philology* 86 (1988), 171–90; Aileen Ward, *Blake: Illustrated Quarterly* 22 (1988–89), 80–92; G. E. Bentley Jr., *Studies in Romanticism* 30 (1991), 657–84; J. M. Mertz, *Modern Philology* 99:1 (2001) 66–77; Bentley, *Stranger from Paradise* (2001); and Alexander S. Gourlay in *Prophetic Character* (2003). On the twelve engraved designs for Blair's *Grave*, see the facsimile edition by Essick and Paley (1982); on the rediscovery of nineteen of the preliminary watercolors, see Martin Butlin, *Blake: An Illustrated Quarterly* 35 (2002), 63–73 and the Blake Archive; on their May 2, 2006, auction, see E. B. Bentley, *Blake Quarterly* 40 (2006), 66–71, and Sotheby's catalogue 8262 by Nancy Bailler, with Essick's assistance.

   Our selection omits most specifics of Blake's attacks on artists and the art establishment to highlight broader aesthetic and social concerns that inform his other writings, especially *Milton* and *Jerusalem*. Our source is the Erdman edition (with Notebook pages indicated in brackets followed as appropriate by Erdman page numbers), compared with the Bentley edition and the Erdman-Moore facsimile edition of the Notebook. Occasionally we have capitalized proper names and inserted periods in run-on sentences.

1. Cromek's prospectus for Blake's illustrations to Blair's *Grave* lists prominent members of the Royal Academy as subscribers and concludes with a joint endorsement of Blake's work by two officials of the academy: Benjamin West, president, and Henry Fuseli, keeper and professor of painting.

And from an Idiots Actions form my rule
Go send your Children to the Slobbering School[2]

I account it a Public Duty respectfully to address myself to The Chalcographic Society & to Express to them my opinion the result of the incessant Practise & Experience of Many Years That Engraving as an Art is Lost in England owing to an artfully propagated opinion that Drawing spoils an Engraver. I request the Society to inspect my Print of which Drawing is the Foundation & indeed the Superstructure. It is Drawing on Copper as Painting ought to be Drawing on Canvas or any other surface & nothing Else. I request likewise that the Society will compare the Prints of Bartollouzzi Woolett Strange[3] &c with the old English Portraits, that is Compare the Modern Art with the Art as it Existed Previous to the Enterance of Vandyke & Rubens into this Country since which English Engraving is Lost & I am sure the Result of this comparison will be that the Society must be of my Opinion that Engraving by Losing Drawing has Lost all Character & all Expression without which The Art is Lost.

[N51/E572] In this Plate Mr B has resumed the style with which he set out in life of which Heath[4] & Stothard were the awkward imitators at that time. It is the style of Alb Durers Histries & the old Engravers which cannot be imitated by any one who does not understand Drawing & which according to Heath & Stothard Flaxman & even Romney[5] Spoils an Engraver, for Each of these Men have repeatedly asserted this Absurdity to me in condemnation [N52] of my Work & approbation of Heaths lame imitation, Stothard being such a fool as to suppose that his blundering blurs can be made out & delineated by any Engraver who knows how to cut dots & lozenges equally well with those little prints which I engraved after him five & twenty Years ago & by which he got his reputation as a Draughtsman.[6]

The manner in which my Character has been blasted these thirty years both as an artist & a Man may be seen particularly in a Sunday Paper cald the Examiner[7] Publishd in Beaufort Buildings & the manner in which I have routed out the nest of villains will be seen in a Poem concerning my Three years Herculean Labours[8] at Felpham which I will soon Publish. [Note:] We all know that Editors of Newspapers trouble their heads very little about art & science & that they are always paid for what they put upon these ungracious Subjects.

✳   ✳   ✳

2. Blake's notes indicate that this poem is to be inserted at this point.
3. Robert Strange's (1721–1792) engravings helped popularize the work of Blake's *bêtes noires* Titian, Correggio, and Van Dyck. Both Anthony Van Dyck (1599–1641) and his mentor, Peter Paul Rubens (1577–1640), spent part of their careers in England as court painters; both were knighted by Charles I, their chief patron. Francesco Bartolozzi (1728–1815), who worked in London for thirty years, established the vogue for stipple (dots and flecks) engraving; Schiavonetti worked in his studio. William Woollett (1735–1785), engraver to the king, was known for landscapes and heroic subjects.
4. James Heath (1757–1834), line and stipple engraver, historical engraver to the king. On Stothard, see the dagger note. On Flaxman, see n. 1, p. 473 herein.
5. George Romney (1734–1802), portrait painter and subject of an 1809 biography by Blake's patron, William Hayley. Albrecht Dürer (1471–1528), German printmaker and painter, master of line engraving. "Histories" refers to his grand subjects. Blake kept Dürer's print *Melencolia I* over his drawing table, according to Palmer, called it *Melancholy: The Mother of Invention* (p. 516 herein).
6. Blake's scores of engravings after Stothard in the 1780s include illustrations for an edition of Chaucer (1782).
7. See p. 497 herein.
8. *Milton a Poem.* See n. 1, p. 483 herein.

[N56/E573] * * * It is very true what you have said [N57] for these thirty two Years I am Mad or Else you are so, both of us cannot be in our right senses. Posterity will judge by our Works. Wooletts & Stranges works are like those of Titian & Correggio, the Lifes Labour of Ignorant journeymen Suited to the Purposes of Commerce no doubt for Commerce Cannot endure Individual Merit. Its insatiable Maw must be fed by What all can do Equally well, at least it is so in England as I have found to my Cost these Forty Years.

* * *

[N57/E574] I do not pretend to Paint better than Rafael or Mch Anglo or Julio Romano or Alb Durer but I do Pretend to Paint finer than Rubens or Remb^t or Correggio or Titian. I do not Pretend to Engrave finer than Alb Durer Goltzius Sadeler or Edelinck but I do pretend to Engrave finer than Strange Woolett Hall^9 or Bartolozzi & All because I understand Drawing which they understand not.

[N58] In this manner the English Public have been imposed upon for many Years under the impression that Engraving & Painting are somewhat Else besides Drawing. Painting is Drawing on Canvas & Engraving is Drawing on Copper & Nothing Else & he who pretends to be either Painter or Engraver without being a Master of Drawing is an Impostor. We may be Clever as Pugilists but as Artists we are & have long been the Contempt of the Continent. Gravelot once said to My Master Basire, De English may be very clever in deir own opinions but dey do not draw De draw.^{1}

Resentment for Personal Injuries has had some share in this Public Address But Love to My Art & Zeal for my Country a much Greater.

* * *

[N39/E575] I do not condemn Rubens Rembrant or Titian because they did not understand Drawing but because they did not Understand Colouring. How long shall I be forced to beat this into Mens Ears? I do not condemn Strange or Woolett because they did not understand Drawing but because they did not understand Graving. I do not condemn Pope or Dryden because they did not understand Imagination but because they did not understand Verse. Their Colouring Graving & Verse can never be applied to Art. That is not either colouring Graving or Verse which is Unappropriate to the Subject. He who makes a Design must know the Effect & Colouring Proper to be put to that Design & will never take that of Rubens Rembrandt or Titian to turn that which is Soul & Life into a Mill or Machine.

[N46] They say there is no Strait Line in Nature this Is a Lie like all that they say, For there is Every Line in Nature. But I will tell them what is Not in Nature. An Even Tint is not in Nature it produces Heaviness. Natures Shadows are Ever varying, & a Ruled Sky that is quite Even never can Produce a Natural Sky; the same with every Object in a Picture: its Spots are its beauties. * * *

9. John Hall (1739–1797), English engraver. Hendrik Goltzius (1558–1617), Dutch printmaker, draftsman, and painter; line engraver who emulated Dürer. Jan Sadeler (1550–1600), Flemish draftsman, engraver, and publisher. Gerald Edelinck (1621–1674), Flemish engraver.
1. Hubert-François Gravelot (1699–1773), French engraver who lived in London for twelve years; influential Rococo illustrator of Shakespeare, Dryden, Pope, Richardson, Fielding, and Gay. Whether or not Blake's master, James Basire, heard the remark directly from Gravelot (who returned to France in 1745, the year Basire became an apprentice), he must have taken it to heart as a boy and passed it down to his pupils.

[N47] * * * Englishmen have been so used to Journeymens undecided bungling that they cannot bear the firmness of a Masters Touch. Every Line is the Line of Beauty[2] it is only fumble & Bungle which cannot draw a Line this only is Ugliness. That is not a Line which Doubts & Hesitates in the Midst of its Course.

* * *

[N61/E576] * * * Englishmen rouze yourselves from the fatal Slumber into which Booksellers & Trading Dealers have thrown you Under the artfully propagated pretence that a Translation or a Copy of any kind can be as honourable to a Nation as An Original, Be-lying the English Character in that well known Saying Englishmen Improve what others Invent. This Even Hogarths Works Prove [N62] a detestable Falshood. No Man Can Improve An Original Invention, Nor can an Original Invention Exist without Execution Organized & minutely Delineated & Articulated Either by God or Man. I do not mean smoothd up & Niggled & Poco Piud[3] and all the beauties pickd out & blurrd & blotted but Drawn with a firm and decided hand at once like Fuseli & Michael Angelo Shakespeare & Milton.

* * *

[N62] I have heard many People say Give me the Ideas, It is no matter what Words you put them into & others say Give me the Design it is no matter for the Execution. These People know Enough of Artifice but Nothing Of Art. Ideas cannot be Given but in their minutely Appropriate Words nor Can a Design be made without its minutely Appropriate Execution. The unorganized Blots & Blurs of Rubens & Titian are not Art nor can their Method ever express Ideas or Imaginations any more than Popes Metaphysical jargon of Rhyming. Unappropriate Execution is the Most nauseous of all affectation & foppery. He who copies does not Execute he only Imitates what is already Executed. Execution is only the result of Invention.

* * *

[N66/E577] It is Nonsense for Noblemen & Gentlemen to offer Premiums for the Encouragement of Art when such Pictures as these can be done without Premiums. Let them Encourage what Exists Already & not endeavour to counteract by tricks. Let it no more be said that Empires Encourage Arts for it is Arts that Encourage Empires. Arts & Artists are Spiritual & laugh at Mortal Contingencies. It is in their Power to hinder Instruction but not to Instruct just as it is in their Power to Murder a Man but not to make a Man.

Let us teach Buonaparte & whomsoever else it may concern That it is not Arts that follow & attend upon Empire but Empire that attends upon & follows The Arts.

* * *

The English Artist may be assured that he is doing an injury & injustice to his Country while he studies & imitates the Effects of Nature. England

---

2. In an engraving of 1749 (from a self-portrait, 1745), William Hogarth (1697–1764) labeled the serpentine or ogee curve (an elongated S) on his palette "THE LINE OF BEAUTY"; he discusses the concept in his *Analysis of Beauty* (1753).
3. Blake makes a verb of "a little more" in Italian, used both in eighteenth-century art commentary (Jean Hagstrum, *Philological Quarterly* 53 [1974], 643–45) and music notation. Hogarth defines *il poco più* as "*the little more* that is expected from the hand of a master" (*Analysis of Beauty*, 66).

will never rival Italy while we servilely copy what the Wise Italians Rafael & Michael Angelo scorned nay abhorred as Vasari[3] tells us

> Call that the Public Voice which is their Error
> Like as a Monkey peeping in a Mirror
> Admires all his colours brown & warm
> And never once percieves his ugly form

What kind of Intellects must he have who sees only the Colours of things & not the Forms of Things? [N71] A jockey that is any thing of a jockey will never buy a Horse by the Colour & a Man who has got any brains will never buy a Picture by the Colour.

When I tell any Truth it is not for the sake of Convincing those who do not know it but for the sake of defending those who Do.

✻　✻　✻

[N17/E578] I wonder who can say Speak no Ill of the Dead when it is asserted in the Bible that the name of the Wicked shall Rot.[4] It is Deistical Virtue I suppose but as I have none of this I will pour Aqua fortis[5] on the Name of the Wicked & turn it into an Ornament & an Example to be Avoided by Some & Imitated by Others if they Please.

Columbus discoverd America but Americus Vesputius finishd & smoothd it over like an English Engraver or Corregio or Titian.

✻　✻　✻

[N18/E579] ✻ ✻ ✻ I hope my Countrymen will Excuse me if I tell them a Wholesom truth. Most Englishmen when they look at a Picture immediately set about searching for Points of Light & clap the Picture into a dark corner. This when done by Grand Works is like looking for Epigrams in Homer. A point of light is a Witticism. ✻ ✻ ✻

Mr B repeats that there is not one Character or Expression in this Print which could be Produced with the Execution of Titian Rubens Coreggio Rembrandt or any of that Class. Character & Expression can only be Expressed by those who Feel Them. Even Hogarths Execution cannot be Copied or Improved. Gentlemen of Fortune who give Great Prices for Pictures should consider the following. [N19] Rubens's Luxembourg Gallery[6] is Confessd on all hands to be the work of a Blockhead. It bears this Evidence in its face. How can its Execution be any other than the Work of a Blockhead? Bloated Gods Mercury Juno Venus & the rattle traps of Mythology & the lumber of an awkward French Palace are thrown together around Clumsy & Ricketty Princes & Princesses higgledy piggledy. On the Contrary Julio Rom[ano's] Palace of T at Mantua is allowed on all hands to be the Production of a Man of the Most Profound sense & Genius & Yet his Execution is pronouncd by English Connoisseurs & Reynolds their Doll to be unfit for the Study of the Painter. Can I speak with too great Contempt of such Contemptible fellows? If all the

---

3. The painter Giorgio Vasari (1511–1574), known for his entertainingly anecdotal *Lives of the Artists* (1550, 1568; trans. William Aglionby [1685, 1719]).
4. Proverbs 10:7.
5. Nitric acid, used for etching.
6. Cycle of twenty-one huge mythographic paintings, now in the Louvre, from Luxembourg Palace in Paris, celebrating Marie de Medici, wife of Henry IV of France and regent for her son Louis XIII after her husband's assassination in 1605. The best-known part of the contrasting work, the duke of Gonzaga's Palazzo del Te—which was both designed and decorated by Raphael's assistant Giulio Romano—is the illusionistic whole-room fresco, *The Fall of the Giants*.

Princes in Europe like Louis XIV & Charles the first were to Patronize such Blockheads I William Blake a Mental Prince should decollate & Hang their Souls as Guilty of Mental High Treason.

✻   ✻   ✻

[N20/E580] The wretched state of the Arts in this Country & in Europe originating in the Wretched State of Political Science which is the Science of Sciences Demands a firm & determinate conduct on the part of Artists to Resist the Contemptible Counter Arts Established by Such contemptible Politicians as Louis XIV & originally set on foot by Venetian Picture traders Music traders & Rhime traders to the destruction of all true art as it is this Day. To recover Art has been the business of my life to the Florentine Original & if possible to go beyond that Original. This I thought the only pursuit worthy of a Man. To Imitate I abhor. I obstinately adhere to the true Style of Art such as Michael Angelo Rafael Jul Rom Alb Durer left it. I demand therefore of the Amateurs of [N21] art the Encouragement which is my due. If they continue to refuse theirs is the loss not mine & theirs is the Contempt of Posterity. I have Enough in the Approbation of fellow labourers this is my glory & exceeding great reward I go on & nothing can hinder my course.

> And in Melodious accents I
> Will sit me down & Cry, I, I.

✻   ✻   ✻

[N23/E581] The Painters of England are unemployd in Public Works, while the Sculptors have continual & superabundant employment. Our Churches & Abbeys are treasures of their producing for ages back, While Painting is excluded. Painting the Principal Art has no place among our almost only public works. Yet it is more adapted to solemn ornament than Marble can be as it is capable of being Placed in any heighth & indeed would make a Noble finish Placed above the Great Public Monuments in Westminster St Pauls & other Cathedrals. To the Society for Encouragement of Arts[7] I address myself with Respectful duty requesting their Consideration of my Plan as a Great Public means of advancing Fine Art in Protestant Communities, Monuments to the dead Painted by Historical & Poetical Artists like Barry & Mortimer.[8] I forbear to name living Artists tho equally worthy. I say Monuments so Painted must make England What Italy is, an Envied Storehouse of Intellectual Riches.

✻   ✻   ✻

7. Society for the Encouragement of Arts, Manufactures and Commerce, founded 1754; or more likely, as Read surmises, the short-lived Society for the Encouragement of the Art of Engraving, through which Cromek attempted to raise seventeen thousand guineas for a series of twenty plates "the size of the larger works of Strange and Woollett."
8. John Hamilton Mortimer (c. 1740–1779), English painter and etcher, known for his theatrical, passion-filled paintings of bandits and scenes from British history and literature. James Barry (1741–1806), Irish history painter in the Grand Manner, the academic style of the late eighteenth century; also an experimental printmaker. Known also for his extreme slovenliness, Barry was expelled in 1799 as professor of painting at the Royal Academy for expressing contempt for his fellow academicians in his *Letter to the Dilettanti Society* (1788). His proposal (with others) to decorate Saint Paul's Cathedral with paintings by British artists (1773) led the Society for Encouragement of the Arts, Manufactures and Commerce to commission his mural series on the progress of human culture for their Adelphi building (1783); while working on this project, he told Blake, he had to live on "Bread & Apples" (annotation to Reynolds; not included in this edition).

[N24/E582] I know my Execution is not like Any Body Else. I do not intend it should be so. None but Blockheads Copy one another. My Conception & Invention are on all hands allowd to be Superior, My Execution will be found so too. To what is it that Gentlemen of the first Rank both in Genius & Fortune have subscribed their Names? To My Inventions. The Executive part they never Disputed.[9] [N25] The Lavish praise I have recieved from all Quarters for Invention & Drawing has Generally been accompanied by this: he can conceive but he cannot Execute. (P. S. I do not believe that this Absurd opinion ever was set on foot till in my Outset into life it was artfully publishd both in whispers & in print by Certain persons whose robberies from me made it necessary to them that I should be hid in a corner. It never was supposed that a Copy Could be better than an original or near so Good till a few Years ago it became the interest of certain envious Knaves.) This Absurd assertion has done me & may still do me the greatest mischief. I call for Public protection against these Villains. I am like others Just Equal in Invention & in Execution as my works shew.

I in my own defence Challenge a Competition with the finest Engravings & defy the most critical judge to make the Comparison Honestly, [N24] asserting in my own Defence that This Print is the Finest that has been done or is likely to be done in England where drawing, its foundation, is Contemnd and absurd Nonsense about dots & Lozenges & Clean Strokes made to occupy the attention to the Neglect of all real Art. I defy any Man to Cut Cleaner Strokes than I do or rougher when I please & assert that he who thinks he can Engrave or Paint either without being a Master of Drawing is a Fool. Painting is Drawing on Canvas & Engraving is Drawing on Copper & nothing Else. Drawing is Execution & nothing Else & he who Draws best must be the best Artist. To this I subscribe my name as a Public Duty.

WILLIAM BLAKE

FROM [THE EVERLASTING GOSPEL] (c. 1818)[†]

There is not one Moral Virtue that Jesus Inculcated but Plato & Cicero did Inculcate before him[1] what then did Christ Inculcate. Forgiveness of Sins This alone is the Gospel & this is the Life & Immortality brought to light by Jesus. Even the Covenant of Jehovah, which is This If you forgive one another your Trespasses so shall Jehovah forgive you That he himself may dwell among you but if you Avenge you Murder the Divine Image & he can-

---

9. According to the carefully worded joint statement by West and Fuseli in Cromek's prospectus for Blair's *Grave*, "the technic Part, and the Execution of the Artist . . . equally claim Approbation, sometimes excite our Wonder, and not Seldom our Fears, when we see him play on the very Verge of legitimate Invention."

† This richly allusive phrase from Revelation 14:6, which Blake inscribed over a set of draft couplets questioning conventional interpretations of Jesus' teachings and example, refers to the ultimate apocalyptic dissemination of the gospel (good news): "And I saw another angel fly in the midst of heaven, having the everlasting gospel to preach unto them that dwell on the earth, and to every nation, and kindred, and tongue, and people." Editors have traditionally applied this title, possibly intended only for one section, to a larger work-in-progress now thought to consist of a prose paragraph and eleven fragmentary verses spread through a four-page folded sheet ("EG," watermarked 1818), a page glued into Blake's Notebook (on 1802 paper), and ten scattered Notebook pages.
　The concept of an "everlasting gospel" that fulfills and transcends (or supersedes) the Old and

not dwell among you because you Murder him he arises Again & you deny
that he is Arisen & are blind to Spirit   [a; EG 1]

    If Moral Virtue was Christianity[2]   [c; EG4]
    Christs Pretensions were all Vanity
    And Caiphas & Pilate Men
    Praise Worthy & the Lions Den[3]
    And not the Sheepfold[4] Allegories   5
    Of God & Heaven & their Glories
    The Moral Christian is the Cause
    Of the Unbeliever & his Laws
    The Roman Virtues Warlike Fame
    Take Jesus & Jehovahs Name.   10
    For what is Antichrist but those
    Who against Sinners Heaven close
    With Iron bars in Virtuous State
    And Rhadamanthus at the Gate[5]

    What can this Gospel of Jesus be   [b; EG 2–3]
    What Life & Immortality
    What was it that he brought to Light
    That Plato & Cicero did not write

New Testaments dates back at least to the twelfth-century visionary Joachim of Fiore, whose writings influenced Boehme, Swedenborg, and such seventeenth-century British dissenters as the Behmenist mystic Jane Lead, the Quakers George Fox and Isaac Pennington, the Muggletonians, the Ranters, and other antinomian sects that persisted underground in Blake's time (some are discussed in A. L. Morton, *The Everlasting Gospel*, 1958). Antinomians believed that they had already received the everlasting gospel that was to convert and reconcile all humanity, and even the fallen angels, under the dispensation of the Holy Spirit (or the risen "spiritual" Christ within); they therefore considered themselves liberated from the moral law that had bound Jews under the Old Testament (dispensation of the Father) and earlier Christians under the New Testament (dispensation of the Son, within the limits of earthly life). Blake was probably aware of these ideas, but in his own writings he simply calls the Everlasting Gospel the "religion of Jesus," the universal original religion of humanity (*Descriptive Catalogue* (p. 429 herein), *Jerusalem* 27, cf. marginalia to Watson, p. 459 herein)—a religion of mutual forgiveness (cf. Matthew 6:14, Colossians 3:13). In the iconoclastic spirit of *The Marriage of Heaven and Hell* (1790), the impudent inquirer behind "The Everlasting Gospel" raises irresistible rhetorical questions in pounding trochaic tetrameter couplets that point to an inescapable (though never finished) conclusion: the Jesus worshiped in churches is the very opposite of the true Jesus, who neither taught nor practiced moral virtue but defied authority, violated taboos, and welcomed the company of sinners. From sections on humility, chastity, and gentility (or gentleness), which counter the sins of pride, lust, and wrath, it can perhaps be inferred that the unfinished structure was to be based on the seven deadly sins.

    For insight into the evolution of the unfinished text, see Erdman in *From Sensibility to Romanticism* (1965), ed. F. W. Hilles and Harold Bloom, and Erdman and Moore, *Notebook* (rev. 1977). On underlying biblical texts, see Michael J. Tolley, *Notes & Queries* n.s. 9 (1962), 171–76, 394, and 15 (1968), 11–19; and Randel Helms, *Blake Studies* 9 (1980), 122–60. For a judicious full commentary, see Morton Paley, *The Traveller in the Evening* (2003). David Owen's hypertext edition (www .english.uga.edu/wblake/EverlastingGospel/) facilitates experimentation with fragment sequences. Our selection and arrangement of striking passages as a cohesive reading text conforms neither to the probable order of composition nor to indications of Blake's evolving ideas for revision. Lowercase alphabetical identifications of selected fragments (a–n) refer to Erdman's text (518–24) and textual notes (874–80); "N" refers to the Notebook, "EG" to the untitled four-page manuscript. The text is packed so full of allusions to familiar Gospel texts that our annotations are necessarily highly selective.

1. Cf. "If Morality was Christianity Socrates was the Saviour" (יה‎ *[Yah]* & *His Two Sons*).
2. Marked "This to come first" in the manuscript, apparently referring to lines 1–14.
3. The high priest Caiphas found Jesus guilty under Jewish law and turned him over to the provincial governor Pontius Pilate to be executed under Roman law (Matthew 26:57 ff., 27:11 ff.). The lions' den, a place of execution, is closed with a stone and sealed with the king's signet (Daniel 6:17).
4. A place of refuge that offers Jesus himself, the Good Shepherd, as the open door (John 10:1–16).
5. One of three judges in Hades who control access to the Elysian Fields; in *Aeneid* VI he presides over the wicked sentenced to Tartarus. Similarly, the moralizing Antichrist (cf. 1 John 2:18, 4:3; 2 John 1:7) blocks the way to Paradise (cf. Covering Cherub: *Milton* 41/37:8, *Jerusalem* 89:9–13). The false Christ is an accuser; the true Christ, a forgiver.

The Heathen Deities wrote them all   5
These Moral Virtues great & small
What is the Accusation of Sin
But Moral Virtues deadly Gin[6]
The Moral Virtues in their Pride
Did oer the World triumphant ride   10
In Wars & Sacrifice for Sin
And Souls to Hell ran trooping in
The Accuser Holy God of All[7]
This Pharisaic Worldly Ball
Amidst them in his Glory Beams   15
Upon the Rivers & the Streams
Then Jesus rose & said to Me
Thy Sins are all forgiven thee
Loud Pilate Howld loud Caiphas Yelld
When they the Gospel Light beheld   20

It was when Jesus said to Me
Thy Sins are all forgiven thee
The Christian trumpets loud proclaim
Thro all the World in Jesus name
Mutual forgiveness of each Vice   25
And oped the Gates of Paradise[8]
The Moral Virtues in Great fear
Formed the Cross & Nails & Spear
And the Accuser standing by
Cried out Crucify Crucify   30
Our Moral Virtues neer can be
Nor Warlike pomp & Majesty
For Moral Virtues all begin
In the Accusations of Sin

*   *   *

I will tell you what Joseph of Arimathea[9]   [m, N52]
Said to my Fairy was not it very queer
Pliny & Trajan[1] what are You here
Come listen to Joseph of Arimathea
Listen patient & when Joseph has done   5
Twill make a fool laugh & a Fairy Fun

---

6. A snare or trap; cf. *Visions* 8/5:18 and *Song of Los* 4:2.
7. Alluding to Satan (literally "adversary") as "the accuser of our brethren . . . before our God day and night" (Revelation 12:10) and the "god of this world" (2 Corinthians 4:4), whose blinding of people's minds shuts out the light of the gospel.
8. Cf. the opening of *For the Sexes: The Gates of Paradise*.
9. The secret follower of Jesus who opposed the Sanhedrin council's condemnation (Luke 50:51) and obtained permission from Pilate to bury him in his own tomb. According to legend, he brought Christianity to Britain, along with the Holy Grail, and founded the first church at Glastonbury. Blake's "Joseph of Arimathea among the Rocks of Albion" (c. 1809; a reworked engraving of a figure from Michelangelo's *Crucifixion of St. Paul*) implies that Joseph witnessed Paul's crucifixion in Rome on his way to England: "This is One of the Gothic Artists who Built the Cathedrals in what we call the Dark Ages Wandering about in sheep skins & goat skins of whom the World was not worthy (Hebrews 11:37–38) such were the Christians in all Ages."
1. Pliny the Younger, governor of Bithynia (111–113 C.E.) corresponded with the emperor Trajan on procedures for trying and executing Christians of all ages and both sexes.

The Everlasting Gospel

Was Jesus Humble or did he   [k; N52]
Give any Proofs of Humility

*   *   *

He did not die with Christian Ease   [k; N52]
Asking Pardon of his Enemies
If he had Caiphas would forgive
Sneaking submission can always live   30
He had only to say that God was the devil
And the devil was God like a Christian Civil
Mild Christian regrets to the devil confess
For affronting him thrice in the Wilderness
He had soon been bloody Caesars Elf   35
And at last he would have been Caesar himself

*   *   *

If he had been Antichrist Creeping Jesus   [k, N53] 55
Hed have done any thing to please us
Gone sneaking into Synagogues
And not usd the Elders & Priests like dogs
But Humble as a Lamb or Ass
Obeyd himself to Caiphas   60
God wants not Man to Humble himself
This is the trick of the ancient Elf
This is the Race that Jesus ran
Humble to God Haughty to Man
Cursing the Rulers before the People   65
Even to the temples highest Steeple
And when he Humbled himself to God
Then descended the Cruel Rod
If thou humblest thyself thou humblest me
Thou also dwellst in Eternity   70
Thou art a Man God is no more
Thy own humanity learn to adore
For that is my Spirit of Life
Awake arise to Spiritual Strife
And thy Revenge abroad display²   75
In terrors at the Last Judgment day
Gods Mercy & Long Suffering
Is but the Sinner to Judgment to bring
Thou on the Cross for them shalt pray
And take Revenge at the Last Day   [k, N54] 80
Jesus replied & thunders hurld
I never will Pray for the World
Once I did so when I prayd in the Garden
I wishd to take with me a Bodily Pardon

*   *   *

---

2. Here God shifts from affirming Jesus' humanity to soliciting his collaboration in bringing sinners
   to judgment.

When the Soul fell into Sleep   [k, N54]
And Archangels round it weep
Shooting out against the Light
Fibres of a deadly night   90
Reasoning upon its own Dark Fiction
In Doubt which is Self Contradiction
Humility is only Doubt
And does the Sun & Moon blot out
Rooting over with thorns & stems   95
The buried Soul & all its Gems
This Lifes dim Windows of the Soul
Distorts the Heavens from Pole to Pole
And leads you to Believe a Lie
When you see with not thro the Eye   100
That was born in a night to perish in a night
When the Soul slept in the beams of Light.[3]

Im sure This Jesus will not do   [l, N54]
Either for Englishman or Jew

Was Jesus Chaste or did he   [f, N48–52]
Give any Lessons of Chastity
The morning blushd fiery red
Mary was found in Adulterous bed[4]
Earth groand beneath & Heaven above   5
Trembled at discovery of Love
Jesus was sitting in Moses Chair
They brought the trembling Woman There
Moses commands she be stoned to Death
What was the sound of Jesus breath   10
He laid his hand on Moses Law
The Ancient Heavens in Silent Awe
Writ with Curses from Pole to Pole
All away began to roll[5]
The Earth trembling & Naked lay   15
In secret bed of Mortal Clay
On Sinai felt the hand Divine
Putting back the bloody shrine
And she heard the breath of God
As she heard by Edens flood   20
Good & Evil are no more
Sinais trumpets cease to roar
Cease finger of God to Write
The Heavens are not clean in thy Sight[6]
Thou art Good & thou Alone   25
Nor may the sinner cast one stone
To be Good only is to be

---

3. Reiterating lines near the end of "Auguries of Innocence."
4. A conflation, common in biblical exegesis of Blake's time, of Mary Magdalene (=from Magdala),
from whom Jesus cast out seven demons (Mark 16:9), and the nameless woman taken in adultery
(John 8:3–11).
5. When the illusion of the old heaven is rolled up like a scroll (Isaiah 34:4, Revelation 6:13–14), the
new heaven and new earth are revealed (Revelation 21:1).
6. Alluding (as does line 36) to the erroneous theology of Job's (25:4–6) false comforter Bildad: "How
then can man be justified with God? or how can he be clean that is of a woman? . . . yea, the stars
are not pure in his sight. How much less man, that is a worm? and the son of man, which is a worm?"

A Devil or else a Pharisee
Thou Angel of the Presence Divine
That didst create this Body of Mine   30
Wherefore has[t] thou writ these Laws
And Created Hells dark jaws
My Presence I will take from thee[7]
A Cold Leper thou shalt be
Tho thou wast so pure & bright   35
That Heaven was Impure in thy Sight
Tho thy Oath turnd Heaven Pale
Tho thy Covenant built Hells Jail
Tho thou didst all to Chaos roll
With the Serpent for its soul   40
Still the breath Divine does move
And the breath Divine is Love
Mary Fear Not Let me see
The Seven Devils that torment thee
Hide not from my Sight thy Sin   45
That forgiveness thou maist win
Has no Man Condemned thee
No Man Lord! then what is he
Who shall Accuse thee. Come Ye forth
Fallen Fiends of Heavnly birth   50
That have forgot your Ancient love
And driven away my trembling Dove
You shall bow before her feet
You shall lick the dust for Meat[8]
And tho you cannot Love but Hate   55
Shall be beggars at Loves Gate
What was thy love Let me see it
Was it love or Dark Deceit
Love too long from Me has fled.
Twas dark deceit to Earn my bread   60
Twas Covet or twas Custom or
Some trifle not worth caring for
That they may call a shame & Sin
Loves Temple[9] that God dwelleth in
And hide in secret hidden Shrine   65
The Naked Human form divine
And render that a Lawless thing
On which the Soul Expands its wing
But this O Lord this was my Sin
When first I let these Devils in   70
In dark pretence to Chastity
Blaspheming Love blaspheming thee

7. In turning aside the Mosaic law from the adulteress, Jesus rejects the Lawgiver as well and with-
   draws his presence from this false deity. When divinity is clearly seen in the human form of Jesus,
   the holy Jehovah enshrined by the churches is cast off as a hollow fraud (called "Nobodaddy" in
   several Notebook poems).
8. Combining allusions to Genesis 3:14 and Micah 7:17 (Stevenson). In lines 49–56, Jesus directly
   addresses Mary Magdalene's seven demons as accusers (line 49; John 8:10–11) and as loveless
   fallen angels (line 50). His questions to Mary herself (lines 57–58) prompt her self-examination
   (lines 59–68) and confession of blasphemy (lines 69–80) as the root cause of her condition (cf.
   Jerusalem 60:62 and the unforgiveable sin against the Holy Ghost, Mark 3:29).
9. The human body, temple of the Holy Spirit (cf. 1 Corinthians 6:19).

Thence Rose Secret Adulteries
And thence did Covet also rise
My Sin thou hast forgiven me   75
Canst thou forgive my Blasphemy
Canst thou return to this dark Hell
And in my burning bosom dwell
And canst thou Die that I may live
And canst thou Pity & forgive   80
Then Rolld the shadowy Man[1] away
From the Limbs of Jesus to make them his prey
An Ever devo[u]ring appetite
Glittering with festering Venoms bright
Crying Crucify this cause of distress   85
Who dont keep the secrets of Holiness
All Mental Powers by Diseases we bind
But he heals the Deaf & the Dumb & the Blind
Whom God has afflicted for Secret Ends
He comforts & Heals & calls them Friends   90
But when Jesus was Crucified
Then was perfected his glittring pride
In three Nights he devourd his prey
And still he devours the Body of Clay
For Dust & Clay is the Serpents meat   95
Which never was made for Man to Eat

Was Jesus Born of a Virgin Pure   [d, N120]
With narrow Soul & looks demure
If he intended to take on Sin
The Mother should an Harlot been
Just such a one as Magdelen   5
With seven devils in her Pen
Or were Jew Virgins still more Curst[2]
And more suckling devils nurst?[3]
Or what was it which he took on   [d, N120]
That he might bring Salvation   10
A Body subject to be Tempted
From neither pain nor grief Exempted
Or such a body as might not feel
The passions that with Sinners deal

✳   ✳   ✳

He mockd the Sabbath & he mockd   [d, N120]
The Sabbaths God & he unlocked
The Evil spirits from their Shrines
And turnd Fisherman to Divines   20
Oerturnd the Tent of Secret Sins
& its Golden cords & Pins
Tis the Bloody Shrine of War

1. The empty negation of Jesus, the Antichrist.
2. The question is whether a harlot or a virgin is possessed by more devils. "Curst" also means "ill-tempered." In *Jerusalem* 61, Jesus' mother is not a virgin.
3. Cf. "Sooner murder an infant in its cradle than nurse unacted desires" (*Marriage* 10:67); not a justification for infanticide but a warning of the toxic effect of cherishing suppressed and unrecognized desires.

Pinnd around from Star to Star
Halls of Justice hating Vice   25
Where the Devil Combs his Lice

Was Jesus gentle or did he   [I, N100–01]
Give any marks of Gentility
When twelve years old he ran away
And left his Parents in dismay
When after three days sorrow found   5
Loud as Sinai's trumpet sound
No Earthly Parents I confess
My Heavenly Fathers business
Ye understand not what I say
And angry force me to obey   10
Obedience is a duty then
And favour gains with God & Men
John from the Wilderness loud cried
Satan gloried in his Pride
Come said Satan come away   15
Ill soon see if youll obey
John for disobedience bled
But you can turn the stones to bread
Gods high king & Gods high Priest
Shall Plant their Glories in your breast   20
If Caiaphas you will obey
If Herod you with bloody Prey
Feed with the Sacrifice & be
Obedient fall down worship me
Thunders & lightnings broke around   25
And Jesus voice in thunders sound
Thus I seize the Spiritual Prey
Ye smiters with disease make way
I come Your King & God to seize
Is God a Smiter with disease   30
The God of this World raged in vain
He bound Old Satan in his Chain
And bursting forth his furious ire
Became a Chariot of fire
Throughout the land he took his course   35
And traced Diseases to their Source
He cursd the Scribe & Trampling down Hipocrisy
Where eer his Chariot took its way
There Gates of Death let in the Day
Broke down from every Chain & Bar   40
And Satan in his Spiritual War
Dragd at his Chariot wheels loud howld
The God of this World louder rolld
The Chariot Wheels & louder still
His voice was heard from Zions hill   45
And in his hand the Scourge shone bright
He scourgd the Merchant Canaanite
From out the Temple of his Mind
And in his Body tight does bind
Satan & all his Hellish Crew   50

And thus with wrath he did subdue
The Serpent Bulk of Natures dross
Till he had naild it to the Cross
He took on Sin in the Virgins Womb
And put it off on the Cross & Tomb   55
To be Worshipd by the Church of Rome
Seeing this False Christ In Fury & Passion   [g, N54]
I made my voice heard all over the Nation

The Vision of Christ that thou dost see   [e, N33]
Is my Visions Greatest Enemy
Thine has a great hook nose like thine
Mine has a snub nose like to mine
Thine is the Friend of All Mankind   5
Mine speaks in parables to the Blind
Thine loves the same world that mine hates
Thy Heaven doors are my Hell Gates
Socrates taught what Melitus[4]
Loathd as a Nations bitterest Curse   10
And Caiphas was in his own Mind
A benefactor of Mankind
Both read the Bible day & night
But thou readst black where I read white

FROM MARGINALIA (1789–1827)[†]

From On Lavater's *Aphorisms on Man* (1788)[*]

[E590]to hell till he[1] behaves better. mark that I do not believe there is such a thing litterally. but hell is the being shut up in the possession of corporeal desires which shortly weary the man for <u>all life is holy</u>

[E592]A vision of the Eternal Now[2]—

* * * Active Evil is better than Passive Good.

[E595]Deduct from a rose its redness. from a lilly its whiteness from a diamond its hardness from a spunge its softness from an oak its heighth from

---

4. One of Socrates' three accusers; cf. *Jerusalem* 93.
† In marginalia that sometimes spilled over onto title pages, endpapers, and any blank space he could find, Blake heckled, cheered, and pitted his wits against books that interested him. In this peculiarly intimate and transgressive medium—a literary genre in which Coleridge surpasses even Blake—the annotator surrounds, invades, and appropriates another author's text as a site for working out corroborative or competing ideas. Occasionally Blake seems aware of a potential reader ("I hope no one will call what I have written cavilling," he notes in a margin of Lavater's *Aphorisms*), but for the most part the uninhibited private voice of his marginalia is closer to that of his Notebook than his letters. His best-known annotations, those on Watson's *Apology for the Bible* (1797–98) and Reynolds's *Discourses* (c. 1798–1809), attack not only the writers' theories but also the writers themselves. Blake is no less intense in his approbations: after annotating Lavater's *Aphorisms*, he added his own name below the author's on the title page and enclosed the paired names in a heart.
  Over a lifetime of marginal jottings, Blake probably left his mark on many more books than can be traced today. For example, he claimed when annotating Reynolds in 1798 to have expressed "exactly Similar" opinions "when very Young" in the margins of Burke's *Treatise on the Sublime*,

a daisy its lowness & rectify every thing in Nature as the Philosophers do. & then we shall return to Chaos & God will be compelld to be Excentric if he Creates O happy Philosopher

[E600]There is a strong objection to Lavaters principles (as I understand them) & that is He makes every thing originate in its accident he makes the vicious propensity not only a leading feature of the man but the Stamina on which all his virtues grow. But as I understand Vice it is a Negative—It does not signify what the laws of Kings & Priests have calld Vice we who are philosophers ought not to call the Staminal Virtues of Humanity by the same name that we call the omissions of intellect springing from poverty

Every mans leading propensity ought to be calld his leading Virtue & his good Angel But the Philosophy of Causes & Consequences misled Lavater as it has all his cotemporaries. Each thing is its own cause & its own effect Accident is the omission of act in self & the hindering of act in another, This is Vice but all Act is Virtue. To hinder another is not an act it is the contrary it is a restraint on action both in ourselves & in the person hinderd. for he who hinders another omits his own duty. at the time

Murder is Hindering Another Theft is Hindering Another Backbiting. Undermining Circumventing & whatever is Negative is Vice

But the origin of this mistake in Lavater & his cotemporaries, is, They suppose that Womans Love is Sin. in consequence all the Loves & Graces with them are Sin

---

Locke's *Essay on Human Understanding*, and Bacon's *Advancement of Learning*. He was still hard at it in 1827, the year of his death, in expressing indignation against Dr. Thornton's "Tory translation" of the Lord's Prayer. As a guide to what triggered Blake's responses, standard editions provide reduced-print excerpts from the original texts, occasionally to the point of swamping a one-word comment with many dull paragraphs of quotation. Facsimile editions of the annotated books give a better sense of the lively dynamics of Blake's interactions with the precursor text, as minor exasperations fuel a head of steam that erupts when he finds a large enough space for a counterattack. As Jason Snart has emphasized in *The Torn Book* (2006) and related essays, facsimile editions can obscure differences between Blake's handwriting and someone else's and between notes he wrote at different times, in pen or pencil, at various stages of reconsideration. As the format of this edition precludes our presenting the give and take of the annotations in full context, we have selected passages that can stand alone, or nearly so, to exhibit Blake's skills as an aphorist, a controversialist, and a terse essayist.

    Our text is based on Erdman (E), collated with Bentley (and with available facsimiles, as individually noted); bracketed references indicate where scattered excerpts begin in the Erdman edition. We add no punctuation but silently remove or alter interrupting periods, add extra spaces between run-on sentences, and supply accidentally dropped letters or words needed for clarity.

* Johann Caspar Lavater, *Aphorisms on Man*, trans. [J. H. Fuseli] (1788); frontispiece by Blake after Fuseli. Huntington Library 57431. Annotated while still in loose sheets (R. J. Shroyer, ed. Scholars Facsimiles edition, 1980; Snart, *The Torn Book*, 2006). Blake's first note is "for the reason of these remarks see the last aphorism," referring to No. 643: "If you mean to know yourself, interline such of these aphorisms as affected you agreeably in reading, and set a mark to such as left a sense of uneasiness with you; and then shew your copy to whom you please." Blake marked many passages "uneasy" but wrote "the best in the book" beside "Keep him at least three paces distant who hates bread, music, and the laugh of a child." Notes in the handwriting of others indicate that Blake followed Lavater's instructions and showed his comments to friends.

1. A fault-finder (No. 309 in Lavater's text). The underlined final phrase is reformulated at the end of *The Marriage* as "Every thing that lives is holy" (cf. *Visions* 8:10, *America* 8:13).

2. Referring to No. 407: "Whatever is visible is the vessel or veil of the invisible past, present, future," which Blake takes as the awakened imagination's opening of the present to eternity; cf. the Bard who "Present Past & Future sees" (*Songs* 30), the perception of "Eternity in an hour" ("Auguries of Innocence" 4); and "Whenever any Individual Rejects Error & Embraces Truth a Last Judgment passes upon that Individual" ("Vision of the Last Judgment"). Cf. Abraham Cowley (1618–1667) on heaven: "Nothing is there To come, and nothing Past, / But an Eternal Now does always last" (*Davideis* 1:360–62).

From On Swedenborg's *Divine Love and Divine Wisdom*
(1788; notes c. 1790)*

[E602]There can be no Good-Will. Will is always Evil It is pernicious to others or selfish If God is any thing he is Understanding He is the Influx from that into the Will Thus Good to others or benevolent Understanding can Work harm ignorantly but never can the Truth. * * *

Understanding or Thought is not natural to Man it is acquired by means of Suffering & Distress i.e Experience. Will, Desire, Love, Rage, Envy, & all other Affections are Natural. but Understanding is Acquired But Observe. without these is to be less than Man. * * *

[E603]Think of a white cloud as being holy you cannot love it but think of a holy man within the cloud love springs up in your thought. for to think of holiness distinct from man is impossible to the affections. Thought alone can make monsters, but the affections cannot

[E605]The Whole of the New Church is in the Active Life & not in Ceremonies at all

Study Sciences till you are blind Study intellectuals till you are cold Yet Science cannot teach intellect Much less can intellect teach Affection

From On Watson's *An Apology for the Bible*
(1797; notes 1798)*

[E611]To defend the Bible in this year 1798 would cost a man his life The Beast & the Whore rule without control[1]

It is an easy matter for a Bishop to triumph over Paines attack but it is not so easy for one who loves the Bible

The Perversions of Christs words & acts are attackd by Paine & also the perversions of the Bible; Who dare defend either the Acts of Christ or the Bible Unperverted?

But to him who sees this mortal pilgrimage in the light that I see it, Duty to his country is the first consideration & safety the last

Read patiently take not up this Book in an idle hour the consideration of

---

* Emanuel Swedenborg, *The Wisdom of Angels, concerning Divine Love and Divine Wisdom*, trans. [N. Tucker] (1788). British Library C.45.e.1. Blake's pencil notes are visible (but illegible) in the images of this copy in Eighteenth Century Collections Online (document CW3320224419).

* R[ichard] Watson, D. D., . . . Bishop of Llandaff, *An Apology for the Bible, in a Series of Letters, addressed to Thomas Paine, Author of . . . The Age of Reason.* 8th ed. (1797). Huntington Library 110 260. For commentary, see G. Ingli James, ed., *William Blake, Annotations to Richard Watson* (facsimile), University College Cardiff (1984); Florence Sandler, *Blake and His Bibles* (1990), ed. Erdman; Robert N. Essick, *Studies in Romanticism* 30 (1991), 189–212; and Morton D. Paley, *Blake: An Illustrated Quarterly* 32 (1998), 32–43. The annotations demonstrate Blake's familiarity with Paine's work and with biblical commentary, especially the controversies touched off in England by German scholars' "higher criticism" of the Bible on historical and textual grounds. Blake had met Paine and, as has recently been recognized, drew his likeness in his Notebook (N74). If Blake began taking notes with the thought of developing a publishable refutation of Watson, which would be tantamount to a public defense of the notorious Paine, he must have realized that such a publication could lead to criminal prosecution: in January 1798 his principal employer, the bookseller Joseph Johnson, was imprisoned for publishing the radical author Gilbert Wakefield.

1. The second sentence is lightly crossed out in pencil, probably by Blake's friend Samuel Palmer, who later owned the book. An illegible seventh letter at the end of "control" was deleted by Blake. On the rule and downfall of the Beast and the Whore of Babylon, see Revelation 17–18.

these things is the whole duty of man & the affairs of life & death trifles sports of time But these considerations business of Eternity

I have been commanded from Hell not to print this as it is what our Enemies wish

[E612]Paine has not Attacked Christianity. Watson has defended Antichrist

Read the XXIII Chap of Matthew & then condemn Paines hatred of Priests if you dare

God made Man happy & Rich but the Subtil made the innocent Poor This must be a most wicked & blasphemous book[2]

If this first Letter is written without Railing & Illiberality I have never read one that is. To me it is all Daggers & Poison. the sting of the serpent is in every Sentence as well as the glittering Dissimulation * * *

I have not the Charity for the Bishop that he pretends to have for Paine. I believe him to be a State trickster

[E612] Mr Paine has not extinguished & cannot Extinguish Moral rectitude. he has Extinguished Superstition which took the Place of Moral Rectitude what has Moral Rectitude to do with Opinions concerning historical fact

To what does the Bishop attribute the English Crusade against France. is it not to State Religion. blush for shame

                        *   *   *

[E613]Conscience in those that have it is unequivocal, it is the voice of God Our judgment of right & wrong is Reason I believe that the Bishop laught at the Bible in his slieve & so did Locke

If Conscience is not a Criterion of Moral Rectitude What is it? He who thinks that Honesty is changeable knows nothing about it

Virtue & honesty or the dictates of Conscience are of no doubtful Signification to any one

Opinion is one Thing. Principle another. No Man can change his Principles Every Man changes his opinions. He who supposes that his Principles are to be changed is a Dissembler who Disguises his Principles & calls that change

Paine is either a Devil or an Inspired man. Men who give themselves to their Energetic Genius in the manner that Paine does are no Examiners. If they are not determinately wrong they must be Right or the Bible is false. as to Examiners in these points they will be spewed out.[3] The Man who pretends to be a modest enquirer into the truth of a self evident thing is a Knave The truth & certainty of Virtue & Honesty i.e Inspiration needs no one to prove it it is Evident as the Sun & Moon He who stands doubting of what he intends whether it is Virtuous or Vicious knows not what Virtue

2. Referring to Watson's *The Wisdom and Goodness of God, in having made both Rich and Poor*, advertised in the endpapers.
3. Like the church at Laodicea, "lukewarm, and neither cold nor hot" (Revelation 3:16).

means. no man can do a Vicious action & think it to be Virtuous. no man can take darkness for light. he may pretend to do so & may pretend to be a modest Enquirer. but he is a Knave

[E614]To me who believe the Bible & profess myself a Christian a defence of the Wickedness of the Israelites in murdering so many thousands under pretence of a command from God is altogether Abominable & Blasphemous. Wherefore did Christ come was it not to abolish the Jewish Imposture Was not Christ murderd because he taught that God loved all Men & was their father & forbad all contention for Worldly prosperity in opposition to the Jewish Scriptures which are only an Example of the wickedness & deceit of the Jews & were written as an Example of the possibility of Human Beastliness in all its branches. Christ died as an Unbeliever. & if the Bishops had their will so would Paine. see page 1 but he who speaks a word against the Son of man shall be forgiven let the Bishop prove that he has not spoken against the Holy Ghost who in Paine strives with Christendom as in Christ he strove with the Jews

[E614]There is a vast difference between an accident brought on by a mans own carelessness & a destruction from the designs of another. The Earthquakes at Lisbon &c were the Natural result of Sin, but the destruction of the Canaanites by Joshua was the Unnatural design of wicked men[4] To Extirpate a nation by means of another nation is as wicked as to destroy an individual by means of another individual which God considers (in the Bible) as Murder & commands that it shall not be done
Therefore the Bishop has not answerd Paine

[E615]That the Jews assumed a right Exclusively to the benefits of God. will be a lasting witness against them. & the same will it be against Christians

Read the Edda of Iceland the Songs of Fingal the accounts of North American Savages (as they are calld)[5] Likewise Read Homers Iliad. he was certainly a Savage in the Bishops sense. He knew nothing of God, in the Bishops sense of the word & yet he was no fool

The Bible or Peculiar Word of God, Exclusive of Conscience or the Word of God Universal, is that Abomination which like the Jewish ceremonies is for ever removed & henceforth every man may converse with God & be a King & Priest in his own house

[E616]The trifles which the Bishop has combated in the following Letters are such as do nothing against Paines Arguments none of which the Bishop has dared to Consider. One for instance, which is That the books of the Bible were never believd willingly by any nation & that none but designing Villains ever pretended to believe That the Bible is all a State Trick, thro which tho' the People at all times could see they never had the power to

---

4. Watson compared the Israelites' extermination of the Canaanites (culminating in Joshua 10:40) to the Lisbon earthquake.
5. Blake knew of the Norse epic *Edda* through Paul Henri Mallet, *Northern Antiquities* (trans. 1770) and the Celtic *Fingal*, supposedly by Ossian, through its "translation" by the author James Macpherson (1762). His source for "accounts" of North American myths is unknown.

throw off Another Argument is that all the Commentators on the Bible are Dishonest Designing Knaves who in hopes of a good living adopt the State religion this he has shewn with great force which calls upon His Opponent loudly for an answer. I could name an hundred such

He who writes things for true which none could write but the actor, such are most of the acts of Moses, must either be the actor or a fable writer or a liar. If Moses did not write the history of his acts, it takes away the authority altogether it ceases to be history & becomes a Poem of probable impossibilities fabricated for pleasure as moderns say but I say by Inspiration.

[E616]Jesus could not do miracles where unbelief hinderd[6] hence we must conclude that the man who holds miracles to be ceased puts it out of his own power to ever witness one The manner of a miracle being performd is in modern times considerd as an arbitrary command of the agent upon the patient but this is an impossibility not a miracle neither did Jesus ever do such a miracle. Is it a greater miracle to feed five thousand men with five loaves than to overthrow all the armies of Europe with a small pamphlet.[7] look over the events of your own life & if you do not find that you have both done such miracles & lived by such you do not see as I do True I cannot do a miracle thro experiment & to domineer over & prove to others my superior power as neither could Christ But I can & do work such as both astonish & comfort me & mine How can Paine the worker of miracles ever doubt Christs in the above sense of the word miracle But how can Watson ever believe the above sense of a miracle who considers it as an arbitrary act of the agent upon an unbelieving patient, whereas the Gospel says that Christ could not do a miracle because of Unbelief
[E617]If Christ could not do miracles because of Unbelief the reason alledged by Priests for miracles is false for those who believe want not to be confounded by miracles. Christ & his Prophets & Apostles were not ambitious miracle mongers

[E617]Prophets in the modern sense of the word have never existed Jonah was no prophet in the modern sense for his prophecy of Nineveh failed Every honest man is a Prophet he utters his opinion both of private & public matters / Thus / If you go on So / the result is So / He never says such a thing shall happen let you do what you will. a Prophet is a Seer not an Arbitrary Dictator. It is mans fault if God is not able to do him good. for he gives to the just & to the unjust but the unjust reject his gift

[E617]Nothing can be more contemptible than to suppose Public RECORDS to be True Read them & Judge. if you are not a Fool.
Of what consequence is it whether Moses wrote the Pentateuch or no. If Paine trifles in some of his objections it is folly to confute him so seriously in them & leave his more material ones unanswered Public Records as If Public Records were True

6. Cf. Matthew 13:58: "And he did not many mighty works there because of their unbelief."
7. Paine's *Common Sense* (1776).

Impossible[8] for the facts are such as none but the actor could tell, if it is True Moses & none but he could write it unless we allow it to be Poetry & that poetry inspired

If historical facts can be written by inspiration Miltons Paradise Lost is as true as Genesis or Exodus. but the Evidence is nothing for how can he who writes what he has neither seen nor heard of be an Evidence of The Truth of his history

[E618]I cannot concieve the Divinity of the books in the Bible to consist either in who they were written by or at what time or in the historical evidence which may be all false in the eyes of one man & true in the eyes of another but in the Sentiments & Examples which whether true or Parabolic are Equally useful as Examples given to us of the perverseness of some & its consequent evil & the honesty of others & its consequent good This sense of the Bible is equally true to all & equally plain to all. none can doubt the impression which he recieves from a book of Examples. If he is good he will abhor wickedness in David or Abraham if he is wicked he will make their wickedness an excuse for his & so he would do by any other book

All Penal Laws court Transgression & therefore are cruelty & Murder The laws of the Jews were (both ceremonial & real) the basest & most oppressive of human codes. & being like all other codes given under pretence of divine command were what Christ pronouncd them The Abomination that maketh desolate.[9] i.e State Religion which is the Source of all Cruelty * * *

[E618]There are no Proofs that Matthew the Earliest of all the Writings of the New Testament was written within the First Century. * * *

They seem to Forget that there is a God of This World. A God Worshipd in this World as God & Set above all that is calld God[1]

[E619]The Bishop never saw the Everlasting Gospel any more than Tom Paine[2]

The Gospel is Forgiveness of Sins & has No Moral Precepts these belong to Plato & Seneca & Nero

Do or Act to Do Good or to do Evil who Dare to judge but God alone

Who does the Bishop call Bad Men Are they the Publicans & Sinners that Christ loved to associate with Does God Love The Righteous according to the Gospel or does he not cast them off. For who is really Righteous It is all Pretension

---

8. Referring to Watson's concession that even if writers later than Moses assembled the first five books of the Bible from public records, "every fact recorded in them may be true." Blake agrees with Paine that the Bible is filled with inconsistencies and is unreliable as history: only Moses could have borne witness to events at the burning bush and on Mount Sinai, yet he could not have described his own death and burial (Deuteronomy 34:5–6).
9. Daniel 11:21, Matthew 24:15; cf. *Milton* 24/22:49; *Jerusalem* 10:16.
1. Attributes of Satan (2 Corinthians 4:4, 2 Thessalonians 2:4).
2. On this timeless dispensation, see dagger note, p. 445 herein.

[E620]It appears to me Now that Tom Paine is a better Christian than the Bishop

I have read this Book with attention & find that the Bishop has only hurt Paines heel while Paine has broken his head the Bishop has not answerd one of Paines grand objections

From On Bacon's *Essays* (1798)*

[E620]Is it True or is it False that the Wisdom of this World is Foolishness with God[1]

This is Certain If what Bacon says Is True what Christ says Is False If Caesar is Right Christ is Wrong both in Politics & Religion since they will divide them in Two

Good Advice for Satans Kingdom [written on the title page]

Every Body Knows that this is Epi[c]urus and Lucretius[2] & Yet Every Body Says that it is Christian Philosophy how is this Possible Every Body must be a Liar & deciever but Every Body does not do this But The Hirelings of Kings & Courts who make themselves Every Body & Knowingly propagate Falshood

[E621]Self Evident Truth is one Thing and Truth the result of Reasoning is another Thing Rational Truth is not the Truth of Christ but of Pilate It is the Tree of the Knowledge of Good & Evil

[E624][A drawing of] The devils arse [with a chain of excrement ending in] A King

[E629]Bacon calls Intellectual Arts Unmanly Poetry Painting Music are in his opinion Useless & so they are for Kings & Wars & shall in the End Annihilate them

[E632]King James was Bacons Primum Mobile

From On Boyd's *Translation of the Inferno in English Verse* (1785; notes c. 1800)*

[E634]the grandest Poetry is Immoral the Grandest characters Wicked. Very Satan. Capanius Othello a murderer. Prometheus. Jupiter. Jehovah, Jesus a wine bibber

---

* Francis Bacon, *Essays Moral, Economical, and Political* (1798); Cambridge University, Keynes. U.4.20.
1. 1 Corinthians 3:19.
2. In *De Rerum Natura* ("On the Nature of Things"), the Latin poet Lucretius (c. 99–55 B.C.E.) celebrated the Greek philosopher Epicurus' (341–270 B.C.E.) materialist theory of a cosmos consisting of atoms randomly colliding in a void.
* Henry Boyd, trans. *Inferno* of Dante Aligheri in English Verse. Cambridge University, Keynes. U.4.13.

Cunning & Morality are not Poetry but Philosophy the Poet is Independent & Wicked the Philosopher is Dependent & Good
Poetry is to excuse Vice & show its reason & necessary purgation

[E635]If it is thus¹ the extreme of black is white & of sweet sower & of good Evil & of Nothing Something

From On Reynolds's *Works* (1798; notes c. 1798–1809)*

[E635]This Man was Hired to Depress Art This is the opinion of Will Blake my Proofs of this Opinion are given in the following Notes

Advice of the Popes who succeeded the Age of Rafael

Degrade first the Arts if you'd Mankind degrade,
Hire Idiots to Paint with cold light & hot shade:
Give high Price for the worst, leave the best in disgrace,
And with Labours of Ignorance fill every place.

[E636]Having spent the Vigour of my Youth & Genius under the Opression of Sr Joshua & his Gang of Cunning Hired Knaves Without Employment & as much as could possibly be Without Bread, The Reader must Expect to Read in all my Remarks on these Books Nothing but Indignation & Resentment While Sʳ Joshua was rolling in Riches Barry¹ was Poor & Unemployd except by his own Energy Mortimer was calld a Madman & only Portrait Painting applauded & rewarded by the Rich & Great. Reynolds & Gainsborough Blotted & Blurred one against the other & Divided all the English World between them Fuseli Indignant almost hid himself—I am hid

The Arts & Sciences are the Destruction of Tyrannies or Bad Governments Why should A Good Government endeavour to Depress What is its Chief & only Support

The Foundation of Empire is Art & Science Remove them or Degrade them & the Empire is No More—Empire follows Art & Not Vice Versa as Englishmen suppose * * *

Who will Dare to Say that Polite Art is Encouraged, or Either Wished or Tolerated in a Nation where The Society for the Encouragement of Art Sufferd Barry to Give them his Labour for Nothing A Society Composed of the Flower of the English Nobility & Gentry—Suffering an Artist to Starve while he Supported Really what They under pretence of Encouraging were Endeavouring to Depress—Barry told me that while he Did that Work—he Lived on Bread & Apples

---

1. That "there are certain *bounds* even to liberty."
* Reynolds, Sir Joshua. *Works*, 2nd ed. (1798). British Library C.45.e.18–20. Blake's annotations (c. 1798–1809) in volume 1, inked over pencil, are clearly visible in the page images of Eighteenth Century Collections Online, document no. CW3303409251.
1. On the painters James Barry and John Hamilton Mortimer and the Society for the Encouragement of Art (founded 1805), see "Public Address."

[E637]The Bible says That Cultivated Life Existed First—Uncultivated Life comes afterwards from Satans Hirelings Necessaries Accomodations & Ornaments are the whole of Life ~~First were Created Wine & Happiness Good Looks & Fortune~~ Satan took away Ornament First. Next he took away Accomodations & Then he became Lord & Master of Necessaries

Liberality! We want not Liberality We want a Fair Price & Proportionate Value & a General Demand for Art

Invention depends Altogether upon Execution or Organization. as that is right or wrong so is the Invention perfect or imperfect. Whoever is set to Undermine the Execution of Art is set to Destroy Art Michael Angelos Art Depends on Michael Angelos Execution Altogether

I am happy I cannot say that Rafael Ever was from my Earliest Childhood hidden from Me. I saw & I Knew immediately the difference between Rafael & Rubens

       Some look to see the sweet Outlines
       And beauteous Forms that Love does wear
       Some look to find out Patches. Paint.
       Bracelets & Stays & Powderd Hair

[E639]The Contradictions in Reynolds's Discourses are Strong Presumptions that they are the Work of Several Hands But this is no Proof that Reynolds did not Write them The Man Either Painter or Philosopher who Learns or Acquires all he Knows from Others Must be full of Contradictions

[E639]I was once looking over the Prints from Rafael & Michael Angelo in the Library of the Royal Academy Moser[2] came to me & said You should not Study these old Hard Stiff & Dry Unfinishd Works of Art, Stay a little & I will shew you what you should Study. He then went & took down Le Bruns & Rubens's Galleries[3] How I did secretly Rage. I also spoke my Mind . . .
I said to Moser, These things that you call Finishd are not Even Begun how can they then, be Finishd? The Man who does not know The Beginning, never can know the End of Art

[E641]To Generalize is to be an Idiot To Particularize is the Alone Distinction of Merit—General Knowledges are those Knowledges that Idiots possess

       When Sr Joshua Reynolds died
       All Nature was degraded;
       The King dropd a tear into the Queens Ear;
       And all his Pictures Faded.

[E642]I consider Reynolds's Discourses to the Royal Academy as the Simulations of the Hypocrite who Smiles particularly where he means to Betray. His Praise of Rafael is like the Hysteric Smile of Revenge His Softness &

---

2. George Michael Moser (1704–1783), Swiss-born enamelist and metalworker, keeper at the Royal Academy from its founding in 1768, and deputy librarian after 1781.
3. Blake thought that neither Charles Le Bruns (1619–1690) nor Peter Paul Rubens (1577–1640) placed enough emphasis on outline.

Candour the hidden trap & the poisoned feast. He praises Michael Angelo for Qualities which Michael Angelo Abhorrd; & He blames Rafael for the only Qualities which Rafael Valued, Whether Reynolds knew what he was doing is nothing to me; the Mischief is just the same, whether a Man does it Ignorantly or Knowingly: I always consider'd True Art & True Artists to be particularly Insulted & Degraded by the Reputation of these Discourses As much as they were Degraded by the Reputation of Reynolds's Paintings. & that Such Artists as Reynolds, are at all times Hired by the Satan's for the Depression of Art A Pretence of Art: To Destroy Art * * *

The Neglect of Fuselis Milton[4] in a Country pretending to the Encouragement of Art is a Sufficient Apology for My Vigorous Indignation if indeed the Neglect of My own Powers had not been. * * *

The Rich Men of England form themselves into a Society to Sell & Not to Buy Pictures The Artist who does not throw his Contempt on such Trading Exhibitions does not know either his own Interest or his Duty.

> When Nations grow Old. The Arts grow Cold
> And Commerce settles on every Tree
> And the Poor & the Old can live upon Gold
> For all are Born Poor. Aged Sixty three

Reynoldss Opinion was that Genius May be Taught & that all Pretence to Inspiration is a Lie & a Deceit to say the least of it For if it is a Deceit the Whole Bible is Madness This Opinion originates in the Greeks Calling the Muses Daughters of Memory

The Enquiry in England is not whether a Man has Talents & Genius? But whether he is Passive & Polite & a Virtuous Ass: & obedient to Noblemens Opinions in Art & Science. If he is; he is a Good Man: If Not he must be Starved

[E643]I do not believe that Rafael taught Mich. Angelo or that Mich. Ang: taught Rafael., any more than I believe that the Rose teaches the Lilly how to grow or the Apple tree teaches the Pear tree how to bear Fruit. I do not believe the tales of Anecdote writers when they militate against Individual Character

Minute Discrimination is Not Accidental All Sublimity is founded on Minute Discrimination

The Lives of Painters[5] say that Rafael died of Dissipation Idleness is one Thing & Dissipation Another He who has Nothing to Dissipate Cannot Dissipate Painters are noted for being Dissipated & Wild.

---

4. Fuseli's exhibitions (1799, 1800) of more than forty paintings of subjects from Milton were commercial failures; the project grew out of an aborted illustrated edition of Milton, for which Blake was to have been among the engravers.
5. According to Giorgio Vasari's *Lives of the Artists* (trans. William Aglionby, 1685; 1719), "following secretly other amorous Delights, it happened, that [Raphael] committed once such an Excess that way, that he came Home with a pritty high *Feaver*" (258), from which he soon died.

[E645]* * * no one can ever Design till he has learnd the Language of Art by making many Finishd Copies both of Nature & Art & of whatever comes in his way from Earliest Childhood

The difference between a bad Artist & a Good One Is the Bad Artist Seems to Copy a Great Deal: The Good one Really Does Copy a Great Deal

* * * Every Eye Sees differently As the Eye—Such the Object

[E646]The Man who asserts that there is no Such Thing as Softness in Art & that every thing in Art is Definite & Determinate has not been told this by Practise but by Inspiration & Vision because Vision is Determinate & Perfect & he Copies That without Fatigue Every thing being Definite & determinate Softness is Produced Alone by Comparative Strength & Weakness in the Marking out of the Forms

I say These Principles could never be found out by the Study of Nature without Con or Innate Science

A Work of Genius is a Work "Not to be obtain by the Invocation of Memory & her Syren Daughters. but by Devout prayer to that Eternal Spirit who can enrich with all utterance & knowledge & sends out his Seraphim with the hallowed fire of his Altar to touch & purify the lips of whom he pleases." Milton[6]

The following Discourse is particularly Interesting to Blockheads. as it Endeavours to prove That there is No such thing as Inspiration & that any Man of a plain Understanding may by Thieving from Others become a Mich Angelo

Without Minute Neatness of Execution The Sublime cannot Exist! Grandeur of Ideas is founded on Precision of Ideas

[E648]Knowledge of Ideal Beauty is Not to be Acquired It is Born with us Innate Ideas are in Every Man Born with him. they are truly Himself. The Man who says that we have No Innate Ideas must be a Fool & Knave Having No Con-Science or Innate Science

All Forms are Perfect in the Poets Mind. but these are not Abstracted nor Compounded from Nature but are from Imagination

The Great Bacon he is Calld I call him the Little Bacon says that Every Thing must be done by Experiment his first principle is Unbelief And Yet here he says that Art must be producd Without such Method. He is Like Sr Joshua full of Self-Contradiction & Knavery

What is General Nature is there Such a Thing
what is General Knowledge is there such a Thing All Knowledge is Particular

6. Quoting *The Reason of Church-government Urg'd against Prelaty* (1641) 41, with minor changes.

[E649]What does this mean "Would have been" one of the first Painters of his Age" Albert Durer Is! Not would have been! Besides. let them look at Gothic Figures & Gothic Buildings, & not talk of Dark Ages or of Any Age! Ages are All Equal. But Genius is Always Above The Age

[E652]Gainsborough told a Gentleman of Rank & Fortune that the Worst Painters always chose the Grandest Subjects. I desired the Gentleman to Set Gainsborough about one of Rafaels Grandest Subjects Namely Christ delivering the Keys to St Peter, & he would find that in Gainsboroughs hands it would be a Vulgar Subject of Poor Fishermen & a Journeyman Carpenter
The following Discourse is written with the same End in View that Gainsborough had in making the Above assertion Namely To Represent Vulgar Artists as the Models of Executive Merit

[E655]To My Eye Rubens's Colouring is most Contemptible His Shadows are of a Filthy Brown somewhat of the Colour of Excrement these are filld with tints & messes of yellow & red His lights are all the Colours of the Rainbow laid on Indiscriminately & broken one into another. Altogether his Colouring is Contrary to The Colouring of Real Art & Science

[E656]Reynolds Thinks that Man Learns all that he Knows I say on the Contrary That Man Brings All that he has or Can have Into the World with him. Man is Born Like a Garden ready Planted & Sown This World is too poor to produce one Seed

[E658]The Ancients did not mean to Impose when they affirmd their belief in Vision & Revelation Plato was in Earnest. Milton was in Earnest. They believd that God did Visit Man Really & Truly & not as Reynolds pretends

[E659]God forbid that Truth should be Confined to Mathematical Demonstration

He who does not Know Truth at Sight is unworthy of Her Notice

Reason or A Ratio of All We have Known is not the Same it shall be when we know More. * * *

[E660]Burke's Treatise on the Sublime & Beautiful is founded on the Opinions of Newton & Locke on this Treatise Reynolds has grounded many of his assertions in all his Discourses I read Burkes Treatise when very Young at the same time I read Locke on Human Understanding & Bacons Advancement of Learning on Every one of these Books I wrote my Opinions & on looking them over find that my Notes on Reynolds in this Book are exactly Similar. I felt the Same Contempt & Abhorrence then; that I do now. They mock Inspiration & Vision Inspiration & Vision was then & now is & I hope will always Remain my Element my Eternal Dwelling place. how can I then hear it Contemnd without returning Scorn for Scorn

From On Spurzheim's *Observations on Insanity* (1817)*

Methodism, &c * * * Cowper[1] came to me & said, "Oh! that I were insane, always. I will never rest. Can you not make me truly insane? I will never rest till I am so. Oh! that in the bosom of God I was hid. You retain health & yet are as mad as any of us all—over us all—mad as a refuge from unbelief—from Bacon Newton and Locke."

From On Berkeley's *Siris* (1744; notes c. 1820)*

[E663]Imagination or the Human Eternal Body in Every Man
Imagination or the Divine Body in Every Man
The All in Man The Divine Image or Imagination
The Four Senses are the Four Faces of Man & the Four Rivers of the Water of Life

[Plato and Aristotle] considerd God as abstracted or distinct from the Imaginative World but Jesus as also Abraham & David considerd God as a Man in the Spiritual or Imaginative Vision
Jesus considerd Imagination to be the Real Man & says I will not leave you Orphanned and I will manifest myself to you he says also the Spiritual Body or Angel as little Children always behold the Face of the Heavenly Father

Harmony [&] Proportion are Qualities & Not Things The Harmony & Proportion of a Horse are not the same with those of a Bull Every Thing has its own Harmony & Proportion Two Inferior Qualities in it For its Reality is Its Imaginative Form

[E664]Knowledge is not by deduction but Immediate by Perception or Sense at once Christ addresses himself to the Man not to his Reason Plato did not bring Life & Immortality to Light Jesus only did this
Jesus supposes every Thing to be Evident to the Child & to the Poor & Unlearned Such is the Gospel
The Whole Bible is filld with Imaginations & Visions from End to End & not with Moral virtues that is the baseness[1] of Plato & the Greeks & all Warriors The Moral Virtues are continual Accusers of Sin & promote Eternal Wars & Domineering over others

God is not a Mathematical Diagram

Man is All Imagination God is Man & exists in us & we in him
What Jesus came to Remove was the Heathen or Platonic Philosophy which blinds the Eye of Imagination The Real Man

---

* J. G. Spurzheim, *Observations on the Deranged Manifestations of the Mind, or Insanity* (1817). Blake's separate sheet of notes (untraced) was transcribed and punctuated by E. J. Ellis and W. B. Yeats (1893).
1. Blake is responding to an observation (153–54) that Methodism supplies "numerous cases" of insanity. The poet William Cowper (1731–1800) suffered two breakdowns during crises of faith.
* George Berkeley, *Siris: A Chain of Philosophical Reflexions and Inquiries Concerning the Virtues of Tar Water* (1744). Trinity College, Cambridge University. RW .35.24.
1. Keynes's transcription, "business," accords with Blake's usage elsewhere, but Trinity College librarians confirm (2005) "baseness," as in Erdman and Bentley.

From On Wordsworth's Preface to *The Excursion* (1814; notes 1826)*

[E666]Solomon when he Married Pharohs daughter & became a Convert to the Heathen Mythology Talked exactly in this way of Jehovah as a Very inferior object of Mans Contemplations he also passed him by unalarmd[1] & was permitted. Jehovah dropped a tear & followd him by his Spirit into the Abstract void it is called the Divine Mercy Satan dwells in it but Mercy does not dwell in him he knows not to Forgive

You shall not bring me down to believe such fitting & fitted[2] I know better & Please your Lordship

does not this Fit & is it not Fitting most Exquisitely too but to what not to Mind but to the Vile Body[3] only & to its Laws of Good & Evil & its Enmities against Mind

From On Wordsworth's *Poems* (1815; notes 1826)*

[E665]One Power alone makes a Poet—Imagination The Divine Vision

I see in Wordsworth the Natural Man rising up against the Spiritual Man Continually & then he is No Poet but a Heathen Philosopher at Enmity against all true Poetry or Inspiration

There is no such Thing as Natural Piety[1] Because The Natural Man is at Enmity with God

This ["To H. C. Six Years Old"] is all in the highest degree Imaginative & equal to any Poet but not Superior I cannot think that Real Poets have any competition None are greatest in the Kingdom of Heaven it is so in Poetry

Natural Objects always did & now do Weaken deaden & obliterate Imagination in Me Wordsworth must know that what he Writes Valuable is Not to be found in Nature Read Michael Angelos Sonnet vol 2 p. 179[2]

* William Wordsworth, Preface to *The Excursion* (1814), which contains a 107-line excerpt from an unpublished poem that Wordsworth offers as a "prospectus" to *the Recluse*, his rejected master work. Blake's notes and transcription of interesting passages are in a four-page manuscript; Dr. Williams's Library, London.
1. "Jehovah—with his thunder, and the choir / Of shouting Angels, & the empyreal thrones, / I pass them, unalarmed" (lines 33–35).
2. "How exquisitely the individual Mind / * * * / . . . to the external World / Is fitted:—& how exquisitely, too / * * * /The external World is fitted to the Mind" (lines 63–68).
3. Cf. "the Saviour . . . shall change our vile body, that it may be fashioned like unto his glorious body" (Philippians 3:20–21).
* Wordsworth, *Poems, Including Lyrical Ballads* . . . (1815). Cornell University. PR5850.E15, copy 5. Borrowed from H. C. Robinson; returned after Blake's death. Robinson inked Blake's penciled notes.
1. Referring to "And I could wish my days to be / Bound each to each by natural piety" ("My heart leaps up").
2. Referring to "No mortal eyes," as translated by Wordsworth: "Heaven-born, the Soul a heaven-ward course must hold; / Beyond the visible world she soars to seek / (For what delights the sense is false and weak) / Ideal Form, the universal mould."

I do not know who wrote these Prefaces they are very mischievous & direct contrary to Wordsworths own Practise

* * * Imagination is the Divine Vision not of The World nor of Man nor from Man as he is a Natural Man but only as he is a Spiritual Man Imagination has nothing to do with Memory

From On Thornton's *The Lord's Prayer, Newly Translated* (1827)*

[E667]I look upon this as a Most Malignant & Artful attack upon the Kingdom of Jesus by the Classical Learned thro the Instrumentality of Dr Thornton The Greek & Roman Classics is the Antichrist I say Is & not Are as most expressive & correct too

Christ & his Apostles were Illiterate Men Caiphas Pilate & Herod were Learned.[1]
The Beauty of the Bible is that the most Ignorant & Simple Minds Understand it Best

If Morality was Christianity Socrates was The Savior.[2]

[E668]O FATHER OF MANKIND, THOU, who dwellest in *the highest of the HEAVENS, Reverenced be* THY *Name!*[3]

May THY REIGN be, *every where, proclaim'd* so that THY *Will* may be *done* upon the Earth, as it is in the MANSIONS of HEAVEN.

Grant unto *me,* and *the whole world, day* by *day*, an abundant supply of *spiritual* and *corporeal* FOOD.

FORGIVE us our TRANSGRESSIONS against THEE, AS WE extend OUR *Kindness,* and *Forgiveness,* TO ALL.

O GOD! ABANDON us *not,* when surrounded, by TRIALS.

But PRESERVE us from *the Dominion* of SATAN: For THINE only, is the SOVEREIGNTY, THE POWER, and THE GLORY, throughout ETERNITY!!!
                    AMEN.

[E668]Lawful Bread Bought with Lawful Money & a Lawful Heaven seen thro a Lawful Telescope by means of Lawful Window Light[4] The Holy Ghost & whatever cannot be Taxed is Unlawful & Witchcraft.

Spirits are Lawful but not Ghosts especially Royal Gin is Lawful Spirit No Smuggling real British Spirit & Truth

---

* Robert John Thornton, M.D., *The Lord's Prayer, Newly Translated* (1827). Huntington Library. HM 113086. Thornton had commissioned—but almost rejected—Blake's wood engravings for a school edition of Virgil's *Pastorals* (1821). For commentary, and some textual corrections that we have adopted, see Morton D. Paley in *Prophetic Character* (2002), ed. Gourlay, revised in *The Traveller in the Evening* (2004).
1. Referring to Thorton's quotation of Samuel Johnson on the difficulty of the Bible: "nor can it be understood at all by the *unlearned,* except through the aid of Critical and Explanatory notes."
2. Reiterated in יה *[Yah]* & *his Two Sons.*
3. The first verse of Thornton's translation (presented in reduced type, with typographical emphases of the original). After the second and third verses, Blake inserted the Greek source texts (Matthew 6:10–11).
4. Referring to the per-window tax on dwellings with more than six windows (1696–1851).

Give us the Bread that is our due & Right by taking away Money or a Price or Tax upon what is Common to all in thy Kingdom

Jesus our Father who art in thy Heavens calld by thy Name the Holy Ghost Thy Kingdom on Earth is Not nor thy Will done but Satans Will who is the God of this World The Accuser His Accusation shall be Forgiveness that he may be consumd in his own Shame

Give us This Eternal Day our own right Bread & take away Money or Debt or Tax a Value or Price as we have all things common among us Every Thing has as much right to Eternal Life as God who is the Servant of Man

Leave us not in Parsimony Satans Kingdom but liberate us from the Natural Man & want or Jobs Kingdom

For thine is the Kingdom & the Power & the Glory & not Caesars or Satans Amen.

[E669]So you See That God is just such a Tyrant as Augustus Caesar & is not this Good & Learned & Wise & Classical

This is Saying the Lords Prayer Backwards which they say Raises the Devil

Doctor Thorntons Tory Translation Translated out of its disguise in the Classical & Scotch language into the vulgar English

Our Father Augustus Caesar who art in these thy Substantial Astronomical Telescopic Heavens Holiness to thy Name or Title & reverence to thy Shadow Thy Kingship come upon Earth first & thence in Heaven Give us day by day our Real Taxed Substantial Money bought Bread & deliver from the Holy Ghost so we call Nature whatever cannot be Taxed for all is debts & Taxes between Caesar & us & one another lead us not to read the Bible but let our Bible be Virgil & Shakspeare & deliver us from Poverty in Jesus that Evil one For thine is the Kingship or Allegoric Godship & the Power or War & the Glory or Law Ages after Ages in thy Descendents for God is only an Allegory of Kings & nothing Else Amen

* * * Spirit is the Ghost of Matter or Nature & God is the Ghost of the Priest & King who Exist whereas God exists not except from their Effluvia

[E670]Here is Signed Two Names which are too Holy to be Written.

Thus we see that the Real God is the Goddess Nature & that God Creates nothing but what can be Touchd & Weighed & Taxed & Measured all else is Heresy & Rebellion against Caesar Virgils Only God See Eclogue i[5] & for all this we thank Dr Thornton

---

5. In which Virgil, who has been saved by Caesar Augustus from exile and the confiscation of his property, affirms the emperor's divinity through the character of Tityrus.

THE LETTERS[†]

To the Reverend Dr. John Trusler,[1] August 23, 1799

Rev[d] Sir

I really am sorry that you are falln out with the Spiritual World Especially if I should have to answer for it. I feel very sorry that your Ideas & Mine on Moral Painting differ so much as to have made you angry with my method of Study. If I am wrong I am wrong in good company. I had hoped your plan comprehended All Species of this Art & Especially that you would not reject that Species which gives Existence to Every other, namely Visions of Eternity. You say that I want somebody to Elucidate my Ideas. But you ought to know that What is Grand is necessarily obscure to Weak men. That which can be made Explicit to the Idiot is not worth my care. The wisest of the Ancients considerd what is not too Explicit as the fittest for Instruction because it rouzes the faculties to act. I name Moses Solomon Esop Homer Plato.

But as you have favord me with your remarks on my Design permit me in return to defend it against a mistaken one, which is, That I have supposed Malevolence without a Cause.—Is not Merit in one a Cause of Envy in another & Serenity & Happiness & Beauty a Cause of Malevolence. But Want of Money & the Distress of A Thief can never be alledged as the Cause of his Thievery, for many honest people endure greater hard ships with Fortitude. We must therefore seek the Cause elsewhere than in want of Money for that is the Misers passion, not the Thiefs.

I have therefore proved your Reasonings Ill proportiond which you can never prove my figures to be. They are those of Michael Angelo Rafael & the Antique & of the best living Models. I percieve that your Eye is perverted by Caricature Prints,[2] which ought not to abound so much as they do. Fun I love but too much Fun is of all things the most loathsom. Mirth is better than Fun & Happiness is better than Mirth—I feel that a Man may be happy in This World. And I know that This World Is a World of Imagination & Vision. I see Every thing I paint In This World, but Every body does not see alike. To the Eyes of a Miser a Guinea is more beautiful than the Sun & a bag worn with the use of Money has more beautiful proportions than a Vine filled with Grapes. The tree which moves some to

---

† Our base text for Blake's letters, except where otherwise noted, is the 1988 Erdman edition, collated with the Bentley edition and, when possible, with facsimiles. We repunctuate most run-on sentences (except in poems) and correct obvious slips of the pen. We draw many facts from Bentley's *Blake Records* (2nd ed, 2004) and Keynes's *Letters of William Blake* (3rd ed., 1980). We leave most biblical allusions unannotated.

1. Trusler (1725–1820), whose many works include *Hogarth Moralized* (1768), *An Easy Way to Prolong Life* (?1775), *The Way to be Rich and Respectable* (?1776), and *A Compendium of Useful Knowledge, Containing a Concise Explanation of Every Thing a Young Man Ought to Know* (1784), commissioned, then rejected Blake's watercolor *Malevolence* (Butlin 341, now in the Philadelphia Museum of Art) and canceled plans for companion pieces *Benevolence, Pride*, and *Humility*. In submitting his design on August 16, 1799 (letter not included in this edition), Blake informed Trusler that he had followed his own "Genius or Angel" rather than his patron's "Dictate." Trusler passed both letters on to his neighbor who had arranged the commission, Blake's old friend George Cumberland (see n. 1, p. 471 herein), who then labeled this letter "Blake Dimd with Superstition" (Bentley, *Blake Records* 2004, 83).

2. Blake wrote to Cumberland on August 26, 1799 (not included in this edition) that Trusler was "so enamored of [Thomas] Rowlandson's [1756–1826] caricatures as to call them copies from life"; "I cannot paint Dirty rags and old Shoes," Blake insisted, "where I ought to place Naked Beauty or simple ornament."

tears of joy is in the Eyes of others only a Green thing that stands in the way. Some See Nature all Ridicule & Deformity & by these I shall not regulate my proportions, & Some Scarce see Nature at all. But to the Eyes of the Man of Imagination Nature is Imagination itself. As a man is So he Sees. As the Eye is formed such are its Powers. You certainly Mistake when you say that the Visions of Fancy are not be found in This World. To Me This World is all One continued Vision of Fancy or Imagination & I feel Flatterd when I am told So. What is it sets Homer Virgil & Milton in so high a rank of Art. Why is the Bible more Entertaining & Instructive than any other book. Is it not because they are addressed to the Imagination which is Spiritual Sensation & but mediately to the Understanding or Reason. Such is True Painting and such was alone valued by the Greeks & the best modern Artists. Consider what Lord Bacon says "Sense sends over to Imagination before Reason have judged & Reason sends over to Imagination before the Decree can be acted." See Advancemt of Learning Part 2 P 47 of first Edition.[3]

But I am happy to find a Great Majority of Fellow Mortals who can Elucidate My Visions & Particularly they have been Elucidated by Children who have taken a greater delight in contemplating my Pictures than I even hoped. Neither Youth nor Childhood is Folly or Incapacity Some Children are Fools & so are some Old Men. But There is a vast Majority on the side of Imagination or Spiritual Sensation.

To Engrave after another Painter is infinitely more laborious than to Engrave ones own Inventions. And of the Size you require my price has been Thirty Guineas & I cannot afford to do it for less. I had Twelve for the Head I sent you as a Specimen, but after my own designs I could do at least Six times the quantity of labour in the same time which will account for the difference of price as also that Chalk Engraving is at least six times as laborious as Aqua tinta. I have no objection to Engraving after another Artist. Engraving is the profession I was apprenticed to, & should never have attempted to live by any thing else If orders had not come in for my Designs & Paintings, which I have the pleasure to tell you are Increasing Every Day. Thus If I am a Painter it is not to be attributed to Seeking after. But I am contented whether I live by Painting or Engraving.

I am Revd Sir Your very obedient servant
William Blake

To George Cumberland,[1] July 2, 1800

* * *

* * * I begin to Emerge from a Deep pit of Melancholy, Melancholy without any real reason for it, a Disease which God keep you from & all good

3. Changing only "sendeth" in Book Two (1605 edition) to "sends," Blake seems to relish citing his intellectual enemy Bacon (cf. *Europe* 13/10:5; annotations to Bacon's *Essays*) on the primacy of the imagination. The section continues: "[I]n matters of *Faith* & *Religion*, we raise our *Imagination* above our *Reason*; which is the cause why *Religion* sought ever access to the *Minde* by Similitudes, *Types, Parables, Visions, Dreames*." In annotating Reynolds, Blake recalls that he read and annotated Bacon's *Advancement* "when very young," but his copy has not been found.
1. Cumberland (1754–1848), Blake's friend from about 1780 (see the chronology), inherited an income that allowed him to pursue his avocations of collecting, engraving, and writing about art. He commissioned work from Blake and lined up other patrons. Blake's last engraving (see n. 4, p. 493 herein) was for Cumberland.

men. Our artists of all ranks praise your outlines[2] & wish for more. Flaxman is very warm in your commendation & more and more of A Grecian. Mr Hayley[3] has lately mentiond your Work on outline in Notes to an Essay on Sculpture in Six Epistles to John Flaxman. I have been too little among friends which I fear they will not Excuse & I know not how to apologize for. Poor Fuseli[4] sore from the lash of Envious tongues praises you & dispraises with the same breath he is not naturally good natured but he is artificially very ill natured yet even from him I learn the Estimation you are held in among artists & connoisseurs.

I am still Employd in making Designs & little Pictures with now & then an Engraving & find that in future to live will not be so difficult as it has been. It is very Extraordinary that London in so few years from a City of meer Necessaries or at least a commerce of the lowest order of luxuries should have become a City of Elegance in some degree & that its once stupid inhabitants should enter into an Emulation of Grecian manners. There are now I believe as many Booksellers as there are Butchers & as many Printshops as of any other trade. We remember when a Print shop was a rare bird in London & I myself remember when I thought my pursuits of Art a kind of Criminal Dissipation & neglect of the main chance which I hid my face for not being able to abandon as a Passion which is forbidden by Law & Religion, but now it appears to be Law & Gospel too, at least I hear so from the few friends I have dared to visit in my stupid Melancholy. Excuse this communication of sentiments which I felt necessary to my repose at this time. I feel very strongly that I neglect my Duty to my Friends, but It is not want of Gratitude or Friendship but perhaps an Excess of both.

✳   ✳   ✳

To George Cumberland, September 1, 1800[1]

My Dear Cumberland

To have obtained your friendship is better than to have sold ten thousand books. I am now upon the verge of a happy alteration in my life which you will join with my London friends in Giving me joy of—It is an alteration in my situation on the surface of this dull Planet. I have taken a Cottage at Felpham on the Sea Shore of Sussex between Arundel & Chichester. Mr Hayley the Poet is soon to be my neighbor he is now my friend. To him I owe the happy suggestion for it was on a visit to him that I fell in love with my Cottage. I have now better prospects than ever. The little I want will be easily supplied, he has given me a twelvemonths work already, & there is a great deal more in prospect. I call myself now Independent. I can be Poet Painter & Musician as

2. *Thoughts on Outline* (1796), a treatise on purity of line in classical art, for which Blake engraved eight plates.
3. On Flaxman, see n. 1, p. 473. William Hayley (1745–1820), fashionable poet and patron of the arts who invited Blake to live near him in Sussex to work on commissions, under his direction.
4. Henry Fuseli (1741–1825), born Johann Heinrich Füssli in Switzerland, unconventional painter, writer, and celebrity who strongly influenced Blake (see the chronology). He moved to England in 1764, studied in Italy (1770–1778), and in 1804 was appointed keeper of the Royal Academy.
1. This letter, discovered in 1997, is excerpted by permission of its owner, Robert N. Essick; for a complete text, photofacsimile, and commentary, see Essick and Morton D. Paley, *Blake: An Illustrated Quarterly* 32:1 (1998), 4 ff. Blake's excitement continued to rise: "My fingers emit sparks of fire with Expectation of my future labours" (to Hayley, September 16, 1800).

the Inspiration comes. And now I take this first opportunity to Invite you down to Felpham. We lie on a Pleasant shore it is within a mile of Bognor to which our Fashionables resort. My Cottage faces the South about a Quarter of a Mile from the Sea, only corn Fields between. Tell Mrs Cumberland that my Wife thirsts for the opportunity to Entertain her at our Cottage.

✻   ✻   ✻

PS. I hope to be Settled in Sussex before the End of September. It is certainly the sweetest country upon the face of the Earth.

Dear Generous Cumberland nobly solicitious for a Friends welfare. Behold me
Whom your Friendship has Magnified: Rending the manacles of Londons Dungeon dark
I have rent the black net & escap'd. See My Cottage at Felpham in joy
Beams over the Sea, a bright light over France, but the Web & the Veil I have left
Behind me at London resists every beam of light; hanging from heaven to Earth   5
Dropping with human gore. Lo! I have left it! I have torn it from my limbs
I shake my wings ready to take my flight! Pale, Ghastly pale: stands the City in fear.

To John Flaxman,[1] September 12, 1800

My Dearest Friend,

It is to you I owe All my present Happiness. It is to you I owe perhaps the Principal Happiness of my life. I have presumd on your friendship in staying so long away & not calling to know of your welfare but hope, now every thing is nearly completed for our removal to Felpham, that I shall see you on Sunday as we have appointed Sunday afternoon to call on Mrs Flaxman at Hampstead. I send you a few lines which I hope you will Excuse. And As the time is now arrivd when Men shall again converse in Heaven & walk with Angels I know you will be pleased with the Intention & hope you will forgive the Poetry.

To My Dearest Friend John Flaxman these lines

I bless thee O Father of Heaven & Earth that ever I saw Flaxmans face
Angels stand round my Spirit in Heaven, the blessed of Heaven are my friends upon Earth[2]
When Flaxman was taken to Italy, Fuseli was giv'n to me for a season.
And now Flaxman hath given me Hayley his friend to be mine such my lot upon Earth.

1. The neoclassical sculptor Flaxman (1755–1826), Blake's friend since 1779 (see the chronology), was known for his Wedgwood pottery designs, funeral monuments, and (especially) his severely linear illustrations of works by Homer and Dante (1793), Aeschylus (1795), and Hesiod (1817, with engravings by Blake). Flaxman recommended Blake to Hayley but warned that his skills extended only to engraving, teaching, and "making neat drawings," for "he is not qualified, either by habit or study" to paint large pictures (Bentley, *Blake Records* 2004, 95).
2. Blake's dual presence in Heaven and Earth, with friends in both, anticipates his multidimensional adventures with Milton in *Milton a Poem*.

Now my lot in the Heavens is this; Milton lovd me in childhood &
   shewd me his face   5
Ezra came with Isaiah the Prophet, but Shakespeare in riper years
   gave me his hand
Paracelsus & Behmen[3] appeard to me, terrors appeard in the Heavens
   above
And in Hell beneath & a mighty & awful change threatend the
   Earth.
The American War began. All its dark horrors passed before my face
Across the Atlantic to France. Then the French Revolution
   commencd in thick clouds   10
And My Angels have told me, that seeing such visions I could not
   subsist on the Earth
But by my conjunction with Flaxman who knows to forgive Nervous
   Fear.

I remain for Ever Yours

William Blake

✢   ✢   ✢

To John Flaxman, September 21, 1800

Dear Sculptor of Eternity

✢ ✢ ✢ Felpham is a sweet place for Study, because it is more Spiritual than
London. Heaven opens here on all sides her golden Gates her windows are
not obstructed by vapours. Voices of Celestial inhabitants are more distinctly heard & their forms more distinctly seen & my Cottage is also a
Shadow of their houses. My Wife & Sister are both well, courting Neptune
for an embrace.

   Our journey was very pleasant & tho we had a great deal of Luggage, No
Grumbling. All was Chearfulness & Good Humour on the Road & yet we
could not arrive at our Cottage before half past Eleven at night, owing to
the necessary shifting of our Luggage from one Chaise to another for we
had Seven Different Chaises & as many different drivers. We set out
between Six & Seven in the Morning of Thursday, with Sixteen heavy
boxes & portfolios full of prints. And Now Begins a New life, because
another covering of Earth is shaken off. I am more famed in Heaven for
my works than I could well conceive. In my Brain are studies & Chambers
filld with books & pictures of old which I wrote & painted in ages of Eternity, before my mortal life & whose works are the delight & Study of
Archangels. Why then should I be anxious about the riches or fame of
mortality. The Lord our father will do for us & with us according to his
Divine will for our Good.
   You O Dear Flaxman are a Sublime Archangel My Friend & Companion
from Eternity, in the Divine bosom is our Dwelling place. I look back into
the regions of Reminiscence & behold our ancient days before this Earth
appeard in its vegetated mortality to my mortal vegetated Eyes. I see our

---

3. Paracelsus and Behmen, or Boehme, also appear in *Marriage*.

houses of Eternity which can never be separated tho our Mortal vehicles should stand at the remotest corners of heaven from Each other. * * *

Your Grateful & Affectionate
William Blake

To Thomas Butts, October 2, 1800[1]

Friend of Religion & Order[2]

I thank you for your very beautiful & encouraging Verses which I account a Crown of Laurels & I also thank you for your reprehension of follies by me fosterd. Your prediction will I hope be fulfilled in me, & in future I am the determined advocate of Religion & Humility the two bands of Society. Having been so full of the Business of Settling the sticks & feathers of my nest, I have not got any forwarder with the three Marys or with any other of your commissions but hope, now I have commenced a new life of industry to do credit to that new life by Improved Works: Recieve from me a return of verses such as Felpham produces by me tho not such as she produces by her Eldest Son. however such as they are. I cannot resist the temptation to send them to you.

To my Friend Butts I write	Astonishd Amazed	20
My first Vision of Light	For each was a Man	
On the yellow sands sitting	Human formd. Swift I ran	
The Sun was Emitting	For they beckond to me	
His Glorious beams 5	Remote by the Sea	
From Heavens high Streams	Saying, Each grain of Sand	25
Over Sea over Land	Every Stone on the Land	
My Eyes did Expand	Each rock & each hill	
Into regions of air	Each fountain & rill	
Away from all Care 10	Each herb & each tree	
Into regions of fire	Mountain hill Earth & Sea	30
Remote from Desire	Cloud Meteor & Star	
The Light of the Morning	Are Men Seen Afar	
Heavens Mountains adorning	I stood in the Streams	
In particles bright 15	Of Heavens bright beams	
The jewels of Light	And Saw Felpham sweet	35
Distinct shone & clear—	Beneath my bright feet	
Amazd & in fear	In soft Female charms	
I each particle gazed	And in her fair arms	

1. For images of this letter and others in the Preston Blake Collection of Westminster Libraries and Arichives, London, follow links from www.motco.com/blake-william/. Butts (1757–1845), a clerk in the office of the Commissary General of Musters (military payroll and records), gave Blake numerous commissions (including Milton and Bible designs) from 1799 on (see the chronology) through his leanest years, allowing the artist to develop the subjects as he saw fit. Besides building a collection of about two hundred pictures and ten illuminated books (some bought from previous owners), Butts also hired Blake to teach his son to engrave.
2. Blake's salutation responds to Butts's reply to Blake's epithet "Friend of my Angels" (September 23, 1800; not in this edition), speculating "whether your Angels are black, white, or grey." More seriously, Butts hoped that Blake would cast off "certain opinions imbibed from reading, nourish'd by indulgence, and riveted by a confined Conversation." The "Eldest Son" in the opening paragraph is Hayley. For document facsimiles, see *Letters from William Blake to Thomas Butts* (1926), ed. Geoffrey Keynes.

My Shadow I knew
And my wifes shadow too   40
And My Sister & Friend.
We like Infants descend
In our Shadows on Earth
Like a weak mortal birth
My Eyes more & more   45
Like a Sea without shore
Continue Expanding
The Heavens commanding
Till the Jewels of Light
Heavenly Men beaming bright   50
Appeard as One Man
Who Complacent began
My limbs to infold
In his beams of bright gold
Like dross purgd away   55
All my mire & my clay
Soft consumd in delight
In his bosom sun bright

I remaind. Soft he smild
And I heard his voice Mild   60
Saying This is My Fold
O thou Ram hornd with gold
Who awakest from sleep
On the sides of the Deep
On the Mountains around   65
The roarings resound
Of the lion & wolf
The loud sea & deep gulf
These are guards of My Fold
O thou Ram hornd with gold   70
And the voice faded mild
I remaind as a Child
All I ever had known
Before me bright Shone
I saw you & your wife   75
By the fountains of Life
Such the Vision to me
Appeard on the Sea

Mrs Butts will I hope Excuse my not having finishd the Portrait. I wait for less hurried moments. * * * We have had but little time for viewing the Country but what we have seen is Most Beautiful & the People are Genuine Saxons handsomer than the people about London.

*   *   *

I am for Ever Yours
William Blake

To Thomas Butts, November 22, 1802[1]

*   *   *

But You will Justly enquire why I have not written All this time to you? I answer I have been very Unhappy & could not think of troubling you about it or any of my real Friends (I have written many letters to you which I burnd & did not send) & why I have not before now finishd the Miniature I promissd to Mrs Butts? I answer I have not till now in any degree pleased myself & now I must intreat you to Excuse faults for Portrait Painting is the direct contrary to Designing & Historical Painting in every respect—If you have not Nature before you for Every Touch you cannot Paint Portrait, & if you have Nature before you at all you cannot Paint History. It was Michael Angelos opinion & is Mine. Pray Give My Wife's love with mine to Mrs Butts. Assure her that it cannot be long before I have the pleasure of Painting from you in Person &

---

1. Blake had last written in the fall of 1801, apologizing for his lack of "steady perseverance" in fulfilling his commissions. Earlier in the letter excerpted here he reports that, after devoting "two years to the intense study of those parts of the art which relate to light & shade & colour," he is confident that his pictures for Butts rival anything done since the age of Raphael; he now considers the linear art of the Roman school superior to the coloristic Venetian school and rejects "the yellow leather flesh of old men the ill drawn & ugly young women & above all the dawbed black & yellow shadows" in pictures preferred by connoisseurs.

then that She may Expect a likeness but now I have done All I could & know she will forgive any failure in consideration of the Endeavour.

And now let me finish with assuring you that Tho I have been very unhappy I am so no longer. I am again Emerged into the light of Day. I still & shall to Eternity Embrace Christianity and Adore him who is the Express image of God but I have traveld thro Perils & Darkness not unlike a Champion. I have Conquerd and shall still Go on Conquering. Nothing can withstand the fury of my Course among the Stars of God & in the Abysses of the Accuser. My Enthusiasm is still what it was only Enlarged and confirmd.

⁂   ⁂   ⁂

Accept my Sincere love & respect

I remain Yours Sincerely,
Willm Blake

⁂   ⁂   ⁂

To Thomas Butts, November 22, 1802 (second letter)

Dear Sir

After I had finishd my Letter I found that I had not said half what I intended to say & in particular I wish to ask you what subject you choose to be painted on the remaining Canvas which I brought down with me (for there were three) and to tell you that several of the Drawings were in great forwardness you will see by the Inclosed Account that the remaining Number of Drawings which you gave me orders for is Eighteen I will finish these with all possible Expedition if indeed I have not tired you or as it is politely calld Bored you too much already or if you would rather cry out Enough Off Off! tell me in a Letter of forgiveness if you were offended & of accustomd friendship if you were not. But I will bore you more with some Verses which My Wife desires me to Copy out & send you with her kind love & Respect they were Composed above a twelvemonth ago while Walking from Felpham to Lavant to meet my Sister.

> With happiness stretchd across the hills
> In a cloud that dewy sweetness distills
> With a blue sky spread over with wings
> And a mild sun that mounts & sings
> With trees & fields full of Fairy elves   5
> And little devils who fight for themselves
> Remembring the Verses that Hayley sung
> When my heart knockd against the root of my tongue
> With Angels planted in Hawthorn bowers
> And God himself in the passing hours   10
> With Silver Angels across my way
> And Golden Demons that none can stay
> With my Father hovering upon the wind
> And my Brother Robert just behind
> And my Brother John the evil one   15
> In a black cloud making his mone

Tho dead they appear upon my path
Notwithstanding my terrible wrath
They beg they intreat they drop their tears
Filld full of hopes filld full of fears   20
With a thousand Angels upon the Wind
Pouring disconsolate from behind
To drive them off & before my way
A frowning Thistle implores my stay
What to others a trifle appears   25
Fills me full of smiles or tears
For double the vision my Eyes do see
And a double vision is always with me
With my inward Eye 'tis an old Man grey
With my outward a Thistle across my way   30
"If thou goest back the thistle said
Thou art to endless woe betrayd
For here does Theotormon[1] lower
And here is Enitharmons bower
And Los the terrible thus hath sworn   35
Because thou backward dost return
Poverty Envy old age & fear
Shall bring thy Wife upon a bier
And Butts shall give what Fuseli gave
A dark black Rock & a gloomy Cave."   40

I struck the Thistle with my foot
And broke him up from his delving root
"Must the duties of life each other cross
Must every joy be dung & dross
Must my dear Butts feel cold neglect   45
Because I give Hayley his due respect
Must Flaxman look upon me as wild
And all my friends be with doubts beguild
Must my Wife live in my Sisters bane
Or my sister survive on my Loves pain   50
The curses of Los the terrible shade
And his dismal terrors make me afraid."

So I spoke & struck in my wrath
The old man weltering upon my path
Then Los appeard in all his power[2]   55
In the Sun he appeard descending before
My face in fierce flames in my double sight
Twas outward a Sun: inward Los in his might.

"My hands are labourd day & night
And Ease comes never in my sight   60
My Wife has no indulgence given
Except what comes to her from heaven

1. Blake's only known references to his mythic figures in private correspondence—one measure of his
ease with Butts. Quotation marks, with minor adjustments, are Blake's.
2. The vision of Los in the sun is further developed in *Milton*, as is the imagery of intellectual combat ("And did those feet," *Milton* i, Copies A and B).

We eat little we drink less
This Earth breeds not our happiness
Another Sun feeds our lifes streams   65
We are not warmed with thy beams
Thou measurest not the Time to me
Nor yet the Space that I do see
My Mind is not with thy light arrayd
Thy terrors shall not make me afraid."   70

When I had my Defiance given
The Sun stood trembling in heaven
The Moon that glowd remote below
Became leprous & white as snow
And every Soul of men on the Earth   75
Felt affliction & sorrow & sickness & dearth
Los flamd in my path & the Sun was hot
With the bows of my Mind & the Arrows of Thought
My bowstring fierce with Ardour breathes
My arrows glow in their golden sheaves   80
My brothers & father march before[3]
The heavens drop with human gore.

Now I a fourfold vision see
And a fourfold vision is given to me
Tis fourfold in my supreme delight   85
And three fold in soft Beulahs night
And twofold Always. May God us keep
From Single vision & Newtons sleep.

I also inclose you some Ballads by Mr Hayley with prints to them by Your
H^{ble} Servt. I should have sent them before now but could not get any thing
done for You to please myself for I do assure you that I have truly studied
the two little pictures I now send & do not repent of the time I have spent
upon them. God bless you.

Yours,
W B

✳   ✳   ✳

To Thomas Butts, January 10, 180[3]

Dear Sir
Your very kind & affectionate Letter & the many kind things you have said
in it: calld upon me for an immediate answer, but it found My Wife & Myself
so Ill & My wife so very ill that till now I have not been able to do this duty.
The Ague & Rheumatism have been almost her constant Enemies which she
has combated in vain ever since we have been here, & her sickness is always
my sorrow of course. But what you tell me about your sight afflicted me not
a little; & that about your health in another part of your letter makes me

3. For Blake's deceased father and brothers, mentioned in lines 13–15, see the chronology.

intreat you to take due care of both it is a part of our duty to God & man to take due care of his Gifts & tho we ought not think *more* highly of ourselves, yet we ought to think *As* highly of ourselves as immortals ought to think.

When I came down here I was more sanguine than I am at present but it was because I was ignorant of many things which have since occurred & chiefly the unhealthiness of the place. Yet I do not repent of coming, on a thousand accounts, & Mᵣ H I doubt not will do ultimately all that both he & I wish that is to lift me out of difficulty, but this is no easy matter to a man who having Spiritual Enemies of such formidable magnitude cannot expect to want natural hidden ones.

Your approbation of my pictures is a Multitude to Me & I doubt not that all your kind wishes in my behalf shall in due time be fulfilled. Your kind offer of pecuniary assistance I can only thank you for at present because I have enough to serve my present purpose here. Our expenses are small & our income from our incessant labour fully adequate to them at present. I am now engaged in Engraving 6 small plates for a New Edition of Mᵣ Hayleys Triumphs of Temper, from drawings by Maria Flaxman sister to my friend the Sculptor and it seems that other things will follow in course if I do but Copy these well. But Patience! if Great things do not turn out it is because such things depend on the Spiritual & not on the Natural World & if it was fit for me I doubt not that I should be Employd in Greater things & when it is proper my Talents shall be properly exercised in Public, as I hope they are now in private, for till then, I leave no stone unturnd & no path unexplord that tends to improvement in my beloved Arts. One thing of real consequence I have accomplishd by coming into the country, which is to me consolation enough, namely, I have recollected all my scatterd thoughts on Art & resumed my primitive & original ways of Execution in both painting & Engraving, which in the confusion of London I had very much lost & obliterated from my mind. But whatever becomes of my labours I would rather that they should be preservd in your Green House (not as you mistakenly call it dung hill), than in the cold gallery of fashion.—The Sun may yet shine & then they will be brought into open air.

But you have so generously & openly desired that I will divide my griefs with you that I cannot hide what it is now become my duty to explain—My unhappiness has arisen from a source which if explord too narrowly might hurt my pecuniary circumstances. As my dependence is on Engraving at present & particularly on the Engravings I have in hand for Mᵣ H. & I find on all hands great objections to my doing any thing but the meer drudgery of business & intimations that if I do not confine myself to this I shall not live. This has always pursd me. You will understand by this the source of all my uneasiness This from Johnson & Fuseli brought me down here & this from Mᵣ H will bring me back again for that I cannot live without doing my duty to lay up treasures in heaven is Certain & Determined & to this I have long made up my mind & why this should be made an objection to Me while Drunkenness Lewdness Gluttony & even Idleness itself does not hurt other men let Satan himself Explain—The Thing I have most at Heart! more than life or all that seems to make life comfortable without, Is the Interest of True Religion & Science & whenever any thing appears to affect that Interest. (Especially if I myself omit any duty to my Station as a Soldier of Christ) It gives me the greatest of torments. I am not ashamed afraid or averse to tell You what Ought to be Told, That I am under the direction of

Messengers from Heaven Daily & Nightly but the nature of such things is not as some suppose, without trouble or care. Temptations are on the right hand & left, behind the sea of time & space roars & follows swiftly, he who keeps not right onward is lost & if our footsteps slide in clay how can we do otherwise than fear & tremble. But I should not have troubled You with this account of my spiritual state unless it had been necessary in explaining the actual cause of my uneasiness into which you are so kind as to Enquire for I never obtrude such things on others unless questiond & then I never disguise the truth—But if we fear to do the dictates of our Angels & tremble at the Tasks set before us, if we refuse to do Spiritual Acts, because of Natural Fears or Natural Desires! Who can describe the dismal torments of such a state!—I too well remember the Threats I heard!—If you who are organized by Divine Providence for Spiritual communion Refuse & bury your Talent in the Earth[1] even tho you should want Natural Bread, Sorrow & Desperation pursues you thro life! & after death shame & confusion of face to eternity—Every one in Eternity will leave you aghast at the Man who was crownd with glory & honour by his brethren & betrayd their cause to their enemies. You will be calld the base Judas who betrayd his Friend!—Such words would make any Stout man tremble & how then could I be at ease? But I am now no longer in That State & now go on again with my Task Fearless, and tho my path is difficult, I have no fear of stumbling while I keep it.

*   *   *

Naked we came here naked of Natural things & naked we shall return, but while clothd with the Divine Mercy we are richly clothd in Spiritual & suffer all the rest gladly. Pray give my Love to Mrs Butts & your family. I am Yours Sincerely

William Blake

*   *   *

To James Blake, January 30, 1803

Dear Brother

Your Letter mentioning Mr Butts's account of my Ague surprized me because I have no Ague but have had a Cold this Winter. You know that it is my way to make the best of every thing. I never make myself nor my friends uneasy if I can help it. My Wife has had Agues & Rheumatisms almost ever since she has been here, but our time is almost out that we took the Cottage for. I did not mention our Sickness to you & should not to Mr Butts but for a determination which we have lately made namely To leave This Place—because I am now certain of what I have long doubted Viz that H is jealous as Stothard[1] was & will be no further My friend than he is compelld by circumstances. The truth is As a Poet he is frightend at me & as a Painter his views & mine are opposite. He thinks to turn me into a Portrait Painter as he did Poor Romney, but this he nor all the devils in hell will never do. I must own that seeing

1. This reference to the familiar parable of the talents (Matthew 25:14–30) sets Blake's decisions as an artist in a religious context, deepened by semisubmerged additional allusions (below): "confusion . . . and shame of my face" (Psalm 44:15), "crowned with glory & honor" (Psalm 8:5), "naked we came . . . naked shall return" (Job 1:21).
1. Thomas Stothard (1755–1834), Blake's friend and rival since his Royal Academy days (see the chronology).

H. like S Envious (& that he is I am now certain) made me very uneasy, but it is over & I now defy the worst & fear not while I am true to myself which I will be. This is the uneasiness I spoke of to Mr Butts but I did not tell him so plain & wish you to keep it a secret & to burn this letter because it speaks so plain. I told Mr Butts that I did not wish to Explore too much the cause of our determination to leave Felpham because of pecuniary connexions between H & me—Be not then uneasy on any account & tell my Sister not to be uneasy for I am fully Employd & Well Paid. I have made it so much H's interest to employ me that he can no longer treat me with indifference & now it is in my power to stay or return or remove to any other place that I choose, because I am getting before hand in money matters. The Profits arising from Publications are immense & I now have it in my power to commence publication with many very formidable works, which I have finishd & ready. A Book price half a guinea may be got out at the Expense of Ten pounds & its almost certain profits are 500 G. I am only sorry that I did not know the methods of publishing years ago & this is one of the numerous benefits I have obtaind by coming here for I should never have known the nature of Publication unless I had known H & his connexions & his method of managing. It now would be folly not to venture publishing. I am now Engraving Six little plates for a little work of M^r H's for which I am to have 10 Guineas each & the certain profits of that work are a fortune such as would make me independent supposing that I could substantiate such a one of my own & I mean to try many. But I again say as I said before We are very Happy sitting at tea by a wood fire in our Cottage the wind singing above our roof & the sea roaring at a distance but if sickness comes all is unpleasant.

✳   ✳   ✳

But I ought to mention to you that our present idea is, To take a house in some village further from the Sea Perhaps Lavant, & in or near the road to London for the sake of convenience—I also ought to inform you that I read your letter to M^r H & that he is very afraid of losing me & also very afraid that my Friends in London should have a bad opinion of the reception he has given to me. But My Wife has undertaken to Print the whole number of the Plates for Cowpers work[2] which she does to admiration & being under my own eye the prints are as fine as the French prints & please every one. In short I have Got every thing so under my thumb that it is more profitable that things should be as they are than any other way, tho not so agreeable because we wish naturally for friendship in preference to interest.—The Publishers are already indebted to My Wife Twenty Guineas for work deliverd. This is a small specimen of how we go on. Then fear nothing & let my Sister fear nothing because it appears to me that I am now too old & have had too much experience to be any longer imposed upon. Only illness makes all uncomfortable & this we must prevent by every means in our power.

✳   ✳   ✳

I write in great haste & with a head full of botheration about various projected works & particularly, a work now Proposed to the Public at the End of Cowpers Life, which will very likely be of great consequence. It is

---

2. Hayley's *Life of Cowper* (1803). The publishing scheme of the previous paragraph (excerpted), if indeed it was feasible, was never executed.

Cowpers Milton[3] the same that Fuselis Milton Gallery was painted for, & if we succeed in our intentions the prints to this work will be very profitable to me & not only profitable but honourable at any rate. The Project pleases Lord Cowpers family. & I am now labouring in my thoughts Designs for this & other works equally creditable. These are works to be boasted of & therefore I cannot feel depress'd tho I know that as far as Designing & Poetry are concernd I am Envied in many Quarters, but I will cram the Dogs for I know that the Public are my friends & love my works & will embrace them whenever they see them. My only Difficulty is to produce fast enough.

I go on Merrily with my Greek & Latin: am very sorry that I did not begin to learn languages early in life as I find it very Easy, am now learning my Hebrew אבג.[4] I read Greek as fluently as an Oxford scholar & the Testament is my chief master. Astonishing indeed is the English Translation it is almost word for word & if the Hebrew Bible is as well translated which I do not doubt it is we need not doubt of its having been translated as well as written by the Holy Ghost.

My wife joins me in Love to you both.

I am Sincerely yours
W Blake

To Thomas Butts, April 25, 1803

* * *

Now I may say to you what perhaps I should not dare to say to any one else, That I can alone carry on my visionary studies in London unannoyd & that I may converse with my friends in Eternity, See Visions, Dream Dreams, & prophecy & speak Parables unobserv'd & at liberty from the Doubts of other Mortals, perhaps Doubts proceeding from Kindness, but Doubts are always pernicious Especially when we Doubt our Friends. Christ is very decided on this Point. "He who is Not With Me is Against Me." There is no Medium or Middle state & if a Man is the Enemy of my Spiritual Life while he pretends to be the Friend of my Corporeal, he is a Real Enemy—but the Man may be the friend of my Spiritual Life while he seems the Enemy of my Corporeal but Not Vice Versa.

What is very pleasant, Every one who hears of my going to London again Applauds it as the only course for the interest of all concernd in My Works, Observing that I ought not to be away from the opportunities London affords of seeing fine Pictures and the various improvements in Works of Art going on in London.

But none can know the Spiritual Acts of my three years Slumber on the banks of the Ocean[1] unless he has seen them in the Spirit or unless he should read My long Poem descriptive of those Acts for I have in these three years composed an immense number of verses on One Grand Theme Similar to Homers Iliad or Miltons Paradise Lost the Person & Machinery

---

3. When Hayley's edition of Cowper's translation of *Latin and Italian Poems of Milton* was published in 1808, it did not contain engravings by Blake.
4. The first three letters of the Hebrew alphabet: aleph, bet, gimel (read right to left).
1. This phrase reappears in "To the Public," *Jerusalem* 3; the "Long Poem" is probably *Milton*.

intirely new to the Inhabitants of Earth (some of the Persons Excepted). I have written this Poem from immediate Dictation twelve or sometimes twenty or thirty lines at a time without Premeditation & even against my Will. The Time it has taken in writing was thus renderd Non Existent, & an immense Poem Exists which seems to be the Labour of a long Life all pro-ducd without Labour or Study. I mention this to shew you what I think the Grand Reason of my being brought down here.

I have a thousand & ten thousand things to say to you. My heart is full of futurity. I percieve that the sore travel[2] which has been given me these three years leads to Glory & Honour. I rejoice & I tremble. "I am fearfully & wonderfully made." I had been reading the CXXXIX Psalm a little before your Letter arrived. I take your advice. I see the face of my Heavenly Father he lays his Hand upon my Head & gives a blessing to all my works why should I be troubled why should my heart & flesh cry out. I will go on in the Strength of the Lord. Through Hell will I sing forth his Praises, that the Dragons of the Deep may praise him & that those who dwell in darkness & on the Sea coasts may be gatherd into his Kingdom. Excuse my perhaps too great Enthusiasm. Please to accept of & give our Loves to Mrs Butts & your amiable Family. & believe me to be——

Ever Yours Affectionately
Will Blake

To Thomas Butts, July 6, 1803

✳   ✳   ✳

Thus I hope that all our three years trouble Ends in Good Luck at last & shall be forgot by my affections & only rememberd by my Understanding to be a Memento in time to come & to speak to future generations by a Sublime Alle-gory which is now perfectly completed into a Grand Poem.[1] I may praise it since I dare not pretend to be any other than the Secretary the Authors are in Eternity. I consider it as the Grandest Poem that This World Contains. Alle-gory addressd to the Intellectual powers while it is altogether hidden from the Corporeal Understanding is My Definition of the Most Sublime Poetry. It is also somewhat in the same manner defind by Plato. This Poem shall by Divine Assistance be progressively Printed & Ornamented with Prints & given to the Public—But of this work I take care to say little to Mr H. since he is as much averse to my poetry as he is to a Chapter in the Bible. He knows that I have writ it for I have shewn it to him & he had read Part by his own desire & has lookd with sufficient contempt to enhance my opinion of it. But I do not wish to irritate by seeming too obstinate in Poetic pursuits But if all the World should set their faces against This, I have Orders to set my face like a flint, Ezekiel iii C 9 v, against their faces & my forehead against their foreheads.

---

2. Travail; labor. This paragraph is a medley of indirect allusions to Psalms: "glory and honour" (8:5); "rejoice with trembling" (2:11); "I am fearfully and wonderfully made" (139:14, the psalm Blake cites to Butts); "laid thine hand upon me" (139:5); "my heart and my flesh crieth out" (84:2); "go in the strength of the Lord" (71:16); "Praise the Lord . . . ye dragons, and all deeps" (148:7); and "hath made me to dwell in darkness" (143:3).

1. Perhaps a very early version of the textual portion of *Milton*, mentioned also in the letter of April 25, 1803. Blake also continued to work on *Vala*, later revised and retitled *The Four Zoas*, but that poem does not concern his "three years trouble."

As to M[r] H I feel myself at liberty to say as follows upon this ticklish subject. I regard Fashion in Poetry as little as I do in Painting. So if both Poets & Painters should alternately dislike (but I know the majority of them will not) I am not to regard it at all but M[r] H approves of My Designs as little as he does of my Poems and I have been forced to insist on his leaving me in both to my Own Self Will, for I am determind to be no longer Pesterd with his Genteel Ignorance & Polite Disapprobation. I know myself both Poet & Painter & it is not his affected Contempt that can move me to any thing but a more assiduous pursuit of both Arts. Indeed by my late Firmness I have brought down his affected Loftiness & he begins to think I have some Genius, as if Genius & Assurance were the same thing.

*   *   *

Yours in truth & sincerity
Will Blake

To Thomas Butts, August 16, 1803

*   *   *

I go on with the remaining Subjects which you gave me commission to Execute for you but shall not be able to send any more before my return tho perhaps I may bring some with me finishd. I am at Present in a Bustle to defend myself against a very unwarrantable warrant from a justice of Peace in Chichester, which was taken out against me by a Private in Capt[n] Leathes's troop of 1st or Royal Dragoons for an assault & Seditious words. The wretched Man has terribly Perjurd himself as has his Comrade[1] for as to Sedition not one Word relating to the King or Government was spoken by either him or me. His Enmity arises from my having turned him out of my Garden into which he was invited as an assistant by a Gardener at work therein, without my knowledge that he was so invited. I desired him as politely as was possible to go out of the Garden, he made me an impertinent answer. I insisted on his leaving the Garden he refused. I still persisted in desiring his departure. He then threatend to knock out my Eyes with many abominable imprecations & with some contempt for my Person it affronted my foolish Pride. I therefore took him by the Elbows & pushed him before me till I had got him out. There I intended to have left him, but he turning about put himself into a Posture of Defiance threatening & swearing at me. I perhaps foolishly & perhaps not, stepped out at the Gate & putting aside his blows took him again by the Elbows & keeping his back to me pushed him forwards down the road about fifty yards he all the while endeavouring to turn round & strike me & raging & cursing which drew out several neighbours. At length when I had got him to where he was Quarterd, which was very quickly done, we were met at the Gate by the Master of the house, The Fox Inn, (who is the proprietor of my Cottage) & his wife & Daughter, & the Mans Comrade, & several other people. My Landlord compelld the Soldiers to go in doors after many abusive threats against me & my wife from the two Soldiers but not one word of threat on account of Sedition was utterd at that

---

1. Private Cock (Cox). The "Private" in Leathes's troop was John Scholfield (Scolfield, Schofield, Skofield). Both are major characters in *Jerusalem*.

time. This method of Revenge was Plann'd between them after they had got together into the Stable. This is the whole outline. I have for witnesses, The Gardener who is Hostler at the Fox & who Evidences that to his knowledge no word of the remotest tendency to Government or Sedition was utterd,— Our next door Neighbour a Millers wife who saw me turn him before me down the road & saw & heard all that happend at the Gate of the Inn who Evidences that no Expression of threatening on account of Sedition was utterd in the heat of their fury by either of the Dragoons. This was the womans own remark & does high honour to her good sense as she observes that whenever a quarrel happens the offence is always repeated. The Landlord of the Inn & His Wife & daughter will Evidence the Same & will evidently prove the Comrade perjurd who swore that he heard me at the Gate utter Seditious words & D—— the K——[2] without which perjury I could not have been committed & I had no witness with me before the Justices who could combat his assertion as the Gardener remain in my Garden all the while & he was the only person I thought necessary to take with me. I have been before a Bench of Justices at Chichester this morning, but they as the Lawyer who wrote down the Accusation told me in private are compelld by the Military to suffer a prosecution to be enterd into altho they must know & it is manifest that the whole is a Fabricated Perjury. I have been forced to find Bail. Mr Hayley was kind enough to come forwards & Mr Seagrave[3] Printer at Chichester. Mr H. in 100L & Mr S. in 50L & myself am bound in 100L for my appearance at the Quarter Sessions which is after Michaelmass. So I shall have the Satisfaction to see my friends in Town before this Contemptible business comes on. I say Contemptible for it must be manifest to every one that the whole accusation is a wilful Perjury. Thus you see my dear Friend that I cannot leave this place without some adventure. It has struck a consternation thro all the Villages round. Every Man is now afraid of speaking to or looking at a Soldier, for the peaceable Villagers have always been forward in expressing their kindness for us & they express their sorrow at our departure as soon as they hear of it. Every one here is my Evidence for Peace & Good Neighbourhood & yet such is the present state of things this foolish accusation must be tried in Public. Well I am content I murmur not & doubt not that I shall recieve Justice & am only sorry for the trouble & expense. I have heard that my Accuser is a disgraced Sergeant his name is John Scholfield. Perhaps it will be in your power to learn somewhat about the Man. I am very ignorant of what I am requesting of you. I only suggest what I know you will be kind enough to Excuse if you can learn nothing about him & what I as well know if it is possible you will be kind enough to do in this matter.

Dear Sir This perhaps was sufferd to Clear up some doubts & to give opportunity to those whom I doubted to clear themselves of all imputation. If a Man offends me ignorantly & not designedly surely I ought to consider him with favour & affection. Perhaps the simplicity of myself is the origin of all offences committed against me. If I have found this I shall have learned a most valuable thing well worth three years perseverance. I have found it! It is certain! that a too passive manner, inconsistent with my active

---

2. Damn the King.
3. Joseph Seagrave, printer of Hayley's and Blake's joint venture, *Ballads*, with engravings by Blake (intended for Blake's benefit) and other works by Hayley.

physiognomy had done me much mischief. I must now express to you my conviction that all is come from the spiritual World for Good & not for Evil.

Give me your advice in my perilous adventure. Burn what I have peevishly written about any friend. I have been very much degraded & injuriously treated, but if it all arise from my own fault I ought to blame myself.

> O why was I born with a different face[4]
> Why was I not born like the rest of my race
> When I look each one starts! when I speak I offend
> Then I'm silent & passive & lose every Friend
>
> Then my verse I dishonour, My pictures despise   5
> My person degrade & my temper chastise
> And the pen is my terror, the pencil my shame
> All my Talents I bury, and Dead is my Fame
>
> I am either too low or too highly prizd
> When Elate I am Envy'd, When Meek I'm despisd   10

This is but too just a Picture of my Present state I pray God to keep you & all men from it & to deliver me in his own good time. Pray write to me & tell me how you & your family Enjoy health. My much terrified Wife joins me in love to you & Mrs Butts & all your family. I again take the liberty to beg of you to cause the Enclosd Letter to be deliverd to my Brother & remain Sincerely & Affectionately Yours

William Blake

Blake's Memorandum [August 1803]

in Refutation of the Information and Complaint of John Scolfield, a private Soldier, &c.[1]

The Soldier has been heard to say repeatedly, that he did not know how the Quarrel began, which he would not say if such seditious words were spoken.—

Mrs. Haynes Evidences, that she saw me turn him down the Road, & all the while we were at the Stable Door, and that not one word of charge against me was uttered, either relating to Sedition or any thing else; all he did was swearing and threatening.—

Mr. Hosier heard him say that he would be revenged, and would have me hanged if he could! He spoke this the Day after my turning him out of the Garden. Hosier says he is ready to give Evidence of this, if necessary.—

The Soldier's Comrade swore before the Magistrates, while I was present, that he heard me utter seditious words, at the Stable Door, and in particu-

---

4. Cf. "Mary," lines 11–14.

1. Not in Blake's handwriting but in his voice; from papers (now in Trinity College, Hartford, Connecticut) drawn up for the barrister Samuel Rose, who was hired by Hayley for Blake's defense (*Blake Records*, 2nd ed., p. 163). According to Scholfield, in the same papers, Blake said that "if Buonapart sho.^d come he wo.^d be master of Europe in an hour's time; . . . he was a strong man and wo.^d certainly begin to cut throats. . . . he Damned the King of England—his Country and his Subjects—that his soldiers were all bound for Slaves & all the poor people in general—that his Wife then came up & said . . . altho she was but a Woman she wo.^d fight as long as she had a Drop of Blood in her."

lar, said, that he heard me D—n the K—g. Now I have all the Persons who were present at the Stable Door to witness that no Word relating to Seditious Subjects was uttered, either by one party or the other, and they are ready, on their Oaths, to say that I did not utter such Words.—

Mrs. Haynes says very sensibly, that she never heard People quarrel, but they always charged each other with the Offence, and repeated it to those around, therefore as the Soldier charged not me with Seditious Words at that Time, neither did his Comrade, the whole Charge must have been fabricated in the Stable afterwards.—

If we prove the Comrade perjured who swore that he heard me D—n the K—g, I believe the whole Charge falls to the Ground.

Mr. Cosens, owner of the Mill at Felpham, was passing by in the Road, and saw me and the Soldier and William standing near each other; he heard nothing, but says we certainly were not quarrelling.—

The whole Distance that William could be at any Time of the Conversation between me and the Soldier (supposing such Conversation to have existed) is only 12 Yards, & W—says that he was backwards and forwards in the Garden. It was a still Day, there was no Wind stirring.

William says on his Oath, that the first Words that he heard me speak to the Soldier were ordering him out of the Garden; the truth is, I did not speak to the Soldier till then, & my ordering him out of the Garden was occasioned by his saying something that I thought insulting.

The Time that I & the Soldier were together in the Garden, was not sufficient for me to have uttered the Things that he alledged.

The Soldier said to Mrs. Grinder, that it would be right to have my House searched, as I might have plans of the Country which I intended to send to the Enemy; he called me a Military Painter; I suppose mistaking the Words Miniature Painter, which he might have heard me called. I think that this proves, his having come into the Garden, with some bad Intention, or at least with a prejudiced Mind.

It is necessary to learn the Names of all that were present at the Stable Door, that we may not have any Witnesses brought against us, that were not there.

All the Persons present at the Stable Door were, Mrs. Grinder and her Daughter, all the Time; Mrs. Haynes & her Daughter all the Time; Mr. Grinder, part of the Time; Mr. Hayley's Gardener part of the Time.—Mrs. Haynes was present from my turning him out at my Gate, all the rest of the Time—What passed in the Garden, there is no Person but William & the Soldier, & myself can know.

There was not any body in Grinder's Tap-room, but an Old Man, named Jones, who (Mrs. Grinder says) did not come out—He is the same Man who lately hurt his Hand, & wears it in a sling—

The Soldier after he and his Comrade came together into the Tap-room, threatened to knock William's Eyes out (this was his often repeated Threat to me and to my Wife) because W—refused to go with him to Chichester, and swear against me. William said that he would not take a false Oath, for that he heard me say nothing of the Kind (i.e. Sedition) Mrs Grinder then reproved the Soldier for threatening William, and Mr. Grinder said, that W— should not go, because of those Threats, especially as he was sure that no Seditious Words were Spoken.—

William's timidity in giving his Evidence before the Magistrates, and his fear of uttering a Falsehood upon Oath, proves him to be an honest Man, &

is to me an host of Strength. I am certain that if I had not turned the Soldier out of my Garden, I never should have been free from his Impertinence & Intrusion.

Mr. Hayley's Gardener came past at the Time of the Contention at the Stable Door, & going to the Comrade said to him, Is your Comrade drunk?— a Proof that he thought the Soldier abusive, & in an Intoxication of Mind.

If such a Perjury as this can take effect, any Villain in future may come & drag me and my Wife out of our House, & beat us in the Garden, or use us as he please, or is able, & afterwards go and swear our Lives away.

Is it not in the Power of any Thief who enters a Man's Dwelling, & robs him, or misuses his Wife or Children, to go & swear as this Man has sworn.—

To William Hayley, October 7, 1803

*   *   *

Art in London flourishes. Engravers in particular are wanted. Every Engraver turns away work that he cannot Execute from his superabundant Employment. Yet no one brings work to me. I am content that it shall be so as long as God pleases. I know that many works of a lucrative nature are in want of hands other Engravers are courted. I suppose that I must go a Courting which I shall do awkwardly in the mean time I lose no moment to complete Romney to satisfaction.

How is it possible that a Man almost 50 Years of Age who has not lost any of his life since he was five years old without incessant labour & study, how is it possible that such a one with ordinary common sense can be inferior to a boy of twenty who scarcely has taken or deigns to take a pencil in hand but who rides about the Parks or Saunters about the Playhouses who Eats & drinks for business not for need how is it possible that such a fop can be superior to the studious lover of Art can scarcely be imagind. Yet such is somewhat like my fate & such it is likely to remain. Yet I laugh & sing for if on Earth neglected I am in heaven a Prince among Princes & even on Earth beloved by the Good as a Good Man this I should be perfectly contented with but at certain periods a blaze of reputation arises round me in which I am considerd as one distinguishd by some mental perfection but the flame soon dies again & I am left stupified & astonishd.* * *

> To Eternity yours
> Willm Blake

To William Hayley, October 23, 1804

*   *   *

Our good and kind friend Hawkins[1] is not yet in town—hope soon to have the pleasure of seeing him, with the courage of conscious industry, worthy of his former kindness to me. For now! O Glory! and O Delight! I have entirely reduced that spectrous Fiend to his station, whose annoyance has

---

1. John Hawkins (1758–1841) of Cornwall, who commissioned work from Blake in the 1790s, had tried to raise funds to send him to Rome for further study.

been the ruin of my labours for the last passed twenty years of my life. He is the enemy of conjugal love and is the Jupiter of the Greeks, an iron-hearted tyrant, the ruiner of ancient Greece. I speak with perfect confidence and certainty of the fact which has passed upon me. Nebuchadnezzar had seven times passed over him; I have had twenty; thank God I was not altogether a beast as he was; but I was a slave bound in a mill among beasts and devils; these beasts and these devils are now, together with myself, become children of light and liberty, and my feet and my wife's feet are free from fetters. O lovely Felpham, parent of Immortal Friendship, to thee I am eternally indebted for my three years' rest from perturbation and the strength I now enjoy. Suddenly, on the day after visiting the Truchsessian Gallery[2] of pictures, I was again enlightened with the light I enjoyed in my youth, and which has for exactly twenty years been closed from me as by a door and by window-shutters. Consequently I can, with confidence, promise you ocular demonstration of my altered state on the plates I am now engraving after Romney, whose spiritual aid has not a little conduced to my restoration to the light of Art. O the distress I have undergone, and my poor wife with me, Incessantly labouring and incessantly spoiling what I had done well. Every one of my friends was astonished at my faults, and could not assign a reason; they knew my industry and abstinence from every pleasure for the sake of study, and yet—and yet—and yet there wanted the proofs of industry in my works. I thank God with entire confidence that it shall be so no longer— he is become my servant who domineered over me, he is even as a brother who was my enemy. Dear Sir, excuse my enthusiasm or rather madness, for I am really drunk with intellectual vision whenever I take a pencil or graver into my hand, even as I used to be in my youth, and as I have not been for twenty dark, but very profitable years. I thank God that I courageously pursued my course through darkness. In a short time I shall make my assertion good that I am become suddenly as I was at first, by producing the *Head of Romney*[3] and the *Shipwreck* quite another thing from what you or I ever expected them to be. In short, I am now satisfied and proud of my work, which I have not been for the above long period.

*   *   *

I remain, with my wife's joint affection,

Your sincere and obliged servant,
Will Blake

To William Hayley, December 11, 1805

*   *   *

It will not be long before I shall be able to present the full history of my Spiritual Sufferings to the Dwellers upon Earth, & of the Spiritual Victories obtaind for me by my Friends—Excuse this Effusion of the Spirit from One

---

2. A collection of German, Dutch, and Flemish art brought to London and exhibited for sale in August 1803 by Joseph, Count Truchsess; not admired by other artists. See Morton D. Paley, *Studies in Romanticism* 16 (1977), 165–76.
3. Blake started the project in August 1803 and finished in late 1804, but Hayley substituted the work of another engraver. Blake's only engraving in Hayley's *Life of Romney* (1809) is *The Shipwreck*.

who cares little for this World which passes away, whose Happiness is Secure in Jesus our Lord, & who looks for Suffering till the time of complete Deliverance. In the mean While, I am kept Happy as I used to be, because I throw Myself & all that I have on our Saviours Divine Providence. O What Wonders are the Children of Men! Would to God that they would Consider it That they would Consider their Spiritual Life Regardless of that faint Shadow Calld Natural Life, & that they would Promote Each others Spiritual Labours, Each according to its Rank & that they would know that Recieving a Prophet As a Prophet is a Duty which If omitted is more Severely Avenged than Every Sin & Wickedness beside. It is the Greatest of Crimes to Depress True Art & Science. I know that those who are dead from the Earth & who mockd & Despised the Meekness of True Art (and such, I find, have been the situations of our Beautiful Affectionate Ballads), I know that such Mockers are Most Severely Punishd in Eternity. I know it for I see it & dare not help.— The Mocker of Art is the Mocker of Jesus. Let us go on Dear Sir following his Cross let us take it up daily Persisting in Spiritual Labours & the Use of that Talent which it is Death to Bury, & of that Spirit to which we are called—

*   *   *

Wishing You & All Friends in Sussex a Merry &
a Happy Christmas I remain Ever Your Affectionate
Will. Blake & his Wife Catherine Blake

To Dawson Turner,[1] June 9, 1818

Sir

I send you a List of the different Works you have done me the honour to enquire after—unprofitable enough to me tho Expensive to the Buyer. Those I Printed for Mr Humphry[2] are a selection from the different Books of such as could be Printed without the Writing tho to the Loss of some of the best things, For they when Printed perfect accompany Poetical Personifications & Acts without which Poems they never could have been Executed.

				£	s	d
America	18 Prints	folio		5£	5.	0
Europe	17	d°. folio		5.	5.	0
Visions &c	8	d°. folio		3.	3.	0
Thel	6	d°. Quarto		2.	2.	0
Songs of Innocence	28	d°. Octavo		3.	3.	0
Songs of Experience	26	d°. Octavo		3.	3.	0
Urizen	28 Prints	Quarto		5.	5.	0
Milton	50	d°. Quarto		10.	10.	0
12 Large Prints Size of Each about 2 feet by 1 & ½						
Historical & Poetical Printed in Colours			Each	5.	5.	0

1. Turner (1775–1858) was a banker, botanist, and antiquarian of Yarmouth, Norfolk. For varying prices over the years, see Blake's 1793 prospectus and his April 12, 1827, letter to Cumberland.
2. Ozias Humphrey (1742–1810), a miniaturist, recommended Blake to the earl of Egremont, who commissioned a *Last Judgment* and a panorama of characters in Spenser's *Fairie Queene*. For Humphrey, Blake made two series of color-printed impressions, c. 1796, of selected plates from the illuminated books; texts, if present, were colored over; now known as the *Large* and the *Small Book of Designs* (Print Room, British Museum).

These last 12 Prints are unaccompanied by any writing.[3] The few I have Printed & Sold are sufficient to have gained me great reputation as an Artist which was the chief thing Intended. But I have never been able to produce a Sufficient number for a general Sale by means of a regular Publisher. It is therefore necessary to me that any Person wishing to have any or all of them should send me their Order to Print them on the above terms & I will take care that they shall be done at least as well as any I have yet Produced.

I am Sir with many thanks for your very Polite approbation of my works

Your most obedient Servant
William Blake

To George Cumberland, April 12, 1827

Dear Cumberland

I have been very near the Gates of Death & have returned very weak & an Old Man feeble & tottering, but not in Spirit & Life not in The Real Man The Imagination which Liveth for Ever. In that I am stronger & stronger as this Foolish Body decays. I thank you for the Pains you have taken with Poor Job.[1] I know too well that a great majority of Englishmen are fond of The Indefinite which they Measure by Newtons Doctrine of the Fluxions of an Atom,[2] A Thing that does not Exist. These are Politicians & think that Republican Art is Inimical to their Atom. For a Line or Lineament is not formed by Chance a Line is a Line in its Minutest Subdivision Strait or Crooked It is Itself & Not Intermeasurable with or by any Thing Else. Such is Job. But since the French Revolution Englishmen are all Intermeasurable One by Another Certainly a happy state of Agreement to which I for One do not Agree. God keep me from the Divinity of Yes & No too The Yea Nay Creeping Jesus from supposing Up & Down to be the same Thing as all Experimentalists must suppose

You are desirous I know to dispose of some of my Works & to make them Pleasing. I am obliged to you & to all who do so. But having none remaining of all that I had Printed I cannot Print more Except at a great loss for at the time I printed those things I had a whole House to range in now I am shut up in a Corner therefore am forced to ask a Price for them that I scarce expect to get from a Stranger. I am now Printing a Set of the Songs of Innocence & Experience for a Friend at Ten Guineas which I cannot do under Six Months consistent with my other Work, so that I have little hope of doing any more of such things. The Last Work I produced is a Poem Entitled Jerusalem the Emanation of the Giant Albion, but find that to Print it will Cost my Time the amount of Twenty Guineas. One I have Finishd[3] It contains 100 Plates but it is not likely that I shall get a Customer for it.

3. A series of twelve large color prints stamped from a reverse image on millboard, in a process similar to monotype, retouched by hand. Three impressions of each subject are known; ten (including *Good and Evil Angels Struggling over a Child*, *God Judging Adam*, *Nebuchadnezzar*, *Newton*) are in the Tate Britain. The place of this series in Blake's oeuvre is clearly summarized in Butlin (1981) 156–77; for reproductions, see Hamlyn and Phillips (2000) 194–221.
1. Cumberland helped line up customers for Blake's print series, *Illustrations to the Book of Job* (1826).
2. See Johnson in *Historicizing Blake* (1994), ed. Clark and Worrall.
3. This is Copy E, the only colored copy of all four chapters of *Jerusalem*, now in the Yale Center for British Art; see color plates 14–16.

As you wish me to send you a list with the Prices of these things they are as follows

	£	s	d
America	6.	6.	0
Europe	6.	6.	0
Visions &/c	5.	5.	0
Thel	3.	3.	0
Songs of Inn. & Exp.	10.	10.	0
Urizen	6.	6.	0

The Little Card[4] I will do as soon as Possible but when you Consider that I have been reduced to a Skeleton from which I am slowly recovering you will I hope have Patience with me.

Flaxman is Gone & we must All soon follow every one to his Own Eternal House Leaving the Delusive Goddess Nature & her Laws to get into Freedom from all Law of the Members into The Mind in which every one is King & Priest in his own House. God Send it so on Earth as it is in Heaven.

I am Dear Sir Yours Affectionately
William Blake

---

4. A calling card with allegorical figures surrounding the name "Mr. Cumberland" (Essick, *Separate Plates* XXI).

CRITICISM

Comments by Contemporaries

ROBERT HUNT

From Mr Blake's Exhibition (1809)[†]

If beside the stupid and mad-brained political project of their rulers, the sane part of the people of England required fresh proof of the alarming increase of the effects of insanity, they will be too well convinced from its having lately spread into the hitherto sober region of Art. I say hitherto, because I cannot think with many, that the vigorous genius of the present worthy Keeper of the Royal Academy[1] is touched, though no one can deny that his Muse has been on the verge of insanity, since it has brought forth, with more legitimate offspring, the furious and distorted beings of an extravagant imagination. But, when the ebullitions of a distempered brain are mistaken for the sallies of genius by those whose works have exhibited the soundest thinking in art, the malady has indeed attained a pernicious height, and it becomes a duty to endeavour to arrest its progress. Such is the case with the productions and admirers of WILLIAM BLAKE, an unfortunate lunatic, whose personal inoffensiveness secures him from confinement, and, consequently, of whom no public notice would have been taken, if he was not forced on the notice and animadversion of the EXAMINER, in having been held up to public admiration by many esteemed amateurs and professors as a genius in some respect original and legitimate. The praises which these gentlemen bestowed last year on this unfortunate man's illustrations of *Blair's Grave*, have, in feeding his vanity, stimulated him to publish his madness more largely, and thus again exposed him, if not to the derision, at least to the pity of the public. That work was a futile endeavour by bad drawings to represent immateriality by bodily personifications of the soul, while its partner the body was depicted in company with it, so that the soul was confounded with the body, as the personifying figure had none of the distinguishing characteristics of allegory, presenting only substantial flesh and

[†] Unsigned review, "Fine Arts" section, *The Examiner*, September 17, 1809, 605–6, with paragraphing and erroneous or obsolete spelling modernized. Most omissions are long quotations from Blake's *Descriptive Catalogue*. Hazard Adams, *Critical Essays on William Blake* (1991), pp. 22–23, reprints somewhat different selections. For full texts (some from manuscript sources) of all known contemporary comments, including those by Wordsworth, Southey, and Lamb, see G. E. Bentley Jr., *Blake Records*, 2nd ed. (2004); for facsimiles of most published texts, see Joseph Anthony Wittreich Jr., ed. *Nineteenth-Century Accounts of William Blake* (1970). Robert Hunt (1773–1851)— the negative inspiration, with his brothers, John and Leigh, for the accusatory Hand in *Jerusalem*—also attacked Blake's designs for Blair's *Grave* (*Examiner*, August 7, 1808, 520–21).

1. Blake's older Swiss-born friend J. H. Fuseli (1741–1825), notorious for *The Nightmare* (1782), gained respectability without giving up his wildness, becoming a full member of the Royal Academy in 1790, professor of painting in 1799, and keeper in 1804; see notes to *Public Address*. Hunt's attack on Fuseli's *Ugolino in Prison* (*Bell's Weekly Messenger* [May 25, 1806]) provoked a defense by Blake (*Monthly Magazine* [July 1, 1806], 520–21).

bones. This conceit was dignified with the character of genius, and the taste-
ful hand of SCHIAVONETTI, who engraved the work, assisted to give it currency by bestowing an exterior charm on deformity and nonsense.

Thus encouraged, the poor man fancies himself a great master, and has
painted a few wretched pictures, some of which are unintelligible allegory,
others an attempt at sober character by caricature representation, and the
whole "blotted and blurred,"[2] and very badly drawn. These he calls an
Exhibition, of which he has published a Catalogue, or rather a farrago of
nonsense, unintelligibleness, and egregious vanity, the wild effusions of a
distempered brain. One of the pictures represents *Chaucer's Pilgrims*, and
is in every respect a striking contrast to the admirable picture of the same
subject by Mr. STOTHARD, from which an exquisite print is forthcome from
the hand of SCHIAVONETTI. "In this Exhibition," Mr. BLAKE very modestly
observes, "the grand style of art is restored; and in it will be seen *real* art,
as left us by RAPHAEL and ALBERT DURER, MICHAEL ANGELO and JULIO
ROMANO, stripped from the ignorances of RUBENS and REMBRANDT, TITIAN
and CORREGIO." * * * That insanity should elevate itself to this fancied
importance, is the usual effect of the unfortunate malady; but that men of
taste, in their sober senses, should mistake its unmeaning and distorted
conceptions for the flashes of genius, is indeed a phenomenon.

A few extracts from Mr. BLAKE's Catalogue will at once amuse the reader,
and satisfy him of the truth of the foregoing remarks. Speaking of his picture of the *Ancient Britons*, in which he has attempted to represent "the
strongest man, the beautifullest man, and the ugliest man," he says—

"It has been said to the artist, take the Apollo for the model of your beautiful man, and the Hercules for your strong man, and the Dancing Fawn for
your ugly man. * * *"

This picture is a complete caricature: one of the bards is singing to his
harp in the pangs of death; and though the colouring of the flesh is exactly
like hung beef, the artist modestly observes—

"The flush of health in flesh, exposed to the open air, nourished by the
spirits of forests and floods, in that ancient happy period, which history has
recorded, cannot be like the sickly daubs of Titian or Rubens. * * *"

SAMUEL TAYLOR COLERIDGE

From Letter to Charles Augustus Tulk
[February 12, 1818][†]

Blake's Poems.—

I begin with my Dyspathies, that I may forget them: and have uninter-
rupted space for Loves and Sympathies.

---

2. Alluding to a passage (not included in this edition) from *Descriptive Catalogue*, Number VI, as a
   picture the artist providentially left "unblotted and unblurred, although molested continually by
   blotting and blurring demons." Blake employed variations of these terms in attacks on Reynolds,
   Gainsborough, Rubens, and Titian.
† Transcribed from a photocopy generously provided by G. E. Bentley Jr. from his photograph (*Blake
   Records* [2004], 865, 92n) of the original document enclosed in a letter to Tulk (1786–1849), a

Title-page and the following emblem contain all the faults of the Drawings with as few beauties, as could be in the compositions of a man who was capable of such faults + such beauties.—The faults—despotism in symbols amounting in the title page to the μισητέον[1] / and occasionally irregular unmodified Lines of the Inanimate, sometimes in the effect of rigidity and sometimes of exosseation[2]—like a wet tendon. So likewise the ambiguity of the Drapery—Is it a garment—or the body incised and scored out—? The <u>Limpness</u> (= the effect of Vinegar on an egg) in the upper one of the two prostrate figures in the Title-page, and the <u>eye</u>-likeness of the twig posteriorly on the second, and the strait line down the waist-coat of pinky goldbeater's skin in the next drawing, with the I don't know whatness of the countenance as if the mouth had been formed by the habit of placing the tongue, not contemptuously, but stupidly, between the lower gums and the lower jaw——these are the only <u>repulsive</u> faults, I have noticed. The figure, however, of the second leaf (abstracted—from the <u>expression</u> of the Countenance, given it by something about the mouth and the interspace from the lower lip to the chin) is such as only a Master, learned in his art, could produce.—

N. B. I signifies, It gave me pleasure. ⧫ still greater—⧫⧫—and greater still. Θ in the highest degree, o[3] in the lowest.

Shepherd ⧫. Spring I (last stanza ⧫) Holy Thursday ⧫⧫. Laughing Song ⧫ Nurses Song I The Divine Image Θ The Lamb ⧫ The little Black Boy Θ: yea, Θ+Θ! Infant Joy ⧫⧫. (N.B. for the 3 last lines I should wish—"When wilt thou smile,["] or O smile o smile! I'll sing the while—. For a Babe two days old does not, cannot <u>smile</u>—and Innocence and the very truth of Nature must go together. Infancy is too holy a thing to be ornamented—. Echoing Green I (the figures ⧫, and of the second leaf ⧫⧫. The Cradle Song I The School boy ⧫⧫. Night Θ On another's sorrow I A dream ?) The little Boy lost I (the drawing ⧫) The little boy found I The Blossom o.—The Chimney Sweeper o. The v. of the ancient Bard o.

Introduction ⧫. Earth's Answer ⧫. Infant sorrow I The clod and the Pebble I The garden of Love ⧫ The fly I The Tyger ⧫ A little Boy lost ⧫ Holy Thursday I.—P. 13.[4] o. Nurse's Song o. The little girl lost. And found— (the ornaments most exquisite! the poem I) Chimney Sweeper in the Snow o. To Tirzah—and The Poison Tree I and yet o. A little girl lost—o. (I would have had it omitted—not for the want of innocence in the poem,

Swedenborgian writer and member of Parliament. In minor details, this text differs slightly from Bentley, *Blake Records* 2004, 336–38; cf. Earl Leslie Griggs, Letter 1116, *Collected Letters of Samuel Taylor Coleridge* (1959), p 4:835–38, based on a Coleridge family transcript. Page references follow the order of Tulk's copy, now known as *Songs* Copy J (1795), collection of Emma Rothschild. In a letter of February 6, 1818, Coleridge refers to Blake's "Poems with very wild and interesting pictures" as the work of "a man of Genius—as I apprehend, a Swedenborgian— certainly a mystic *emphatically*," and he claims to be "in the very mire of common-place common-sense compared with Mr Blake, apo- or rather ana-calyptic Poet, and Painter!" (*Blake Records*, 336). See Michael Ferber, *Modern Philology* 76 (1978), 189–93, and, on Coleridge's rating system, B. R. McElderry, *Modern Language Quarterly* 9 (1948), 293–32; and David M. Baulch, *Coleridge Bulletin* 16 (2000), 5–14. For Wordsworth's, Southey's, Hazlitt's, and Lamb's opinions of Blake, see the *Blake Records* index.

1. *Miseteon*; to be hated, odious.
2. Coinage from *exossate*, to remove bones; thus bonelessness.
3. "o means that I am perplexed—and have no opinion——" [Coleridge's note]. This symbol for disapproval or perplexity becomes progressively larger as the letter continues. We have uniformly used boldface for the *o*, which is usually darkly inked, and standardized its size.
4. "The Angel." Or perhaps the whole two-page spread that includes page 12, the otherwise unmentioned three-flower plate. "My Pretty Rose Tree," "Ah! Sunflower," and "The Lilly" (Bentley, *Blake Records*, 337). Also unmentioned are "Introduction" to *Innocence* and "The Human Abstract."

but for the too probable want of it in many readers. [)] London **I** The sick
Rose **I** <u>The little Vagabond</u>.—Tho' I cannot approve altogether of this last
poem and have been inclined to think that the error, which is most <u>likely</u>
to beset the Scholars of Em[anuel] Sw[edenborg] is that of utterly demerg-
ing the tremendous incompatibilities with an evil will, that arise out of the
essential Holiness of the abysmal Aseity,[5] in the Love of the eternal <u>Per-
son</u>—and thus giving temptation to <u>weak</u> minds to sink this Love itself into
<u>good nature</u>—yet still I disapprove the mood of mind in this wild poem so
much less than I do the servile, blind-worm, wrap-rascal Scurf-coat <u>fear</u>
of the <u>modern Saints</u> (whose whole Being is a Lie, to themselves as much
as to their Brethren) that I should laugh with good conscience in watching a Saint of the new stamp, one of the Fixt Stars of our eleemosynary
Advertisements, groaning in—wind-pipe! and with the Whites of his Eyes
upraised, at the <u>audacity</u> of this poem!—Any thing rather than <u>this</u> degra-
dation[6] of Humanity, and therein of the incarnate Divinity!—

S.T.C.

JOHN THOMAS SMITH

From Nollekens and His Times (1828)[†]

Much about this time [1780], Blake wrote many other songs, to which
he also composed tunes. These he would occasionally sing to his friends;
and though, according to his confession, he was entirely unacquainted
with the science of music, his ear was so good, that his tunes were sometimes most singularly beautiful, and were noted down by musical professors. As for his later poetry, if it may be so called, attached to his plates,
though it was certainly in some parts enigmatically curious as to its application, yet it was not always wholly uninteresting; and I have unspeakable
pleasure in being able to state, that though I admit he did not for the last
forty years attend any place of Divine worship, yet he was not a Free-
thinker, as some invidious detractors have thought proper to assert, nor
was he ever in any degree irreligious. Through life, his Bible was every
thing with him. * * *

In his choice of subjects, and in his designs in Art, perhaps no man had
higher claim to originality, nor ever drew with a closer adherence to his
own conception; and from what I knew of him, and have heard related by
his friends, I most firmly believe few artists have been guilty of less pla-
giarisms than he. It is true, I have seen him admire and heard him expatiate upon the beauties of Marc Antonio[1] and of Albert Durer; but I verily

5. Coinage from *a se*. By itself or himself, i.e., not proceeding from, or created by something more
   basically real . . . than itself" (Wicksteed in Keynes, ed., *Blake Studies*, 2nd ed. [1971], 84).
6. "[W]ith which how can we utter 'Our Father'?" [Coleridge's note].
† From *Nollekens and his Times* . . . , 2 vols. (London: H. Colburn, 1828), 2:457–158, 459–61,
   467–68, 472–73, 474, 480–82, 485–87. Smith (1766–1833), who had been a friend of Blake's
   brother Robert, extended his biography of the fashionable portrait sculptor Joseph Nollekens
   (1737–1823) with memoirs of artists from Hogarth to Flaxman. The most influential early biography of Blake, based on interviews with Smith, Tatham, Linnell, and others, was Allan Cunningham, *Lives of the Most Eminent British Painters, Sculptors, and Architects* (1830; rpt. Bentley, *Blake
   Records* [2004], 626–60).
1. Marcantonio Raimondi (c. 1480–c. 1534), Italian engraver and inventor of a standardized
   method of crosshatching (shading by fine criss-crossed lines). As an engraver after three of Blake's

believe not with any view of borrowing an idea; neither do I consider him at any time dependent in his mode of working, which was generally with the graver only; and as to printing, he mostly took off his own impressions.

After his marriage, which took place at Battersea, and which proved a mutually happy one, he instructed his *beloved*, for so he most frequently called his Kate,[2] and allowed her, till the last moment of his practice, to take off his proof impressions and print his works, which she did most carefully, and ever delighted in the task: nay, she became a draughtswoman; and as a convincing proof that she and her husband were born for each other's comfort, she not only entered cheerfully into his views, but, what is curious, possessed a similar power of imbibing ideas, and has produced drawings equally original, and, in some respects, interesting.

Blake's peace of mind, as well as that of his Catherine, was much broken by the death of their brother Robert, who was a most amicable link in their happiness; and, as a proof how much Blake respected him, whenever he beheld him in his visions, he implicitly attended to his opinion and advice as to his future projected works. I should have stated, that Blake was supereminently endowed with the power of disuniting all other thoughts from his mind, whenever he wished to indulge in thinking of any particular subject; and so firmly did he believe, by this abstracting power, that the objects of this compositions were before him in his mind's eye, that he frequently believed them to be speaking to him. This I shall now illustrate by the following narrative.

Blake, after deeply perplexing himself as to the mode of accomplishing the publication of his illustrated songs, without their being subject to the expense of letter-press, his brother Robert stood before him in one of his visionary imaginations, and so decidedly directed him in the way in which he ought to proceed, that he immediately followed his advice, by writing his poetry, and drawing his marginal subjects of embellishments in outline upon the copper-plate with an impervious liquid, and then eating the plain parts or lights away with aquafortis considerably below them, so that the outlines were left as a stereotype. The plates in this state were then printed in any tint that he wished, to enable him or Mrs. Blake to colour the marginal figures up by hand in imitation of drawings.

*   *   *

An Engraver of the name of Cromek, a man who endeavoured to live by speculating upon the talents of others, purchased a series of drawings of Blake, illustrative of Blair's 'Grave,' which he had begun with a view of engraving and publishing. These were sold to Mr. Cromek for the insignificant sum of one guinea each, with the promise, and indeed under the express agreement, that Blake should be employed to engrave them; a task to which he looked forward with anxious delight. Instead of this negotiation being carried into effect, the drawings, to his great mortification, were put into the hands of Schiavonetti. During the time this artist was thus employed, Cromek had

---

favorite artists, Dürer, Giulio Romano, and Raphael, he influenced Blake profoundly. English artists—who had little access to originals—knew the Old Masters mainly through engravings.

2. "A friend [probably Tatham] has favoured me with the following anecdotes, which he received from Blake, respecting his courtship. He states that 'Our Artist fell in love with a lively little girl, who allowed him to say every thing that was loving, but would not listen to his overtures on the score of matrimony. He was lamenting this in the house of a friend, when a generous-hearted lass declared that she pitied him from her heart. "Do you pity me?" asked Blake. "Yes; I do, most sincerely."—"Then," said he, "I love you for that."—"Well," said the honest girl, "and I love you." The consequence was, they were married, and lived the happiest of lives'" [Smith's note].

asked Blake what work he had in mind to execute next. The unsuspecting artist not only told him, but without the least reserve showed him the designs sketched out for a fresco picture; the subject Chaucer's 'Pilgrimage to Canterbury'; with which Mr. Cromek appeared highly delighted. Shortly after this, Blake discovered that Stothard, a brother-artist to whom he had been extremely kind in early days, had been employed to paint a picture, not only of the same subject, but in some instances similar to the fresco sketch which he had shown to Mr. Cromek. The picture painted by Stothard became the property of Mr. Cromek, who published proposals for an engraving from it, naming Bromley as the engraver to be employed. However, in a short time, that artist's name was withdrawn, and Schiavonetti's substituted, who lived only to complete the etching; the plate being finished afterwards by at least three different hands. Blake, highly indignant at this treatment, immediately set to work, and proposed an engraving from his fresco picture, which he publicly exhibited in his brother James's shop window, at the corner of Broad-street, accompanied with an address to the public, stating what he considered to be improper conduct.[3]

*   *   *

* * * Whatever may be the public opinion hereafter of Blake's talents, when his enemies are dead, I will not presume to predict;[4] but this I am certain of, that on the score of industry at least, many artists must strike to him. Application was a faculty so engendered in him that he took little bodily exercise to keep up his health: he had few evening walks and little rest from labour, for his mind was ever fixed upon his art, nor did he at any time indulge in a game of chess, draughts, or backgammon; such amusements, considered as relaxation by artists in general, being to him distractions. His greatest pleasure was derived from the Bible,—a work ever at his hand, and which he often assiduously consulted in several languages. Had he fortunately lived till the next year's exhibition at Somerset-house, the public would then have been astonished at his exquisite finishing of a Fresco picture of the Last Judgment, containing upwards of one thousand figures, many of them wonderfully conceived and grandly drawn. The lights of this extraordinary performance have the appearance of silver and gold; but upon Mrs. Blake's assuring me that there was no silver used, I found, upon a closer examination, that a blue wash had been passed over those parts of the gilding which receded, and the lights of the forward objects, which were also of gold, were heightened with a warm colour, to give the appearance of the two metals.

As to Blake's system of colouring, which I have not hitherto noticed, it was in many instances most beautifully prismatic. In this branch of the art he often acknowledged Apelles to have been his tutor. * * *

*   *   *

Blake's modes of preparing his ground, and laying them over his panels for painting, mixing his colours, and manner of working, were those which he considered to have been practised by the earliest fresco-painters, whose productions still remain, in numerous instances, vivid and permanently

3. Smith continues with Cromek's side of the story: that Blake had seen Stothard's treatment of the subject before designing his own; for more on this quarrel, see notes to *Public Address.*
4. "* * * The predictions of Fuseli and Flaxman may hereafter be verified,—'That a time will come when Blake's finest works will be as much sought after and treasured up in the portfolios of men of mind, as those of Michel Angelo are at present'" [Smith's note].

fresh. His ground was a mixture of whiting and carpenter's glue, which he passed over several times in thin coatings: his colours he ground himself, and also united them with the same sort of glue, but in a much weaker state. He would, in the course of painting a picture, pass a very thin transparent wash of glue-water over the whole of the parts he had worked upon, and then proceed with his finishing.

This process I have tried, and find, by using my mixtures warm, that I can produce the same texture as possessed in Blake's pictures of the Last Judgment, and others of his productions, particularly in Varley's curious picture of the personified Flea.[5] Blake preferred mixing his colours with carpenter's glue, to gum, on account of the latter cracking in the sun, and becoming humid in moist weather. The glue-mixture stands the sun, and change of atmosphere has no effect upon it. Every carpenter knows that if a broken piece of stick be joined with good glue, the stick will seldom break again in the glued parts.

That Blake had many secret modes of working, both as a colourist and an engraver, I have no doubt. His method of eating away the plain copper, and leaving his drawn lines of his subjects and his words as stereotype, is in my mind perfectly original. Mrs. Blake is in possession of the secret, and she ought to receive something considerable for its communication, as I am quite certain it may be used to the greatest advantage both to artists and literary characters in general.

❊   ❊   ❊

Blake and his wife were known to have lived so happily together, that they might unquestionably have been registered at Dunmow.[6] 'Their hopes and fears were to each other known,' and their days and nights were passed in each other's company, for he always painted, drew, engraved and studied, in the same room where they grilled, boiled, stewed, and slept; and so steadfastly attentive was he to his beloved tasks, that for the space of two years he had never once been out of his house; and his application was often so incessant, that in the middle of the night, he would, after thinking deeply upon a particular subject, leap from his bed and write for two hours or more; and for many years, he made a constant practice of lighting the fire, and putting on the kettle for breakfast before his Kate awoke.

During his last illness, which was occasioned by the gall mixing with his blood, he was frequently bolstered-up in his bed to complete his drawings, for his intended illustration of Dante; an author so great a favourite with him, that though he agreed with Fuseli and Flaxman, in thinking Carey's translation superior to all others, yet, at the age of sixty-three years, he learned the Italian language purposely to enjoy Dante in the highest possible way. For this intended work, he produced seven engraved plates of an imperial quarto size, and nearly one hundred finished drawings of a size considerably larger; which will do equal justice to his wonderful mind, and the liberal heart of their possessor,[7] who engaged him upon so delightful a

5. *The Ghost of a Flea*, Tate Gallery, London; Butlin 750. On John Varley, see dagger note, p. 514.
6. An Augustinian priory in Little Dunmow, Essex, annually awarded a "flitch" (side) of bacon to any couple who proved that they had lived in perfect harmony for the first year and a day of their marriage. From the sixteenth century a jury of six bachelors and six maids heard the cases. The quotation is a variation on "Our Griefs and Joys, be to each other known" in Lady Mary Lee Chudleigh's "To Clorissa" (1722).
7. John Linnell, one of the young artists who befriended Blake in his later years, commissioned the Dante designs.

task at a time when few persons would venture to give him employment, and whose kindness softened, for the remainder of his life, his lingering bodily sufferings, which he was seen to support with the most Christian fortitude.

On the day of his death, August 12th, 1827, he composed and uttered songs to his Maker so sweetly to the ear of his Catherine, that when she stood to hear him, he, looking upon her most affectionately, said, 'My beloved, they are not mine—no—they are not mine.' He expired at six in the evening, with the most cheerful serenity. Some short time before his death, Mrs. Blake asked him where he should like to be buried, and whether he would have the Dissenting Minister, or the Clergyman of the Church of England, to read the service: his answers were, that as far as his own feelings were concerned, they might bury him where she pleased, adding, that as his father, mother, aunt, and brother, were buried in Bunhill-row, perhaps it would be better to lie there, but as to service, he should wish for that of the Church of England.

*   *   *

FREDERICK TATHAM

From The Life of William Blake (c. 1832; 1906)[†]

William, the artist, appears to have possessed from a child that daring, impetuous, and vigorous temper which was in latter life so singularly characteristic both of him and his sublime inventions. Although easily persuaded, he despised restraints and rules, so much that his father dared not send him to school. Like the Arabian horse, he is said to have so hated a blow that his father thought it most prudent to withhold from him the liability of receiving punishment. He picked up his education as well as he could. His talent for drawing manifesting itself as spontaneously as it was premature, he was always sketching; and, after having drawn nearly everything around him with considerable ability, he was sent to draw with Pars, a drawing master in the Strand, at ten years of age. He used also at this time to frequent Langford's, the auctioneer, where he saw pictures and bought prints from Raphael, Michael Angelo, Albert Durer, Julio Romano, and others of the great designers of the Cinquecento, and refused to buy any others, however celebrated. Langford favoured him by knocking down the lots he bought so quickly, that he obtained them at a rate suited to the pocket savings of a lad. Langford called him his little connoisseur. Even at this time he met with that opposition and ridicule from his contemporaries

---

[†] Composed 1832. From *The Letters of William Blake together with a Life by Frederick Tatham*, ed. Archibald G. B. Russell (London: Methuen, 1906), 3–4, 10–11, 13–16, 18–24, 27, 31–35, 37–39. Blake's young disciple Tatham (1805–1878), an aspiring sculptor, wrote this not entirely reliable memoir when he was trying to sell *Jerusalem* (Copy E) after Catherine Blake's death in 1831. As a widow, Catherine had lived briefly and unhappily with the Linnells as their housekeeper before accepting a similar arrangement with Tatham and his wife, who helped care for her as her strength declined. Because neither of the Blakes left a registered will and William had asked Tatham to handle his affairs, Tatham considered all of Blake's copper plates and unsold works his property, despite Linnell's objections on behalf of Blake's impoverished unmarried sister. After Tatham became an Irvingite, a follower of the charismatic preacher Edward Irving (1792–1834), he burned an unknown number of Blake's works, believing them inspired by Satan (Bentley, *Blake Records* [2004], 731).

(many of whom have since become men of note) that harassed him afterwards: they laughed at his predilection for these great masters.

*   *   *

About this time [1783] Blake took to painting, and his success in it being a matter of opinion, it will require some care to give a fair account. Oil painting was recommended to him as the only medium through which breadth, force, and sufficient rapidity could be obtained. He made several attempts, and found himself quite unequal to the management of it. His great objections were that the picture, after it was painted, sunk so much that it ceased to retain the brilliancy and luxury that he intended, and also that no definite line, no positive end to the form could, even with the greatest of his ingenuity, be obtained: all his lines dwindled and his clearness melted. * * * Desiring that his colours should be as pure and as permanent as precious stones, he could not with oil obtain his end.

*   *   *

* * * Very singular it is to know that many of the best painters do not paint with the oil vehicle, or, if they do, in a very small quantity. Fuseli painted with very little oil, but then oil painters consider Fuseli no colourist. What is colouring? It is a most vague term, and is generally used in a still more vague manner. * * *

*   *   *

Because Fuseli coloured a witch like a witch, and Michael Angelo coloured a prophet like a prophet, these men are called no colourists. That the greatest men should colour worst is an enigma perfectly inexplicable; but after apologising for the digression, if the reader should want any more light upon this obscure subject, he must ask the picture dealers or their fry: it will of them be learnt that nobody can colour well but those that can draw ill, in an equivalent ratio. Blake painted on panel or canvas covered with three or four layers of whiteing and carpenter's glue, as he said the nature of gum was to crack; for as he used several layers of colour to produce his depths, the coats necessarily in the deepest parts became so thick that they were likely to peel off. Washing his pictures over with glue, in the manner of a varnish, he fixed the colours, and at last varnished with a white hard varnish of his own making. It must, however, be confessed that his pictures mostly are not very deep, but they have an unrivalled tender brilliancy. He took infinite pains with them, coloured them very highly, and certainly, without prejudice, either for or against, has produced as fine works as any ancient painter. He can be excelled by none where he is successful. Like his thoughts, his paintings seem to be inspired by fairies, and his colours look as if they were the bloom dropped from the brilliant wings of the spirits of the prism. * * *

*   *   *

It is now necessary to mention somewhat concerning the fanciful representations that Blake asserted were presented to his mind's eye. Difficult as this subject is, it cannot be omitted without a sacrifice to the memory of this great man. He always asserted that he had the power of bringing his imaginations before his mind's eye, so completely organised, and so perfectly formed and evident, that he persisted that while he copied the vision (as he called it) upon his plate or canvas, he could not err, and that error and defect could only arise from the departure or inaccurate delineation of this unsubstantial scene. He said that he was the companion of spirits, who taught, rebuked, argued, and advised with all the familiarity of personal intercourse. What appears more odd still, was the power he contended he had of calling up any personage of past days, to delineate their forms and features, and to converse upon the topic most incidental to the days of their own existence. How far this is probable must be a question left either to the credulity or the faith of each person. It is fair, however, to say that what Blake produced from these characters, in delineating them, was often so curiously original, and yet so finely expressed, that it was difficult, if prejudices were cast away, to disbelieve totally this power. * * *

* * *

* * * All that is necessary to prove now is, that other men, other sensible men, such as scarcely could be designated as mad or stupid, did see into an immaterial life denied to most. All that is proposed here, further, is that it is a possible thing, that it does not require either a madman to see or an idiot to believe that such things are. Blake asserted, from a boy, that he did see them; even when a child, his mother beat him for running in and saying that he saw the prophet Ezekiel under a tree in the fields. In this incredulous age it is requisite, before this possibility is admitted, even as a doubt or question, that it should be said that he who inefficiently attempts to defend this power, never has been accustomed to see them, although he has known others besides Blake, on whose veracity and sanity he could equally well rely, who have been thus favoured. The Cock Lane ghost story,[1] the old women's tales, and the young bravo who defies the ghost in the tap-room, that he shudders at in his walk home, are foolishly mixed up with Blake's visions. They are totally different; they are mental abstractions, that are not necessarily accompanied with fear, such as ghosts and apparitions, which either appear to be, or are, seen by the mortal eyes, which circumstance alone horrifies. These visions of Blake seem to have been more like peopled imaginations and personified thoughts; they only horrified where they represented any scene in which horrors were depicted, as a picture or a poem. * * *

Again, in reference to the authenticity of Blake's visions, let anyone contemplate the designs in this book.[2] Are they not only new in their method and manner, but actually new in their class and origin? Do they look like the localities of common circumstances, or of lower worlds? The combinations are chimerical, the forms unusual, the inventions abstract; the poem not only abstruse, but absolutely, according to common rules of criticism, as near ridiculous as it is completely heterogeneous. With all that is incomprehensible in the poem, with all that might by some be termed ridiculous in the plan, the designs are possessed of some of the most sublime ideas, some of the most lofty thoughts, some of the most noble conceptions possible to the mind of man. You may doubt, however, the means, and you may criticise the peculiarity of the notions, but you cannot but admire, nay, "wonder at with great admiration,"[3] these expressive, these

1. "Scratching Fanny," a famous hoax perpetrated in 1762 by landlord William Parsons, with the aid of his eleven-year-old daughter, to accuse a tenant of murder. Even Dr. Johnson joined the investigation, and Samuel Foote's *The Orators* (1762) includes a trial scene with the ghost as witness.
2. *Jerusalem*, Copy E, the only complete colored copy.
3. From Revelation 17:6, John's response to the Whore of Babylon.

sublime, these awful diagrams of an eternal phantasy. Michael Angelo, Julio Romano, or any other great man, never surpassed Plates 25, 35, 37, 46, 51, 76, 94, and many of the stupendous and awful scenes with which this laborious work is so thickly ornamented. * * * Even supposing the poetry to be the mere vehicle or a mere alloy for the sake of producing or combining these wonderful thoughts, it should at all events be looked upon with some respect.

* * *

Blake was standing at one of his windows,[4] which looked into Astley's premises (the man who established the theatre still called by his name), and saw a boy hobbling along with a log to his foot, such an one as is put on a horse or ass to prevent their straying. Blake called his wife and asked her for what reason that log could be placed upon the boy's foot. She answered that it must be for a punishment for some inadvertency. Blake's blood boiled, and his indignation surpassed his forbearance. He sallied forth, and demanded in no very quiescent terms that the boy should be loosed, and that no Englishman should be subjected to those miseries, which he thought were inexcusable even towards a slave. After having succeeded in obtaining the boy's release in some way or other, he returned home. Astley by this time, having heard of Blake's interference, came to his house and demanded, in an equally peremptory manner, by what authority he dare come athwart his method of jurisdiction. To which Blake replied with such warmth, that blows were very nearly the consequence. The debate lasted long, but, like all wise men whose anger is unavoidably raised, they ended in mutual forgiveness and mutual respect. Astley saw that his punishment was too degrading, and admired Blake for his humane sensibility, and Blake desisted from wrath when Astley was pacified. As this is an example truly worthy of imitation to all those whose anger is either excited by indignation or called forth by defence, it may not be out of place to say, if all quarrels were thus settled, the time would shortly come when the lion would lie down with the lamb, and the little child would lead them.

* * *

* * * About this time [1790–99] he taught drawing, and was engaged for that purpose by some families of high rank; which, by the bye, he could not have found very profitable, for after his lesson he got into conversation with his pupils, and was found so entertaining and pleasant, possessing such novel thoughts and such eccentric notions, together with such jocose hilarity and amiable demeanour, that he frequently found himself asked to stay to dinner, and spend the evening in the same interesting and lively manner in which he had consumed the morning.[5] * * *

* * *

He was a subject of much mental temptation and mental suffering, and required sometimes much soothing. He has frequently had recourse to the following stratagem to calm the turbulence of his thoughts. His wife being

---

4. At Hercules Buildings, Lambeth, Bentley notes that Astley's theater (see map) was "perhaps a quarter mile from number 13 Hercules Buildings, but Astley's own house was built in behind number 11 in the next garden but one to Blake's" (*Blake Records*, 675).
5. According to Tatham, Blake abruptly stopped teaching so that he would not be obligated to accept an invitation to teach drawing to the royal family.

to him a very patient woman, he fancied that while she looked on at him as he worked, her sitting quite still by his side, doing nothing, soothed his impetuous mind; and he has many a time, when a strong desire presented itself to overcome any difficulty in his plates or drawings, in the middle of the night risen, and requested her to get up with him and sit by his side, in which she as cheerfully acquiesced.[6]

*   *   *

He was a subject often of much internal perturbation and over-anxiety, for he has spoilt as much work (which every artist knows is not only easy, but common) by over-labour as would take some a whole life of ordinary industry to accomplish. Mrs. Blake has been heard to say that she never saw him, except when in conversation or reading, with his hands idle; he scarcely ever mused upon what he had done. Some men muse and call it thinking, but Blake was a hard worker; his thought was only for action, as a man plans a house, or a general consults his map and arranges his forces for a battle. His mental acquirements were incredible; he had read almost everything in whatsoever language, which language he always taught himself. His conversation, therefore, was highly interesting, and never could one converse on any subject with him, but they would gain something quite as new as noble from his eccentric and elastic mind. It is a remarkable fact that among the volumes bequeathed by Mrs. Blake to the author of this sketch, the most thumbed from use are his Bible and those books in other languages.[7] He was very fond of Ovid, especially the *Fasti*. He read Dante when he was past sixty, although before he never knew a word of Italian, and he drew from it a hundred such designs as have never been done by any Englishman at any period or by any foreigner since the fifteenth century, and then his only competitor was Michael Angelo.[8]

*   *   *

It has been supposed his excessive labour without the exercise he used formerly to take (having relinquished the habit of taking very long walks) brought on the complaint which afterwards consumed him. In his youth he and his wife would start in the morning early, and walk out twenty miles and dine at some pretty and sequestered inn, and would return the same day home, having travelled forty miles. Mrs. Blake would do this without excessive fatigue. Blake has been known to walk fifty miles in the day, but being told by some physicians that such long walks were injurious, he discontinued them, and went * * * to the other extreme.

*   *   *

About a year before he died, he was seized with a species of ague (as it was then termed), of which he was alternately better and worse. He was at times very ill, but rallied and all had hopes of him; indeed, such was his energy that

6. Cf. Tatham's account in Gilchrist (1863; 1945, p. 315): "She would get up in the night, when he was under his very fierce inspirations, which were as if they would tear him asunder, while he was yielding himself to the Muse, or whatever else it could be called, sketching and writing. And so terrible a task did this seem to be, that she had to sit motionless and silent; only to stay him mentally, without moving hand or foot: this for hours, and night after night."
7. Blake studied Latin, Greek, and Hebrew before 1803, quoted Voltaire in French about 1808, and taught himself Italian about 1824.
8. Michelangelo did not illustrate *The Divine Comedy*, but Tatham may have had in mind Botticelli's great illustrations (c. 1490), most of which were in the Hamilton Palace collection in Blake's time.

even then, though sometimes confined to his bed, he sat up drawing his most stupendous works. In August he gradually grew worse and required much more of his wife's attention; indeed, he was decaying fast. His patience, during his agonies of pain, is described to have been exemplary.

Life, however, like a dying flame, flashed once more, gave one more burst of animation, during which he was cheerful, and free from the tortures of his approaching end; he thought he was better, and, as he was sure to do, asked to look at the work over which he was occupied when seized with his last attack. It was a coloured print of the Ancient of Days striking the first circle of the Earth,[9] done expressly by commission for the writer of this. After he had worked upon it he exclaimed: "There, I have done all I can! It is the best I have ever finished. I hope Mr. Tatham will like it." He threw it suddenly down and said: "Kate, you have been a good wife; I will draw your portrait." She sat near his bed, and he made a drawing which, though not a likeness, is finely touched and expressed. He then threw that down, after having drawn for an hour, and began to sing Hallelujahs and songs of joy and triumph which Mrs. Blake described as being truly sublime in music and in verse; he sang loudly and with true ecstatic energy, and seemed so happy that he had finished his course, that he had run his race, and that he was shortly to arrive at the goal, to receive the prize of his high and eternal calling. * * * [H]is spirit departed like the sighing of a gentle breeze, and he slept in company with the mighty ancestors he had formerly depicted.[1]

William Blake in stature was short, but well made, and very well proportioned; so much so that West, the great history painter, admired much the form of his limbs; he had a large head and wide shoulders. Elasticity and promptitude of action were the characteristics of his contour. His motions were rapid and energetic, betokening a mind filled with elevated enthusiasm; his forehead was very high and prominent over the frontals; his eye most unusually large and glassy, with which he appeared to look into some other world. * * *

In youth he surprised everyone with his vigour and activity. In age he impressed all with his unfading ardour and unabated energy. His beautiful grey locks hung upon his shoulders; and dressing as he always did in latter years in black, he looked, even in person, although without any effort towards eccentricity, to be of no ordinary character. In youth, he was nimble; in old age, venerable. His disposition was cheerful and lively, and was never depressed by any cares but those springing out of his art. He was the attached friend of all who knew him, and a favourite with everyone but those who oppressed him, and against such his noble and impetuous spirit boiled, and fell upon the aggressor like a water-spout from the troubled deep. Yet, like Moses, he was one of the meekest of men. His patience was almost incredible: he could be the lamb; he could plod as a camel; he could roar as a lion. He was everything but subtle; the serpent had no share in his nature; secrecy was unknown to him. He would relate those things of

---

9. A separate impression of the frontispiece to *Europe* (Butlin, 261), now in the Whitworth Art Gallery, University of Manchester. The deathbed portrait of Catherine (Butlin, 685) is untraced.

1. The young artist George Richmond, who was not present at Blake's death, told his grandson that he closed Blake's eyes "to keep the vision in" (Ruthven Todd, *Blake Newsletter* #21 [1972]). Recent investigators have debunked stories of the glorious final hours witnessed only by Catherine Blake; see Aileen Ward, "William Blake and the Hagiographers" in *Biography and Source Studies* (1994), ed. Frederick R. Karl; and Lane Robeson and Joseph Viscomi, *Blake: An Illustrated Quarterly* 29 (1996).

himself that others make it their utmost endeavour to conceal. He was possessed of a peculiar obstinacy, that always bristled up when he was either unnecessarily opposed or invited out to show like a lion or a bear. Many anecdotes could be related in which there is sufficient evidence to prove that many of his eccentric speeches were thrown forth more as a piece of sarcasm upon the inquirer than from his real opinion. If he thought a question were put merely for a desire to learn, no man could give advice more reasonably and more kindly; but if that same question were put for idle curiosity, he retaliated by such an eccentric answer as left the inquirer more afield than ever. He then made an enigma of a plain question: hence arose many vague reports of his oddities. He was particularly so upon religion. His writings abounded with these sallies of independent opinion. He detested priestcraft and religious cant. He wrote much upon controversial subjects, and, like all controversies, these writings are inspired by doubt and made up of vain conceits and whimsical extravagances. A bad cause requires a long book. Generally advocating one in which there is a flaw, the greatest controversialists are the greatest doubters. They are trembling needles between extreme points. Irritated by hypocrisy and the unequivocal yielding of weak and interested men, he said and wrote unwarrantable arguments; but unalloyed and unencumbered by opposition, he was in all essential points orthodox in his belief. But he put forth ramifications of doubt, that by his vigorous and creative mind were watered into the empty enormities of extravagant and rebellious thoughts.

HENRY CRABB ROBINSON

From Reminiscences (1852; 1907)[†]

[1825] I was aware of his idiosyncracies and therefore to a great degree prepared for the sort of conversation which took place at and after dinner, an altogether unmethodical rhapsody on art, religion—he saying the most strange things in the most unemphatic manner, speaking of his *Visions* as any man would of the most ordinary occurrence. He was then 68 years of age. He had a broad, pale face, a large full eye with a benignant expression—at the same time a look of languor, except when excited, and then he had an air of inspiration. But not such as without a previous acquaintance with him, or attending to *what* he said, would suggest the notion that he was insane. There was nothing *wild* about his look, and though very ready to be drawn out to the assertion of his favourite ideas, yet with no warmth as if he

---

† Composed 1852. From "Crabb Robinson's Reminiscences" in Arthur Symons, *William Blake* (London: Archibald Constable, 1907), 285–86, 287–88, 291, 292–94, 296–98, 301–5, with minor typographical adjustments. Symons was the first to publish in full the narrative that Robinson prepared from his diary entries of 1825–1827. The genial, long-lived Robinson (1775–1869) filled thirty-three volumes with anecdotes of celebrity writers and artists. His interest in Blake, whom he met in 1825, dates from 1810, when he attended Blake's exhibition twice, the second time with Charles and Mary Lamb in tow, in preparation for writing the first essay of substance ever published about Blake (*Vaterländisches Museum* [January 1811]; *Blake Records* [2004], 571 ff.). Taken aback by Blake's odd remarks, Robinson admired his genius but questioned his sanity, as did most contemporaries. But cf. Tatham's statement that "many of his eccentric speeches were thrown forth more as a piece of sarcasm upon the inquiry than from his real opinion" (p. 510 herein); Samuel Palmer's remark that he would answer a materialist "according to his folly, by putting forth his own views in their most extravagant and starting aspect" (p. 517 herein); and Linnell's affirmation that "I never saw anything the least like madness for I never opposed him spitefully" (*Blake Records*, 341).

wanted to make proselytes. Indeed one of the peculiar features of his scheme, as far as it was consistent, was indifference and a very extraordinary degree of tolerance and satisfaction with what had taken place. A sort of pious and humble optimism, not the scornful optimism of Candide. But at the same time that he was very ready to praise he seemed incapable of envy, as he was of discontent. * * *

* * * As I had for many years been familiar with the idea that an eternity *a parte post* was inconceivable without an eternity *a parte ante*,[1] I was naturally led to express that thought on this occasion. His eye brightened on my saying this. He eagerly assented: 'To be sure. We are all coexistent with God; Members of the Divine body, And partakers of the Divine nature.' Blake's having adopted this Platonic idea led me on in our *tete-a-tete* walk home at night to put the popular question to him, concerning the imputed Divinity of Jesus Christ. He answered: 'He is the only God'—but then he added—'And so am I and so are you.' He had before said—and that led me to put the question—that Christ ought not to have suffered himself to be crucified. 'He should not have attacked the Government. He had no business with such matters.' On my representing this to be inconsistent with the sanctity of divine qualities, he said Christ was not yet become the Father. It is hard on bringing together these fragmentary recollections to fix Blake's position in relation to Christianity, Platonism, and Spinozism.

*   *   *

* * * He declared his opinion that the earth is flat, not round, and just as I had objected the circumnavigation dinner was announced. But objections were seldom of any use. The wildest of his assertions was made with the veriest indifference of tone, as if altogether insignificant. * * *

*   *   *

On the 17th I called on him in his house in Fountain's Court in the Strand. The interview was a short one, and what I saw was more remarkable than what I heard. He was at work engraving in a small bedroom, light, and looking out on a mean yard. Everything in the room squalid and indicating poverty, except himself. And there was a natural gentility about him, and an insensibility to the seeming poverty, which quite removed the impression. Besides, his linen was clean, his hand white, and his air quite unembarrassed when he begged me to sit down, as if he were in a palace. There was but one chair in the room besides that on which he sat. On my putting my hand to it, I found that it would have fallen to pieces if I had lifted it, so, as if I had been a Sybarite, I said with a smile, 'Will you let me indulge myself?' and I sat on the bed, and near him, and during my short stay there was nothing in him that betrayed that he was aware of what to other persons might have been even offensive, not in his person, but in all about him.

His wife I saw at this time, and she seemed to be the very woman to make him happy. She had been formed by him. Indeed, otherwise, she could not have lived with him. Notwithstanding her dress, which was poor and dirty,

---

1. From the part before (Latin, literal trans.); referring in theological and philosophical discourse to eternity as extending before time as well as after (*a parte post*).

she had a good expression in her countenance, and, with a dark eye, had remains of beauty in her youth. She had that virtue of virtues in a wife, an implicit reverence of her husband. It is quite certain that she believed in all his visions. And on one occasion, not this day, speaking of his Visions, she said, 'You know, dear, the first time you saw God was when you were four years old, and he put his head to the window and set you a-screaming.' In a word, she was formed on the Miltonic model, and like the first Wife Eve worshipped God in her husband. He being to her what God was to him. Vide Milton's *Paradise Lost—passim*.

*   *   *

On the 24th [December 1825] I called a second time on him. And on this occasion it was that I read to him *Wordsworth's Ode* on the supposed pre-existent State, and the subject of Wordsworth's religious character was discussed when we met on the 18th of Feb., and the 12th of May. I will here bring together Blake's declarations concerning Wordsworth, and set down his marginalia in the 8vo. edit. A.D. 1815, vol i. I had been in the habit when reading this marvellous Ode to friends, to omit one or two passages, especially that beginning:

But there's a Tree, of many one,

lest I should be rendered ridiculous, being unable to explain precisely *what* I admired. Not that I acknowledged this to be a fair test. But with Blake I could fear nothing of the kind. And it was this very stanza which threw him almost into a hysterical rapture. His delight in Wordsworth's poetry was intense. Nor did it seem less, notwithstanding the reproaches he continually cast on Wordsworth for his imputed worship of nature; which in the mind of Blake constituted Atheism.

The combination of the warmest praise with imputations which from another would assume the most serious character, and the liberty he took to interpret as he pleased, rendered it as difficult to be offended as to reason with him. The eloquent descriptions of Nature in Wordsworth's poems were conclusive proofs of atheism, for whoever believes in Nature, said Blake, disbelieves in God. For Nature is the work of the Devil. On my obtaining from him the declaration that the Bible was the Word of God, I referred to the commencement of Genesis—In the beginning God created the Heavens and the Earth. But I gained nothing by this, for I was triumphantly told that this God was not Jehovah, but the Elohim; and the doctrine of the Gnostics repeated with sufficient consistency to silence one so unlearned as myself.

The Preface to the *Excursion*, especially the Verses quoted from book i. of the *Recluse*, so troubled him as to bring on a fit of illness. These lines he singled out:

Jehovah with his thunder, and the Choir
Of shouting Angels, and the Empyreal throne,
I pass them unalarmed.

'Does Mr Wordsworth think he can surpass Jehovah?'[2] * * *

---

2. Cf. Blake's annotation of these lines (pp. 467–468. herein).

[1826] *19ᵗʰ Feb.* It was this day in connection with the assertion that the Bible is the Word of God and all truth is to be found in it, he using language concerning man's reason being opposed to grace very like that used by the Orthodox Christian, that he qualified, and as the same Orthodox would say wholly nullified, all he said by declaring that he understood the Bible in a Spiritual sense. As to the natural sense he said *Voltaire* was commissioned by God to expose that. 'I have had,' he said, 'much intercourse with Voltaire, and he said to me, "I blasphemed the Son of Man, and it shall be forgiven me, but they" (the enemies of Voltaire) "blasphemed the Holy Ghost in me, and it shall not be forgiven to them."' I asked him in what language Voltaire spoke. His answer was ingenious and gave no encouragement to cross-questioning: 'To my Sensations it was English. It was like the touch of a musical key; he touched it probably French, but to my ear it became English.' I also enquired as I had before about the form of the persons who appeared to him, and asked why he did not *draw* them. 'It is not worth while,' he said. 'Besides there are so many that the labour would be too great. And there would be no use in it.' In answer to an enquiry about Shakespeare, 'he is exactly like the old engraving—which is said to be a bad one. I think it very good.' I inquired about his own writings. 'I have written,' he answered, 'more than Rousseau or Voltaire—six or seven Epic poems as long as Homer and 20 Tragedies as long as *Macbeth*.' He shewed me his 'Version of Genesis,' for so it may be called, as understood by a Christian Visionary. He read a wild passage in a sort of Bible style. 'I shall print no more,' he said. 'When I am commanded by the Spirits, then I write, and the moment I have written, I see the words fly about the room in all directions. It is then published. The Spirits can read and my MS. is of no further use. I have been tempted to burn my MS., but my wife won't let me.' 'She is right,' I answered; 'You write not from yourself but from higher order. The MSS. are their property, not yours. You cannot tell what purpose they may answer.' This was addressed *ad hominem*. And indeed amounted only to a deduction from his own principles. He incidentally denied *causation*, every thing being the work of God or Devil. 'Every Man has a Devil in himself, and the conflict between his *Self* and God is perpetually going on.' I ordered of him today a copy of his *Songs* for 5 guineas. My manner of receiving his mention of price pleased him. He spoke of his horror of money and of turning pale when it was offerd him, and this was certainly unfeigned.

In the No. of the *Gents. Magazine* for last Jan. there is a letter by *Cromek* to Blake printed in order to convict Blake of selfishness. It cannot possibly be substantially true.

✻　✻　✻

13ᵗʰ June. I saw him again in June. He was as wild as ever, says my journal, but he was led today to make assertions more palpably mischievous, if capable of influencing other minds, and immoral, supposing them to express the will of a responsible agent, than anything he had said before. As, for instance, that he had learned from the Bible that Wives should be in common. And when I objected that marriage was a Divine institution, he referred to the Bible—'that from the beginning it was not so.' He affirmed that he had committed many murders, and repeated his doctrine, that reason is the only sin, and that careless, gay people are better than those who think, etc., etc.

It was, I believe, on the 7th of December that I saw him last. I had just heard of the death of Flaxman, a man whom he professed to admire, and was curious how he would receive the intelligence. It was as I expected. He had been ill during the summer, and he said with a smile, 'I thought I should have gone first.' He then said, 'I cannot think of death as more than the going out of one room into another.' And Flaxman was no longer thought of. He relapsed into his ordinary train of thinking. Indeed I had by this time learned that there was nothing to be gained by frequent intercourse. And therefore it was that after this interview I was not anxious to be frequent in my visits. This day he said, 'Men are born with an Angel and a Devil.' This he himself interpreted as Soul and Body, and as I have long since said of the strange sayings of a man who enjoys a high reputation, 'it is more in the language than the thoughts that the singularity is to be looked for.' And this day he spoke of the Old Testament as if it were the evil element. 'Christ,' he said, 'took much after his mother, and in so far was one of the worst of men.' On my asking him for an instance, he referred to his turning the money-changers out of the Temple:—'He had no right to do that.' He digressed into a condemnation of those who sit in judgment on others. 'I have never known a very bad man who had not something very good about him.'

Speaking of the Atonement in the ordinary Calvinistic sense, he said, 'It is a horrible doctrine; if another pay your debt, I do not forgive it.'

✦   ✦   ✦

SAMUEL PALMER

Letter to Alexander Gilchrist[†]

Kensington, Aug. 23rd, 1855.

My Dear Sir,

I regret that the lapse of time has made it difficult to recall many interesting particulars respecting Mr. Blake, of whom I can give you no connected account; nothing more, in fact, than the fragments of memory; but the general impression of what is great remains with us, although its details may be confined; and Blake, once known, could never be forgotten.

His knowledge was various and extensive, and his conversation so nervous and brilliant, that, if recorded at the time, it would now have thrown much light upon his character, and in no way lessened him in the estimation of those who know him only by his works.

---

† From Alexander Gilchrist, *Life of William Blake: Pictor Ignotus* (1863; rpt., ed. Ruthven Todd [London: J. M. Dent, 1945]), 301–4. In May 1824, when Palmer (1804–1881) was nineteen years old, the artist John Linnell (1792–1882), his future father-in-law, introduced him to Blake. Palmer, drawn especially to Blake's series of eighteen small woodcuts for Thornton's translation of Virgil's *Pastorals* (1821), was the most distinguished of a youthful band that included Edward Calvert (1799–1883) and George Richmond (1809–1896), who called themselves "The Ancients" and Blake "The Interpreter"; see *Essays on the Blake Followers* (1983), ed. G. E. Bentley Jr. Through Holman Hunt (1827–1910), who with Linnell studied watercolor with Blake's astrologer friend John Varley (1778–1842), Blake influenced artists of the Pre-Raphaelite brotherhood (fl. 1849–53) and the international movement of art nouveau (fl. 1884–1914), and reached artists, illustrators, and graphic novelists as diverse as Paul Nash (1889–1945), Bill Everett (1917–1973), Leonard Baskin (1922–2000), Maurice Sendak (1928–), Alan Moore (1953–), Walton Ford (1960–), Matthew Ritchie (1964–), and Chris Ofili (1968–), and comics studies scholars: *ImageTexT* 3.2 (2007), ed. Roger Whitson and Donald Ault, www.english.ufl.edu/imagetext/.

In him you saw at once the Maker, the Inventor; one of the few in any age: a fitting companion for Dante. He was energy itself, and shed around him a kindling influence; an atmosphere of life, full of the ideal. To walk with him in the country was to perceive the soul of beauty through the forms of matter; and the high gloomy buildings between which, from his study window, a glimpse was caught of the Thames and the Surrey shore, assumed a kind of grandeur from the man dwelling near them. Those may laugh at this who never knew such an one as Blake; but of him it is the simple truth.

He was a man without a mask; his aim single, his path straight-forwards, and his wants few; so he was free, noble, and happy.

His voice and manner were quiet, yet all awake with intellect. Above the tricks of littleness, or the least taint of affectation, with a natural dignity which few would have dared to affront, he was gentle and affectionate, loving to be with little children, and to talk about them. 'That is heaven,' he said to a friend, leading him to the window, and pointing to a group of them at play.

Declining, like Socrates, whom in many respects he resembled, the common objects of ambition, and pitying the scuffle to obtain them, he thought that no one could be truly great who had not humbled himself 'even as a little child.' This was a subject he loved to dwell upon, and to illustrate.

His eye was the finest I ever saw: brilliant, but not roving, clear and intent, yet susceptible; it flashed with genius, or melted in tenderness. It could also be terrible. Cunning and falsehood quailed under it, but it was never busy with them. It pierced them, and turned away. Nor was the mouth less expressive; the lips flexible and quivering with feeling. I can yet recall it when, on one occasion, swelling upon the exquisite beauty of the parable of the Prodigal, he began to repeat a part of it; but at the words, 'When he was yet a great way off, his father saw him,' could go no further; his voice faltered, and he was in tears.

I can never forget the evening when Mr. Linnell took me to Blake's house, nor the quiet hours passed with him in the examination of antique gems, choice pictures, and Italian prints of the sixteenth century. Those who may have read some strange passages in his *Catalogue*, written in irritation, and probably in haste, will be surprised to hear, that in conversation he was anything but sectarian or exclusive, finding sources of delight throughout the whole range of art; while, as a critic, he was judicious and discriminating.

No man more admired Albrecht Dürer, yet, after looking over a number of his designs, he would become a little angry with some of the draperies, as not governed by the forms of the limbs, nor assisting to express their action; contrasting them in this respect with the shaped antique, in which it was hard to tell whether he was more delighted with the general design, or with the exquisite finish and the depth of the chiselling; in works of the highest class, no mere adjuncts, but the last development of the design itself.

He united freedom of judgment with reverence for all that is great. He did not look out for the works of the purest ages, but for the purest works of every age and country—Athens or Rhodes, Tuscany or Britain; but no authority or popular consent could influence him against his deliberate judgment. Thus he thought with Fuseli and Flaxman that the Elgin Theseus, however full of antique savour, could not, as ideal form, rank with the

very finest relics of antiquity. Nor, on the other hand, did the universal neglect of Fuseli in any degree lessen his admiration of his best works.

He fervently loved the early Christian art, and dwelt with peculiar affection on the memory of Fra Angelico, often speaking of him as an inspired
inventor and as a saint; but when he approached Michael Angelo, the Last
Supper of Da Vinci, the Torso Belvedere, and some of the inventions preserved in the Antique Gems, all his powers were concentrated in admiration.

When looking at the heads of the apostles in the copy of the *Last Supper*
at the Royal Academy, he remarked of all but Judas: 'Every one looks as if
he had conquered the natural man.' He was equally ready to admire a contemporary and a rival. Fuseli's picture of *Satan building the Bridge over
Chaos* he ranked with the grandest efforts of imaginative art, and said that
we were two centuries behind the civilization which would enable us to
estimate his *Aegisthus*.

He was fond of the works of St. Theresa, and often quoted them with
other writers on the interior life. Among his eccentricities will, no doubt,
be numbered his preference for ecclesiastical governments. He used to ask
how it was that we heard so much of priest-craft and so little of soldier-craft
and lawyer-craft. The Bible, he said, was the book of liberty, and Christianity the sole regenerator of nations. In politics a Platonist, he put no
trust in demagogues. His ideal home was with Fra Angelico: a little later he
might have been a reformer, but after the fashion of Savonarola.

He loved to speak of the years spent by Michael Angelo, without earthly
reward, and solely for the love of God, in the building of St. Peter's, and of
the wondrous architects of our cathedrals. In Westminister Abbey were his
earliest and most sacred recollections. I asked him how he would like to
paint on glass, for the great west window, his *Sons of God shouting for Joy*,
from his design in the *Job*. He said, after a pause, 'I could do it!' kindling at
the thought.

Centuries could not separate him in spirit from the artists who went
about our land, pitching their tents by the morass or the forest side, to build
those sanctuaries that now lie ruined amidst the fertility which they called
into being.

His mind was large enough to contain, along with these things, stores of
classic imagery. He delighted in Ovid, and, as a labour of love, had executed
a finished picture from the *Metamorphoses*, after Giulio Romano. This
design hung in his room, and, close by his engraving table, Albert Dürer's
Melancholy the Mother of Invention, memorable as probably having been
seen by Milton, and used in his *Penseroso*. There are living a few artists,
then boys, who may remember the smile of welcome with which he used
to rise from that table to receive them.

His poems were variously estimated. They tested rather severely the imaginative capacity of their readers. Flaxman said they were as grand as his
designs, and Wordsworth delighted in his *Songs of Innocence*. To the multitude they were unintelligible. In many parts full of pastoral sweetness, and
often flashing with noble thoughts or terrible imagery, we must regret that
he should sometimes have suffered fancy to trespass within sacred precincts.

Thrown early among the authors who resorted to Johnson, the bookseller, he rebuked the profanity of Paine, and was no disciple of Priestly;
but, too undisciplined and cast upon times and circumstances which
yielded him neither guidance nor sympathy, he wanted that balance of the

faculties which might have assisted him in matters extraneous to his profession. He saw everything through art, and, in matters beyond its range, exalted it from a witness into a judge.

He had great powers of argument, and on general subjects was a very patient and good-tempered disputant; but materialism was his abhorrence: and if some unhappy man called in question the world of spirits, he would answer him 'according to his folly,' by putting forth his own views in their most extravagant and startling aspect. This might amuse those who were in the secret, but it left his opponent angry and bewildered.

Such was Blake, as I remember him. He was one of the few to be met with in our passage through life, who are not in some way or other, 'double-minded' and inconsistent with themselves; one of the very few who cannot be depressed by neglect, and to whose name rank and station could add no lustre. Moving apart, in a sphere above the attraction of worldly honours, he did not accept greatness, but confer it. He ennobled poverty, and, by his conversation and the influence of his genius, made two small rooms in Fountain Court more attractive than the threshold of princes.

I remain, my dear Sir,
Yours very faithfully,
Samuel Palmer.

Twentieth- and Twenty-First-Century Perspectives

ALLEN GINSBERG

[My Vision of Blake]†

* * * [A]nd suddenly I realized that the poem was talking about *me*. "Ah, Sun-flower! weary of time, / Who countest the steps of the Sun; / Seeking that sweet golden clime, / Where the traveller's journey is done." Now, I began understanding it, the poem while looking at it, and suddenly, simultaneously with understanding it, heard a very deep earthen grave voice in the room, which I immediately assumed, I didn't think twice, was Blake's voice; it wasn't any voice that I knew, though I had previously had a conception of a voice of rock, in a poem, some image like that—or maybe that came after this experience.

And my eye on the page, simultaneously the auditory hallucination, or whatever terminology here used, the apparitional voice, in the room, woke me further deep in my understanding of the poem, because the voice was so completely tender and beautifully . . . ancient. Like the voice of the Ancient of Days. But the peculiar quality of the voice was something unforgettable because it was like God had a human voice, with all the infinite tenderness and anciency and mortal gravity of a living Creator speaking to his son. "Where the youth pined away with desire, / And the pale Virgin shrouded in snow / Arise from their graves, and aspire / Where my Sun-flower wishes to go." Meaning that there *was* a *place*, there was a sweet golden clime, and the *sweet golden*, what was that . . . and simultaneous to the voice there was also an emotion, risen in my soul in response to the voice, and a sudden *visual* realization of the same awesome phenomena. That is to say, looking out at the window, through the window at the sky, suddenly it seemed that I saw into the depths of the universe, by looking

† From an interview by Thomas Clark, "The Art of Poetry VIII: Allen Ginsberg," *The Paris Review* 37 (1966), 13–55, excerpts from 36–40, 42–43, 44–45, 50–51. By permission of Regal Literary, Inc. as agent for *The Paris Review*. © 1966 by *The Paris Review*. Ginsberg's quotations from memory deviate from Blake's texts. Of distinguished writers who have admired or emulated Blake—among them D. G. Rossetti, A. C. Swinburne, W. B. Yeats, G. B. Shaw, James Joyce, Joyce Cary, Dylan Thomas, Theodore Roethke, Kenneth Patchen, Philip Pullman and even T. S. Eliot (1920, rpt. in his *Selected Essays* [1932], 317–22, and in our 1979 edition)—only Ginsberg claims to have experienced Blake's presence directly. The poet Alicia Ostriker discusses Blake's influence on Ginsberg in Bertholf and Levitt's *William Blake and the Moderns* (1982) and on her own life and work in *The Romantics and Us* (1990), ed. Gene W. Ruoff. Ginsberg's liner notes to his Verve recording (1970) with Peter Orlofsky are reprinted as "To Young or Old Listeners: Setting Blake's *Songs* to Music, and a Commentary on the *Songs, Blake Newsletter* 4 (1971), 98–103; other notable settings of *Songs* may be found in Donald Fitch, *Blake Set to Music* (1989). (Our own favorites are Greg Brown [Red Label, 1986] and William Bolcom [Naxos, 2004]). For visual artists inspired by Blake, see dagger note on p. 514.

simply into the ancient sky. The sky suddenly seemed very *ancient*. And this was the very ancient place that he was talking about, the sweet golden clime, I suddenly realized that *this* existence was *it!* And, that I was born in order to experience up to this very moment that I was having this experience, to realize what this was all about—in other words that this was the moment that I was born for. This initiation. Or this vision or this consciousness, of being alive unto myself, alive myself unto the Creator. As the son of the Creator—who loved me, I realized, or who responded to my desire, say. It was the same desire both ways.

Anyway my first thought was this was what I was born for, and second thought, never forget—never forget, never renig, never deny. Never deny the voice—no, never *forget* it, don't get lost mentally wandering in other spirit worlds or American or job worlds or advertising worlds or war worlds or earth worlds. But the spirit of the universe was what I was born to realize. What I was speaking about visually was, immediately, that the cornices in the old tenement building in Harlem across the back yard court had been carved very finely in 1890 or 1910. And were like the solidification of a great deal of intelligence and care and love also. So that I began noticing in every corner where I looked evidences of a living hand, even in the bricks, in the arrangement of each brick. Some hand placed them there— that some hand had placed the whole universe in front of me. That some hand had placed the sky. No, that's exaggerating—not that some hand had placed the sky but that the sky was the living blue hand itself. Or that God was in front of my eyes—existence itself was God. Well the formulations are like that—I didn't formulate it in exactly those terms, what I was seeing was a visionary thing, it was a lightness in my body . . . my body suddenly felt *light*, and a sense of cosmic consciousness, vibrations, understanding, awe, and wonder and surprise. And it was a sudden awakening into a totally deeper real universe than I'd been existing in. So, I'm trying to avoid generalizations about that sudden deeper real universe and keep it strictly to observations of phenomenal data, or a voice with a certain sound, the appearance of cornices, the appearance of the sky say, of the great blue hand, the living hand—to keep to images.

But anyway—the same . . . *petite sensation* recurred several minutes later, with the same voice, while reading the poem *The Sick Rose*. This time it was a slightly different sense-depth-mystic impression. Because *The Sick Rose*—you know I can't interpret the poem now, but it had a meaning—I mean I can interpret it on a verbal level, the sick rose is my self, or self, or the living body, sick because the mind, which is the worm "that flies in the night, in the howling storm," or Urizen, reason; Blake's character might be the one that's entered the body and is destroying it, or let us say death, the worm as being death, the natural process of death, some kind of mystical being of its own trying to come in and devour the body, the rose. Blake's drawing for it is complicated, it's a big drooping rose, drooping because it's dying, and there's a worm in it, and the worm is wrapped around a little sprite that's trying to get out of the mouth of the rose.

But anyway, I experienced *The Sick Rose*, with the voice of Blake reading it, as something that applied to the whole universe, like hearing the doom of the whole universe, and at the same time the inevitable beauty of doom. I can't remember now, except it was very beautiful and very awesome. But a little of it slightly scary, having to do with the knowledge of death—my death and also the death of being itself, and that was the great pain. So, like a prophecy, not only in human terms but a prophecy as if Blake had penetrated the very secret core of the *entire* universe and had come forth with some little magic formula statement in rhyme and rhythm that, if properly heard in the inner inner ear, would deliver you beyond the universe.

So then, the other poem that brought this on in the same day was *The Little Girl Lost*, where there was a repeated refrain,

> Do father, mother, *weep*,
> Where can Lyca *sleep?*
>
> How can Lyca *sleep*
> If her mother *weep?*
>
> 'If her heart does *ache*
> Then let Lyca *wake*;
> If my mother *sleep*,
> Lyca shall not *weep.*'

It's that hypnotic thing—and I suddenly realized that Lyca was me, or Lyca was the self; father, mother seeking Lyca, was God seeking, Father, the Creator; and "If her heart does ache / Then let Lyca wake"—wake to what? *Wake* meaning wake to the same awakeness I was just talking about—of existence in the entire universe. The total consciousness then, of the complete universe. Which is what Blake was talking about. In other words a breakthrough from ordinary habitual quotidian consciousness into consciousness that was really seeing all of heaven in a flower. Or what was it, eternity in a flower . . . heaven in a grain of sand. As I was seeing heaven in the cornice of the building. By heaven here I mean this imprint or concretization or living form, of an intelligent hand—the work of an intelligent hand, which still had the intelligence molded into it. The gargoyles on the Harlem cornices. What was interesting about the cornice was that there's cornices like that on every building, but I never noticed them before. And I never realized that they meant spiritual labor, to anyone—that somebody had labored to make a curve in a piece of tin—to make a cornucopia out of a piece of industrial tin. Not only that man, the workman, the artisan, but the architect had thought of it, the builder had paid for it, the smelter had *smelt* it, the miner had dug it up out of the earth, the earth had gone through eons preparing it.

* * * And God knows how many people made the moon. Or what spirits labored . . . to set fire to the sun. As Blake says, "When I look in the sun I don't see the rising sun I see a band of angels singing holy, holy, holy." Well his perception of the field of the sun is different from that of a man who just sees the sun sun, without any emotional relationship to it.

*   *   *

Then, I was walking around Columbia and I went in the Columbia bookstore and was reading Blake again, leafing over a book of Blake, I

think it was *The Human Abstract*: "Pity would be no more . . ." And suddenly it came over me in the bookstore again, and I was in the eternal
place *once more*, and I looked around at everybody's faces, and I saw all
these wild animals! Because there was a bookstore clerk there who I
hadn't paid much attention to, he was just a familiar fixture in the bookstore scene and everybody went in the bookstore every day like me,
because downstairs there was a café and upstairs there were all these
clerks that we were all familiar with—this guy had a very *long* face, you
know some people look like giraffes. So he looked kind of giraffish. He
had a kind of a long face with a long nose. I don't know what kind of sex
life he had, but he must have had something. But anyway I looked in his
face and I suddenly saw like a great tormented soul—and he had just
been somebody whom I'd regarded as perhaps a not particularly beautiful or sexy character, or lovely face, but you know someone familiar, and
perhaps a pleading cousin in the universe. But all of a sudden I realized
that *he* knew also, just like I knew. And that everybody in the bookstore
knew, and that they were all hiding it! They all had the consciousness, it
was like a great *un*conscious that was running between all of us that
everybody *was* completely conscious, but that the fixed expressions that
people have, the habitual expressions, the manners, the mode of talk, are
all masks hiding this consciousness. Because almost at that moment it
seemed that it would be too terrible if we communicated to each other
on a level of total consciousness and awareness each of the other—like
it would be too terrible—it would be the end of the bookstore, it would
be the end of civ . . . not civilization, but in other words the position that
everybody was in was *ridiculous*, everybody running around peddling
books to each other. Here in the universe! Passing money over the
counter, wrapping books in bags and guarding the door, you know, steal-
ing books, and the people sitting up making accountings on the upper
floor there, and people worrying about their exams walking through the
bookstore, and all the millions of thoughts the people had you know, that
I'm worrying about, whether they're going to get laid or whether anybody
loves them, about their mothers dying of cancer or you know the complete death awareness that everybody has continuously with them all the
time—all of a sudden revealed to me at once in the faces of the people,
and they all looked like horrible grotesque masks, grotesque because *hiding* the knowledge from each other. Having a habitual conduct and forms
to prescribe, forms to fulfill. Roles to play. But the main insight I had at
that time was that everybody knew. Everybody knew completely everything. Knew completely everything in the terms which I was talking
about.

     * * * The twisted faces of all those people, the faces were twisted by
rejection. And hatred of self, finally. The internalization of that rejection.
And finally disbelief in that shining self. Disbelief in that infinite self. Partly
because the particular . . . partly because the *awareness* that we all carry is
too often painful, because the experience of rejection and lacklove and cold
war—I mean the whole cold war is the imposition of a vast mental barrier
on everybody, a vast anti-natural psyche. A hardening, a shutting off of the
perception of desire and tenderness which everybody *knows* and which is
the very structure of . . . the atom! Structure of the human body and

organism. That desire built in. Blocked. "Where the youth pined away with desire, the Virgin shrouded in snow." Or as Blake says, "On every face I see, I meet / marks of weakness, marks of woe." So what I was thinking in the bookstore was the marks of weakness, marks of woe. Which you can just look around and look at anybody's face right next to you now always—you can see it in the way the mouth is pursed, you can see it in the way the eyes blink, you can see it in the way the gaze is fixed down at the matches. It's the self-consciousness which is a substitute for communication with the outside. This consciousness pushed back into the self and thinking of how it will hold its face and eyes and hands in order to make a mask to hide the flow that is going on. Which it's aware of, which everybody is aware of really! So let's say, shyness. Fear. Fear of like total feeling, really, total being, is what it is.

So the problem then was, having attained realization, how to safely manifest it and communicate it. Of course there was the old Zen thing, when the sixth patriarch handed down the little symbolic oddments and ornaments and books and bowls, stained bowls too . . . when the *fifth* patriarch handed them down to the sixth patriarch he told him to hide them and don't tell anybody you're patriarch because it's dangerous, they'll kill you. So there was that immediate danger. It's taken me all these years to manifest it and work it out in a way that's materially communicable to people. Without scaring them or me. Also movements of history and breaking down the civilization. To break down everybody's masks and roles sufficiently so that everybody has to face the universe *and* the possibility of the sick rose coming true and the atom bomb. So it was an immediate Messianic thing. Which seems to be becoming more and more justified. And more and more reasonable in terms of the existence that we're living.

So. Next time it happened was about a week later walking along in the evening on a circular path around what's now I guess the garden or field in the middle of Columbia University, by the library. I started invoking the spirit, consciously trying to get another depth perception of cosmos. And suddenly it began occurring again, like a sort of breakthrough again, but this time—this was the last time in that period—it was the same depth of consciousness or the same cosmical awareness but suddenly it was not blissful at all but it was *frightening*. Some like real serpent-fear entering the sky. The sky was not a blue hand anymore but like a hand of death coming down on me—some really scary presence, it was almost as if I saw God again except God was the Devil. The consciousness itself was *so* vast, much more vast than any idea of it I'd had or any experience I'd had, that it was not even human any more—and was in a sense a threat, because I was going to die into that inhuman ultimately.

*   *   *

* * * There was a cycle that began with the Blake vision which ended on the train in Kyoto when I realized that to attain the depth of consciousness that I was seeking when I was talking about the Blake vision, that in order to attain it I had to cut myself off from the Blake vision and renounce it. Otherwise I'd be hung up on a memory of an experience. Which is not the actual awareness of now, now.

NORTHROP FRYE

Blake's Treatment of the Archetype†

The reader of Blake soon becomes familiar with the words "innocence" and "experience." The world of experience is the world that adults live in while they are awake. It is a very big world, and a lot of it seems to be dead, but still it makes its own kind of sense. When we stare at it, it stares unwinkingly back, and the changes that occur in it are, on the whole, orderly and predictable changes. This quality in the world that reassures us we call law. Sitting in the middle of the lawful world is the society of awakened adults. This society consists of individuals who apparently have agreed to put certain restraints on themselves. So we say that human society is also controlled by law. Law, then, is the basis both of reason and of society: without it there is no happiness, and our philosophers tell us that they really do not know which is more splendid, the law of the starry heavens outside us, or the moral law within. True, there was a time when we were children and took a different view of life. In childhood happiness seemed to be based, not on law and reason, but on love, protection, and peace. But we can see now that such a view of life was an illusion derived from an excess of economic security. As Isaac Watts says, in a song of innocence which is thought to have inspired Blake:

> Sleep, my babe; thy food and raiment,
> House and home, thy friends provide;
> All without thy care or payment:
> All thy wants are well supplied.

And after all, from the adult point of view, the child is not so innocent as he looks. He is actually a little bundle of anarchic will, whose desires take no account of either the social or the natural order. As he grows up and enters the world of law, his illegal desires can no longer be tolerated even by himself, and so they are driven underground into the world of the dream, to be joined there by new desires, mainly sexual in origin. In the dream, a blind, unreasoning, childish will is still at work revenging itself on experience and rearranging it in terms of desire. It is a great comfort to know that this world, in which we are compelled to spend about a third of our time, is unreal, and can never displace the world of experience in which reason predominates over passion, order over chaos, Classical values over Romantic ones, the solid over the gaseous, and the cool over the hot.

The world of law, stretching from the starry heavens to the moral conscience, is the domain of Urizen in Blake's symbolism. It sits on a volcano in which the rebellious Titan Orc, the spirit of passion, lies bound, writhing and struggling to get free. Each of these spirits is Satanic or devilish to the other. While we dream, Urizen, the principle of reality, is the censor, or, as Blake calls him, the accuser, a smug and grinning hypocrite, an impotent

---

† From *English Institute Essays: 1950*, ed. Alan S. Downer (Columbia University Press, 1951), pp. 170–196. By permission of Victoria University in the University of Toronto. Cf. *The Collected Works of Northrop Frye*, ed. Alvin A. Lee (1996–), vol. 16, ed. Angela Esterhammer (University of Toronto Press, 2005), pp. 190–206. Frye's Olympian archetypal overview—often challenged in feminist, new historicist, deconstructive, and other more recent work—has profoundly influenced Blake studies since the appearance of *Fearful Symmetry* in 1947 (see "Selected Bibliography").

old man, the caricature that the child in us makes out of the adult world that thwarts him. But as long as we are awake, Orc, the lawless pleasure principle, is an evil dragon bound under the conscious world in chains, and we all hope he will stay there.

The dream world is, however, not quite securely bound: every so often it breaks loose and projects itself on society in the form of war. It seems odd that we should keep plunging with great relief into moral holidays of aggression in which robbery and murder become virtues instead of crimes. It almost suggests that keeping our desires in leash and seeing that others do likewise is a heavy and sooner or later an intolerable strain. On a still closer view, even the difference between war and law begins to blur. The social contract, which from a distance seems a reasonable effort of cooperation, looks closer up like an armed truce founded on passion, in which the real purpose of law is to defend by force what has been snatched in self-will. Plainly, we cannot settle the conflict of Orc and Urizen by siding with one against the other, still less by pretending that either of them is an illusion. We must look for a third factor in human life, one which neets the requirements of both the dream and the reality.

This third factor, called Los by Blake, might provisionally be called work, or constructive activity. All such work operates in the world of experience: it takes account of law and of our waking ideas of reality. Work takes the energy which is wasted in war or thwarted in dreams and sets it free to act in experience. And as work cultivates land and makes farms and gardens out of jungle and wilderness, as it domesticates animals and builds cities, it becomes increasingly obvious that work is the realization of a dream and that this dream is descended from the child's lost vision of a world where the environment is the home.

The worker, then, does not call the world of experience real because he perceives it out of a habit acquired from his ancestors: it is real to him only as the material cause of his work. And the world of dreams is not unreal, but the formal cause: it dictates the desirable human shape which the work assumes. Work, therefore, by realizing in experience the child's and the dreamer's worlds, indicates what there is about each that is genuinely innocent. When we say that a child is in the state of innocence, we do not mean that he is sinless or harmless, but that he is able to assume a coherence, a simplicity and a kindliness in the world that adults have lost and wish they could regain. When we dream, we are, whatever we put into the dream, revolting against experience and creating another world, usually one we like better. Whatever in childhood or the dream is delivered and realized by work is innocent; whatever is suppressed or distorted by experience becomes selfish or vicious. "He who desires but acts not, breeds pestilence."

Work begins by imposing a human form on nature, for "Where man is not, nature is barren."[1] But in society work collides with the cycle of law and war. A few seize all its benefits and become idlers, the work of the rest is wasted in supporting them, and so work is perverted into drudgery. "God made Man happy & Rich, but the Subtil made the innocent, Poor."[2] Neither idleness nor drudgery can be work: real work is the creative act of a free man, and wherever real work is going on it is humanizing society as well as

---

1. *Marriage of Heaven and Hell* 10, Proverb 68. The previous paragraph concludes with *Marriage* 7, Proverb 5. [*editors' note*].
2. Marginalia to Watson [*editors' note*].

nature. The work that, projected on nature, forms civilization, becomes, when projected on society, prophecy, a vision of complete human freedom and equality. Such a vision is a revolutionary force in human life, destroying all the social barriers founded on idleness and all the intellectual ones founded on ignorance.

So far we have spoken only of what seems naturally and humanly possible, of what can be accomplished by human nature. But if we confine the conception of work to what now seems possible, we are still judging the dream by the canons of waking reality. In other words, we have quite failed to distinguish work from law, Los from Urizen, and are back where we started. The real driving power of civilization and prophecy is not the mature mind's sophisticated and cautious adaptations of the child's or the dreamer's desires: it comes from the original and innocent form of those desires, with all their reckless disregard of the lessons of experience.

The creative root of civilization and prophecy can only be art, which deals not only with the possible, but with "probable impossibilities"[3]—it is interesting to see Blake quoting Aristotle's phrase in one of his marginalia. And just as the controlling idea of civilization is the humanizing of nature, and the controlling idea of prophecy the emancipation of man, so the controlling idea of art, the source of them both, must be the simultaneous vision of both. This is apocalypse, the complete transformation of both nature and human nature into the same form. "Less than All cannot satisfy Man"; the child in us who cries for the moon will never stop crying until the moon is his plaything, until we are delivered from the tyranny of time, space, and death, from the remoteness of a gigantic nature and from our own weakness and selfishness. Man cannot be free until he is everywhere: at the center of the universe, like the child, and at the circumference of the universe, like the dreamer. Such an apocalypse is entirely impossible under the conditions of experience that we know, and could only take place in the eternal and infinite context that is given it by religion. In fact, Blake's view of art could almost be defined as the attempt to realize the religious vision in human society. Such religion has to be sharply distinguished from all forms of religion which have been kidnapped by the cycle of law and war, and have become capable only of reinforcing the social contract or of inspiring crusades.

When we say that the goal of human work can only be accomplished in eternity, many people would infer that this involves renouncing all practicable improvement of human status in favor of something which by hypothesis, remains forever out of man's reach. We make this inference because we confuse the eternal with the indefinite: we are so possessed by the categories of time and space that we can hardly think of eternity and infinity except as endless time and space, respectively. But the home of time, so to speak, the only part of time that man can live in, is now; and the home of space is here. In the world of experience there is no such time as now; the present never quite exists, but is hidden somewhere between a past that no longer exists and a future that does not yet exist. The mature man does not know where "here" is: he can draw a circle around himself and say that "here" is inside it, but he cannot locate anything except a "there." In both time and space man is being continually excluded from his own home. The dreamer, whose space is inside his mind, has a better

---

3. Marginalia to Watson. Frye next quotes *There Is No Natural Religion* [6] V. [*editors' note*].

notion of where "here" is, and the child, who is not yet fully conscious of the iron chain of memory that binds his ego to time and space, still has some capacity for living in the present. It is to this perspective that man returns when his conception of "reality" begins to acquire some human meaning.

> The Sky is an immortal Tent built by the Sons of Los:
> And every Space that a Man views around his dwelling-place
> Standing on his own roof or in his garden on a mount
> Of twenty-five cubits in height, such space is his Universe:
> And on its verge the Sun rises & sets, the Clouds bow
> To meet the flat Earth & the Sea in such an order'd Space:
> The Starry heavens reach no further, but here bend and set
> On all sides, & the two Poles turn on their Valves of gold . . . [4]

If the vision of innocence is taken out of its eternal and infinite context, the real here and now, and put inside time, it becomes either a myth of a Golden Age or a Paradise lost in the past, or a hope which is yet to be attained in the future, or both. If it is put inside space, it must be somewhere else, presumably in the sky. It is only these temporal and spatial perversions of the innocent vision that really do snatch it out of man's grasp. Because the innocent vision is so deep down in human consciousness and is subject to so much distortion, repression, and censorship, we naturally tend, when we project it on the outer world, to put it as far off in time and space as we can get it. But what the artist has to reveal, as a guide for the work of civilization and prophecy, is the form of the world as it would be if we could live in it here and now.

Innocence and experience are the middle two of four possible states. The state of experience Blake calls Generation, and the state of innocence, the potentially creative world of dreams and childhood, Beulah. Beyond Beulah is Eden, the world of the apocalypse in which innocence and experience have become the same thing, and below Generation is Ulro, the world as it is when no work is being done, the world where dreams are impotent and waking life haphazard. Eden and Ulro are, respectively, Blake's heaven or unfallen world and his hell or fallen world. Eden is the world of the creator and the creature, Beulah the world of the lover and the beloved, Generation the world of the subject and the object, and Ulro the world of the ego and the enemy, or the obstacle. This is, of course, one world, looked at in four different ways. The four ways represent the four moods or states in which art is created: the apocalyptic mood of Eden, the idyllic mood of Beulah, the elegiac mood of Generation, and satiric mood of Ulro. These four moods are the tonalities of Blake's expression; every poem of his regularly resolves on one of them.

For Blake the function of art is to reveal the human or intelligible form of the world, and it sees the other three states in relation to that form. This fact is the key to Blake's conception of imagery, the pattern of which I have tried to simplify by a table.

---

4. *Milton* 31/29:4–11 [editors' note].

EXPERIENCE		CATEGORY	INNOCENCE	
Individual Form	*Collective Form*		*Collective Form*	*Individual Form*
sky-god (Nobodaddy)	aristocracy of gods	(1) Divine	human powers	incarnate God (Jesus)
a) leader and high priest (Caiaphas)	tyrants and victims	(2) Human	community	*a*) one man (Albion)
b) harlot (Rahab)				*b*) bride (Jerusalem)
dragon (Covering Cherub)	beasts of prey (tiger, leviathan)	(3) Animal	flock of sheep	one lamb (Bowlahoola)
tree of mystery	forest, wilderness (Entuthon Benython)	(4) Vegetable	garden or park (Allamanda)	tree of life
a) opaque furnace or brick kilns	*a*) city of destruction (Sodom, Babylon, Egypt)	(5) Mineral	city, temple (Golgonooza)	living stone
b) "Stone of Night"	*b*) ruins, caves			
(not given)	salt lake or dead sea (Udan Adan)	(6) Chaotic	fourfold river of life	"Globule of Blood"

Let us take the word "image" in its vulgar sense, which is good enough just now, of a verbal or pictorial replica of a physical object. For Blake the real form of the object is what he calls its "human form." In Ulro, the world with no human work in it, the mineral kingdom consists mainly of shapeless rocks lying around at random. When man comes into the world, he tries to make cities, buildings, roads, and sculptures out of this mineral kingdom. Such human artifacts therefore constitute the intelligible form of the mineral world, the mineral world as human desire would like to see it. Similarly, the "natural" or unworked form of the vegetable world is a forest, a heath or a wilderness; its human and intelligible form is that of the garden, the grove, or the park, the last being the original meaning of the word Paradise. The natural form of the animal world consists of beasts of prey: its human form is a society of domesticated animals of which the flock of sheep is the most commonly employed symbol. The city, the garden and the sheepfold are thus the human forms of the mineral, vegetable, and animal kingdoms, respectively. Blake calls these archetypes Golgonooza, Allamanda and Bowlahoola, and identifies them with the head, heart, and bowels of the total human form. Below the world of solid substance is a chaotic or liquid world, and the human form of that is the river or circulating body of fresh water.

Each of these human forms has a contrasting counterpart in Ulro, the world of undeveloped nature and regressive humanity. To the city which is the home of the soul or City of God, the fallen world opposes the city of destruction which is doomed through the breakdown of work described by Ezekiel in a passage quoted by Blake as "pride, fullness of bread and abundance of idleness." Against the image of the sheep in the pasture, we have the image of the forest inhabited by menacing beasts like the famous tiger, the blasted heath or waste land full of monsters, or the desert with its fiery serpents. To the river which is the water of life the fallen world opposes the image of the devouring sea and the dragons and leviathans in its depths. Blake usually calls the fallen city Babylon, the forest Entuthon Benython, and the dead sea or salt lake Udan Adan. Labyrinths and mazes are the only patterns of Ulro; images of highways and paths made straight belong to the world informed with intelligence.

The essential principle of the fallen world appears to be discreteness or opacity. Whatever we see in it we see as a self-enclosed entity, unlike all others. When we say that two things are identical, we mean that they are very similar; in other words "identity" is a meaningless word in ordinary experience. Hence in Ulro, and even in Generation, all classes or societies are aggregates of similar but separate individuals. But when man builds houses out of stones, and cities out of houses, it becomes clear that the real or intelligible form of a thing includes its relation to its environment as well as its self-contained existence. This environment is its own larger "human form." The stones that make a city do not cease to be stones, but they cease to be separate stones: their purpose, shape, and function is identical with that of the city as a whole. In the human world, as in the work of art, the individual thing is there, and the total form which gives it meaning is there: what has vanished is the shapeless collection or mass of similar things. This is what Blake means when he says that in the apocalypse all human forms are "identified." The same is true of the effect of work on human society. In a completely human society man would not lose his individuality, but he would lose his separate and isolated ego, what Blake calls his Selfhood. The prophetic vision of freedom and equality thus cannot stop at the Generation level of a Utopia, which means an orderly molecular aggregate of individuals existing in some future time. Such a vision does not capture, though it may adumbrate, the real form of society, which can only be a larger human body. This means literally the body of one man, though not of a separate man.

Everywhere in the human world we find that the Ulro distinction between the singular and the plural has broken down. The real form of human society is the body of one man; the flock of sheep is the body of one lamb; the garden is the body of one tree, the so-called tree of life. The city is the body of one building or temple, a house of many mansions, and the building itself is the body of one stone, a glowing and fiery precious stone, the unfallen stone of alchemy which assimilates everything else to itself, Blake's grain of sand which contains the world.

The second great principle of Ulro is the principle of hierarchy or degree which produces the great chain of being. In the human world there is no chain of being: all aspects of existence are equal as well as identical. The one man is also the one lamb, and the body and blood of the animal form are the bread and wine which are the human forms of the vegetable world. The tree of life is the upright vertebrate form of man; the living stone, the glowing transparent furnace, is the furnace of heart and lungs and bowels in the animal body. The river of life is the blood that circulates within that body. Eden, which according to Blake was a city as well as a garden, had a fourfold river, but no sea, for the river remained inside Paradise, which was the body of one man. England is an island in the sea, like St. John's Patmos; the human form of England is Atlantis, the island which has replaced the sea. Again, where there is no longer any difference between society and the individual, there can hardly be any difference between society and marriage or between a home and a wife or child. Hence Jerusalem in Blake is "A City, yet a Woman," and at the same time the vision of innocent human society.

On the analogy of the chain of being, it is natural for man to invent an imaginary category of gods above him, and he usually locates them in what is above him in space, that is, the sky. The more developed society is, the more clearly man realizes that a society of gods would have to be, like the society of man, the body of one God. Eventually he realizes that the intelligible forms of man and of whatever is above man on the chain of being must be identical. The identity of God and man is for Blake the whole of Christianity: the adoration of a superhuman God he calls natural religion, because the source of it is remote and unconquered nature. In other words, the superhuman God is the deified accuser or censor of waking experience, whose function it is to discourage further work. Blake calls this God Nobodaddy, and curses and reviles him so much that some have inferred that he was inspired by an obscure psychological compulsion to attack the Fatherhood of God. Blake is doing nothing of the kind, as a glance at the last plate[s] of *Jerusalem* will soon show: he is merely insisting that man cannot approach the superhuman aspect of God except through Christ, the God who is Man. If man attempts to approach the Father directly, as Milton, for instance, does in a few unlucky passages in *Paradise Lost*, all he will ever get is Nobodaddy. Theologically, the only unusual feature of Blake is not his attitude to the person of the Father, but his use of what is technically known as pre-existence: the doctrine that the humanity of Christ is coeternal with his divinity.

There is nothing in the Ulro world corresponding to the identity of the individual and the total form in the unfallen one. But natural religion, being a parody of real religion, often develops a set of individual symbols corresponding to the lamb, the tree of life, the glowing stone, and the rest. This consolidation of Ulro symbols Blake calls Druidism. Man progresses toward a free and equal community, and regresses toward tyranny; and as the human form of the community is Christ, the one God who is one Man, so the human form of tyranny is the isolated hero or inscrutable leader with his back to an aggregate of followers, or the priest of a veiled temple with an imaginary sky-god supposed to be behind the veil. The Biblical prototypes of this leader and priest are Moses and Aaron. Against the tree of life we have what Blake calls the tree of mystery, the barren fig tree, the dead tree of the cross, Adam's tree of knowledge, with its forbidden fruit corresponding to the fruits of healing on the tree of life. Against the fiery precious stone, the bodily form in which John saw God "like a jasper and a sardine stone," we have the furnace, the prison of heat without light which is the form of the opaque warm-blooded body in the world of frustration, or the stone of Druidical sacrifice like the one that Hardy associates with Tess. Against the animal body of the lamb, we have the figure that Blake calls, after Ezekiel, the Covering Cherub, who represents a great many things, the unreal world of gods, human tyranny and exploitation, and the remoteness of the sky, but whose animal form is that of the serpent or dragon wrapped around the forbidden tree. The dragon, being both monstrous and fictitious, is the best animal representative of the bogies inspired by human inertia: the Book of Revelation calls it "the beast that was, and is not, and yet is."

Once we have understood Blake's scheme of imagery, we have broken the back of one of the main obstacles to reading the prophecies: the difficulty in grasping their narrative structure. Narrative is normally the first thing we look for in trying to read a long poem, but Blake's poems are presented as a series of engraved plates, and the mental process of following a narrative sequence is, especially in the later poems, subordinated to a process of comprehending an interrelated pattern of images and ideas. The plate in Blake's epics has a function rather similar to that of the stanza with its final alexandrine in *The Faerie Queene*: it brings the narrative to a full stop and forces the reader to try to build up from the narrative his own reconstruction of the author's meaning. Blake thinks almost entirely in terms of two narrative structures. One of these is the narrative of history, the cycle of law and war, the conflict of Orc and Urizen, which in itself has no end and no point and may be called the tragic or historical vision of life. The other is the comic vision of the apocalypse or work of Los, the clarification of the mind which enables one to grasp the human form of the world. But the latter is not concerned with temporal sequence and is consequently not so much a real narrative as a dialectic.

The tragic narrative is the story of how the dream world escapes into experience and is gradually imprisoned by experience. This is the main theme of heroic or romantic poetry and is represented in Blake by Orc. Orc is first shown us, in the "Preludium" to *America*, as the libido of the dream, a boy lusting for a dim maternal figure and bitterly hating an old man who keeps him in chains. Then we see him as the conquering hero of romance, killing dragons and sea monsters, ridding the barren land of its impotent aged kings, freeing imprisoned women, and giving new hope to men. Finally we see him subside into the world of darkness again from whence he emerged, as the world of law slowly recovers its balance. His rise and decline has the rotary movement of the solar and seasonal cycles, and like them is a part of the legal machinery of nature.

Blake has a strong moral objection to all heroic poetry that does not see heroism in its proper tragic context, and even when it does, he is suspicious of it. For him the whole conception of κλέα ἀνδῶν[5] as being in itself, without regard to the larger consequences of brave deeds, a legitimate theme for poetry, has been completely outmoded. It has been outmoded, for one thing, by Christianity, which has brought to the theme of the heroic act a radically new conception of what a hero is and what an act is. The true hero is the man who, whether as thinker, fighter, artist, martyr, or ordinary worker, helps in achieving the apocalyptic vision of art; and an act is anything that has a real relation to that achievement. Events such as the battle of Agincourt or the retreat from Moscow are not really heroic, because they are not really acts: they are part of the purposeless warfare of the state

---

5. *Klea andon*: famous deeds of heroes [*editors' note*]. Frye's next quotation is from *[Yah] & His Two Sons*.

of nature and are not progressing towards a better kind of humanity. So Blake is interested in Orc only when his heroism appears to coincide with something of potentially apocalyptic importance, like the French or American revolutions.

For the rest, he keeps Orc strictly subordinated to his main theme of the progressive work of Los, the source of which is found in prophetic scriptures, especially, of course, the Bible. Comprehensive as his view of art is, Blake does not exactly say that the Bible is a work of art: he says "The Old & New Testaments are the Great Code of Art." The Bible tells the artist what the function of art is and what his creative powers are trying to accomplish. Apart from its historical and political applications, Blake's symbolism is almost entirely Biblical in origin, and the subordination of the heroic Orc theme to the apocalyptic Los theme follows the Biblical pattern.

The tragic vision of life has the rhythm of the individual's organic cycle: it rises in the middle and declines at the end. The apocalyptic theme turns the tragic vision inside out. The tragedy comes in the middle, with the eclipse of the innocent vision, and the story ends with the re-establishment of the vision. Blake's major myth thus breaks into two parts, a Genesis and an Exodus. The first part accounts for the existence of the world of experience in terms of the myths of creation and fall. Blake sees no difference between creation and fall, between establishing the Ulro world and placing man in it. How man fell out of a city and garden is told twice in Genesis, once of Adam and once of Israel—Israel, who corresponds to Albion in Blake's symbolism, being both a community and a single man. The Book of Genesis ends with Israel in Egypt, the city of destruction. In the Book of Exodus we find the state of experience described in a comprehensive body of Ulro symbols. There is the fallen civilization of Egypt, destroyed by the plagues which its own tyranny has raised, the devouring sea, the desert with its fiery serpents, the leader and the priest, the invisible sky god who confirms their despotic power, and the labyrinthine wanderings of a people who have nothing but law and are unable to work. Society has been reduced to a frightened rabble following a leader who obviously has no notion of where he is going. In front of it is the Promised Land with its milk and honey, but all the people can see are enemies, giants, and mysterious terrors. From there on the story splits in two. The histories go on with the Orc or heroic narrative of how the Israelites conquered Canaan and proceeded to run through another cycle from bondage in Egypt to bondage in Babylon. But in the prophecies, as they advance from social criticism to apocalyptic, the Promised Land is the city and garden that all human effort is trying to reach, and its conqueror can only be the Messiah or true form of man.

The New Testament has the same structure as the Old. In the life of Jesus the story of the Exodus is repeated. Jesus is carried off to Egypt by a father whose name is Joseph, Herod corresponds to Pharaoh, and the massacre of the innocents to the attempts to exterminate the Hebrew children. The organizing of Christianity around twelve disciples corresponds to the organizing of the religion of Israel among twelve tribes, the forty days wandering of Jesus in the desert to the forty years of Israel, the crucifixion to the lifting of the brazen serpent on the pole, and the resurrection to the invasion of Canaan by Joshua, who has the same name as Jesus. From there on the New Testament splits into a historical section describing the beginning of a new Christian cycle, which is reaching its Babylonian phase in Blake's own time, and a prophetic section, the Book of Revelation, which deals with what it describes, in a phrase which has fascinated so many apocalyptic thinkers from Joachim of Floris to Blake, as the "everlasting gospel," the story of Jesus told not historically as an event in the past, but visually as a real presence.

The characters of Blake's poems, Orc, Los, Urizen, Vala, and the rest, take shape in accordance with Blake's idea of the real act. No word in the language contains a greater etymological lie than the word "individual." The so-called undivided man is a battleground of conflicting forces, and the appearance of consistency in his behavior derives from the force that usually takes the lead. To get at the real elements of human character, one needs to get past the individual into the dramatis personae that make up his behavior. Blake's analysis of the individual shows a good many parallels with more recent analyses, especially those of Freud and Jung. The scheme of the Four Zoas is strikingly Freudian, and the contrast of the Orc and Los themes in Blake is very like the contrast between Jung's early book on the libido and his later study of the symbols of individuation. Jung's anima and persona are closely analogous to Blake's emanation and spectre, and his counsellor and shadow seem to have some relation to Blake's Los and Spectre of Urthona.

But a therapeutic approach will still relate any such analysis primarily to the individual. In Blake anything that is a significant act of individual behavior is also a significant act of social behavior. Orc, the libido, produces revolution in society: Vala, the elusive anima, produces the social code of *Frauendienst*;[6] Urizen, the moral censor, produces the religion of the externalized God. "We who dwell on Earth can do nothing of ourselves," says Blake: "every thing is conducted by Spirits." Man performs no act as an individual: all his acts are determined by an inner force which is also a social and historical force, and they derive their significance from their relation to the total human act, restoration of the innocent world. John Doe does nothing as John Doe: he eats and sleeps in the spirit of Orc the Polypus: he obeys laws in the spirit of Urizen the conscience; he loses his temper in the spirit of Tharmas the destroyer; and he dies in the spirit of Satan the death-impulse.

Furthermore, as the goal of life is the humanization of nature, there is a profound similarity between human and natural behavior, which in the apocalypse becomes identity. It is a glimmering of this fact that has produced the god, the personalized aspect of nature, and a belief in gods gradually builds the sense of an omnipotent personal community out of nature. As long as these gods remain on the other side of nature, they are merely the shadows of superstition: when they are seen to be the real elements of human life as well, we have discovered the key to all symbolism in art. Blake's Tharmas, the "id" of the individual and the stampeding mob of society, is also the god of the sea, Poseidon the earth shaker. His connection with the sea is not founded on resemblance or association, but, like the storm scene in *King Lear*, on an ultimate identity of human rage and natural tempest.

In the opening plates of *Jerusalem* Blake has left us a poignant account of one such struggle of contending forces within himself, between his creative

---

6. Service to women. The next quotation is from "To the Public," *Jerusalem* 3 [editors' note].

powers and his egocentric will. He saw the Industrial Revolution and the great political and cultural changes that came with it, and he realized that something profoundly new and disquieting was coming into the world, something with unlimited possibilities for good or for evil, which it would tax all his powers to interpret. And so his natural desire to make his living as an engraver and a figure in society collided with an overwhelming impulse to tell the whole poetic truth about what he saw. The latter force won, and dictated its terms accordingly. He was not allowed to worry about his audience. He revised, but was not allowed to decorate or stylize, only to say what had to be said. He was not allowed the double talk of the sophisticated poet, who can address several levels of readers at once by using familiar conceptions ambiguously. Nothing was allowed him but a terrifying concentration of his powers of utterance.

What finally emerged, out of one of the hottest poetic crucibles of modern times, was a poetry which consisted almost entirely in the articulation of archetypes. By an archetype I mean an element in a work of literature, whether a character, an image, a narrative formula, or an idea, which can be assimilated to a larger unifying category. The existence of such a category depends on the existence of a unified conception of art. Blake began his prophecies with a powerfully integrated theory of the nature, structure, function, and meaning of art, and all the symbolic units of his poetry, his moods, his images, his narratives and his characters, form archetypes of that theory. Given his premises about art, everything he does logically follows. His premises may be wrong, but there are two things which may make us hesitate to call them absurd. One is their comprehensiveness and consistency: if the Bible is the code of art, Blake seems to provide something of a code of modern art, both in his structure of symbols and in his range of ideas. The other is their relationship to earlier traditions of criticism. Theories of poetry and of archetypes seem to belong to criticism rather than to poetry itself, and when I speak of Blake's treatment of the archetype I imply that Blake is a poet of unique interest to critics like ourselves. The Biblical origin of his symbolism and his apocalyptic theory of perception have a great deal in common with the theory of anagoge which underlies the poetry of Dante, the main structure of which survived through the Renaissance at least as late as Milton. Blake had the same creative powers as other great poets, but he made a very unusual effort to drag them up to consciousness, and to do deliberately what most poets prefer to do instinctively. It is possible that what impelled him to do this was the breakdown of a tradition of criticism which could have answered a very important question. Blake did not need the answer, but we do.

The question relates to the application of Blake's archetypes to the criticism of poetry as a whole. The papers delivered to this body of scholars are supposed to deal with general issues of criticism rather than with pure research. Now pure research is, up to a point, a coordinated and systematic form of study, and the question arises whether general criticism could also acquire a systematic form. In other words, is criticism a mere aggregate of research and comment and generalization, or is it, considered as a whole, an intelligible structure of knowledge? If the latter, there must be a quality in literature which enables it to be so, an order of words corresponding to the order of nature which makes the natural sciences intelligible. If criticism is more than aggregated commentary, literature must be somewhat more than an aggregate of poems and plays and novels: it must possess some kind of total form which criticism can in some measure grasp and expound.

It is on this question that the possibility of literary archetypes depends. If there is no total structure of literature, and no intelligible form to criticism as a whole, then there is no such thing as an archetype. The only organizing principle so far discovered in literature is chronology, and consequently all our larger critical categories are concerned with sources and direct transmission. But every student of literature has, whether consciously or not, picked up thousands of resemblances, analogies, and parallels in his reading where there is no question of direct transmission. If there are no archetypes, then these must be merely private associations, and the connections among them must be arbitrary and fanciful. But if criticism makes sense, and literature makes sense, then the mental processes of the cultivated reader may be found to make sense too.

The difficulty of a "private mythology" is not peculiar to Blake: every poet has a private mythology, his own formation of symbols. His mythology is a cross-section of his life, and the critic, like the biographer, has the job of making sure that what was private to the poet shall be public to everyone else. But, having no theory of archetypes, we do not know how to proceed. Blake supplies us with a few leading principles which may guide us in analyzing the symbolic formation of poets and isolating the archetypal elements in them. Out of such a study the structure of literature may slowly begin to emerge, and criticism, in interpreting that structure, may take its rightful place among the major disciplines of modern thought. There is, of course, the possibility that the study of Blake is a long and tortuous blind alley, but those who are able to use Blake's symbols as a calculus for all their criticism will not be much inclined to consider it.[7]

The question that we have just tried to answer, however, is not the one that the student of Blake most frequently meets. The latter question runs in effect: you may show that Blake had one of the most powerful minds in the modern world, that his thought is staggeringly comprehensive and consistent, that his insight was profound, his mood exalted, and his usefulness to critics unlimited. But surely all this profits a poet nothing if he does not preserve the hieratic decorum of conventional poetic utterance. And how are we to evaluate an utterance which is now lucid epigram and now a mere clashing of symbols, now disciplined and lovely verse and now a rush of prosy gabble? Whatever it is, is it really poetry or really great and good poetry? Well, probably not, in terms of what criticism now knows, or thinks it knows, about the canons of beauty and the form of literary expression.

Othello was merely a bloody farce in terms of what the learned and acute Thomas Rymer knew about drama. Rymer was perfectly right in his own terms; he is like the people who say that Blake was mad. One cannot refute them; one merely loses interest in their conception of sanity. And critics may be as right about Blake as Rymer was about Shakespeare, and still be just as wrong. We do not yet know whether literature and criticism are forms or aggregates: we know almost nothing about archetypes or about any of the great critical problems connected with them. In Dante's day

7. In this passage Frye adumbrates ideas developed in his *Anatomy of Criticism* (Princeton: Princeton University Press, 1957) [editors' note].

critics did know something about the symbols of the Bible, but we have
made little effort to recover that knowledge. We do not know very much
even about genres: we do not know whether Blake's "prophecy" form is a
real genre or not, and we certainly do not know how to treat it if it is. I leave
the question of Blake's language in more competent hands, but after all,
even the poets are only beginning to assimilate contemporary speech, and
when the speech of *Jerusalem* becomes so blunt and colloquial that Blake
himself calls it prosaic, do critics really know whether it is too prosaic to be
poetic, or even whether such an antithesis exists at all? I may be speaking
only of myself, for criticism today is full of confident value-judgments, on
Blake and on everyone else, implying a complete understanding of all such
mysteries. But I wonder if these are really critical judgments, or if they are
merely the aberrations of the history of taste. I suspect that a long course
of patient and detailed study lies ahead of us before we really know much
about the critical problems which the study of Blake raises, and which have
to be reckoned with in making any value-judgment on him. Then we shall
understand the poets, including Blake, much better, and I am not concerned with what the results of that better understanding will be.

W. J. T. MITCHELL

Dangerous Blake†

The future of Blake studies is likely to be quite different from its past. We
have gone through, roughly, three periods in the reception of Blake, and are
about to enter the fourth. The first period was that of preservation of basic
documents, a period of biographical and archival interests, often rather private or amateur, in which Blake was treated as something between a house-
hold god and a familiar spirit. The second phase was that of appropriation
and interpretation, Blake's employment by writers like Joyce, Yeats, and
Lawrence as a precursor for modernism, a progenitor in an avant garde
canon of unjustly neglected works. The third phase, which we are still in, has
been the professionalization of Blake studies, the disinterested, technical justification of his work, his assimilation into the canon of mainstream English
literature (the line of Chaucer, Spenser, and Milton) and the demonstration
that his work conforms to what I will call (very loosely) "formalist" aesthetic
canons. Whether these forms are grounded in large structures of myth and
imagery, the New Critic's matrices of tension and ambiguity, or the mastery
of rhetoric and reader response, the tendency in the last twenty years of Blake
criticism has been to work from the assumption that "every word and every
letter" (and every graphic mark) "is in its fit place."

Northrop Frye has been, of course, the father of the third phase Blake, the
Blake of sweetness and light, the centrally English poet, of the master craftsman whose writings are not to be seen simply as religious texts, as prophecies, but as *poems* in the grand national style. A similar effort, pioneered by

† From *Studies in Romanticism* 21 (1982), 410–16. Mitchell's section titles refer to (I) Letter to Hayley, October 23, 1804 (not in this edition; Erdman 756); (II) "I saw a chapel all of gold"; and (III)
Jerusalem 98:14. His first quotation is from *Jerusalem* 3. For Mitchell's work on Blake as a "composite artist" and for other contributors to this journal's special issue on the "Blake industry," edited
by Morris Eaves, see "Selected Bibliography."

Anthony Blunt, Jean Hagstrum, David Bindman, and Martin Butlin, has been made to justify Blake's graphic art. Since my own work on Blake's composite art has been primarily in this formalist mode I'm naturally a bit reluctant to admit that it is in danger of being left behind. You can be sure, therefore, that by the end of this essay I will have found some way of reaffirming the continued centrality of formalism, even as many of its achievements are called into question.

What, then, is the major shift that seems to be occurring in the study of Blake? I would summarize it in the mode of antithesis: where we have seen some twenty years of attempts to justify Blake as a great formal artist, we will now see a kind of criticism that tends to deface the monument we have erected. Everything suggests to me that we are about to rediscover the dangerous Blake, the angry, flawed Blake, the crank who knew and repeated just about every bit of nonsense ever thought in the eighteenth century; Blake the ingrate, the sexist, the madman, the religious fanatic, the tyrannical husband, the second-rate draughtsman. We will also in this process rediscover a historical Blake, and begin to build on the work of David Erdman.

Blake has, of course, been through all this before. For outsiders to the institutions of Blake criticism, the nasty figure I've just described has always been the character of Blake. It's only the Blake Mafia that regards their Prophet as above reproach, unerring in his judgments on art and life, passing on sacred words of unimpeachable doctrine, or achieving a rhetorical and formal mastery of language that anticipates the great experimental texts of modernism. But Blake is now safely canonized; his poems are part of the curriculum of romantic poetry, his engravings are on the way to being certified as masterpieces, and he has achieved a place in popular literary sensibility that would have seemed inconceivable a century ago. Like Wordsworth, he is now ready to take a little abuse and spring back with renewed vigor.

What sort of abuse? The obvious things are already well under way: the feminists are busy exposing the problems in Blake's sexual opinions, and the art historians will rightly never accept him into the pantheon of painting (as distinct from engraving). I would like to reopen three issues here that, for the last twenty years at least, have been taboo, or at least neglected, areas in the criticism of Blake, and which will soon be rediscovered: madness, obscenity, and incoherence.

I. MADNESS: "Dear Sir, excuse my enthusiasm or rather madness, for I am really drunk with intellectual vision . . ."

Northrop Frye observed in 1966 that "the complaints that Blake was 'mad' are no longer of any importance, not because anybody has proved him sane, but because critical theory has realized that madness, like obscenity, is a word with no critical meaning."[1] We hardly need to invoke the work of R. D. Laing and Michel Foucault to sense that there is something a bit odd about Frye's banishment of madness from the critical lexicon, not just for Blake, but for any writer. We are inevitably provoked to ask what sort of discourse denies meaning to a term like madness. It sounds as if the phenomenon were threatening to infect the name, as if the incoherent, the

---

1. *Some British Romantics* (Columbus, Ohio: Ohio State University Press, 1966), p. 3.

irrational, the meaningless, the sick were so dangerous to criticism—or so
alien to it—as to be unnameable and unutterable. For Frye, one can speak
of madness as a physician or perhaps as a "naive biographer," but not as a
critic; to speak of madness in Blake or any other artist is to renounce the
claim to speak critically.

Two ways of reinstating Blake's madness within the discourse of criticism
immediately suggest themselves. The first would be to use Laing's roman-
ticized version of schizophrenia to reconcile Frye and what he calls "critical theory" with the irrational and deranged. On this view, true art and true
criticism *are* madness: they reveal an unrepressed, Dionysian perspective
whose distance from normality and sanity is precisely the distance required
for a telling criticism of ordinary life. Critical and poetic furor unite in the
passionate, methodical exposure of normal consciousness as repression
and neurosis, and give intellectual vision and enthusiasm the status of
healthy, divine madness. If this alternative seems a bit too predictable, it
may be because Frye has already anticipated it himself in his treatment of
the Orc-cycle as a neo-Freudian allegory in which Urizen plays the role of
"reality principle." Despite his banishment of madness as a critical term,
Frye has always smuggled the notion into his understanding of the critical
function of art. For Frye, madness has a meaning in the criticism which art
makes of life (i.e., art shows that ordinary life is madness) but it has no
meaning in the criticism of art, which is understood as intrinsically healthy,
sane, and coherent by virtue of its artistry.

A more radical critical recognition of Blake's madness would, I suspect,
take its inspiration from Foucault, and it would not try to reconcile Blake's
madness with his art. Foucault notes that from the time of the romantics,

> from the time of Hölderlin and Nerval, the number of writers, paint-
> ers, and musicians who have "succumbed" to madness has increased;
> but let us make no mistake here; between madness and the work of art,
> there has been no accommodation, no more constant exchange, no
> communication of languages; their opposition is much more danger-
> ous than formerly; and their competition now allows no quarter;
> theirs is a game of life and death. . . . Madness is the absolute break
> with the work of art; it forms the constitutive moment of abolition,
> which dissolves in time the truth of the work of art; it draws the exte-
> rior edge, the line of dissolution, the contour against the void.[2]

There is no lack of evidence that Blake experienced what he regarded as a
madness destructive to his work. "Nebuchadnezzar," he tells Hayley, "had
seven times passed over him" before his "understanding" was restored (see
Daniel 4); "I have had twenty." The "spectrous fiend" that Blake subdues
in *Jerusalem* is no easy conquest, but a foe "even as a brother who was my
enemy" who contrives to ruin Blake's labor for twenty years of his life. Blake
occupies an often ambiguous borderline between the divine madness of
inspiration, and the demonic madness of incapacity and false or fruitless
labor, a madness of irrationality, slavery, and compulsive repetition. If this
latter kind of madness is an "aspersion . . . Cast on the Inspired by the tame
high finisher of paltry Blots / Indefinite," (*M* 41:9–11), it is also an aspersion which Blake did not hesitate to cast on himself.

2. Michel Foucault, *Madness and Civilization*, trans. Richard Howard (New York: Random House, 1973), pp. 286–87.

Foucault speaks of madness as something which "draws the exterior edge, the line of dissolution, the contour against the void." How would this remark change the way we see Blake's "wirey bounding lines" which he "reengraved time after time" till not only motifs, figures, and postures, but even abstract linear patterns became a kind of overdetermined code? Would it not suggest that this code is not a code of art, but rather a code of desperation, incapacity, and compulsive repetition? The formalist aesthetic likes to think of Blake working deliberately and consciously, in the light of a higher understanding of his work, and it finds evidence for this sanity in the coherence and methodical, systematic character of his work. It finds the method in his madness and calls it sanity. But what if we began to see the method *as* the madness? What if we took coherence and diagrammatic consistency as evidence, not of a higher rationality at work, but of obsession and compulsive repetition?

The results, in my view, would not be very interesting unless we took one more step which is also suggested by Foucault, and that would be to deepen and particularize our historical sense of madness and Blake's place in it. It is all too easy for us to pronounce Blake sane from the safe remove of almost two centuries, and to see our ability to acknowledge his sanity as evidence of how far we have come from those dark times that failed to recognize his genius. Yet how many of us, in the terms afforded by our present critical and aesthetic canons, could recognize Blake if he walked in the door today? If we could take a time capsule to Felpham in 1802, just how many of us would be more comfortable talking to Hayley than to Blake? As long as we insist that "madness, like obscenity, is a word with no critical meaning," we will be unable to make either of these confrontations, and we will have only a safe and sanitized Blake, not the dangerous, difficult figure he really was.

II. OBSCENITY: "So I turnd into a sty / And laid me down among the swine"

The term that Frye banishes from criticism along with madness is obscenity, that which, according to the *OED* is "offensive to the senses, or to taste or refinement; disgusting, repulsive, filthy, foul, loathsome, abominable . . . offensive to modesty or decency, expressing or suggesting unchaste or lustful ideas; impure, indecent, lewd." Like his madness, Blake's obscenity has been domesticated and sanitized in the name of higher sublimations: Christian *agape,* free love, and more recently, Norman O. Brown's "polymorphous perversity." Perhaps now that he has passed safely by the Victorian censors and the modernist strategies of desublimation we can return to Blake's images of rape, lust, sado-masochism, and other scenes of abnormal sexuality with a keener sense of the precise relation of these episodes to the norms they violate. What are the winged vaginas and menstrual chariots of *Jerusalem* showing us? Why are there scenes of homosexual fellatio in *Milton,* and what do they have to do with the presentation of Satan-Hayley's effeminacy in the Bard's Song? (For a partial answer, see my essay on *Milton* in *Blake Studies* 6:1.) Precisely how do we read Oothoon's offer to catch for Theotormon "girls of mild silver" for orgies of "lovely copulation" which she will watch in delight? And if Blake could express all these things when he sat down to write, consider what he did when he sat down to shite, doodling in his notebook, interlacing his manuscripts with obscene drawings, scrawling graffiti in the margins of his Reynolds, throwing acid on the names of his enemies. Blake was not a nice man: he was filthy with work and visionary conviction. Despite Catherine's famous claim that "Mr. Blake don't durt," he could wipe his ass on the poem of a competitor and compare the shadows in Rubens' paintings to excrement.

III. INCOHERENCE: "And the dim Chaos brightend beneath, above, around! Eyed as the Peacock."

The greatest challenge and the most threatening scandal for the formalist appropriation of Blake is the threat of incoherence, nonsense, failure to communicate; the presence of accident, random sloppiness, lack of technical facility; the cranky miscalculation of audience; the self-defeating strategies of isolation; the self-fulfilling prophecies of paranoia; the megalomania of "Giants & Fairies" and the solipsistic absorption in the silent, solitary obsession with "Writing" for no audience but oneself. The hermeneutic imperative of formalism is that every word and every letter be studied and put in its fit place; it asks us to take Blake's word that he knows what he is doing, or that poetry and painting, through him, know what *they* are doing.

But suppose that Blake, like the rest of us, is a weak vessel, a flawed instrument. Suppose that, as both poet and painter, he nods as often as he awakens us or himself. May it not be time to consider the hypothesis that *Jerusalem* is a botched poem? Every sophisticated formal analysis of this poem in the last twenty years has tried to rescue it with some paradoxical and quasi-modernist formula of "form in anti-form," treating the failure of the poem to conform to any narrative or rhetorical scheme as part of a master design to disrupt our reliance on narrative, causal, and temporal order, and to replace it with a non-linear, visionary, diagrammatic and "eternal" aesthetic. Now the fact that this anti-Aristotelian sense of form has a traditional pedigree in the texts of sacred literature, particularly prophecy and apocalypse, helps to secure our confidence in its integrity and offers the best hope for a formalist recuperation of Blake's literary art. But we will also need to remind ourselves that religious justification of Blake's strange and difficult art is not the same thing as an aesthetic justification. To demonstrate that Blake is a great prophet is not equivalent to showing that he is a first-rate English poet. At least not yet. We have to make Blake strange again, which at the present time will not be to make him a modernist. It will be to distance him historically, to see his difference from us, and *then* to see what his poems are and do. We have appropriated him and familiarized him, made him safe for modern consumption through Freud, Jung, and Marx; employed the strategies of formalism, the discourses of phenomenology, existentialism, modernism, aestheticism, and even romanticism, which as Northrop Frye pointed out long ago, takes him out of his proper milieu, the Age of Sensibility.

It is time for the pendulum to swing back toward defamiliarization and the rediscovery of Blake's exotic, archaic, alien, and eccentric character, toward the recovery of his difficulty, the recognition of his involvement in contingencies which may erode the truth (by whatever standard) of his art. As we swing back on this pendulum, however, it will be important for us not to suffer amnesia, not to forget the accomplishment of Frye and the classical era of Blake criticism. If we hope to preserve continuity with what may be called the "professional" era of Blake studies, we will need a way of assimilating formalism even as we criticize its conclusions.

Deconstruction has come along at just the right moment to rescue the formalist Blake, for it provides a new and more subtle formalism: a hermeneutics of the text as something that dissolves its own authority and breaks open into unresolved contradictions, suppressed psychic and political motives, unsublimated energies, and symptomatic, pathological behavior. Blake's authority will be called into question in a variety of ways, e.g., his power over his art and his audience; his claims to inspiration; his status as an "original" and an originator. And we will in turn be moved to question the kind of authority which has been given to him by generations of interpreters: his status as prophet and seer, as the central figure in an anti-Wordsworthian reinterpretation of romanticism; as precursor of the avant garde in modernism. If some of Blake's authority seems to be lost in this process, we will need to watch carefully where the power is being transferred—to a Nietzchean reader who imposes his will to power in critical texts which aspire to rival and surpass Blake's own? or to the historicality of Blake's work, its place in a network of concrete and specific conditions?

Finally, I think we can predict that Blake will not merely survive deconstruction; he will prevail over it, and provide a new leavening for critical theory in the process—perhaps one as profound as the one which emerged from the last great critical struggle with his work, Frye's *Anatomy of Criticism*. This will be so because Blake anticipates so many of the strategies of deconstruction, and offers such powerful antidotes to its skeptical and nihilistic tendencies. Blake will offer us the critical power to meet the threat of doubt and nothingness because his work is one long struggle with the forces of negation. He will provide ways of harnessing the energy of textual freeplay because he gave himself so completely to his "Writing" (as opposed to clinging to his "Voice," the ghostly desire for authentic presence which haunted the romantics). Blake eludes the trap of logocentrism because he already calls into question the binary oppositions which privilege spirit over body, mind over matter, voice over writing, signified over signifier, poetry over painting. He gives us a text which is literally the play of differences between our most fundamental modes of signification, words and images, providing us with an icono-logo-machia which dramatizes a fundamental struggle in western concepts of mind and representation. In short, wherever critical theory goes, Blake will be out there waiting for it to catch up with his imagination, waiting for criticism itself to reunite with prophecy.

JOSEPH VISCOMI

[Blake's Relief Etching Process: A Simplified Account]†

In 1788 William Blake began to experiment with relief etching, the innovative printmaking process he used to create the *Songs of Innocence and of Experience* (1794) and most of his other beautiful illuminated books. In *The Marriage of Heaven and Hell* (ca. 1790–93), he called it the "infernal

† Condensed and adapted from *The Art of William Blake's Illuminated Prints* ([New York]: Manchester Etching Workshop, 1983 [edition of 200, accompanying "Facsimile and Monochrome Editions

method" and described it as "melting apparent surfaces away, and displaying the infinite which was hid." Put less symbolically, Blake drew a design on a copper plate with an acid-resistant varnish and etched away the unprotected metal to bring the design in relief. He printed the plates on an etching press and colored the impressions by hand; each copy of each book is unique.

It has often been suggested that Blake used relief etching because it enabled him either to combine text and illustration on one plate or to escape the division of labor inherent in reproductive engraving. That the medium appealed to Blake technically and aesthetically is no doubt true, but text and illustration can be combined, and complete control of production secured, in intaglio printing also, as the etched plates to *The Gates of Paradise* (1793) and *The Book of Ahania* (1795) demonstrate.[1] On the other hand, only in relief etching could Blake write and draw autographically and reproduce certain book conventions, such as facing pages. Blake's choice of relief etching may have been based on the kinds of tools and materials he preferred to work with and not only on the kinds of visual effects he hoped to create.

*   *   *

In ordinary etching, a ball of "ground" consisting of wax and resins is melted and spread over a warm degreased plate. The plate is smoked with waxed tapers to darken and harden the ground, and the design is then cut through the ground with a needle. The metal thus exposed is bitten below the surface with acid. In relief etching, however, the design is not cut out or incised by any metal instrument; rather, it is drawn on a bare copper plate with pens and brushes using a liquid medium. This medium must be acid resistant like an etching ground, but also must flow easily, adhere when dry, not spread or blot on the plate, and, like writing ink, be usable in pens and brushes. John Linnell, Blake's friend and patron, identified his "impervious liquid" as being "the usual stopping as it is called by the engravers made chiefly of pitch and diluted with Terps."[2] In the fine arts, the term *pitch* usually referred to rosin or to natural bitumens like asphaltum. Such resinous substances dissolve in volatile solvents like turpentine to form "simple-solution varnishes," which are acid resistant and used to paint over lines sufficiently etched to "stop" the acid from biting them deeper.

---

of . . . *Songs of Innocence and of Experience*]), 1, 3, 4, 8–9, 10–12, 14–15, 16, 19–20, with adapted footnotes and page references. By permission of the author. For an expanded account of Blake's methods, with illustrations, see Viscomi's contribution to *The Cambridge Companion to William Blake* (2003), ed. Morris Eaves available in The William Blake Archive (www.blakearchive.org). See also Viscomi's *Blake and the Idea of the Book* (1993) and his articles with Robert N. Essick in *Blake: An Illustrated Quarterly* 35 (2001–2), 74–103 and 36 (2002), 49–64, which challenge aspects of Michael Phillips's technical analyses in his *William Blake: The Creation of the Songs from Manuscript to Illuminated Printing* (2000 [reaffirmed in *Print Quarterly* 21 (2004) 18 ff. and 22 (2005) 138 ff.]), and supported by Martin Butlin, *BIQ* 36 (2002). This intense debate is accessible online from the *BIQ* home page (www.blakequarterly.org). Also important are Essick, *ELH* 52 (1985) 833–72 and (on the copper plates) Bentley, *University of Toronto Quarterly* 76 (2007), 714–65.

1. See Michael Phillips, "William Blake's *Songs of Innocence* and *Songs of Experience* from Manuscript Draft to Illuminated Plate," *The Book Collector* (Spring 1979), pp. 35–36; Robert N. Essick, "Blake and the Tradition of Reproductive Engraving," *Blake Studies*, vol. I, no. 5 (Fall 1972), p. 66; Essick, *Relief Inventions of William Blake* (Los Angeles, 1978), p. 31; Kay Easson, "Blake and the Art of the Book," *Blake in His Time*, ed. Essick and Donald Pearce (Bloomington: Indiana University Press, 1978), p. 35; and Morris Eaves, "What is the History of Publishing?" *Publishing History*, vol. 2 (1977), p. 61ff.

2. *Blake Records*, 2d. ed. G.E. Bentley, Jr. (2004), p. 609 n.

* * * [Blake] probably used one of the stopping-out varnishes then available, perhaps adding a little lampblack for color and oil to prevent coagulation. An "impervious liquid" on a copper plate makes the design positive and direct: the marks of the tool are dark on a light background and are the marks that print. This is not the case in woodcut, a relief process in which the design is produced indirectly and the marks of the tool do not print. For Blake, such a liquid used with pens and brushes made the execution of the design autographic, a quality unique to the graphic arts of the day—and one that may have been as attractive to a poet as to a graphic artist.

❀   ❀   ❀

The technical difficulty in illuminated printing lies not in writing backward, but in giving the letters the proper slant and mastering the writing varnish and instruments. Varnish was normally used from a shell, which exposed the solvent to the air and, as Linnell noted, made it "glutinous." Although it can still be used as a stop-out in this state, for writing it had to be kept "diluted with terps," or mixed with a little linseed oil. Blake probably dipped the brushes directly in the shell but loaded the pen with a small brush, a method used by illuminators to keep pens from clogging.

It seems that Blake wrote his text with a quill pen and not a brush; the lettering style and the variations between horizontal and vertical strokes do not show the variety that is typical of a brush—or, for that matter, of a formal pen hand.[3] Technically, writing a ten- or twelve-point Roman and italic script backward with a brush is far more difficult than writing with a quill. In fact, lettering with a brush was a very uncommon skill. According to Thomas Astle's *Origin and Progress of Writing* (1784), brushes were not used in the West except in making very large letters.[4] We do not know if writing with a brush was one of Blake's skills, but he had certainly mastered writing with a quill—even in a medium more viscous than writing ink. Indeed, in *Jerusalem*, plate 37 (**41**, p. 261 herein), Blake pictures himself writing backward with a quill. On the other hand, Blake used fine brushes to execute the broad lines and solid areas of the illustrations and, of course, to paint the impressions.

Blake wrote Roman and pseudoitalic scripts, both of which we see in *Songs*, though the latter, probably for technical as well as aesthetic reasons, came to dominate. Italic script looks more difficult to execute, but to connect letters and to give them a slant in the direction the pen is moving is actually easier than to write one letter at a time with a vertical axis while moving from right to left. Because there are fewer letter ends to coordinate, an italic script makes it easier to keep lines straight and words the same size. Besides simplifying the writing of the text, italic script also simplifies biting the plate: words are better protected against foulbiting and undercutting when fewer letter ends are exposed to acid.

3. Graily Hewitt, Percy Grassby, and "most calligraphers would maintain [the script] could not be accomplished with any instrument other than a pen" (Grassby, "William Blake as Printer and Engraver: A Note," *The American Printer*, "Craftsman Number," vol. 79, no. 3, 1924, unnumbered). Hewitt, one of the twentieth-century's finest calligraphers, found Blake's script "commonplace" and "undistinguished," for which he partly faults the technique: writing backward directly on the plate with a quill pen (as noted in Mona Wilson's *The Life of Blake*, 1927, rpt. London: Oxford University Press, 1971, pp. 382–83).

4. (London, 1784; rev., 2nd ed. 1803), p. 208; the illustrations demonstrating letter brush writing are on plate VIII and are over seventy-two points [a measure of size].

Another example of Blake's thinking in terms of the process, of his knowing that one material or stage can affect, or be affected by, a later one, is
his breaking up space with ascenders, descenders, and interlinear decorations. A tightly composed design needs to be etched less deeply than one
with open areas and thus spends less time in acid. It also keeps the ink dab-
ber on the surface and thus helps to prevent ink from being deposited in
the shallows, those areas that are bitten below the surface and are supposed
to print white. By filling out lines, interlinear decorations are part of this
line system, and by breaking up space, they decrease the number of open
areas, or shallows. This is not to say that the pictograms in *The Marriage of
Heaven and Hell* and other books are not significant, but only that marks
on any given plate may function as part of the composition or as part of the
line system, and not necessarily, or only, as arcane symbols.

The illuminated prints look as though they were written and drawn, not
necessarily because Blake was intent on making prints in imitation of illuminated pages—had that been his sole objective, he could have used other
media—but because the materials and tools of relief etching allowed him
to actually write and draw. Pens and brushes exercise less dictatorial control over hand and eye than do burins and needles, the use of which was
heavy with technique, convention, and translation. In relief etching, unlike
engraving, Blake could freely conceive, compose, and execute in terms of
the same medium. All of this made relief etching technically and aesthetically appealing but not inherently more creative than engraving, nor did it
make engraving a medium that Blake despised or sought to avoid. In any
event, it is not fair to compare engraving with an autographic medium that
seems to have appealed to the poet and painter in Blake as well as to the
graphic artist. For Blake, multiple styles and different media were never
mutually exclusive, and if his working in unconventional media reflects
anything, it is not a desire to escape reproductive engraving but rather a
desire to experiment and explore. "My business," he said, "is to Create."[5]

* * *

For the design to retain its autographic quality, it had to be bitten accu-
rately and sensitively. Controlling the bite required knowledge of acid and
additives and much skill. Blake probably used nitric acid, the acid "commonly employed by engraving" in his day.[6] Because of nitric acid's strength,
though, it can pit or lift the etching ground, and because it bites laterally
(that is, as it bites down, it also bites sideways, thus forming a rounded cav-
ity), it can undercut and thus collapse fine cross-hatching. To avoid the
problem of using this strong acid on a plate with fine and precise line work,
seventeenth- and eighteenth-century manuals often advised etching with
a weaker, vinegar-based acid. This advice, however, did not apply to Blake;
in his relief plates the areas to be bitten were not delicate and fine, but open
and broad, and had to be bitten deeply.

* * *

The borders of the plates [visible in proof impressions] were caused by
the sides of the plate being embedded in strips of bordering wax. The wax
formed a walled-in area to hold the acid, which was poured on the surface

5. *Jerusalem* 10:21.
6. Robert Dossie, *The Handmaid to the Arts* (London, 1764, 2 vols.), I. 147.

about a quarter inch deep, turned blue, and bubbled along the varnished lines. * * * During the biting, the design appears dark brown on the reddish copper plate in its blue-tinted bath. Hours later, a relief plate, or cast, is produced.

*   *   *

After a forty-five- to ninety-minute etch puts the design in slight relief, the plate can be rinsed and dried, and the words (not the individual letters) can be carefully painted over with stopping-out varnish. This will save details such as serifs, ascenders, and descenders. * * *

Just how long—and thus, how deeply—Blake's plates were bitten is a matter of debate. Based on the striations in electrotypes made from the original relief plates (1861–63), it has been suggested that the plates were bitten very deeply and stopped out three times, which would have made the biting and repainting processes quite complicated.[7] But an electrotype, though it exactly reproduces the surface appearance of the original plate, does not record its depth. The method by which the electrotype is made includes preparing an intermediate matrix and then building up the relief areas of the matrix, so that its cast, the electrotype, is deep enough to be commercially printed.

The depth of plates executed before 1793 was probably greater than of those executed afterwards. There are fewer broken lines in the later prints, a sign that the plates spent less time in acid, as well as of Blake's increased designing and biting skills. Plates to *The Book of Urizen* (1794) seem quite shallow.[8] They were probably executed with color printing in mind; a shallowly bitten plate does, in fact, facilitate the simultaneous printing of colors from the lower and raised levels of the plate. The first six of the seven copies of *Urizen* were color printed, which supports the idea that Blake conceived the product in terms of the process. It is probably a mistake, however, to deduce from the *Urizen* plates that color printing necessitated a shallow bite, or from the *Innocence* plates that Blake ordinarily etched his plates deeply. As in most technical matters, Blake did not seem to adopt any rigidly standard practice, but continued to experiment from book to book and plate to plate.

*   *   *

Unlike letterpress printers, Blake printed the plates of his books one at a time, not in forms, and, it seems, on paper cut to page size, not on large sheets that were folded in gatherings. By being printer as well as artist and etcher, Blake retained full artistic control over impressions; he could conceive of the design in terms of its entire execution, and make choices in earlier and later stages accordingly. For example, a dark ink is neither easily washed over nor harmonious with an elaborate coloring style, whereas a bright ink is more suitable for this kind of illumination. The variants among impressions from the same plate resulted not only from coloring but also from the way the plate was printed and the kind of ink used.

7. John Wright, "Blake's Relief-Etching Method," *Blake Newsletter,* vol. 9, no. 4 (Spring, 1976), p. 95.
8. In relief etching, *deep* and *shallow* are relative terms. The plates themselves were probably between 16- and 18-gauge, and with both sides etched, such plates could not structurally support depths of even 1/32nds of an inch. Essick has carefully measured the depth of the *America* fragment and platemakers' marks and has concluded that Blake's plates, at least the later ones, were quite shallow (Essick, *Printmaker,* p. 92).

*   *   *

Because Blake printed with relatively light pressure, his prints are usually free of any pronounced platemarks. Thus, unlike intaglio printers, Blake could print on both sides of the paper, which made it possible for illuminated books to have facing pages, like conventional books. Facing pages and continuous paging in illuminated books seem to have been part of Blake's original conception.

* * * He changed his printing format after the color-printing experiments of 1794, perhaps because the opaque colors printed simultaneously from surface and lower levels changed the appearance of the page so dramatically that a facing page created tension and distraction. As graphic art, Blake's prints are most effective when viewed independently of other pages—when they are seen as prints and not just as pages. By reprinting his books on only one side of the sheet, Blake changed the focus of attention. He forced the reader to experience the book as a physical, beautiful artifact, not just as a vehicle for narrative and pictorial ideas.

*   *   *

There are, of course, many interrelated reasons for Blake's producing so few copies of his books. Two or three weeks is not much time to print a copy—even if it is only eleven or eighteen pages—but considering how few copies Blake could produce during the "run" of multiple copies of the same title, we can see that his was a labor-intensive, and not cost effective, means of production. Printing relief-etched plates is not technically difficult, but inking and printing plates on a rolling press is slow. And so, Blake was "never . . . able to produce a Sufficient number for a general Sale by means of a regular Publisher," as he told Dawson Turner in 1818.[9]

Blake came to see his illuminated books as more than symbols and as something other than symbolic in their function as communicative vehicles. The evolution from print-as-page to print-as-painting reflected Blake's perceiving of the book as an art object. Indeed, when late in his life Blake reprinted the plates, he was not only republishing books of poems but also issuing series of prints or miniature paintings. The poems on the metal plates were unchangeable and could have been twenty-five or more years old, whereas the appearance of the impression was not fixed by the plate image but could be worked up fresh each time—"at least as well as any . . . yet produced." It was the illuminated book as artifact, not as an edition of poems, that his friends and patrons were buying. And it seems that he, a poet who believed his books had given him a "great reputation as an artist," was also chiefly selling on those terms.

Blake's work in relief etching belongs not only to the history of books and bookmaking, but also to the *peintre-graveur* tradition in the fine arts. His experiments in relief etching not only anticipate developments in the industrial arts, such as zincos and process blocks, but also the deep etch and viscosity printing methods used by graphic artists today. The illuminated books are not books or publications in any conventional sense. They do not consist of "exact repeatable images," since the plate image is invariably altered in each impression. They are, each and every copy, works of original pictorial and graphic art.

9. See p. 491 herein.

STEPHEN C. BEHRENDT

[The "Third Text" of Blake's Illuminated Books]†

William Blake's illuminated poems naturally invite the hard questions about the relation of visual texts and verbal texts in any illustrated book, and in his in particular. I should like to revisit a few of the more trouble-some problems that continue to face us as readers and viewers of Blake's illuminated pages, and to pose some questions about those pages and the ways in which Blake may or may not have intended us to proceed in digest-ing them. I say 'digesting' deliberately, for it seems to me that Blake asks us to 'consume' his texts in a manner analogous to that of John of Patmos, by means of a distinctively *physical* process through which we quite literally internalize the texts. This is 'informed consumerism' with a peculiarly Blakean twist. The account in Revelation is that the voice from heaven commanded John to 'Go and take the little book which is open in the hand of the angel which standeth upon the sea and upon the earth' (Rev. 10.8). The result is just what the angel predicts: 'And I took the little book out of the angel's hand, and ate it up; and it was in my mouth sweet as honey: and as soon as I had eaten it my belly was bitter' (Rev. 10.10). Significantly, the angel makes it clear what must transpire next: 'And he said unto me, Thou must prophesy again before many peoples, and nations, and tongues, and kings' (Rev. 10.11).

Much as John was told to consume and thereby internalize the visions revealed to him in an act replete with sacramental overtones of the Eucharist, Blake asks us to treat his texts with comparable appetite and fer-vency, their often inherent bitterness notwithstanding. * * * [F]or Blake the act of reading is to be regarded in fact as essentially sacramental in nature, at least when that act is performed correctly, for it is a prelude both to indi-vidual insight and to social—or community—prophecy and redemption. When done incorrectly, however, whether frivolously or with deliberate intent to misread, the sacrilegious treatment of the text is certain to pro-duce intellectual and imaginative indigestion. This is not to imply that Blake's notion of 'reading' is ever entirely consistent, nor is it to disregard his irreverent and often deliberately perverse rendering of everything from physical and imaginative myopia to the immensely fruitful polyvalence (and polysemy) that at once tantalizes and frustrates modern poststructuralist approaches to his verbal and visual texts alike. We shall need, therefore, to proceed from the outset with some care.

But first a problem of taxonomy: what are we to call Blake's texts? This question is not so frivolous as it may at first appear, even in the wake of Joseph Viscomi's thorough examination of Blake's books (Viscomi 1993).[1] We usually call them 'illuminated texts', but every time I teach Blake's *Songs of Innocence and of Experience*, students almost without exception talk about 'the texts and the pictures'. Nor are the students alone in instinc-tively prioritizing the verbal text over the visual in this fashion. Writing in

† From "'Something in My Eye': Irritants in Blake's Illuminated Texts," chapter 3 in *Blake in the Nineties*, ed. Steve Clark and David Worrall (Basingstoke: Macmillan Press Ltd.; New York: St. Martin's Press, 1999), 78–81, 82–83, 84–85, 86–88, 90–91, 93–94, with adjustments in citations of sources. Abridgement approved by the author.
1. See the "Selected Bibliography" for works cited parenthetically [*editors' note*].

Engaging English Art, for example, Michael Cohen refers to Blake's *Songs* in terms of 'text and picture' or 'design and poem', while David Bindman, writing earlier, likewise calls the illuminated works essays in 'combining text and design'.[2] Indeed, this dichotomous and apparently mutually exclusive terminology recurs with surprising frequency in much of recent post-structuralist commentary on Blake's work.[3] Language of this sort implies that only a literary text can be a real 'text' and that the visual text is at best the weak and subservient sister art whose function is not *textually* significant and whose nature *as art* is only minimally and marginally important in the generation of meaning. Even so perennially perceptive a student of Blake as David Erdman seems to have been driving along this one-way street, if we are to take at face value his comment in *The Illuminated Blake* that 'every graphic image has its seed or root in the poetry' (Erdman 1974, p. 16). Yet as Molly Anne Rothenberg has noted this sort of bifurcation blurs the distinction that exists between Blake's illuminated poems as 'works' and as 'texts', and between the opposing tendencies towards restriction and liberation, or demarcation and freedom, that customarily typify the two (Rothenburg 1993, p. 1).[4] In reminding us of the strongly performative—and therefore communitarian—nature of Blake's illuminated poems, Rothenberg helps to redirect our attention to what is transpiring on the pages (as aesthetic entities or 'wholes') and in the individual consciousnesses of a varied (and varying) readership.

My quibble here is less with the terminology than with the logocentric bias it betrays. Blake offered us at least partial guidance when in his advertising prospectus of 1793 he described the *Songs* and the early prophetic poems as works executed 'in Illuminated Printing', each 'with [*n*] designs' (E693). Blake says, 'The Illuminated Books are Printed in Colours', but he goes no further in defining what he means by 'illuminated', either here or anywhere else in his writings. The *OED* tells us that in eighteenth-century usage 'illumination' commonly referred to rich adornment of the page with gold, silver or colour, and to the use of 'tracery and miniature designs, executed in colours', as for instance in illuminated medieval manuscripts. This more modern and technically specific meaning of the term had in Blake's time become concurrent with its older and clearly relevant connotations of enlightenment and elucidation. It would seem that the 'designs' to which Blake refers in his prospectus are therefore those substantial visual images that range in size from a quarter-page to a full page; presumably the interlinear and minor marginal visual details do not in themselves add up to

2. Michael Cohen, *Engaging English Art: Entering the Work in Two Centuries of English Painting and Poetry* (Tuscaloosa: University of Alabama Press, 1987), pp. 65, 76; David Bindman, *Blake as an Artist* (Oxford: Phaidon; New York: E. P. Dutton, 1977), p. 43.
3. See essays in the following collections: Nelson Hilton and Thomas A. Vogler, eds., *Unnam'd Forms: Blake and Textuality* (Berkeley: University of California Press, 1986); Dan Miller, Mark Bracher, and Donald Ault, eds., *Critical Paths: Blake and the Argument of Method* (Durham: Duke University Press, 1987). More helpful—and probably more faithful historically and intellectually to Blake's aesthetic in the context of his times—is the notion of the sort of 'composite' art discussed some time ago by W. J. T. Mitchell, *Blake's Composite Art: A Study of the Illuminated Poetry* (Princeton: Princeton University Press, 1978); and, still earlier, the encompassing tradition of the 'sister arts' invoked by Jean H. Hagstrum, *William Blake: Poet and Painter. An Introduction to the Illuminated Verse* (Chicago and London: University of Chicago Press, 1964). I have discussed this matter in some detail, in a somewhat different context, in Behrendt, *Reading William Blake* (London: Macmillan Press, 1992), esp. Chapters 1 and 2.
4. Rothenberg here draws the distinction which Roland Barthes examines most specifically in 'From Work to Text', in *Textual Strategies: Perspectives in Post-Structuralist Criticism*, ed. Josué V. Harari (Ithaca: Cornell University Press, 1979) pp. 72–81.

what Blake means by 'designs',[5] though they do come remarkably close to the 'tracery and miniature designs' to which the *OED* refers.

We can, however, say with greater certainty what Blake's inter-disciplinary texts are *not*. They are not texts-with-illustrations in the fashion of the eighteenth-century printed book adorned with engraved full- or partial-page illustrations, books in which the areas devoted to verbal and visual texts not only are kept separate by physical means but also are typically executed by different hands (the typesetter who 'sets' the author's verbal text, the illustrator who engraves a design—perhaps from a sketch supplied by yet another hand, and the printer-bookmaker who assembles the package under the supervision of the editor, publisher or bookseller). In producing his illuminated books Blake either saw to every one of these tasks himself or oversaw the work that his wife Catherine did when she worked with him to print, colour and otherwise prepare copies. In this respect, either alone or—as frequently happened—in creative partnership with his wife, Blake was able to maintain virtually absolute control over every aspect of the aesthetic nature of the final interdisciplinary product.

Blake's texts are not simply verbal texts with illustrations 'to' or 'of ' them, and their verbal / visual interplay is of quite a different nature from that which governs his designs for, most notably, Milton, Gray, Young, Woll-stonecraft, Dante and the Bible. Nor are they the sort of text that he seems to have envisioned for *Tiriel* (c. 1788), for which work the verse and the pictures seem to have been conceived as firmly separate (and separated) components—more in the manner of the conventional eighteenth-century typeset book with full-page illustrations. Nor are they essays in the familiar form of the later eighteenth-century illustrated children's book, although Blake also tried his hand at a variant on that form (*For Children*, subsequently reworked as *For the Sexes: The Gates of Paradise*).

Blake's illuminated poems generate what is essentially a 'third text', a meta-text that partakes of both the verbal and the visual texts, but that is neither the sum of, nor identical with either of, those two texts. The verbal and visual texts stimulate different varieties of aesthetic, intellectual and affective responses which are firmly grounded in the disciplinary natures of the two media and in the tradition and 'vocabulary' (or reference-systems) particular to each. Certainly one would scarcely think of suggesting that Blake's pages are in the manner of Hogarth, whose productions are insistently and inescapably *visual* texts—pictures—no matter how much verbal material the artist introduces into them in the form of inscriptions, bits of printed matter lying about, and so forth. When we say that we 'read' a Hogarth print, we are well aware that we are using the verb 'read' in a very special way to suggest a process of perception and cognition (or recognition) that finds an analogue—and only an *analogue*, however near a one—in the largely sequential activity by which we read a conventional printed verbal text. Even the powerful *narrativity* of many of Hogarth's pictures—and certainly of sequences like his 'progresses'—is nevertheless intrinsically different from Blake's art. Perhaps the more historically apt point of contrast is furnished by the popular caricature art of Blake's time, where the striking visual textures of images by Gillray, Woodward, Rowlandson, Isaac Cruikshank and others are regularly interrupted by inscriptions,

5. Comparing Blake's counts of the 'designs' with the numbers of pages containing such large-scale visual images appears to corroborate this claim.

speech balloons and undemarcated lines of dialogue that seem to float in
the visual space.

*   *   *

With pictures, viewers typically begin with an overall impression that
forms quickly upon first apprehension of the picture and gradually work
their way into the image, letting their eyes explore the full image in
response to the artist's prompting. Readers, on the other hand, must proceed in just the opposite fashion, putting the subject together like a jigsaw
puzzle, in linear, chronological fashion, in order to construct the overall
image with its attendant impressionistic, imaginative shadings. The actual
process, of course—as contemporary phenomenologies of perception, cognition and interpretation quickly remind us—is a good deal more complicated, involving as it does simultaneously ongoing activities of recognizing,
sorting, comparing, reconciling, rejecting, retaining and modifying data
and 'meaning' literally with every piece of information that is encountered
and registered. Nevertheless, there remain profound differences in the
nature and the effect of the linearity involved in apprehending the content
of information conveyed in each medium, differences that are a direct consequence of the nature of the individual artistic medium.

Not surprisingly, these two very different ways of presenting their materials and thus engaging their audiences indicate the extent to which the two
arts are both grounded in, and directed towards, different sorts of aesthetic,
intellectual and affective modes of creation and response. The really crucial difference, it seems to me, is not that of the opposition between the
inherently powerful initial dramatic impact of the stunning visual image,
on one hand, and the accumulative, prolonged crescendo of impact generated on the other by the verbal passage. Rather, the crux of the matter lies,
I believe, in what the responding mind is asked to do in dealing with the
two arts.

The visual artist controls the picture's system of references, presenting—
typically—a representational image of something or someone about which
(or whom) we may or may not know anything in advance. The artist also
provides—and we respond to—a variously coded set of contextual indicators that might include visual conventions, specific iconography, historical
or cultural references, along with what might be called 'tonal' indicators
(colours, textures, 'technique' and, of course, size) that demonstrably influence our affective response to the pictorial image.

*   *   *

Given one of Blake's illuminated pages, like *Europe*, plate 9 [**12**, p. 102
herein], for instance, one almost without exception first 'sees' the visual text
and—unavoidably—formulates an initial response to that visual statement.
I choose this page deliberately, since it effectively demonstrates one of the
most characteristic and challenging intellectual 'problems' we face in dealing with Blake's illuminated poems. This lovely, graceful, visual image por-
trays a pair of figures whose apparent function it is to blight the crops, an act
that is in fact recounted not in *Europe* at all but rather in the poem that preceded it, *America*. The visual image is an intellectual and aesthetic trap for
the unwary: its seductively attractive visual aspect disguises what subsequent
investigation reveals as evil, as menace, as a force of destruction.

Is a page of this sort primarily a verbal or a visual text? That seems to me just one of the many *wrong questions* that critical commentary often permits to distract us from the real matter at hand in Blake's art. These heterogeneous pages, with their decidedly differing and often contradictory aesthetic and intellectual demands, constitute deliberately interdisciplinary physical representations intended to put us in touch with a body of meaning, or signification, of which each text—taken both separately and in tandem—is at best merely an approximation, an analogue. Robert Essick is certainly on the right track when he observes that Blake seems in his art to be aiming at creating 'a hermeneutic community whose members share a common language' (Essick 1989, p. 223). But that community—and its language—is only partly physical, and it is only partly subject to or restricted by the limitations of the verbal and visual media that seek to convey what they in fact cannot contain.

Blake offered a useful guide when he wrote in *A Vision of the Last Judgment* of the obligations that rest on the cooperating (and thus collaborating) ideal viewer:

> If the Spectator could Enter into these Images in his Imagination[,] approaching them on the Fiery Chariot of his Contemplative Thought[;] if he could Enter into Noahs Rainbow or into his bosom or could make a Friend & Companion of one of these Images of wonder which always intreats him to leave mortal things as he must know[;] then would he arise from his Grave[,] then would he meet the Lord in the Air & then he would be happy. (E560 [p. 435 herein])

An act of perception of this sort sets up a different dynamic than does the standard gallery picture, for it requires that the viewer be both participant and co-creator. It also dictates that the communication that is the object of *both* parties (artist and viewer) is of a sort that transcends the limitations of the physical medium and approaches a sort of telepathic communication that transpires 'in the air', where the viewer leaves the 'grave' of vegetable, human sensory activity and enters directly into the world of pure vision, pure Idea, which transcendent activity the artist endeavors to mediate (and, to be sure, also to *manipulate*) through the materials and the nuances of his art. For as Viscomi observes, for Blake 'the drawn line is analogous to the word of God; the inspired line is itself inspirating [*sic*] and true art is by nature sublime' (and hence capable of producing the sort of 'transport' we have come to associate with eighteenth-century notions of the Sublime) (Viscomi 1993, p. 42).

✳   ✳   ✳

One often hears that the verbal texts of various of the *Songs of Innocence and of Experience* appear to exploit ostensible emotional and intellectual differences, or distances, that exist between the 'naive' speakers of *Innocence* or the cynical speakers of *Experience* and the knowledgeable, intellectually mature *reader* of those texts. Analogous suggestions have been made about the verbal texts of the longer narrative poems as well. Much less consideration seems to have been given, however, to whether the *visual* texts of Blake's illuminated poems engage in any of the same deadly earnest playfulness with the viewer. Commentators may *describe* the formal visual aspects of 'The Lamb' or 'The Tyger', for instance; they may note that the asymmetrical tiger is anything but fearful or that the pastoral scene depicted on the plate of 'The Lamb' is Edenic. But despite some early and passing inquiry into the functional relation of verbal and visual components, it has taken until fairly recent years for Blake scholarship to yield really detailed and systematic examination of the nature of the intellectual and aesthetic manipulations the illuminations invite us—even compel us—to pursue as part of the act of reading.

In 'The Tyger', for instance, are we asking anything like the right question when we debate (as many have) the relative realism or ferocity of the tiger? That is, we may well submit that the earnestly playful Blake offers us a visual image that shatters our expectations of a standard zoo tiger. But would we be thinking about a zoo tiger in any case? Certainly it would require an impossibly naive reader to read the verbal text in that fashion. Then why should we expect otherwise in the *visual* text? Nor does it help, for that matter, to call to mind the supposedly simplified visual vocabulary of the traditional children's book, for the child is in any event more likely than the rationalizing adult to accept that Blake's odd-looking creature actually *is* a tiger. One need only think of the imaginative paradigm behind the immensely popular American comic strip, *Calvin and Hobbes*. That is, the child is both more credulous and more imaginatively generous *by nature* than is the reasoning, Urizenic adult who can see only what is 'there'. Is the *image* of Blake's tiger, perhaps, itself a physical representation of the consequences (or the workings) of the same failed *vision* that struggles to see aright the tiger of the verbal text? If so, might we then attribute to the design (and by extension to the 'painter'—NOT necessarily Blake himself but some persona of an 'illustrator') the same sort of bound and faulty vision that informs the verbal texts (and by extension their speakers—*also* NOT Blake but rather personae who inhabit Experience)? Notice the number of plates in *Experience*, especially ('Earth's Answer' or 'A Poison Tree', for example), whose bleak designs begin to make greater sense when we consider them in this way. Much the same can be said about *Innocence*, for that matter, but with a nod instead to the positive, fertile, energetic vision the designs share with the verbal texts (e.g., 'Night' or 'Spring').

Suppose we come at the matter from still another angle and consider what happens when we regard the visual image of the entire illuminated *page* of 'The Tyger' to be the text—the 'third text' or meta-text I mentioned earlier. Suppose, too, that we nevertheless view the page with the conditioned, traditionalist eyes whose powers of observation are rooted in our *expectations* rather than in the truths that the page attempts to disclose. Given the page's small scale, the reader / viewer necessarily sees top and bottom more or less at once, picture and title serving in this relatively instantaneous apprehension reinforce one another. Or so it seems. The title encourages us to identify as a tiger that creature which we might otherwise puzzle over. What the eye first 'sees' on and in this page is this double reference, verbal and visual, tied together by the heavy tree-trunk on the right whose upper and lower lines, like its attenuated bare branches, extend out to title and picture.

Within this engineered but nevertheless problematic bracketing of equivalency the reader next begins seriously to 'enter into' the poem's verbal text. As we proceed through the verses of 'The Tyger'—continuously building and modifying 'meaning' by interconnected processes of comparing, choosing, deleting, retaining and reformulating—the words come to seem less and less applicable to either our preconception of a tiger (which the title asks us to call up) or the beast represented by and in the image at the bottom of the page. Lies abound. The page is too well lit to square with 'the forests of the *night*', and in most copies the tiger's colours cannot honestly be called 'bright'. Most significantly, neither the beast *nor the illuminated page* is symmetrical: indeed the whole notion of 'fearful symmetry' is almost laughable, given the insistent asymmetry of the page and the absurdly mild aspect of the tiger.

When we approach this page 'on the Fiery Chariot of [our] Contemplative Thought' (VLJ, E560 [p. 435 herein])—when we follow that initial reading with one or more increasingly sophisticated and self-reflexive rereadings (each of which proceeds in light of—*illuminated* by—all the previous readings and the various responses and insights those readings have generated)— we begin to recognize how the intellectual and aesthetic complexity of the text-as-a-whole is generated in significant measure by the interaction among the expected and the unexpected, the conventional and the unconventional. This sophisticated, studious variety of reading, rereading *and contemplation* is, of course, that which historically attended the study of the medieval illuminated manuscript, in which verbal and visual texts likewise worked in mutual cooperation, even when it might appear otherwise at first glance.

*   *   *

None of this is to take the easy way out and suggest that Blake's texts are simply—even randomly—indeterminate, or that they shirk the responsibility we typically place upon the author / artist (and certainly upon the 'illustrator') to be reliable and reasonably direct. Rather, Blake characteristically invokes and manipulates our expectations about determinacy (of word, of image, of 'meaning') to force us to recognize and appreciate the multiplicity of *potential* signification that resides in seemingly every word, every line, every suggestion. As he put it in *A Vision of the Last Judgment*, 'not a line is drawn without intention & that most discriminate & particular . . . as Poetry admits not a Letter that is Insignificant so Painting admits not a Grain of Sand or a Blade of Grass "Insignificant"' (E560, [p. 435 herein]). Indeterminacy is not the point, then, nor is the accidental ambiguity that stems from mere carelessness; the point lies instead that unconventional sort of determinacy that rests upon the intellectual and imaginative compact that Blake takes for granted between himself and his responsive, contemplative reader, a compact mediated physically by the illuminated pages. This compact, as Joseph Viscomi (most recently) has noted, is founded upon Blake's conviction that line (rather than colour or other tonal effects) is 'the foundation of art', because 'the line that discriminates and particularizes is the line that finds and fixes form in the initial chaos of lines, marks, and blurs' (Viscomi 1993, p. 167). This is why the many apparent 'variations' among copies of the illuminated works—especially variations in printing characteristics—are not the calculated and ideologically meaningful differences for which some critics have taken them,[6] but are, rather, essentially 'accidentals' resulting from the mechanical process of producing the copy:

6. See Jerome J. McGann, "The Text, the Poem, and the Problem of Historical Method," *New Literary History* 12 (1981), pp. 269–288; Stephen Leo Carr, "Illuminated Printing: Toward a Logic of Difference," in Hilton and Vogler (1986), pp. 177–196; Stewart Crehan, *Blake in Context* (Dublin: Gill and Macmillan, 1984); Morris Eaves, "Blake and the Artistic Machine: An Essay in Decorum and Technology," *PMLA* 92 (1977), 903–927; and his *The Counter-Arts Conspiracy: Art and Industry in the Age of Blake* (Ithaca and London: Cornell University Press, 1992).

they do not in this respect 'deviate' from the 'line' (of vision) the artist placed on the original plate to indicate 'real' (or Eternal) signification.

* * * Blake's campaign against worldly materialism—and against the seductive appeal of the material world in general—was intended not to reconcile us to the natural world, or it to us, but rather to draw us away from it and towards the imaginative and spiritual world of Eternity, itself a comparatively reactionary concept that likewise hearkened back to earlier times. Blake directed his art towards engendering in his audience the sort of accession to vision that had been Elisha's part. In this sense Blake's is a deliberately and radically iconoclastic *political* art in its distrust of—indeed its attack upon—the easy, conditioned 'answers' to complex problems that are the stock-in-trade of all Establishments bent upon maintaining control not just of individuals but indeed of all the artifacts and institutions of national culture. Blake's texts foster independence of mind and vision precisely because they deny us the comfort and intellectual leisure offered by determinacy. The more I return to Blake's illuminated poems, the more compelling is the evidence I find there of Blake's particular challenge to our expectations as readers. In the subversive, oppositional intent of his art generally lies much of the aesthetic and intellectual 'agenda' that is tangibly represented in the meta-text that emerges from Blake's illuminated pages.

MARTIN K. NURMI

[On *The Marriage of Heaven and Hell*]†

One of the best places to see Blake the philosophical poet at work is in *The Marriage of Heaven and Hell*. This work * * * displays on every page the man who chooses to create instead of reason and compare, but who nevertheless has something to say to the reasoners.

* * * Two conceptions * * * form its main themes: the idea of expanded "spiritual sensation" and the doctrine of "contraries."

I. Blake's Ideal of Expanded Sense Perception

* * * "If the doors of perception were cleansed," as Blake writes in *The Marriage*, and everything appeared to man "as it is, infinite" (*MHH* 14, p. 75 herein) there would not only be a general transformation of men's view of this world. There would also, as a consequence of this new view, be a literal transformation of this world itself, an apocalypse. Viewing this world as "One continued Vision or Fancy" (p. 471) and knowing that life is truly a divine—and human—unity in Christ, men would re-establish society on a new foundation, forming laws of freedom and love instead of repression, abolishing every kind of tyranny that prevents man from realizing his potentialities, and celebrating the divinity that is in every man.

† From Martin K. Nurmi, *Blake's Marriage of Heaven and Hell: A Critical Study*, Research Series 3, Kent State University Bulletin, 45: 4 (April 1957), pp. 14–23, 28–29, 59–61; abridgements approved by the author. Abbreviated references (followed by plate number) are to *Jerusalem* (J), *There Is No Natural Religion* (NNR), *The Marriage of Heaven and Hell* (MHH), *A Vision of The Last Judgment* (VLJ), *Europe* (E), *Everlasting Gospel* (EG), *The Four Zoas* (FZ), and *Milton* (M). The first paragraph alludes to J 10:21. Page numbers refer to this edition.

Spiritual perception, therefore, is obviously not merely a superior kind of physical sense perception such as Locke conjectured spirits to possess, enabling them to see "secondary qualities" directly, as if with microscopic or X-ray vision.[1] Blake explicitly rejects as useless for his purpose any kind of improvement in perception like that afforded by the telescope or microscope, which merely "alter / The ratio of the Spectator's Organs, but leave Objects untouch'd" (*M* 29:17–18, p. 184). Spiritual perception transforms objects. And it does so imaginatively, making them into symbolic forms which reveal the significance of those objects to the life of man, and thus shows their "real" form. The real form of the sun to Blake, for instance, is not that of a "round disk of fire somewhat like a Guinea," but "an Innumerable company of the Heavenly host crying, 'Holy, Holy, Holy is the Lord God Almighty'" (VLJ, p. 439).

There is no use in objecting, "But surely the sun *is* more like a guinea than like a chorus of angels." To ordinary perception, yes, it appears so. But even ordinary perception departs from the abstract ideal of a noumenal sun independent of perception, for ordinary perception too is imaginative, whether we like it or not. In fact, as Blake suggests in the second "Memorable Fancy" of *The Marriage* (*MHH* 12, p. 74), imagination is "the first principle" of human perception. Some imagination is necessary to any kind of perception, if only to synthesize discrete sense data into objects, synthesizing the brightness, warmth, roundness, etc. of the sun into the physical sun. (Modern psychology would agree, boggling only at the term imagination.) The chief difference between seeing the sun as a guinea and as a chorus of angels, Northrop Frye points out, is that the one requires only a limited amount of imagination, whereas the other requires a great deal. "The guinea-sun," writes Frye, "is a sensation assimilated to a general, impersonal, abstract idea. Blake can see it if he wants to, but when he sees the angels, he is not seeing more 'in' the sun but more of it."[2] He sees it, that is, not merely in relation to the growth of cabbages, but, to adapt Spinoza's famous phrase, *sub specie humanitatis*, under the aspect of a cosmic Humanity.

Such a way of seeing is philosophical, because it takes into account the order of all things and the nature of the Real. Spiritual perception is most philosophical, of course, when it apprehends the cosmic order directly, as it does in Blake's vision on the sands at Felpham (p. 479). But Blake has too much common sense to insist that one should always see with a fourfold eye: Spiritual perception is flexible. He does hold, nevertheless, that if man is going to realize his potentialities for beauty and joy, individually and socially, he must keep the larger order of things in mind. Man must do so even when using the practical vision needed for everyday life, so that even his ordinary actions are at least consistent with a Human conception of life in which every man participates in the divinity of Christ, and in which "every particle of dust breathes forth its joy" (*E* 3/iii.18, p. 98). When man can do this, "the whole creation," as Blake predicts in *The Marriage*," will be consumed and appear infinite and holy, whereas it now appears finite & corrupt" (*MHH* 14, p. 75). It will only *appear* so. To the visionary the creation appears infinite and holy now. But when all men learn to see aright,

---

1. Secondary qualities are the imperceptible powers in objects; these qualities produce primary or perceptible qualities. Locke, *Essay Concerning Human Understanding*, Bk. II, ch. xxiii, sec. 13.
2. Northrop Frye, *Fearful Symmetry: A Study of William Blake* (Princeton, 1947), p. 21.

and act according to an expanded vision, life in "this" world will in fact become infinite and holy and man will return to Eden.

II. His Doctrine of Contraries

Spiritual perception will return man to Eden; the doctrine of contraries, the other main theme of *The Marriage*, explains what life will be like there. It will not be insipid. "How wide the Gulf and Unpassable," exclaims Blake in mirror writing on a title page in *Milton*, "between Simplicity & Insipidity" (*M*33/30, p. 187). The simplicity of Eden is the simplicity of wisdom when combined with vision, or, in short, "innocence," in Blake's special meaning of the word. It also has a surpassing vigor: "As the breath of the Almighty such are the words of man to man / In the great Wars of Eternity" (*M*33/30:18–19). These mighty words are spoken in war, but it is a war that is a creative enterprise "in fury of Poetic Inspiration, / To build the Universe stupendous, Mental forms Creating" (*M*33/30:19–20). for the wars are "intellectual wars."

The theoretical basis for the dynamic creativeness of Edenic "Human" life is stated in essence in another distinction which appears on the same page of *Milton*: "Contraries are Positives / A Negation is not a Contrary" (*M*33/30 [epigram]). Or as Blake states it in *The Marriage*, "Without Contraries is no progression. Attraction and Repulsion, Reason and Energy, Love and Hate, are necessary to Human existence" (*MHH*3, p. 69). That is, a Human world must be informed by opposed yet positive and complementary forces which, when allowed to interact without external restraint, impart to life a motion and a tension that make it creative.

Since contraries have appeared in the speculations of many ages, in many forms, a few illustrative distinctions may be helpful.

Blake is not a Hegelian. Though he uses the word "progression" in *The Marriage*, his contrary forces do not, like Hegel's "thesis" and "antithesis," constitute a world process of "becoming." Indeed, Blake's Human world, in which the contraries freely interact, is not one of becoming at all, for it is perfect; the only "progression" there is in it is that of continued creativeness. And, of course, Blake would have nothing to do with anything as abstractly systematic as Hegel's dialectic.[3]

Nor, on the other hand, does Blake's doctrine resemble that of Nicholas of Cusa (1401–1464), the skeptic who taught that the contraries of this world become identical in God. For though Blake's cosmos has ultimately the form of One Man, or Christ, the contrary forces of life do not become in any sense identical in the cosmic man, but remain as oppositions which give the cosmos its Human vitality.

Finally, Blake's contraries are not like "Yin" and "Yang," the cosmological principles of Tsao Yen (3rd century B.C.). For "Yin" and "Yang" function alternatively somewhat as do the alternations of electrical waves, whereas Blake's contraries interact simultaneously.

Blake's contraries neither progress, disappear, nor alternate because they polarize human life. They are cosmic forces to be seen in every "individual." Not, however, as forces external to individuals, but as immanences. Tigers and horses are contraries, but that which makes them contraries is not sep-

---

3. The distinction between Blake and Hegel, and other matters relating to Blake's contraries, are treated in relentless detail in my dissertation, "Blake's Doctrine of Contraries: A Study in Visionary Metaphysics," unpubl. diss. (Minnesota, 1954).

arable from them, for their contrariety is in everything they are and do. Everything, moreover, has an eternal "identity" in the cosmic scheme as either active or passive contrary: tigers and horses, male and female, poets and philosophers, plowmen and harrowers. And active and passive contraries exist in "every Nation & every Family," in every "Species of Earth, Metal, Tree, Fish, Bird & Beast" (*M*27/25:41, p. 178). The tension of opposition is in every fibre of Blake's world.

But this opposition is not mere opposition, for "Contraries are Positives / A Negation is not a Contrary" (*M*33/30). The contraries of Blake's world are opposed but not in such a way that they hinder or deny each other, for such an opposition would produce only destruction, or a kind of cold war, or a state of trembling impotence. Rather, they act positively in opposed but complementary directions, and their opposition is like that between expansion and contraction, between the creative imagination and the ordering reason, or between idea and form. To use the key terms of *The Marriage*, the contraries are "energy" and "reason," by which Blake means the desire for creation and the desire for order. And by "reason" here he intends an ideal reason which strives to supply the form and order which raw energy lacks.

"Negations," on the other hand, are not "contraries," because they simply deny and seek to destroy each other, as the false reason of the materialistic rationalists seeks to destroy imagination by denying it any validity as a means to knowledge, and as a tyrannical king seeks to destroy liberty by oppression and war.

The distinction between contraries and negations is crucial. For to see the qualities of things as vital, necessary contraries is to live in a Human world of vision and imagination, whereas to see them as negations is to live in the fallen world of materialism and repressive social, religious, and political laws, a world in which the contraries are distorted and given the crude normative designations "good" and "evil." * * * The great task is to restore the abstractions which the "religious" call Good and Evil to their true and original identities as contraries. Good and evil, as the religious understand them, do not exist, says Blake. Good is simply "the passive that obeys Reason. Evil is the active springing from Energy" (*MHH*3, p. 69). * * *

* * * Humanity must reject the divisive moral categories which now pit one half of creation against the other half in destructive conflict. Conflict there must be, but it must be the creative conflict of the contraries in "intellectual war" (*FZ IX*, p. 421).

* * * The most important application of the doctrine of contraries is the social one: The contraries Blake is most interested in are the two classes of men, the energetic creators and the rational organizers, or the "devils" and the "angels," as he calls them in *The Marriage*. Both classes are necessary, and both must strive positively and vigorously each in its own way if man is to live the Human life.

III. On the Structure of The Marriage

Entirely Blake's own is the structure of *The Marriage*. One of the reasons, I think, why this work has been misunderstood lies in its unorthodox structure. For though it expounds philosophical conceptions, it does not do so in any of the modes usual for such a purpose. It is developed according to no traditional logical or rhetorical plan. More than anything else, the structure of *The Marriage* seems to resemble the A-B-A' of the ternary form in music, in which a first theme and its development are followed by a second theme and its development, followed in turn by a return to the first section or a modification of it. If a little intermingling of themes be allowed, *The Marriage* could be thought of as a rich philosophical rondo. Indeed, even the mode of development employed by Blake here is closer to musical than to rhetorical modes. For he does not rely upon argument, but uses the discursive expository sections of the work as "variations" of his theme, as it were, alternating them with "memorable fancies" and the other symbolic sections. In general, the first or "A" section deals with the idea of contraries, the second or "B" section with spiritual perception, and the third or "A'" section with the contraries again. So that the ternary structure of the work may be kept in mind the three main sections of the explication have been labeled A, B, and A'.

The first or "A" part (pp. 69–71), comprised of the first expository section (*MHH* 3,), "The Voice of the Devil" (*MHH* 4), and the second expository section (*MHH* 5–6), states the theme of the doctrine of contraries and introduces as a sort of counter-subject Swedenborg, who is to be the symbol of the angels who do not perceive the necessity of the contraries to Human existence. The main theme is first stated in the first expository section. It is then developed by the dramatic commentary of the devil, who, preaching partisan doctrine, presents the arguments against the angels. In the second expository section, Blake develops further the idea of contraries by explaining how one half of existence came to try to restrain the other half: he gives the history of that restraint which obscures the contraries, and gives as well both the angels' and the devils' versions of the story.

The tone of the "A" part is rather drier than that of the rest of the work, since this part contains two expository sections and only "The Voice of the Devil" as a variation. The middle or "B" part (p. 71–75), however, comprising the first memorable fancy (*MHH* 6–7) the "Proverbs of Hell" (*MHH* 7–10), the third expository section (*MHH* 11) the second memorable fancy (*MHH* 12–13) and the fourth expository section (*MHH* 14), relies more on symbolic development. The main theme of this part is enlarged sense perception, introduced dramatically but quite formally in the short first memorable fancy. It is developed contrapuntally, as it were, in the "Proverbs of Hell," with the general theme of energy, as it is seen by the devils. Thus the "Proverbs" are parallel in the structure of this part of the work to "The Voice of the Devil" in the first part. Now follows in the third expository section another history, this time of the growth of abstract systems through the corruption of the enlarged sense perceptions of the ancient poets. This history is also parallel to the history of restraint given in the first part, since it shows the role of abstraction in the development of restraint. Now the second memorable fancy develops the other side of the question by associating enlarged sense perception with excess and energy, in the lives of Isaiah and Ezekiel. Finally, the fourth expository section ends this part of the work in a prophetic tone by announcing that men's perceptions will be enlarged, and it also provides a kind of musical bridge passage in the figures of the cavern and printing, which are picked up in the third part of "A'" part.

The "A'" part (pp. 75–80) is the richest part of *The Marriage*, compris-ing the third memorable fancy (*MHH* 15), the fifth expository section (*MHH* 16–17), the fourth memorable fancy (*MHH* 17–20), the sentence "Opposi-tion is true Friendship" (*MHH* 20), the sixth expository section (*MHH* 21–22), and the climactic fifth memorable fancy (*MHH* 22–24), besides the final aphorism (*MHH* 24). In this part in general Blake returns to the doc-trine of contraries and brings the work to a close by joining the angel and the devil. But he also keeps the idea of enlarged perception in mind.

The doctrine of contraries, together with the idea of enlarged sense per-ception, is reintroduced allegorically, in this part, in the very meaty third memorable fancy, which also shows how enlarged perception leads to the free interaction of the contraries and subsequently to the creativeness that is characteristic of Human life. In the fifth expository section, which follows, Blake employs demonstration to show that there are two classes of men and that they must remain contraries. Returning to Swedenborg, who had been a counter-subject in the "A" part of *The Marriage*, Blake then shows in the remarkable fourth memorable fancy the true character of the angelic meta-physics that endeavors through fear and monsters of the mind to prevent cre-ative strife by suppressing imaginative energy in all spheres of life. And he follows this in the last expository section by a direct and serious attack on Swedenborg as one of the angels, which should be read against the back-ground of the robust comedy of the preceding satirical memorable fancy as in part a transitional change of mood leading to the climactic and prophetic debate that brings *The Marriage* to a close. This debate, in which the two contraries embrace and become one in the person of the prophet Elijah, effects the apocalyptic resolution toward which *The Marriage* has moved throughout its last part and which was announced at the beginning of the work ("Now is the dominion of Edom, & the return of Adam into Paradise") and again at the end of the "B" part ("The cherub with his flaming sword is hereby commanded to leave his guard at tree of life"). By marrying the angels and devils of this world, it prophesies that Human life, which was allegori-cally portrayed in the "Printing house in Hell," will actually come to pass.

Though not, perhaps, at once. *The Marriage* moves, like Blake's great epics—and indeed his prophetic lyric "The Tyger"—toward an apocalyptic conclusion, but in the last part there sounds a slightly less positive note, in the shift back to ironic point of view in which anyone who embraces energy becomes a "devil." It reminds one of Beethoven's tempering the positive resolution of his song cycle, *An die Ferne Geliebte*, by a brief snatch of its plaintive first theme. Perhaps even in the exultant mood in which Blake wrote *The Marriage*, he was not quite sure that the oppositions of this world could in fact become the contraries of the mental war.

And, indeed, the great synthesis of *The Marriage* was not to be a final one. Blake found that the dialectics of his initial formulation of the doc-trine of contraries, in which he would simply transform into fruitful con-traries all oppositions now splitting this world, could not bring about the Eden he envisaged for man. After his initial excitement at the possibilities suggested by such a synthesis had lessened somewhat, he no doubt saw that the intellectual battles of an Edenic mental war of art and science were not to be fought as long as corporeal wars were waged by "spectres" such as George III. Evidently something very like evil did after all have a real exis-tence, though it was still not what the religious call evil. And accordingly we find Blake becoming more uncompromisingly apocalyptic, demanding a more radical revolution in the modes of thought and life. In the next statement of his doctrine of contraries, in the so-called "Lambeth Books," we find that he has sharply distinguished the oppositions of this world and those of the Human world into negations and contraries; or rather, that he has applied to the idea of opposites the distinction between the positive virtue of "act" and its negative "hindering," which he had set forth at the end of his annotations to Lavater in 1789 (p. 454). Not all of the angels are capable of becoming contraries, for some of them can never do anything but hinder. There is no place for them in Eden.

ALICIA OSTRIKER

From Desire Gratified and Ungratified: William Blake and Sexuality†

To examine Blake on sexuality is to deal with a many-layered thing. Although we like to suppose that everything in the canon "not only belongs in a unified scheme but is in accord with a permanent structure of ideas,"[1] some of Blake's ideas clearly change during the course of his career, and some others may constitute internal inconsistencies powerfully at work in, and not resolved by, the poet and his poetry. What I will sketch here is four sets of Blakean attitudes toward sexual experience and gender relations, each of them coherent and persuasive if not ultimately "systematic"; for convenience, and in emulation of the poet's own method of personifying ideas and feelings, I will call them four Blakes. First, the Blake who celebrates sexuality and attacks repression, whom we may associate with Freud and even more with Reich. Second, a corollary Blake whom we may associate with Jung, whose idea of the emanation—the feminine element within man—parallels Jung's concept of the anima, and who depicts sexual life as a complex web of gender complementarities and interdependencies. Third, a Blake apparently inconsistent with Blake number one, who sees sexuality as a tender trap rather than a force of liberation. Fourth, and corollary to that, the Blake to whom it was necessary, as it was to his patriarchal precursor Milton, to see the female principle as subordinate to the male.

Blake number one is perhaps the most familiar to the common reader, although professional Blakeans have paid little attention to him lately. He is the vigorous, self-confident, exuberant advocate of gratified desire, writing in his early and middle thirties (that is, between the fall of the Bastille and the execution of Louis and the declaration of war between England and

---

† From *Blake: An Illustrated Quarterly* 16 (1982–83), 156–65; abridged with minor changes approved by the author. Page numbers refer to this edition. Ostriker, along with Anne K. Mellor (e.g. 148–55 in the same issue of *BIQ* and in *Nineteenth-Century Studies* 2 [1988]), Irene Tayler, *Bulletin of the Midwest Modern Language Association* 6 (1973; reprinted in our first edition), Susan Fox, *Critical Inquiry* 3 (1977), and Diana Hume George (1980), opened an ever-proliferating feminist line of inquiry taken up by critics of a greater variety of persuasions, talents, and schools of thought than we can recognize, among them Brenda Webster, Margaret Storch, Claire Colebrook, Eugenie R. Freed, Laura Ellen Haigwood, Catherine McClenahan, David Punter, and Helen Bruder. See also "Sources Cited in Editorial Notes."
1. Northrop Frye, *Fearful Symmetry* (Princeton: Princeton Univ. Press, 1947), p. 14.

France) the early Notebook poems, the *Songs, The Marriage of Heaven and Hell* and the *Visions of the Daughters of Albion.* A few texts will refresh the memory. Among the Notebook epigrams we are told that

> Love to faults is always blind
> Always is to joy inclind
> Lawless wingd and unconfind
> And breaks all chains from every mind
> (p. 384)

> Abstinence sows sand all over
> The ruddy limbs & flaming hair
> But Desire Gratified
> Plants fruits of life & beauty there
> (p. 389)

> What is it men in women do require?
> The lineaments of Gratified Desire
> What is it Women do in men require?
> The lineaments of Gratified Desire
> (p. 389)

It was probably these lines that converted me to Blake when I was twenty. They seemed obviously true, splendidly symmetrical, charmingly cheeky— and nothing else I had read approached them, although I thought Yeats must have picked up a brave tone or two here. Only later did I notice that the epigrams were tiny manifestoes announcing an identity of interest between sexuality and the human imagination.

During these years Blake wrote numerous minidramas illustrating how possessiveness and jealousy, prudery and hypocrisy poison the lives of lovers. He pities the chaste ("The Sunflower") and depicts the pathos of chastity relinquished too late ("The Angel"), looks forward to a "future Age" when "Love! Sweet Love!" will no longer be thought a crime, while protesting its repression by Church and State in his own time. One of his two major statements about sexual repression in *Songs of Experience* is the deceptively simple "The Garden of Love," in which the speaker discovers a Chapel built where he "used to play on the green." The garden has a long scriptural and literary ancestry * * * [in which it symbolizes] at once the earthly paradise and the body of a woman. Probably Blake saw it so. Later he would draw the nude torso of a woman with a cathedral where her genitals should be. The briars at the poem's close half-suggest that the speaker is being crowned with something like thorns, somewhere about the anatomy, and it anticipates Blake's outraged demand, near the close of his life, in the *Everlasting Gospel:* "Was Jesus chaste? Or did he / Give any lessons of chastity?" Since the design for "The Garden of Love" depicts a priest and two children kneeling at an open grave beside a church, the forbidden love may be a parent as well as a peer, and the speaker might be of either sex: all repression is one. It is important that the tone here is neither angry nor self-righteous, but pathetic and passive—indeed, pathetically passive, for after the opening "I went," the governing verb is "saw." That the speaker only "saw . . . my joys and desires" being bound with briars and did not "feel" anything, should shock us into realizing that this speaker, at least by the poem's last line, has been effectively self-alienated. Repression has worked not merely from without, but from within.[2]

The other major statement is "London," where Blake hears the clanking of the mind-forg'd manacles (chains such as "Love . . . breaks from every mind") he will later associate with Urizen. Economic exploitation sanctioned by blackening churches and political exploitation sanctioned by bleeding palace walls are grievous, but "most" grievous is sexual exploitation, perhaps because it is a denial of humanity's greatest virtue, charity, as sweep's cry and soldier's sigh are denials of faith and hope; or perhaps because, to Blake, sexual malaise precedes and produces all other ills:

> But most thro' midnight streets I hear
> How the youthful Harlots curse
> Blasts the newborn Infants tear
> And blights with plagues the Marriage hearse
>
> (p. 41)

That final stanza is Blake's most condensed indictment of the gender arrangements in a society where Love is ruled by Law and consequently dies; where virtuous females are pure, modest, and programmed for frigidity, so that healthy males require whores; where whores have ample cause to curse; and where their curses have the practical effect of infecting young families with venereal disease as well as with the more metaphoric plague of unacknowledged guilt.[3] Through his hissing, spitting and explosive alliteration Blake creates an ejaculatory harlot who is (and there are analogues to her in Spenser, Shakespeare, Milton) not the garden but the snake. That a syntactic ambivalence common in Blake makes her one who is cursed by others, as well as one who curses, does not diminish the point.

The point recurs polemically in *The Marriage of Heaven and Hell*, where, according to Auden, "the whole of Freud's teachings may be found.[4] Here "Prisons are built with stones of Law, brothels with bricks of Religion," "Prudence is a rich ugly old maid courted by Incapacity," and we are exhorted: "Sooner murder an infant in its cradle than nurse unacted desires" (pp. 71–73). Here too is the famous pre-Freudian précis of Freud's theories on suppression: "Those who restrain desire, do so because theirs is weak enough to be restrained; and the restrainer or reason usurps its place and governs the unwilling. And being restrained it by degrees becomes passive till it is only the shadow of desire" (p. 70). . . . But Blake— and this is what makes him more Reichian than Freudian—joyfully foresees the end of discontent and civilization too: "For the cherub with his flaming sword is hereby commanded to leave his guard at tree of life, and

2. I am disagreeing at this point with Morris Dickstein's otherwise excellent essay, "The Price of Experience: Blake's Reading of Freud" in *The Literary Freud*, ed. Joseph Smith (New Haven: Yale Univ. Press), pp. 67–111. * * * A persuasive reading of the poem's Oedipal dimension is in Diana Hume George, *Blake and Freud* (Ithaca: Cornell Univ. Press, 1980), pp. 104–106.
3. For a harrowing account of the phenomenon of the youthful harlot in nineteenth-century England, see Florence Rush, *The Best-Kept Secret: Sexual Abuse of Children* (Englewood Cliffs, NJ: Prentice-Hall, 1980), ch. 5.
4. W. H. Auden, "Psychoanalysis and Art To-day" (1935), in *The English Auden*, ed. Edward Mendelson (New York: Random House, 1977), p. 339.

when he does, the whole creation will be consumed, and appear infinite, and holy whereas it now appears finite & corrupt. This will come to pass by an improvement of sensual enjoyment" (p. 75)

In all such texts Blake is not only attacking the powers of repression, particularly institutional religion, which in the name of reason and holiness attempts to subdue desire. He is also asserting that gratified desire *does* what religion *pretends* to do: gives access to vision, the discovery of the infinite. Moreover—and this is a point to which I will return—Blake in these texts does not stress the distinction between male and female, or assign conspicuously different roles to the two sexes. Youth and virgin suffer alike under chastity, man and woman have identical desires, and the "ruddy limbs and flaming hair" of which an ardent imagination makes a garden, and an abstinent imagination makes a desert, may belong interchangeably to a lover or a beloved, a male or a female.

The poem in which Blake most extensively elaborates his celebration of love and his critique of repression is *Visions of the Daughters of Albion*, printed in 1793. *Visions* is also the poem most clearly delineating male sexual aggressiveness as a component of Urizenic patriarchy, and illustrating the kinds of damage it does to both males and females. First of all, Bromion is a number of things which to Blake are one thing. He is the slaveowner who converts humans into private property and confirms his possession by impregnating the females, the racist who rationalizes racism by insisting that the subordinate race is sexually promiscuous, the rapist who honestly believes that his victim was asking for it; and, withal, he does not actually experience "sensual enjoyment." But if Bromion represents the social and psychological pathology of sexual violence, Theotormon represents its pitiable underside, sexual impotence. "Oerflowd with woe," asking unanswerable questions, weeping incessantly, Theotormon does not respond to Bromion's insult to his masculinity ("Now thou maist marry Bromions harlot" (5/2:1, p. 58). Playing the hesitant Hamlet to Bromion's rough Claudius, intimidated slave to coarse slave-master, Theotormon has been victimized by an ideology that glorifies male aggressiveness, as much as by that ideology's requirement of feminine purity. Dejected and self-flagellant (design, p. 64), he cannot look Oothoon in her intellectual and erotic eye as she maintains her spiritual virginity and offers him her love, not only because she is damaged goods but because she is taking sexual initiative instead of being "modest." Only with incredulity and grief does Oothoon realize this (9/6:4–20, p. 63).

Most of *Visions* is Oothoon's opera. Raped, enslaved, imprisoned, rejected, the heroine's agonized rhapsody of self-offering rushes from insight to insight. Though she begins by focusing on her individual condition, her vision rapidly expands outward. She analyzes the enchainment of loveless marriage and the unhappy children it must produce, she praises the value of infant sexuality and attacks the ethos which brands joy whoredom and sublimates its sexuality in twisted religiosity. She also bewails other ramifications of the tyranny of reason over desire, such as the abuse of peasant by landlord, of worker by factory owner, of the faithful by their churches. For Oothoon life means being "open to joy and to delight where ever beauty appears," and the perception of any beauty is an erotic activity in which eye and object join "in happy copulation." Made desperate by her lover's unresponsiveness, she cries out for "Love! Love! Love! Happy

happy Love! Free as the mountain wind! / Can that be Love, that drinks another as a sponge drinks water?" Though remaining herself "bound" to Bromion, she nevertheless concludes with a vision of the vitality of all free things:

> Arise you little glancing wings, and sing your infant joy!
> Arise and drink your bliss, for every thing that lives is holy!
> (11/8:9–11, p. 65)

Blake in *Visions* has created a heroine unequalled in English poetry before or since. Oothoon not only defines and defends her own sexuality rather than waiting for Prince Charming to interrupt her nap, and not only attacks patriarchal ideology root and branch, but outflanks everyone in her poem for intellectuality and spirituality, and is intellectual and spiritual precisely because she is erotic.* * *

Blake number two appears later than Blake number one, and shifts his psychological principles from an essentially socio-political to an essentially mythic base. Beginning with *The Book of Urizen*, engraved in 1794, and throughout his major prophecies, the poet relies on an idea of humanity as originally and ultimately androgynous, attributing the fall of man and what John Milton called "all our woe" not to female narcissism but to specifically male pride, male competitiveness, or male refusal to surrender the self, and depicting a fallen state in which sexual division—lapse of unity between male and female as one being—is the prototype of every division within the self, between self and other, and between humanity and God.

The mythology of these poems posits a hero who is both Great Britain and all mankind, and who lives in Eternity or Eden as one of a family of Eternals who collectively compose One Man, Christ. Albion's "Human Brain," the equivalent of Jung's collective unconscious, houses four energetic Jungian Zoas, each of whom has a feminine counterpart or emanation. At Man's Fall, precipitated in *Urizen* by Urizen's pride, in *The Four Zoas* and *Milton* by rivalry between Urizen and Luvah, and in *Jerusalem* by Albion's selfish refusal to maintain erotic union with his Saviour and his insistence on moral virtue, Albion lapses into what Blake variously calls sleep, death and disease, and what the rest of us call human history. The Zoas simultaneously lapse into lower forms and mutual conflict instead of harmony, and are disastrously divided from their emanations. As the late Blake formulaically puts it, "The Feminine separates from the Masculine & both from Man." Bodies grow around them, inimical "to the embrace of love":

> that no more the Masculine mingles
> With the Feminine, but the Sublime is shut out from the Pathos
> In howling torment, to build stone walls of separation, compelling
> The Pathos, to weave curtains of hiding secresy from the torment.
> (*Jerusalem* 90:10–14, p. 330)

At the close of his three longest poems Blake imagines an apocalypse in which selfhood is relinquished and male and female are reunified (*Jerusalem* 97:12–15, p. 333).

To say that Blake's emanations resemble what Jung calls the anima is to say that they represent a man's interior "female part," the "life-giving aspect of the psyche" and the "a priori element in his moods, reactions and impulses," and whatever else is spontaneous in psychic life."[5] As a positive figure the Blakean emanation like the Jungian anima is a benevolent guide to the unconscious life. As a negative figure she is seductive and destructive. She seems also to represent a man's emotionality, sensuousness, sensitivity, receptivity—all that makes him potentially effeminate—which in a fallen state he rejects or believes to be separated from himself, and must recover if he is to gain psychic wholeness. According to Jung, of course, an individual man changes and develops during the course of his lifetime but "his" anima does not. She remains static, and his only problem is to accept her existence as a portion of himself. What is particularly fascinating about Blake, then, is that he invents not one but a set of female beings, each appropriate to the Zoa she belongs to, each with her own personality and history of transformations, not radically different from the personalities in highly symbolic fiction and drama, and able to shed light very often on characters we thought we knew as well as on larger issues of sexual complementarity.

The first figures we encounter in *The Four Zoas*, for example, are Tharmas and Enion—humanity's Sensation—in the midst of a marital quarrel. Tharmas and Enion are bucolic characters of the sort that the wheels of history run over: good but not too bright, easily confused. We may recognize their like in mythic pairs like Baucis and Philemon, Deucalion and Pyrrha, and the Wakefield Noah with his farcically shrewish wife.

✳   ✳   ✳

Enion gives birth to Los and Enitharmon, the Eternal Prophet and his Muse, who from the start are as arrogant and self-absorbed as their parents are humble and selfless. [Enitharmon becomes] a seductive and maddening tease. She is the muse who won't come across, taunting the poet with failure and giving her alliance to Reason (Neoclassicism, let us say) instead of Prophecy, while forbidding the poet to love anyone but herself.

✳   ✳   ✳

A third couple is Urizen and Ahania: Reason and the Faith or Idealism necessary to it. Early in *The Four Zoas*, Urizen as cosmic architect places Ahania in a zodiacal shrine and burns incense to her. Here we have Blake's version of the "pedestal," and of that neo-Platonically inspired sexual reverence which prefers ladies pure, exalted and static rather than adjacent and active. When Ahania is uncomfortable in her shrine and tires to give her spouse some advice about returning to Eternity, he seizes her by the hair, calling her "Thou little diminutive portion that darst be a counterpart," and throws her out of heaven, declaring "Am I not God? Who is equal to me?" (*Four Zoas* III, 42:21–43:9, Erdman p. 328). Without Ahania,

---

5. C. F. Jung, "Archetypes of the Collective Unconscious," *Collected Works*, ed. Herbert Read, Michael Fordham, Gerhard Adler and W. McGuire, trans. R.F.C. Hull, (Princeton: Princeton Univ. Press, Bollingen Series XX, 1967–78), vol. 9, part 1, p. 27. Jung also discusses the anima and the anima-animus "sacred marriage" in "Two Essays on Analytical Psychology" (vol. 7) and "Aion: Researches into the Phenomenology of the Self" (vol. 9, part 2). ✳ ✳ ✳ Among the critics who identify anima with emanation are June Singer, *The Unholy Bible: A Psychological Interpretation of William Blake* (New York: Putnam, 1970), p. 212, and W. P. Witcutt, *Blake: A Psychological Study* (Port Washington, NY: Kennikat Press, 1945), pp. 43ff. Christine Gallant, in *Blake and the Assimilation of Chaos* (Princeton: Princeton Univ. Press, 1978) disagrees, arguing that ✳ ✳ ✳ Blake's emanations are not animae because "if they were . . . they would have characteristics as differentiated as those of their Zoas" (pp. 53–54). It is my contention that they do. ✳ ✳ ✳

Urizen is Doubt instead of Faith, and degenerates in the course of *The Four Zoas* from Prince of Light, to tyrannic parody of Milton's God, to William Pitt opposing the Bread Bill of 1800, to the Dragon Form of Antichrist. Ahania falls from being a sky goddess who opened her mouth once too often to "the silent woman" about whom feminist critics are presently writing a good deal.[6] Until just before the end of *The Four Zoas* Ahania has nothing further to say. As "the furrowed field" she is a figure of complete submission.

*   *   *

Luvah and Vala, last of the Zoas and Emanations, are in their unfallen form lover and beloved, the Eros and Psyche of Man. Luvah is born into this world as the revolutionary babe and flaming youth who must become a sacrificed god in epoch after epoch, while Vala is the *dolorosa* who, believing she loves him, always sacrifices him.

As all Blake readers know, Vala is one of Blake's most complicated characters. Her name means "vale" as in "valley," and as Nature she is the valley of the shadow of death, the declivity of the female genitals, and the membranous "veil" which preserves virginity, as well as the "veil" covering the tabernacle of the Old Testament. Like the chapel in "The Garden of Love" and the "chapel all of gold" (p. 388), she stands at the intersection between corrupt sexuality and institutional religion; thus she is also the veil of the temple which was rent when Jesus died, for Vala is the Nature we worship when we should worship Christ, she is Fortuna, Babylon, the Great Whore, enemy of Jerusalem. Where Enitharmon is a tease and a betrayer, Vala is the "Female Will" incarnate as killer. She is the chaste mistress who withholds favors so that her lovers will become warriors, and she is the blood-spattered priestess who with a knife of flint cuts the hearts out of men—all the while protesting that she craves nothing but Love. So powerful a figure is she that I expect we see at least as much of her in popular culture—where she is the voluptuous pinup on barracks walls, and she is the lady in black leather who will punish you—as in conventional fiction and drama. Pornography magazines offer us endless reproductions of Vala-Babylon, and, in the most high-chic phases of fashion design, the ideal fashion model is "cruel" Vala.

*   *   *

Late in *Jerusalem*, one of Vala's avatars has a warrior-lover whom she craves to possess completely. "O that I could live in his sight," she says; "O that I could bind him to my arm" (*Jerusalem* 82:44, p. 320). Concealing him under her veil, she wishes him to become "an infant love" at her breast. When she opens the veil, revealing "her own perfect beauty," her lover has become "a winding worm." Blake hopes at this moment to show that Female Will is ultimately self-defeating. The winding worm is a further degeneration of helpless infancy, so that her wish has come true beyond her intention, as in folktales. The worm is also the phallic worm . . . and the devouring worm of the grave.

6. See, for example, Mary Daly, *Beyond God the Father* (Boston: Beacon Press, 1973), Marcia Landy, "The Silent Woman," in *The Authority of Experience*, ed. Arlyn Diamond and Lee Edwards (Amherst: Univ. of Massachusetts Press, 1977), Susan Griffin, *Woman and Nature: The Roaring Inside Her* (New York: Harper and Row, 1978), Sandra M. Gilbert and Susan Gubar, *The Madwoman in the Attic* (New Haven: Yale Univ. Press, 1980), chaps. 1 and 2. * * *

*   *   *

For the Blake who conceived of humanity as androgynous, the division of Zoas from Emanations signified human disorder and disaster. His poetry describing sexual division is some of the most anguished in the language. By the same token, re-couplings precipitate and are accompanied by all the images for joy and order Blake knew: a seasonal cycle culminating in harvest, vintage, and communal feast; a painful bread-making and wine-making which issues in happiness; music and "vocal harmony" concluding in human "conversing"; and a beaming morning sun.

To trace the lineaments of Blake number three, we must return to the very outset of the poet's career, and the extraordinary lyric "How sweet I roamed from field to field" (p. 357), where an unidentified winged speaker is lured and trapped by "the prince of love."

*   *   *

Although the theme of romantic enthrallment of a woman by a man is relatively unusual in English poetry, Irene H. Chayes argues convincingly that the speaker is Psyche and the manipulator of "silken net" and "golden cage" is Eros.[7]

But in later versions of this scenario, the instruments of entrapment and enclosure—net, cage, locked box—will be the sexually symbolic props of females who imprison males. "The Crystal Cabinet," "The Golden Net," and "The Mental Traveller" (p. 397 ff.) are all versions of this theme, and the "Woman Old" of the last of these is a brilliant portrayal of the *vagina dentata* in action, for she torments male vitality simultaneously by nailing and piercing, and by binding and catching.

*   *   *

Among the engraved poems, "To Tirzah" is a furious repudiation of female sexuality in its maternal aspect as that which encloses and divides man from Eternity. To appreciate the impact of "To Tirzah" in its original context we should probably see it as the contrary poem to "A Cradle Song" in *Innocence* (p. 20). Where in *Innocence* a mother sings lullingly to a sleeping infant of the "sweet" smiles and tears that Jesus as "an infant small" sheds and shares with herself and the child, in *Experience* the child responds, ironically using Jesus' adolescent rejection of Mary (John 2:4) for his punch line: . . . . "Then what have I to do with thee" [see full text, p. 45)].

A second strong repudiation is *Europe*, where erotic entrapment both maternal and sexual, the former expressing itself as possessive, the latter as seductive manipulation of male desire, takes place so that "Woman, lovely Woman! May have dominion" during the corrupt centuries of Enitharmon's reign. Here Enitharmon's "crystal house" is analogous to the crystal cabinet, and within it there is a constant claustrophobic movement of nocturnal binding, circling, cycling, broken only by the dawn of European revolution.

How well do these poems fit the Blake who praises "gratified Desire" and insists that "Energy is the only life and is from the body"? Rather poorly, I think. However allegorically we interpret the thing, sexual love in these poems is neither gratifying nor capable of gratification, and the poet

---

7. Irene H. Chayes, "The Presence of Cupid and Psyche," in *Blake's Visionary Forms Dramatic*, ed. David V. Erdman and John E. Grant (Princeton: Princeton Univ. Press, 1970), pp. 214–43.

consistently associates "sensual enjoyment" with cruelty, imprisonment, illusion and mortality instead of liberation, vision and immortality. Morton Paley has pointed out that Blake's Lambeth books involve "a sort of involuntary dualism, a myth with implications that in some ways conflicted with his own beliefs. Blake's intuition of the goodness of the body in general and of sexual love in particular had not weakened . . . but . . . the Lambeth myth seems to imply that physical life is inherently evil."[8] If, in other words, we have one Blake for whom physical life is type and symbol of spiritual life and fulfilled joy in one leads us to the other, there is also a Blake for whom body and spirit are as irreconcilably opposed as they are for any Church Father. But the contradiction is exacerbated rather than resolved in the later books, where the anatomical image of the enclosure vastly expands to become a whole world, the realm of Beulah, a dreamy moony place presided over by tender females, which is both comfort and trap.

＊　＊　＊

Love in Beulah inevitably brings a depletion of energy and the advent of jealousies, murders, moral law, revenge, and the whole panoply of inhuman cruelties the poet has taught us to struggle against.

＊　＊　＊

If the Blake who celebrates desire sees it as equally distributed between genders, the Blake who fears desire sees sexuality in general and sexual threat in particular as a female phenomenon. This third Blake gives us an array, culminating in *Jerusalem*, of passive males subject to females who seduce, reject, betray, bind, lacerate, mock and deceive them. After *Visions of the Daughters of Albion*, though Blake continues strenuously to oppose the idea that woman's love is *sin*, he increasingly describes it as *snare*. There is no comparable depiction of males seducing and betraying females.

This brings me to Blake number four, who is perhaps not quite a classic misogynist—though he sometimes sounds like one—but someone who believes that the proper study of woman is the happiness of her man, and who cannot conceive of a true woman in any but a supportive, subordinate role. ＊ ＊ ＊

Examining Blake from this point of view, and returning to *Visions*, we notice that Oothoon is good, and she is wise, but she is completely powerless. So long as her menfolk refuse enlightenment, she will be bound hand and foot, imprisoned in a passivity which she does not desire but to which she must submit. Looking at *The Four Zoas*, we see that Enion and Ahania are likewise good—indeed, they represent precisely the goodness of selfless love and compassion—but passive, while Enitharmon and Vala are active and evil. In *Milton* and *Jerusalem* the story is the same: female figures are either powerful or good; never both. The late prophecies may even constitute a retreat from the point Blake arrived at in *Visions*, for the better the late females are, the more passive, the more submissive and obedient they also are.[9] When Ololon finds Milton, she tearfully apologizes for being the

8. Morton D. Paley, *Energy and the Imagination: A Study of the Development of Blake's Thought* (Oxford: Clarendon, 1970), p. 90.
9. A partial exception is the prophetic figure of Erin in *Jerusalem*, yet in a sense Erin is an exception that proves the rule; for though her voice is inspirational without passivity or subordination, she remains undeveloped as a character, lacking the internal struggles and self-transformations of the other major figures in the poem.

cause of Natural Religion. And when Milton concludes his splendid final speech on "Self-annihilation and the grandeur of Inspiration" with a peroration against the "Sexual Garments, the Abomination of Desolation," Ololon responds by dividing into the six-fold Virgin who dives "into the depths / Of Miltons Shadow as a Dove upon the stormy sea" and a "moony Ark" who enters into the fires of intellect

> Around the Starry Eight: with one accord the Starry Eight became
> One Man Jesus the Saviour. Wonderful! Round his limbs
> The Clouds of Ololon folded as a Garment dipped in blood
>   (*Milton* **49**/42:9–11, p. 203)

At the climax of *Jerusalem* there is a similar self-immolative plunge when "England" awakes on Albion's bosom. Having blamed herself for being "the Jealous Wife" who has caused all the troubles of the poem:

> England who is Brittania enterd Albions bosom rejoicing
> Rejoicing in his indignation! adoring his wrathful rebuke.
> She who adores not your frowns will only loathe your smiles
>   (*Jerusalem* 95:22–4, p. 336)

But this somewhat gratuitous-seeming passage lacks—since we have not met "England" until now—the systematic quality of Blake's treatment of his chief heroine.

The poet's final and most fully-idealized heroine "is named Liberty among the sons of Albion" (*J* 26:3–4) yet we seriously mistake Blake's intention if we think Jerusalem is herself a free being, or even a being capable of volition. She is the City of God, bride of Christ, and man's Christian Liberty, to be sure, but that is only in Eden, and even there she does not act; she simply is. What happens to Jerusalem within the body of the poem at no point involves her in action or in protest. At its outset she is withheld by Albion from "the vision & fruition of the Holy-one" (*J* 4:17) and is accused of sin by Albion and Vala. Unlike Oothoon she does not deny the accusation, nor does she defend her own vision with anything like Oothoon's exuberance. Patiently, meekly, she explains and begs Love and Forgiveness from her enemies. That is her last initiative. Subsequently she is rejected as a whore, cast out, imprisoned, driven finally to insanity, and becomes wholly incapable even of remembering her original self without being reminded of her origins by the voice of her pitying and merciful God. Even this comfort does not help; for at the poem's darkest moment, just before the advent of the Covering Cherub, Jerusalem passively receives a cup of poison from the conquering Vala (*J* 88:56).

The final movement of *Jerusalem* evokes its heroine twice, when "the Universal Father" speaking through "the vision of Albion" echoes the Song of Solomon: "Awake! Awake Jerusalem! O lovely Emanation of Albion / . . . / For lo! The Night of Death is past and the Eternal Day / Appears upon our hills: Awake Jerusalem and come away" (*J* 97:1–3), and when the poet's vision of "All Human Forms" is complete: "And I heard the Name of their Emanations they are named Jerusalem" (*J* 99:5). Yet * * * we do not and cannot encounter the "awakened" Jerusalem directly. As *A Vision of the Last Judgment* explicitly tells us, and as the whole of *Jerusalem* implies, "In Eternity Woman is the Emanation of Man; she has no Will of her own. There is no such thing in Eternity as a Female Will" (p. 436). If we wonder what the Emanative role in Eternity is, Blake has already told us:

When in Eternity Man converses with Man, they enter
Into each others Bosom (which are universes of delight)
In mutual interchange, and first their Emanations meet . . .
For man cannot unite with Man but by their Emanations . . .
(*Jerusalem* 88:3–9, p. 326)

Is femaleness, then, ideally a kind of social glue? Susan Fox argues that
although "in his prophetic poems Blake conceives of a perfection of
humanity defined by the complete mutuality of its interdependent genders," he nevertheless in these same poems "represents one of these equal
genders as inferior and dependent . . . or as unnaturally and disastrously
dominant," so that females come to represent either "weakness" or "power-
hunger."[1] Anne Mellor has observed that Blake's ideal males throughout the
major prophecies are creative and independent while his ideal females "at
their best are nurturing . . . generous . . . compassionate . . . all welcoming
and never-critical, emotional supporters," and that "in Blake's metaphoric
system, the masculine is both logically and physically prior to the feminine."[2] But at its most extreme, Blake's vision goes beyond proposing an
ideal of dominance-submission or priority-inferiority between the genders.
As a counter-image to the intolerable idea of female power, female con-
tainment and "binding" of man to mortal life, Blake wishfully imagines that
the female can be re-absorbed by the male, be contained within him, and
exist Edenically not as a substantial being but as an attribute. Beyond the
wildest dreams of Levi-Strauss, the ideal female functions as a medium of
interchange among real, that is to say male, beings.

And what are we as readers to make of Blake's contradictions?[3] Morris
Dickstein, noting the shift from the "feminism" of *Visions* to his later stress
on "female Will," calls it "a stunning change that seems rooted less in politics than in the nearly unknown terrain of Blake's personal life" (pp. 77–78).
Diana George believes that Blake became entrapped in a culturally mandated
sexual typology which he initially intended to "redeem."[4] Although all our
anecdotal material about the Blakes indicates that Catherine adored her
visionary husband even when he was not bringing home the bacon, much
less adorning her in gems and gold, marital friction looks like a reasonable
source for many Notebook and other poems. Perhaps, too, Blake had a model
for Oothoon in Mary Wollstonecraft, whose vigorous equal may not have
been encountered in his other female acquaintances after Wollstonecraft's
death.[5] At the same time, we should recognize that the shift in Blake's sexual
views coincides with other ideological and doctrinal transformations: from a
faith in political revolution perhaps assisted or exemplified by Art to a faith
in Imagination as that which alone could prepare humanity for its harvest
and vintage; from what looks like a love of nature that makes him one of the

1. Susan Fox, "The Female as Metaphor in William Blake's Poetry," *Critical Inquiry* 5 (1977), 507.
2. Anne K. Mellor, "Blake's Portrayal of Women," *Blake: An Illustrated Quarterly* 26:3 (1982–83),
   148–155.
3. For some readers, of course, no contradiction worth noticing exists. ° ° ° Such is Jean Hagstrum's
   pleasant conclusion in "Babylon Revisited, or the Story of Luvah and Vala," in *Blake's Sublime Allegory*, ed. Curran and Wittreich (1973), p. 188. David Aers, in "William Blake and the Dialectic of
   Sex," *ELH* 44 (1977), 500–514, feels that in *Visions* Blake "may have slipped toward an optimistic,
   idealistic illusion in his handling of Oothoon's consciousness." ° ° °
4. *Blake and Freud*, chap. 6, includes this argument in a larger discussion of Blake's treatment of "the
   feminine."
5. See Alicia Ostriker, "Todd, *Wollstonecraft Anthology*," *Blake: An illustrated Quarterly* 14 (1980–81),
   129–131.

great pastoral poets in the English language and extends as far as *Milton*, to a growing and finally absolute rejection of nature and all fleshly things; and from an immanent to a transcendent God.

Yet to say that Blake's views moved from X to Y would be an absurd over-simplification. It would be truer to say that X and Y were with him always—like his Saviour—in varying proportions, and that the antagonism between them is the life of his poetry. One of the idols of our tribe is System, a Blakean term signifying a set of ideas bounded by an adhesive inflexible consistency, cognate of the "bounded" which its possessor soon loathes, the "Circle" that any sensible God or Man should avoid, and the "mill with complicated wheels." If "Unity is the cloke of Folly" in a work of art, we might make it our business as critics not only to discover, but also to admire, a large poet's large inconsistencies—particularly in an area like the meaning of sex, where the entire culture, and probably each of us, in the shadows of our chambers, feel profound ambivalence.

If "without contraries is no progression," I think we should be neither sur-prised nor dismayed to find in Blake both a richly developed anti-patriarchal and proto-feminist sensibility, in which love between the sexes serves as a metaphor for psychic wholeness, integrity, and more abundant life, and its opposite, a homocentric gynophobia in which heterosexual love means human destruction.[6] "If the doors of perception were cleansed everything would appear to man as it is, infinite." What then if we concede that Blake's vision, at least part of the time, was fogged to the degree that he could per-ceive Man as infinite but could not perceive Woman as equally so? Blake understood that it is impossible for any prophet finally to transcend histor-ical time. He understood so of Isaiah and Ezekiel, he understood the same of John Milton. "To give a Body to Error" was, he believed, an essential ser-vice performed by mighty intellects for posterity. We might, with gratitude for this way of comprehending great poetry, see him as he saw his precur-sors. To paraphrase Emerson and the *Gita*, when him we fly, he is our wings.

NELSON HILTON

From Some Polysemous Words in Blake[†]

APPALLS / APPALL'D

The aged sun rises appall'd from dark mountains, and gleams a dusky beam
[*French Revolution*, 270]

How the Chimney-sweepers cry
Every blackning Church appalls
["London," 9–10]

Even from other poems in the *Songs*, it is clear that no church—certainly not the main church "of Pauls" (cf. "Holy Thursday" [SI])—is concerned, still less appalled by the "blackning" urchins' cry. Rather the cries, borne on

---

6. The mirror image of this view appears in a number of contemporary lesbian feminist works. See, for example, Griffin, pp. 207–227.

† From *Literal Imagination: Blake's Vision of Words* (Berkeley: University of California Press, 1983), Appendix One: "Some Polysemous Words in Blake," 240–41, 244–45, 251, 254–44. The serious

the wind like incessant soot, are darkening every church, revealing them to be dead and awaiting a pall-bearer. Their *cry* could initiate the reign of Christ. Realizing the moral façade of the first reading offers a paradigm for the deepening vision the poem presses toward—it is the church's lack of social concern that is truly appalling. The obvious question "How do these lines make sense?" mirrors the social question.

The earlier instance, with the unsettling conception of an aged rising Sun with an already dusky dawn-beam, offers a nice example of referents fusing into polysemy. Prepared by the unusual personification "aged" (and the context), the Sun and the French "sun-king" tradition it represents is imagined as "appall'd" at the sight of the rising lights of the republican army. The old light is giving out—to the people as a pall before the new day, to the aristocrats as appalling, and for the reader as both.

COVERING CHERUB / SELFHOOD

Jerusalem is his Garment & not thy Covering Cherub O lovely

[*M* 18.37]

I saw he was the Covering Cherub & within him Satan
And Raha[b], in an outside which is fallacious! within
Beyond the outline of Identity, in the Selfhood deadly

[*M* 37.8–10]

Thus was the Covering Cherub reveald majestic image
Of Selfhood

[*J* 89.9–10]

The Marriage of Heaven and Hell, in a revision of Genesis 3:24, says that "the cherub with his flaming sword is hereby commanded to leave his guard at the tree of life, and when he does, the whole creation will be consumed, and appear infinite and holy whereas it now appears finite & corrupt" (pl. 14). Thirteen of the remaining seventeen "epic" instances of the word refer to "the Covering Cherub," a figure appearing only once in the Bible. It is evident that the Covering Cherub is important not only for its mention in Ezekiel 28:16 (and as the "cherub that covereth," 28:14) but more so because its name identifies it as a "covering"—a useful clarification of the original "cherub" who covered the infinite. Banishing the cherub, as plate 14 continues, is identical with "melting apparent surfaces away, and displaying the infinite which was hid." This cherub offers the parallel to Blake's Boehme-influenced vision of "selfhood," where the suffix "-hood" has become, in Blake's vision, an expression of the covering, a part of the garment. This verbal felicity is probably the major motivating force behind Blake's widespread yet "isolated" (*OED*, s.v. "selfhood") use of the word. In Spenser, for example, a priest of Isis tells Britomart, "in queint disguise":

---

wordplay that Hilton detects in Blake, part of a larger "vision of the word as object, as other, and as divine, . . . an eternal living form with its own personality, family, and destiny" (*Literal Imagination* 3), is a provocative extreme in "textuality" studies (see Robert F. Gleckner, *Cithara* 15 [1976], 75–85, and Hazard Adams, *New Literary History* 5 [1973], 135–46) that gained momentum in the 1980s; for example, in the essays of Hilton and Thomas Vogler's *Unnam'd Forms* (1986); W. J. T. Mitchell's contribution to *Romanticism and Contemporary Criticism* (1986), ed. Morris Eaves and Michael Fischer; Robert N. Essick's historically informed semiotic study, *Blake and the Language of Adam* (1989); and books by De Luca (1991), Otto (1991), Rothenberg (1993), Pierce (2003), and Kathleen Lundeen, *Knight of the Living Dead* (2000).

> *How couldst thou weene, through that disguized hood,*
> *To hide thy state from being understood?*
> *Can from th'immortall Gods aught hidden bee?*
> [*The Faerie Queen,* 5.7.21.4–6]

The self and selfhood, we see, are two different things. In *The Four Zoas*, the most common covering is the "covering veil," a slightly different hood. Covering is concealing, whether with a "husk," "opake hardnesses," or "Bacon, Locke & Newton" (*J* 98.19; 65.5; *M* 51.5). One of the marvelous touches in *Milton*, plate 18/16, where Milton steps through and out of the word "self-hood" [p. 167 herein], is that the Urizenic figure before him on the plane of the page surrounds his head like a hood to be lifted off. In Ezekiel, the "Covering Cherub" is invoked only for comparison to the commerical giant, "the prince of Tyrus," the quintessence of selfhood: "Thine heart was lifted up because of thy beauty, thou hast corrupted thy wisdom by reason of thy brightness" (28:17).

OBJECTING

> *. . . it is the Reasoning Power*
> *An Abstract objecting power, that Negatives every thing*
> [*J* 10.13–14]

A capsule dose of philosophy: the concept of "objecting" reveals the twin birth of individualism and alienation. To say "no" is to objectify; when "I object," I make myself something thrown in the way (Lat. *ob-iacere*). Negations are passive, reasoning, ultimately selfish, while contraries are active and wrathful, so asserting their existence and that which they oppose (not object). Los says that "Exceptions & Objections & Unbeliefs / Exist Not" (*J* 17.34–35)—the negation, the world of objects and objectors is "as a distorted & reversed Reflexion in the Darkness" (17.42).

TYPES

> *Therefore I print; nor vain my types shall be*
> [*J* 3.9]

At the beginning of *Jerusalem*, Blake sites us firmly in the universe of his engraver's "types" and his visionary typology (the inscription on one etched plate, the "Chaining of Orc," reads, "Type by W Blake" [Erdman edition, 682]).

URIZEN

No discussion of Blake's vision of words would be complete without an example of his inventiveness in naming characters. "Urizen," the most remarked, suggests "your reason"; the "horizon," our physical-perception limit; "your eyes in," a form of self-contemplation; "ur-reason," a primary model; "you risen," marking the ascendancy of the faculty that even now reads; "err-reason," this is only too human—to forgive is to reason not. This list is, of course, not complete: Urizen, like "Reason" [*There Is No Natural Religion*], is not the same that he shall be when we know more.

574

JON MEE

From Blake the Bricoleur†

Part of the complexity of Blake's work from the 1790s onwards stems from the fact that he drew on disparate discourses to create a bricolage which has features in common with the work of Spence, Paine, and other radicals.[1] Initially, at least, two separate aspects of Blake's eclecticism can be identified.

The first * * * is a matter of seemingly disparate discourses operating in a single text. * * * From interactions between discourses Blake constructed a rhetoric that was alive with political resonances. At the same time he was also responding to developments which, especially in the intensely ideological decade of the 1790s, were already emergent in the discourses themselves. Biblical criticism, for instance, which might seem the very stuff of dry scholarship, was taken to be intimately involved with the ideological struggles of the Revolution controversy.

* * *

The second aspect of Blakian bricolage to which I want to draw attention is the facility with which it produced forms, plots, and figures which stand at significant confluences between discourses. Sometimes these confluences preceded Blake's own formulations. The association of the Celtic bard with the Hebrew prophet, for instance, was a well-established product of syncretic tendencies in literary primitivism, biblical studies, and historiography. But even given these larger trends, Blake seems to have taken a particular interest in such confluences, extending those which were already established, and evolving others which seem uniquely Blakian. A typical example is the complex referentiality of Blake's Tree of Mystery.[2] * * * By placing the Tree in a context which links druidism with Christian priestcraft this configuration suggests, like Paine's *The Age of Reason* (1794–5), that Christianity perpetuated barbaric pagan practices. Perhaps less obviously, the image also takes up one of the most emotive and contentious configurations of the Revolution controversy. Burke had presented the British

† From *Dangerous Enthusiasm: William Blake and the Culture of Radicalism in the 1790s* (Oxford: Clarendon Press, 1992), "Introduction: Blake the Bricoleur," 5, 6–8, 9–10, 11–12, 13–14, 17–18. Excerpts approved by the author. Footnotes have been adjusted, and citations of Blake's works have been altered to refer to the present edition. Since David V. Erdman's *Blake: Prophet against Empire* (1954; 3rd ed., 1977), historicist studies, more materialist in orientation, have abounded; see especially Michael Ferber (1985), E. P. Thompson (1993; also his *The Making of the English Working Class*, 2nd ed. [1968]), and essays and collections of David Worrall; Makdisi (p. 576 herein) and Wright (p. 583 herein) are investigating yet-unexplored areas. For a critique of Mee's application of the Structuralist term *bricoleur* to Blake, see Morton D. Paley's otherwise favorable review in *Blake: An Illustrated Quarterly* 27, no. 3 (1993–94), 86 ff.
1. A "bricolage" is something made by a "bricoleur," a "person . . . who constructs or creates something from a diverse range of materials or sources" (*OED Online*). In discussing his use of the term, Mee refers to Claude Lévi-Strauss, *The Savage Mind*, 2nd ed. Weidenfeld and Nicolson, 1972), pp. 16–20, and Jacques Derrida, *Writing and Difference*, trans. Alan Bass (Chicago and London: University of Chicago Press, 1978), 279–95. He also cites, as precedents for applying the concept to Blake, Ronald Paulson, *Representations of Revolution* (New Haven, CT: Yale University Press, 1983), 18, and the oral version of Iain McCalman, "The Infidel as Prophet: William Reid and Blakean Radicalism," in *Historicizing Blake*, ed. Steve Clark and David Worrall (Houndmills: Macmillan Press / New York: St. Martin's Press, 1994), 24–42. Thomas Spence (1750–1814), radical activist publisher of the serial *Pig's Meat* (1793–95) and Thomas Paine (1737–1809), author of *The Rights of Man* (1791–92), blended secular and religious rhetoric in their writings [*editors' note*].
2. See *Ahania* (3:60–4:8) [*editors' note*].

state as the product of an organic and legitimate evolutionary process; in doing so he gave new life to the traditional symbol of the English oak. For radicals this image of natural maturation was a mystification of 'the tree of feudal tyranny' which Paine sought to cut down and replace with the Tree of Liberty. The secret noxious growth of Blake's Tree of Mystery reveals his sense of the corrupt reality hidden by Burke's rhetoric. The point is made even more explicitly in the later works where the image transmutes into 'Tyburn's fatal tree', the gallows on which the power of Burke's established order was most nakedly displayed.[3]

The organisation of an account of Blake's rhetoric around the notion of bricolage provides for a dialectical approach. Aspects traceable to the issues and language of one discourse can also be made sense of in other discursive contexts so that simplistic notions of sources and influence have to be abandoned.

*   *   *

* * * Blake took full advantage of the potential the complex nexus of languages he inherited opened up for subversion and parody. Many radicals in the 1790s took up the role of the bricoleur; they relished breaking down those discourses which had cultural authority and creating from them new languages of liberation. Blake's attachment to this poetic of transgression receives one of its clearest statements in Plate 14 of his *The Marriage of Heaven and Hell*. There he wrote of his 'printing in the infernal method, by corrosives, which in Hell are salutary and medicinal, melting apparent surfaces away, and displaying the infinite which was hid.' So taken have many critics been with the figural allusion to the engraving process which produced the plate that they have often failed to give due weight to the fundamentally subversive nature of the method declared here.

* * * Blake's conception of the Bible involved him in a struggle to liberate its poetic aspects from the legalistic Word.

At the root of Blake's attitude to the Bible lies a hostility to the very notion of the pure text, the text which gains authority from its claim to be sacred, invariable, and original. In his annotations to Bishop Watson's *Apology for the Bible* (1798) Blake described 'the Bible or <Peculiar> Word of God' as an 'Abomination'. Perhaps the paradigmatic expression of Blake's attitude to the whole notion of the sacred text lies in Plate 11 of *The Marriage of Heaven and Hell*, which offers a telescoped account of the origins of 'forms of worship' in the corruptions of 'poetic tales'.[4]

* * * This plate invokes in stark terms an opposition which functions throughout Blake's work: the opposition between scripture, represented as an oppressive mode of writing associated with the law, and poetry, a mode of writing which is open, multiform, and seeks the imaginative participation of the reader. The same opposition is personalized in the conflict between bard-prophet and druid-priest in the figures of Los and Urizen.

Blake's work seeks to reverse the process whereby priestly authority usurped the poetic function and maintained the Bible as a moral allegory. It was a politically sensitive tactic in the 1790s, when, as Robert Hole has recently shown, there was a new emphasis on religion as the teaching of

---

3. The phrase 'the tree of feudal tyranny' is taken from J. Gerrald's *A Convention the Only Means of Saving us from Ruin* (London, 1793), p. 89.
4. For the text Mee quotes at this point, see p. 74 herein [editors' note].

'Moral Virtues' which would function as the guarantors of political and social stability. Although Blake's mythopoesis is often taken to approximate to allegory, it is more accurate to say that this similarity is an invocation of allegorical form which is subverted or parodied as part of a process of contesting the hegemony of Moral Virtues.[5] Whereas strict allegory depends on a stable relationship between signifier and signified, each term consistently standing, say, for some moral principle, Blake's metaphorical procedures are more complex. His vocabulary is often reversible. Particular images have positive and negative variants. An example is Blake's use of the serpent as a signifier in *Europe*. The fiery serpent of the poem's title-page seems to be associated with the liberating energy of revolt. It is akin to the serpentine Orc of *America*. The 'temple serpent-form'd' described in the poem itself represents the petrifaction of that energy into the oppressive authority of State Religion. The latter, of course, is analogous to the rigidity of scripture; the former has the fluidity Blake associates with poetic tales.

The indeterminate relationship between text and design opens up the illuminated book to the reader. The same is true of other aspects of Blakian indeterminacy. * * * The text is not offered as a univocal and invariable authority. It is contingent and contradicts itself, other copies of itself, and elements similar to itself which appear in other poems. In total these features are part of Blake's attempt to achieve a style which 'rouzes the faculties to act' [p. 470 herein]. They seek to promote the rights of the living reader against manuscript authority. The reader is enfranchised within the text, a development which could be compared to Daniel Eaton's decision to publish his readers' contributions in the pages of his *Politics for the People* (1794). Indeed the reader might be seen as the keystone of the Blakian bricolage.

SAREE MAKDISI

From Fierce Rushing: William Blake and the Cultural Politics of Liberty in the 1790s[†]

"*America,*" wrote Henry Crabb Robinson in an 1811 essay, "appears in part to give a poetical account of the [American] Revolution, since it contains the names of several party leaders. The actors in it are a species of guardian angels. We give only a short example, nor can we decide whether it is intended to be in prose or verse." Like its sister book *Europe: A Prophecy*, Robinson concluded, *America* is a "mysterious and incomprehensible rhapsody, which probably contains the artist's political visions of the future, but is wholly inexplicable."[1] * * *

Reading *America* a little later in the nineteenth century, Blake's first major biographer, Alexander Gilchrist, found himself dazzled by the "unquestionable

---

5. W. J. T. Mitchell has written of the 'schematic, allegorical surface of Blake's prophetic books', *Blake's Composite Art* (Princeton: Princeton University Press, 1978), 118. For Robert Hole's discussion, see *Pulpits, Politics, and Public Order in England 1760–1832* (Cambridge: Cambridge University Press, 1989), 101–2.

† From *William Blake and the Impossible History of the 1790s* (Chicago: University of Chicago Press, 2003), 16–22, 23–24, 28–29, 34–35, 39–40, 77. Abridgement of chapter 3 approved by the author. Footnotes have been adapted for this edition.

1. Henry Crabb Robinson, "William Blake, Artist, Poet, and Religious Mystic," in *Blake Records* (2004), ed. G. E. Bentley, p. 602. [Makdisi also quotes from Alan Cunningham's account in *Blake Records*, p. 656, para. 51—*editors' note*.]

power and design" of the plates: "Turning over the leaves, it is sometimes like an increase of daylight on the retina, so fair and open is the effect of particular pages. The skies of sapphire, or gold, rayed with hues of sunset, against which stand out leaf or blossom, or pendant branch, gay with bright plumaged birds; the strips of emerald sward below, gemmed with flower and lizard and enamelled snake, refresh the eye continually."[2] But even Gilchrist found the text "hard to fathom; with far too little Nature behind it;—the fault of all this class of Blake's writings; too much wild tossing about of ideas and words." * * * Through the chaotic storm clouds of prophecy, he writes, "the merely human agents show small and remote, perplexed and busied in an ant-like way."

Given the perplexed early reception history of Blake's *America*, it is striking that this prophecy, of all of Blake's work, is the one around which a fairly clear consensus has emerged in modern scholarship, a consensus which has only in the past few years faced systematic questioning.[3] There has been much discussion of the various divisions in Blake studies, but on the question of *America* there has been a rare convergence of the conflicting strands of scholarship.[4] Although it is often argued that it was the unfinished piece *The French Revolution*, due to have been printed in 1791 by Joseph Johnson—the publisher of William Godwin, Tom Paine, Mary Wollstonecraft, Joseph Priestley, and other well-known radicals—that confirmed Blake's position in the 1790s struggle for "liberty," according to the critical consensus it was in *America* that Blake produced his most political work.[5]

This view has largely developed from a tendency to see Blake, in Gilchrist's

2. Alexander Gilchrist, *The Life of William Blake* (1863; reprint, Mineola, N.Y.: Dover, 1998), pp. 109–13.

3. Most recent accounts of *America* are derived in one way or another from David Erdman's magnificent study *Blake: Prophet against Empire* (Princeton, N.J.: Princeton University Press, 1977). According to Erdman, *America* tells the story of the American War of Independence and celebrates the goals of the American Revolution and the American Declaration of Independence. John Howard questions Erdman's reading of the significance of Barlow's *Visions of Columbus* as a source for *America* but confirms Erdman's argument that Blake's prophecy "recounts the struggle in America of the contrary forces during the 1770s." See John Howard, *Infernal Poetics: Poetic Structures in Blake's Lambeth Prophecies* (Cranbury, N.J.: Associated University Presses, 1984). Also see Stephen Behrendt, *Reading William Blake* (New York: St. Martin's Press, 1992), and "History When Time Stops: Blake's *America, Europe*, and *The Song of Los,*" *Papers on Language and Literature* 28, no. 4 (1992); Michael Ferber, *The Social Vision of William Blake* (Princeton, N.J.: Princeton University Press, 1985), and "Blake's *America* and the Birth of Revolution," in *History and Myth: Essays on English Romantic Literature*, ed. S. Behrendt (Detroit: Wayne State University Press, 1990); Nicholas Williams, *Ideology and Utopia in the Poetry of William Blake* (Cambridge: Cambridge University Press, 1998); and James Swearingen, "William Blake's Figural Politics," in *ELH*, vol. 59 (1992). Other critics have questioned the extent to which *America* can be read simply as a celebration of the War of Independence: Minna Doskow questions such optimistic readings, as does James McCord. See Minna Doskow, "William Blake's *America*: The Story of a Revolution Betrayed," *Blake Studies* 8, no. 2 (1978); and James McCord, "West of Atlantis: William Blake's Unromantic View of the American War," *Centennial Review* 30, no. 1 (1986).

4. See Doskow, "William Blake's *America*," pp. 169–77. Nicholas Williams argues that "the apocalyptic joy of the poem must always be read in the light of this historical deconfirmation, not indeed as an exercise in pessimism but as a way of suggesting that the promises of that earlier struggle have yet to be fulfilled, a fulfillment that they will find only in the medium of history, as Blake's continuation of the line from *America* to *Europe* . . . eventually serves to show." See Nicholas Williams, *Ideology and Utopia*, pp. 116–17.

5. Critics interested in politics often pay more heed to *America* and its sister prophecies from the mid-1790s than to the later works, while those interested in psychic themes generally do the opposite. Erdman's work continues to be the reference point for politically and historically oriented scholarship on Blake. *Blake: Prophet against Empire*, Jackie DiSalvo argues, "definitively established" Blake's place in the political struggles of the era of the French Revolution (though DiSalvo herself is one of the critics who have taken the study of Blake's politics beyond *America*). There is a prevailing consensus, even among such thoroughgoing critics as Helen Bruder, that the task of historicizing Blake in the political context of the 1790s "has been largely completed." See Jackie DiSalvo, *War of Titans: Blake's Critique of Milton and the Politics of Religion* (Pittsburgh: University of Pittsburgh Press, 1983), p. 12; and Helen Bruder, *William Blake and the Daughters of Albion* (New York: St. Martin's Press, 1997), p. 91.

words, as "an ardent member of the New School, a vehement republican and
sympathiser with the Revolution, hater and contemner of kings and kingcraft. . . . To him, at this date, as to ardent minds everywhere, the French
Revolution was the herald of the Millennium, of a new age of light and reason." Blake has often been made to fit seamlessly into a respectable company
of rational, sensible, judicious, and essentially (if not actually) secular intellectuals, for whom revolution was first and foremost a matter for ardent
minds. His class position—that of a small tradesman, an independent
artisan—has been repeatedly invoked as a more or less sure indicator of the
extent to which he must have conformed to the standards of secular radicalism, as they supposedly filtered down from the ideologues who attended
Johnson's dinner parties to the cadres of the London Corresponding Society
(LCS), which was made up largely of tradesmen and artisans occupying the
same social stratum as Blake. Radicalism in this context has often been taken
to imply a mobilization of light and reason to peer into the dark recesses and
gloomy mysteries of the old regime. This, of course, is explicitly the Enlightenment role that Tom Paine and Mary Wollstonecraft claimed for themselves
in their confrontations with Edmund Burke, and many modern scholars have
taken their position for granted as definitive of all radicalism in the period,
including Blake's. As a result, the complex political positions of both Blake's
early work and his later work have often been read reductively, either—in the
case of the early work—as a conformist celebration of "liberty," or—in the
case of the later work—as a kind of apolitical quietism.[6] Thus, Blake has been
configured as a soft liberal who was buoyed by the false hopes of a foreign
revolution only to soften into respectable quietism in later years when that
revolution supposedly revealed its true nature.

[I propose that although] *America* is indeed concerned with Blake's commitment to the radical struggles of the 1790s, as well as with the relationship
between the events that unfolded in the American War of Independence and
the events defining London radicalism in the 1790s, Blake's concern has
nothing to do with a gratuitous celebration of either the American War or the
notion of liberty being heralded by Tom Paine and his followers. While I con-
cur with David Erdman's reading of Blake as a "prophet against empire" and
as a constant opponent of the forces of tyranny and what he would call oppressive codes (such as the iron laws of "State Religion, which is the source of all
Cruelty"),[7] I am not convinced that there is much evidence of Blake's sharing
the fundamental conceptual and political assumptions of the advocates of liberty. *America*, which was written at a crucial turning point during the political struggles of the 1790s, confirms both Blake's attack on the old regime *and*
his disruption of the philosophical, conceptual, and political narratives underlying the discourse of "liberty," and in particular his critique of the narrow
conception of freedom animating much of 1790s radicalism.[8] * * *

The academic understanding of the 1790s as a crystalline moment of
struggle between two highly polarized forces—on the one hand, the defend-

6. Indeed, in * * * one of the most thorough studies of Blake's radicalism, Jon Mee argues that [Erd-
   man's] *Prophet against Empire* may ironically have led scholars astray to the extent that its engage-
   ment with *America's* politics makes the other prophetic books seem less political by contrast
   (*Dangerous Enthusiasm: William Blake and the Culture of Radicalism in the 1790s* [Oxford: Oxford
   University Press, 1994]).
7. Blake, annotations to Watson, p. 459 herein.
8. See David Worrall, "Blake and 1790s Plebeian Radical Culture," in *Blake in the Nineties*, ed. Steve
   Clark and David Worrall (New York: St. Martin's, 1999); and Jon Mee, "The Strange Career of
   Richard 'Citizen' Lee" in *Radicalism in British Literary Culture*, ed. T. Morton (2002).

ers of the old regime (e.g., Edmund Burke, Hannah More, Patrick Colquhoun), and on the other, the rational and secular advocates of a new-found liberty (e.g., Tom Paine, Mary Wollstonecraft, William Godwin)—has been complicated in recent scholarship. Iain McCalman, Jon Mee, David Worrall, Mark Philp, E. P. Thompson, and others have demonstrated the extent to which the decade of the 1790s was characterized, especially among radicals, by a complex and heterogeneous network of forces and tendencies, making such straightforward polarizations difficult to plot. In particular, critical attention has been drawn to the resurgence during the 1790s of forms of popular enthusiasm and radical antinomianism, explicitly reaching back to the writers and activists of that earlier moment of revolutionary crisis in the seventeenth century, many of whose tracts were reprinted in fresh editions during the 1790s.[9] Richard Brothers, the ex–Navy officer who in 1792 began prophesying earthquakes and revolutions and the fall of monarchies (as well as a quasi-colonialist fantasy in which he, the Nephew of God, would lead the Hebrews to Palestine, where they would "rebuild" Jerusalem) until he was arrested and declared to be insane and consequently locked up from 1795, is only one of the many colorful figures of late-eighteenth-century London radicalism of whom we are now more aware, [and whose] activities and publications * * * complicate the often-invoked polarization between the educated spokespersons of a secular and rational radicalism on the one hand and the tradition-bound defenders of the old regime on the other. * * *

The fact that various seventeenth-century currents had resurfaced in 1790s London allows us to more fully appreciate the extent to which Blake (whose antinomian affiliations had been recognized as early as 1958 by A. L. Morton and were amplified in Michael Ferber's 1985 study, before being further elaborated by E. P. Thompson and Jon Mee)[1] was not alone in his faith in the "everlasting gospel," that key concept in antinomian thought linking Blake and other 1790s enthusiasts to seventeenth-century heretics like Abiezer Coppe and Laurence Clarkson.[2] "For all his individual genius," McCalman points out, "William Blake was a more typical figure in his day than many scholars have realized."[3]

However, the recent scholarly emphasis on the heterogeneity of 1790s radicalism, and on the extent to which popular enthusiasm could be combined with secular rationalism in a pungent revolutionary blend, should not prevent us from discerning the presence of a strand of radicalism that sought to rise above the fray and to assert its own legitimacy, partly by making its own claims on "respectable" political discourse, partly by denying, excluding, and disassociating itself from other forms and subcultures of radicalism (which it regarded as inarticulate, unrespectable, unenlightened, and hence illegitimate), and partly by working to assimilate as many grievances as possible into its own agenda for reform, rearticulating them when necessary—and thereby exercising, in effect, a form of hegemony, albeit one whose dominance was

9. See Jon Mee, "Is There an Antinomian in the House? William Blake and the After-life of a Heresy," in *Historicizing Blake*, ed. S. Clark and D. Worrall (New York: St Martin's Press, 1994).
1. See A. L. Morton, *The Everlasting Gospel: A Study in the Sources of William Blake* (London: Lawrence and Wishart, 1958); Michael Ferber, *The Social Vision*; and E. P. Thompson, *Witness against the Beast: William Blake and the Moral Law* (New York: New Press, 1993).
2. The concept of the "everlasting gospel" is invoked both by Blake and the Ranters. See Blake, *Everlasting Gospel*, E518–25 [p. 445 herein]; also see Abiezer Coppe, *A Fiery Flying Roll* (1649), reprinted in *A Collection of Ranter Writings from the Seventeenth Century*, ed. Nigel Smith (London: Junction Books, 1983).
3. Iain McCalman, "Introduction," in *The Horrors of Slavery and Other Writings by Robert Wedderburn*, ed. Iain McCalman (New York: Marcus Wiener, 1991), p. 11.

still very much in question at the time and would fade altogether amid the deepening crises of 1796–97, only to return early in the nineteenth century. This strand of radicalism enjoyed the allegiance of many of the best-known radical intellectuals as well as relatively broad-based popularity among the artisan class whose members constituted the core of London's radical culture. * * * [It] centered almost exclusively on what are by now familiar ideas, namely, demands for universal (male) suffrage and annual parliaments, or in other words for an extension of the political franchise through more adequate representation in parliament. These demands would reemerge in modified form after the end of the Napoleonic Wars and would gather strength under the banner of Chartism.⁴ The persistence of what may usefully be thought of as this liberal-radical tendency is what tied together, for example, the great open-air meetings organized by the London Corresponding Society at Copenhagen Fields in October and November 1795 (which according to some drew up to two hundred thousand participants) and the now more famous Peterloo gathering of 1819. * * *

Both in the 1790s and in the early nineteenth century, however, the spokesmen of this liberal-radical tendency had to articulate their own position, and reinforce their claims to legitimacy, by focusing attention on certain questions—principally those concerning political representation—and suppressing those questions that were seen to be incompatible with their own epistemological and philosophical foundation. * * *

Thus, the liberal-radical position very carefully distinguished the political rights of the property-owning and [the] individual from collective or communal rights of any kind. "Assured that man, Individual man, may justly claim Liberty as his birthright," one of the earliest declarations of the London Corresponding Society begins, "we naturally conclude that, as a member of Society, it becomes his indispensable duty to preserve inviolate that Liberty for the benefit of his fellow citizens and of his and their posterity.⁵ * * * [T]he early leadership of the LCS had to wage two continuous struggles: on the one hand, against the state, and, on the other, against those radicals and enthusiasts [who formulated] very different—and far more "excessive"—political demands, and, moreover, far more excessive means to achieve them. Political arguments here merged with philosophical, religious, and epistemological ones, for these different political demands grew out of different conceptual frameworks, different understandings of identity, being, and community. Hence, what might on one level seem like a narrowly political gesture often had an epistemological or conceptual motivation. * * *

*   *   *

* * * In considering the 1790s, then, we need to keep sight of distinctions among varieties of radical ideology, some of which would not only ultimately rise to respectability, but would develop into the very bases of the modern liberal democracy and the free market that we presently inhabit, while others would continue—and still continue—to be thought of as mad, bad, and dangerous to know. The spokesmen of the former position tended

---

4. See Craig Calhoun, *The Question of Class Struggle: Social Foundations of Popular Radicalism during the Industrial Revolution* (Chicago: University of Chicago Press, 1982).
5. London Corresponding Society, *Address to the Nation*, 24 May 1792, in *Selections from the Papers of the London Corresponding Society*, ed. Mary Thale (Cambridge: Cambridge University Press, 1982), p. 10.

to formulate their arguments around the concept of the sovereign individual (the modern subject first systematized by Locke),[6] they tended to draw on rationalist arguments and natural law for their justification, and as a result they were to a certain extent, as Lottes observes, "unable to break free from the political language of the established system in which their political consciousness had been formed."[7] The advocates of the latter position, often though not always drawing their strength and inspiration from an older radical subculture, sought to question the primacy of individual rights and the very status of the individual as a transcendent metaphysical category, a unit granted ontological privilege as the alpha and omega of all historical processes and political developments.

*   *   *

* * * [W]ith such lines in mind,[8] we can see in the illuminated books a joyous form of freedom—that is a political formulation—utterly incompatible with the doctrine of individual rights and opening up a radically different set of concepts concerning subjectivity, temporality, identity, and community.

*   *   *

[T]he only revolutionary "action" that can properly be said to take place in *America* is carried out not by Washington, Franklin, and company (and their revolutionary army, with whom the sacred cause of liberty celebrated by the hegemonic radicals of the 1790s is to be associated), but by ordinary citizens: "Fury! rage! madness! in a wind swept through America / And the red flames of Orc that folded roaring fierce around / The angry shores, and fierce rushing of th' inhabitants together" (*America* 16/14:10–12). * * * [T]he decisive scene in *America* is this collective action of a crowd of angry citizens surging through city streets in precisely the sort of spectacle of urban mayhem which the radicals in London were at the time of the prophecy's appearance desperate to avoid, and which they avoided all the more desperately the more the situation in Paris got out of control.

In *America* it is only "the fierce rushing of th' inhabitants together," who "all rush together in the night in wrath and in raging fire" (*America* 16/14:19), and not the frozen and almost comical posturing of the revolution's "real" leaders (who never come to power in Blake's prophecy), that apparently could keep Earth from "losing another portion of the infinite." Afterward, "the millions sent up a howl of anguish and threw their hammerd mail / And cast their swords & spears to earth, & stood a naked multitude." (*America* 17/15: 4–5).[9] * * *

6. According to Etienne Balibar, "the key philosophical notions which are still in use today when dealing with individual rights and personality were actually invented or systematized by Locke." Thus, Balibar says, "we may suggest that the best way of reading Locke is not to characterize him as a 'forerunner' of any of the particular modern ideologies which have become projected into the past (for example, as a supporter of 'possessive individualism,' in a Marxist paradigm, or as a representative of 'natural political virtue,' in a conservative-liberal paradigm), but rather to understand how he made all these different ideologies possible, by creating their common ground." See Etienne Balibar, "What Is 'Man' in Seventeenth-Century Philosophy? Subject, Individual, Citizen," in *The Individual in Political Theory and Practice*, ed. J. Coleman (Oxford: Oxford University Press, 1996), p. 215–41, esp. pp. 233–39.
7. See Gunther Lottes, "Radicalism, Revolution and Political Culture," in *The French Revolution and British Popular Politics,* ed. Mark Philp (Cambridge: Cambridge University Press, 1991), p. 85.
8. "He who sees the Infinite in all things sees God. He who sees the Ratio only sees himself only. Therefore God becomes as we are, that we may be as he is" (*There Is No Natural Religion*, p. 7 herein).
9. Cf. Constantin Volney's depiction of revolution as a mass phenomenon, "a numberless people, rushing in all directions, pour through the streets and fluctuate like waves in the public places" (*The Ruins of Empires* 1792; rpt. Baltimore: Black Classics Press, 1991), p. 63.

[T]he fierce rushing toward the end of *America* is quite inconsistent with
those readings of the prophecy which, following David Erdman's magisterial
account, see it either as a narrative of the American War of Independence,
as it unfolded following the intervention of the colonial elite into what had
begun as a mass uprising, or as a more or less straightforward celebration of
the radical struggle for liberty in 1790s London as articulated in the work of
Tom Paine or the LCS.

*   *   *

* * * Those 1790s radicals who followed Paine and were inspired by the
struggle for American independence adopted as their conceptual and philosophical foundation the Lockean formula of the transhistorical individual
(which Rousseau and the Enlightenment would confirm as "born free but
everywhere in chains"), whose eternal liberty Paine's *Rights of Man* would in
one stroke confirm and guarantee for all time. While Blake accepted the radical attack on the ancien régime, and on priestcraft and kingcraft and patriarchal tyranny in general, he was very far from accepting the radical notion
that the Paineite/Lockean individual—developing autonomously through the
progressive linear time of modernity—could possibly be the basis for genuine
freedom, or even that such an individual could be assumed to have a eternal
validity, an ontological priority outside human history, to be taken for granted
as it was by Paine and others, as an eternal reference point for all human
struggles.
   * * * [In] the scene of fierce rushing, the individuals are absorbed into the
crowd that they constitute, not simply losing but altogether detonating their
prior individuality. For the fierce rushing collective is sharply distinguished
from "the citizens of New York" who "close their books & lock their chests,"
the "mariners of Boston" who "drop their anchors and unlade," the "scribe of
Pennsylvania" who "casts his pen upon the earth," and "the builder of Virginia" who "throws his hammer down in fear" (*America* 16/14:13–16). The
condition of possibility for the constitution of the rushing multitude is, in
other words, the loss—the annihilation—of the individual specificity of the
little units, the citizens, who together make up the revolutionary crowd. It is
only when they cease ("close," "drop," "cast," "throw") their individual occupations, which are figured here as their hastily abandoned occupational
materials and tools, that the fierce rushing collective is brought into being.
And, in another, quite different, sense, the rushing multitude—the urban revolutionary crowd par excellence—might be seen to challenge the sturdy independence and frugal individuality of the craftsmen who drop their tools in
fear. This collective is much more than the sum of its little constituent parts.
It is a form of belonging—a community—whose very existence is predicated
upon the annihilation of those parts as self-sufficient, independent, sovereign
units (i.e., citizens). While these sovereign units are being broken up and dissolved into a collective body whose parts have no ontologically prior existence, "fierce desire" and "lusts of youth" also dissolve the "bonds of religion."
Now with "the doors of marriage open," these reborn sprits, who are depicted
as largely female, "Run from their fetters reddening, & in long drawn arches
sitting, / They feel the nerves of youth renew" (*America* 17/15: 24–25).
   In its uniquely Blakean slippage between political and biological language,
this moment in the prophecy highlights the mutually constitutive relationship between political forms and the subjective categories—literally, the

psychological and biological forms of identity—to which they correspond. Here, the breakdown of the one is inseparable from the breakdown of the other. For what seems to take place toward the end of the prophecy is the dissolution of one mode of existence, that of the property-owning individual, as well as the political institutions associated with it; and the constitution of a new mode of being, a new sense of community that is no longer commensurate with the political, psychological, or even biological units that brought the transformation about. The "fierce desire" associated with the "fierce rushing" is productive of the surging energy of the revolutionary crowd. This fierce energy is quite incompatible with the discourse of liberty associated with Paine. Indeed, it is reminiscent instead of that "wild democratical fury that leads nations into the vortex of anarchy, confusion and bloodshed,"[9] which most radical activists of the 1790s were desperate to avoid. * * *

No "fierce rushing" took place in London's streets in the 1790s, and the closest things to mass mobilization were the quite peaceful though very well attended open-air demonstrations organized by the LCS in 1794–95. *America* concerns itself not with a celebration of the cause of liberty, but rather with a critique of its conceptual and practical limitations with regard to popular politics and the question of labor. If it subverts the discourse of liberty with questions that most London radicals and reformers preferred not to discuss, Blake's prophecy does not do so because this discourse goes too far, but because it does not go far enough. The prophecy utterly resists being made to conform to the grand narrative of bourgeois revolution, in which critics have attempted to locate it. Much of the significance of Blake's prophecy is derived from its capacity to disrupt a certain kind of logic, a certain kind of philosophy, along with its attendant politics, temporality, subjectivity, and epistemology. What *America* opens up is the confusion and "animated absurdity" of history, rather than the reassurance and order often provided by historians and critics. For it is in just such "animated absurdity" that *America's* prophetic power lies. "Strange" indeed, as Gilchrist himself points out, "to conceive that a somewhat associate of Paine [was] producing these 'Prophetic' volumes!"[1]

JULIA WRIGHT

From "How Different the World to Them": Revolutionary Heterogeneity and Alienation[†]

Los's declaration "I must Create a System, or be enslav'd by another Mans" (*J*, 10.20) contains both an imperative ("must") and a threat ("or be enslav'd"). The warning does more than establish Blake's belief that rational systems are limiting; it describes them as "enslav[ing]," a term that connotes institutionalized subjugation and abuses of power (particularly in the charged climate of the abolition debate of the early Romantic period), and it alienates the speaker from any preexisting system by defining it as

9. From a printed declaration of the Association of Weavers to the public in Bolton, 13 May 1799 (Public Records Office, HO 42/47).
1. Gilchrist, *Life of William Blake*, p. 111. On "animating absurdity," see *Blake Records* (2004), 656.
† From *Blake, Nationalism, and the Politics of Alienation* (Athens: Ohio University Press, 2004), 57, 85–89. Excerpts approved by the author. Footnotes have been adapted and renumbered; citations of Blake's text refer to this edition.

"another Mans."[1] To function within a system that one has not created is to belong to someone else. Conversely, to create one's own system is to be isolated from all community, unless, of course, one creates a system that enslaves others—an option that Los does not seem to entertain.

*   *   *

Locating the Alienated Reader

By including different systems in these poems [*Visions of the Daughters of Albion, America, Europe*], Blake produces a text that is radically different from the Urizenic model. The examples of Urizenic texts offered in *Europe* involve commands that are addressed directly to the reader: "Thou shalt not" and "Fear" (*Europe* 14/12.28). Such dictates seek to bring the reader under the text's control, not only by seeking to alter the reader's behavior, but also by making the reader an implied one, already anticipated within the text and contained by its pre(in)scription. In *Visions* and *Europe*, however, the reader is placed in an alienated position, from which it can be seen that the assumptions that govern the homogenous societies that are represented do not operate naturally or totalize the field; the reader is a spectator of mutually exclusive systems and, in being able to see the different systems that are fundamentally unable to recognize each other, is placed on the edges of them all. The reader has access to the *Visions'* "three-sided soliloquy," eavesdropping on the speeches unheard by characters within the text, while the reader of *Europe* is placed outside of the mythological and historical domains that the narrative perspective tries to separate.[2] In *America,* the reader is even more alienated by the constantly marked, but never limiting, boundaries between myth and history, as well as the reversals of power that reveal the symbolic, rather than essential, nature of authority. This alienation does not create a new system, but it does mark that crucial first step toward the recognition that the prevailing system is "another Mans."

In this context, the sympathetic construction of Oothoon is something of a trick. Fox suggests, "It is certainly true that Oothoon speaks for Blake in this poem, that she is as noble in its context as ever Los is in the final poems (more noble: she does not make mistakes)," and Ostriker declares that Oothoon is "a heroine unequalled in English poetry before or since."[3] These qualities (nobility, the apparent coincidence of views with the author, heroism, intelligence, courage, and so forth), particularly when juxtaposed with those of an unrepentant rapist like Bromion and a self-indulgent whiner like Theotormon, invite the reader who is looking for a figure with whom to identify to take Oothoon's part. The reader, like the Daughters, is thus placed in a position outside of all three systems, as well as nudged toward sympathizing with Oothoon as she moves through different, mutually exclusive perspectives, so that the reader can follow at once the narrator's and Oothoon's unfamiliar perspectives on fundamental social institutions. But then Oothoon declares, in a line that has long troubled Blake scholars, that she will "catch for thee girls of mild silver, or of furious gold" (*Visions* 10/7.24). Where is the reader now? While Oothoon speaks of Theotormon in the third person and herself (usually) in the first person, it is easy for the reader to follow conventional literary

---

1. For a psychological, rather than a political, view of alienation in Blake's works, see Steven Shaviro, "'Striving With Systems': Blake and the Politics of Difference," *boundary* 2.10 (1982): 229–50.
2. Erdman, *Prophet against Empire,* 236.
3. Fox, "Female as Metaphor," 512–13; Ostriker, "Desire Gratified and Ungratified," 158 [564 herein].

practice by searching for a figure with whom to identify and select the most sympathetic character, Oothoon. But in turning to the second-person form of address, Oothoon not only implicates the reader—just as commandments of the form "thou shalt not" or gestures such as "gentle reader" do—but locates the reader elsewhere. On plate 10/7, she asks, "Why dost thou seek religion" and "Why hast thou taught my Theotormon this accursed thing," as well as declares, "thou seekest solitude," "be thou accursed from the earth," and "I'll lie beside thee on a bank" (*Visions* 10/7.9, 13, 10, 12, 25), before closing with a return to Theotormon's proper name (*Visions* 10/7.26). This referent, "thou" / "thee," is characterized, in series, as one who seeks confining structures, one who criminally imposes confining structures, and one who accepts the avails of Oothoon's confining structures, "silken nets and traps of adamant" (*Visions* 10/7:23). If Blake is positing a (heterosexual) male reader, if only implicitly (as well as practically, given the rarity of his manuscripts and the select distribution of them), Oothoon's offer to "catch for thee girls" and "lie beside thee" is at once a compromise of her heroic status, because she is serving Theotormon's desires and denying her own, and an inscription of the reader into Theotormon's Bromion-like position in her fantasy. (Theotormon's position is like Bromion's because of Oothoon's use of the commodification of women that marks Bromion's speech about his proprietorial rights.) Our identification with Oothoon, already problematic because of the different perspectives that she expresses, from her plea to Theotormon that she is "pure" (*Visions* 5/2.28) to her critique of marriage and other social institutions that define purity to her offer to trap women for him, is thus further compromised by her use of pronouns that implicitly include the reader in the male positions that she decries. It is here that Blake comes closest to Brecht's "alienation effect," prohibiting the audience's easy identification with characters and, in doing so, subverting the pervasive, familiar practice of identification.[4]

In *Europe,* there is no figure with whom to identify. The indefinite assignment of the speeches in the first mythic section, the overwhelming violence of the historic section, the quick descriptions of Enitharmon's children in the final mythic section, and the inarticulateness of Orc prohibit the identification of a clear protagonist or hero. The reader is instead faced with an alternation between extremes of familiar dichotomies, as the narratorial perspective switches abruptly from one set of characters to another. The reader is thus shown that each system is self-contained and unaware of its alternative, functioning as a homogeneous society like that defined by Georges Bataille.[5] But the reader, aware of the alternative, is also shown that neither totalizes the

4. In a time of increasingly gendered reading, in which the boundaries of proper reading for each gender, as well as the classification of writing (especially novels) by women as reading for women, were being more rigorously policed, Blake offers an interesting gendering of readers and writers: Oothoon speaks, even though she does not recognize it, to a female audience (the Daughters) as well as a male one (Theotormon), but the text is written by a man and for a generally male readership (insofar as Blake controlled the circulation of his texts at this time through personal sales of hand-produced illuminated prints). In other words, *Visions* offers a scene of women writing and reading, but in a text that circulates outside of the boundaries of "women's writing," not only in the material conditions of its production and circulation, but also in its non-novelistic form.
5. "*Homogenity* signifies here the commensurability of elements and the awareness of this commensurability: human relations are sustained by a reduction to fixed rules based on the consciousness of the possible identity of dileneable persons and situations," so that "*Homogeneous* society is productive society, namely, useful society. Every useless element is excluded, not from all of society, but from its *homogeneous* part" ("The Psychological Structure of Fascism," *Visions of Excess: Selected Writings, 1927–1939,* ed. Allan Stoekl, trans. Allan Stoekl with Carl R. Lovett and Donald M. Leslie Jr., vol. 14 of *Theory and History of Literature* [Minneapolis: University of Minnesota Press, 1991], 137–38). See also Bertholt Brecht's "alienation effect" (*Brecht on Theatre: The Development of an Aesthetic,* ed. and trans. John Willett [New York: Hill and Wang, 1964]).

field, as it believes it does. The reader, moreover, in being aware of both, is placed outside of both, and occupies a liminal space in which she is aware of myth and history but is part of neither. This is crucial, because it is at the points at which revolution approaches that the boundary between the two domains is compromised and the reader is placed in the position of always seeing those domains as compromised. In *America,* this liminal space is all-inclusive, as there is no homogeneous space in which the reader can rest except briefly. The rape depicted in the preludium also unsettles any alignment with Orc, particularly since he appears to be as hypocritical as the God of which Boston's Angel complains, because Orc seizes the female in the preludium and condemns bonds in the prophecy. (And his assertion in the prophecy that a woman is "undefil'd tho' ravish'd in her cradle night and morn" [10/8.12] looks uncomfortably like a denial that his rape could have detrimental effects on his victim.) The marginality of the reader places the reader in a potentially liberating place, as long as the reader is not drawn to the center through an identification that incorporates the reader into a single ideological perspective.

Blake's reader thus sees and is alienated from both halves of the "sympathy-antipathy pair." The strange language and names, the revision of history, and the articulation of radical viewpoints are defamiliarizing and estranging, placing the reader, like all spectators, on the margins of the domains being represented. This is finally what we can take from Blake's description of *A Vision of the Last Judgment:* "I have represented it as I saw it[.] to different People it appears differently . . . as every thing else does" (p. 433). Besides referring to fallen vision as fractured and fallible, Blake sets apart his vision, and the vision of every other individual, denying, in a fundamentally alienating way, the possibility of a shared vision. This is not, as I have argued with reference to alienation in *Visions of the Daughters of Albion,* necessarily negative, because it also operates as a liberation from the perspective of others. Blake's discomfort with simple equality is noted by Ferber, who suggests, "Perhaps equality bore connotations offensive to his love of uniqueness, the minute particularity, of each individual."[6] Pluralism is, in one sense, a condition of the fallen world, but it is also a diversity worth celebrating and engaging. By dramatizing this plurality of vision and perspective in *Visions, Europe,* and *America,* Blake places the reader not only outside of one system, but outside of a set of systems, disrupting any simple binaries. The reader necessarily occupies the intersection of the different systems represented in Blake's poems, at the margins of all and included in none. Blake's work retains its unfamiliarity, its strangeness, and its estranging effect, leaving the reader in the space in which revolutionary transgressions of homogeneous societies are possible.

MORRIS EAVES

The Title-Page of The Book of Urizen†

Around the time of the 1793 Prospectus that Blake addressed 'To the Public' as an advertisement for the works that he had spent the previous five

---

6. Ferber, "Blake's Idea of Brotherhood," *PMLA* 93 (1978) 438.
† From *William Blake: Essays in Honour of Sir Geoffrey Keynes* (Oxford: Clarendon Press, 1973), 225–30. Page numbers have been changed to refer to this edition; for works not included herein, references are to the 1988 Erdman (E) edition.

years creating in his new medium, he was naturally thinking more than ever not about his art only, but also about the art of his countrymen in his century. He compacted much of that thinking into a single etched plate, the title-page of *The Book of Urizen* (see color plate 11), which is Blake's report on the state of the arts—which is the state of the nation—in 1794.

The principal object of the satire is Law. The appropriate text is from *The Marriage of Heaven and Hell*: 'One Law for the Lion & Ox is Oppression' (p. 80 herein). One way of looking at the title-page design is as a study of the effect of law on art. The vertical aspect of the design is almost equally divided between the top spaces and the bottom; the script of the title is the focus of the top, the bearded patriarch of the bottom. The spaces are equally divided but unequally filled; the lower part of the design is far denser. The unusual balance of forces is dictated by Newton's Law of Gravity, which earthward drags lion, ox, and man alike. Newton's Law tugs so strongly at the design that nothing but the stone tablets of the Law can stand upright. One who wishes to be most comfortable in such a universe will lie prone on a dead level, like a corpse, a posture suggested by the vertical tablets behind the patriarch, which are not only tablets of the Law, but also tombstones. The horizontal tablets on which the patriarch is writing with one hand and etching with the other are also sepulchral, and they may be seen in several ways: as two separate and more or less square tablets, as a single long tablet extending from left to right, or perhaps as two long tablets extending from the patriarch in the foreground to the upright tablets in the background.

The force of the Law has tugged the trees into earthbound arches, and the arches are deathly, like everything else in the design. We might say that the trees have been brought into line, as they have in more ways than one, for in their arrangement Blake seems to have used the 'laws' of perspective to suggest a corridor of arched, dead trees endlessly receding. It has been said that the effort to transfer the third dimension to the pages of books helped to exhaust the medieval illuminated book,[1] and the use of Newtonian space may be unusual for Blake,[2] but it is apt in a design whose subject is the effect of Laws of the Universe on art.

Urizen, who has sunk to the bottom of the design like a stone, is depicted as a man unable to stand erect in a universe of his own creating. His flesh weighed down by the heaviness of his thought, inward drawn he squats. If we enlarge the scope of our vision, he becomes the fleshy pistil of a huge stone flower with petals of geometric shape. The roots that start out to the left and right belong as much to the flowering monument of Urizen, book, and tablets as to the arching trees; all are tightly rooted to earth. In fact, both the Urizenic flower and the arching trees are made parts of a single organism by the vertical aspect of the design, which is a stack of convex curves. The lowermost curve is the implied dome formed by the roots. The other curves are implied by the outline of Urizen's beard and head, the outline of

---

1. See David Diringer, *The Illuminated Book: Its History and Production*, Faber, London, 1958, p. 25; also David Bland, *The Illustration of Books*, Pantheon Books, New York, 1952, p. 242.
2. See Nikolaus Pevsner, 'Blake and the Flaming Line', ch. 5 of *The Englishness of English Art*, Praeger, New York, 1956, pp. 117–46; ch. 4 of Robert Rosenblum, 'The International Style of 1800: A Study in Linear Abstraction', Diss. New York University, Institute of Fine Arts, 1956; and Rosenblum's *Transformations in Late Eighteenth Century Art*, Princeton University Press, Princeton, N.J., 1967, pp. 154–9, 189–91. W. J. T. Mitchell, in 'Poetic and Pictorial Imagination in Blake's *The Book of Urizen*', *Eighteenth-Century Studies*, 3 (Fall 1969), 104, speaks of Blake's 'systematic refusal to employ the techniques of three-dimensional illusionism which had been perfected in Western art since the Renaissance'.

his body and the right and left edges of the book on which he squats, the standing stones, and finally the succession of tree arches. Thus the vertical aspect of the design is marked by its unity under the Law.

The horizontal aspect, on the other hand, is strictly divided into left and right halves by the implied line down the centre of the page. But then, this aspect has the symmetry of an ink-blot, or, more to the point, of a printed book, as the open book at the bottom of the page suggests. Thus the strict division is a division of sameness. Blake emphasized this aspect of the design when, upon its inclusion in a 'Small Book of Designs' apart from the rest of *The Book of Urizen,* he gave it a caption: 'Which is the Way / The Right or the Left' (E, p. 673). Diversified monotony, a confusion that Blake thought necessary to Newtonian science, is the Urizenic reflection in the mirror of the natural world of various unity, which is one of Blake's own artistic principles. One Law—the wisdom of experimental science— reduces all phenomena to some common unit that makes them 'intermeasurable'. The result is uniformity in fragments—atoms, for instance. In 1827, the year he died, Blake stated his opinion to George Cumberland:

> I know too well that a great majority of Englishmen are fond of The Indefinite which they Measure by Newton's Doctrine of the Fluxions of an Atom. A Thing that does not Exist. These are Politicians & think that Republican Art is Inimical to their Atom. For a Line or Lineament is not formed by Chance: a Line is a Line in its Minutest Subdivisions: Strait or Crooked It is Itself & Not Intermeasurable with or by any Thing Else. Such is Job, but since the French Revolution Englishmen are all Intermeasurable One by Another, Certainly a happy state of Agreement to which I for One do not Agree. God keep me from the Divinity of Yes & No too. The Yea Nay Creeping Jesus, from supposing Up & Down to be the same Thing as all Experimentalists must suppose. (p. 492).

Those preliminary remarks help us to understand the squatting patriarch, whose activities are the central enigma of the design. He is sitting on a book with his legs pulled under him and crossed, his right foot showing through his long beard. His arms are extended sideways along horizontal stone tablets, and each hand grips some kind of writing instrument. From these few facts we move into another order of doubt to ask what Urizen is doing. He may be writing with one hand and engraving with the other.[3] But since there is no sign of handwritten or engraved script on either tablet, and no sign of life or motion in either arm (both arms rest on the tablets), Urizen may have sat down only intending to write. Pascal may be applied to my purpose here: 'Reason acts slowly and with so many views upon so many principles which always must be present, that at any time it may fall asleep or get lost, for want of having all its principles present.'[4] Urizen's eyes are closed. His book may have put him to sleep, or into a hypnotic trance. He may be blind, or he may be dead. At any rate inaction, not action, blind or otherwise, is the over-all effect of the design, from its rigid symmetry without contraries, to its dead vegetation. Urizen's closed eyes, and the lifeless pull of gravitational forces that order the design as a magnet orders iron shavings.

---

3. This is Mitchell's suggestion, op. cit., p. 84. He also suggests that Urizen is holding a 'burin'; but the instrument in the squatting patriarch's left hand bears no resemblance at all to a burin. It is probably an etching needle, though it might also be a 'pencil', i.e. the kind of paintbrush used for fine work.
4. Quoted in Marshall McLuhan, *The Gutenberg Galaxy: The Making of Typographic Man,* 1962; rpt. New American Library, New York, 1969, p. 295.

Urizen is depicted as a composite of reader, writer, and etcher. The only person who reads and writes at the same time is a scribe. A scribe is a professional copyist. As a satire on Law in eighteenth-century writing and engraving, then, the design is directed first against imitation. Urizen copies his Law from a book, that is, from authority, from the ancients, no doubt, since they have the most authority, and most obviously from the Hebrew ancients, since the Tables of the Law are the most oppressive symbols of ancient authority, though also possibly from the Greek and Roman ancients, since their authority in artistic matters superseded that of the Bible in the Enlightenment minds of Pope and Joshua Reynolds.[5] He might just as easily be shown copying nature, since, as Pope declared, nature and the ancients are the same. Before Urizen dropped off to sleep, he was obeying the first rule of the copyist, which is to pay attention to what has been written rather than what is being written.

But Urizen as a copyist does not even possess the virtue of being what we would call a transparent medium. Instead, from one book he makes two stone tablets, one written and one engraved. Acts of division, translation, and rigidification are characteristic of the reasoning intellect. The disposition of Urizen's limbs emphasizes the division of one into two: he needs one foot to keep his place in the book, but two hands to write down what he finds. His foot, which acts as book-mark for his mind, also reveals the pedestrian nature of his intellect, whose operations are limited to the linear and the step-by-step only. These, however, are the operations of literacy itself, the mental movements necessary to get a reader through a book. The act of reading a printed page embodies all that Blake despises in schooling. The pupil, whose drudgery is the subject of 'The School-Boy' in *Songs of Experience*, is imprisoned in the modes of conventional literacy. When a child beginning to read moves his eyes with his place-marker across the line and down the page of print, he scans the lineaments of Urizen word by word and line by printed line. The lineaments of Urizen are the modes of conventional literacy, and the lineaments are complete when the education is complete, by which time the student has become what he beheld.[6]

It is here worth noting of the title-page design that if Urizen's book contains true Vision he will miss it, not because his eyes are closed, but because he will be sitting on it. His posture is the product of his intellect. It tells him to accept the pages passively one word and one line at a time, left to right, top to bottom, first page to second to third, a method well suited to copying, less well to illumination.

A discussion of the squatting patriarch must eventually include a discussion of the apparatus of death that surrounds him. Urizen and his environment are of a piece, and for two reasons: a man becomes what he beholds, and 'As a man is, So he Sees' (p. 471).[7] These principles operate jointly to fuse subject and object in a cycle of perception that gives the power of creation to the taker. Thus either man makes his environment or it makes him. Urizen has clearly not taken control of his environment; he has been put to sleep, entranced, or blinded by it. Nature has made him over in her image, which is the image of Natural Law. The first of Nature's

5. There may be the suggestion of an aleph near the end of Urizen's beard at the viewer's left.
6. 'Terrified at the Shapes / Enslavd humanity put on he became what he beheld' (*The Four Zoas* 53. 23–4; Erdman 336). This is Blake's first use of an idea that he used many times. [cf. M 3:29, p. 150]
7. Cf. 'A fool sees not the same tree that a wise man sees' (*MHH* 7, p. 72) and 'As the Eye—Such the Object' (Annotations to *The Works of Sir Joshua Reynolds*, p. 464).

laws is the inevitability and finality of death, of which the title-page design is an elaborate study.

As it pertains to the health of eighteenth-century art, the apparatus of death in the design shows both a hopeful and a less hopeful side. The sides are condemnation and remedy, a familiar pair in satire, which Blake displays in a corresponding pair of paradoxical Christian symbols, the grave and the cross. He has ingeniously incorporated the grave into the cross and made the cross emerge from the configuration of book, stones, and Urizen, who is ignobly crucified, crouching on the ground. His arms are nailed to the arms of the cross by quill and etching needle, though the force of gravity and the sleep of reason would be sufficient to fasten him.

The remedial side of Blake's meaning is beyond the range of this essay, though the remedy seems to grow out of the condemnation. If we take as evidence the amalgamated cross and tomb on the title-page of *Urizen*, the English arts of writing and engraving were crucified, dead, and buried in 1794. The design also shows that the crucified arts crucify; Urizen is his own victim. 'He became what he beheld' should be his epitaph. Whatever he is writing and engraving on the arms of his cross indeed is his epitaph, since his cross is also his tomb.

HAROLD BLOOM

[On the Theodicy of Blake's *Milton*]†

Like the Book of Job and *Paradise Regained*, Blake's *Milton* is a study in gathering self-awareness. Job and Milton's Son of God come to recognize themselves in their true relation to God. Blake's Milton recognizes himself as God or imaginative Man and proceeds to purge from himself everything opposed to that recognition. But where the Book of Job and *Paradise Regained* identify sonship to God with obedience to Him, Blake's *Milton* urges us to "seek not thy heavenly father then beyond the skies" but rather "obey thou the Words of the Inspired Man." Job and Milton's Son of God overcome their temptations, which in Job are deeply involved with inner conflicts. Blake's Milton is close to Job in that he must rid himself of the conviction of his own righteousness before he can resolve the conflict within his own self.

The clearest link between the Book of Job, *Paradise Regained*, and *Milton* is that the protagonist of each work must overcome Satan, or a condition brought on by Satan's activity. Here *Milton* occupies a kind of middle position with respect to both the earlier works. Like Job, Blake's Milton must overcome his Satanic situation or inwardness, rather than Satan himself. But like the Son of God, Blake's Milton must resist overt Satanic temptations as well. Blake's Milton is both a suffering man, like Job, and a Son of God, very like Milton's Christ.

Something of the beauty of *Milton*'s form ought to be evident by now, and I would make the claim that it is a poem worthy of a place beside the Book of Job and *Paradise Regained*. One question remains: is it a theodicy in as

† From *Blake's Apocalypse: A Study in Poetic Argument* (1963; Ithaca: Cornell University Press, 1970), 362–64. By permission of the author c/o Writers Representatives, LLC, New York, NY. All rights reserved. Aside from his formidable body of literary and cultural criticism, Bloom influences Blake studies through collections of reprinted essays in the "Bloom's Literary Criticism" series published by Chelsea House.

clear a sense as they are? Does it earn its Miltonic motto: "To Justify the Ways of God to Men?" It does, if one remembers exactly how the Bard's Song, that extraordinary transfiguration of a biographical incident, finds its place in the poem. Just as *Paradise Regained* afforded Milton the opportunity to explore the Jobean problem within himself, so Blake's *Milton* allows the later poet to advance his personal solution to the problem of evil as it confronted him in his own life. The historical Milton indeed became a Rintrah in the wilderness, and a lonely prophet is an excellent prospect for Satan. *Paradise Regained* concludes with the Son of God returning to his mother's house, to wait again upon the will of God. So John Milton, at the end, learned to wait, comforted by a paradise within himself, happier far than the outer one he had failed to bring about in his England. Blake's temptation, in the Bard's Song, is an instructive contrast to this pattern of painfully acquired patience and prophetic hope. Under the "mild" self-imposition of a subtler Satan than the ones who tried Job and Christ, Blake is tempted to forsake prophecy altogether. He has ranged against him not only the desert silence where he should have auditors, but all the subtle pressures of conformity, the persuasiveness of Moral Virtue. Rescued by Milton's descent, and realizing that he is the reincarnation of Milton, Blake is strengthened to the spiritual audacity by which he transvalues the entire notion of theodicy. What justifies the ways of God to men in *Milton* is finally just and only this: that certain men have the courage to cast out what is not human in them, and so become Man, and to become Man is to have become God.

The ways of God can be justified to men only insofar as men can and do put themselves beyond the "cloven fiction" that creates the initial problem of theodicy. To Job man and God were radically divided, one from the other, and to the historical Milton this otherness was bridged only by a historical Incarnation. To Blake all dualities are spectral, and Christ and the human imagination in the freedom of its power are as one. The greatness of Blake's *Milton* is a poetic greatness; the poem excels in design and execution, and yields to few other poems in its rhetorical art. Yet the greatness of Blake's argument counts for much also, and the lasting beauty of *Milton* is partly due to the moving passion with which Blake believed in the truth of the awakened imagination, and the holiness of the affections of the altogether human as opposed to merely natural heart. Even if, with Keats, we have more faith in the natural heart than Blake did, we can feel the critical force of so energetic and human a prophecy.

V. A. DE LUCA

From A Wall of Words: The Sublime as Text[†]

> I give you the end of a golden string,
> Only wind it into a ball:
> It will lead you in at Heavens gate,
> Built in Jerusalems wall.

(J 77)

† From *Unnam'd Forms: Blake and Textuality*, ed. Nelson Hilton and Thomas A. Vogler (Berkeley: University of California Press, 1986), 218–20, 226–27, 230–36, 237–39, 240–41. By permission of Nelson Hilton. See also De Luca's *Words of Eternity* (1991). Adjusted citations of Blake's text refer to this edition.

Blake is still conspicuously difficult to read, even in a critical climate in which all readings are said to be problematic. This difficulty is my theme. I want to concentrate on those elements of Blake's texts that tend to withdraw from referential function altogether. Where these elements operate, the text becomes iconic, a physical *Ding an sich*, not a transparent medium through which meaning is easily disseminated. In *Jerusalem*, particularly, the thread of thematic continuity is subject to snagging on these verbal outcroppings, and there are indeed passages in the poem where such outcroppings mass themselves into a solid wall of words. Most readers of Blake have spent a lot of time pacing before these ramparts, the golden string slack in their hands.

I want to pursue this notion of a Blakean "wall of words" in the context of the Romantic sublime, in which natural walls, steep and lofty cliffs, have a preeminent place. For the Romantics, these towering forms interpose a barrier to the continuities of travel, substituting elevation for the planned destination. In the theory of the period the sublime experience is typically presented as a three-fold moment: an encounter with the stimulating object, an episode of discontinuity (usually described as vertigo or blockage or bafflement), and a sudden and ecstatic exaltation. In all sophisticated theories of the sublime, this outer confrontation betokens an inner drama; the sublime experience is said to sift the mind, dividing it into two unequally privileged faculties, one consigned to pain and deprivation, the other admitted to an exalted sphere of delight. The terms for these faculties vary from writer to writer—for Wordsworth "the light of sense" goes out as "Imagination, dread power" rises up; for Kant the Imagination is itself the faculty of deprivation, and Reason the faculty of plenitude—but their relative functions remain the same. Although he is not often included among the theorists of the sublime, Blake also gives us a psychology of the sublime as constituted from a similar division of faculties. Speaking of his own work as a "Sublime Allegory," Blake goes on to amplify his terms: "Allegory addressed to the Intellectual powers while it is altogether hidden from the Corporeal Understanding is My Definition of the Most Sublime Poetry" (p. 484). The barrier to the faculty allied with sense is an avenue to its more privileged counterpart. Conceived dynamically, the sublime stimulus operates as a kind of psychic traffic light that directs energy denied to the Corporeal Understanding into the released Intellectual Powers. Such a barrier is needed to channel and concentrate energy, and this economy explains why Blake deems a privilege afforded to one of two faculties as more sublime than privileges afforded to both.

At the barrier is a point of indeterminacy, a moment between stop and go, a state of incomplete disengagement between the Corporeal Understanding and the Intellectual Powers. The barrier seems to flicker before the eyes, now opaque, now translucent, at once forbidding and yielding. The sublime object presents a towering face and yet offers a conspicuous invitation to ascent, or it holds back and teases with the promise of penetration, or it hints at ineffable possibilities of Presence and then defers them. It is not surprising therefore that recent critics, increasingly sensitive to the perplexed role of language as both a conductor of meaning and an agency of blockage, have, like Blake, described the sublime experience as if it were an encounter with a difficult text.[1] For even the material world affords objects that function as signs or the settings for them. The walls and their aggrandized equivalents so prominent in the literature of the sublime—lofty cliffs, great architectural piles, monumental slabs, standing stones, ruins, and the like—seem to beg to be read, blank as they are. For this reason, many artists working in the tradition of the sublime betray a fascination with inscription, as if responding to a call latent in their grand but mute material. The point where writing begins to appear on the wall is the point of indeterminacy, the point where the flicker of opacity and translucence starts, of presentation and deferral. Before the *mise en abyme* of recent deconstructionist talk became a scene of reading and writing, it was literally a scene of the eighteenth-century and Romantic material sublime with its steep drops and dizzying heights. Blake's own textual sublime, to be fully understood, should also be located within the larger tradition of walls and inscriptions that prevailed in his age.

*   *   *

The task of a sublime artist and poet such as Blake is to liberate the signifier from the signified, word from surface—and the Intellectual Powers, reflected in words, from the grip of death toward which the Corporeal Understanding tends. * * *

*   *   *

[T]he etched words of Blake's illuminated books often seem to hover in space against a background of cloudy grandeur or stony height. This visual foregrounding is in itself a kind of statement of the preeminence of language, yet even in late Blake it is rarely an uncontested eminence. What kind of visual statement, for example, does plate 70 of *Jerusalem* make (p. 302)? The design of the huge Druidic trilithon is surely preeminent; * * * on one level it signifies the material sublime towering high over natural man. Does this image not usurp the midway position, thrusting the text to the peripheries above and below, with the text blocks themselves functioning almost as elaborate captions? (The first words on the plate are "And this the form of," the last, "the mighty limbs of Albion." The limbs seem to be shown in petrified form here.) Yet a counterreading asserts itself against this baleful triumph of the material sublime, bringing with it different questions. How triumphantly does this image tower, when for all its "height" it does not even tower up to the top of the page? Is it not significant that language floats above the trilithon in a space precisely analogous to the space occupied by the naked youth above the lintel of Death's Door?[2] (We are reminded of the etymology of the word *sublime*, "the lintel [raised] from beneath.") In short, the same visual schema produces antithetical readings and a see-sawing domination

---

1. See, e.g., Geoffrey H. Hartman, *The Fate of Reading* (Chicago: University of Chicago Press, 1975) 120: "The structure of the act of reading . . . is the structure of the sublime experience in a finer mode"; Neil Hertz, "The Notion of Blockage in the Literature of the Sublime," in *Psychoanalysis and the Question of the Text*, ed. Geoffrey H. Hartman (Baltimore: Johns Hopkins University Press, 1973) 68–70; and, most elaborately, Theodore Weiskel, *The Romantic Sublime: Studies in the Structure and Psychology of Transcendence* (Baltimore: Johns Hopkins University Press, 1976) 26–31and passim.
2. In Schiavonetti's twelfth engraving (1808) after Blake's designs for Blair's *Grave*. See n. 9, p. 79 [*editors' note*].

of rival sublimes.[3] Such equivocal competitions of text and image are of course found everywhere in Blake, and they fuel much of the energy of his composite art. But as long as an element of material "height" is present in the competition we never proceed entirely beyond equivocation into the transcendent certainty of the Intellectual Powers.

As his creative enterprise proceeds to its culmination in *Milton* and *Jerusalem*, Blake's own sublime becomes increasingly an affair of the text and the text alone. The reading experience supplies all the essential ingredients of the sublime experience, without reference to any external sublime. Initially offering threads of thematic and narrative continuity that lure the reader onward, the text presents a refractory iconicity, a wall or steep, that halts or dizzies the Corporeal Understanding. At the same time it displays an exuberance in its own self-referential play that provides the leap of *jouissance*, as Barthes would say, for the Intellectual Powers. In short the text provides its own golden string, its own walls, its own gates, its own heaven.

*   *   *

* * * In its most developed state, Blake's sublime of the text is no longer a matter of words on walls, inscriptions on indeterminate ground, but of walls made out of words. To be sure, in the Keynes proof of the frontispiece of *Jerusalem* actual inscriptions cover the arch of the gate and the walls on either side,[4] but Blake suppressed these inscriptions in all finished copies of the poem as if to encourage us to read the inscribed text within the work as embodying its own iconic ground. There is no danger in this kind of iconicity that the text will merge with its ground * * * for there is no material ground. The iconicity of Blake's late prophetic texts functions both as an opaque barrier to meaning and also as an exhilarating window into a textuality where riches of meaning are generated and stored.

A number of specific devices in Blake's late works contribute to this effect of words as textual walls; I shall confine myself here to mentioning four. First, visual illuminations, often occupying a block of half a plate or larger (as in *Jerusalem* 70), introduce pictorial signifiers in the midst of alphabetic ones, with the inevitable effect of inducing the eye to pictorialize the rest of a plate. The attention of the reader is diverted from a sequential pursuit of words and lines to a visual contemplation of the whole block of text as a single unit, a panel. Blake criticism is just beginning to investigate the significance of the layout of his illuminated books and to attend to such matters as the size of the designs, their situation on the plate, the intervals between them, and the patterns that combinations of these elements may produce. To look at Blake's text this way—and it is inevitable once we accept the implications of the notion of a composite art as elaborated by W.J.T. Mitchell and others—is to see it as blocks of light space, adorned with little dark figurations, played off against blocks of dark space, figured with light bounded shapes. Not only do the meanings of the individual words recede in importance in this visual perspective but so does the continuity of meaning from plate to plate; the plates become mural panels, movable units in a hundred-panelled wall.

---

3. I have elaborated on this rivalry elsewhere (see De Luca, *Studies in Eighteenth-Century Culture* 11 (1982), 93ff.), particularly with reference to Burke * * *.
4. See n. 1, p. 210 [*editors' note*].

Second, Blake frequently increases the density of inscription to the point of visual strain. *Jerusalem* provides many examples, but plate 16 is particularly notorious, crammed as it is with sixty-nine lines of verse that run virtually from one edge of the copperplate to the other, with scarcely more than a squiggle or two of visual decoration. To compound this impediment to easy reading, the text is packed with proper nouns, 140 of them in the lower half of the plate alone. Although such a crowding of characters and of reference inevitably irritates those who come to texts for smooth communication, the effect of this impediment to the reading eye is precisely to reify the signifier and so provoke the tension necessary for the sublime experience. Suddenly, at the turn of a page, row upon row of verses piled high strike the reader's eye, each row composed of discrete horizontal slabs of letters, like so many bricks. The text presents itself, in short, as a solid wall of words over which the eye slips, unable to find fastening. A second glance discriminates bristling ranks of capital letters, verse without syntax, nouns without predication, names without context ("Levi. Middlesex Kent Surrey. Judah Somerset Glouster Wiltshire. / Dan. Cornwal Devon Dorset, Napthali" [*J* 16.45–46]). At the very start, then, the reader feels fatigue, a vertigo, and even though he may proceed through the text word by word, his ordinary, or corporeal, understanding never succeeds in comprehending or retaining the whole. The reader experiences something like Kant's sublime of magnitude, "for there is here a feeling of the inadequacy of his Imagination [a purely sense-related faculty in Kant] for presenting the Idea of a whole, wherein the Imagination reaches its maximum, and in striving to surpass it, sinks back into itself."[5] Frequently in *Jerusalem*, the alternative for the Corporeal Understanding to the text as spatial barrier is the text as linear labyrinth, which leads the understanding, after much travail, back to the cold and obdurate exterior of the structure.

Third, with less dire effect, Blake enhances the iconicity of his text by favoring regular, periodic repetition of words and phrases and rectilinear arrangements of these reiterations on the plate:

> And every Month, a silver paved Terrace builded high:
> And every Year, invulnerable Barriers with high Towers.
> And every Age is Moated deep with Bridges of silver & gold.
> And every Seven Ages is Incircled with a Flaming Fire.
> (*M* 28.54–57)

> And sixty-four thousand Genii, guard the Eastern Gate:
> And sixty-four thousand Gnomes, guard the Northern Gate:
> And sixty-four thousand Nymphs, guard the Western Gate:
> And sixty-four thousand Fairies, guard the Southern Gate:
> (*J* 13.26–29)

> All Human Forms identified even Tree Metal Earth & Stone. all
> Human Forms identified, living going forth & returning wearied
> Into the Planetary lives of Years Months Days & Hours reposing
> (*J* 99.1–3)

---

5. Immanuel Kant, *Critique of Judgment*, trans. J. H. Bernard (London: Macmillan, 1914), p. 112.

The perfect vertical alignment of the repeated phrases in the first two passages is immediately apparent to the eye, indeed, more immediately apparent than the meanings of the lines. In the extract from *Jerusalem* 13 verticality moves into rectangularity as the horizontal structure "And sixty-four thousand . . . guard the . . . Gate" quadruplicates itself in symmetrically spaced columns with a variation in terms filling the lacunae like mortar. The alignments in *Jerusalem* 99 are more complex: the repetition of the word "all" at the beginning and end of the first line squares off the slab of text like a pair of quoins, but the alignments of other repeated terms are not strictly rectilinear. In the paired phrases "Human Forms identified," for example, the lower phrase slips slightly to the left of perfect vertical alignment. The metrically and syntactically congruent phrase "Years Months Days & Hours" in the third line echoes "Tree Metal Earth & Stone" in the first but shows a similar leftward slippage in its respective position in the line; on the other hand, "reposing" in line 3 moves to the right of a vertical alignment with the congruent "returning" in the line above. Here the effect is rather like the cross-hatch layering of bricks in a wall: the mortar spaces are always obliquely aligned. More precisely, the interplay of repetition and displaced position creates a kind of visual syncopation as well as a misalignment of eye and ear (the former defeated in an expectation of periodic return that is made good for the latter). The effect is a small tension or disequilibrium that provokes, on a larger scale, the energy of the sublime experience.

The isolation of text blocks as panels in a larger visual design, the crowding of words on a plate into an opaque mass, the distribution of replicated terms along rectilinear axes all serve to induce in the text a resistance to discursive reduction. More powerful even than these three modes of inducing resistance is the massive proliferation of proper names, which we have already glimpsed in *Jerusalem* 16. Names are intrinsically irreducible, hard givens, unavailable for paraphrase. The irreducibility of the name can take two contrary forms: either it brings transparently to mind the unique signified it denotes and, in a sense, collapses into it * * * or else it hides an unknown referent that cannot be made present through paraphrase or synonym, whereupon the name signifies itself as signifier and nothing else. * * * [T]he particular power of the autonomous name in Blake is that in confronting its opacity we are never unaware that it also transparently denotes a unique signified whose presence is tantalizingly deferred; psychic energy is generated in the tension between the apparent opacity and the possible transparency. This tension may best be seen not in those passages in Blake where the names are pure inventions, hermetically sealed, but where the names hover at the remote margins of the known:

> A wine-press of Love & Wrath double Hermaph[r]oditic
> Twelvefold in Allegoric pomp in selfish holiness
> The Pharisaion, the Grammateis, the Presbuterion,
> The Archiereus, the Iereus, the Saddusaion, double
> Each withoutside of the other, covering eastern heaven
> (*J* 89.4–8)

We know, vaguely, that there are real referents behind these formidable names, or rather we are induced to make that assumption because of the relative familiarity of some of them. Yet even the more familiar are orthographically distorted, estranged, as if read in a dream. Such familiarity as they have is like the faint tracing of an inscription on the cliff face of their obscurity. We labor to read but keep sliding away: a dreadful trade.

*   *   *

It is time to speak of these Intellectual Powers, and of what lies on the other side of the wall. It should be said at once that there is no other side; there is only an opacity that becomes a translucence once the intellectual order of the text is grasped. * * * [I]n the visionary conclusion of *Jerusalem*, the delight of Eternity, the form of its fulfilled desire, is conceived as discourse—the word is Blake's own (98.35)—in which "every Word & Every Character Was Human" (98.35–36). * * *

*   *   *

"And the Writing/Is the Divine Revelation in the Litteral expression (*M* 42.13–14). This is a writing whose "woven letters" compose history and fallen time, the "Woof of Six Thousand Years" (42.15). But if we detach these words from their contextual bed, allowing them to articulate the range of their syntactic and semantic possibilities, they assert a revelation about the Divine Vision itself as nothing other than transcendent writing: the Writing IS the Divine Revelation (what is revealed about the Divine); the Writing IN THE LITTERAL EXPRESSION is the Divine Revelation (that is, the Divine Revelation inheres in the characters of the Writing, not the meaning of the Writing). God is the Word, but the Word as Written; in the Eternity every Word and every Character is human, but without losing the properties of words and characters.[6] It is thus not surprising that when Blake apostrophizes his reader in *Jerusalem* as "*lover* of books! *lover* of heaven" (plate 3), his syntax induces us to consider the terms as appositive and the two loves as one and the same: heaven is a form of text.[7]

Behind this equation of divinity and textuality there are religious sanctions from traditional sources, both orthodox and unorthodox. The Kabbalistic tradition of creation as an emanation of the Tetragrammaton or four letters of the Divine Name is one possible source; another is the representation of the godhead as Alpha and Omega in Revelation. The Book of Revelation, furthermore, is essentially about the revelation of a book, sealed at first and opaque, then burst open to reveal a new textuality, visible letters both read and seen—a paradigm of the sublime experience that perhaps informs all its later secular versions.[8] But however much he draws

---

6. Nelson Hilton articulates these points in a fundamental way: "Words," he says, "are the building-blocks of Blake's 'universe stupendous'—which is language. The words are not signs for what is seen (*idea*); rather, what appears is a *phainomenon* or showing-forth of words, a *logosophany*" (*Literal Imagination: Blake's Vision of Words* [Berkeley and Los Angeles: University of California Press, 1983] 9). Hilton defines "literal imagination" as one that "would, in keeping with its etymology (*littera*), identify itself in letters, that is to say, in the word and in writing" (*Literal* 2).
7. Paul Mann ("*The Book of Urizen* and the Horizon of the Book," in *Unnam'd Forms: Blake and Textuality*, ed. Nelson Hilton and Thomas A. Vogler [Berkeley, Los Angeles, London: University of California Press, 1986]) 170ff.; argues the contrary position: "Eternity is bookless, a perspective from which the book is seen as a hole torn in the seamless fabric of Eternity." For Mann, all inscription is constriction and obliteration of life. One might reply that it is not so much a case of language doing violence to Eternity as of Urizen doing violence to language, by limiting its endless potentialities to reductive descriptiveness and prescriptive flat. But the living Words of Eternity still form collectively Eternity's ideal, unfallen book.
8. On the Name of God in the Kabbalah, see Gershom Scholem, *Kabbalah* (New York: New York Times Book Company, 1974) 170ff.; for a survey of older commentary on Revelation pertinent to themes mentioned here, see Joseph Anthony Wittreich, Jr., *Visionary Poetics: Milton's Tradition and His Legacy* (San Marino: Huntington Library, 1979) 3–54.

on the imagery of scriptural revelation (and inscription as the revealed), Blake himself is a secularist of the sublime, if we understand "secularist" to mean one who seeks to demystify the conception of the all-creating, transcendental inscription as glowing characters suspended in the void, originating in an unapproachable Other, a mystery of mysteries. Blake understands language not only as having human origin but also as being the quintessence and the glory of our humanity. Allegory means "other-speaking," but in the state of transcendence and sublimity there is no "other." "Sublime allegory" is thus an "other-speaking" that cancels its own otherness and becomes simply speaking; "Allegory addressed to the Intellectual powers" refers therefore to a scene of self-recognition.

*   *   *

[In Blake's sublime of the text,] the Intellectual Powers perceive [the] text as a concentration of minute particulars gathered to a presence, taking it in as a conclave of signifiers—each particular a word, each word a determinate form though bristling with polyvalent possibilities. The words are sometimes servants of meaning, sometimes lords of their own autonomy, in kaleidoscopically shifting patterns of order. * * * The Intellectual Powers do not address themselves to meaning as such. The text is generous in its inclusion of meanings, which are there to be found sooner or later. Interpretation is deferred, but delight is immediate. In that sphere of delight the wall of words becomes a reticulated wall, and every word a window yielding prospects of our sovereign powers.

A critique of Blake's sublime and an exposition of textuality's role in his work come, then, to much the same thing. But, a final word of critic's caution. The terminology of our present-day discourse on textuality easily lends itself to the discussion of Blake. The ease of application, however, depends largely on the fact that this terminology, with its imagery of blocks, gaps, abysses, labyrinths, deferrals, and the like, is itself a sublime rhetoric, one that hints at common intellectual roots between the antipositivism of Blake's time and of our own. But a historical sense serves not only to indicate those points of *rapprochement* between Blake's theoretical concerns and our own but also to draw the limits of their compatibility. The sublime is inherently an idealizing mode. Although Blake would recognize much in our current discourse as part of the vocabulary of sublimity, he would see this vocabulary as stuck in the intermediate or deprivative phase of the sublime moment without a promise of the fulfillment that makes the sublime worth its name. For Blake Presence is available, and the transcendental subject exists; these are in fact the cornerstones of his faith. The experience of transcendence, moreover, leads him to an earnest preoccupation with other concerns currently unfashionable in some quarters—with truth and error, moral persuasion, and an unsparing analysis of the world we live in every day. The sublimity of the text is not the text's only value, and it is of no value if it serves only to lead us into an endless labyrinth of linguistic traces and differences. In that sublimity we breathe heaven's air, but as a gift to sustain us in our return to the continuities of the common day—the samphire-man[9] back on the beach with his burden, the birds of the airy way homing in to the nest.

---

9. Referring to a figure in "Edgar's imaginary recreation of Dover Cliff in *King Lear*" (4.4.15), discussed at length in a section not included in this edition (pp. 220–222) [*editors' note*].

Textual Technicalities

Because Blake himself controlled his illuminated books at every stage, from composition to etching to printing to touching up or coloring the printed pages, it may seem that he left nothing for an editor to do. Even misprints in the ordinary sense are impossible. But all printmakers make mistakes, and Blake produced his share of malformed, missing, or repeated letters, to say nothing of stray marks, faint impressions, and underinked words that require editorial attention. Furthermore, most of Blake's illuminated books exist in more than one version, so that the fundamental scholarly concept of a "copy-text"—which emphasizes in its most traditional form the authority for typeset punctuation—cannot readily be applied. A technically exact mark-for-mark transcription of Blake's punctuation, even in an ideal impression, cannot produce a reading text in conventional typography appropriate for the Norton Critical Edition series. Accordingly, in translating Blake's handmade work to a machine-operated medium, we have adjusted standard editorial principles to suit our author and nudged special features of his work in the direction of our principles. In choosing base texts, we have benefited from Joseph Viscomi's discovery of "editions" consisting of all known copies produced during a single printing session, as elucidated in *Blake and the Idea of the Book* (1993). We usually base our text on a prime exemplar of the earliest edition that contains all or most plates appertaining to a given work, always a copy that is accessible in facsimile (usually both online and in print) so that readers can conveniently check our sources. With certain exceptions explained below, we preserve Blake's highly irregular spelling and capitalization but alter his most problematic punctuation. All in all, our editorial trade-offs, on a case-by-case basis, are wickedly complicated to explain: this appendix may be most useful if consulted only when questions arise about why a word or a line is printed in a certain way.

Source texts. For most illuminated works, by special arrangement with the William Blake Archive (www.blakearchive.org) edited by Morris Eaves, Robert Essick, and Joseph Viscomi (1996–), our base text is the archive's transcription of the specific copy named in our headnotes, checked against the archive's corresponding images and against printed facsimiles of the same and other versions of the same book. This set of transcriptions we have compared with the comprehensive scholarly editions (not necessarily based on the same source texts) of David V. Erdman, *The Complete Poetry and Prose of William Blake* (1982; 1988) and G. E. Bentley Jr., *William Blake's Writings* (1978), as well as with the transcriptions, variants, and textual notes of the scholarly facsimile editions in the Blake Trust series produced under the general editorship of David Bindman (1991–95). For Blake's writings that appeared in conventional typography and for those that remained in manuscript, we generally follow Erdman's edition, with alterations based on our own study of the originals, the facsimiles, and the findings of other editors, especially Bentley. For a few Notebook poems, in order to recover an earlier realization of a work in progress, we occasionally restore Blake's canceled words and relegate later alterations to footnotes.

Copy designations, plate numbers, and line numbers. Because almost all of Blake's illuminated books exist in more than one version, often varying in page sequences, those who write about Blake use a standardized reference system that identifies each copy by an alphabetical letter and assigns a number to each plate, no matter where the page printed from that plate happens to appear in a specific copy. For example, the four known copies of *Milton* are designated A, B, C, and D. A citation of "*Milton* 11: 28–30" refers to lines 28 through 30 on plate 11, a plate that appears as the twelfth page in Copy D, the base text for this edition. The Erdman edition, the key text for literary criticism, employs this standard system, slightly modified from that of Geoffrey Keynes's 1966 edition, *Complete Writings with Variant Readings* (corr. rpt. 1979)

This edition adheres to standard designations for copies but identifies pages by boldface arabic numbers throughout, almost always corresponding to those in the Bentley edition and the Blake Archive, to avoid the standard system's occasional anomalies and inconsistencies in treatment of frontispieces, title pages, and introductory elements (often identified by lowercase Roman numerals) and full-page designs (sometimes left unnumbered). In this edition, page, that is "plate," numbers appear in a box at the right of the text in boldface type. If the Erdman number is different, it appears in ordinary type after a forward slash. For example, "Thel's Motto" in *The Book of Thel* is plate "i" in the standard ordering; in this edition it is identified as "**2**/i," and the first page of the poem proper is "**3**/1." As for line numbers, we follow the Keynes-Erdman-Bentley and Blake Trust convention of beginning with the first line of poetry after the title, leaving prose lines unnumbered, and ignoring overflow lines and catchwords (the Blake Archive assigns a number to *all* lines, including titles, page and section numbers, carry-over lines, and catchwords).

Fonts, layout, capitalization, and spelling. We standardize references to Blake's titles in the table of contents, headnotes, and footnotes but present, in the text proper, Blake's own preferences ("SONGS Of *INNOCENCE* and *Of EXPERIENCE*," for example). Within texts, we retain all of Blake's irregular capitalization, all of his nonstandard spellings, except for obvious slips, and most of his odd punctuation, and we preserve most indentations and inset lines of his verse. Even though we recognize the importance and integrity of the aesthetic and physical unit of the copper plate, a fundamental building block of the illuminated books, we focus instead in this reading text on Blake's rhetorical units of poetic lines, stanzas, and verse paragraphs, regardless of plate boundaries. We respect the argument that Blake achieves special visual and verbal effects by hyphenating words at strategic points and carrying the remainder over to short lines above or below the main text (the solitary Urizen's "books formd of me- / -tals," p. 117 herein), but because we do not reproduce all pages with accompanying designs, we follow typographical convention in keeping poetic lines together, space permitting, and in printing most lines of prose continuously, regardless of length.

Punctuation. In translating Blake's nonstandard punctuation into rough typographical equivalents, we acknowledge our inability to do justice to such phenomena as hybrid question marks over comma bases, oblong periods, or elongated colons (or are they short exclamation points? lopped-off question marks?). Nor can we reproduce more than a sampling of the minuscule birds, butterflies, fish, squiggles and plant tendrils that serve as animated textual markers. In general, we omit punctuation marks that seriously interrupt units of thought and sparingly alter or add punctuation elsewhere, mainly at the ends of major grammatical units, without further gestures toward regulating or normalizing Blake's practice. Except for gently clarifying sentence boundaries, we make no alterations to Blake's unpublished letters, marginalia, and manuscript poems. And we scarcely lay an editorial finger on his best-known published work, *Songs of Innocence and of Experience*, in which rhythms, line breaks, and stanza divisions serve as unmarked rhetorical indicators. Blake usually dispenses with quotation marks and apostrophes, for example, and readers of these short poems can manage without them. Other seemingly random variations, such as "gatherd," "gather'd," and "gathered," deserve a closer look: in poems of regular meter, the full "-ed" spelling often (but not always) indicates that an additional final syllable should be sounded, as in "kisséd me" ("The Little Black Boy") and "lapséd soul" ("Introduction" to *Songs of Experience*)—but not in "piped with merry chear" ("Introduction" to *Innocence*). If pronunciation is in doubt, even with proper names, the rhythm of the line is a surer guide than Blake's spelling.

In all other illuminated works, we have altered punctuation just enough to smooth the way for readers. Because the dialogue, especially in Blake's later poems, can be extremely difficult to follow, we supply quotation marks. We also supply apostrophes for nouns in the possessive case, even when either the singular or the plural would fit the context. (Is the "fool's" reproach or the "fools'" [*Marriage* 9:47] a kingly title?) Conversely, for "Zoa's," a plural, we retain Blake's consistent apostrophe. Blake's periods, or dots, cannot be treated consistently: they appear unexpectedly, sometimes indicating pauses or breathing stops (which we mark by commas), sometimes marking the ends of clauses, or questions (which in the longer poems we often punctuate conventionally), and sometimes serving no discernible purpose at all (and so we remove them). In providing all these amenities, we acknowledge having sometimes spoiled such special effects as the surprise of discovering at the end of an expository passage that it is a quotation (as in *Europe* 3/iii:7), or the puzzlement of deciding which of several speakers has delivered a speech of ambivalent attribution (as in *Europe* 7/4:10–14). We have also broken up Blake's "swinging door" units of grammar such as participial phrases that could modify either the previous or the following main clause, or nouns or noun clusters that could be either an object in one sentence or a subject in the next. And we have interfered with the precision and delicacy of Blake's hovering dots, as in his punctuation of Oothoon's new start in *Visions of the Daughters of Albion* 9/6:21: "But Oothoon is not so. a virgin fill'd with virgin fancies." Because Blake kept Oothoon's old and new states within the same sentence, instead of setting the last part off as an emphatic fragment, we changed this dot to a semi-colon, rather than capitalizing the "a" to start a new sentence. For an exercise that forces fresh thought about any given passage, we recommend printing it out from a Blake Archive transcription and penciling in do-it-yourself punctuation.

Throughout, our aim has been to balance accuracy with readability. In our experience, Blake's expressive idiosyncrasies are not so much to be tolerated as to be enjoyed. We trust that this edition will prove less formidable in actual use than in our description of its making, and we wish our readers as absorbing a journey through Blake's texts as we have had in editing them.

William Blake's Life and Times: A Chronology

1757 (November 28) Born at 28 Broad Street, Carnaby Market, London (see map); baptized at St. James's Church, Piccadilly. Second of five surviving children of James Blake, a hosier and haberdasher, and his wife, born Catherine Wright, widow of Thomas Armitage (also a hosier), with whom she had joined the Fetter Lane Moravian Church (evangelical sect in communion with the Church of England).

1759 Voltaire, *Candide*.

1761 First vision of God (at age four); later sees a tree full of angels in a field at Peckham Rye (see map).

1762 Birth of favorite brother Robert (baptismal record: "Richard").
   Rousseau, *The Social Contract*.

1765 Percy, *Reliques of Ancient English Poetry*.

1768 After being taught at home, enters Henry Pars's Drawing School in the Strand (see map).

1769 Begins composing lyrics later printed in *Poetical Sketches* (1783).

1770 Poet Thomas Chatterton (b. 1752) commits suicide.

1772 Begins seven-year apprenticeship; (at fourteen) to James Basire on Great Queen Street (see map), engraver to London Society of Antiquaries; begins purchasing old prints from auctioneer Langford (see map).

1773 Earliest known independent engraving, after a figure in Michelangelo's *Crucifixion of St. Peter*; reworked (1810) and titled *Joseph of Arimathea among the Rocks of Albion*.

1774 Basire sends Blake to draw tombs in Westminster Abbey, where he develops a taste for the Gothic style. Probably engraves plates (signed by Basire) for Jacob Bryant, *A New System, Or an Analysis of Ancient Mythology*.

1775 Battles of Lexington and Concord and Bunker Hill. Artist J. M. W. Turner born.

1776 Declaration of Independence; war between Britain and the American colonies. Paine, *Common Sense*. Adam Smith, *Wealth of Nations*. Artist John Constable born.

1778 Death of Voltaire (b. 1694) and Rousseau (b. 1712).

1779 (October 8) Enrolls (at twenty-one) in the Royal Academy, Somerset House, for six years, as an engraver; attends lectures; draws from plaster casts of classic statues and live models; meets John Flaxman, sculptor. Engraves for Joseph Johnson, bookseller (who later publishes Priestley, Paine, Wollstonecraft, Godwin).

603

1780   Exhibits *Death of Earl Goodwin* at Royal Academy, favorably noted by "Candid" (i.e., George Cumberland, amateur etcher, insurance firm employee) in the May 27 *Morning Chronicle*. Caught up in anti-Catholic Gordon Riots (June 1–8), witnesses burning of Newgate Prison. Meets Cumberland (probably) and artist Thomas Stothard. Arrested with Stothard and another artist while sketching on the River Medway, under mistaken suspicion of spying for France.

1781   British surrender at Yorktown. Barbauld, *Hymns in Prose for Children.* William Herschel discovers Uranus.

1782   (August 18) Marries Catherine Boucher (b. 1762), daughter of a market gardener in Battersea (see map); they move to 23 Green Street, Leicester Fields. Catherine signs her marriage papers with an "X" but later reads, writes, draws, operates a press, and colors prints for her husband.

Swiss émigré artist Henry Fuseli (Johann Heinrich Füssli) exhibits *The Nightmare* (first version) at the Royal Academy. Fanny Burney, *Cecilia.* James Watt improves steam engine.

1783   *Poetical Sketches* printed at the expense of John Flaxman and the Reverend Mr. and Mrs. A. S. Mathew but not sold. In Harriet Mathew's salon (and throughout his life), Blake sings his verses to tunes of his own composition (not preserved).

Peace between Britain and the United States. Barry's mural series, *The Progress of Human Knowledge and Culture*, in Royal Society of Arts. Galvani experiments with electricity.

1784   Blake's father dies. Blake and James Parker (fellow apprentice at Basire's) open a print shop next door, at 27 Broad Street; both couples live above the shop. Purchases his own wooden rolling press about this time. Exhibits *War Unchained* and *A Breach in a City Wall* at Royal Academy. Satirical prints, engraved after Stothard, published in *Wit's Magazine*. About this time annotates Burke's *On the Sublime*, Locke's *On Human Understanding*, and Bacon's *Advancement of Learning* (present whereabouts unknown). Flaxman sends *Poetical Sketches* to popular poet William Hayley.

Handel festival in London. (September) Lunardi's hot air balloon ascent. (December) Death of Samuel Johnson.

1785   Manuscript satire, "An Island in the Moon" (editorial title), refers to Dr. Johnson's death and contains poems later appearing in *Songs of Innocence*. Exhibits three watercolors on the Joseph story and one on Gray's *Bard* at Royal Academy; teaches brother Robert to engrave. Parker & Blake shop fails; Blakes move to 28 Poland Street (see map).

1786   Burns, *Poems Chiefly in the Scottish Dialect.* "Sons of Africa" abolition campaign.

1787   (February) Brother Robert (at twenty-four) dies of tuberculosis; Blake, sleepless for two weeks at his bedside, sees his spirit ascend through the ceiling, clapping his hands for joy; later claims idea of relief etching revealed by Robert's spirt. Adopts Robert's sketchbook as his own *Notebook* for sketches and drafts. Meets Fuseli (see 1782), a profound influence (who also found Blake "d——d good to steal from").

1788   Produces first verbal-visual works in relief etching (illuminated printing): *All Religions Are One* and *There Is No Natural Religion*.

Engraves, after Fuseli's design, the frontispiece for Lavater's *Aphorisms on Man* (trans. Fuseli). Annotates this book and Swedenborg's *Wisdom of Angels Concerning Divine Love and Divine Wisdom*. Engraves four plates for fascicles of Lavater's *Essays on Physiognomy*, vol. 1.

> George III suffers dementia attack. Law (unenforced) sets eight as minimum working age for chimney sweepers. Olaudah Equiano, *Interesting Narrative* . . . ; abolitionist William Wilberforce campaigns (see 1807).

1789   Writes and illustrates *Tiriel* (never published); issues *The Book of Thel* and *Songs of Innocence*. (April) Signs document approving doctrines of New Jerusalem Church (Swedenborgian); does not attend this or any other church thereafter.

> (June–July) French Revolution begins. Richard Price, *A Discourse on Love of our Country*.

1790   Begins *The Marriage of Heaven and Hell*; engraves, after Hogarth, a climactic scene in Gay's *Beggar's Opera*; annotates Swedenborg's *The Wisdom of Angels Concerning Divine Love and Providence*. Moves across the Thames to 13 Hercules Buildings, Lambeth (see map), with ample space for printing, coloring, exhibiting, and selling his illuminated books.

> Burke, *Reflections on the Revolution in France*. Bligh, Narrative of the Mutiny on the Bounty (event of 1789).

1791   *The French Revolution*, Book I, commercially typeset proof; never published. Illustrates Wollstonecraft's *Original Stories from Real Life* (engraved by an anonymous artist); engravings, after Chodowiecki, for C. G. Salzmann's *Elements of Morality* (trans. Wollstonecraft); engravings for Darwin's *Botanical Garden* (1791–92), including two after Fuseli and details of the Portland Vase; begins engravings for Stedman's *Narrative* (1796) concerning slavery in Surinam.

> Paine, *The Rights of Man*, Part 1. John Wesley dies (b. 1703).

1792   Blake's mother dies. Completes *The Marriage of Heaven and Hell*; four plates for Stuart and Revett's *Antiquities of Athens*.

> Paine's *Rights of Man*, Part 2 (February) prompts indictment for seditious utterance; he goes to France (September)—warned by Blake?—as a member of the National Convention. Wollstonecraft, *Vindication of the Rights of Woman*. Prussian invasion of France halted at Valmy. France proclaimed a republic; Year One of Revolutionary calendar. Reynolds dies. Benjamin West becomes president of the Royal Academy.

1793   *Songs of Experience* (advertised as separate book), *Visions of the Daughters of Albion*, *America a Prophecy*, *For Children: The Gates of Paradise*; engraves *Edward & Elenor*, *Albion Rose*, twelve plates for Gay's *Fables*.

> (January 21) Louis XVI executed; (February 1) France declares war on Great Britain, the Dutch Republic, and Spain; (February 11) Britain declares war on France; (September) Marie Antoinette executed; Reign of Terror; (November) Goddess of Reason enthroned on high altar at Notre Dame; (December) Paine imprisoned in Paris. Wordsworth, *An Evening Walk*; Godwin, *Political Justice*.

1794   *Songs of Innocence and of Experience* (brought together under a new title page), *Europe: A Prophecy*; *The First Book of Urizen*. Engravings for Cumberland's *Thoughts on Outline*.

(July) Fall of Robespierre; death of Danton (April); Paine released from prison; trials (and acquittals) of Hardy, Holcroft, Thelwell, and Horne Tooke (London Corresponding Society, urging Parliamentary reform). Paine, *The Age of Reason*, Part 1; Wollstonecraft, *An Historical and Moral View of the Origin and Progress of the French Revolution*.

1795   *The Book of Ahania, The Book of Los, The Song of Los*, twelve large color prints (including *Elohim Creating Adam, Satan Exulting over Eve, God Judging Adam, Nebuchadnezzar, Newton, Good and Evil Angels Struggling for Possession of a Child*). (September) Blake is "mobbed and robbed."
    Treasonable and Seditious Meetings Act ("Pitt's terror"); famine, war-weariness, civil unrest: "No King, no war, no famine, and no Pitt." Napoleon puts down royalist insurrection; Constitution of Year III establishes (unstable) five-man Directory. France adopts metric system.

1796   Produces 537 watercolor drawings surrounding mounted text of Young's *The Complaint, and Consolation; or Night Thoughts . . .* (1742–46), commissioned by Edwards; enters fifteen-year hiatus in issuing new illuminated books (see 1811); eight engravings for Cumberland's *Thoughts on Outline*.
    Paine, *Age of Reason*, Part 2; Stedman, *Narrative of a Five Years Expedition against the Revolted Negroes of Surinam* (cf. 1791).

1797   Forty-three engravings for Edwards's edition of *Night Thoughts* I–IV. Begins using leftover paper and prints for for much-revised epic-scale illustrated poem *Vala*, retitled *The Four Zoas* (never published); 116 watercolors for Gray's *Poems* (for Flaxman).
    (April–June) Mutinies in the British Navy at Spithead and the Nore. Bank crisis. Wollstonecraft dies of complications of childbirth (on her daughter, Mary, see 1817).

1798   Probably annotates Watson's *An Apology for the Bible . . . Addressed to Thomas Paine* and Bacon's *Essays*; begins annotating Reynolds's *Discourses*.
    (Summer) Wolf Tone Rebellion in Ireland, suppressed; (August) Battle of the Nile: Nelson's naval victory halts French conquest of the Middle East. Wordsworth and Coleridge, *Lyrical Ballads*. Malthus, *Essay on the Principle of Population*.

1799   Exhibits *The Last Supper* at the Royal Academy. "Even Johnson and Fuseli have discarded my Graver." Thomas Butts, a civil servant, commissions fifty "small Pictures from the Bible" (thirty temperas and more than eighty watercolors are extant).
    (November 9) Napoleon's *coup d'etat* of 18 Brumaire; Consulate established. French remove Rosetta Stone from Egypt. Fall of Seringipatam concludes fourth Mysore-British war in India. Britain conquers Surinam. Goya publishes (and withdraws) *Los Caprichos*.

1800   (Spring) Exhibits *The Loaves and Fishes* at the Royal Academy. (September) Blakes move to Felpham, in Sussex, on English Channel near Chichester, taking "Sixteen heavy boxes & portfolios full of prints" and the printing press, to accept commissions from William Hayley.
    Act of Union with Ireland (Great Britain). Wordsworth, "Preface" to second edition of *Lyrical Ballads*. Poet William Cowper dies. Volta develops electric battery.

1801   Paints portraits of eighteen poets for Hayley's library and miniature portraits for others; begins watercolors on Milton's *Comus* for new patron, the Reverend Joseph Thomas; studies Greek, Latin, and Hebrew; works on *The Four Zoas*.

(April) Admirals Nelson and Parker victorious in first Battle of Copenhagen; George III rejects Catholic emancipation.

1802   Designs and engraves fourteen illustrations for Hayley's *Ballads*; engraves portrait of Cowper after Romney. Probably begins composing poems in Manuscript "Auguries" (through c. 1807).

(March 27) Peace of Amiens, briefly ending English-French hostilities (see 1803). Napoleon named consul for life. Coleridge, "Dejection: An Ode." Painter George Romney dies.

1803   Works on biblical watercolor series for Butts. (August 12) Evicts drunken soldier from his garden; indicted for sedition and assault; (September) returns to London, to 17 South Molton Street (see map); two engravings after Fuseli for Chalmers's edition of Shakespeare.

1804   (January 11–12) Acquitted of all charges at Chichester Quarter Sessions, to cheers of spectators. Sets up press, returns to illuminated books; dates title pages of *Milton* and *Jerusalem*. (October) Visits Truchsessian Gallery of Pictures; is "again enlightened with the light I enjoyed in my youth."

Napoleon becomes emperor, taking crown from the pope and placing it on his own head (painted by David).

1805   Designs and expects to engrave illustrations for R. H. Cromek's edition of Blair's *Grave* (published 1808); Cromek gives the lucrative engraving commission to the popular Louis Schiavonetti. More biblical watercolors for Butts.

Nelson defeats French at Battle of Trafalgar, near Gibraltar; dies heroically. Scott, *The Lay of the Last Minstrel*.

1806   Designs frontispiece (engraved by Cromek) for B. H. Malkin's *A Father's Memoir of His Child* (Malkin's prefatory remarks on Blake include texts of six poems). Defends Fuseli in *Bell's Weekly Messenger*. Hiatus in commercial engraving (until 1815); steady income from Butts: *A Vision of the Last Judgment* (other extant versions, 1808–09), first set of designs for the Book of Job (1806–07), lessons for young Tommy Butts.

1807   Watercolor series on *Paradise Lost* for the Reverend Joseph Thomas; *The Fall of Man* [or *Descent of Humanity*] for Butts. Cumberland reports that Blake has engraved "60 Plates of a new Prophecy" (*Jerusalem*). Blake believes Cromek has stolen his idea for *The Canterbury Pilgrims* and given it to Stothard.

Thomas Phillips exhibits his portrait of Blake (engraved by Schiavonetti as frontispiece to Blair's *Grave*, 1808) at Royal Academy. Stothard exhibits *The Canterbury Pilgrims*. Wordsworth, *Poems in Two Volumes*. British slave trade abolished.

1808   Exhibits *Jacob's Dream*, *Christ in the Sepulchre*, and (possibly) *Vision of the Last Judgment* (attributed to "B. Blake") at Royal Academy; makes second set of *Paradise Lost* illustrations; probably begins *The Canterbury Pilgrims*. (August) Robert Hunt mocks Blake's *Grave* designs in *The Examiner*.

Sir Arthur Wellesley, later duke of Wellington, leads Peninsular Campaign in Portugal and Spain (1808–13).

1809   (May) Opens first and only one-artist show in his brother's shop, 28 Broad Street; accompanied by *A Descriptive Catalogue* of sixteen paintings, including *Canterbury Pilgrims* and his huge *The Ancient Britons* (now lost); (September) viciously reviewed by Robert Hunt. Illustrates Milton's *On the Morning of Christ's Nativity* for the Reverend Joseph Thomas. Drafts *Public Address* and explication of *A Vision of the Last Judgment* (largest version, now lost).

Byron, *English Bards and Scotch Reviewers*. Stothard, engraving of *The Canterbury Pilgrims*.

1810   Engraves *The Canterbury Pilgrims*. Robert Southey, Charles and Mary Lamb, H. C. Robinson visit Blake's show.

1811   *An Allegory of the Spiritual Condition of Man*, Blake's largest surviving painting (five feet by four feet); *The Judgment of Paris* (for Butts); prints three copies of *Milton a Poem* (first new title since 1795). Henry Crabb Robinson's article on Blake, in German, published in *Vaterlandisches Museum*.

George III declared incompetent; the Prince of Wales becomes Prince Regent. Austen, *Sense and Sensibility*.

1812   *Philoctetes and Neoptolemos on Lemnos*. Exhibits three works from his show (*Canterbury Pilgrims*, *Pitt*, *Nelson*) and "Detached Specimens" of *Jerusalem* at Associated Painters in Water Colour; reviewed (June) in *The Lady's Monthly Museum*.

(June) United States declares war on Britain. Napoleon invades and retreats from Russia. Luddites attack British textile industry (framebreaking). Byron, *Childe Harold's Pilgrimage* I–II.

1813   Austen, *Pride and Prejudice*; P. B. Shelley, *Queen Mab*.

1814   (March) Fall of Paris; Napoleon exiled to Elba; (April) restoration of French monarchy: Louis XVIII. War of 1812 ends in *status quo ante*. Wordsworth, *The Excursion*.

1815   More Milton watercolors for Butts (through c. 1820). Engraves 185 dishes for Wedgwood catalog; visits Royal Academy to draw the *Laocoön* for Rees's *Cyclopedia*.

(March–June) Napoleon's Hundred Days, ending at Waterloo (June 18); economic depression in Britain. Wordsworth, *Poems*. Turner exhibits *Dido Building Carthage*. Caricaturist James Gillray (b. 1757) dies.

1816   Coleridge, *Christabel, Kubla Khan* . . . (composed 1797); P. B. Shelley, *Alastor*. Byron, *Childe Harold III*.

1817   Engraves Flaxman's designs for Hesiod's *Works and Days*.

Byron, *Manfred*. Coleridge, *Biographia Literaria*. Mary Wollstonecraft Shelley, *Frankenstein*. Austen, *Emma*. Elgin marbles (from the Parthenon) exhibited at British Museum.

1818   Resumes illuminated printing: reissues *Thel, Visions, Marriage, Songs, Urizen, Milton*; revises *The Gates of Paradise* ("For the Sexes"); begins "The Everlasting Gospel" (uncompleted). Meets the young painter John Linnell, who becomes a patron. Dines at Lady Caroline Lamb's, with the painter Sir Thomas Lawrence and others.

Keats, *Endymion*. Hazlitt, *English Poets, English Comic Writers*. Scott, *Heart of Midlothian*. Byron, *Childe Harold IV*. Jane and Ann Taylor, *City Scenes* (includes Blake's "Holy Thursday," *Innocence*).

1819 Draws "Visionary Heads" and "The Ghost of a Flea" for occultist astrologer John Varley.

"Peterloo Massacre," Manchester: mounted troops charge into sixty thousand peaceful demonstrators for Parliamentary reform. Byron, *Don Juan I–II*. Gericault exhibits *The Raft of the Medusa* in Paris.

1820 Issues first edition of *Jerusalem* (three copies) and (c. 1820–25) *For the Sexes: The Gates of Paradise* (see 1793). *Epitome of Hervey's Meditations on the Tombs*.

George III dies; Prince Regent becomes George IV. Keats, *Lamia, Isabella, The Eve of St. Agnes*. Shelley, *Prometheus Unbound*. Southey, *A Vision of Judgment*. Venus de Milo discovered. Sir Thomas Lawrence becomes president of the Royal Academy.

1821 Moves to 3 Fountain Court, The Strand (see map), small rooms with a narrow view of the Thames, owned by Catherine's brother-in-law. Sells print collection to raise money. Woodcuts for Virgil's *Pastorals*, ed. R. J. Thornton. Paints *The Arlington Court Picture* (*The Sea of Time and Space*).

Keats dies in Rome. Shelley, *Adonais*. Byron, *The Vision of Judgement, Cain, Heaven and Hell, Don Juan III–IV*. Constable exhibits *The Hay-Wain*.

1822 *On Homer's Poetry*, on same sheet with *On Virgil*. *The Ghost of Abel*. Royal Academy makes £25 charitable grant to Blake as "an able Designer & Engraver labouring under great distress."

Shelley drowns off coast of Italy.

1823 Begins attracting a following of young artists (Samuel Palmer, Edward Calvert, George Richmond, Frederick Tatham, F. O. Finch) who call themselves "The Ancients" and name Blake's apartment the "House of the Interpreter" (from Bunyan's *Pilgrim's Progress*, also the subject of a separate Blake print). Phrenologist James S. Deville takes cast of Blake's head.

Byron, *Don Juan VI–XIV*; Lamb, *Essays of Elia*.

1824 Begins 29 watercolors for *Pilgrim's Progress* and 103 watercolors and seven engravings for Dante's *Divine Comedy* (through 1827).

Byron, *Don Juan XV–XVI*; Byron dies in Greece, a champion of Greek independence from the Ottoman Empire.

1825 *The Characters in Spenser's Faerie Queene* (format similar to *Canterbury Pilgrims*, 1809); meets H. C. Robinson and (probably) Coleridge at salon of Charles and Elizabeth Aders.

Hazlitt, *The Spirit of the Age*. Fuseli dies in England.

1826 *Illustrations of the Book of Job* (twenty-two engravings, most derived from earlier watercolor designs) for Linnell; יה *[Yah]* & *his two Sons Satan and Adam* (the *Laocoon* figures [1815], surrounded by inscriptions of 1826–27). Annotates Wordsworth's *Excursion* (1814) and *Poems* (1815).

Flaxman dies (b. 1755). M. W. Shelley, *The Last Man*.

1827 *The Wise and Foolish Virgins* and *Queen Katherine's Dream* for Lawrence (£31/10 for both); annotates Thornton's *New Translation*

WILLIAM BLAKE'S LIFE AND TIMES: A CHRONOLOGY

of the Lord's Prayer; continues working on Dante project, propped up in bed; makes separate print of *Europe* frontispiece: "The Ancient of Days"; engraves a calling card for Cumberland; sketches Catherine Blake. (August 12) Dies, aged sixty-nine, probably of gallbladder and liver failure, reportedly singing of what he sees in heaven. Buried with the rest of his family in Bunhill Fields (behind the label of the "Blake's London" map), the Dissenters' cemetery in London, with a Church of England clergyman officiating.

Selected Bibliography

Because Blake's original illuminated books are fragile and highly sensitive to light, museums and research libraries rarely allow them to be exhibited; ordinarily they are accessible only to scholars, only by special arrangement. The most comprehensive repositories of these precious books are the Department of Prints and Drawings, British Museum (London), the Fitzwilliam Museum (Cambridge), the Yale Center for British Art, the Henry E. Huntington Library (San Marino, California), the Pierpont Morgan Library (New York), the Houghton Library of Harvard University, and the Lessing J. Rosenwald Collection, Library of Congress. Works in other media are sturdier, as may be seen in the rich Blake collection of the Tate Britain (London). Images from these and many other institutions, and from the collection of Robert N. Essick, are always on view in the online William Blake Archive (www.blakearchive.org), a treasure trove most quickly navigated in "non-Java" mode, for those with slower machines and Internet connections.

The master bibliographer of all things Blakean is G. E. Bentley Jr., author of *Blake Books* (BB, 1978), *Blake Books Supplement* (BBS, 1995), and the annual checklist in *Blake: An Illustrated Quarterly* (1994–); Bentley is also the world's greatest authority on Blake's life, work, and reputation (culminating in *Blake Records*, 2nd ed., 2004). The Blake Archive offers an extensive nonannotated bibliography covering reference works; standard and useful editions; literary, historical, and biographical studies; art historical studies; studies of color-printed drawings; commercial book illustrations; drawings, watercolors, and paintings; illuminated books; manuscripts; separate plates and plates in series; typographic works; and works by and about Blake's circle. The standard text for scholarly citation, *The Complete Poetry and Prose of William Blake*, edited by David V. Erdman ("E", rev. ed., 1988), is available electronically at the Blake Archive and at Nelson Hilton's Blake Digital Text Project (www.english.uga.edu/wblake).

The longest-running publication devoted to the poet is *Blake: An Illustrated Quarterly* (1967–)—formerly *Blake Newsletter*—ed. Morris Eaves and Morton D. Paley. So comprehensive is this journal of record, covering all aspects of Blake's work from microscopic to gargantuan, that an article on a particular subject, though indexed annually and online by author, may be difficult to retrieve. Because Bentley records the entire contents of *Blake* (*BIQ*) and other special publications chronologically by issue, substantial articles are easier to spot in the alphabetical listings, within categories, of the Blake Archive. The nine volumes of *Blake Studies*, ed. Roger R. Easson and Kay Parkhurst Long Easson, published irregularly from 1969 to 1983 (also listed by issue in Bentley), contain much criticism of merit. Also noteworthy is the far less broadly distributed *Blake Journal*, published annually by the Blake Society, London (1986–).

Our all-too-brief bibliography, heavily weighted toward recent and general criticism, and necessarily slighting the visual arts, is intended to offer students and nonspecialized readers an overview of Blake's achievement as a poet. In favoring often-cited, recent, or controversial literary studies in English that deal with more than one work, we omit much that we admire (to say nothing of our own essays). For more specialized criticism, studies of writings absent from this edition (such as *Tiriel*), and investigations of the paintings and designs, see Bentley's bibliographical listings and the Blake Archive bibliography; for important older studies, see these resources and Johnson's 1985 survey.

For studies of specific works, see facsimiles, editions, and criticism noted in our editorial apparatus, indexed by author on p. 617, and the Blake Archive bibliography.

I. STANDARD TEXTUAL AND GRAPHIC EDITIONS; SELECTED FACSIMILES AND REPRODUCTIONS

Bentley, G. E., Jr., ed. *William Blake's Writings*. 2 vols. Oxford: Clarendon Press, 1978 [including some 700 images in vol. 1, *Engraved and Etched Writings*.]

Bentley, G. E., Jr. ed. *William Blake's Works in Conventional Typography*. Delmar, N.Y.: Scholars' Facsimiles and Reprints, 1984.

Bindman, David, gen. ed. *Blake's Illuminated Books*. 6 vols. Princeton: The William Blake Trust and Princeton University Press and London: The William Blake Trust and Tate Gallery Publications, 1991–95; paperback 1994–98 [meticulously edited, annotated, moderately priced facsimile editions of the illuminated corpus].

Vol. 1. Morton D. Paley, ed. *Jerusalem: The Emanation of the Giant Albion*. 1991/1997.

Vol. 2. Andrew Lincoln, ed. *Songs of Innocence and of Experience*. 1991/1994.

Vol. 3. Morris Eaves, Robert N. Essick, and Joseph Viscomi, eds. *The Early Illuminated Books: All Religions Are One and There Is No Natural Religion; The Book of Thel; The Marriage of Heaven and Hell; Visions of the Daughters of Albion*. 1994/1998.

Vol. 4. D. W. Dörrbecker, ed. *The Continental Prophecies: America a Prophecy; Europe a Prophecy; The Song of Los.* 1994/1998.

Vol. 5. Robert N. Essick and Joseph Viscomi, eds. *Milton a Poem and The Final Illuminated Works: The Ghost of Abel, On Homer's Poetry [and] on Virgil, Laocoön.* 1993/1998.

Vol. 6. David Worrall, ed. *The Urizen Books: The First Book of Urizen; The Book of Ahania; The Book of Los.* 1995/1998.

[The earlier limited-edition Blake Trust series of handcolored collotype facsimiles edited by Geoffrey Keynes and produced by the Trianon Press under the direction of Arnold Fawcus contains all eighteen of the illuminated books (1951–76), some in more than one version, designs for the Bible (1957), for Gray (1972), for Dante (1979) and for the Book of Job (1982, 1987); as well as fine photographic reproductions of *Songs of Innocence and of Experience* and *The Marriage of Heaven and Hell,* with commentary by Keynes, in association with Oxford University Press (and Orion Press). Dover Press has issued inexpensive photographic copies of Trianon Press facsimiles since 1971. See also Dent / Dutton photographic color facsimiles of *The Marriage of Heaven and Hell* (1927), ed. Max Plowman and *The Book of Urizen* (1929), ed. Dorothy Plowman and facsimiles of *Songs* included in critical studies by Phillips and Gardner; facsimiles of individual works are cited in headnotes and footnotes.]

Bindman, David. intro. *William Blake: The Complete Illuminated Books.* London: The William Blake Trust and the Tate Gallery; New York: Thames & Hudson, 2000 [the entire set of facsimiles, minus editorial apparatus].

Eaves, Morris, Robert N. Essick, and Joseph Viscomi, eds. The William Blake Archive (www .blakearchive.org). 1996– [images and transcriptions of at least one copy of every illuminated work; annotations; the Erdman edition, and much more].

Easson, Kay Parkhurst and Roger R. Easson, eds. *William Blake: The Book of Urizen.* Boulder: Shambhala; New York: Random House, 1978; and *William Blake: Milton.* Boulder: Shambhala; New York: Random House, 1978.

Erdman, David V., ed. Commentary by Harold Bloom. *The Complete Poetry and Prose of William Blake.* 1965. Rev. ed. Berkeley: University of California Press, 1988 [affordable, portable, standard edition for scholarly citations]. Available also online (Eaves et al; Hilton)

Erdman, David V., annot. *The Illuminated Blake: All of William Blake's Illuminated Works with a Plate-by-Plate Commentary* 1974; New York, Dover, 1992.

Erdman, David V., ed. With the assistance of Donald K. Moore. *The Notebook of William Blake: A Photographic and Typographic Facsimile.* 1973; rev. Readex, 1977.

Fuller, David, ed. *William Blake: Selected Poetry and Prose.* Harlow: Longman; New York, Pearson Education Ltd., 2000.

Hilton, Nelson, ed. Blake Visual Text Project. www.english.uga.edu/wblake/home1.html. [includes an excellent concordance of "eE," the Erdman edition].

Keynes, Geoffrey, ed. *Blake: Complete Writings with Variant Readings.* 1966. Corr. rpt. Oxford: Oxford University Press, 1979.

Keynes, Geoffrey, ed. *The Letters of William Blake.* 3rd ed. Oxford: Oxford University Press, 1980.

Ostriker, Alicia, ed. *William Blake: The Complete Poems.* Harmondsworth, Middlesex: Penguin, 1977 [bibliography updated through 1986].

Stevenson, W. H., ed. *Blake: The Complete Poems* 3rd. ed. London: Pearson Longman, 2007.

II. BASIC REFERENCE WORKS, BIBLIOGRAPHIES, AND BIOGRAPHICAL RESOURCES

Ackroyd, Peter. *Blake.* London: Sinclair-Stevenson, 1995 [skillful popularization].

Bentley, G. E., Jr. *Blake Books: Annotated Catalogues of William Blake's Writings in Illuminated Printing, in Conventional Typography and in Manuscript.* Oxford: Clarendon Press, 1978. *Blake Books Supplement: A Bibliography of Publications and Discoveries . . . 1971–1992.* Oxford: Clarendon Press, 1995 [the riches of *BB* and *BBS* include judicious introductory surveys, detailed physical descriptions of Blake's writings (see also Viscomi), and annotated listings of everything written about him].

Bentley, G. E., Jr. *Blake Records.* 2nd ed. New Haven and London: Yale University Press, for the Paul Mellon Centre for Studies in British Art, 2004 [encompassing and superseding *Blake Records* (1969) and *Blake Records Supplement.* (1988)].

Bentley, G. E. *The Stranger from Paradise; A Biography of William Blake.* New Haven: Yale University Press, 2001.

Bentley, G. E. "William Blake and His Circle: A Checklist of Publications and Discoveries" [annual annotated checklist (sporadic in early years, under various titles) compiled by Thomas Minnick, *Blake Newsletter,* 1976; by Minnick and D. W. Dörrbecker, *Blake: An Illustrated Quarterly,* 1978–82; by Dörrbecker (beginning with 1984–86), 1986–93; and by Bentley (beginning with 1992), 1994–].

Damon, S. Foster. *A Blake Dictionary: The Ideas and Symbols of William Blake.* Rev. ed. with a new foreword and annotated bibliography [and all-important index] by Morris Eaves. Hanover, N.H.: University Press of New England, 1988.

Davies, Keri and Marsha Keith Schuchard. "Recovering the Lost Moravian History of William Blake's Family." *Blake/An Illustrated Quarterly* 38 (2004): 36–57.

Essick, Robert N. "William Blake." In *Oxford Dictionary of National Biography.* Oxford: Oxford University Press, 2004. [Available online.]

Erdman, David V., with John E. Thiesmeyer, Richard J. Wolfe, et al. *A Concordance to the Writings of William Blake.* 2 vols. Ithaca: Cornell University Press, 1967 [keyed to the 1966 Keynes edition; for an easy-to-use concordance keyed to the 1988 Erdman edition, see Hilton listing].

Gilchrist, Alexander. *Life of William Blake, Pictor Ignotus.* 2 vols. London: Macmillan, 1863. 2nd ed., 1880. Rpt. New York: Phaeton, 1969; Bristol : Thoemmes Press ; Tokyo: Kinokuniya, 1998.
Hilton, Nelson et al. *Concordance to the Complete Poetry and Prose of William Blake.* Athens, Ga.: Department of English, University of Georgia. (www.english.uga.edu/Blake_Concordance/).
Johnson, Mary Lynn. "William Blake." *The English Romantic Poets: A Review of Research and Criticism.* 4th ed. Ed. Frank Jordan. New York: Modern Language Association, 1985. 113–252 [survey through c. 1983].
Keynes, Geoffrey, and Edwin Wolf, eds. *William Blake's Illuminated Books: A Census.* New York: Grolier Club, 1953 [though factually superseded by Bentley's *Blake Books* and *Supplement,* the *Census* remains valuable because of its ease of use].
Miner, Paul. "William Blake's London Residences." *Bulletin of the New York Public Library* 62 (1958), 535–50.
Paley, Morton D. "The Truchsessian Gallery Revisited." *Studies in Romanticism* 16 (1977): 165–76.
Patenude, Troy. "'The Glory of a Nation': Recovering William Blake's 1809 Exhibition." *British Art Journal* 4 (2003), 52–63.
Phillips, Michael. "No. 13 Hercules Buildings, Lambeth: William Blake's Printmaking Workshop and Etching-painting Studio Recovered." *British Art Journal* 5 (2004), 13–21.
Summerfield, Henry. *A Guide to the Books of William Blake for Innocent and Experienced Readers* [based on criticism through 1984]. Gerrards Cross, Bucks, UK: Colin Smythe, 1998.
Viscomi, Joseph. *Blake and the Idea of the Book.* Princeton: Princeton University Press, 1993 [evidentiary analysis of Blake's processes (fits also in sections 3 and 4 of this bibliography)].
Whitehead, Angus. "William Blake's Last Residence . . . ," *British Art Journal* 6 (2005), 21–30.
Wilson, Mona. *The Life of William Blake.* 1927. 3rd ed. Oxford: Oxford University Press, 1971.
Wittreich, Joseph Anthony, Jr. *Nineteenth Century Accounts of William Blake.* Gainesville: Scholars' Facsimiles and Reprints, 1970.

III. BROAD STUDIES OF ILLUMINATED BOOKS AND OTHER WRITINGS
• Indicates works included or excerpted in this Norton Critical Edition.

Books

Adams, Hazard. *William Blake: A Reading of the Shorter Poems.* Seattle: University of Washington Press, 1963.
Ault, Donald D. *Visionary Physics: Blake's Response to Newton.* Chicago: University of Chicago Press, 1974.
Baine, Rodney M., with the assistance of Mary R. Baine. *The Scattered Portions.* Athens, Ga.: Distributed by the author, 1986.
Beer, John. *William Blake: A Literary Life.* London: Palgrave, 2005 [by the author of *Blake's Humanism* (1968) and *Blake's Visionary Universe* (1969)].
Behrendt, Stephen C. *Reading William Blake.* London: Macmillan Press, 1992.
• Bloom, Harold. *Blake's Apocalypse: A Study in Poetic Argument.* Garden City: Doubleday, 1963. Reissued Ithaca: Cornell University Press, 1970.
Bruder, Helen P. *William Blake and the Daughters of Albion.* Basingstoke: Macmillan; New York: St. Martin's Press, 1997.
Connolly, Tristanne J. *William Blake and the Body.* Basingstoke and New York: Palgrave Macmillan, 2002.
Cox, Stephen. *Love and Logic: The Evolution of Blake's Thought.* Ann Arbor: University of Michigan Press, 1992.
Damrosch, Leopold, Jr. *Symbol and Truth in Blake's Myth.* Princeton: Princeton University Press, 1980.
De Luca, Vincent Arthur. *Words of Eternity: Blake and the Poetics of the Sublime.* Princeton: Princeton University Press, 1991.
Di Salvo, Jackie. *War of Titans: Blake's Critique of Milton and the Politics of Religion.* Pittsburgh: University of Pittsburgh Press, 1983.
Erdman, David V. *Blake: Prophet against Empire: A Poet's Interpretation of the History of His Own Times.* 1954. 3rd ed. Princeton: Princeton University Press, 1977.
Essick, Robert N. *William Blake and the Language of Adam.* Oxford: Clarendon Press, 1989.
Esterhammer, Angela. *Creating States: Studies in the Performative Language of John Milton and William Blake.* Toronto: University of Toronto Press, 1994.
Ferber, Michael. *The Poetry of William Blake.* Harmondsworth: Penguin Books, 1991.
Ferber, Michael. *The Social Vision of William Blake.* Princeton: Princeton University Press, 1985.
Frosch, Thomas. *The Awakening of Albion.* Ithaca: Cornell University Press, 1974.
Frye, Northrop. *Fearful Symmetry: A Study of William Blake.* 1947. *The Collected . . . Works of Northrop Frye.* Vol. 14. Ed. Nicolas Halmi. Toronto: University of Toronto Press, 2005.
• Frye, Northrop. "Essays on Blake" [22 items] in *Northrop Frye on Milton and Blake, The Collected . . . Works of Northrop Frye.* Vol. 16. Ed. Angela Esterhammer. Toronto: University of Toronto Press, 2005.
George, Diana Hume. *Blake and Freud.* Ithaca: Cornell University Press, 1980.
Gallant, Christine. *Blake and the Assimilation of Chaos.* Princeton: Princeton University Press, 1978.
Gleckner, Robert F. *Blake and Spenser.* Baltimore: Johns Hopkins University Press, 1985.
Hagstrum, Jean H. *William Blake: Poet and Painter. An Introduction to the Illuminated Verse.* Chicago and London: University of Chicago Press, 1964.
Howard, John. *Infernal Poetics: Poetic Structures in Blake's Lambeth Prophecies.* Rutherford, N.J.: Fairleigh Dickinson University Press, 1984.

• Hilton, Nelson. *Literal Imagination: Blake's Vision of Words*. Berkeley: University of California Press, 1983.

Hobson, Christopher Z. *The Chained Boy: Orc and Blake's Idea of Revolution*. Lewisburg, Pa.: Bucknell University Press, 1999.

Hobson, Christopher Z. *Blake and Homosexuality*. New York and London: Palgrave, 2000.

Hutchings, Kevin. *Imagining Nature: Blake's Environmental Poetics*. Montreal: McGill-Queen's University Press, 2002.

Keynes, Geoffrey. *William Blake: Poet Printer Prophet. A Study of the Illuminated Books*. New York: Orion, 1964.

• Makdisi, Saree. *William Blake and the Impossible History of the 1790s*. Chicago: University of Chicago Press, 2003.

• Mee, Jon. *Dangerous Enthusiasm: William Blake and the Culture of Radicalism in the 1790s*. Oxford: Clarendon Press, 1992.

Mellor, Anne K. *Blake's Human Form Divine*. Berkeley: University of California Press, 1974.

Michael, Jennifer Davis. *Blake and the City*. Lewisburg: Bucknell University Press, 2006.

Mitchell, W. J. T. *Blake's Composite Art: A Study of the Illuminated Poetry*. Princeton: Princeton University Press, 1978.

Moskal, Jeanne. *Blake, Ethics and Forgiveness*. Tuscaloosa and London: University of Alabama Press, 1994.

Ostriker, Alicia. *Vision and Verse in William Blake*. Madison: University of Wisconsin Press, 1965.

Otto, Peter. *Constructive Vision and Visionary Deconstruction: Los, Eternity, and the Productions of Time in the Later Poetry of William Blake*. Oxford: Clarendon Press, 1991.

Paley, Morton D. *Energy and the Imagination: A Study of the Development of Blake's Thought*. Oxford: Clarendon Press, 1970.

Paley, Morton D. *The Traveller in the Evening: The Last Works of William Blake*. Oxford: Oxford University Press, 2003.

Paley, Morton. *William Blake*. Oxford: Phaidon; New York: E. P. Dutton, 1978.

Peterfreund, Stuart. *William Blake in a Newtonian World: Essays on Literature as Art and Science*. Norman: University of Oklahoma Press, 1998.

Pierce, John B. *The Wond'rous Art: William Blake and Writing*. Madison, N.J.: Farleigh Dickinson University Press, 2003.

Raine, Kathleen. *Blake and Tradition*. 2 vols. Princeton: Princeton University Press, 1968.

Richey, William. *Blake's Altering Aesthetic*. Columbia: University of Missouri Press, 1996.

Rothenberg, Molly Anne. *Rethinking Blake's Textuality*. Columbia and London: University of Missouri Press, 1993.

Spector, Sheila A. *"Wonders Divine": The Development of Blake's Kabbalistic Myth*. Lewisburg, Pa.: Bucknell University Press; London: Associated University Presses, 2001; [and its companion volume, by the same publishers] *"Glorious Incomprehensible": The Development of Blake's Kabbalistic Language*, 2001.

Tannenbaum, Leslie. *Biblical Tradition in Blake's Early Prophecies: The Great Code of Art*. Princeton: Princeton University Press, 1982.

Thompson, E. P. *Witness against the Beast: William Blake and the Moral Law*. Cambridge: Cambridge University Press, 1993.

Vine, Steven. *Blake's Poetry: Spectral Visions*. London: Macmillan, and New York: St. Martin's Press, 1993.

Weir, David. *Brahma in the West: William Blake and the Oriental Renaissance*. Albany: State University of New York, 2003.

Wittreich, Joseph Anthony, Jr. *Angel of Apocalypse: Blake's Idea of Milton*. Madison and London: University of Wisconsin Press, 1975.

• Wright, Julia M. *Blake, Nationalism, and the Politics of Alienation* (Athens: Ohio University Press, 2003).

Essays and Collections

[Most collections are of previously unpublished work; most editors are also contributors, though not so listed here.]

Adams, Hazard, ed. *Critical Essays on William Blake*. Boston: G. K. Hall, 1991 [reprints Frye, Erdman, Hagstrum, Frosch, • Ostriker, Mitchell, Fox, Paley, Shaviro, Essick].

Adams, Hazard. "Blake and the Philosophy of Literary Symbolism." 1973; rev. in *Philosophy of the Literary Symbolic*. Tallahassee: Florida State University Press, 1983 [see also his *Antithetical Essays in Literary Criticism and Liberal Education* (Tallahassee, 1990).

Bertholf, Robert J. and Annette S. Levitt, eds. *William Blake and the Moderns*. Albany: State University of New York Press, 1982 [Adams, Pease, Searle, Parini, Ostriker, Gleckner, Glazer, Susan Levin, Doskow, Sanzo, Horn].

Bruder, Helen P., ed. *Women Reading William Blake*. London: Palgrave Macmillan 2006 [Chevalier, Colebrook, Connolly, Dent, Erle, Freed, Goslee, Greer, Ima-Izumi, Johnson, Kruger, Labbe, Linkin, McClenahan, McCreery, Michael, Norvig, O'Donoghue, Ostriker, Rajan, Schuchard, Spector, Stephen, Sturrock, Tayler, Warner, Webster, Wolfson, Wright].

Clark, Steve, and David Worrall, eds. *Historicizing Blake*. Basingstoke: Macmillan, 1994 [McCalman, Mee, Larrissy, Lincoln, Philip Cox, Johnson, Dörrbecker, Bruder, Beer]; *Blake in the Nineties*. Basingstoke: Macmillan, 1999 [Essick, Viscomi, Larrissy, • Behrendt, Hilton, Esterhammer, Ferber, Schuchard, K. Davies]; *Blake, Nation, and Empire*. Houndmills and New York: Palgrave Macmillan, 2006 [Makdisi, Mee, Matthews, Chandler, Eaves, Hobson, Lincoln, Whittaker, Essick, Viscomi].

Colby Library Quarterly 13 (1977), 78–157 [Heppner, Warner, Warren Stevenson, Rose, Sutherland].

Curran, Stuart, and Joseph Anthony Wittreich Jr., eds. *Blake's Sublime Allegory: Essays on Milton, Jerusalem, and The Four Zoas*. Madison and London: University of Wisconsin Press, 1973 [McGann, Grimes, Rose, Hagstrum, Paley, Grant, Johnson and Wilkie, Tayler, Rieger, Mitchell, R. Easson, Kroeber].

DiSalvo, Jackie, G. A. Rosso, and Christopher Z. Hobson, eds. *Blake, Politics, and History*. New York: Garland, 1998. [Behrendt, Chandler, Swearington, Mee, Schuchard, Wittreich, Hutton, Worrall, Lincoln, Richey, Ferber, Otto, Rubenstein, Townsend, McClenahan, Linkin, Sturrock, Mellor].

Eaves, Morris, ed. *The Cambridge Companion to William Blake*. Cambridge: Cambridge University Press, 2003 [Ward, Viscomi, Wolfson, Bindman, Makdisi, Mee, Ryan, D. Simpson, Hilton, Lincoln, Johnson, Essick, Gourlay].

Erdman, David V., ed. *Blake and His Bibles*. West Cornwall, Conn.: Locust Hill Press, 1990 [J. M. Q. Davies, Sandler, Grant, Johnson, M. T. Smith, Spector].

Erdman, David V., and John E. Grant, eds. *Blake's Visionary Forms Dramatic*. Princeton: Princeton University Press, 1970. [England, Halloran, Mitchell, Hagstrum, Tolley, Simmons, Warner, Bass, Chayes, Sutherland, Quasha, Tayler, Nelms, Wilkie, McNeil, Lesnick, Johnston, Rose].

Essick, Robert N., ed. "William Blake: Images and Texts," *Huntington Library Quarterly* 58 (1995), 277–458 [Viscomi, Mellor, Bindman, Rajan, Eaves, Mitchell].

Essick, Robert N., and Donald Pearce, eds. *Blake in His Time*. Bloomington and London: Indiana University Press, 1978 [La Belle, Tannenbaum, K. P. Easson, Mellor, Butlin, Bindman, Wittreich, Carothers, Adams, R. Easson, Rose, Paley, Hagstrum, Bentley].

Fox, Susan. "The Female as Metaphor in William Blake's Poetry." *Critical Inquiry* 3 (1976–77), 507–19.

Gleckner, Robert F. "Blake and the Senses." *Studies in Romanticism* 5 (1966), 1–15.

Gleckner, Robert F. "Most Holy Forms of Thought: Some Observations on Blake and Language." *ELH* 41 (1974), 555–75.

Goslee, Nancy Moore. "Soul in Blake's Writing: Redeeming the Word." *The Wordsworth Circle* 33 (2002), 18–23; also " 'Soul-Shudd'ring Vacuum': Space for Subjects in Later Blake," *European Romantic Review* 15 (2004), 391–407.

Gourlay, Alexander S., ed. *Prophetic Character: Essays on William Blake in Honor of John E. Grant*. West Cornwall, Conn.: Locust Hill Press, 2002 [Behrendt, Davies, Ferber, Frost, McClenahan, Mee, Michael, Otto, Paley, Rosso, Spector, Squibbs].

Hagstrum, Jean H. " 'What Seems to Be: Is': Blake's Idea of God." *Johnson and His Age*. Ed. James Engell. Cambridge, Mass. and London: Harvard University Press, 1984.

Hilton, Nelson. "Blakean Zen." *Studies in Romanticism* 24 (1985): 183–200.

Hilton, Nelson, ed. *Essential Articles for the Study of William Blake, 1970–1984*. Hamden, Ct.: Archon Books, 1986 [reprints Adams, Curran, Sandler, Riffaterre, Fox, Gleckner, De Luca, Ault, Eaves, • Ostriker, R. C. Taylor, Shaviro, Santa Cruz Study Group].

Hilton, Nelson, and Thomas A. Vogler, eds. *Unnam'd Forms: Blake and Textuality*. Berkeley: University of California Press, 1986. [Simpson, Edwards, Mann, Ault, Carr, Essick, • De Luca, Hartman].

Keach, William. "Blake Violence, and Visionary Politics." *Representing the French Revolution*. Ed. James A. W. Heffernan. Hanover, N.H.: University Press of New England, 1992.

McGann, Jerome J. "The Idea of an Indeterminate Text: Blake's Bible of Hell and Dr. Alexander Geddes." *Studies in Romanticism* 25 (1986), 303–24.

Miller, Dan, Mark Bracher, and Donald Ault. *Critical Paths: Blake and the Argument of Method*. Durham: Duke University Press, 1987 [Adams, Horn, Hilton, Bracher, Webster, Langland, Aers, Vogler, Wagenknecht].

Miner, Paul. "William Blake's Divine Analogy." *Criticism* 3 (1961): 46–61.

Phillips, Michael, ed. *Interpreting Blake*. Cambridge: Cambridge University Press, 1978 [Parisi, Kittel, Beer, Glen, Butler, Ferguson, Thompson].

Paley, Morton D. and Michael Phillips, eds. *William Blake: Essays in Honour of Sir Geoffrey Keynes*. Oxford: Clarendon Press, 1973 [Bindman, Tolley, Hagstrum. Knight, Erdman et al., Warner, Eaves, Beer, Butlin, Lister, Hoover, Bentley, Essick, Miles].

Rose, Edward J. "Blake's Biblical Consciousness and the Problem of Interpretation of Text and Design." *Bucknell Review* 31 (1988), 113–23; "Blake's Human Root: Symbol, Myth, and Design." *Studies in English Literature* 20 (1980), 579–90; "Blake's Metaphorical States." *Blake Studies* 4 (1971): 9–31; "The Spirit of the Bounding Line: Blake's Los." *Criticism* 13 (1971), 54–61.

Rosenfeld, Alvin, ed. *William Blake: Essays for S. Foster Damon*. Providence: Brown University Press, 1969 [Adams, Bloom, Fisch, Hartman, Hughes, de Sola Pinto, Butlin, Kostelanetz (later Mellor), Harper, Miner, Nanavutty, Nurmi, Gleckner, Grant, Hagstrum, Raine, Paley, Roe, Ansari, Frye, Erdman, Keynes].

Studies in Romanticism 13 (1974), 89 ff. [Roger, Murray, Goslee, G. J. Taylor, Wardle].

Studies in Romanticism 16 (1977), 145 ff. [Mitchell, Paley, Erdman, Worrall, Deck, Gallagher; Eaves reviewing Howard, Brisman reviewing Fox; Minnick reviewing Erdman].

Studies in Romanticism 21 (1982), 389–443: "Inside the Blake Industry: Past, Present, and Future," ed. Morris Eaves [Erdman, Essick, Adams, Viscomi, Mitchell, Hilton, Paley, Kroeber, Gleckner, Grant].

Studies in Romanticism 41 (2002), 143–348: "The Once and Future Blake." [20th anniversary follow-up to vol. 21, Kari Kraus interview with Eaves, Essick, and Viscomi; Paley, Vine, Yoder, Miner, Wagenknecht].

Williams, Nicholas M., ed. *Palgrave Advances in William Blake Studies*. Houndmills and London: Palgrave Macmillan, 2006 [Jones, Otto, Esterhammer, Hilton, Prickett and Strathman, Bruder, Punter, Lussier, Lincoln, Makdisi, Larrissy].

IV. ART REFERENCE WORKS AND OTHER STUDIES

Behrendt, Stephen C. *The Moment of Explosion: Blake and the Illustrations of Milton*. Lincoln and London: University of Nebraska Press, 1983.

Bindman, David. *Blake as an Artist*. Oxford: Phaidon; New York: E. P. Dutton, 1977 [and see his exhibition catalog, *William Blake: His Art and Times*, 1982].

Bindman, David. *The Divine Comedy: William Blake*. Paris: Bibliotheque de l'Image, 2000.

Bindman, David. "William Blake and Popular Religious Imagery." *Burlington Magazine* 128 (1986): 712–18.

Bindman, David, ed. *William Blake's Illustrations of the Book of Job*. The Engravings and related material with Essays, Catalogue of the states and printings, Commentary on the plates and Documentary record [Bryant, Essick, Keynes, Lindberg]. 2 vols. London: The William Blake Trust, 1987.

Bindman, David, assisted by Deirdre Toomey. *The Complete Graphic Works of William Blake*. London: Thames and Hudson, 1978.

Blunt, Anthony. *The Art of William Blake*. New York: Columbia University Press, 1959.

Butlin, Martin. *The Paintings and Drawings of William Blake*. 2 vols. New Haven: Yale University Press, 1981 [illustrated catalog with commentary; indispensable!].

Chayes, Irene H. "Blake's Ways with Art Sources [I]: Michelangelo's *The Last Judgment*." *Colby Library Quarterly* 20 (1984): 60–89; "Blake's Ways with Art Sources II: Some Versions of the Antique." *CLQ* 26 (1990): 28–58.

Damon, S. Foster. *Blake's Job: William Blake's Illustrations of the Book of Job*. Providence, R.I.: Brown University Press, 1966; New York: Dutton, 1969.

Davies, J. M. Q. *Blake's Milton Designs: The Dynamics of Meaning*. West Cornwall, Conn.: Locust Hill, 1993.

Dunbar, Pamela. *William Blake's Illustrations to the Poetry of Milton*. Oxford: Clarendon Press, 1980.

Eaves, Morris. *The Counter-Arts Conspiracy: Art and Industry in the Age of Blake*. Ithaca: Cornell University Press, 1992.

Eaves, Morris. *William Blake's Theory of Art*. Princeton: Princeton University Press, 1982.

Essick, Robert N. "Blake in the Marketplace." [Annual checklist of sales, occasionally revealing lost or untraced works, *Blake Newsletter* 1974–1976; *Blake: An Illustrated Quarterly*, 1978–.

Essick, Robert N. *William Blake's Commercial Book Illustrations: A Catalogue and Study of the Plates Engraved by Blake after Designs by Other Artists*. Oxford: Clarendon Press, 1991.

Essick, Robert N. *William Blake Printmaker*. Princeton: Princeton University Press, 1980.

Essick, Robert N. *The Separate Plates of William Blake: A Catalogue*. Princeton: Princeton University Press, 1983.

Essick, Robert N., ed. *The Visionary Hand: Essays for the Study of William Blake's Art and Aesthetics*. Los Angeles: Hennessey and Ingalls, 1973 [reprints Todd, Binyon, Blunt, Brown, Collins Baker, Nanavutty, Frye, Erdman, Adams, Roe, Merchant, Burke, Butlin, Rose, Mitchell, Helmstadter, Grant, Rhodes, Simmons and Warner, La Belle].

Essick, Robert N. and Morton D. Paley. *Robert Blair's The Grave illustrated by William Blake: A Study with Facsimile*. London: Scolar Press, 1982.

Fuller, David. "Blake and Dante." *Art History* 11 (1988): 349–73.

Gleckner, "Blake, Gray, and the Illustrations." *Criticism* 19 (1977)

Grant, John E. and Robert E. Brown. "Blake's Vision of Spenser's *Faerie Queene*: A Report and an Anatomy." *Blake Newsletter* 8 (1975), 58–85.

Grant, John E., Edward J. Rose, and Michael J. Tolley; with David V. Erdman, eds. *William Blake's Designs for Edward Young's Night Thoughts*. 2 vols. Oxford: Clarendon Press, 1980.

Hamlyn, Robin, commentary. *Night Thoughts: The Poem by Edward Young Illustrated with Watercolours by William Blake*. London: Folio Society, 2005.

Heppner, Christopher. *Reading Blake's Designs*. Cambridge: Cambridge University Press, 1995.

Klonsky, Milton. *Blake's Dante*. New York: Harmony Books, 1980 [see also Albert S. Roe, *Blake's Illustrations to the Divine Comedy*, 1953].

LaBelle, Jenijoy, "Michelangelo's Sistine Frescoes and Blake's 1795 Color-Printed Drawings," *Blake: An Illustrated Quarterly* 14 (1980), 66–84.

Lindberg, Bo. *William Blake's Illustrations to the Book of Job*. Acta Academiae Aboensis, ser. A: Humaniora 46. Abo, Finland: Abo Akademi, 1973.

Norvig, Gerda S. *Dark Figures in the Desired Country: Blake's Illustrations to The Pilgrim's Progress*. Berkeley: University of California Press, 1993.

Tayler, Irene. *Blake's Illustrations to the Poems of Gray*. Princeton: Princeton University Press, 1971.

Townsend, Joyce H., ed. *William Blake: The Painter at Work*. Princeton: Princeton University Press, 2004. [Anderson, Bower, Cahaner McManus, Dean, Hamlyn, Ormsby, Singer, Townshend.]

Vaughan, Frank A. *Again to the Life of Eternity: William Blake's Illustrations to the Poems of Thomas Gray*. Selinsgrove: Susquehanna University Press; London: Associated University Presses, 1996.

Vaughan, William. *William Blake*. Princeton: Princeton University Press, 1999.

Warner, Janet. *Blake and the Language of Art*. Kingston and Montreal: McGill / Queen's University Press, 1984.

Werner, Bette Charlene. *Blake's Vision of the Poetry of Milton: Illustrations to Six Poems*. Lewisburg, Pa.: Bucknell University Press, 1986.

See also catalogs of major exhibitions (e.g., Bindman, 1982; Gert Schiff, 1990; Hamlyn, Serraller, and Diego, 1996; Hamlyn and Phillips, 2000–01) and of such repositories as the Tate Galley (Butlin, 1978, 1990) Huntington Library and Art Gallery (Essick, 1994) and the Yale Center for British Art: Mellon Collection (Patrick Noon, 1997).

Sources Cited in Editorial Notes†

† See "Abbreviations" (p. xvii) for often-cited work by Bentley, Bindman, Butlin, Damon, Dörrbecker, Erdman, Eaves, Essick, Lincoln, Ostriker, Paley, Stevenson, Viscomi, and Worrall, and "Selected Bibliography" (p. 611) for other important studies.

Index of Titles and First Lines